Art Dept.

ART EDUCATION

HARPER'S SERIES ON TEACHING
UNDER THE EDITORSHIP OF
ERNEST E. BAYLES

ART EDUCATION

ITS MEANS AND ENDS

ITALO L. DE FRANCESCO

DIRECTOR OF ART EDUCATION
STATE TEACHERS COLLEGE
KUTZTOWN, PENNSYLVANIA

HARPER & BROTHERS, PUBLISHERS, NEW YORK

CONTENTS

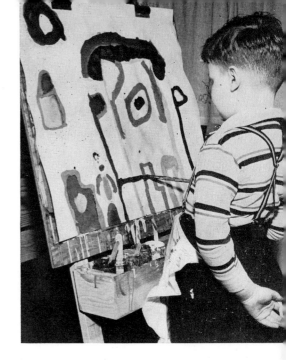

EDITOR'S INTRODUCTION

Dr. ITALO DE FRANCESCO, AN EMINENT FIGURE IN ART EDUCATION, HAS long owed his profession a book setting forth his ideas. This is it: a book significant because it places on record the thinking of one whose influence has been, and is, widespread.

Whether one does or does not agree with everything Dr. de Francesco has to say, one can confidently state that what follows represents momentous advancement in the field. Copy work has long been decried, but in practice creativity has been little more than an empty though impressive word. Integration has lacked definition. It has been far from clear how much children's productions should be criticized and pointed to better things, or even if they should be criticized at all. Teachers have been admonished to draw out what is within their pupils' budding personalities, but have been left in the dark as to how they might recognize a real self when it should emerge.

To say that these and other vagaries in art and art education are now history is hardly justified. But Dr. de Francesco has addressed himself diligently to the task of writing himself clear on such matters and has moved distinctly ahead in his field. Moreover, although the personal qualities of an author may not be directly pertinent to the merits of a book, I do wish to express my gratification for the opportunity to work with the author during the final stages of preparation of his manuscript. Never have I experienced a finer spirit of coöperation nor more discerning response to criticism; the author has used what seemed to him valid and his rejections were always thoughtful and considered. This is an important book in its field and I am confident that it will receive the recognition which it deserves.

ERNEST E. BAYLES

FOREWORD

During the last few years a gratifying flow of publications which deal with art education has appeared. Their very number is a testament to the current vitality of the field and its growing importance within all of education. Excellent as many of these statements have been, each has tended to deal with only a part of the field, such as art instruction at one or more levels, growth and development as exhibited in art activities, or its historic background. No publication has appeared in recent years which examines art education in its entirety.

It is to a comprehensive study of art education that Dr. I. L. de Francesco has addressed himself. His manuscript is probably the most broadly conceived approach to the field which has been undertaken. He deals not only with the social backgrounds of art education but with specific practices at varying levels. Supervision, a highly important activity and one which concerns a large percentage of art educators, is also critically studied and presented. Dr. de Francesco has also shown his awareness of new and significant developments within the field by his consideration of art education for adults and nonschool groups generally.

Of particular importance is the fact that Dr. de Francesco sees art education both in a broad cultural and educational setting. He is aware of the essentiality of art in a democracy—a point of view which needs strong statement at this time of preoccupation with science and technology. Furthermore, he sees the implications and applications of democratic practices for instructional and supervisory practices in art education. In Dr. de Francesco's view, art education is not something which is apart from other interests and aspects of growth of young students, adolescents, and adults, but a vital part of all of them. It is characteristic that he has not presented his own viewpoints only, but has drawn upon the thinking and practices of a widely divergent group of art educators, general educators, and educational philosophers. This approach gives his writing a texture and richness not often encountered.

By virtue of his lifetime endeavor in art education, Dr. de Francesco is uniquely able to present this authoritative statement. He has for a number of years been the chairman of an influential department of art education which has graduated students now teaching throughout the country. In addition to these generally academic activities, he has been intensely active in professional associations at the state, regional, and national levels. In all of them he has held important officerships. He has also given unstintingly of his time and energy on a wide variety of professional problems.

This book is a statement of the working philosophy of its author. It should be a landmark in the field to which he has devoted his life.

EDWIN ZIEGFELD

ACKNOWLEDGMENTS

I AM INDEBTED TO MANY INDIVIDUALS AND SOURCES FOR HELP RECEIVED IN planning, writing, and securing illustrations for this work.

Particular thanks are due Dr. Q. A. W. Rohrbach, president of the State Teachers College at Kutztown, for the initial stimulation and continual encouragement of the project. To Dr. Edwin Ziegfeld, head of the Department of Fine and Industrial Arts at Teachers College, Columbia University, I owe deep personal and professional appreciation for many valuable criticisms and for his willingness to write an introduction to this text.

Dr. Ernest E. Bayles, professor of Education at the University of Kansas, has read every page of the manuscript; his objective and challenging criticisms and his meticulous attention to the slightest details have added clarity and logic to the text. Whatever is lacking or faulty is the author's responsibility. To Dr. Bayles I wish to express not only gratitude but profound respect.

My associates, Dr. Elizabeth Hurwitz, Dr. Horace Heilman, Professor Josef Gutekunst, and Mrs. de Francesco, read the typescript and offered significant criticisms; to them I give sincere thanks. Lastly, I owe much to Mrs. Eleanor Leimbach for her patience in transcribing the original manuscript on her own narrow margin of time.

A large number of art educators and school administrators from many parts of the nation shared their thoughts and resources in this venture. To them I extend my gratitude. Specific contributions come from the following:

Allentown, Pa., Dr. John Cartwright and Miss Clarissa Breinig; Alliance, Ohio, Mr. Henry W. Ray; Atlanta, Ga., Miss Katherine Comfort; Baltimore, Md., Dr. Leon L. Winslow; Boise, Idaho, Mr. Paul Dalzell;

xiv   Boston, Mass., Boston Boys' Club; Brooklyn, N.Y. (Pratt Institute), Mr. Vincent Roy and Professor Charles Robertson; Buffalo, N.Y. (S.T.C.), Dr. Stanley Czurles; Cleveland, Ohio, Mr. Alfred Howell; Easton, Pa., Dr. Edward Tracy and Miss Edith Sturtevant; Edinboro, Pa. (S.T.C.), Dr. Wellington Gray; Hazleton, Pa., Mr. Karl Wallen; Indiana, Pa. (S.T.C.), Dr. Orval Kipp; Jackson, Mo., Miss Mary Dell Buford; Kanahwa County, W.Va., Mrs. Gratia B. Groves; Kansas City, Mo., Miss Rosemary Beymer; Kutztown, Pa., Mr. John Driebelbis; Livingston, N.J., Mrs. Margaret La Morte; Long Beach, Calif., Dr. John Olsen; Minneapolis, Minn., Dr. Edward Del Dosso; Needham, Mass., Mr. John Sawyer; New Paltz, N.Y. (S.T.C.), Dr. Ernest Ziegfeld; Normal, Ill. (S.N.U.), Dr. F. Louis Hoover; Oak Ridge, Tenn., Mr. George Wilson; Oklahoma City, Okla., Miss Grace Chadwick; Philadelphia, Pa., Dr. Earl Milliette; Pittsburgh, Pa., Miss Mary Adeline McKibbin; Portland, Ore., Miss Ruth E. Halvorsen; Reading, Pa., Dr. Thomas Ford and Mr. Frederick R. Schenk; Richmond, Va., Miss Helen Cynthia Rose; Rio Vista, Calif., Miss Idella Church; Seattle, Wash., Mr. Dale Goss; Snyder County, Pa., Mr. Michael Weader; Stratford, Conn., Mrs. Glenn Ketchum Maresca; Toronto, Can., Mr. Howard Dierlam; University Park, Pa. (P.S.U.), Professor Viktor Lowenfeld; Wallkill, N.Y., Mrs. Nuvart Bedrosian; Washington, Pa., Mr. John Grossman; West Point, N.Y., Mr. Dudley Lytle; Worcester, Mass. (Museum), Miss Minnie Levenson; West Reading, Pa., Mr. James Waldron.

Identification of the four part-title illustrations is as follows: Part I, 12th grade, Langley Senior High School, Pittsburgh, Pa.; Part II, 1st grade, Kansas City, Mo.; Part III, evening class, Allentown, Pa.; Part IV, student teaching seminar, State Teachers College, Buffalo, N.Y.

Finally, appreciation is expressed to the many publishers who have granted permission to quote from sources copyrighted by them.

I. L. DE FRANCESCO

TO THE READER

THIS TEXT HAS BEEN WRITTEN TO MEET THE NEEDS OF TWO TYPES OF educational workers: art personnel in the field and students preparing to become teachers or coördinators of art. General classroom teachers and administrators will also find the contents of interest and, it is hoped, of value.

In fulfillment of this purpose, a reasonable exploration and some answers to the following questions have seemed important throughout the development of the text:

What are the claims of art education for a place in the school program?

What constitutes a tenable philosophy of art education?

What is the nature and what are the needs of those to be educated?

What are the professional means available to accomplish the task?

What are the ends sought through art experiences?

What is the proper function of the art teacher, of the coördinator?

What are some promising practices in art education?

The teaching or supervision of art is a fairly complex task because the art teacher must work closely, constantly, and harmoniously with a variety of people at the same time. These, normally, include classroom teachers, administrators, parents, and public. The complexity is easily grasped as one considers that in better-art-staffed states there is but one art coördinator for every 60 elementary teachers. The proportion of elementary-school personnel is even greater in all other states and surely in large school systems. The condition indicates that art teachers must have adequate command of several facets of their own field in addition to being as broadly prepared as other educational workers. At the same time, they must be conversant with the field of education in general.

With due admiration for the artist and for the psychologist, the situation suggests that neither will suffice for the task. The art teacher must be a dedicated educational worker in whom a blend of both is clearly discerned.

It is for these reasons that the means of art education as well as its ends have seemed equally significant in the preparation of this book. The *means* of art education include the scope of education in a democracy, the function of art in total education, foundations of method, the nature of creative experience, the use of resources, the use of evaluative criteria, the function of the teacher, and the nature of the curriculum. These tools, adequately understood and properly utilized, may bring about a satisfactory accomplishment of the ends of art education.

The *ends* may be conceived as the optimum creative growth and the best general development of all individuals through art. The definition applies equally at all levels of the public schools, with adults, and with those referred to as *exceptional*. The achievement of the ends calls for an understanding of the nature of the learner, his many-sided pattern of growth, possibilities of behavior changes, and the establishment of flexible, yet attainable, standards of expression.

Aside from the considerations just mentioned, observation of good practices in teaching or coördinating art raises important issues which also relate to the use of the means and the accomplishment of the ends of education. These need to be recognized and harmonized with the philosophical counterparts.

The first issue is implicit in the term *change*. Changes from traditional art-school curricula have been evident in art education since the 1800's. Those changes became dramatic deviations from the prevailing pattern at the beginning of the present century, and the last 25 years have witnessed a far-reaching reëxamination of the philosophy, method, content, and principal aims of the field. Academic perfectionism has been superseded by self-discovery, and step-by-step exercises have been replaced by experiencing and experimenting. Fixed methods and procedures have been supplanted by positive guidance, and stereotyped subject matter has given way to personal interpretations of man and environment. The application of adult concepts and aesthetic standards in the evaluation of children's work has been replaced by a fresh insight into the nature and meaning of the art of children. Lastly, the aim of art education has shifted from technical precision and visual representation to the encouragement of interpretation in which individual perception finds a large sphere.

The major change, however, is best seen in the gradual recognition of art as a basic element in the development of all individuals. Art education has ceased to be a "special" field and is today regarded as an integral part of the total curriculum. The new concept, *art as education,* owes much to a broadening of the social function of education in our democratic society and to the importance attached to freedom of expression and creative action in that society. A complete understanding of the changes and of their implications can only be achieved over a long period of time and through experience in the art of teaching itself. However, it is conceivable that the substance of what constitutes a valid point of view in art education for our time can be reasonably delineated. Then it should be possible to stimulate the reader to arrive at a synthesis of contemporary thinking in art education. In the process, a more dynamic art program should evolve.

The second issue deals with the effect of the science of education upon art teaching and learning. The prevalent pattern of undergraduate teacher education permits only limited study of psychology and foundations of education. As a consequence, the study of the nature and stimulation of the creative impulse, of experience, of child development, and of the crucial problems of adolescence are, of necessity, abridged. But, it is both important and feasible to establish a basic acquaintance with these aspects of education as they affect art and to make suggestions for their implementation in the classroom. In the text, an attempt is made to point up such basic understandings, not as entities in themselves, but in relation to the structure and function of art as education. To accomplish this a relational point of view has been stressed. In it, three elements are deemed equally significant: the creator, the object created, and the value of the object to the individual or to society.

The method of arriving at a unified view of problems in art education has also been considered significant; therefore, an endeavor has been made to weave a consistent pattern from the following elements:

1. A background in the history and philosophy of art education in order to gain appreciation of the field
2. A foundation in psychology, method, and other professional means to under-

stand the multiple task: guiding young people, organizing the art program, dealing effectively with classroom teachers

3. A knowledge of educational procedures, professional technics, and practices from which to evolve a personal method and a tenable point of view for the accomplishment of the ends of art education

The early chapters are devoted to an overview of the total task of art education. The basis of a philosophy of art education is projected against the background of the social ideals and the unique character of American education. At the same time, the nature of art and its potentials as education are explored with regard to its effect on the needs and values of individuals and of society. The teacher is made aware of the evolutionary character of the changes that have occurred, of the shifts in emphasis, and of the relationships of changes in art education to those in education in general. Historic highlights provide the perspective necessary to understand current trends and help to bolster the faith that art education is a widening interest.

The second element in the pattern is significant because it will profoundly affect the further growth of the teacher. Whenever possible, the method of analysis has been used to interpret the means of education. There are many trends in art education and many of them seem valid, to a degree. There are many methods which have proved successful in the hands of their originators and there are many practices which, under certain circumstances, may be considered worth while. But trends, beliefs, methods, and practices cannot be imposed upon anyone. An educational theory, no matter how sound, if automatically imposed on students or teachers, becomes a denial of the very freedom advocated on other occasions. Objective appraisal is the only road to understanding. This is especially true of professional relationships between classroom teachers and art coördinators, curriculum committees, in-service education, and other aspects involving human relations. Therefore, the nature and needs of the learner, the role of art in the cultivation of the senses, the function of art in social living, the meaning of experience, the meaning of freedom in creative work, the utilization of evaluative technics, and the character and use of resources are usually analyzed.

The next element of the pattern concerns knowledge of professional technics and practices. Curriculum guides, units, and special programs are related to the characteristics of the pupils involved, their needs at various age levels and their stages of development. What constitutes valid subject matter, standards of achievement, and an adequate appreciation of the meaning of integration has been clarified.

The art programs in the self-contained classroom, in the junior high school and the senior high school, with exceptional children, and for adults have been viewed not only from the standpoint of art and of the learner but also in relation to typical school situations and successful practice.

Unquestionably, art educators need to be conversant with what constitutes an ideal program. The ideal is, however, regarded as a goal and as a challenge rather than an existing situation. Chapter 17, "Programs of Promise," shows what is being done across the nation by good teachers and coördinators, while the chapters on the art program at various levels, when possible, include reported or personally observed conditions. By implication the reader should be able to discover how similar problems may be solved in his locality.

Sustained effort has been made to evoke reader reactions through suggested readings and questions for discussion and activity at the end of each chapter.

The illustrations have been gleaned from a wide geographic area and have been interpreted in relation to the chief concern of each chapter rather than as illustrations of specific types of artistic achievement. This should minimize the danger of stereotypes.

Finally, the spirit and thoughts that have guided the author in this task should clarify these central ideas: (1) art education is the birthright of every individual in a democratic society; (2) the final end of art education is to help each individual achieve maximum growth through self-discovery and self-development; (3) educational means are "tools" through which pupils are led toward ultimate harmonization, but never ends in themselves; and (4) the teacher's role is one of constant, positive guidance of learners toward personal fulfillment and social integration.

ITALO L. DE FRANCESCO

State Teachers College
Kutztown, Pennsylvania
June, 1957

PART I

BACKGROUND AND PHILOSOPHY

ART EDUCATION FOR OUR TIME

It is not enough, therefore, to fix attention on professional conceptions of education alone. Observation must
also be taken from the center of society, for education,
government, economy, and culture are parts of the same
thing.

Educational Policies Commission,
*The Unique Function of Education
in American Democracy*

TOWARD A PHILOSOPHY

THE PRIMARY PURPOSE OF THIS CHAPTER IS TO PRESENT AND TO CLARIFY CER-
tain premises and the general point of view which underlie the thesis of this
text, namely, that art education is not a fringe subject, but an integral part
of the total education of the citizens of a democracy.

Elaboration of the premises should lead to the second purpose, which is
the proposal of a philosophy of art education for a democratic society.
Ultimately, it is hoped that such a philosophy may help the reader achieve
a personal basis for a program adequate to the times.

As a starting point, it must be accepted that what comprises art education today is neither a new phenomenon nor a development of the last decade. Rather, it is the result of a long and slow evolution, compounded of
tradition, some history, frequent reforms, and, more lately, some experimentation.

Philosophers from Plato to Dewey have concerned themselves, among
other things, with art and, in a sense, with the kind of art education children should have. Professional art educators of the past and, especially of

4   the last half-century, have continued the interest in both problems. They have made pronouncements and have engaged in studies, some of them empirical, to discover better ways and sounder methods for a more effective program in the arts. Art as it affects the individual and art as it affects society have been considered singly and in relation to each other. The training of producing artists, the development of general taste and appreciation, and the preparation of art teachers have also continuously occupied the minds of art educators, general educators, and social scientists.

EVOLUTION OF A DYNAMIC PHILOSOPHY

More recently, the findings of experimentation in the fields of education, aesthetics, and psychology have begun to be made available to those who teach art. The findings have had and will continue to have tangible effects in refined thinking, improved practices, and clearer concepts of the task. *Art as education* for growth and development, not merely to foster exhibitionism, is both the result and the evolution of continuous study and effort to make art an affective element in the life of the people.

These facts indicate that the character of a philosophy of art education for our time must be dynamic, and that it must take into account several factors. Among them the following seem essential:

1. Utilization of available knowledge of the nature and functions of art and of education.
2. Knowledge of the character of the social setting in which art and education have developed and are developing.
3. Clarification of the specific contributions of art to the growth of individuals.
4. Recognition of the social values of art as an integrating agent.

A closer look at what is suggested above discloses that even the deepest concern with any one of the four factors could yield only a limited outlook insofar as the total task of art education is concerned. All factors need to be recognized simultaneously and in relation to each other. Then it may be possible to see the wholeness of the problem: art-man-society.

THE ART AND SCIENCE OF TEACHING

Art education, when thought of as a branch of the profession of teaching, must view the problem not only philosophically but from the point of view of the operation of art in the education of people. Being a teacher, or wanting to become one, implies acceptance of the responsibility to know. Among other things, a teacher must know the nature of art, its meaning in expression and appreciation, its various manifestations and modes, and its developmental values in education. The responsibility further implies knowledge of human beings, of how and why they behave as they do, and of the role which guidance plays in the process of growth. Even if considered simply as tools for teaching, these aspects of education represent a wide segment of total knowledge. Actually, they encompass the fields of art, education, psychology, sociology, and biology.

But teaching means even more. It means acceptance of the responsibility to understand the character of the educational service to be rendered, its scope, its ends, its organizational structure, and the means available for accomplishing the whole task. Implicit in these responsibilities are several important facts which have direct bearing on the practice of teaching. The first is that art and education, when considered as institutions, are subject to various uses by the supporting society. Education and art in a primitive culture have one meaning; in a communistic society they serve certain ends; in a democratic society, their scope is an entirely different matter. Obviously, such varying situations demand equally different methods and points of view. Eventually, a teacher and his teaching can be productive only if the underlying social concepts are clear and there is harmony between teaching and the goals of the supporting society.

A second fact is that knowledge, of itself, is of limited value. It becomes meaningful only when it is organized for use. There is a distinction between science, or the product of knowledge, and the *method* of science. The science of education makes use of pertinent knowledge from a variety of fields, and through experimentation, testing, and other professional technics arrives at certain hypotheses. When the hypotheses have been tested and their validity has been proved, they become a part of the. science of education and are made available to teachers. But there is no guarantee that proven methods will necessarily ensure desirable results; it is the skillful use of the method that brings about the desirable ends of teaching. Therefore, in addition to a science, there is an *art* of teaching.[1]

---

[1] Ernest E. Bayles, *The Theory and Practice of Teaching*, New York, Harper & Brothers, 1950, Chapter 1.

A PERSONAL PHILOSOPHY

In a later discussion (Chapter 16), such teaching has been called "creative," and its characteristics have been identified as skill, excellence, and quality of performance. The achievement of artistry in teaching implies growth: in knowledge, in insights, concepts, and outlooks. In reality one begins with what appears adequate at a given time and builds along the way, changes, adds, eliminates what is not valid, and eventually arrives at a broad point of view. It is that point of view which is called a philosophy of art education or of any other field of human activity.

It is safe to assume that, by interest and professional intention, art

FOR ALL THE CHILDREN. The universality of the art impulse and the principle of universality in American education suggest that all children, not the few, are entitled to education in the arts (6th grade, Pittsburgh, Pa.).

teachers or supervisors, and those who are preparing to teach art, have accumulated or are acquiring a reasonable amount of knowledge about art and education. This should, unquestionably, be useful in arriving at a point of view. But the whole of knowledge is vast; the mastery of even a fraction of it requires endless labor and a great deal of experience in living and teaching. Therefore, in practice, it seems wise to focus attention principally on those concerns which are immediately allied to the task on hand. A teacher will then build on that foundation until his philosophy has developed. Reference to the basic elements which eventually lead to a philosophy brings the realization that any one of them could well become a specialized study for a lifetime of endeavor. Indeed, each has had the benefit of the wisdom of philosophers, scientists, artists, and educators.

The present work is an attempt to lead the reader to reach a synthesis, a sound if telescoped one, regarding the total problem of education through art for use in the classroom. In consequence, the many ramifications and relationships which are bound to appear in the process of seeing the elements of the philosophy as a unified whole must, of necessity, be left to the intellectual yearning and to the reflective capacity of the reader. The significant fact is that the elements are interdependent and indeed integral one with the other. It must also follow that the art of teaching depends on a proper and adequate assimilation and integration of the relevant knowledge back of it.

RELEVANT KNOWLEDGE OF ART AND EDUCATION

The remainder of this chapter is devoted to clarification of terms and to the raising of pertinent issues so that the purposes and functions of art education may be delineated. Furthermore, the reader will find statements of hypotheses and attempts to test their validity for the field.

A great deal of needless confusion in art education, between art education and professional education, and among lay people, is due to lack of effective communication. What does the art educator mean by the term *art?* Is the same meaning accepted by the professional educator? Do teachers in general and the public share the definition of the educator and of the art teacher? The same questions apply to such terms as experience, creative expression, integration, appreciation, con-

8 ceptualization, and others commonly used in the literature of art, education, and psychology.

It would be presumptuous to assume that by mere definition of words all problems of communication could be solved. But it is conceivable that by clarifying the larger meanings of professional terms a way is opened, at least with respect to the use made of them in the present context. In this limited sense, therefore, the immediate problem will be to interpret certain pertinent areas of knowledge in the hope that they may shed light on what seems basic to arrive properly at a tenable philosophy. Other equally important areas and issues are discussed in the further development of this chapter or in subsequent chapters where the need for clarification seems apparent.

THE NATURE OF ART

It was indicated above that one of the chief difficulties in the path of art education is the great variety of meaning given to art itself. There is no decrying difference. But it seems that persons working in the same area of education should share the significance of this basic term. The reader will find that Dewey expresses himself on the matter in these words:

Art is a quality of doing and of what is done. Only outwardly then, can it be designated by a noun substantive. Since it adheres to the manner and content of doing, it is adjectival in nature. When we say that tennis playing, singing, acting, and a multitude of other activities are arts, we engage in an elliptical way of saying that there is art in the conduct of these activities, and that this art so qualifies what is done and made as to induce activities in those who perceive them in which there is also art. The product of art—temple, painting, statue, poem—is not the work of art. The work takes place when a human being cooperates with the product so that the outcome is an experience that is enjoyed because of its liberating and ordered properties.[2]

The principal value of the above statement lies in the fact that it determines what art is and what it is not. An adequate understanding of these concepts has direct bearing on what teachers will expect from their pupils in the classroom. Analyzed, the definition appears to say that art is a quality; that art involves action; that art is not the product of action alone but of the quality of the experience which pupils undergo in the doing. Of course, it also indicates that there is art in human activities

---

[2] John Dewey, *Art as Experience*, New York, Minton, Balch and Company, 1934, p. 214.

of various types and not only in the visual arts, as is sometimes assumed.

Beyond the definition, however, Dewey[3] explains the process of art in production as organically related to the perception, or the inner vision of the doer. Perception itself goes beyond intellect and outside judgments, as will be seen later. This is a fact which establishes the autonomy of the individual as artist, and should have meaning in the evaluation and guidance of his growth.

THE MEANING OF EXPERIENCE

Another significant area which needs understanding is that of experience. What is it? How does it operate? What are its characteristics? How does education profit by its use? Chapter 5 is devoted to an elaboration of the workings of this extremely important aspect of education, but a clarification of its meaning at this point may pave the way.

First of all, it should be clear that a real experience is a result of the creative urge. Dewey's interpretation seems useful in establishing the relationship of an experience to art. He says: "Experience is the result, the sign, and the reward of that interaction of organism and environment which, when it is carried to the full, is a transformation of interaction into participation and communication."[4]

One cannot but be impressed by the organic nature of the expressive act as described. The process of creation is like a chain in which the creator's entire being, the process (what he is doing), his way of perceiving, and the results he achieves are inseparable, connecting links. If one link breaks, the experience is incomplete. In terms of teaching, the meaning is that art is more than doing; it is living through, feeling, and sensing the *whole* act. In the later discussion of this subject, the various types of experience and the selection of meaningful aspects of it are detailed for practical use in the art laboratory.

THE BASIS OF CREATIVE EXPRESSION

An additional term much used in art education is expression—more particularly, *creative expression*. Precisely, what does it mean? In simplest terms one may say that it means to push out or to bring forth. It has been indicated that experience begins from an inner urge, or an

---

[3] *Ibid.*, p. 214.
[4] *Ibid.*, p. 22.

impulsion, and that it is an act which originates in need and involves the whole being. As such, expression is a need of the living organism. But not all expression is necessarily creative. For example, one may contrast yelling with singing; aimless, even joyful jumping with dancing; smearing paint to give vent to anger with composing a pattern. In Dewey's words, one finds that ". . . what is evoked is not just quantitative, or mere energy, but is qualitative, a transformation of energy into thoughtful action, through assimilation of meanings from the background of past experience."[5] Now, if to the meaning of *art* one adds Dewey's qualifications of action, it seems quite defensible to say that creative expression is the result of reflective action upon a medium. In other words, past and recent experiences, insights, and concepts are brought to bear upon the tools and materials of expression with purpose and quality. Once again, one realizes the inescapable unity of creative expression and, consequently, of its potential in education, not only in the visual arts but in other modes of human behavior.

As one understands the dominant role which the emotions play in the creative act, it becomes clear that the spontaneity and vitality found in the art of young people is not a result of mere impulsive swinging of a brush, but of a thought-out, even calculated creative act. Of course, there is excitement in creative expression. Such excitement, when it is genuine, is a natural and healthy sign of buoyancy; indeed, it is a prelude to the successful completion of the creative experience. Yet evidence of excitement in children and young people usually calls for examination and, perhaps, wise guidance on the part of the teacher.

THE SIGNIFICANCE OF INTEGRATION

It has been pointed out that the way of creation, or art, is an organic, indivisible process. The same holds true for aesthetic appreciation or enjoyment of art. This truth becomes more important when attention is focused on the ultimate function of art, namely, its effect on man; here one deals with the integration of his personality. Bayles, following a critique of what is generally spoken of as "core" curricula, makes this interesting observation: "And we can say that, if the term integration has any significant meaning for democratic education, it is exactly what is

---

[5] *Ibid.*, p. 60.

meant by our term harmonization. But, it is integration or harmonization—oneness—of student outlook which is important for democratic
education, etc. . . ."[6] Harmony within the individual also involves identification and oneness of relationship to the environment, which includes
understanding of people, things, situations, facts, causes, and effects.
It must be stressed that personal outlooks are the result of the integrative
process, which is compounded of knowledges, concepts, and insights.
The total effect is seen in the harmonious working of mind-body-emo-
tions and is itself an example of integrated behavior.

Harmonization, then, becomes a real potential of art because it shares
and is inherent in the creative experience. As such, it requires sympathy,
permissiveness, experimental attitude, and positive guidance. In practice,
the process of integration must anticipate successes, failures, and repeated performance. And all these need to be viewed as valuable if the
outlooks of the learners are to be complete and satisfying.

The method referred to as "integrated teaching" is analyzed elsewhere; what matters now is that its worth be recognized and that its
meaning be heightened by reflective thinking. Bayles expresses a necessary corollary to the whole idea of integration thus: "We must, in the
interest of democratic education, continually be cognizant of the need
for integrating or helping to integrate student outlooks, both transversely
and longitudinally."[7] The implication for a philosophy of art education
seems to be that, in order to get reflective thinking and doing from
pupils, teacher-pupil planning must also be of a reflective type. This is
another way of saying that a teacher must identify himself with the
needs and aspirations of his pupils.

THE IMPORTANCE OF APPRECIATION

The production of art and the development of a feeling of warmth
toward and genuine enjoyment of art objects on the part of all individuals are closely related activities. In practice, however, the problem of
aesthetic appreciation has often been considered an activity independent
of production. There is both logic and lack of it in this popular understanding of the situation. If one accepts the full meaning of art and of
experience which has been delineated, it will appear that creation and

---

[6] Bayles, *op. cit.*, p. 179.
[7] *Ibid.*, p. 180.

appreciation derive from the same organic process. In the case of an individual who is impelled to act—to draw, paint, compose, or model—the result of action is in the form of an object. The result may be a poem, a melody, a painting, a carving, or a similar artistic outcome. In the case of an individual who is not a creator in the sense of being a doer, action assumes the form of enjoyment, of judgment, and of communion with the creator as well as the object. It is also true that the individual who is impelled to create constantly reacts or evaluates his own work. In the process of evaluating, shaping, and reshaping there is enjoyment. Furthermore, a doer is often capable of appreciating, passing judgment on, or evaluating the art productions of others. Actually, there is no such thing as passive and active appreciation. They are both active, and the same basic perception, the same insights, and concepts are basic to both types of activity. It must be repeated that the elements cannot be separated if the oneness of *an* experience is to be maintained. Referring to Dewey once more, he sums up the matter in these words: "What is true of original production is true of appreciative perception. We speak of appreciation and its object. But perception and its object are built up and completed in one and the same continuing operation."[8] And again: "For to perceive, a beholder must create his own experience. And his creation must include relations comparable to those which the original

ACTION and the feeling for pattern and rhythm are effectively expressed by a junior-high-school girl. The technic of ink resist offers opportunity for experimentation (10th grade, Boise, Idaho).

---

[8] Dewey, *op. cit.*, p. 177.

producer underwent. They are not the same in a literal sense. But with the perceiver, as with the artist, there must be an ordering of the elements of the whole that is in the form, although not in detail, the same as the process of organization the creator of the work consciously experienced."[9]

In consequence of what has been presented, there can be no argument as to whether to "teach" appreciation or to assume that there is constant appreciation going on as part of the creative process. The fact remains that there are two types of experiences, one leading to or from creative action, the other, largely constructing its own experience by reliance on conceptual and perceptual reactions to the object of art. But if art education is to affect the lives of *all,* especially children, then it seems fair to say that appreciation must be attacked deliberately. Its broad purposes should encompass discriminating consumership, intelligent citizenship, and the raising of the level of taste of all individuals. The subject matter, on the other hand, must be wide: appreciation of painting, sculpture, architecture, and the many types of design that affect life and living.

Obviously, the teaching of appreciation will be effective only in the degree of understanding of what it is and how it is developed. Because it has been intimated that a direct effort needs to be made to induce appreciation, the term "teaching" is used here. However, real appreciation is a matter of personal conviction; indeed, the old dictum that appreciation is not taught but caught would seem to contain a great deal more truth than is sometimes suspected. For example, exposure to works of art will not necessarily induce appreciation, although rarely it may; but to let the matter rest with chance acquaintance alone hardly fulfills a teacher's obligation.

Anecdotes, dates, schools, even characteristic technics, may be learned as bits of interesting data which may bring the observer a bit closer to the object of art, yet even then there is no assurance that appreciation is taking place. This is precisely why the old-fashioned appreciation lessons failed; they were perfunctory, quasi-literary exercises.

Is there a sounder approach to this problem which should influence the lives of immense numbers in the schools? Without pretense of being *the* answer, what follows is offered for consideration.

---

[9] *Ibid.,* p. 54.

First, there are cognitive elements in the appreciational experience; these need to be considered carefully in order that mental, rather than superficial, acquaintance with art may be established. But, in addition, there are certain affective elements in any form of art. The latter must be considered equally as well because, in a real way, they involve the values inherent in the art object. This second element takes on the form of evaluation, not of facts or of biographical data, but of the sensitiveness of the use of elements and principles, in a unique manner chosen by the artist. As the observer beholds the work of art he relives the experience of the creator; and only in so doing can he arrive at a point where he would like to own, or senses the purpose of, the art object in his life.

The final question in this consideration is whether or not the teacher sets the "standard" of what is to be appreciated. Even though it has been intimated, it seems plausible to conclude that any imposed, dictated, dominated teaching is ineffective and undemocratic. It is well to hope that young people may "appreciate" Rembrandt, Cézanne, or Picasso; it is well to hope that they may enjoy the music of Bach or Ravel; but it is utter futility to say that they *must*. In the final analysis, the proof of the pudding is in the eating. The obligation of teaching is to present opportunities, stimulate interest, encourage evaluation, and hope that genuine enjoyment of what is good may result.

THE DEVELOPMENT OF PERCEPTION

One of the oldest and most persistent claims of art teaching has been "the development of the faculty of sight." Unfortunately, in the past such a claim could be based only on the belief that the purpose of art was to "represent" and that artistic merit could be measured by one's ability to reproduce, photographically, the world of nature. Perception, therefore, could be said to be largely a matter of good eyesight, coupled to a gift called art.

How erroneous such a conclusion is must be obvious, in view of the diversity of styles and schools in the art of the past and more particularly since expressionism has given rise to the many modes referred to as "modern." Yet there is partial truth in the "development of the faculty of sight" if by that is meant an increase in sensitiveness to the world of objects as well as to kinesthetic experience. Such sensitiveness is usually shown in the individual's response to visual stimuli, and its development ranges from the early drawings of a child to the complex works of mature expressionists.

Today, psychology has fairly well defined the nature and operation of perception and can suggest how it may be developed. From the standpoint of contemporary art education, it is essential to understand what this psychological attribute of man is, how it works, and what its refinement means in terms of growth and behavior.

Human beings do things, act and learn, in the process of living. Such behavior, however, is impossible unless man senses, or perceives, the world about him, other human beings, situations, and occurrences that make up life. Perception, to use Newman's words, "is the first event in the chain which leads from stimulus to action."[10]

It could be argued that the physical world, people, and the things which are seen and touched are real, or tangible, and, therefore, exist just as man perceives them. This is neither true nor quite as simple as may be suspected, because man is the most complicated living organism and his reactions are just as complex. For example, when a pupil uses a pigment he may think of it merely as a color, but to the scientist the same mixture represents many kinds of light. This discrepancy between man's experience and the fullness of reality indicates that they are two different things. The statement does not contradict what has been previously said about experience; it rather emphasizes the existence of a world aside from man's visual or tactile or auditory experience of it. Yet both need to be understood if they are to be utilized. The definition further distinguishes between perception and sensation. The latter refers to those facts in experience which depend on how the sense organs act.

To understand what it is that one perceives, it may be useful to think as scientists do. The psychologist, for example, says that the most common perception is an object. An object has a *figuration;* it occupies a certain amount of space in a field, and has a contour which encloses a shape. In addition, objects have depth, solidity, and surface qualities. When seen in terms of *planes,* objects produce a stimulus pattern in the eye and the beholder senses light, shade, and perspective. This total

---

[10] Edwin B. Newman, "Perception," in Edwin Boring, Herbert Langfeld, and Harry Weld, *Foundations of Psychology,* New York, John Wiley and Sons, Inc., 1948, Chapter X, p. 215.

16 visual effect results into perception of depth. Many of these terms are commonly used in art education and perhaps taken for granted. Actually, they represent steps in growth which need much attention and nurturing.

There are a number of important facts concerning perception which may be of help to teachers. The first is that a perception is often the result of coöperation between several senses; in fact, it is very seldom that one sense alone yields all one needs to know about an object. If this is understood, then Dewey's concept of perception augments and enhances the meaning of visual perception by endowing it with sensory intelligence, personal meaning and values, and intellectual reactions. Perhaps it is Dewey's broad concept that prompts Barkan to say that "Perception is the embodiment of meaning derived from an individual's prior experiences and retained for future sensory reception."[11]

Scientific studies of perception reveal that in operation it is selective, organized, and based on change. Briefly, these qualities indicate that the individual responds to differences in the environment, that he selects the particular aspect to which he will give attention, and that he links together a number of stimuli into a group so that a single response results in a complex pattern. These are indications of the significance of perception as part of total growth; they also point to a major opportunity as well as to a responsibility in art education.

Lastly, it must be stated that a real relationship exists between meaning and perception; even more, between perceiving and thinking. Altogether, these are essential factors in the behavior pattern and cannot be separated. In art education, acting upon or with materials, implies giving form to an idea.

The present discussion has centered on the visual aspect of the subject for the purpose of clarity. Actually, all the sense organs are involved in an individual's reaction to the environment. Later in this chapter the matter of cultivation of the senses is further detailed.

THE IMPORTANCE OF CONCEPTS AND INSIGHTS

The term self-expression is, perhaps, the most widely used term in art education. Indeed, it seems that its fostering is the major objective of

---

[11] Manuel Barkan, *A Foundation for Art Education*, New York, The Ronald Press Company, 1955, p. 132.

the field. Certainly, it is the chief preoccupation of art teachers in the implementation of activities in the classroom. Having set down a tentative definition for the term, it can be agreed that there is no questioning the matter of self-expression. However, some questions may well be raised regarding the validity of the usual interpretation of the term, of what is "expressed," and whether all sources from which expression derives have been fully considered.

Even when reasserting the presence of the creative impulse, it must be realized that a work of art does not spring, full blown, from a void. It could be argued that occasionally the subconscious mind, the apperceptive mass, gives rise to artistic expression without the usual thinking-feeling preludes. Such a notion is incomplete because the subconscious operates on remote, personal, and hidden sources. Yet their existence is certain; therefore, the subsequent action reverts to the normal organic pattern of creative expression and results in the activation of the thinking-feeling pattern of an individual. In Dewey's words, one finds that it is "a transformation of energy into thoughtful action, through assimilation of meanings from a background of experience."[12] Herein, it seems, is the heart of teaching and learning in art education. Unless action is accompanied by realization of what the action accomplishes, and unless concepts are clear, insights are not called up and creation is impeded rather than facilitated. All this calls for a clarification of what is meant by concepts and insights in education; it may reveal the tremendous importance of these elements in creativity.

A *concept* is a generalized idea of a whole classification of people, objects, animals, things, or situations. Through learning, concepts expand by the inclusion of additional common elements of the classification and by the exclusion of differences. In addition, a concept brings to mind pertinent situations and associations. For example, the term *paint* refers, among other things, to water-color painting, oil painting, landscape, still-life, figure, mural, and portrait painting. But it also refers to house painting, painting a fence, or it may refer to the phrase "painting the town" or "painting a beautiful picture" with words. To pupils in the art class it immediately suggests color names; to pupils in science and in art it may readily suggest light, rainbow, refraction, and other physical phenomena.

---

[12] Dewey, *op. cit.*, p. 60.

Thus it is plain that concepts are component parts of what is called knowledge. It follows that clarity of concepts makes for clarity of thinking and perceiving. To the contrary, poor concepts lead to fallacies and, therefore, to inaccurate or faulty thinking and perceiving. A second point in this connection is that as a pupil's knowledge advances, clearer concepts and better patterns of thinking are likely to result, and the development of insights may be facilitated.

The significance of insights and concepts further suggests that what-

REACTION TO ENVIRONMENT and to situations is part of the education of the senses. "Confusion at the Fair" is the impression portrayed by a child artist (Age 12, 6th grade, Boise, Idaho).

ever else teachers may "teach," their most important function is to guide pupils in the development of these basic processes. An individual's outlook on life becomes increasingly more wholesome as his insights and concepts broaden and become integral with his behavior in all circumstances.

The pattern of thinking used by boys and girls is at the bottom of their interpretations and selections in things and in situations. Choosing materials suitable to solve an art problem, choosing the right tools, developing the technic that will enhance the materials, conceiving the compositional arrangement which will best convey the idea—all these involve concepts and insights related to creation. Self-expression, therefore, is facilitated when teachers lead pupils to arrive at wise conceptualizations prior to proceeding to the final product.

Theoretically, when pupils are "thinking" about their work, they are sorting out the many pertinent concepts they have acquired. Their insight may suggest which concepts are most suitable in the situation and, by acting upon material, they solve their problem. Obviously, the activation of the knowledge that pupils have accumulated through experiences in learning is a most effective way of guiding their conceptual development. Another effective way is to think of experimentation not merely as an interesting game, but as a serious way of arriving at tentative solutions. These are then examined, and while some will be accepted, others will be rejected.

In creative education, the best thinkers are less rigid in their uses of old concepts; new ways, new arrangements, and new uses for old concepts are evidences of discrimination and of a sense of how a concept applies to a new situation. The inference for teaching is to avoid sustained, rigid requirements, directions, and predetermined results. The value of creative education rests on the nurturing of the desire to find new ways of using concepts in new situations and on altering them as occasion demands and the insights justify. Then new concepts are formed, insights arise, outlooks are broadened, and creative growth takes place. Errors may and will occur, but that is part of growing.

An additional important fact regarding conceptualization is that children, adolescents, youth, and adults extend their concepts through life experiences and through learnings of various types. As the extension takes place, the level of understanding rises. The first level of understanding may be a simple fact, such as "the name of this color is red." Color names are learned very early by many children. But a second and higher level of understanding is reached when the properties of red are realized: light red, deep red, red-orange; or red and yellow will make orange, and there are values and intensities of orange. The third level of understanding, or the highest, is reached when the pupil recognizes that a *principle* comes out of his earlier understandings: two colors, when mixed, produce a third one, or, all colors have values and intensities. The foregoing may be simple examples, but the connotations are easily applied to other and more difficult learning situations. It may be concluded then that such levels of understanding, when appropriate to the age, endowment, and experience of pupils, are reasonable expectancies as well as evaluations of teaching and learning.

An *insight* is the key to the solution of a problem. The problem may be one in arithmetic or in science or in art; there is no difference in the basis of thinking required. If one restricts the meaning of insight by saying that it is a flash of genius that comes instantaneously, it may be possible to gain a first glimpse into its deeper significance. For example, a pupil is thinking over the idea of a painting on a subject of his own choosing. As he reflects over the matter, a number of concepts, situations, and associations come to the fore. Then, quickly, so it seems, he begins to paint and finds that he likes the composition, the color tones, in fact the whole idea. It may be said that he has solved a creative problem, aided by his insights.

Croce, the Italian aesthete, referred to such solutions as being intuitional, or the result of a "sixth sense." Regardless of terminology, in human experiences such inspired solutions are common to all who have learned to do reflective thinking.

Another example of insight is to think of an individual who examines a situation, selects the correct method or recognizes the principle involved, and arrives at a solution to the problem. Obviously, activated knowledge, past experience, clear thinking, and the "feel" for what is involved have bearing on the apparent "flash" or insight.

A celebrated example of insight is found in one of Köhler's[13] experiments with apes. Originally, the chimpanzee had learned how to pull a banana through a fence by making use of a stick. But sometime later the ape was given two sticks, neither of which was long enough to reach the banana. The shorter sticks were so designed that one would fit into the other and thus make a long stick. In playing with the two sticks, the ape accidentally fitted them together; suddenly it realized that it now had a long stick, ran to the fence, and pulled in the banana. Prior experience led to the insight, and from then on the chimpanzee knew how to use two short sticks to make a longer one.

However, not all learning comes with the first flash of insight. Some of it is achieved by trial and error. For example, in the solution of a problem several hypotheses may be tried; then suddenly, by insight, the one hypothesis is recognized as the solution.

---

[13] Wolfgang Köhler, *The Mentality of Apes*, New York, Harcourt, Brace and Company, 1925.

Especially applicable to art education, although in no sense differing from other interpretations, is Bayles' further qualification of insight. He says: "Insight often comes without going through the motion (repetition), and whenever this happens, repetition is unnecessary. Thus, the term insight when taken in this sense represents the essential factor which makes experience effectual in influencing subsequent behavior."[14]

This discussion points out the fallacy of assuming that creative work requires no effort; that it is only a matter of inspiration; that it results from mysterious sources. Art education is education in thinking, in seeing, in sensing, and finally in acting. Teaching, therefore, cannot assume a passive attitude; it must be in the form of active guidance, stimulation, and motivation. Then the thinking and the conceptualization of pupils become natural links in the process of creative self-expression.

THE IMPROVEMENT OF OUTLOOKS

If art education were mainly a matter of teaching skills, as was the case many years ago, then there would be little point in the present concern with psychology, educational method, and other sciences considered to have a relationship to the education of individuals. But since the function of art is to educate the whole man, not just separate parts of him, it is essential that whatever he learns, whatever he creates, whatever he does, should have a clear-cut relationship to his view of himself and of the world of which he is a part. That view may be called his *outlook*. A widely accepted educational premise is that when outlooks are refined, a degree of harmonization, or integration, is achieved.

In Bayles'[15] judgment, if a pupil realizes his lack of adequacy, or disharmony, in one area or another, he has a problem. As he proceeds, willingly, to solve the problem and as he arrives at partial solutions, he is also approaching adequacy. Eventually, he may solve the whole problem, and when that happens his harmonization increases and his outlooks are changed. Furthermore, from that point on, the pupil can reconstruct outlooks independently because of prior experience, successes, and even some failures.

In art education the problems encountered by pupils may be in the direction of ideas, concepts, technics, composition, figure drawing, or

---

[14] Bayles, *op. cit.*, p. 51.
[15] *Op. cit.*, p. 135.

whatever other area is being explored by him. Guidance in seeking solutions, through an evaluation of the pupil's former accomplishments, or the examination of masterworks, or the work of classmates—any or all of these are ways of searching for the adequacy the pupil needs.

The measure in which the pupil grows in perceptive power, in clarity of conceptualization, and in reflective thinking, in that measure will his outlooks broaden and deepen. In a real way, this is one of the purposes of teaching. The obligation is a recurring theme throughout these pages.

SOCIAL FORCES AND ESTABLISHMENT OF GOALS

In addition to a utilization of knowledges and a clarification of meanings, a philosophy of art education must consider the fact that beyond the sphere of the learning process itself, and beyond educational philosophy, certain social, economic, and political beliefs have always operated to affect the course of art and of education profoundly.

The development of public education in the United States shows this quite plainly. After the struggle to conquer the wilderness, establish a nation, set up a government, and insure the general welfare, the people of America turned their attention to the education of the masses. Knight, in a discussion of the early history of education in America, describes the endeavors of some of the more potent forces which, especially during the early nineteenth centruy, helped to awaken national consciousness of the need for public education. He states: "These forces were economic and industrial, political, religious, and humanitarian. Through their influence, the way of public education became somewhat clearer, but it was to brighten also through the influence of other agencies and of some fervid educational leaders."[16]

Noble, another educational historian, again referring to conditions of environment and to social forces, puts it very plainly: ". . . it is freely conceded that the history of education has been and will continue to be, largely, the history of its institutions. Society has long recognized its stake in the educative process. . . ."[17]

---

[16] Edgar W. Knight, *Education in the United States,* New York, Ginn & Company, 1951, p. 188.

[17] Stuart G. Noble, *A History of American Education,* New York, Farrar & Rinehart, 1938, p. 15.

James B. Conant, former president of Harvard University, expresses himself on this point in these words: "Our educational system reflects the social structure of this free and fluid nation. Our free tax-supported schools are the sinews of our society; they are the product of our special history, a concrete manifestation of our ideals, and the instrument by which the American concept of democracy may be transmitted to our future citizens."[18]

An additional pertinent point which refers especially to art and its manifestations comes from the literature of art education itself. Payant, in a discussion of the social background of American art, says quite appropriately: "Rarely in history has a people been composed of a greater variety of nationalities and accompanying influences than has the United States. This has meant a rich kaleidoscopic inheritance of art that from the very beginning was filled with the vigor, adventure, and freedom of expression peculiar to this heterogeneous population."[19]

Lastly, the words of R. L. Duffus, a cultural historian, may indicate the concern of the people and the determination to seek cultural advancement. In his introduction to *The American Renaissance,* he says: "We have attained to economic maturity. We have made locomotives, automobiles, bridges and skyscrapers, and sometimes have stumbled upon beauty. Is there any reason why we should not now go deliberately forth to seek it? And need we be ashamed to seek it in our own way and our own places, not alone in quietness but amid the sweat and dust, fire and molten metal?"[20]

Beyond these statements, it would be a simple task to suggest many more similar ones from current professional and lay literature to reinforce the point that all facets of education in America have a clear function and an equally clear responsibility.

A philosophy of art education for our time, therefore, must take cognizance of social forces and beliefs in addition to marshaling its own special claims and interests if it is to be educationally effective and of utmost worth for the individual and for contemporary society.

---

[18] James B. Conant, "Strengthen Education to Strengthen Democracy in a Divided World," *School Life,* January, 1949, p. 13.

[19] Felix Payant, "The Social Background of American Art," in National Society for the Study of Education, Fortieth Yearbook, *Art in American Life and Education,* Bloomington, Ill., Public School Publishing Company, 1941, p. 32.

[20] R. L. Duffus, *The American Renaissance,* New York, Alfred A. Knopf, 1928, p. 14.

SOME BASIC PREMISES

The next advance in American art education will likely rest on greater harmony between what is educationally sound and what is consonant and feasible within the framework of American education as a whole. For this reason, a number of basic premises which grow out of the social setting are proposed and examined. The scope will be to determine what social foundations must underlie an art program for the present and the immediate future. The premises themselves are not offered in the spirit of finality. They are intended to serve as guideposts which, it is hoped, will point to the goals and clarify the methods which hold the best hope for art education in a democracy. Briefly, the premises which are proposed for analysis are these: (1) American education is unique; (2) art education contributes to growth and development; (3) art education implies effective social living.

FREEDOM OF EXPRESSION with exuberant enjoyment of medium and a feeling for form are evident in this still life by a young junior-high school boy (8th grade, Jackson, Miss.).

An elaboration of these basic premises should not only result in an understanding of their broad implications for the field but also clarify the functions of art as education for our time.

These functions have been variously interpreted at various periods, but they have always furnished the bases for the aims of art education. The evolution of such aims is presented in Chapter 2.

UNIQUENESS OF AMERICAN EDUCATION

Even a cursory review of the literature of education, and more especially that part which deals with trends in curriculum thinking, reveals some fundamental directions peculiar to our society and, consequently, to our education. Because we believe in democracy, the functions of our education have assumed a special, even though evolving, character. It follows that the relation between education in general and art education must grow out of these unique directions.

An examination of the beliefs inherent in American education raises these questions: How do they apply to, and how do they affect art education? Further inquiries could also deal with the question of whether art education is taking full advantage of the broad opportunities offered by such an educational philosophy, and what its orientation ought to be for the improvement and extension of the art program as it exists today.

Education and Democracy

Obviously, the first consideration deals with the relation of American education to democracy. Before attempting to establish this much-discussed relationship, it may be profitable to attempt a definition of democracy. One of the most lucid statements on what democracy is has been furnished by Bayles: *"It is a form of socio-governmental organization in which there is equality of freedom or opportunity to participate in making decisions on matters of group or individual concern, and equality of obligation or responsibility to abide by such decisions and carry them out."* [21] The inference of the definition seems to be that the sovereignty of the state is vested in the people and is exercised, either directly or indirectly, by means of representative institutions. In effect, the citizens of a democracy have a large share in its political life, and civic consciousness extends over the mass of the people. Two major characteristics of a democracy seem to be civil liberty and political liberty. The first implies equality before the law; the second, equality in the legal right to determine the state's will. Futhermore, it must follow that the operational aspects of democracy depend on the high motives, on the wisdom, and on the ideals of the people. Social democracy, as a corollary of political democracy, would then include the equalization of educational and other cultural opportunities.

In America, the basic characteristics of democracy have been at work since the early days of its founding. Its history reveals a continual struggle to extend and make more effective the sovereignty of the people in all areas of activity. Education has invariably been regarded as an

---

[21] Bayles, *op. cit.*, p. 33.

instrument for improving personal and group living and for the promotion of democratic ideals. The President's Commission on Higher Education expresses itself as follows:

Equal educational opportunity for all persons, to the maximum of their individual abilities and without regard to economic status, race, creed, color, sex, national origin or ancestry, is a major goal of American Democracy. Only an informed, thoughtful, tolerant people can maintain and develop free society.

Equal opportunity for education does not mean equal or identical education for all individuals. It means, rather, that education at all levels should be available to every qualified person.[22]

At this point, one may ask what concepts may be derived from a democratic philosophy with reference to education. They are clearly discerned, at least in spirit, in the literature of the field. In practice, they are becoming more evident with the years. Such concepts suggest both the scope of education and the method of achieving its goals. An analysis of this problem by Ziegfeld brings him to a conclusion that seems appropriate here. He states the functions which education assumes in a democratic society thus:

1. Every individual is to be regarded as an end and never as a means.
2. In this respect, all men are to stand equal.
3. The ultimate purpose of the democratic society is the liberation of the individual's potentialities for creative, intelligent, self-disciplined living.
4. There is an interdependent relationship between individual living and group living whereby each contributes to the richness and the vitality of the other and, conversely, neither can prosper without the other.
5. The individual and the group likewise bear a mutual responsibility each for the welfare of the other.[23]

Early American schools were not unlike those of Europe, which in turn had been influenced by the medieval system, itself founded on the Greek and Latin systems. However, even from the very outset American schools adopted aims peculiarly suited to the social needs of constituents and based on the central concepts upon which the nation had been founded. The Eleventh Yearbook of the Department of Supervisors and Directors of Instruction of the National Education Association declares that the early functions of American education were "promotion of democratic

[22] President's Commission on Higher Education, *Higher Education for American Democracy*, Washington, D.C., Government Printing Office, 1947, Vol. II, p. 3.

[23] Ernest Ziegfeld, *Art in the College Program of General Education*, New York, Teachers College, Columbia University, 1953, p. 40.

ideals; assimilation of aliens; and assurance of economic opportunity."[24] Those early functions have undergone changes in emphasis and in interpretation; actually they have been extended and broadened in scope. The most recent function of education is characterized by its emphasis upon the obligation to improve social living, and upon the imperative that it is an instrument for training in coöperative group living.

Reflected in the functions of education for democratic living one finds the major ideals of American education. A brief mention of these may throw light on the present problem.

Equal educational opportunity is a democratic goal which places the benefits of education at the disposal of every person, the sole limitation being the individual's capacity to avail himself of these opportunities. The prevalence of compulsory school attendance and the widespread advantages for education point to the fact that an educated citizenry is considered essential to the maintenance and advancement of democratic government. Local sovereignty in control embodies the privilege of determining policies and the responsibility of providing adequately for public education.

The fuller meaning of the functions and ideals of public education is perhaps best expressed in the "Children's Charter," which reads in part: *"For every child an education which, through the discovery and development of his individual abilities prepares him for life; and through training and vocational guidance prepares him for a living which will yield him the maximum of satisfaction."*[25]

Further light on the more recent concept of education in America is gleaned from the *Unique Function of Education in American Democracy.* While distinguishing between the intrinsic and the extrinsic features of education, its authors make it clear that the program of education is never completed and that the ideas of "completed formalism and perfect practice handed down by the past are ruled out." On the other hand they make it equally clear that while teachers are bound to preserve the heritage of past culture, they must be aware of advancing knowledge, "add to it, sift, and create as well as accumulate."[26]

[24] Department of Supervisors and Directors of Instruction, *Cooperation,* Eleventh Yearbook, Washington, D.C., National Education Association, 1938, p. 39.

[25] Educational Policies Commission, *The Structure and Administration of American Education,* Washington, D.C., National Education Association, 1938, p. viii.

[26] Educational Policies Commission, *The Unique Function of Education in American Democracy,* Washington, D.C., National Education Association, 1937, pp. 75–76.

Beyond the above statement on the general nature of education, the Commission offers a number of significant statements concerning the scope and character of education for the schools of America. The far-reaching impact of those statements compels the art educator to ponder them anew in our time:

1. Its [education's] source is not merely books and laws.
2. Education embraces knowledge, training, and aspiration.
3. Knowledge includes the practical arts, the social arts, the fine arts.
4. Knowledge alone is not enough—ethics is indispensable.
5. Education includes the training of the body and spirit.
6. Education fosters the social virtues by example.
7. Education is committed to the maintenance and improvement of American society.
8. The American society is democratic.
9. American society repudiates government by sheer force.
10. Democracy nourishes the free spirit of science.
11. Democracy rests on ideals, institutions, and economy of education.
12. The philosophy of democracy enters into the definition of education.
13. Education lays emphasis on its social obligations.
14. Education must serve an associational economy.
15. Education must prepare youth for associational life and activities.
16. Education must prepare citizens for participation in associational government.
17. Education must aid in upholding social values.
18. Education is distinguished from propaganda.[27]

Paralleling these pronouncements, in spirit and in substance, are the *Implications of Social Economic Goals for Education,* in which the characteristics desired for the individual American indicate that the public schools are regarded as agents of society for the attainment of the goals. These are some pointed suggestions for public education:

The school must increasingly become an agency for applying the best in the culture of the past to the solution of our civic, social, and economic problems.

Art is universal. Beauty appeals to everyone. The major purpose of art education is to help individuals in their capacity as consumers.

The school must seek to encourage a more balanced view, a more judicious balancing of course and consequence, a grasp of underlying relations.

---

[27] *Ibid.,* pp. 71–100.

The kind of education necessary is group experience in study, discussion, and activity supplemented by individual guidance.[28]

The recommendations particularly directed at public education are summarized thus: education must be universal (1) in its implications and applications, (2) in its materials and methods, and (3) in its aims and spirit.

It is clear then that the function of education in a democratic society goes beyond the narrow limits of subject-matter teaching and learning. It is a workshop for democratic ideals, a community in which the problems and aspirations of learners find coöperative outlets for independent thinking which may lead to creative solutions.

Therefore, the implementation of the program of the schools, including art education, in order that the functions of American education may be realized, becomes a chief concern for administrators and teachers.

[28] *Ibid.,* pp. 71–100.

PERSONAL SATISFACTION is conducive to emotional well-being. Personality development is significant in a democratic education (1st grade, Allentown, Pa.).

For the moment, it may be well to look at the specific *values* that determine the goals of American education. These are stated in *Education for All American Youth*, thus:

1. Development of those basic skills and that sturdy independence and initiative which will enable our citizens to attack the problems that face them and to press forward toward ever improving solutions.
2. The discovery and full development of all humane and constructive talents of each individual.
3. Emphasis on social responsibility and the cooperative skill necessary to the progressive improvement of social institutions.[29]

But since principles, to a large extent, control practice, the major values are interpreted as follows: "First, development and growth are continuous; second, behaviour is learned; third, learning and growth are stimulated by both security and adventure; fourth, each individual is unique; fifth, we learn what we live; sixth, we always learn a great deal and learn it rather permanently, by example."[30]

IMPLICATIONS FOR ART EDUCATION

A careful examination of the statements which have been chosen from the vast literature dealing with the social beliefs of American education should make it possible to arrive at a number of important meanings which apply equally to all areas of the curriculum. Such meanings may be expressed in the form of axioms, or truths, which should undergird a philosophy of art education based on relevant knowledge as well as on the character of the social setting.

Briefly, what has been discussed so far reveals that American education is based, among others, upon the following axioms:

1. We believe in education for all.
2. We believe in the worth of the individual.
3. We believe in a democratic society.
4. We believe in freedom.

---

[29] Educational Policies Commission, *Education for All American Youth*, Washington, D.C., National Education Association, 1948, pp. 1–8.

[30] *Ibid.*, p. 8.

When applied to art education for the boys and girls in the schools of the nation, the same axioms take on special meaning. They are paraphrased and discussed hereafter.

Art Education for All Children

The first axiom may be phrased to read as follows: *We believe in education for all, therefore, art education is for "all the children of all the people."*

This is perhaps the most unique and, at the same time, the most fundamental element in American education because upon it depends the maintenance of the democratic society. The ideal of a full educational opportunity for all children and youth with particular reference to art education means that every child in the nation's schools is afforded an art education that will help him to grow to the fullest possible stature —mentally, emotionally, creatively, aesthetically, socially, and physically.

A wider appreciation of the significance of growth and development is realized as one ponders how much boys and girls experience before reaching school and during the early years at school. Psychology further indicates that what is done, or is not done, for children at the beginning of their educational career is vastly more significant than what is done for them as they advance toward maturity. The education of the emotions, feelings, attitudes, habits, and a sharpening of the senses constitute the birthright of all American children. Therefore, art education in the schools, which by its very nature lends itself to the task, must become an instrument which will aid in the growth of young people. This is imperative, especially because the school years represent the age span most significant in the life of any being, and because art expression, in any form, derives from the urges, the emotional yearnings, and the creative potentialities with which all men are endowed in some degree. The ultimate harmonization of an individual rests on the proper nurture of these basic components of human personality and behavior.

The axiom, furthermore, holds certain meanings with regard to method and procedures. This fact can neither be overlooked nor overemphasized if teachers are to be concerned with the fostering of democratic living. Wherever this is the ideal, teacher-pupil planning, group dynamics, the thoughtful reaching of shared goals and values, and the climate of the classroom will need to be considered seriously. It will also follow that the selection of experiences, the pupil's relationship to the group, and all other interactions must come immediately to the fore and demand a teacher's considered attention and conviction. Details and the implementation of these problems are developed in later chapters of this text; for the present they must be accepted as fundamental to the proper functioning of the art program in the classroom.

A final important implication of this axiom seems to be that not the few but *all* the children are the concern. The ways of democracy must be learned by all because the business of living and the practice of democratic principles involved in it affect all social strata. The children from rural communities, those from industrial areas, those who live in cities, and those who live in suburban areas, all are the citizens of today and tomorrow. Art education must, therefore, have meaning for all of them and the art teacher must conceive of art as all-pervading rather than as a specialized form of education. The ultimate effectiveness and full impact of the aesthetic response will vary with each child, but the belief that art expression is for all must be central to the philosophy and practice of the arts in the schools. Conceived otherwise, art is only for an elite, for the privileged. If such were the case, art education would forfeit the right to social and financial support as well as to its claim as an agent for the growth and development of boys and girls.

Significance of the Individual

The second axiom may be stated as follows: *We believe in the worth of the individual; therefore, one of the major tasks of art education is to develop individual potentialities and unique personal expression.*

There seems to be a happy relationship between the principle of universality in American education and the universality of the artistic impulse. Upon closer examination the significance of this relationship is heightened by the fact that democracy and art expression derive from an identical urge: self-expression. Kenneth Holmes says quite appropriately that one of the aims of art education "is to encourage creative expression and at the same time to foster imagination. Art is a language and the natural birthright of a child, by which he can tell us about *the world around him,* and, of more importance, *the world within himself.*"[31]

Ziegfeld,[32] in discussing art experience in relation to general education, enumerates the benefits that may accrue to the individual who is exposed to art. Among them are these: art is a vehicle for aesthetic experience; art is essentially creative because it is based on personal factors; art activity refines emotional and intuitive perception; art activity

SOCIAL LIVING is fostered by art activities in which children share ideas, materials, plans, and the eventual success of the enterprise (3rd grade, Stratford, Conn.).

involves not only intelligence but imagination and capacity for experimentation. It is benefits such as these that lift an individual's life from a base existence to that of an enlightened man. Man is changed by aesthetic experiences, his horizons are broadened, and his spiritual resources are deepened. Man, through art, becomes highly sensitive and, perchance, may produce works of art for the enjoyment of others.

---

[31] Kenneth Holmes and Hugh Collison, *Child Art Grows Up,* New York and London, Studio Publications, 1952, p. 7.
[32] Ziegfeld, *op. cit.,* Chapter 4.

But the development of individuals in a democracy implies a twofold task. The first directs attention to all the children; the second directs attention to the maximum development of the potential leaders and creators of today and tomorrow. Herein lies a major difficulty as well as a great challenge: how to do an adequate piece of work for all amid the limitations of the typical educational system, and still be mindful of those individuals whose creative potential is high.

Persons who are currently teaching, as well as the young people who have recently come from high schools into art-teacher education, are aware of the difficulties of the present situation. They are aware of the heterogeneity of the pupils, of the broad tenor of the school program, of the large size of classes, and of the cocurricular demands made on teachers and on pupils. To all this there may be added the healthy yet complicating factor of communal interest and pride in the schools, coöperative curriculum planning, and the participation of lay people in the determination of educational policies. The schools, by far and large, are the people's schools, in which parents, teachers, administrators, social agencies, business, and industry are deeply concerned.

Recognizing the circumstances and even the added duties, still the twofold task must be accomplished. Tentatively, the problem may be answered by affirming that teachers of art must think of themselves primarily as *educators* whose particular contribution is the development of self-expression in all children to the end that, as individuals, they may assume an intelligent role in the emerging pattern of national culture. The question of special talent is significant and must be solved. However, it seems hardly defensible, in the typical classroom, to devote unwarranted attention to the *special* task. In Chapter 11, specific suggestions are made for the solution of this phase of art education. For an answer to the general task, it may be well to refer to the *Statement of Beliefs* of the National Art Education Association. In it the broad concepts of art education are stressed:

As an Art Teacher, I Believe That

Art experiences are essential to the fullest development of all people at all levels of growth because *they promote* self-realization of the whole individual by integrating his imaginative, creative, intellectual, emotional and manual capacities, and social maturity and responsibility through cultivating a deepened understanding of the problems, ideals, and goals of other individuals and social groups.

Art is especially well suited to such growth because it: encourages freedom of expression, emphasizes emotional and spiritual values, integrates all human capacities, and universalizes human expression.

Art instruction should encourage: exploration and experimentation in many media, sharpened perception of aesthetic qualities, increased art knowledge and skills, and the creative experience in significant activities, and the realization that art has its roots in everyday experience.

Art classes should be taught with full recognition that: all individuals are capable of expression in art, individuals vary markedly in motivations and capacities, and art is less a body of subject matter than a developmental activity.

Because art experiences are close to the core of individual and social development and because they pervade all phases of living, THE NATIONAL ART EDUCATION ASSOCIATION believes that *all* teachers should have basic training in art.[33]

Appropriate to this discussion is the section on art of the Report of the National Commission on Cooperative Curriculum Planning. It reflects the opinions of the then existing bodies of art educators and has this to say: "Unfortunately there has been a tendency on the part of some educators to limit the meaning of the 'esthetic experience' only to such activities as 'creative' drawing and painting, or those pursuits not closely related to the ordinary stuff of existence. This results in a separation of art from other daily activities and *smacks strongly of the Ivory Tower concept of art.*"[34]

It could be claimed by some that this is no longer the case, that much progress has been made toward bringing art to the masses, and similar other statements. Observations in the field indicate that, unfortunately, much of art education still belongs to the ivory-tower type.

The proper guidance of the instinctive urge to create is indeed ill served by traditional, preconceived, and specialized compartments of art. Moreover, if freedom of expression is assumed as a desirable method in the development of boys and girls, it is absurd to impose upon them

---

[33] National Art Education Association, *Statement of Beliefs,* Kutztown, Pa., the Association, 1949.

[34] National Commission on Cooperative Curriculum Planning, John DeBoer (ed.), *The Subject Fields in General Education,* New York, D. Appleton-Century Company, 1941, p. 188.

only certain modes of expression. They may or may not have meaning for them.

Art education in the schools must, furthermore, face the problems and share the responsibilities of general education together with other subject fields. This can be done only through a broad-based art program which will involve each individual. Meantime, it is plausible to search for adequate solutions to those problems that arise from the peculiar nature of art and the physical conditions under which it is administered. It also seems logical to think that the chief function of art in general education is not merely to uplift man but to make him an intelligent consumer of the common things of life. Public taste is shaped by the cultivation of the sensitiveness of each individual to sound design, color, and arrangement as well as through the understanding of a variety of art forms. It is safe to conclude that the aim of art in the schools is not the making of artists but rather personal expression, education in the use of art, and its appreciation. Through such education, the potential artist is usually discovered and further provisions may then be made for his further development.

Another important fact in connection with the education of individuals is that they differ considerably from one another. Perhaps the most significant contribution of psychology to the art of teaching is the vast amount of evidence it has presented on this very point. The value of the contribution is heightened in democratic education because a realization of differences resolves what seems paradoxical: equal opportunity for all and at the same time diverse guidance for each individual.

Boring and his associates state that "Individual differences in behavior are characteristic of all living organisms," then they show how important it is to realize this fact in education: "It has become increasingly evident in recent years that the more we know about individual differences in intelligence, aptitudes for particular tasks and in the ability to make good adjustments in social living, the better able we shall be to train and guide the individual in making the most of his physical and mental equipment."[35]

What is it that causes individuals to differ as they do? The answer is

[35] Edwin Boring, Herbert Langfeld, and Harry Weld, *Foundations of Psychology,* New York, John Wiley & Sons, Inc., 1948, Chapter 18.

indeed involved, but for the moment it may suffice to say that it involves all the elements of heredity and all the forces of environment. Biological inheritance determines the basic capacity for art expression, while environmental forces may cause the creative capacity either to develop or to lie dormant. Environmental forces are conditioning factors. The strange fact is that the effect of surroundings can act either way. A fine environment, if not properly utilized, may act negatively; a poor environment, or an environment generally judged not too conducive to the best aesthetic development, may only act as a temporary barrier. Given a favorable atmosphere, proper guidance, and encouragement, a child from a poor environment may develop to full expectation. A complete account of case studies along this line is recorded by Starch[36] and others, and may be worthy of investigation.

In addition to these broad aspects of differences there are more subtle ones which are of particular concern to art education. Lowenfeld[37] makes it clear that at the extremes there are two distinct perceptive types: the *visual* and the *haptic*. These basic distinctions affect an individual's work in both the graphic and the three-dimensional area and indicate a strong direction that needs to be borne in mind in planning activities for individual pupils as well as an entire program. It is, therefore, extremely important in art education, in spite of any existing difficulties, that the individual be magnified and developed along the lines of his major strengths. Associational life may then be stressed to effect a balance and bring about harmonization.

Social Relationships and Responsibilities

The third axiom may be expressed as follows: *We believe in a democratic society; therefore, art education must foster a wholesome relationship and a feeling of responsibility to the social group.*

Social living is one of the more recent emphases in American education and one that bids fair to have a profound effect on the generations that will feel its impact. Stated simply, social living refers to education for social integration. In a sense, it is education for what is real; for

---

[36] Daniel Starch, Hazel Stanton, and Wilhelmina Koerth, *Psychology in Education*, New York, D. Appleton-Century Company, 1941, Chapter 19.

[37] Viktor Lowenfeld, *The Nature of Creative Activity*, New York, Harcourt, Brace and Company, 1939, Chapters 4 and 5.

what people do, how they do it, why they do it; and for the ultimate good they all desire to achieve through shared enterprises.

Since this discussion deals with children and youth in the schools, there would seem to be little argument about the validity of an approach which utilizes the energies of all members of a group, points up the importance of all contributions, and still gives significance to individual gifts. As a tenet for art education, such a procedure increases in value because it emphasizes the great variety of aesthetic gifts which may be brought out of individual pupils as contributing members of a group. In a sense, this also seems worth while as democratic education.

A more detailed consideration of correlation in art, often erroneously referred to as "integrated" teaching, is reserved for later (Chapter 4). However, it seems important here to be cautioned about a fact which art education needs to recognize, namely that some pupils give evidence of superior talent, some are sensitive to form and color, others are meticulous performers but are not imaginative, a few have average talent, and still others are weak and emotionally maladjusted. But they are all in the art classes! What types of activities will bring out the best in each pupil? Here is a realistic question that confronts art teachers everywhere.

The crucial relationship of this axiom to democracy suggests that children must learn to live, play, and work harmoniously with their associates. They must learn to appreciate the work of others, and to participate in group undertakings by making whatever contributions they can. They must learn to share ideas, accept responsibility, examine the point of view of others, and evaluate fairly so that all may benefit by the experience. These early experiences may seem unimportant, yet they are preludes to the associational life which children will live as they grow into adulthood. Planning, making decisions, and allocating work according to ability and personal inclination are components of the democratic way. Leadership and followership are discovered in these processes, and through practice coöperative behavior is learned. While developing each child to his fullest capacity through art, and while encouraging individual differences of expression, how can art education socialize the child? One answer may be that group activities should become as much a part of the program as activities of an individual type. Those who look askance at correlated art activities may need to reappraise their position in the light of accomplishments in elementary education, or in the core curriculum of secondary education. Art that functions in the solution of problems which relate to life or to learning has value and deserves a definite place in the total program.

Additional significant questions follow. Is the art program differentiated, or are all pupils made to engage in the same outward experiences? Have pupils shared in planning? Are the activities suited to the level of the group? Are the activities valid as art or are they busy work? Answers to these questions may test whether or not the teaching-learning situation is meaningful or perfunctory, and whether it is teacher-dominated or coöperatively developed.

A balanced program implies not only variety of activities, some in the graphic and some in the three-dimensional area. It implies also that some will be purely developmental art experiences and some may be complementary to other learnings which stimulate conceptual growth and reflective thinking. If the child of today is to become the effective citizen of tomorrow, he must learn the ways of associational life as well as how to develop as an individual.

Importance of Freedom

The fourth axiom may be expressed as follows: *We believe in freedom; therefore, one of the tasks of art education is to foster freedom of expression.*

In the vital relationship between art and the way of life called democratic, freedom is the most essential element. It is central to the survival of all that democratic man believes, hopes for, and shares as common values. But, unfortunately, the very importance of freedom has caused many to overwork the phrase to the extent that it is abused and misused, as indicated hereafter.

The discussion on art in relation to the individual pointed out that it is only through freedom of expression that democracy can survive the most cunning sophistry of totalitarian thinking and triumph over it. However, the anxieties of the times and the misguided zeal for this foundation stone of democracy have tended to confuse freedom with unbridled and purposeless individualism. Eric Fromm distinguishes between the two types: positive and negative freedom. His elaboration makes it clear that as individuals think of their freedom as relating

FULFILLMENT. Buoyancy and the pleasure of accomplishment contribute to the healthy growth of boys and girls (6th grade, Pittsburgh, Pa.).

them constructively to their environment, or to the social group, they exercise positive freedom; when they construe freedom as setting them apart from the social group, they perpetrate negative freedom. Obviously, the latter is neither the intent nor the desirable goal of democratic society.

In art education for the children in the nation's schools this misconception needs pointing up and clearing up. In the name of freedom of expression, and largely due to lack of understanding of the true significance of freedom, a great deal of disservice has been rendered to children and to the growth of art. It should be clear to those who administer the art program that the function of all education is to harmonize individual and environment, individual and society. On this score Read quotes Freud as saying:

> The function of education . . . is to inhibit, forbid and suppress, and it has at all times carried out this function to admiration. But we have learnt from analysis that it is this very suppression of instincts that involves the danger of neurotic illness. . . . Education has therefore to steer its way between the Scylla of giving the instincts fair play and the Charybdis of frustrating them. Unless the problem is altogether insoluble, an optimum of education must be discoverable, which will do *the most good and the least harm*. It is a matter of finding out how much one may forbid, at which times, and by what methods.[38]

Holmes and Collison of the Leicester College of Art, England, are blunt on this point, perhaps due to their nearness to actual classroom situations. They say quite unequivocally: "Nor must it be thought that children should be allowed to do just what they please in the interest of freedom and imagination, with no guidance or discipline. We are aware that this may be heresy to some."[39] Indeed it would be heresy if the authors did not clarify what they have in mind, and did not indicate the way they move between Freud's Scylla and Charybdis.

In principle, American education believes in freedom of choice among several possible options. It is conceivable that boys and girls, through guided and sympathetic education, may learn to exercise the principle as basic to all activities in life. Ziegfeld says in regard to this problem: "The most common misconception has been that freedom is achieved to

---

[38] Herbert Read, *Art and Society*, New York, The Macmillan Company, 1937, p. 220.
[39] Holmes and Collison, *op. cit.*, p. 8.

the extent that the restraints of the physical and social environment are removed—an idea of freedom *from* the environment. The fallacy of this concept becomes obvious when it is pushed to the extreme, for the individual who is completely freed from his environment is separated from it and when this happens he ceases to exist."[40]

The creation of works of art, or their appreciation, depends quite as much on firsthand contacts and experiences of the past as they do on one's capacity to feel or sense those same experiences. Good art results from personal imagination guided by newly realized insights and concepts of form; it never is the result of uncontrolled action. Therefore, meaningless manipulation or aimless action has little relationship to art. The conclusion, therefore, is that art education must develop in growing boys and girls a concept of freedom consistent with thoughtful activity. Such activity will then result in a limitation of one's freedom and in qualitative action.

To summarize, the implications of the first premise may be restated thus: art as education, to be most effective and to serve its proper ends, must strive to harmonize with the general philosophy of democratic education. Furthermore, as the uniqueness of American education is understood, four elements become significant: the individual, society, freedom, and equality of opportunity.

CONTRIBUTION OF THE ARTS TO GROWTH AND DEVELOPMENT

Implicit in the second basic premise, and one that merits serious consideration, is that art education is not a pastime. It is a serious educational undertaking, with special functions to perform, much as other subjects and other activities in the school curriculum. To make clear the specific contributions of the program in art, it is well to examine it from at least two points of view—first, the universality of the creative impulse; second, its relation to the nature and function of art itself.

Universality of the Creative Impulse

Philosophy and psychology have dealt and continue to deal with this subject in a scientific manner. But they have done so in terms that are not always easily related to school situations. Only occasionally, although

---

[40] Ernest Ziegfeld, "Human Values in a Democracy," in *Art and Human Values,* 1953 Yearbook, Kutztown, Pa., National Art Education Association, 1953, p. 11.

more frequently in recent years, have art teachers been able to study the essential findings or conclusions of psychology in a form that readily points to general classroom conditions. By way of stimulation, then, and without pretense of exhausting either of the fields, it may be profitable to glance at both psychology and philosophy to establish a basis for the understanding of the role of art teaching and of art expression to personal growth.

The first essential fact is that what is called the artistic impulse is universal. Read puts it this way: "For common sense as well as psychology tells us that the aesthetic impulses which are the normal possession of children, and which children all over the world and throughout all time have possessed in striking uniformity, are merely dormant in so-called educated people."[41] Another affirmation of this fact is offered by Murphy: "We know from watching children in progressive schools that the desire to create must be almost universal and that almost everyone has some measure of originality which stems from his fresh perception of life and experience, and from the uniqueness of his own fantasy when he is free to share it."[42]

If one proceeds to analyze the implications of the universal nature of the art impulse as reported above, it will be possible to gain a fairly clear concept of how to implement art programs in harmony with school situations.

First of all, it will be sensed that all pupils are potential creators, but in varying degrees and in varying modes. Nevertheless, they are all capable and eager to express themselves if given the chance, proper motivation, and a friendly atmosphere. The creative urge is in fact so strong a factor in the total growth of individuals that, when given freedom for expression, it furnishes answers to the partial solution of many other problems which individuals seem to face: fear, lack of confidence, lack of individuality.

Lowenfeld,[43] Naumburg,[44] and other modern writers on psychology as

---

[41] Read, op. cit., p. 223.

[42] Gardner Murphy, Personality, A Biosocial Approach to Origins and Structure, New York, Harper & Brothers, 1937, p. 453.

[43] Viktor Lowenfeld, Creative and Mental Growth, rev. ed., New York, The Macmillan Company, 1952, pp. 60, 77, 188.

[44] Margaret Naumburg, The Art of the Schizophrenic, New York, Grune and Stratton, Inc., 1950, pp. 3–34.

44   it relates to art point to a large number of cases, ordinarily referred to as emotionally blocked, frustrated, maladjusted, or retarded, for whom art expression has furnished the clue and has been a partial cure. The lack of opportunity for artistic outlet sows seeds antithetical to what education purportedly wishes to cultivate. The deep-seated reasons for this devastating fact may be attributed to all situations which ignore the structure of every individual's emotional nature and the will to express oneself.

Psychology and experimental education explain, as far as it is possible to explain at present, the nature of the creative impulse. It is generated in the innermost recesses of human consciousness (the id); it is restrained by the experiences of life, the moral code of society, the mystical and material beliefs and acceptances of society (the ego); finally, it is refined and given expression in an idealized form (the superego). To put it more simply: there is within each individual a deep well of chaotic, powerful, and fantastic force that needs outlet and guidance.

It is this "deep well," to use Read's words, that needs to be tapped, that needs opportunity for fulfillment, through sympathetic understanding, cultivation, and occasional redirection.

But the will and wish to express oneself have other implications which must be heeded if art education is to be generally successful. If the education of the instincts is one of the serious tasks of art teaching at all levels, the uniqueness of American education suggests that the problem must be equated in terms of the greatest good to the greatest number. Read recognizes this problem in discussing the education of the gifted. Yet it seems to apply even at this point. He says: "If ideally the number of those who are to be trained as artists should be restricted, on the other hand the number of those to be trained in the appreciation of art should be vastly increased; indeed no person should be exempt from such training except those hopelessly disqualified by stupidity or mental atrophy."[45]

This universal impulse seeks expression for a number of reasons, and is set into motion by various forces which are a part of the individual's reaction to the external world. Regardless of the reasons or the reactions,

---

[45] Read, *op. cit.*, p. 223.

art education is one vehicle through which all children may discover
themselves, if the impulse is wisely guided.

The Functions of Art as Education

Irwin Edman, writing about art as education, says: "I am submitting
the hypothesis that art, or the arts, adequately taught, are perhaps in
our day the most central and important means of education."[46] Upon
further reading, one finds the following as components of Edman's
concept of the functions of art: art is education in and for the senses;
art educates the sense of form; art is the teaching to the inexperienced
of the habits of attention, discrimination, and exactitude; art is the education of the emotions; the arts are a kind of therapy and, at the same
time, a kind of fulfillment; art is escape, in the sense that it liberates
the individual from the rigidity and regimentation of society.

It may be profitable to ponder the words of this eminent contemporary
philosopher and teacher in an attempt to arrive at a cognition of what
art in the schools should be doing for young people.

Refinement of the Senses. The first of Edman's reminders is that art is
education which can be aimed at the senses. He is talking, frankly, about
the physical senses, sight, sound, hearing, touch, and smell, but with a
heightened meaning. He implies sensitiveness or awareness to sound,
color, movement, texture, and the like. It is this awareness of qualities that
distinguishes mere looking from "seeing," mere hearing from "listening,"
mere touching an object from registering its "feel" (smoothness, rough-
ness, coarseness, fineness). Awareness, in the fullest sense, is what is generally called appreciation. As such it becomes a primary function of art as
education, and is closely related to, if not identical with, perceptual
growth.

But Edman goes beyond the senses and speaks of art as education in
the sense of *form.* Here one could easily become involved in the meaning of the term "form." Let it simply mean the felt objectification of an
idea, which, incidentally, no two persons will sense in the same manner. Let it mean what the individual *perceives* with the inner eye, so

---

[46] Irwin Edman, "Art as Education," in *Art Education Today,* New York, Teachers
College, Columbia University, 1951–1952, pp. 11–18.

46 to speak. Then it may be seen that "form" implies conceptualization and interpretation in terms of line, form, color, texture, sound, or movement. Interestingly enough, Edman indicates that there are many angles to be pointed out to the inexperienced so that this perception of form

HUMAN NEEDS. The problem of human needs was perhaps the earliest motivation for creative activity. Art education continues to recognize the necessity of creating beautiful as well as useful things (Richmond, Va.).

may become "second nature and first rate delight."[47] Not all art experiences are play; some of them are painful, some of them depend on endurance, on mastery, or on plain hard work. These elements of the experience, in turn, become parts of a pupil's growth.

Education of the Emotions. The education of the emotions is the next function of art. Some reference has already been made to this important aspect, but it deserves fuller development. Art is not an affair of idle moments; indeed, its activities encompass all of life. They involve

---

[47] *Ibid.*, p. 13.

the individual and society through all the inevitable complications of a machine age, a much-shrunken world, global thinking, planned living, and atomic power. The present world is a complex one in which the individual is likely to be submerged. It is true that it is possible to point with pride to "modern" housing, new and more efficient machinery, public parks and playgrounds, community centers, and other types of quasi-public institutions. All these are intended to make life more pleasant, to lengthen its span, to lessen its strain, to supply leisure-time recreational opportunities, and in general to make life and living more bearable.

But although all these attempts are well-intentioned and in the proper direction, and although in a measure they aid toward the attainment of vast social goals, they nevertheless seem feeble in the face of the gigantic task of social integration. One of the chief obstacles to the achievement of that goal is lack of opportunities for education of the emotions.

The significant role of feelings and emotions in the learning situation and in patterning the behavior of individuals is such that art teachers must strive to understand it. Since the present concern is with utilization of the emotions, it may not be amiss to call attention to their nature and functions. In the first place, it should be remembered that the emotions are useful to man if he is in control of them. But they are injurious to him if he is unable to control them, as in fear, anger, and similar other manifestations. Second, emotions can be altered by learning; but uncontrolled, they interfere with learning and are productive of behavior which society regards as inappropriate and harmful.

Hunt, reflecting the generally cautious attitude of most psychologists, points out that "They [emotions and feelings] range from the milder feelings which we call pleasantness and unpleasantness to stronger emotions like fear and anger. We do not know what the exact relationship may be between the *affective* states, as pleasantness and unpleasantness are called, and the stronger emotions, but this we do know: they both involve general reaction attitudes of the organism toward something in its environment."[48]

Hence, one is reminded that reaction infers stimulation, and that the

---

[48] William A. Hunt, "Feelings and Emotions," in Boring, Langfeld, and Weld, *op. cit.*, p. 90.

kind of stimulation used can be an effective means at the disposal of teachers. Again one is reminded of the fact that the whole biological being is involved in the reaction which causes an emotional manifestation. More than the so-called physical senses are involved; these often are the external signs which indicate the internal reactions. But the internal reactions involve the complex autonomic nervous system and all its functions, sympathetic and parasympathetic. For example, unpleasantness may be followed by fear or anger, pleasantness by joy or even mirth. In any case, an emotion is a complete experience (see Chapter 4) and, therefore, very significant in the teaching-learning situation. What is called *hedonic tone* may determine the rapport between teacher and pupils, motivations, and, consequently, behavior.

In this discussion, it is interesting to note that although the emotions are of concern to all education and all of life, some recent psychologists have attempted to identify *aesthetic* emotions. Lund [49] admits that the determination of the qualities that make an emotion aesthetic are not adequate, even though they exist. Munro,[50] on the other hand, has assembled an impressive bibliography of experimental studies dealing with aspects of the aesthetic, including reactions and emotions. The latter may shed light on the problem.

The arts offer a sense of adequacy which in turn makes the individual capable of coping with the problems of living even in a complicated society. Adults have learned, with varying degrees of success, how to get along. But children and young people are the ready prey of confusion and frustration because they must grow simultaneously in many directions in addition to adjusting themselves to a world designed by and for adults. What follows is a significant statement that reaffirms the need for strengthening the individual through emotional development: "These are confusing times. The daily headlines, evidence of fear and anxiety in high places, fill us with these same feelings of fear and anxiety."[51]

---

[49] Frederick Lund, *Emotions, Their Psychological, Physiological and Educative Implications,* New York, The Ronald Press, 1939, Chapter II, pp. 49–51.

[50] Thomas Munro (ed.), National Society for the Study of Education, Fortieth Yearbook, *Art in American Life and Education,* Bloomington, Ill., Public School Publishing Company, 1941, Section II.

[51] Association for Supervision and Curriculum Development, *Growing Up in an Anxious Age,* 1952 Yearbook, Washington, D.C., National Education Association, 1952, pp. 4–5.

It may be contended that creation is often promotive of anxieties and frustrations. But in human experience, in all fields of serious endeavor, and more so in the arts, anxieties are preludes to fulfillment and satisfaction. Therefore, one answer to the dilemma of the age may be found in the cultivation of the emotional energies and drives common to most individuals. The seriousness of the task suggests once more that teaching and learning in art education must be of a reflective kind in order that pupils may look upon their anxieties not as insurmountable barriers but as problems which can be and must be solved. Fear can be a wholesome stimulus when regarded as a challenge; frustrations, likewise, are banished by the success which inevitably attends effective thinking and acting upon problems.

Methods of teaching, therefore, would also seem to require more than ordinary concern. Above all, they must be evocative in order that originality of solutions and freshness of expression may result. Whatever the method, whatever the activities, whatever the medium, a paramount function of art education is to provide stimulating opportunities through which pupils will express themselves in the pursuit of personal security, self-confidence, and eventual integration.

Art activities of many types are the natural vehicles for the expression of the feelings and the emotions of the individual. Properly guided and understood, such activities become dynamic and energizing. Repressed or unheeded, they become hindrances to growth. Hunt furnishes a glimpse into the tremendous importance of the emotions when he states: "Few areas of human experience and behavior are as vital and interesting to the individual as his feelings and emotions. They occur in situations of special importance to him, when his interest is aroused, his attention held, and his energy increased and directed toward a definite goal."[52]

Art as Therapy and Fulfillment. The arts, as interpreted by Edman, are a kind of therapy and, at the same time, a kind of fulfillment. The simple completion of an ordinary task gives one a feeling of relief and a sense of achievement. The ego experiences satisfaction in having accomplished what was required, but even greater satisfaction in having had the capacity to achieve it. How much pleasure the artist, young or

---

[52] Hunt, *op. cit.*, p. 90.

old, must experience at being able to say: "This is my own," or "I have done it!" Those who have achieved, and art teachers in particular, will agree that such feeling defies description. The effect on the whole being is equally indescribable. In young people, who have yet to master their emotions, extra buoyancy, added vigor, and exuberant mental health become very obvious signs. The joy of the accomplishment of a work of art thus becomes what psychology calls a *conscious experience*.

The therapeutic effect on the individual may be interpreted in terms of the good feeling and the new courage. The fulfillment may be interpreted in terms of having mastered, objectified, communicated an idea or even a dream. Again, referring to the anxious age in which men live, it is imperative that art education strive to affirm the good and the true in life. And while these are anxious times, they are also times replete with possibilities and opportunities for new contributions to the achievement of the highest goals of man and society.

Art as Liberation. Lastly, art may be construed as escape. Edman emphasizes that he is using the term "not in the usual ivory tower sense" but rather as meaning liberation. Liberation from what? From the too-well-ordered and highly mechanized life that people must live. Liberation from fallacious social restraints and, finally, liberation from the regimentation of everyday pursuits. Children and young people, infinitely more than grown-ups, feel the frustrations of the adults' world; hence they seek and welcome avenues which may lead them to freedom through expression. Thomas Jefferson is credited with the statement: "I have sworn upon the altar of God eternal hostility against every form of tyranny over the mind of man." Perhaps the statement is a major clue to the method needed in art education in the schools of America. In it one also discerns the danger of interference with expression. For practical purposes, it may be stated that art education for growth and development must recognize that one of its functions is to make possible the liberation of the creative powers of pupils. In this instance, the pupil who enters the portals of the schools is, in a very real sense, the citizen of a democracy. His thinking, his actions, his ideals, and his values and purposes are being formed even now. It is the pupil of today that shall uphold and advance the cultural heritage of the nation. And, more significantly, preserve for himself and for future generations the democratic institutions which will continue to guarantee an opportunity for a universal education which is concerned with maximum development in an atmosphere of freedom.

ART EDUCATION AND SOCIAL LIVING

Art and Civilization

The third basic premise is that art education for a democratic society implies harmonious social living. The history of civilization, and by that is meant *all* civilization, not simply the western version, owes a great debt to the artist, be he bushman, Negro, cave dweller, Egyptian, Greek, Roman, or early American. Regardless of origin or geographic environment, artists have left, leave now, and always will leave examples of their work which will make the writing of history possible.

Temple and tomb, utensil and weapon, costume and house, a carving on stone or a painting on a wall, a mystical symbol or a utilitarian tool, comprise the "sacred ruins." It is from these that the story of the struggles and the achievements, the joys and the sorrows, the play and the worship of man, are reconstructed. Read comments on this point thus: "No kind of human activity is so permanent as the plastic arts, and nothing that survives from the past is so valuable as a clue to the history of civilization."[53]

Understanding Cultural Patterns

The value of the study of history, and of art history in particular, is that it shows quite clearly the movement and rhythm of cultural patterns. Such study points out the direction that each pattern takes. It indicates why the spirit of Gothic art, for example, differs from the spirit of Renaissance art or Egyptian art, or, for that matter, from the art of any other period or culture. Thus the individuality of patterns and the achievements of each are properly appraised, understood, and appreciated. Art appreciation, beyond its value as general education, throws light on the relation of the artist to his society. Ziegfeld gives an indication of what is here intimated when he says: "One of the most striking examples of this variation [of patterns] may be found in a comparison of the function of the arts in Soviet Russia with the role which they [the arts] played in medieval Europe. In the latter, artistic expression

[53] Read, *op. cit.*, p. 164.

resulted largely from religious motivation, whereas in the former it is dominated by a political and economic idealogy, and religion is not recognized as a valid area of experience."[54]

Both Dewey and Read, using the same technic, that of assaying certain periods of art history, arrive at similar conclusions. Among them are the universality of the art impulse, the difference in the character of each culture, the nature of symbols and forms, and the functions of art in each of the societies explored. Dewey says in this respect: "But the arts by which primitive folk commemorated and transmitted their customs and institutions, arts that were commercial, are the sources out of which all fine arts have developed." And then again: "Each of these communal modes of activity united the practical, the social and the educative in an integrated whole having aesthetic form."[55] A contemporary writer, Mumford, states quite appropriately that "Man truly lives only to the extent that he transforms and creates out of the raw materials of life a world whose meanings and values outlast his original experience and its limitations."[56]

A recent unfortunate tendency in the field of art education indicates a direction away from what may be termed "practical," or "useful," or "related" in the resulting work of children. The fallacy of such a position is attested not only by history and philosophy but by the uniqueness of American education which has just been discussed. It is quite difficult to determine whether a child gets his full measure of satisfaction and self-expression by creating a painting, by collaborating on a mural, or by building a model of a settler's cabin. The strained effort to be "pure" is in reality depriving growing boys and girls of many experiences through which they might find themselves, and quite naturally at that. The insecurity and futility which children experience in being unable to do acceptable work in the "fine" arts might well be compensated by the success and pleasure which they may achieve along other creative avenues.

D'Amico takes this position when he proposes an art program which envisions the child as potter, the child as stage artist, the child as graphic artist, the child as sculptor, the child as muralist. The question,

---

[54] Ziegfeld, *op. cit.*, p. 95.
[55] Dewey, *op. cit.*, p. 327.
[56] Lewis Mumford, *Art and Technics,* New York, Columbia University Press, 1953, p. 141.

therefore, is not of making art experience subservient to other human activities but rather of recognizing the creative capacity of the individual child, no matter what its mode, and guiding it in the direction that assures fullest development for him. D'Amico says: "The sensitive art teacher guides the child into experiences most suited to his ability and most satisfying to his individual concepts at a rate of learning natural to him."[57] It seems logical to conclude that when the art activity is meaningful to the child, it will develop wholesome outlooks in him and lead him to personal and social integration.

There is no intention here of suggesting that art should be subservient to any other discipline or any other form of expression. Art has its own contributions to make, as has been pointed out; art has its own *raison d'être*. That might suffice, but the thesis thus far maintained indicates that art as general education and as a means of integration calls for a tangible relationship to the world in which boys and girls live. It would appear more cogent to think that art activity is motivated by the social milieu rather than adorning it; that art, in return, vitalizes social living and makes it more and more in its own image.

Art and Human Needs

There is another point of view, just as tenable, namely, that art arises from the needs of humankind. It could very well be assumed, as it must be in many instances, that the supreme human need is for expression, for creation, for identification, and for release. Surely this is a fundamental need which can be largely supplied by picture making, carving, shaping, and building activities for their own sake in every classroom.

However, human needs are of two general types: there are emotional needs which are nonmaterial, and then there are material needs. To this latter category belong such earthy things as food, clothing, and shelter and all derivations and extensions which one might wish to add to those three. Melvin Haggerty pointed out a very significant fact when he stated that "Art as cult may be a hindrance rather than an aid to art as a way of life, and it clearly seems to be so in many cases. The teacher's

---

[57] Victor D'Amico, "Are We Jeopardizing the Child's Creative Growth?" *The Art Education Bulletin,* April, 1953, p. 1.

54 art must be that of the broad and crowded avenues of life, the home,
the factory and the market place. It is this conception that must be clarified and dramatized in concrete ways, if art is to take its place in the
schools as a major and vital instrument of cultural education."[58]

Edwin Ziegfeld,[59] writing about his own experience with the Owatonna
Art Project, reaffirms this position in a detailed discussion of what constitutes a functional basis for art education. The inferences of Ziegfeld's
statement, as well as the entire contents of *Art Today*,[60] attest to this
widely held and extremely practical point of view. Its chief concern is
with activities that revolve around such areas of living as the home, the
community, religion, industry, recreation, the individual, and other areas
that are integral with life. This point of view vitalizes art creation and
at the same time gives boys and girls unbounded opportunity for experiences that lead to personal growth and development in all their
facets.

Social Goals and Values

To assume that the transfer of individually reached goals and values
to the social group is automatic would be a gross misconception. Aside
from the relatedness of art activities to life, there is an extremely important fact that one dares not overlook, namely, the recognition of
group goals and values. How will children come to recognize common
goals and shared values unless they are permitted to practice the ways
of democracy? Such valuable educational practices as core teaching and
the philosophy of integration are discussed and analyzed fully in a later
chapter, where the advantages of such procedures are presented. For
the moment, however, it may be safe to state that art activities which
grow out of the problems of group education are quite likely to parallel
those situations from which arise the values and goals of American life
and education.

To quote Read again: "The notion of an art, then, divorced from the

[58] Melvin Haggerty, *Art as a Way of Life*, Minneapolis: University of Minnesota Press,
1935, p. 43.

[59] Edwin Ziegfeld, "Developing a Functional Program of Art Education," in *Enriching
the Curriculum of the Elementary School Child*, 18th Yearbook, Washington, Department
of Elementary School Principals, National Education Association, 1939, pp. 284–295.

[60] Ray Faulkner, Edwin Ziegfeld, and Gerald Hill, *Art Today*, New York, Henry Holt
and Company, 1956.

general process of social development, is an illusion, and since the artist cannot escape the transformation of life which is always in progress, he had better take stock of his position and play his part in the process. If he believes in the reality and importance of the artistic activity in itself, he must see that activity is integrated with other social activities which constitute the active totality of social development."[61]

The implications for art education in the schools are indeed very clear. Teaching technics may change; methods may evolve; new tools and materials may be developed and new uses found. The art program itself may be adapted to harmonize with prevalent philosophy, yet a fact that must be generally accepted is that human values in a democracy have an unquestioned and a large place. Self-acceptance, integrity, pride, individuality, personal security, creative autonomy, and all the other attributes of the integrated personality are soon lost in the face of mechanization, mass production, mass media, and, more lately, mass education. These are the by-products of industrial growth and economic development in which one may take just pride, yet they need the antidotes suggested above in order to achieve a balanced view and sound social living.

A most significant and exhaustive statement on this subject is presented by Feldman[62] in a recent yearbook of the National Art Education Association. It indicates that there are at least two areas of concern in this respect: the development of individual values and the development of social values. Art functions in the first area primarily as the truest expression of individual values. It functions as a means of revelation of the world and the self; it affords a means for the development of personal security; and finally, it functions as a perfect vehicle for the development of integrity.

However, it must be recognized that individuals do not live unto themselves. They are part of a social group, hence the importance of group values. Here again it is safe to suggest that art is a vehicle for the communication of those values; that art activity and freedom of expression are interrelated. Art can and does express individual relationships, but art expresses social relationships as well.

---

[61] Read, *op. cit.*, p. 255.
[62] Edmund Feldman, "Art as the Expression of Individual Values," in *Art and Human Values*, 1953 Yearbook, Kutztown, Pa., National Art Education Association, 1953, pp. 15–25.

In the last analysis, individual and social goals and values find their way into the totality of a culture, and it is there that creative action and creative teaching find their acid test.

A Synthesis

Now it seems reasonable to review the major characteristics of the philosophy of art education which has been projected and partially supported. They appear to be these:

1. Art is action. Action in and of itself may be meaningless; but when it is the result of sound conceptualization and is organically linked to all the doing and undergoing of an experience, it becomes meaningful. It is meaningful because it will have involved the creator, body and soul, as it were.

2. Art and its fullest development are encouraged or delimited by the social setting to which they are related. American democracy, if viewed as a social philosophy, makes available the opportunities of education to all who can profit by it. Meantime, the ways of democracy have direct implications for the working out of the art program in the classroom. Specifically, art education prizes the individual, recognizes individual responsibility to the group, fosters freedom of expression, and guides growth and development by methods and procedures which are in harmony with the beliefs of democratic society.

3. The creative impulse is recognized as a universal human trait. Properly guided and nurtured, it is a vehicle for the development of reflective thinking and doing. Emotional satisfactions and balance, the fulfillment of individual goals, and eventual integration are the desirable ends that may be achieved through creative activity. Art education cannot claim to do this alone, yet by its very nature it is a recognized, powerful instrument for the accomplishment of these educational ends.

4. Art education can be a socializing medium. This is true of all creative education. The history of art and the study of cultural patterns show that the rituals, play, and institutions of man reflect his creative endeavors. The needs of life, whether material or emotional, as well as the whole environment, are the subject matter of art. The artist, young or old, is an interpreter. Thus society is improved and life is enhanced by the work of the creative thinker and doer.

But it should be crystal clear that, to realize fully the unique functions of education in American democracy, to utilize the intrinsic values of art for growth and development, and to attain optimum social and individual integration, the art program must recognize the totality of the task rather than any one of its facets to the exclusion of the others.

In practice, the great need is for an evolving philosophy, one that shares the broad goals of society while transforming and renewing itself. When an individual sets his own limits in consonance with social values, then it may be said that proper interaction has been achieved. This is, in a sense, the democratic pattern. Ziegfeld summarizes the matter by saying: "The art of a democratic society is the positive affirmation of the creative spirit of man and the human values by which he lives."[63] Indeed, the ultimate test of the soundness of a philosophy of art education for the nation's schools is in terms of the appreciations, the aesthetic standards, and the general values which are developed and accepted in the process of creating. Finally, the capacity to conceptualize, the habit of refined thinking, and the growth in perceptive capacity which art can inspire may harmonize boys and girls as persons as well as with the social group. Thus, art education will have served its own ends as well as the broader goals of a democratic society.

SUMMARY

In this chapter an effort has been made to lead the reader to think about the many aspects which together may form a basis, or philosophy, for art education in the schools of our time. The nature of art, of experience, of creative expression, of integration, and other foundational matters have been reviewed as background for the determination of reasons why art is taught in the schools. Such a review furnishes a partial background of pertinent knowledge for the further study of the problems of art education. It has been concluded that *art as education* is not a fringe subject, a dispensable area, but one which is integral with all education.

This point of view is supported and related to the fundamental beliefs of American democracy. The direct bearing of those beliefs on education include the following: education is for all individuals, to the extent

---

[63] Ernest Ziegfeld, *op. cit.*, p. 122.

to which they can avail themselves of it; the worth of the individual and, therefore, his optimum development are central; associational life is basic to the common welfare; maximum freedom, within the limitations agreed upon by society, is paramount. Interpreted in relation to art education, these beliefs indicate that art education is for all and not a privileged few; that individual expression and individual development are deemed highly significant; that relationships and responsibilities to the social group must be recognized. The implications for the conduct of teaching in the classroom seem to indicate that freedom of expression rather than formalism and dictation is most conducive for the achievement of maximum growth for the individual pupil and his harmonization to the group. Carried to their proper conclusion, the implications have far-reaching effects on the growth and development of children and youth, indicate the nature of method, and demonstrate their bearing on the perpetuation of democratic ideals.

In this chapter it has also been pointed out that the creative impulse is universal. As such, creative expression is viewed as a necessary vehicle for the achievement of desirable educational ends. Art then becomes a means to cultivate and refine the senses, to foster the education of the emotions, to lead to personal fulfillment and, consequently, to the liberation of the creative spirit of man. Furthermore, the art experience has been shown to be an organic process which involves perception, insights, concepts, and appreciations. Through action or reaction, through shaping the media of expression, the creator or appreciator expresses himself. These characteristics of an art experience lead to integration. The latter is the central purpose of all education.

A study of history shows that man has always expressed himself creatively. His worship, his work, his play, his communal life, and all other achievements have involved art in some form. Upon this historic foundation, art education claims its place in the scheme of education for successful living. Further, basic human needs, which have remained constant throughout the history of civilization, are satisfied through the work of creative genius, whether in art or other fields of endeavor. Utensils, weapons, temples, tombs, and other forms of art which satisfy human needs are the gifts of creative minds and hands.

Lastly, it has been stressed that the elements which lead to a tenable philosophy of art education must recognize the value of pertinent knowledge of art and education, the conditions, the goals, and the values of the social setting, the specific contributions which art can make to education, and the significance of art experience in effective social living.

For Discussion and Activity

1. What forces, beyond education itself, often affect the art program? Apply to a typical local situation.
2. Build the argument for art education in answer to a Superintendent's question.
3. What is the meaning of the terms *fulfillment* and *liberation* in connection with art education? Be specific in terms of children.
4. Do you believe that art education should be limited to those who show talent? Depending on your answer, present evidences for your position.
5. In what specific ways is art education allied to the democratic way of life? How does art sustain democratic living?
6. Visit an exhibition and make your personal analysis of the work you see. How do the artists seem to differ among themselves?
7. Examine a group of children's paintings and describe what seem to be differences among the young artists as evidenced by their creations.
8. In what respects does art education contribute to social living? Cite situations in which this phase of development could be promoted through art education.
9. What does the history of man, and of art especially, indicate that is of value to the art educator?
10. How can art education help children establish personal values and goals? How can art make them conscious of group values and goals?

For Further Reading

Cane, Florence, *The Artist in Each of Us,* New York, Pantheon Books, Inc., 1951, Chapters III and XXIV.

Gotshalk, D. W., *Art and the Social Order,* Chicago, University of Chicago Press, 1947, Chapters IX and X.

Harrison, Elizabeth, *Self-Expression Through Art,* Toronto, W. J. Gage and Company, Ltd., 1951, Part I.

Keiler, Manfred L., *Art in the Schoolroom,* Lincoln, University of Nebraska Press, 1951, Chapter I.

Logan, Frederick M., *Growth of Art in American Schools,* New York, Harper & Brothers, 1954, Chapters I and II.

Lowenfeld, Viktor, *Creative and Mental Growth,* rev. ed., New York, The Macmillan Company, 1952, Chapter I.

60   McDonald, Rosabel, *Art as Education,* New York, Henry Holt and Company, 1941, Chapter I.

Mendelowitz, Daniel M., *Children Are Artists,* Stanford, Stanford University Press, 1954, Chapter I.

Read, Herbert, *Education Through Art,* 2nd ed., New York, Pantheon Books,ʹ Inc., 1945, Chapters I and II.

Shultz, Harold, and Shores, Arlan, *Art in the Elementary School,* Urbana, University of Illinois Press, 1948, Chapter II.

Whitford, William G., *An Introduction to Art Education,* rev. ed., New York, D. Appleton-Century Company, 1937, Chapters I and IV.

Winslow, Leon L., *The Integrated School Art Program,* New York, McGraw-Hill Book Company, 1949, Chapter I.

Ziegfeld, Ernest (ed.), "Human Values in a Democracy," in *Art and Human Values,* 1953 Yearbook, Kutztown, Pa., National Art Education Association, 1953, Chapters I and IV.

2

EVOLUTION OF CONCEPTS

> A major premise now established, is that a true grasp of
> reality requires the widest possible envelopment of past—
> leading into present with no breaks to mar the continuity
> that is the prime characteristic of being and becoming.
>
> Richard Guggenheimer,
> *Creative Vision*

HISTORY OF ART EDUCATION

THE FUNCTION OF HISTORY IS TO GIVE PERSPECTIVE. IF KNOWING THE PAST
can help one to solve contemporary problems, the purpose of history is
fulfilled. Without perspective, wasted effort and many illusions are likely
to impede progress.

Professional art educators have always sought to improve art instruction on the basis of new needs, the findings of psychology, of education,
and the demands of society. Changes, improvements, and progress call
for a flexible mind. Therefore, in this chapter an endeavor will be
made to trace the evolution of the larger objectives in art education
from the time the subject appeared as an element in American public
education to the present day. It is hoped that by pointing out the changes
that have occurred at various periods, the implications for the art program of our time may be made clear. It is also possible to recognize that
certain directions have always been present and that certain emphases
are inherent in the nature of American educational philosophy.

EARLY AIMS AND OBJECTIVES

The aims of art education for the public schools, much as the aims of other subjects, have undergone evolutionary changes. These appear to have been in two general directions: in relation to the field of art expression itself and in relation to the aims of education in general.

Whitford, a pioneer in the scientific study of art education, summarizes the various trends of art in the schools thus: "We have had as slogans for art education 'Art for Art's Sake,' 'Art for Industry's Sake,' and now we have 'Art for Life's Sake.'[1]

Formal art instruction, on a large scale, does not appear in any American public school system until 1821. It was then that it was introduced on an experimental basis in the schools of Massachusetts by William Bentley Fowle. However, there are instances prior to that date when some form of art instruction was available. Benjamin Franklin was one of the earliest, if not actually the first person, in the United States to pronounce some sort of aims for art education. In those early days it was referred to as "drawing." It was in connection with his "Proposed Hints for an Academy" that Franklin felt the importance of "drawing" in a scheme of education. He wrote: "It is therefore proposed that they learn those things that are likely to be most useful and most fundamental, regard being had to the several professions for which they are intended. All should be taught a fair hand, and swift, as that is useful to all. And with it may be learned *something of drawing by imitation of prints and some of the first principles of perspective.*"

Franklin's prescription of drawing for all, and his further comment on the fact that due regard should be given to the intended vocations, leads one to believe that his concern, and therefore his aim for "drawing," might be stated in terms of utilitarian value. In the days of colonization and empire building that aim was both defensible and natural. Further evidences of that spirit, in regard to art as a vocational aid, are reported by Farnum. In his brief essay on the beginning of art education in America, he calls attention to the fact that "In the early decades of the nineteenth century we find drawing taught as a special and somewhat detached subject, advertised in the local newspaper on the one hand by

---

[1] William G. Whitford, *An Introduction to Art Education*, rev. ed., New York, D. Appleton-Century Company, 1937, p. 3.

professional artists, who offered such instruction in limited classes with a definite vocational intent, and on the other hand by boarding school mistresses who 'respectfully solicit' a share of the public patronage for such ornamental branches as 'Drawing, Embroidery, Music, and Making a variety of fancy articles.' "[2]

While the vocational aim is clearly revealed in the above quotation, a new element makes its appearance, namely, that drawing was considered to be a cultural asset for young ladies, along with other things also deemed desirable. It is interesting to note that these teaching services were available to those who could afford to pay the price.

Vocation and Culture

So far, then, two of the earliest aims of art education may be said to have been art for vocational ends and art for cultural ends. Such art instruction was essentially undemocratic because it was available only to those who could afford to pay the price and it addressed itself only to the "talented" few. While it would be deplorable today, that situation was natural, if not plausible. The forces which were making their impact upon art education were traceable to the Renaissance and to the Industrial Revolution. The first placed emphasis on individualism and catered to those with a high degree of talent. At the same time, it gave rise to the unfortunate separation of the crafts from the fine arts. The second force placed emphasis on mass production and was largely concerned with reproducing historic motifs.

It seems clear that early American art education was characterized by graphic activities based on copies of the classics, and the term "drawing," which was generally used, referred largely to cast drawing or copying from nature. So conceived, the sphere of art education was narrow in extent and in scope since "drawing" confined the activities to graphic representation. That system was perpetuated by most art schools and persisted, with some of them, until the recent past.

Introduction of Art in the Schools: Various Movements

As early as 1838, Henry Barnard, who eventually became the first United States Commissioner of Education, promoted art as a common-

---

[2] Royal B. Farnum, "The Early History of American Art Education," in *Art in American Life and Education,* National Society for the Study of Education, Fortieth Yearbook, Bloomington, Ill., Public School Publishing Company, 1941, pp. 445–447.

THE TWO CHILDREN on this page are a study in contrast. The young girl at the top shows the restraint and precision which was induced by the adult-determined behavior of the mid-nineteenth century (*Peterson's Magazine*, Philadelphia, Pa., June, 1876). The happy child of 1955, as shown below, expresses herself freely in an atmosphere of understanding and freedom in which growth and development are encouraged (3rd-grade child, Pittsburgh, Pa.).

school subject. Horace Mann advocated art instruction in his famous report as secretary of the Board of Education in Massachusetts in 1843. By 1848 William Minife likewise encouraged drawing in the schools of Baltimore. Interestingly enough, however, to the prevalent utilitarian purpose there was added another, the cultivation of taste. Art was advocated for training in taste and for art in American industry.

In 1870, an act of the Massachusetts legislature made it mandatory to teach drawing "in towns of over 10,000 population." The type of drawing taught was industrial and mechanical and the general method of teaching is described thus: "Drawing, taught as an isolated subject, was dictated, geometric, and mechanical."[3]

The Massachusetts Normal Art School was founded in 1873. It was the first state-supported school of its kind, and its purpose was definitely to train teachers of "industrial drawing." A similar school, the Philadelphia School of Design for Women, now the Moore Institute, was established in 1844 on the premise that American industry needed workers and teachers who could understand applied design. The "Art in Industry" movement which began with

[3] *Ibid.*, p. 446.

Benjamin Franklin has had an almost continuous history except for inter-
mittent periods. Occasionally new emphases entered the field, either permanently or for a short duration. Up to that time, the subject matter and
approach to "drawing" evolved approximately in the following manner:
imitation of prints, mechanical drawing, rendering of geometric solids,
historic ornaments copied or adapted, and antique drawing from plaster
casts. The general aims were either to produce art for industry or to train
artists. The prevailing method of instruction was later characterized as
"academic" by Arthur Wesley Dow.

Two events of importance in connection with the next advance in art
education in America were the Philadelphia Centennial of 1876 and the
Chicago World's Fair of 1893. These expositions, showing the arts and
crafts of many lands, were a clear stimulus to those engaged in art and
in education at the time. Color, an element scarcely seen before in art
education, made itself felt. The drabness and flatness of work in drawing
assumed gaiety and opened up a new world of expression. To be sure,
even this was not uncontested. By the end of the century, "Art for
Technique's Sake" was fading in the background, but the industrial and
applied design emphases were evident. Yet it was clear that a new day
was dawning for American art education. The next movement was dedicated to "Art for Art's Sake." It was inspired by increased wealth and
an expanding culture. The Paris Exposition of 1800 and the first International Art Congress were held contemporaneously. They gave American art-education leaders a new vision, somewhat broader than before,
even if not complete.

In 1899 the National Education Association appointed a committee
of ten on drawing in the public schools. That committee's report was, in
some respects, prophetic. With slight revisions, what it advocated then
is practically what art education stands for today. After years of confusion, of contradictions, of overlapping statements of aims, art education was falling in line with general thinking in other areas of education. The committee's report stated the aims of art education as follows:

1. To develop an *appreciation* of the beautiful.
2. To develop the *creative* impulse.
3. To offer a consistent development of the faculty of sight.
4. To acquire *ability* to represent.
5. To prepare pupils for manual industry is purely incidental.

6. The development of professional artists is in no sense the aim of art education in the public schools.[4]

It is significant that objectives (5) and (6) are stated negatively. The committee squarely declared itself for what art education was and what it was not.

The Art for Art's Sake movement had made its inroads. While it was responsible for freeing art as a servant of the machine, it also brought about a number of ills. The worst was overemphasis on technical skill, which automatically made art a subject of awe on the part of the masses. It actually fostered admiration for exhibitionism, but made no provision for art as related to the life of the people. As for method, Hilpert points out that "Little or no recognition was given to experimental procedures or the development of originality."[5]

Art was an end in itself. Art as a cultural pursuit was considered worthwhile, elevating, capable of affecting an individual's moral and ethical character. These were the fundamental beliefs of the period. They still have their adherents.

BROADER INFLUENCES FROM EDUCATION AND PSYCHOLOGY

At this point, it may be helpful to take a retrospective as well as a forward glance at the field to indicate the influence exerted on art teaching and upon its objectives by professional education and by the psychology prevalent at various periods of time. A fact that is not often realized by contemporary art educators is the amazing evolution which has attended what appears to be new or altogether revolutionary thinking in the art field.

Obviously, it is impossible within the compass of this study to single out all influences and all contributors to the evolving scope of art education. Only the major forces can be itemized.

Rousseau (1712–1778), for example, was the forerunner of the child-centered school. His *Émile* is worthy of renewed study because much so-called modern method is revealed therein. Froebel (1782–1852), who

---

[4] Walter H. Klar, Leon L. Winslow, and C. Valentine Kirby, *Art Education in Principle and Practice*, Springfield, Mass., Milton Bradley Company, 1933, p. 27.

[5] Robert S. Hilpert, "Changing Emphases in School Art Programs," in *Art in American Life and Education*, National Society for the Study of Education, Fortieth Yearbook, Bloomington, Ill. Public School Publishing Company, 1941, p. 443.

is considered the father of the kindergarten movement, and consequently of the deep concern with very young children, insisted that the school must be less artificial, less conventional, and much closer to home or natural conditions. Pestalozzi (1746–1827) advanced the idea of experiencing when he insisted that a way must be found to achieve the natural and systematic development of all the powers of the individual. He also foresaw what today is termed sensory education by insisting that observation is the basis of knowledge; in fact, he developed what were called, in his time, object lessons and demonstration teaching. He insisted that the best education is achieved in a "homelike" atmosphere. Herbart (1776–1841) affected both philosophy and education in his time and in the decades that followed. He pointed out that the main purpose of education was the molding of character. To accomplish the task he advanced by many years the idea of correlation of subjects in order to capture the interests of all pupils, whom he believed to be many-sided and differing in apperception. What today is called unit teaching stems from Herbart's point of view. His influence on Charles and Frank McMurray, who studied in Germany, is one of the most significant chapters in American education. Likewise, the Morrison revival of the unit concept, developed at Chicago in the mid-twenties is based on Herbartian philosophy. The McMurrays were influential in establishing what today is the National Society for the Study of Education.

Horace Mann (1796–1859), often referred to as the "father" of common schools, exercised a powerful influence on American education generally, through his writing, speaking, and as secretary for the Massachusetts Board of Education. It was through his efforts that the first formal type of teacher education was organized in the establishment of the Lexington Normal School in 1839. It was through Mary Peabody's relationship to Mann that what is today termed "art" was introduced in the schools of Massachusetts. Henry Barnard (1811–1900) fostered the Pestalozzian ideals as Commissioner of Education in Connecticut. He was an ardent and early advocate of art in education.

Another significant figure in American education, one who exerted a strong influence, was Colonel Frank Parker (1837–1902). In a sense he is one of the founders of what later became the progressive movement. As superintendent of schools in Quincy, Massachusetts, he championed the Froebelian ideal of less formalism in the school room. He believed

68 in experiencing as a basis for learning in science and thus advocated taking children outdoors to study nature. He believed, intensely, in teaching "from the standpoint of the child." Some educational historians credit the Quincy experiment and, therefore, Parker as being the forerunner of Dewey. Colonel Parker organized the earliest teachers' institutes and was instrumental in the founding of the College of Education at the University of Chicago.

Decorative Landscape Compositions. These may be Traced and Filled in with Color Schemes

TRACING, COPYING, and filling in with color were common practices in 1914 (*How to Teach Drawing, A Teacher's Manual*, Boston, Prang Company, 1914, pp. 11–12). By contrast, the lower photograph shows direct reference to environment, freedom of interpretation of a mood of nature, and keenness of observation as stressed today (2nd grade, Livingston, N.J.).

William T. Harris (1835–1909) was superintendent of schools of St. Louis, Missouri, in 1873. While revolting against the systematic approach suggested by Froebel, he nevertheless accepted his major premises and established the first public-school kindergarten in America. He advocated flexible promotions, individualized instruction, and special attention for gifted children. Harris became U.S. Commissioner of Education in 1889; in that position he was able to exert wide influence on American education.

William Rainey Harper (1850–1906), president of the University of Chicago, encouraged Dewey in the establishment of an experimental school at that university. During his lifetime he pioneered many movements which are widely accepted today, among them the junior college and the idea of general education.

G. Stanley Hall (1845–1924), widely educated in America and in Germany, is one of the earliest students of adolescence and its problems. As president of Clarke University he emphasized the study of psychology and thus had a deep influence on the thinking of educators of his time.

John Dewey (1859–1953) is at once the most influential as well as the most controversial figure in American education. Instrumentalism, pragmatism, experience, and experimentation are key words in the educational philosophy of Dewey. First at the University of Chicago and later at Columbia University, his teaching and his influence deeply affected thousands of men and women in education. The progressive movement in general received the impetus of his point of view as well as his personal support. *Art as Experience* is perhaps the best known of his works to affect art education in America. Among Dewey's closest associates in the progressive-education movement were such men as Boyd Bode and William Kilpatrick. The latter became the chief exponent of the project method, in fact of foundations of method in general. His emphasis on the life activities of children as a source of motivation made a profound impression on thousands of his disciples. As a balancing wheel and force William Bagley at the same time stressed what is often referred to as essentialism in the schools. Thomas Briggs, also of Columbia University, became a force in the direction of secondary education, while Edward Thorndike made extensive contributions from the point of view of new psychological findings. Lester Dix, on the other hand, spoke clearly for the progressives in *A Charter for Progressive Education*.[6]

Among other strong influences in the broader field of education which have had direct bearing on art education, the work of Maria Montessori, a physician and educator, needs to be recognized. She advocated sense education through the use of proper teaching materials. Above all she emphasized the need of freedom for the child to express himself. Her "system" of education for young children had a powerful effect on American educational thinking during the early part of the century.

It is not possible to conclude this summary of contributors without mention of the experimental work of Carleton Washburn at Winnetka, or the extensive and devoted attention given by Leta Hollingsworth to the field of the "exceptional" child. The controlled studies of the learning of young children undertaken by the psychologist Arnold Gesell are

---

[6] Lester Dix, *A Charter for Progressive Education*, New York, Teachers College, Columbia University, 1939.

paramount. The results obtained with animals by Koffka and Köhler, on the other hand, have pointed out many new directions in the study of the nature of the child and his modes of learning.

But the totality of the forces and of the men and women who have contributed to the present inheritance cannot be accounted for in the present work. Certainly men such as Charles Eliot of Harvard, a political philosopher such as Jefferson, and, more recently, Hutchins of Chicago and Conant of Harvard have exercised far-reaching influence on American education and, indirectly, on art education.

DOW'S INFLUENCE

As late as 1890 Arthur Wesley Dow speaks of "the prevailing method of nature copying" and of his search for a new and better method of teaching. The new method of teaching art was introduced to him by Professor Ernest Fenellosa, a curator in the Boston Museum of Fine Arts. The distinct difference in Fenellosa's approach to art education was that, while the prevailing system had realism as its cornerstone, the leading thought of the new approach was "the expression of Beauty, not Representation."[7]

The subsequent fortunes of the new approach were such that it revolutionized American art education. Its major departure lies in what has been called the synthetic method of teaching as opposed to the academic. The chief premise of the new scheme is contained in the dictum attributed to Dow, "The true purpose of art teaching is the education of the whole people for appreciation." It was contended and accepted by a host of teachers trained under Dow that "A better understanding of the true usefulness of art recognizes *creative power* as a divine gift, the natural endowment of every human soul, showing itself at first in the form that we call appreciation. This appreciation leads a certain number to produce actual works of art, greater or lesser, perhaps a temple, perhaps only a cup, but it leads the majority to desire finer form, and more harmony of tone and color in surroundings and things for daily use. It is the individual's right to have full control of these powers."[8] Dow

---

[7] Arthur Wesley Dow, *Composition*, New York, Doubleday, 1913, pp. 5–6.

[8] Arthur Wesley Dow, *Theory and Practice of Teaching Art*, New York, Teachers College, Columbia University, 1908, p. 1.

went farther than merely presenting a more effective method and new aims for art education. He attacked the old system: "This lack of appreciation is responsible for an immense waste of labor, skill, and money in the production of useless and ugly things."[9]

The diagrams on page 72 are reproduced from Dow's *Theory and Practice of Teaching Art.* They are introduced here because they clarify the essential differences between the new and the old at the beginning of the present century.

Dow's influence is felt even to this day. Yet, while his approach to art education was acknowledged as being directed toward personal expression and power, the impact of industrial expansion continued to influence art education. In 1907 the industrial-arts movement was given impetus, and the 1912 International Art Congress at Dresden made America conscious of the fact that even in our public schools art must take cognizance of the following needs: better-designed products, greater color discrimination, discovery of talent for further training.

The cultural movement gradually gave impetus to art appreciation by taking within its sphere of interest not only painting but architecture,

---

[9] *Ibid.,* p. 1.

1

Draw two lines lightly with your pencil. Notice that they slant down in the same direction. Be sure to get them the right distance apart

2

Put a dot straight above the beginning of the front line. Draw the ear in front of this dot and from the ear draw the long curved line of the back

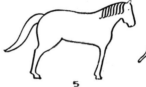

3

Now let us finish the back leg. Notice that it is rather large at the top

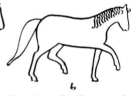

4

Let us make a line for the under part of the head. Notice that it ends straight under the ear

5

Draw the front line of the horse's head. Finish the front leg. Draw the tail, mane, eye, and stomach line. This gives a standing horse

6

To make a walking horse, one of the forelegs and one of the rear legs must be extended. Draw the tail, mane, and stomach line

Steps in Drawing a Horse

DIRECTED, STEP-BY-STEP instructions in drawing, painting, and other forms of art persisted even as late as 1930 (*The Classroom Teacher,* Vol. 4, p. 64). The lower photograph shows the freedom and creativity of contemporary art expression (*Progressive Education,* October, 1935).

The Academic Method

Emphasis: "Learn to Draw"

Representation
{
Drawing from casts and other objects
Perspective
}
Pencil drawing
Pen drawing
Charcoal line drawing
Brush drawing, etc.

Light and shade
Color study from nature

Painting
Picture study
Composition incidental
}
Charcoal
Water color
Oil

Design
{
Historic ornament
Structure of pattern
Perspective of pattern
Color exercises
Wash drawing
Composition in same style or period
}

The Synthetic Method

Emphasis: Composition

Line
{
Spacing-line structure
Character of line, expression
Principles of design
Composition of line
Representation
}
Drawing and modeling

Dark and Light
{
Massing, values
Quality of tone
Composition of dark and light
Light and shadow in representation
}
Painting

Color
{
Hue, value, intensity
Color harmony
Color composition
}

sculpture, and the industrial arts. By 1920, American art education was beginning to show a threefold direction. It admitted of:

1. *Fine arts:* drawing, painting, sculpture.
2. *Appreciation:* art as culture, taste and discrimination.
3. *Industrial art:* crafts, art for industry.[10]

The broadening base of art education was beginning to be quite impressive. In many localities, especially in the larger school systems, progressive teachers were attempting to balance the offerings of the art program along the lines indicated above. The grave difficulty seemed to be one of standards. Indeed, much of the work in the three broad areas referred to was stereotyped. The type of design used in the crafts followed what was published in the art-education magazines of the time without much compunction.

THE SCIENTIFIC MOVEMENT

Modern art education in America may be said to date from 1920. Progress was largely due to a widespread interest in art as education, to new social needs, and to a scientific attitude in education such as had never been witnessed before. The new attitude toward art parallels the general interest in education for the same period. In his report for the year indicated, Farnum states: "Probably the outstanding mark of progress in art is the serious effort in many cities to study the problem from a scientific standpoint."[11] And again: "Being a more or less tryout stage the new phase of art education is unsettled, but some of the general objectives would include: (a) Drawing primarily for self-expression; (b) Close relation to community needs; (c) Training in appreciation; (d) Development of orderly habits; (e) Education for the profitable use of leisure; (f) Art as expressed in the industrial and commercial development of the race; (g) Self-expression in the life needs of the child; (h) Discovery and encouragement of special abilities."[12]

It becomes apparent at this stage that the role of art had broadened and that its function included more than mere technics. Tastes, skills, ap-

---

[10] Dates and data adapted and extended from Farnum's *Biennial Report* of 1931.

[11] Royal B. Farnum, *Art Education in the United States,* Washington, D.C., Department of the Interior, Bureau of Education, Bulletin 1925, No. 38, p. 1.

[12] *Ibid.,* p. 2.

preciations, correct habits, community needs, and the worthy use of leisure were given a place. The term *self-expression* now entered the scene
and the child became important.

SYSTEMATIC ORGANIZATION OF ART

In 1924 Whitford, largely influenced by Dewey, brought from the
field of general education a term seldom heard up to that time. He
sought to achieve the functions of art through *experience*, an idea which
undoubtedly stemmed from the Pestalozzian philosophy of a century before. Accordingly, he listed the graphic experience (drawing), the ornamental experience (design), the motor experience (construction), the
mental experience (appreciation), and the chromatic experience
(color).[13] At the same time, Boas made bold to state: "Few children are
ever going to be either singers or writers or painters, but all are human
beings and it is for them that singers, writers, and painters produce their
work."[14] Today art educators refer to the implication of her statement as
"consumer education" in art. In elaborating, she states that the aims of
art in the public schools should be intelligent consumership—appreciation and taste; proper use of leisure; interest in order; and use of the imagination.

STUDIES OF THE FEDERATED COUNCIL

In 1925 the Federated Council on Art Education was established
through the financial assistance of the Carnegie Corporation of New
York. The following year the Council appointed ten committees of three
members each to discover trends and practices in art education throughout the United States. The committees were so chosen geographically as
to represent the various sections of the country: the eastern, southern,
central, northwestern, mountain, and Pacific states. The committees were
asked, among other things, to gather data and formulate statements on
general objectives in art for the elementary school. They were also to
outline minimum-content essentials for courses of study. The various
committees, after debate and evaluation, assembled their findings into
a report. That report states the purposes of art education for the elementary schools as follows:

---

[13] William C. Whitford, "Problem of Differentiation and Standardization of Art Work
in Modern High Schools," *The School Review*, May, 1924, pp. 333–341.

[14] Belle Boas, *Art in the Schools*, New York, Doubleday, Page & Company, 1924, pp. 1–3.

A. Broad Objectives: Appreciation, Skills, Knowledge
B. Specific Objectives: Appreciations, Skills, Habits, Attitudes, Ideals, Outstanding Abilities
C. Minimum Content Essentials: Formal drill and instruction in the main elements of art: (a) design, (b) lettering, (c) color, (d) form, (e) narrative illustration, (f) construction, (g) appreciation, (h) creative and individual expression[15]

How important the Council's report was may be judged by the variety of fields suggested as minimum content, and by the similarity of the objectives prevalent in other areas of education during the same period.

ART AND DEMOCRACY

Meantime the National Education Association, through its Department of Superintendence, was also attempting to formulate objectives for art education. William McAndrew's report reads in part:

The purposes of the public schools are conditioned by the source of their support, taxation of all the community. The object of the public schools is the same as the object of the United States itself: Equal right to Life, Liberty, Happiness, duties of a More Perfect Union, Justice, Domestic Tranquillity, Common Defense, General Welfare. The right to life means the right to a full complete life *which must include appreciation of beauty and art.* To contribute toward National Defense and the General Welfare *we look to the teaching of art in the public schools.*

Life: Our fathers considered it a self-evident truth that all men are entitled to their lives. We interpret it as meaning more than mere existence: a full, complete, well-developed life, enjoying the beauties of nature, of works of literature, and the graphic arts.

Happiness: We hold that the course of study in art should conduce directly to a happy life, and that the exercises throughout the courses of study should give enjoyment.

Liberty: We believe that *the lessons in art should free the spirit from oppressive obsessions, that freedom, initiative, originality, governed by order, law, and beauty should be developed.*

Common Defense: We conceive it to be the duty of public schools *through art cultivation to create more beautiful homes,* cities and countryside, and thus, indirectly, perhaps make the Common Defense more worthwhile.

General Welfare: We hold that the refining influence of art study on the whole community brings it under this national objective.[16]

---

[15] Federated Council on Art Education, *Report of the Committee on Elementary School Art,* 1926, Sanduski, Ohio, The American Crayon Co., pp. 5–6, 9–10.

[16] *Ibid.,* pp. 5–6.

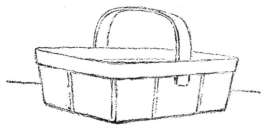

A Perspective Sketch from the Object

Showing Grouped Objects Treated in Outline
Note the Composition and Spacing

PERSPECTIVE AND COMPOSITION taught in a
formal manner, by means of similar objects, in
classrooms all over the country are the subject
of the upper drawings, which come from a
drawing book published in 1914 and widely
used (*How to Teach Drawing, A Teacher's Manual,* Boston, Prang Company, 1914, p. 53). The
lower photograph shows the experimental and
personalized drawing of a still life by a sixth-
grader of today (6th grade, Hazleton, Pa.).

McAndrew's statement as to the
aims and functions of art in the general scheme of American education
was prophetic. The tendency since
1925 has been to harmonize the objectives of art education with those
of general education. This tendency
will be more evident as further statements of aims are brought to light.

What has gone into art-education
history as a memorable date is the
1927 meeting of the N.E.A. in Dallas, Texas. It was then that for the
first time art education was accorded
general recognition as a fundamental in the curriculum of public education. The McAndrew report just
referred to and the work of the Federated Council on Art Education
had a fruitful culmination at that
convention. Among the chief protagonists for art education at that
time were Kirby, Winslow, and
Klar; their impact was to be felt for
the next two decades.

ART AS INTEGRATION

Subsequent developments in art
education have been marked by earnest coöperation on the part of the
general educator and a feeling of
genuine responsibility by leaders in
the art field. Such approaches as the
project method, correlation with
other subject fields, the core curriculum, and integration have become
bywords in public-school art much

as they are in education in general. The following statements of aims show conclusively that art is no longer considered a "special" department, but a normal activity through which the personalities of boys and girls may grow more completely.

Gambril, in her introduction to Margaret Mathias' *Art in the Elementary Schools,* presented these as the aims of art education:

1. To foster and develop the child's natural impulses to express the feelings about his experiences through the use of materials.
2. It seeks to give him control over the skillful use of materials for the practical purpose of social intercommunication as well as for the satisfaction and personal enrichment which results from the shaping of matter to new form in response to a creative impulse.
3. It strives to extend the range of materials which he knows and can use with sufficient skill to carry out adequately his purposes.
4. Perhaps its most universally recognized function is the stimulation and fostering of sensitiveness to beauty in its varied manifestations.[16]

Nyquist approached the entire question of aims from a historical point of view. He classified them under three categories: (1) cultural aims, (2) pedagogical aims, (3) economic aims. He pointed out that the cultural objectives aim toward liberalizing the learner by broadening and deepening his interests and knowledge along art lines and by providing for heightened appreciation of nature and objects of fine and industrial arts."[17] Further, he stated that the pedagogical aims consist mainly of three divisions and these are "chiefly utilitarian and industrial in character." In summary, Nyquist stated the following as the objectives of art in the elementary curriculum: "communication, observation, construction and appreciation." It is significant that all writers on art education after 1900 recognize an activity which prior to that time was totally absent from the school art program, namely, the manipulative activity. Manipulative activities have, in the course of time, become more important. Under the name of crafts, they now occupy a prominent place in the program of art education.

---

[16] Margaret E. Mathias, New York, Charles Scribner's Sons, 1929, *Art in the Elementary Schools,* pp. 7–10.

[17] Frederick V. Nyquist, *Art Education in Elementary Schools,* Baltimore, Warwick and York, 1929, pp. 13–28, 34.

STRESS ON SOCIAL OBLIGATIONS

The next stage in the evolution of concepts appeared when art educators began to think in terms of the broad educational objectives which are applicable to and should be sought in art education. For instance, Whitford states: "The field of modern art education may be [further] divided into three major objectives: the social objective, the vocational objective, and the leisure-time."[18] The objectives were based on a survey of art needs in American life. This fact was even more significant in that it was a new procedure in determination of objectives.

In 1932 Tannahill was able to assert that the aims of education and those of art education were in "happy harmony." The purpose of the fine arts in the schools, according to her view, were the creative (self-expression, freedom, release), the appreciative (taste, critical judgment, emotional expression), the technical (skills and techniques).[19]

Hopkins and Burnett conceived the purposes of art education thus:

1. First among the underlying purposes is to aid the individual to improve his daily living by helping him to discover in it more and varied insights, deeper feelings, and broader understanding.
2. A second purpose is to help the individual to grow in range and depth of interest.
3. A third cluster of values sought lies in the field of social attitudes and abilities.
4. The fourth type of aim lies in the realm of skills.[20]

Later, Nicholas, Mawhood, and Trilling stated the general objectives of art education as being creative self-expression, personal enrichment, social worth, recreational resource, vocational training.[21]

In 1937 several statements of objectives were published by the regional art associations. They differed in words but not in spirit:

1. To provide sense training and a natural outlet for the child's creative impulse and imagination.

---

[18] Whitford, *An Introduction to Art Education*, New York, D. Appleton and Company, 1929, p. 19.

[19] Sallie B. Tannahill, *Fine Arts for Public School Administrators*, New York, Teachers College, Columbia University, 1932, p. 43.

[20] L. T. Hopkins and M. H. Burnett (eds.), *Enriched Community Living*, Dover, Delaware, State Department of Education, 1936, pp. 13–14.

[21] Florence W. Nicholas, N. C. Mawhood, and M. B. Trilling, *Art Activities in the Modern School*, New York, The Macmillan Company, 1937, pp. 4–12.

2. To cultivate taste and sound aesthetic judgment.
3. To administer to the particular needs of the community.
4. To train all to a degree of self-expression.
5. To discover, guide, and conserve those with exceptional aptitudes and gifts.

Obviously, then, the art program so conceived and so administered takes care of a variety of abilities, a variety of responses, and a variety of needs.

Prescott, who is concerned chiefly with the emotions and their affective role in education, presents a point of view in which art educators have believed for a long time, but on which· they have not expressed themselves in as eloquent a fashion. He states that aesthetics may contribute directly to personality development as follows:

A. The use of the arts to bring children into the stream of our own culture, to aid them in appreciating how the present has grown out of the past and to assist them in understanding and appreciating other contemporary cultures.
B. The use of the arts as vehicles for self-expression and for organizing and unifying the personality by giving opportunities for the expression of personal convictions and feelings.
C. The use of aesthetic productions of young people by teachers and personnel workers to gain insights into their fantasies and needs on the basis of which they may be understood more sympathetically and guided more effectively.
D. The use of aesthetic expression and experience as a cathartic for relieving emotional tension and for the conscious development of morale.[22]

In 1939 Winslow saw the aims of art education as identical with those of all education. His aims are of two types: those of art in relation to the curriculum as a whole, and those of art in relation to the child. He states: "From the standpoint of school organization art should serve to motivate and enrich the entire curriculum and it should contribute generously to the integration of school experience." And again: "Art in the modern school should aim both to stimulate in the child the experience of creating and to help him improve the manner in which he expresses himself through creative processes, at the same time it should aim to stimulate in him the experience of appreciating by acquainting him sys-

---

[22] Daniel Prescott, *Emotion and the Educative Process,* Washington, D.C., American Council on Education, 1938, p. 289.

8 0

tematically with fine examples of the arts of various peoples, both of the present and the past."[23]

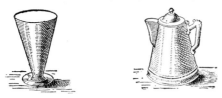

CLAY MODELING IN THE SCHOOLROOM. 63

A wineglass is made by adding a base to the frustrum, and the addition of a handle and a spout makes a coffee-pot.

WINEGLASS.   **COFFEE-POT.**

Connect two similar frustra by a short rope of clay and the result is a pair of opera glasses.

OPERA GLASSES.

With normal pupils the cone may be cut to show the parabola, hyperbola and ellipse, the latter being an interesting connection with the spheroids.

Pyramids of all kinds may be derived from the cone and are formed by flattening the cone from point to base, upon three or any number of sides.

MODELING and other types of three-dimensional work were recognized as early as 1892, but the language used and the "type solid" notion were barriers to creative unfolding. (*Clay Modeling in the Schoolroom* by Ellen Stephen Hildreth, Springfield, Mass., Milton Bradley Company, 1892, p. 63). Today art education stresses free modeling and design in general. The lower photograph shows modeling as done by third-graders from Philadelphia. Children are encouraged to make things that have purpose and meaning for them (modeling by 3rd-grade pupils, Philadelphia, Pa.).

Welling, preferring to think in terms of what art education does rather than in terms of what it is, puts it in this manner: "The arts are definitely concerned with: the growth of individuals, the relationships among the arts themselves, and the culture of communities."[24]

Another view that has recently gained favor is that presented by Pauline Johnson. She contends that the art program should keep clearly in mind the needs of living, the emotional experience and its use in the development of sensitivities, and an understanding of what constitutes art, including a knowledge of its principles.[25]

RECOGNITION OF GROWTH AND DEVELOPMENT

The Commission on Secondary School Curriculum of the Progressive Education Association stated a point

[23] Leon L. Winslow, *The Integrated School Art Program*, New York, McGraw-Hill Book Company, 1939, pp. 25–48.

[24] Jane Betsey Welling, *Art Education in the Elementary School, An Analysis of Trends and Implications*, Washington, D.C., Department of Art Education, National Education Association, Bulletin 1939, pp. 12–20.

[25] Pauline Johnson, *Art in the Core Curriculum*, Washington, D.C., Department of Art Education, National Education Association, Bulletin 1940, p. 57.

of view which is widely accepted in art-education circles. After tracing the evolution of concepts, the following were given as the "conceptions" of art education:

First, the most important concern of art education is the growth of personality, the cultivation of persons who are widely sensitive and aware in all aspects of living, who strive to bring satisfyingness into life and to eliminate ugliness, who are adequate to the demands of such a large task. . . .

Second, art experiences are the right of every person. If art has values to contribute to living, then in a democracy all should enjoy them and profit by them.

Third, art should be an inherent element in the total living drama, etc. . . .[26]

The Commission concludes that "The aim of art education in the secondary school is to further the growth of individuals in rich enjoyment and effectiveness and to encourage them to create a society where such living is possible."

Actually, what the Commission points out could be referred to, in terms of recency, as the last word in the objectives of art education: art education fosters personality; art experiences are the right of every person; art should be the inherent element in the total drama of living.[27]

LIFE AS SUBJECT MATTER OF ART

At this point it seems that a functional definition of art as education becomes quite clear, and that its component elements are equally well delineated. A definition might take a form such as this: Art is the personal expression of feelings, thoughts, and ideas growing out of experience with the environment or generated by the imagination and the perceptive powers, in forms and technics adequate to the individual. Appreciation, of the environment or of the creations of man, is likewise an aesthetic reaction, either complete in itself or the generative force of personal expression.

Obviously, in a broader sense, art involves all of life and all of living. It is a way, and not a thing. The visual arts, literature, drama, the dance, and the myriad crafts would then fall within the scope of the definition.

---

[26] Commission on the Secondary School Curriculum, Progressive Education Association, *The Visual Arts in General Education*, New York, D. Appleton-Century Company, 1940, pp. 15–16.

[27] *Ibid.*, p. 20.

For the present concern, however, one must focus on what is generally understood as comprising the broad program of art in the schools. How to implement the definition in the schoolroom and how it may leaven the culture of the community, the state, and the nation is the task of the teacher and, particularly, of the art consultant.

Some further statements may illuminate the path. Ziegfeld writes: "These findings [of the Owatonna Project] have important implications for art instruction in the schools. They imply, first of all, that an art program should be organized in terms of life areas of experience, or areas of activity in order that the learning situation be as meaningful as possible." And again: "A program of art conceived in terms of life situations will have a vitality and a meaning that is not approximated by one conceived in terms of art principles or art skills."[28]

Faulkner and his collaborators explain the function of art thus: "Art in spite of the haze which often obscures its nature, is no mysterious activity to be understood by a few. It is one of several fields of human activity in which all men use their powers and abilities to communicate their experiences to fellow men and to transform the materials of the natural world for human use. Art always arises out of human needs, and these demand first study."[29] While Faulkner does not set down aims as such, he points out clearly the direction in which art education should move and what its goals ought to be, namely, (1) art for all, (2) art as communication of experiences, (3) art as an answer to human needs.

McDonald,[30] on the other hand, is not so much concerned with general and immediate objectives. She believes that art education (for junior and senior high schools) needs a solid educational foundation. She calls attention to two major concepts, namely, appreciation and expression. Through these, she believes, such general objectives as (1) building faith in the potential ego, (2) development of individual initiative, and (3) development of group initiative in relation to social responsibility,

[28] Edwin Ziegfeld, *A Community Project in Art Education*, Washington, D.C., Department of Art Education, National Education Association, Bulletin 1940, pp. 222–229.

[29] Ray Faulkner, Edwin Ziegfeld, and Gerald Hill, *Art Today*, New York, Henry Holt and Company, 1956, p. xxxii.

[30] Rosabel McDonald, *Art as Education*, New York, Henry Holt and Company, 1941, pp. 1–7.

can be achieved, it is possible to relate school and life, and to integrate creative activity and social understanding.

Winslow,[31] in a later statement of the aims of art education, points to the fact that "specifically, the objectives of art teaching relate to the meeting of educational needs through art." He states the following objectives: self-realization, human relationship, economic efficiency, civic responsibility, and instruction. These are identical to the pronouncements of the Educational Policies Commission.

SELF-DEVELOPMENT THROUGH SELF-DISCOVERY

Further light on the function of art in the schools is found in the report of the National Commission on Cooperative Curriculum Planning.[32] The statement on art education is the result of the opinions of art educators representing the following groups: the Department of Art Education, N.E.A.; the Eastern Arts Association; the Southeastern Arts Association; and the Western Arts Association. That statement is significant in that it points up a definite shift of emphasis—the emphasis on personal growth and expression.

Lowenfeld[33] summarizes the newer position of art education not in terms of specific aims but rather as broad psychological concepts which emphasize the two major roles of art: self-expression and self-adjustment. He further stresses the identification of the pupil with the art experience and through art media. These involve, as they must, subject matter and personalized means of expression, and culminate in social adjustments and in the integration of the individual.

Kainz and Riley state definitely that "The ultimate aim of secondary school education is to develop a complete and rounded personality. How does the Art Education program contribute to this goal? We believe that its most important contribution lies in making the student realize that he must (1) observe keenly and react vividly; (2) develop meaning and

---

[31] Leon L. Winslow, *Art in Secondary Education*, New York, McGraw-Hill Book Company, 1941, pp. 32–36.

[32] John J. DeBoer (ed.), *The Subject Fields in General Education*, New York, D. Appleton-Century Company, 1941, pp. 187–204.

[33] Viktor Lowenfeld, *Creative and Mental Growth*, rev. ed., New York, The Macmillan Company, 1956, Chapter I.

imagination; (3) exercise judgement and discrimination; (4) express ideas courageously and logically; and (5) construct with power and with vision."[34] To be noted here is that the only shift in emphasis from elementary to secondary art education is *in terms of the heightened value of the art product*. Otherwise, the individual pupil maintains his preëminent position.

Finally, an examination of recent literature, including state and local guides for the development of courses in art education, may prove rather profitable. Except for a few isolated instances, the reader will find a reiteration of similar, current concepts. This does not necessarily prove that theory and practice today go hand in hand. However, it does indicate that statements such as the following, even though general, are, in a sense, symptomatic of the new thinking:

DECORATIVE DESIGN, largely of conventionalizations of nature (have from flowers and seed pods), was done by formulas based on "principles" and "elements" until quite recently. (*Classroom Practice in Design* by James Parton Haney, 1907). By contrast, expressive design, based on felt rhythm and original forms, is advocated today. The latter is calculated to bring out the individuality of the young artist. (Decorative design by a 12th-grade pupil of New Orleans, La.).

Teachers [of art] are recognizing more clearly the close relationship between the commonplace human activities and art activities.

. . . art activities in the school should be organized so that the students will receive a foundation which they can draw upon later.

If art work is organized in such terms as the home, the community, the school, and the individual, the program will have vitality and be applied to real experiences and situations.

[34] Louise C. Kainz and Olive L. Riley, *Exploring Art,* New York, Harcourt, Brace and Company, 1951, pp. iii-ix.

These functions or experience areas are: art in personal living (including correct dress, poise, skill in social dancing), enjoyment of the fine arts, and expression as a leisure time activity; art in the planning, equipping, and beautifying the home; art in the selection of consumers' products; and art in community life.

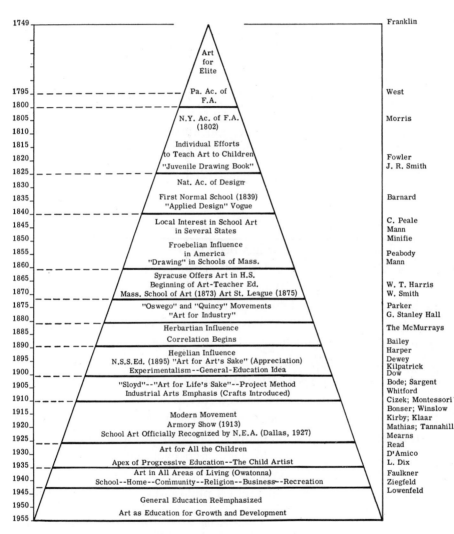

THE BROADENING BASE OF ART EDUCATION

NOTE: Names of educators are placed in position approximating date of their influence.

In 1948 Shultz and Shores[35] restated the aims of art education for the elementary schools in these significant statements: Art is not for artists only; art is life; good art is functional; genuine art is original. The implications of the statements reveal that a creative approach is essential; that technical achievement is commensurate with the individual's growth; that art has a function as an educative agent and that art experience is akin to life.

THE BROADENING BASE OF ART EDUCATION

The chart on page 85 is an attempt to epitomize, graphically, the major currents, contributions, and contributors that together culminate in the present position of art education. It is in the form of a pyramid with an ever-widening base. The pyramid shows a continuous evolution from art for an elite to art for all; from art education with specific and ulterior purposes to an art education for human growth and development. The chart itself is an elaboration and an extension of the author's original scheme published some years ago.[36]

SUMMARY

In this chapter the endeavor has been to present the high spots in the growth of aims, concepts, and functions of art in the public schools. While it cannot be assumed that certain influences and trends were born or died out completely at definite points, the review should lead to a reconstruction of these developments as presented in the diagram on page 85. The symbolic pyramid is used because objectives and procedures in art education, from their inception to this day, have tended to broaden the basic concept of art education. From art for the talented few, or art for industry, or art for its own sake to art as enjoyment and to art for all the children are steps in the evolution. Likewise, from copybooks and historic ornaments, copied or badly applied, to drawings of solids and casts, to nature study, hence to color, and eventually to a method in which experience and personal expression play a large role, there also seems to be a wide difference. From a philosophy of awkward utilitari-

---

[35] Harold Shultz and J. Harlan Shores, *Art in the Elementary Schools*, Urbana, University of Illinois, Bureau of Research and Service, Bulletin 1948, pp. 5–6.

[36] I. L. de Francesco, *An Evaluation of Curricula for the Preparation of Teachers of Art*, doctoral dissertation, New York University, 1943, p. 70.

anism, or even one of servilism to "Art for Art's Sake," to a point of view that recognizes art as a broad area of human activity common to all men and basic to personal growth and happiness, there would seem to be a large contrast. Yet this has been the evolution of art education for the public schools from about 1800 to this day.

Some further deductions to be drawn from this review seem to be these:

1. While even the most recent statements do not show total agreement, there are many common denominators in all of them:
   A. Art expression is a means of education.
   B. Art experience is a way toward personal growth and development.
   C. The development of appreciation and taste for all is desirable.
   D. Art is related to areas of living.
   E. Discovery and cultivation of talent is an imperative.
2. The aims show that art education has tended to divorce itself from definite alliances as such; preparation for professional art fields or for industry is sought as a natural by-product of the broad program which centers on individual growth rather than on predetermined, specific goals.
3. Art education is conceived as integral with all education. Through the use of experiences as an educational means, art contributes to the social, creative, mental, aesthetic, and emotional needs of every pupil whether as consumer of art or as a potential artist.
4. The experiences advocated for the art program tend toward the recognition of personal expression, communal life and regional interests. Thus art becomes a living expression of American democracy.

In conclusion, the newer concepts are not concerned with the development of technical facility and the achievement of professional standards as such. Each child, given opportunity and proper guidance, will grow to his own creative stature.

For Discussion and Activity

1. How were the earlier aims of art education formulated and what influences affected the direction of what was taught? How did the aims change over a period of time? Develop a time chart showing the changes in emphasis.
2. What is your understanding of Dow's reform in art education? Are the traces of that change still operative today?
3. Is a systematic organization or a sequential development of the art program desirable? What are the dangers of adult logic in relation to children's creative development?

4. To what extent have European thinking and other cultural influences affected the art program in American schools? Cite specific events and evaluate their effects.

5. How does art education today reflect the views expressed by McAndrew? Attempt a specific answer that will clearly show the extent to which democratic ideals and art education parallel.

6. What is your understanding of *integration?* How is it achieved, especially through art in the schools? How is it recognized in children and in adults?

7. What social-living values can you ascribe to art activities? Make a history of art activities that promote effective social living for an elementary grade, a junior-high-school grade, and a senior-high-school grade.

8. Growth and development seem to be the chief objectives of all education today. What are the contributions of art to child growth and development? Gather evidences from the classroom and from teachers in service.

9. On the basis of the present study what do you consider to be the subject matter of art? Is it perspective, color theories, devices for producing decorative design, charts on lettering, and other art processes?

10. If the theory of self-identification has value in art education, what behavior changes could be reasonably expected in children as evidences of growth and development?

For Further Reading

Commission on Secondary School Curriculum, Progressive Education Association, *The Visual Arts in General Education,* New York, D. Appleton-Century Company, 1940, Chapters I, III, VI.

DeBoer, John J. (ed.), *The Subject Fields in General Education,* New York, D. Appleton-Century Company, 1941, Chapter XI.

DeYoung, Chris A., *Introduction to American Public Education,* New York, McGraw-Hill Book Company, 1950, Part II, Units V–IX.

Kainz, Louise, and Riley, Olive, *Exploring Art,* New York, Harcourt, Brace and Company, 1951, Chapter I.

Logan, Frederick M., *Growth of Art in American Schools,* New York, Harper & Brothers, 1954, Chapter VIII.

Lowenfeld, Viktor, *Creative and Mental Growth,* rev. ed., New York, The Macmillan Company, 1952, Chapter I.

McDonald, Rosabel, *Art as Education,* New York, Henry Holt and Company, 1941, Chapter I.

Moholy-Nagy, Ladislaus, *The New Vision,* New York, W. W. Norton and Company, 1938, Chapter I.

Whitford, William G., *An Introduction to Art Education,* rev. ed., New York, D. Appleton-Century Company, Chapter II.

CURRENT TRENDS

> A trend is much more important to understand than is
> any particular content of thought or any particular skill.
> . . . Knowledge of a trend of civilization carries the edu-
> cator forward. It gives him a standard of selection, a guid-
> ing principle.
>
> Charles H. Judd,
> "The Place of Research in a
> Program of Curriculum De-
> velopment," *Journal of Edu-
> cational Research.*

DESIRABILITY OF VARIETY

THAT THERE SHOULD BE A VARIETY OF POINTS OF VIEW IN ART EDUCATION
is only natural. It results from the American tradition of freedom and, at
the same time, it is consistent with the nature of art itself. In a sense, it
is part of the genius of democratic education; the opposite would be authoritarian uniformity, which has been and is one of the earmarks of to-
talitarianism.

However, this very freedom of opinion places on teachers and students
of art education the responsibility of studying and appraising the various currents before determining on a course of action or establishing
their own philosophy and related methods.

CONSONANCE WITH AMERICAN TRADITION

Aside from the more idealistic reasons for the existence of many points
of view, there are practical ones, which can only be mentioned briefly

here, but which will become clearer as the totality of the program of art education is studied. The current and unprecedented growth of interest in this field on the part of school administrators, professional educators, parents, and classroom teachers is at once encouraging and bewildering. Most art educators agree that the function of art in the schools is to help children develop into mentally healthy, integrated individuals. Most of them would agree to the personal and social potentials of the art experience; all of them will agree that art is a way of life and, as a consequence, that it is the inalienable right of all children to have the advantages of a sound art education. These are the encouraging facts.

However, the healthy variety of opinions to which reference has just been made has raised many questions in the minds of those concerned with art education in the schools. Those questions are a natural outcome of the rapidity of recent changes in the aims of art education and of the diverse interpretations of them by authorities in the field.

Administrators who sincerely believe in the worth of art experiences for all children must rely on the thinking and beliefs of the art consultants and art teachers whom they employ. Therefore, unless these individuals have a clear concept of what constitutes sound method, and unless they can clarify the purposes of art education to classroom teachers

GROUP WORK dealing with the community emphasizes the social living possibilities of art. Two- and three-dimensional outcomes may be developed from the same source. In upper grades and at the secondary level, collaboration develops democratic ideals and satisfying personal relationships (2nd grade, Millersburg, Pa.).

and resolve the seeming conflict of authoritative opinions, the program will suffer.

Art consultants and teachers of art in junior and senior high schools must accept this condition as a challenge and as a problem to be resolved. This may be best accomplished within the framework and through the means of democratic educational statesmanship, that is to say, recognition of coöperative solutions of the problem.

LAG OF PRACTICE BEHIND THEORY

As one observes the results of art teaching across the nation, he is impressed with the fact that the method and the point of view that motivate the teaching of art do not always reflect the essential aims reviewed in the previous chapter. There is evidence, nevertheless, that, under the aegis of existing professional organizations, art educators are coming together on essentials. It has been indicated that terms are being clarified, that aims are being defined, and that clear hypotheses are emerging. Research, which is much needed, will undoubtedly aid in pointing the way to better art education. However, the task is vast and the full effects of a shared point of view, if such were desirable, would be slow. Changes in beliefs rest with the individuals who administer the art program, the teachers themselves. Some feel assured in their accustomed ways; others have come into the profession with meager resources; some have come with adequate backgrounds in psychology and art; still others have come by devious ways. Thus the personal equation in the classrooms is a factor, and it must be realized that its heterogeneity and power can and do resist or advance art education. The situation is further complicated by the contentions among conservatives, modernists, and middle-of-the-roaders.

To the presence of these groups there must be added the aggravating doubts which arise from the strong appeal of various major points of view, all vying for attention and adherents. This fact has caused many a teacher of art to say: "I wish we could make up our mind," or "Today it is this; next year it is something else." The truth is that change indicates professional growth, and growth requires flux and exchange and, finally, synthesis. In many instances the teacher has resorted to the adoption of a coalition of several points of view in order to meet the local situation. In some cases the general tenor of a school district has suggested to the art teacher how best to adapt the program. In other instances the teacher's professional background and inclination have determined the complexion of the art offering. Fortunately, there are, in all this wide variety of types and adaptations, enough excellent art situations to warrant the hope that sound art education is an emerging reality.

The problem of educational lag is one that consultants and teachers of art must recognize as an inevitable which must be faced and solved. The advancement of the program cannot be forced, but it can be accomplished through in-service education of classroom teachers and by the implementation of other professional activities in which all teachers have a part. Only through these can lag be reduced and broader understandings achieved.

NEED FOR RESEARCH

Art education in America is not yet fortunate enough to have developed a respectable corpus of indigenous research to which one may turn to check, evaluate, compare, and test theories with regard to their validity or applicability to the classroom. It may be apropos here to distinguish between pure research and informational studies. There is available a considerable amount of informational material, some of it based on doctoral and master's theses, independent studies, or as the result of the work of groups and committees of the regional art associations, the National Art Education Association, and the Committee on Art Education. A large part of this material, helpful though it may be, must be classified as empirical and awaiting more scientific treatment.

INACCESSIBILITY

Pure research in art education is, as yet, inaccessible. What exists is still largely shrouded in the terminology of psychology and aesthetics, and is published mainly in journals that seldom reach the masses of teachers.

However, the scientific work of Thomas Munro and of Norman Meier has set the stage for serious research and has called attention to a fairly large amount of experimental endeavor on the part of others. But again, their bibliographies show that the bulk of research in the psychology

and aesthetics of the art of children is either in foreign language or is
published in foreign publications. Munro[1] cites over seventy significant
sources in his consideration of the psychological and aesthetic aspects
of art education, Faulkner's[2] survey of the entire area of research points

USE OF THE ENVIRONMENT as a source of inspiration, for observation, and for the development of
individual responses to the world is becoming common practice (Northeast Senior High School, Kansas
City, Mo.).

up nearly one hundred sources, and Meier[3] indicates over one hundred
and fifty studies dealing with psychological research in the field. Lowenfeld's study in the nature of creative activity was originally published in

---

[1] Thomas Munro, "The Psychological Approach to Art and Art Education," National
Society for the Study of Education, Fiftieth Yearbook, *Art in American Life and Education*,
Bloomington, Ill., Public School Publishing Company, 1941, pp. 286–288; 321–322.

[2] Ray Faulkner, "A Survey of Recent Research in Art and Art Education," National
Society for the Study of Education, Fiftieth Yearbook, *Art in American Life and Education*, Bloomington, Ill., Public School Publishing Company, 1941, pp. 372–377.

[3] Norman C. Meier, "Recent Research in the Psychology of Art," National Society for
the Study of Education, Fiftieth Yearbook, *Art in American Life and Education*, Bloomington Ill., Public School Publishing Company, 1941, pp. 393–400.

German, and until its translation it was little known in this country. This is a problem that young teachers and students in graduate schools may well face and accept as a challenge because on it depends the further significant growth of the field.

These, then, are the bewildering facets of the situation which gives rise to diverse points of view. The task, therefore, of appraising trends and philosophies is an arduous and dangerous one. Nevertheless, if it is possible to present in the form of synthesis what appears to be significant in each major philosophy for the further and exhaustive investigation by teachers and students of art education, the venture will have been justified.

The purpose of what follows will be to analyze those trends, among many more, that have achieved prominence. Some points of view have secured a substantial following because they contain sound, recognizable elements; others because they present a new emphasis. It will be for the teacher to determine which of the approaches more nearly satisfies the demands of a particular situation, just as it will be for him to decide how quickly or how slowly changes may be effected in the direction of the most desirable program for the children involved. There is a feeling in certain quarters that the evolutionary approach is slow and, therefore, not satisfactory. Yet all too many young teachers have failed and too many art programs have suffered due to the lack of will or the ability on the part of those teachers to adjust to certain local situations.

EARLY EXPERIMENTATION

In Chapter 2 it was pointed out that the major turn in American art education was brought about by Dow's[4] synthetic method of teaching art. For a long time that point of view has dominated school art and, indeed, has had serious effects on academies and art schools in general. Today its influence remains a force in so far as the basic elements of perception are involved. It is a high tribute to Dow that after over fifty years the impact of his contribution is still felt.

But Dow's approach was more in the nature of the organization of the elements, as has been pointed out, than in terms of a philosophy re-

---

[4] Arthur Wesley Dow, *Theory and Practice of Teaching Art*, New York, Teachers College, Columbia University, 1908, pp. 1–5.

lated to child development through art, although he referred to his method as a "natural" one and insisted on general appreciation for consumership.

Another early experiment which has had considerable effect on American art education during the last quarter-century is the one referred to as the "free expression" approach spearheaded by Franz Cizek of the Vienna School of Arts and Crafts. At the same time, Rothe, also of Vienna, believed in the universality of the art impulse, but his method insisted on a rational mode of teaching first; freedom of expression would follow. Thetter, a third teacher in Vienna, discounted any intellectual approach, but rather emphasized the stimulation of creative imagination into art activity.[5] For present purposes, only the Cizek point of view will be further touched upon. The chief contribution of Professor Cizek's emphasis rests in the fact that it points up a most important element in art teaching, that reservoir of creative power that lies within the child's consciousness, the source of all true spontaneity. The prominence of the approach was and is a salutary one in spite of the fact that after a brief success it died out. The weakness of Professor Cizek's theory lay not in the spirit but rather in the practicality of the premises. Children, theoretically, were not permitted to see or study art works in museums, nor prints of them. But they did see the works of their fellow students, all of them highly selected. Therefore, the results of the Vienna School soon became stereotyped and the very purpose with which Cizek started out was defeated by human nature. Nevertheless, the sincerity of the Cizek experiment and its psychological bases are worthy of study and application under certain practical classroom adaptations.[6] Teachers and coördinators of art will do well to familiarize themselves with the interpretation of the work of Cizek as presented by Viola.[7] He, perhaps more adequately than anyone else, has brought together the major aspects of the method and point of view of Franz Cizek in the true light of their original intent. Viola, in answer to thousands of questions propounded by teachers of art in England, makes it clear that the Old Master was not as

---

[5] George Cox, "Modern Trends in Art Education," *Teachers College Record*, May, 1930, pp. 511–521.

[6] A complete account of the Cizek School can be found in *Art and Education*, Merion, Pa., The Barnes Foundation Press, pp. 311–316.

[7] Wilhelm Viola, *Child Art*, London, University of London Press, 1944.

passive a teacher as certain critics would make it appear. He was constantly stimulating, always asking questions of children, sometimes showing displeasure at what was happening, often clearly forbidding certain procedures adopted by children, but eternally vigilant to spot the creative and encourage it.

CURRENT EMPHASES

Coming now to present conditions and current emphases, it should be noted that most of these points of view lean heavily on psychological foundations. In general, they are concerned less with the technical perfection of the results than they are with expression as an index of the growth and development of the individual pupil. They are concerned with method, but chiefly in so far as it relates to the discovery of the emerging personality of the pupil. This fact is of supreme importance for teachers to understand because teachers are the guiding spirit; and unless they understand and feel the implications of the various interactions of pupil environment, they will fail in the stimulation of maximum growth no matter how well-intentioned they may otherwise be.

CREATION-CREATOR RELATIONSHIP

The first of the prevalent trends proposed for analysis is the point of view which has been stressed by Lowenfeld.[8] He conceives of creative development and expression as being intimately related to other types of growth in the same individual. Such a point of view naturally emphasizes the dual role of art activities: *self-discovery* on the one hand and cumulative *self-adjustment* on the other. The types of growth referred to are intellectual, emotional, social, perceptual, physical, aesthetic, and creative. The point of view, furthermore, places great importance on knowing the needs, the thinking, the emotional drives, and the creative type represented by each child. In general, children fall into three broad categories: the visually minded, the haptic, and those who are somewhere between the two main categories. The visual type reacts optically to environment: color, space, shape, and other elements; as Lowenfeld puts it, "Visual types feel as spectators, looking at their work from out-

---

[8] Viktor Lowenfeld, *Creative and Mental Growth,* New York, The Macmillan Company, 1952, Chapter I.

PROBLEMS OF HOUSING, interior design, and others of equal importance are used today not only to develop the abilities of boys and girls but also to give them opportunities to see the relationships of art to life (Shenley Senior High School, Pittsburgh, Pa.).

side."[9] The haptic type is subjective; children in this category are the expressionists; they "feel involved in their work"[10] and are more sensitive to the emotional contents of the experience than they are to visual appearance. A fact that has been grossly misunderstood is that by far the largest number are not at the extremes of the types but rather in between. Awareness of these perceptual types will reveal quite readily the children who lean in one or the other direction. Another central point in this theory is the self-identification of the child with his work. If he does not feel the meaning of the situation, he cannot express himself adequately. To quote Lowenfeld again: "It is, therefore, imperative that

[9] *Ibid.*, p. 189.
[10] *Ibid.*, p. 184.

every child be able to face his own experience. If he cannot identify himself with it, the motivation of his experience must be boosted *and not the drawing activity.*"[11] It is clear then that technics, materials, aesthetic considerations of composition, and mechanics of art in general must be subordinated to the child's own expression, adequate to his perceptual development, and with which he can identify himself. Problems of evaluation and of motivation naturally must take into account the individual *as he is* and as he grows and develops.

Obviously, such a point of view is in direct opposition to teaching by means of formulas, charts, perspective accuracy, anatomical precision, and other conceptions of refinement unless the child artist is conscious of them from within and wishes to express them from conviction. The point of view does not countenance imposition but guidance; there is no teaching for the teacher's sake. And, even more significantly, there is one standard of achievement and that is determined by the child's natural development.

Properly appraised and properly implemented the psychological understanding of children presages that not only art itself but children and youth will grow and flourish into integrated personalities if unhampered and unhindered. While personal growth and development seem to be stressed in this point of view, it is obvious that social integration is assumed as a by-product of well-adjusted individuals. In connection with this point of view, it seems extremely important for teachers to realize that, while art expression does reveal the individual, to psychoanalyze every child through his art and to place unwarranted weight on what his drawings show constitute dangerous practice.

Lastly, the implications growing out of this trend for teacher education and for the spirit of the classroom are of decided importance. These are discussed in Chapters 7 and 14.

ART AS MEANINGFUL EXPERIENCE

The point of view expressed by Mildred Landis is fully discussed in her *Meaningful Art Education.*[12] The basic thesis of this contribution

---

[11] Viktor Lowenfeld, "The Significance of Self-Identification," *The Art Education Bulletin,* February, 1951. Italics are the author's.

[12] Mildred Landis, *Meaningful Art Education,* Peoria, Charles A. Bennett Company, 1951.

may be expressed in the form of a question: How meaningful to the child are the art activities undertaken? To answer the question the author reviews the chief methods employed in the practice of art teaching, appraises them, and rejects them as falling short of being proper avenues for the meaningful experiencing of art.

Thus the directing method, the free-expression method, and the eclectic method are found wanting. The directing method suffers from the "spatial adjacency" of elements that just happen to be together; the free-expression method falls short due to lack of conscious purpose; the eclectic method is inadequate because it "shares the characteristics of the first two." In Landis' words, meaningful art education "is concerned with immediate as well as broad purposes, and with the unity of means and end. It allows the individual sufficient freedom for emotion and reflection. These factors accompanied by ever widening experience may enable the individual to develop a sense of values essential to art and living."[13]

DRAMATIZATION of games and plays acts as springboards for drawing and painting activities. Often children represent themselves as the actors, sometimes as spectators (1st grade, Boise, Idaho).

Furthermore, meaningful art education must distinguish between aesthetic and nonaesthetic principles. The aesthetic principles are beauty of material, beauty of form, and beauty of meaning. The process of understanding these principles will involve empathy, perception, and intuition. For the sake of clarity the last three terms will be defined here.

Empathy is the feeling of relatedness of the individual with the object of regard. In art education a great deal has been said about self-identification. Empathy may be realized either as one creates or as one looks upon a work of art. On looking at a painting, or a piece of sculpture, or an architectural structure, one may sense the rhythm, or the gesture or the unusual height, or the weight represented in the work of art. The

---

[13] *Ibid.,* p. 27.

mental or emotional reaction of the individual is often accompanied by such physical accompaniments as swaying of the body, standing on tiptoe, or assuming the pose suggested by the work of art. It is this mental-emotional-physical response that is referred to as empathy.

Perception and its importance were discussed in Chapter 1. By way of review, it is defined as the experience of objects which are here and in the present. It is the ability to see shape, size, depth, surface, direction, color, texture, and the rest. But the ability and the quality of what is seen are not the same in all individuals even though they may have equally effective eyesight. The totality of perception goes beyond "seeing" and involves comprehension. For examples of this fact one might consider the significance of such popular phrases as "seeing through" something, or the existence of "more than meets the eye." Such phrases imply the sensing of time, space, and meaning of objects. Psychology indicates that the basis of perception is change: intensity, novelty, repetition, intention, and others. Finally, it should be made clear that perception involves not only the visual but all other sense responses.

Intuition is a more elusive term. It is compounded of highly personalized feelings about something or someone. It is knowledge without proof; it is closely associated with empathy and with perception. Croce, the Italian aesthetician, referred to it as the sixth sense. It is rather penetratingly catching a pattern. Artists in general, and very young artists in particular, often rely on this type of feeling in their work.

Meaningful art education, furthermore, is of value to the individual in that "it can be a unifying process," "it has the advantage of tangibility," and it "can be a pervasive element in the life of the individual." By the same token there are social gains to be derived from meaningful art education in terms of the acquisition of values and social integration which are contingent upon unity.

Finally, in *Meaningful Art Education* some basic postulates are presented. Landis suggests three stages of growth: the manipulative stage, the form-experimental stage, and the early-expressive stage. To the recognition of these stages is assigned a major importance in the total development of the child. Teachers are warned about clichés and stereotypes and the improper use of visual materials. The value of proper stimulation at the right time is emphasized. Essentials of a meaningful art program would seem to be:

1. That the child have something to express.
2. That the child be made aware of the possibility of expressing his ideas and feelings in art materials, and
3. That he be helped to understand, enjoy, and appreciate the material organization and the meanings of his work and the work of others."[14]

SENSE EDUCATION

A point of view based on the beliefs of Pestalozzi, yet less prevalent because least understood, was revived by the late Moholy-Nagy.[15] Together with Read and with many psychologists, he believed that every human being is biologically endowed with some capacity for developing a visual mode of expression that will adequately relate him to his environment. When such articulation occurs the individual tends to be more unified, and to develop a sense of adequacy. Thus viewed, the arts are not esoteric activities that may or may not occur; they become integral with life itself. The problem then becomes one of sense education in the free development of the creative impulse so that individuals may become conversant in the language of the emotions. What man needs, therefore, is the opportunity to explore. He may explore many media and many tools and materials to discover how they may become tangible means for his intangible feelings. This point of view is not unlike what Frank Lloyd Wright proposed much earlier. He insisted that the machine is a legitimate tool for artists of a machine age.

Moholy-Nagy went so far as to propose a series of exercises calculated to offer acquaintance and release. The most interesting fact about these exercises is that they follow an alternating pattern of freedom and restraint. Not all art is play; some art experiences are hard and disheartening.

The imagination, fantasy, inventiveness, organization and significant relationships of a social, technical, and scientific nature are part of the set of exercises. The theory, when understood, becomes a living element in its applications to problems of an industrial character. The approach reveals the Bauhaus point of view which, in its extensive applications to the education of industrial designers and architects, had already been

---

[14] *Ibid.*, p. 108.
[15] Ladislaus Moholy-Nagy, *The New Vision*, New York, W. W. Norton and Company, 1938.

demonstrated in Germany. It was later transplanted to the Chicago Institute of Design and is now incorporated in the work at the Illinois Institute of Technology.

How the plan could be implemented for use with children in crowded classrooms is a larger problem. The handling of a variety of tools and materials has received attention for some time, but not to the extent suggested by Moholy-Nagy. When the point of view is coupled to the belief that there is a natural way of developing and that children have things to say, there is reason to believe that in time children would acquire the literacy which they require to relate themselves to their environment.

There has been and there still is a tendency among art teachers to shun experiences in the crafts: weaving, woodwork, plaster, metal, and the rest. These, in addition to graphic experiences, are part and parcel of sense education. To continue such imbalance in the art program is to deny thousands of children the opportunity to find *their* way of expression and, therefore, of complete fulfillment. The necessity of a balanced program is reiterated at various points throughout this book because of the conviction that tools, materials, and technics are natural means of self-discovery for many children.

THE THEORY OF NATURAL UNFOLDING

In contrast to intuitional approaches to art, Schaeffer-Simmern[16] presents the challenging results of an experiment which includes individuals as varied as possible in biological and environmental backgrounds. Three factors remain constant in the experiment:

1. Individuals are at all times free to choose the manner of expression and the subject matter.
2. Self-criticism is the sole basis for continuing effort and progress.
3. Group efforts and criticism are used only when several individuals are recognized as being at the same level of artistic growth.

A number of questions arise in surveying the results of the experiment. The first is concerned with the self-criticism of individuals. There is here a personal element that the best teachers of art would want to possess; it was evident in the work of Cizek's classes. The master was ex-

---

[16] Henry Schaeffer-Simmern, *The Unfolding of Artistic Activity*, Berkeley and Los Angeles, University of California Press, 1948.

ercising, without wanting to, a tremendous influence on what children did. This reinforces the importance of the teacher as a guide. As a technic of teaching it is most desirable to bring children to the point where they will seek after self-improvement by self-analysis. But how this can be accomplished is a question which each teacher must determine. The present tendency to have children work in committees, to have discussions, to bring in demonstrators, to evaluate personal work or the work

ADVENTURE, physical activities, and other daily experiences of significance to children may be utilized at all levels, but especially with junior- and senior-high-school pupils (7th grade, Druid Junior High School, Baltimore, Md.).

of others in the spirit of fellowship, is a possible answer to how this may be accomplished in crowded classrooms.

A second question arises from the examples of the results of the experiment, namely, the similarity of subject matter and styles. Is it possible that, as in the Cizek classes, a few individuals, stronger than the rest, will in the long run influence others? The cloistered atmosphere of the experimental laboratory, and even the strong personality of the teacher, obviously are insufficient to offset group reaction which conspires against the artistic autonomy with which the individual begins.

A third question is in regard to the evident retrogression in the work of some normal individuals in the experiment at the point of their highest development. They seek after the "classic" and academic in art rather than progress in the direction of expressionism. Whether this is an intermediate stage which will later flourish in more significant form is difficult to tell.

The significance of the experiment, however, is not lessened by the questions posed above; rather, they enhance it. In the case of the "concept stage" one finds that definite and steady progress has been made: from the "intentional figure with ground" the individual moves to "greatest contrast of direction of lines," later to "variability of direction of lines," and thence to "borderless transition from parts with figural meaning to parts with ground meaning." This shows conclusively the power of the individual to grow in visual perception and thus in greater facility to produce artistic configurations. The independent growth in artistic concepts and the striving after order is bound to affect the individual as a whole, and to lead him to a reconstuction and integration of his total personality.

The value of the experiment and its contribution to art education would seem to be rather indirect because there exists a sharp difference in situations: classroom versus experimental laboratory. The significance lay in asserting that each individual is an autonomous being and that he has his own way of developing and his own style, due to his own drives, needs, and aspirations. It will help teachers to realize these facts even when confronted with large groups of children for a relatively few minutes of the day. Great significance should be attached to the value of self-criticism and to the making of individual decisions on mode of expression and choice of materials. Schaeffer-Simmern emphasizes the *self:* self-choice, self-development, self-improvement, and self-discipline, eventually. As a tenet for art education, this emphasis can not be denied. Its implementation in the typical classroom is a matter to ponder.

THE FUNCTIONAL APPROACH

Ziegfeld and Smith,[17] reporting on the Owatonna Art Education Project, an experiment now well known, present a picture of art education

---

[17] Edwin Ziegfeld and Mary Elinore Smith, *Art for Daily Living: The Story of the Owatonna Art Education Project,* Minneapolis: University of Minnesota Press, 1944.

quite in tune with the times. Slightly over twenty years ago, educators believed and advocated that the daily living of poeple should be the basis of curriculum planning. The project in Owatonna, therefore, set for itself specific goals: to discover the art needs of a community, to develop a practical course of study in art suited to those needs, and to develop interest in art in the daily life of the community. The study revealed that all people, in some way, use art in the satisfaction of some daily need and that, therefore, it is important to include all phases of art in a functional program. Art needs give rise to art problems when situations are meaningful, thus tapping the inner springs of creative activity. It follows that the art program for the schools should be organized in terms of areas of living. The study of local examples of art of all types is useful in making people aware of art in their immediate surroundings and in establishing a vital point of contact. The project further revealed that, since art is usually compartmentalized, the art program should establish relationships between various modes of art expression and between art and other subject fields. It was also discovered that interest in and acquaintance with a special area of art are closely related; this fact should indicate that in planning the art program the interests of those to be taught should be central. Experience with adults showed little interest in technical skills; this fact indicates that in art education it is important to develop expression without overemphasis on technic.

The implications of Ziegfeld's point of view, it may be well to note, are reflected in the approach used in *Art Today*,[18] of which he is a co-author. Basically intended for the appreciation of art, the volume reflects the meaning of art in relation to life. The problem of human needs manifests itself in terms of food, clothing, and shelter at first. Later, as these needs are satisfied, the artistic refinements of decoration as well as of structure arise and must be satisfied. Beyond the elemental needs, however, man has emotional or nonmaterial needs: religion, patriotism, and the pure urge to create. All these are accounted for in this point of view. Specifically, the areas covered are these: art in the home, art in the community, art in religion, art in industry, and art in commerce. The problems of organization and of materials find their place in the scheme

[18] Ray Faulkner, Edwin Ziegfeld, and Gerald Hill, *Art Today*, rev. ed., New York, Henry Holt and Company, 1955.

quite naturally, and the specific understandings essential for the appreciation of each major art are given due attention.

In attempting a critique of this point of view one is conscious of a prevalent notion in the field, namely, that it is too realistic as an approach or that it sounds too earthy. In reply one may ask whether a functional program need be less creative than one concerned with remote experiences, and whether a functional program need be oblivious of individual expression and growth. When is an individual fully integrated and unified within himself? The answers to these questions are probably obvious. It would seem that from the standpoint of the classroom the functional approach should lend itself admirably to the task of developing genuine creative power because its motivations inhere in the problems of life. The dangers of subservience to other purposes and of being too "practical" are minimized when the pupil's interest is made central to the program. Perhaps in no other approach can social goals and values be realized more fully.

THE INDIVIDUAL AS CREATOR

Victor D'Amico in his *Creative Teaching in Art*[19] stresses development of the individual's capacities in relation to basic skills and technics. The point of view has a great deal to offer because, in essence, it affirms the integrity of the person, or the child, and at the same time uses what art and history recognize as sound. In a sense this point of view may be extremely worth while in that the psychological approach to education is blended with the development of those skills essential to adequate self-discovery. The words of the exponent of this point of view may clarify the preëminent position of the child as artist: "The concept of the child as artist implies that every child is a potential creator endowed with those sensibilities that characterize the artist. It does not claim that every child will become an accomplished artist and produce masterpieces. The concept transcends the idea of art as performance or a product and looks upon art as a way of living—the means of enjoying and enriching life through creative expression."[20] But D'Amico wants the child to develop art values while he is expressing himself freely. There are stages of de-

---

[19] Victor D'Amico, *Creative Teaching in Art*, rev. ed., Scranton, International Textbook Company, 1953.
[20] *Ibid.*, p. 1.

velopment, which is another way of saying that there is a proper time and proper approach, but the child artist must, in the long run, become design-conscious if his growth is not to be stunted. The establishment of art values is not superimposed, nor can it be achieved by rules, tricks, and exercises. Values, rather, depend on timing and on the intensity of the child's awareness of his need for developing the mode of expression desired. This is also true of the teaching of technics. Again: "Teaching in response to the need, and through understanding, requires an individual approach, for every child in a group will not meet the same problems at the same time because each child develops at his own rate of speed."[21]

This point of view recognizes the true artist in the child and his felt need to develop values and technics at appropriate junctures in his development. Life experiences are acknowledged as the chief source of "what to do" rather than fictitious, preconceived schemes and stereotyped programs. Major areas of activity are investigated: the child as painter, as muralist, as sculptor, as potter, as graphic artist, as stage artist, as designer, and as craftsman. The length and breadth of the art program are thus presented, but with the caution that these compartments are used only for convenience and that all of them should be at the disposal of the growing child. He will be either a consumer or an artist, but in either case a better-integrated person because of the art experience.

Finally, this point of view conceives of the child as a center, but, at the same time, envisions the teacher as an ever-present, fully understanding, and continually stimulating guide.

THE INTEGRATED ART PROGRAM

Man is a living organism and as such possesses a variety of potential characteristics. Adequately and harmoniously developed, such characteristics result in the "whole" man and the successful citizen. It is this process of harmonious growth that is called integration. The term itself has been applied to that type of education that best facilitates the process of unifying. The interpretations and ramifications of that educational process are discussed at length in Chapter 4.

---

[21] *Ibid.*, p. 17.

Winslow, who has followed the gradual development of art education for over thirty years, has written copiously on various phases of school art, particularly from the standpoint of education in general. He has concluded that an *integrated* program in art is emerging.[22] What Winslow presents is an organization and adaptation of what seemed, at the time, to be the best thinking in curriculum organization. That point of view is still very strong in many sections of the country where correlated and "core" teaching obtain. The term "organization" is used in the sense of educational sequence, of systematic and logical follow-up, of planned units and activities believed suitable at certain age and grade levels. Extreme organization may even show preconceived though desirable outcomes, related information deemed worth while for all pupils, and certain types of art information and technics considered essential for adequate expression.

UNUSUAL EVENTS, such as the circus, the fair, a fire, a wedding, a party, the school assembly, a football game, and similar occurrences, often form the basis for creative work in painting and drawing (4th grade, Hazleton, Pa.).

Philosophically, Winslow attaches himself to the idea of integrated learning and presents, lucidly, its place in art education for a changing world. He points out the *why* of art in the schools, how it affects living, the function of art as a liberal pursuit, its contributions to vocations, the relationships of materials to processes, and the transformation of emotion into expression. Examined critically, it is difficult to discount such a point of view. Its lack, it seems, is a verbal omission of proper emphasis on the developmental aspects of art education. This, however, may be assumed as a logical by-product of art expression. In fact, considerations such as "art as experience," "the creative aspects of art activity," and the "motivation" of art expression are suggested as essential considerations in the planning of the art program.

[22] Leon L. Winslow, *The Integrated School Art Program*, New York, McGraw-Hill Book Company, 1939.

The proponent of this point of view believes that activities should be both directed and free. The latter would be resultants of the former. In fact, the former should act as stimulants for the latter. A parallel is Moholy-Nagy's emphasis on freedom and restraint, the restraint being largely in the nature of discipline.

It should be remembered that the idea of "justifying" art as a subject in the curriculum was rife at the time when integrated curricula were advocated. Only by showing art's relatedness to other subject fields, and by setting up a logical organization, could it be demonstrated that art is a body of workable subject matter, and that it serves as a useful means toward the ends of American education. Only thus could art establish its legitimacy. Winslow, furthermore, demonstrates that art can and should be a "major" curriculum in those senior high schools where the number of pupils, interested and capable, would justify the expenditures involved.

A critique of this point of view, in the light of the times, raises the following questions: (1) Does the program tend to be fixed? (2) Does the program concern itself too much with established sequences of subject matter? (3) Does it place art too much on a "service" basis? (4) Does it sufficiently emphasize the pupil in actual planning? (5) Does it stress the effect of art on the individual's growth and development?[23]

EXPERIMENTAL APPROACHES

In concluding this survey and analysis of current trends and points of view, it seems proper to single out some highly personal, yet noteworthy efforts by well-known teachers who have chosen to set down a record of what they have accomplished or discovered.

The study of these experimental methods indicates to teachers the value of undertaking experimentation, of testing procedures, and of deepening their insights of the art of teaching. Such enterprises are not only worth while for personal growth and more satisfying teaching, but actually may add to the knowledge which comprises the science of teaching. The only caution which seems of import is that the experimenter should be in possession of valid facts, that his own hypotheses

---

[23] Winslow readily recognizes these facts in an article, "Stages of Growth and Development in Art," *Educational Administration and Supervision*, January, 1952, pp. 18–24.

110 should be tested, and that results or conclusions should be based on sufficient data before generalizing.

The Artist in Each of Us

Florence Cane,[24] a successful teacher who pioneered many experiments in the field of art teaching, believes firmly that there is the germ of creative power in each individual. The creative process involves from the very beginning a combination of two opposites: an active and a receptive stage. The significance of these elements might well be pondered, for too often teachers are prone to think that there must be "work" going on always, and that pupils must be "busy." This may be a way of maintaining a sort of discipline, but it is not necessarily a good way of bringing out the creative. The opposite situation, of course, would be an abuse of what is intended by the term *receptive*. Contemplation, listening, seeing, and absorbing are conditions of preparation for creativity. But since children are generally ready for activity, one must ask oneself whether the situation has meaning for the pupil.

Mrs. Cane recognizes three major developmental periods of growth and has some simple suggestions on how to motivate for these periods. The predominance of muscular and sensory activity of the early years is followed by the period of emotional self-expression: "This looks just the way I feel inside." Then follows the period of observation and of setting down the world as the pupil perceives it. Later comes the adolescent age with critical awareness, a sense of third dimension, and a deepening of feelings which need not be lost if properly understood and nurtured. She says quite aptly that "Youth deserves teachers with psychological understanding, artistic ability and simple, direct method of supplying the technique demanded by hungry minds and searching hearts."[25]

Mrs. Cane lists the following as conditions favorable to creative work: outer factors of physical comfort, proper materials and tools arranged for convenience, and then the inner conditions, which, of course, are the basic ones because they deal with the spirit of the child artist. The process of creating is conceived as an integrating force as well as an expression of the self.

---

[24] Florence Cane, *The Artist in Each of Us*, New York, Pantheon Books, 1951.
[25] *Ibid.*, p. 29

Regarding method, three avenues are explored: release of creative faculties through basic experiences of the *body,* and basic experiences
of the *mind* and *spirit*. Thus, movement, feeling, and sound are proposed
as means of releasing and harmonizing with the creative impulse. Each
of these means is explained and the application to the stirring of the im-

MODELING in clay, plaster, papier-mâché, wire, string, and other three-dimensional work, develop
coördination and the imagination at all levels. The teacher's guidance as shown in the illustration is
intended to stimulate pupils and leads to fuller creative growth (4th grade, Richmond, Va.).

agination, the awakening of the mind, the sensitizing of the feelings, and
the development of observation, recollection, and perception is illustrated
by her practices in teaching.

Case histories are finally presented as evidences of the effectiveness of
the method. The true significance of this contribution may be discovered only by careful understanding of its author's philosophy and method,
followed by personal experimentation in both.

How effective can this be in the typical classroom? There is the question! The answer may be given only by those teachers brave enough, under auspicious conditions, to try and find out for themselves.

The Arts in the Classroom

Another significant personal effort that has borne abundant fruits is Natalie Cole's approach. In this instance the term "arts" is used in the plural because Mrs. Cole uses more than the visual arts to evoke from her children the excellent work that they produce. The chief values of her method, it seems, may be best understood if some of the captions from her book are reproduced in capitals for emphasis:

1. A CHILD'S PICTURE TRAVELS ON ITS INTEREST
2. FROM AMONG THE MOST TIMID WILL COME SOME OF THE FINEST PAINTERS
3. "WHY WORRY ABOUT HOW A COW REALLY OUGHT TO BE?"
4. "I CLOSED MY EYES AND SEEN AN ANGEL AND MADE ONE LIKE I SEEN IT"
5. IT IS NOT THE LINOLEUM—IT IS THE SPIRIT
6. "DON'T WORRY HOW OTHERS ARE DOING IT"
7. "IT IS HOW MUCH WE FEEL ON THE INSIDE THAT COUNTS"

It is worthy of note that the statements used by Mrs. Cole have the same human quality, lilt, and freshness as those used by children (the statements in quotation marks). At once one is aware of a communion between teacher and pupils, of an understanding of home and personal life, of the need for the free expression of deep-seated feelings such as arise from life situations. Then, again, one senses that not every one could accomplish what Mrs. Cole has accomplished unless the same spirit animates the teacher who attempts to utilize her method.

An analysis of the statements reproduced above reveals that children's interests are paramount; that visual realism is not the sole criterion; that fantasy and dreams count; that materials and tools are simply means, not ends in themselves. It is individuality that matters; and how one feels *inside* is true expression. Finally, it is clear that art expression is evoked rather than forced out of children.

Art Has Many Faces

Lastly, it seems proper to recognize a contribution which contains powerful suggestions for art teachers. The suggestions seem particularly significant because they focus on the importance of the teacher in the teaching-experiencing situation. Katharine Kuh[26] states in the Introduction to her book: "My hope is to *show* rather than tell, to combine *looking* with reading by limiting the text to statements which can be verified through visual examples, comparisons or contrasts. The reader is asked to take nothing on faith, though he must remember that certain emotional reactions to art cannot always be explained." As she proceeds, it becomes clear that nature reveals itself dramatically to eyes "sensitized by art," and that one may find art in commonplace surroundings if one but looks "searchingly." Here, then, is a clue, an answer to where one may find subject matter of interest. Art, indeed, does have "many faces." By means of photographs, reproductions of paintings, drawings, and charts, Kuh points them out. Actually, it is an elucidation of what art is, in terms of art. While devoid of educational terms, and while not intended as a book on method, this personal contribution does much to answer the query as to why there are so many modes of expression often encountered in the work of young people. To be able to see in the variants a true spark of creativity is to recognize the worth of the individual artist.

PICTUREMAKING in various media is encouraged not only as art expression of a general nature but also as a means through which pupils communicate personal interests, impressions, and feelings (Junior High School, Toronto, Canada).

The further significance of this personal point of view lies in the fact that it underscores for teachers the vast resources which act as stimulants. A group of teacher-education students were dealing with the element of texture and were advised to locate not "pictures" of many surface qualities but actual materials. They brought in a variety of stones, barks, swatches of textile, leaves, fruits, and other available objects. A study of these collections clarified the problem and made *real* the element itself. Similar experiences were utilized in dealing with form and line. Nature

---

[26] Katharine Kuh, *Art Has Many Faces*, New York, Harper & Brothers, 1951.

in its many modes, and the world in general, offer an abundance of art sources which may remain unknown to children until they are awakened to the variety and wealth of the surroundings.

HARMONY IN DIVERSITY

It will be obvious to anyone that many more trends are at work and, consequently, that many more could have been included in this review. Yet, from those chosen for analysis, it may be worth while to attempt a reconciliation, which indeed is present and easily discoverable. What are the common elements in these seemingly different points of view?

First, they are all relatively concerned with the individuality of the pupil, his development into an integrated being, and his rapport to the social group.

Second, all indicate a belief in the creative endowment of human beings in varying degrees, and in the urgency within each individual to express himself adequately.

Third, they are all committed, in varying degrees, to freedom with regard to choice of technic, medium, mode, and subject matter.

Fourth, they are all agreed that technical perfectionism of an academic character is not significant; proper growth at the proper level for each individual is important.

Fifth, they all recognize that experience is basic to expression and that a program, to be vital, must be of interest to those who undertake creative activity.

How do the various points of view differ? It would seem that the chief differences are in terms of emphasis rather than in basic beliefs.

Some points of view are largely based on psychology and seem to be mainly concerned with the free and natural development of the creative impulse and of the senses without direct concern for technics and for the functional use of the art object. Undoubtedly, it is inferred that as the individual grows his creative development will be commensurate to his endowment. Furthermore, he will adjust to whatever problems may arise because of inner strength. Other points of view are more pragmatic in nature and, in differing degree, are concerned with problems and activity areas that are real in the sense that they occur in daily life to most people. But, functional aspects do not preclude the education and development of the senses, or the development of the potential artist.

All proponents believe in the integration of the individual and of society in terms of life relationships; in fact, it is through the creation and use of art in daily tasks that life and art find their true significance.

It is clear that all points of view consider the teacher's position in the classroom as the most crucial element in the implementation of the art program. The teacher's understanding of the pupil's limitations and abilities, and the appreciation of the pupil's needs and emotional drives, become the determinants of the success or failure of the art experience.

A RELATIONAL POINT OF VIEW

There are some final questions concerning the whole matter. How shall teachers choose from this array of trends? To which school of thought shall they attach themselves? Which is most effective? Is it possible to arrive at a synthesis? As a possible answer, a relational point of view is suggested. It recognizes three basic factors which need to be considered of equal importance in the process of arriving at a satisfactory working philosophy of art education. These factors are the process of creation, including the individual; the created object; and the worth of the created object to the creator and/or to his social group. These factors were analyzed in detail in Chapter 1.

What has been discussed thus far leads to the conclusion that art teachers must conceive of an art program based on a broad pattern of development if it is to be of utmost validity and effectiveness for the pupil and if it is to be in harmony with present concepts of education.

To clarify the meaning of the proposed relational point of view, it may be profitable to set down propositions somewhat as follows:

1. Art is a normal human activity which functions most adequately when the individual (creator) establishes rapport with his environment (including society).
2. The object created (art expression) must have aesthetic qualities appropriate to the age and to the creative level of the creator.
3. The individual as well as the social group should benefit from or be affected by the production or consumption of the art object.

It will be remembered that Dewey's first concern in his *Art as Experience* is with "The Live Creature" and further, in the same work, with

"The Human Contribution." Below are some of his statements apropos of this relationship:

> When artistic objects are separated from both conditions of origin and operation in experience, a wall is built around them that renders almost opaque their general significance, with which aesthetic theory deals.[27]
>
> The self acts as well as undergoes, and its undergoings are not impressions stamped upon an inert wax but depend upon the way the organism reacts and responds. There is no experience in which the human contribution is not a factor in determining what actually happens. The organism is a force, not a transparency.[28]
>
> Any psychology that isolates the human being from the environment also shuts him off, save for external contacts, from his fellows.[29]
>
> Art is the extension of the power of rites and ceremonies to unite men, through a shared celebration, to all incidents and scenes of life. This office is the reward and seal of art.[30]

The meaning of Dewey's statements, when applied to this consideration, cannot but evoke a sense of inherent relationships in the total act of creating. The necessity in art education is for a point of view that considers all elements rather than stressing one to the exclusion of the others. The child is the most significant element in the process, but what he undergoes is equally as important. And surely, what happens as a result of what he undergoes is of supreme importance to him and to society.

The soundness of a relational concept may be further affirmed as one considers art from the standpoint of how it has functioned or what it has been ever since man painted on the walls of caves. Man made tools with which to support life itself; and when he created, he did so in response to the ideas and the ideals of his time and his social group. This latter aspect has been especially stressed in the preceding chapters. Dewey's concept of experience is detailed in Chapter 4.

But to proceed with the argument, it may be of value to remember that art has many moods. Herbert Read describes them as hedonistic, purposive, and expressive.[31] The existence of these moods reinforces the

---

[27] John Dewey, *Art as Experience*, New York, Minton, Balch and Company, 1935, p. 3.
[28] *Ibid.*, p. 246
[29] *Ibid.*, p. 270.
[30] *Ibid.*, p. 271.
[31] Herbert Read, *Art and Society*, New York, The Macmillan Company, 1937, Chapter II.

value of relationalism as a very logical position calling attention to the constant need for awareness of the total structure of the art experience. As this structure is clearly understood, it should be possible to harmonize the many points of view just discussed. It should also be possible to analyze opinions expressed in the literature of art education and to examine, objectively, the variety of approaches and results that one observes on examining children's work. Finally, the structure should clarify the place and function of art in the schools and thus relieve the bewilderment and insecurity prevalent among teachers, parents, and administrators.

As indicated a moment ago, the relational theory recognizes three elements in the creative experience: (1) the process of creation, (2) the created object, (3) the value of the object to the creator or to his fellow men.

The first element refers to the universal will to create which has been touched upon in the first chapter. It may now be accepted as an assumption that every boy and girl, or every adult, for that matter, is endowed with some degree of plastic sensibility. The genetic basis and the psychological implications of this fact have been the subject of special studies, of research, and of experimentation. Every art teacher may wish to examine available sources for affirmation and for a more complete understanding of the nature of the creative impulse, its manifestations, and its nurturing. The refinements of method and the increased personal effectiveness of the teacher suggest extended acquaintance with the psychology and the philosophy of art as they relate to childhood and adolescence.

An important point to remember with regard to the child as creator seems to be this: while his activity must be unhampered and not dictated, and while his expression must be free from adult interference, nevertheless, such activity must account for its coming into being. Unless the art activity is meaningful to the creator and at the same time valid as a mode of expression, at the creator's level of growth, it is to be recognized, at best, not as art but as pastime. There are aesthetic measures which show whether adequate growth and development are taking place or whether the youthful artist is at a standstill. It should be considered the duty of the art teacher to ask whether the work of art shows qualities of perception and whether it evidences those controls appropriate to the level of the child. Evaluation will then have meaning for the child and for the teacher (see also Chapter 7).

The second element involved in the trilogy deals with what is created, or the objectification of the will to create. Much misunderstanding has arisen in the ranks of art education over "progressive" methods. It is a matter of record that many have misunderstood freedom for laissez faire: uncontrolled, unguided, uninhibited activity and atmosphere. At its worst, that misunderstanding made of every scrawl a work of art. And for a brief time any sense of order or resemblance to the visual world, or an intelligible idea in child art, was condemned as ordinary or unworthy. The precious soul of the child was hallowed to the point of absurdity, and the function of the teacher was reduced to that of a pedant who looked on to ensure that the artistic instinct would not bubble over and result in physical conflict. To be sure, that point of view may have been a just antidote to the precise, imitative, and dictated exercises of the era immediately proceeding it. But, unfortunately, the salutary effects of progressive education were nullified by misunderstandings and by the quasi-religious fervor of its adherents.

The truth of the matter, supported by the several points of view examined, is that the created object should have aesthetic merit in relation to the level of growth and creative development of the individual who creates it. As the level rises, or as the child matures, the futile controversy over process and product is resolved by a realization that children cease babbling as they master words and sentences. As a young artist grows he acquires a maturer idiom and more should be expected of him. This element of the trilogy points up for teachers the significance of understanding stages of development in art. The latter are discussed in detail in Chapter 8, "Art Education in the Elementary School," as well as in connection with the consultant's work.

The third element of the relational point of view is best expressed in the form of questions: What good has been served by the work of art? Does it have value for the individual who created it, or for his group? Has the expression served as personal communication? Does it help the individual in a vocational sense? Does it serve as an emotional stabilizer? Has it been worth while as general education?

Whatever the case, no purpose is demeaned if it leads the child artist toward the development of a harmonious outlook on the life of which he is a part. Furthermore, the point of view becomes significant when considered in relation to practice in the classroom. Specifically, art activities for the lower grades of the elementary school may be assigned a preëminently developmental role. Similar activities in the junior high school may be intended to serve a guidance function. In the senior high school, the activities may be directed toward the more realistic task of discovering and fostering vocational or avocational interests and abilities, in art or other fields of human endeavor.

It should not be construed, however, that each element of the trilogy can or should be pursued singly at any one level. They remain as constants in the total development of the child artist and as flexible guides that will help teachers determine when one or another element should be given justifiable emphasis.

Of greater importance will be the teacher's answers to questions that determine whether or not the art activity has served as an integrating medium. Has the young artist found himself? Has he discovered relationships? Has art experience improved his behavior as a member of the group? Has art supplied him with a tool with which better to establish himself in relation to the world in which he lives?

It seems clear that a relational theory, as it applies to art education, is in perfect harmony with sound psychology, and that it does not preclude any worthy practice or method. It advocates, unequivocally, a purposeful program that is widely adaptable. It implies that art education for all children has a definite task to perform quite outside the realm of the esoteric and the sophisticated. It further implies that art education for the schools of the nation has specific goals and functions. It discounts the notion of art for its own sake or as being a meaningless pastime. In contrast, it seeks after a program that may bring about an organic unity: creator-creation-society.

SUMMARY

In this chapter, it was noted that there is a great deal of diversity in points of view with regard to the *what* and *how* of art education. That differences should exist is natural. Democratic ideals and ways invariably admit of differences. Differences are healthy indexes when considered as issues to be discussed or as problems to be solved intelligently. On the other hand, the existence of too many and too varied points of view tends to confuse. It also indicates that theory and practice do not always parallel each other.

A way of reducing professional lag and of arriving at a broadly shared point of view is to promote research, to participate in it, to disseminate its results, and to test its findings. Every classroom can, in a sense, become a laboratory for better art education. Continued experimentation and research constitute one of the major needs of the field.

It was noted that there has been some experimentation in art, both in Europe and in America. The influence of Cizek on art education in this country is a matter of record. It was also noted that the criticisms of Cizek made by Munro and others were justified. On the other hand, the best interpreter of the Viennese master, Professor Wilhelm Viola, now in England, more than vindicates the intent of the great teacher.

Dow's revolutionary forward step in art teaching was also noted, as well as subsequent reports of the National Art Education Association and its regional affiliates. Reports of committees on curriculum and method were recognized.

But the major purpose of this chapter has been to analyze contemporary major points of view with the intention of determining how each differs from the others and to what extent they agree on basic principles. That there is harmony in diversity has been amply shown.

The author's own point of view has been expressed in the *relational theory:* creator-creation-society. It has been indicated that equal attention to these three facets should bring about satisfying results in art and, at the same time, develop in all children a wholesome way of seeing the world of which they are a part.

For Discussion and Activity

1. To what extent and for what specific reasons is a variety of point of view in art education a desirable situation?
2. What is the value of analysis in determining the significant elements of a philosophy of art education?
3. Through readings, develop a comprehensive analysis of the work of early experimenters, such as Cizek, Thetter, or others. Compare their findings and beliefs with the point of view held in art education today. To what

extent are the earlier points of view tenable today? How applicable are they to classroom situations?

4. What are the chief contributions of each of the following: D'Amico, Lowenfeld, Winslow, Ziegfeld, Landis, Schaeffer-Simmern, Moholy-Nagy?

5. Develop your own synthesis from the study of the points of view prevalent today; test its validity in relation to the basic premises presented in Chapter 1.

6. What is the significance of self-identification in art experience? Develop a number of concrete situations, and, if possible, attempt actual applications in the classroom.

7. What are the implications for the art program of the point of view that conceives of the child as painter, the child as potter, etc.?

8. When is an art activity meaningful? Elaborate on the point of view and develop examples that would be applicable to a specific grade in school.

9. What value do you attach to materials and tools of expression? How are they significant? How far would you go in directing children in their use?

10. Do you agree or disagree with the relational point of view presented in this chapter? Develop arguments for and against it.

For Further Reading

Cane, Florence, *The Artist in Each of Us*, New York, Pantheon Books, 1951, Chapters II, III.

D'Amico, Victor, *Creative Teaching in Art*, rev. ed., Scranton, International Textbook Company, 1953.

Faulkner, Ray; Ziegfeld, Edwin; and Hill, Gerald, *Art Today*, rev. ed., New York, Henry Holt and Company, 1955, Part I.

Gotshalk, D. W., *Art and the Social Order*, Chicago, University of Chicago Press, 1947, Chapters III, IX, X.

Landis, Mildred M., *Meaningful Art Education*, Peoria, Charles A. Bennett Company, 1951, Chapters I, III.

Logan, Frederick M., *Growth of Art in American Schools*, New York, Harper & Brothers, 1954, Chapters V, VI.

Lowenfeld, Viktor, *Creative and Mental Growth*, rev. ed., New York, The Macmillan Company, 1952, Chapters I, II.

McDonald, Rosebel, *Art as Education*, New York, Henry Holt and Company, 1941, Chapter I.

Rannells, Edward W., *Art in the Junior High School*, Lexington, University of Kentucky, College of Education, 1946, Chapters VII, IX, X.

Schaeffer-Simmern, Henry, *The Unfolding of Creative Activity*, Berkeley and Los Angeles, University of California Press, 1948.

122   Shultz, Harold, and Shores, Harlan, *Art in the Elementary School*, Urbana, University of Illinois Press, 1948, Chapter II.

Starch, Daniel; Stanton, Hazel M.; and Koerth, Wilhelmine, *Psychology in Education*, New York, D. Appleton-Century Company, 1941, Chapter XIX.

Whitford, William G., *An Introduction to Art Education*, rev. ed., New York, D. Appleton-Century Company, 1937, Chapter III.

Winslow, Leon L., *The Integrated School Art Program*, rev. ed., New York, McGraw-Hill Book Company, 1949, Chapters I, II, III.

Ziegfeld, Edwin (ed.), *Education and Art, A Symposium*, Paris, UNESCO, 1953, Section I.

PART II
CONSIDERATIONS
OF METHOD

NATURE AND FUNCTION
OF METHOD

> The best procedure will depend on several factors, none
> of which can be neglected, namely, the genius of the
> teacher, the intellectual type of the pupils, their prospects
> in life, the opportunities offered by the immediate sur-
> roundings of the school, and allied factors of this sort.
> Alfred North Whitehead,
> *The Aims of Education*

MEANING OF METHOD

A DISCUSSION OF METHOD INEVITABLY RAISES A NUMBER OF QUESTIONS
because the *who, why, what, when, where,* and *how* that are involved
in such a consideration must include the pupil, the teacher, what is to
be taught, the physical environment, the climate of the classroom, technics, and other related factors.

By setting down specific prescriptions for what good method is, one
is likely to run the danger of limiting freedom. Yet by being too vague,
the whole effort may be wasted. Therefore, in order that the nature
and purposes of method may be clearly understood and its applications
made functional, a number of the broad aspects and of the scope of
method will be analyzed. Briefly, what will be attempted is a consideration of those means of education, those professional technics, and
those tools generally employed by teachers in their guidance of pupils
which may obtain the most beneficial results for them.

In the present case, since art is the area through which it is hoped to induce proper growth, it is in terms of art education that this consideration should be especially interpreted.

EVOLUTION OF METHOD

From the earliest days of formalized education, and surely since the introduction of art as an activity in the school curriculum, certain *ways* of teaching have developed. Some have persisted for a long time, some have disappeared as their usefulness waned, and some still linger with us. In the course of events other means and other ways must be found to meet more adequately the new needs of individuals and the contemporary goals of education. In general, today one hears of directed, free-expression, correlated, integrated, and "core" methods of teaching. Just what do these terms imply? Are they sound? Do the methods they describe help young people achieve maximum development? Are they dangerous devices that frustrate individuals and kill the creative spark?

In addition to the methods mentioned above, certain approaches which are inherent in all good methods have been developed through experimental education and through the wider application of psychological findings, and have proved to be worth-while aids in teaching. One hears of motivation, stimulation, evaluation, teacher-pupil planning, sensory aids, and curriculum resources as effective means of teaching and learning. What is their significance? What is their educational foundation? How may they be used with profit? How are they abused?

Beyond this enumeration, because tools and materials play such an important role in the visual arts, attention must be given to their appropriate use and to best ways of introducing them at the proper time and level. Technics and processes are significant factors in art education; hence, their place, function, and value need to be understood in order that pupil guidance in the arts may be conducive to the best development of the pupil.

Method, therefore, is, in a primary sense, compounded of all these factors. Properly understood, well organized, and skillfully used by the teacher, they become a part of his working philosophy. But method is much more. It is a way, or a state of mind, in which all significant elements are fused into an organic approach in the teaching and guiding of young people.

REFLECTIVE TEACHING

It is a truism to say that good method is synonymous with creative teaching. But Herbert Read suggests that he studiously avoids the term "creative" in his writing because the word has suffered serious abuses. A similar conclusion is reached by Munro in connection with the preparation of the Fortieth Yearbook.[1] Observation over the years has sustained the opinion that the term "creative" is badly or at least variously understood, poorly applied, and indescriminately used, so that its meaning and value are now rather dubious. One hears and reads of "creative art education," "creative work" of and by children, "creative method," that a child is more "creative" than another, and so on. At one period the term was used to distinguish the progressive approach to art education from the more academic type. Some call "creative" any work that appears casual, unplanned, and even unintelligible, as if the term were synonymous with spontaneous, uninhibited, or meaningful. This unfortunate situation has robbed the field of art education of a term and of a prerogative that rightfully belong to it. To avoid the pitfall, this discussion will instead use the term *reflective* teaching or reflective method. To deny that real thinking, or that all the thinking that a pupil may be capable of doing, is involved in the creative experience would be a fallacy of the first order. The spontaneity which one sometimes finds among young artists cannot be mistaken for lack of "thought behind it"; it is just the opposite. In the second place, if, as contended in Chapter 1, a sound point of view in art education must involve both the science (knowledge) and the art (the application) of teaching, thinking cannot be ignored in the development of dynamic method. Finally, if art education is truly to fulfill its ends, namely, to develop insights, appreciations, emotions, and the formulation of concepts in pupils, again thinking cannot be excluded from the teaching-learning process. All this does not imply hard-and-fast sequence of operation; it does not imply schemes that never change; it does not imply drill as such. What it means, however, is that to achieve the ends of art as education, the teacher and the pupil must engage in reflection on the problems they decide to solve.

---

[1] Thomas Munro, "Creative Ability in Art," in National Society for the Study of Education, Fortieth Yearbook, *Art in American Life and Education*, Bloomington, Ill., Public School Publishing Company, 1941, pp. 289–322.

Bayles[2] describes the process of thinking as proceeding on three levels: recollection-level thinking, understanding-level thinking, and reflection-level thinking. Of the three levels, the third seems most essential to complete readiness for valid expression. Bayles defines it in this way:

"The secret of vital, challenging, interest-provoking teaching is to make it reflective. Reflective teaching means that problems are raised which both class and teacher together proceed to solve."[3] He then describes how a class conducted reflectively really operates. The picture he gives has been described in this book as *teacher-pupil planning* and relationships from the choosing of the problem to the achievement of expression. But most significant is what Bayles concludes: "As a natural and inevitable result of the insights so gained, certain feeling tones, attitudes, or dispositions develop which are the emotional accompaniment of insight. It is the insights which a child actually gains, the actual relationships which he recognizes his school activities to bear toward the pattern of genuinely-accepted goals and insights representing the real self that control and determine the true attitude of the child."[4]

METHOD BEGINS WITH THE INDIVIDUAL. The pupil's needs, abilities, and general growth pattern determine the teacher's initial approach and continued guidance (5th grade, Laboratory School, State Teachers College, Kutztown, Pa.).

What does all this mean with regard to learning? Simply that there is rote or mechanical learning, and that there is learning which becomes a permanent element in the thinking-acting pattern of pupil behavior. Such learning might well be described as creative or reflective learning.

---

[2] Ernest E. Bayles, *The Theory and Practice of Teaching*, New York, Harper & Brothers, 1950, p. 104.

[3] *Ibid.*, p. 111.

[4] *Ibid.*, p. 113.

In art education, a major need is for a method that leads from thinking to action. Ruch[5] describes the process quite clearly and in a manner that will be quickly recognized by teachers and others who have experienced art. Paraphrased, the introspection of artists suggests the following steps in creative effort:

1. *The Problem.* The artist must have a task to perform or an artistic problem to solve. During this period, ideas come quickly, shift rapidly; new ideas are examined and accepted or discarded.
2. *Incubation.* During this period an idea recurs spontaneously and from time to time; this phase may last from a few minutes to a year or several years.
3. *Illumination.* The recurring idea which has been incubating for sometime is now set down as a sketch, a model, for the first time.
4. *Verification.* At this stage, the artist has contemplated the sketch or model, changes, adds details, eliminates what is unwanted, and refines until his idea has been perfected.

It seems quite clear that the method of the artist follows the organic unity and sequence which Dewey attributes to creative expression and which was described in Chapter 1. What needs to be mentioned here is that preparation, incubation, and illumination fuse in the art of thinking. They represent a kind of data gathering, of testing ideas and concepts. The last step, verification, is the acting or doing.

The analogies that follow are attempts to show that scientific thinking and creative action are very similar to one another and that, ultimately, both depend on the quality of thinking. Quality is art, art in the sense of sensitive performance.

THE EXPERIMENTAL ATTITUDE

When a scientist works in his laboratory, methodically, painstakingly, patiently, in search of a solution to his problem, he is working creatively. When a mathematician ponders and works over formulas, symbols, or geometric configurations to reach a conclusion or to advance a mathematical theory, he works creatively. When a craftsman prepares to produce an article for the market and studies his tools and materials, develops suitable design, and then executes his task, he is working creatively. And so one might continue to cite a limitless array of human

---

[5] Floyd L. Ruch, *Psychology and Life*, Chicago, Scott, Foresman and Company, 1941, p. 381.

activities, performed daily by many persons, which are or may be performed reflectively. What distinguishes reflective teaching and reflective experience from the nonreflective is not so much a matter of "what" one is doing or performing, as it is "how" he is performing the task.

All good teaching is an art; it is never a chore. It is a daring and challenging pursuit, not a mere vocation. When viewed in this light, teaching assumes all the characteristics of the reflective act. What, then, is reflective teaching? It is a mental attitude, a way of working with human resources; it is intelligent self-identification with the nature, the needs, the drives, and the interests of those to be educated.

A CONCEPT OF METHOD

When the art of guiding young people is defined as indicated above, the concept of method becomes a dynamic one and one of organic relationships throughout the teaching-learning situation. Actually, it becomes identical with the superior performance just discussed.

Method does not mean the step-by-step of a process, nor how-to-do-it. It is broader, deeper, farther reaching than all that. A point that should be emphasized is that there is no such thing as *one* method, which once conceived and adopted will automatically furnish solutions to all the educational problems that a teacher may encounter. Method is first and always determined by the nature of the task and the nature of those to be taught.

Prescott indicates quite clearly the true nature of method in this fashion:

The best method of maturing children is to provide them with situations in which they can work out behavior that will satisfy their personality needs as the latter appear. This does not mean stressing drill for mastery of fundamental processes; it does not mean rote learning and recitation; it does not imply the use of regimentation to teach good habits and conformity; it does not permit indoctrinating all children with arbitrarily chosen emotionalized concepts; it does not suggest that teachers should have a bag of tricks for motivating pupils. These methods produce psychological immaturity.[6]

---

[6] Daniel Prescott, *Emotions and the Educative Process,* Washington, D.C., American Council on Education, 1938, p. 194.

FOUNDATIONAL ELEMENTS

There are certain foundational elements that distinguish good from poor, appropriate from inappropriate, and effective from ineffective method. A fuller comprehension and appraisal of method itself may be achieved by examining those elements. For the sake of clarity they are stated rather tersely below:

1. Method *emphasizes* the fullest possible growth and integration, personal and social, of each individual to be taught.
2. Method *realizes* and is concerned with the nature and endowment of each individual in the group.
3. Method *recognizes* that standards are not fixed, but flexible, for each individual according to his endowment.
4. Method *utilizes* experiences, content, materials, and other resources adaptable to the contemporary needs and interests of pupils.
5. Method *evokes* those modes of expression suited to the psychological nature and the growth level of the pupils concerned.

Here again, one comes face to face with the fact that each child is an entity of utmost worth. He cannot and should not be made to fit into a preconceived pattern merely for the sake of uniformity or even to make the teacher's task easier. The individual's needs are the clue to a method for *him*.

Except for those children who deviate sufficiently from the accepted norm and, therefore, are in need of specialized attention or even institutionalization, a method must be discovered by the teacher to make the most of each child's inborn capabilities but, at the same time, take into account his limitations.

Evaluation of growth, adjustment of behavior, outright expectancy of attainments, and productivity in general, whether in art or other areas of learning, cannot be fixed quantities. The pupil must be motivated to seek and achieve his own optimum standard. Then only will the method have proved to be successful.

A method that relies only on the stereotyped approaches to teaching and learning has little claim. When it utilizes all the available resources to evoke the best from each pupil, then it may be admitted as worth while and effective. The most important aspect of method is characterized by the fact that it is adjusted to the psychological bent of the pupil.

1 3 2   In art education, good method will seek to encourage the perceptive powers, the mode of expression, and the particular tendencies of each child.

INTERACTION BETWEEN THEORY AND PRACTICE

A brief elaboration of the suggested foundational elements in relation to the most widely used approaches to teaching art seems appropriate because reflective teaching manifests itself rather concretely in its func-

DISCUSSIONS, panels, demonstrations, and other means of activating learning are worth-while ways of stimulating pupils. Growth is often evident in the pupil's responses and his ability to relate himself to the situation. Invariably, art action is enriched (Laboratory School, State Normal University, Normal, Ill.).

tioning within the typical classroom. The final test of any theory is its applicability in terms of the purposes to be accomplished. It is true that a wide gap often exists between one's understanding of theory and one's practice. But this should not be discouraging to anyone or act as a deterrent to a sincere teacher. Rather it must become a stimulus for experimentation and for testing theory. Experimentation is the surest road to professional growth and personal integration; in turn it will be reflected in the art expression of pupils. Disparity between theory and practice, it was pointed out elsewhere, is due to lack of interaction between the two elements. Therefore, the professionally minded teacher evaluates his work in terms of foundations of method. The purpose will not be to reach a compromise but rather to establish a frame of reference looking toward improvement. In the final analysis, the adequacy of an art program in a school depends on the teacher's awareness and judicious adoption of the essential elements of democratic social philosophy and of the best findings of educational experimentation. These, in turn, are reflected in effective method.

ANALYSIS OF CURRENT METHODS

Among the more popular methods employed by teachers of art today one finds these: directed, correlated, integrated, free-expression, and "core" teaching. The fact that none of these procedures finds universal approval among teachers of art education suggests the value of an analysis of them. By pointing up the strengths as well as the weaknesses in each it may be possible to throw light on the better way to guide children through art. Perchance, the teacher or coördinator may find a personal solution to his problem and arrive at a satisfying personal point of view. Without such an experience, no one may honestly claim validity for his method of teaching.

DIRECTED TEACHING

This is perhaps the oldest approach. Its persistence, in spite of progress in educational philosophy, suggests the need for close scrutiny. The academies and art schools of the past, and even some of today, taught by prescribed steps, by graduated exercises, and by progressive levels of technical achievement. Such teaching was and is analytical and systematic, but also formal and authoritarian. The inference in such an approach is that the pupil is in school to learn; the teacher is there to impart knowledge, prescribe technics, dictate procedures, and deal with facts. The main objective is the mastery of technic in design, color,

134 painting, drawing, modeling, lettering, perspective, and such other areas of art as may be thought desirable by those who determine the course of study in art. The chief virtue of this method is that it is hallowed by time and tradition. Such teaching, if judged on the basis of the major objective prevalent in the past, mastery of technics, was justifiable. But art education has evolved. It now recognizes as its objective the self-development of children and youth. It believes that mastery of skills and technics is achieved as a natural and gradual by-product of experience with each individual. Therefore, it is inconceivable that the educational aims of today can be served by the sterile and short-sighted approach under consideration. Such a method may hope to keep children busy, and it may even ensure that they may be made to produce identical and precise results. But evidences indicate that the creative powers of pupils may be stunted, their aesthetic sense warped, and their personal development deferred or completely unrealized.

The further implications of a critique regarding the directed method would indicate that courses of study of a fixed and final nature have little place in contemporary art education; that consistently formalized instruction is inimical to individual growth; that closely compartmentalized instruction in color, design, drawing, and other phases of art instruction, treated as specialized pursuits, should be deferred for late-high-school or post-high-school education. Lastly, the implication is that activities preplanned only by the teacher are generally unsuited to the interests and, therefore, to the proper artistic unfolding of young people.

The question may arise as to whether directed teaching is ever defensible. A categorical *never* might be the best answer. However, teachers should be ready to help, directly, whenever the critical needs and best interests of pupils demand it. When such occasions arise, teaching assumes the form of suggesting a better tool, of demonstrating a particular technic, or of leading to specific information. Creative teachers generally anticipate the needs of their pupils; at the same time they are ready to help at the point where it is most effective. A laissez-faire attitude is not to be confused with creative teaching. Such a confusion would be detrimental to the proper encouragement of boys and girls and, instead of inspiring self-confidence and promoting integration, would produce feelings of inadequacy and of discouragement.[7]

---

[7] Munro, *op. cit.*, pp. 314–321.

The directed method may be of value in certain types of vocational and adult-education programs, but it is largely unwarranted in the elementary and junior high school. If ever, it should be used sparingly and understandingly at the senior-high-school level where technical problems arise and it appears imperative that the teacher aid the pupil by demonstration or by suggesting practice.

FREE EXPRESSION

This method has been alluded to in connection with the discussion of current trends in Chapter 3. At this point the concern is with its appraisal as a way of teaching. In contrast to the directed approach this method suggests that the work of pupils is spontaneous, that it originates with them, that it is not teacher-dominated, and that it is concerned with the pupils' genuine ideas and personal mode of expression. Advocates of this method easily fall in line with whatever new point of view may come along in growth and development because the chief virtue of free expression is that it has few, if any, limitations. "Let the child express himself"; "do not restrain him"; "do not interfere, allow maximum latitude." These and similar phrases are the stock in trade of the followers of this approach to teaching.

On the surface it seems as a most defensible method; but when examined in the light of its own past history and achievements, its fallacies appear. It will be claimed, quite appropriately, that the teacher is the key to the method; but that is true of all methods, the best and the worst.[8] The misunderstandings and misinterpretations of this manner of working with children have become evident in art education of the recent past. It is obvious that few teachers, great teachers, can use this methodology without falling into its inherent errors.

Limitations and Advantages

There are, furthermore, certain psychological reasons for the limitations of this approach. The first of these is that although education and psychology suggest freedom of expression for complete development, neither denies the role of guidance. The second limitation is that, admittedly, the creative development of children requires careful stimulation and sound motivation at almost every step. It could be argued then

---

[8] Munro, *op. cit.*, p. 317.

136 that any type of adult guidance or interference with free expression automatically nullifies the very heart of the method and renders it not as free as it claims. When it is completely free, in the hands of children and over a period of time, it becomes purposeless and meaningless manipulation. Children, unguided, tend to repeat themselves, to find the line of least resistance, and to become stereotyped. The purpose of guidance or of motivation is to keep them from falling into habits which are antagonistic to proper growth and development.

It may be well to ponder that negative freedom is just as strong as positive freedom. The former may set in motion forces which eventually destroy the true intention of democratic education and may drive an individual to disregard all restraints. The legal restraints created by society, the physical limitations of institutionalized education, and the prohibitions of the moral code are intended to uphold positive freedom

PHYSICAL ACTIVITY, often of an aesthetic nature, stimulates creative expression. The rhythm of the body and the resulting kinesthetic sensation are reflected in the pupil's work in art (5th grade, Tucson, Ariz.).

for all. This difficult distinction as well as a critical attitude must be developed early in formal education.

These are sufficient indications to suggest that what has been termed "free expression" in art education is, under most classroom conditions, not a profitable method. Sooner or later, a teacher must enter the scene to infuse new life and vigor into the program lest the true creative growth of children be arrested or forever atrophied.

Nevertheless, individuality of expression and originality, which are the chief claims of the free-expression method, are qualities that art education must prize. Dewey clarifies the values and the problems inherent in the development of individuality in these words:

Individuality itself is originally a potentiality and is realized only in interaction with surrounding conditions. In this process of intercourse, native capacities, which contain an element of uniqueness, are transformed and become a self. Moreover, through resistances encountered, the nature of the self is discovered. The self is both formed and brought to consciousness through interaction with environment. The individuality of the artist is no exception. If his activities remained mere play and merely spontaneous, if free activities were not brought against the resistance offered by actual conditions, no *work* of art would ever be produced. From the first manifestation by a child to draw, up to the creations of a Rembrandt, the self is created in the creation of objects, a creation that demands active adaptation to external materials, including a modification of the self so as to utilize and thereby overcome external necessities by incorporating them in an individual vision and expression.[9]

Obviously, then, the essential philosophy underlying the free-expression method is most significant. It must be retained and advanced at all levels of art education, more particularly at the early stages of education. The freshness and spontaneity of wisely guided and properly stimulated pupils will stand as the supreme achievement of every creative teacher of art.

CORE TEACHING

The core pattern is, in a sense, as old as American education itself. In fact, if the history of education as a whole is examined, it will be realized that every society, in every age, has deemed certain learnings

---

[9] John Dewey, *Art as Experience,* New York, Minton, Balch and Company, 1934, pp. 281–282.

on the part of their young people to be central in importance or value. The so-called three R's are an example of the belief that, whatever else may be taught in the schools, reading, writing, and arithmetic must form the "core" of teaching and learning. In other words, certain subjects, because of their value in further learning, have been considered centers around which all other activities should revolve.

Another and more recent view has suggested that there are certain "common learnings" which are valuable to all; therefore, they should be at the core of the situation. For varying reasons, educational leaders have assumed that there are certain learnings, certain subjects, certain skills, and certain areas of knowledge of sufficient value to all people that they should all be exposed to them. Hence a *core* or a center of learning has always existed in the schools.

The recent revivals are not as hard and fast as the older versions. Core curriculums today, although centering around certain common learnings, are, nevertheless, intensely concerned with needs, interests, abilities, and growth of pupils. They recognize that in a democratic society there are both individual and social goals and values which need to be identified and developed. They recognize that pupils differ in many ways but that at the same time they live, play, and work as a social group. In brief, even when a core is established, in operation it employs all areas of learning that will bring out of pupils the very best contributions of which they are capable.

Anderson explains the core curriculum thus: "And here is the significance of this development: the core curriculum deals with social and personal problems, organizing the classroom work around the *solution of the problems* and drawing upon subject matter from any area needed to solve these problems."[10] Such fields as music, art, drama, the dance, and others, when not a part of the pattern, are not outlawed but are used functionally. Where it is adopted, "core" teaching makes use of the best educational procedures. Such technics as teacher-pupil planning, committee work, "resource unit" planning, the community; and historic resources are common elements. A pupil may participate as an individual or as a member of a group.

---

[10] Vernon E. Anderson, "Things are Happening in Secondary Education," *Journal of the National Education Association,* March, 1956, pp. 167–169.

The literature of this method of teaching shows that there are several ways of accomplishing the job as well as several types of organization: "fusion" of subject matter, "dominant fields," and "common learnings." These are all in vogue. Yet they all aim at the achievement of the common goal, which is better teaching and better learning, with desirable changes in behavior.

A Unified Approach

By whatever name it may be called, the procedure implies a unified approach to learning by relating areas such as history, science, and English. While these subject-matter areas seem to establish a foundation, they do not preclude the introduction, whenever students feel the need of it, of other areas of learning. This is particularly true of the arts, for they are recognized as the enriching and binding media.

For purposes of present concern, it may be well to ask several questions: How does art function in a core situation? Is it true that art loses its identity? Does art serve ends other than its own? Are the results satisfying to children? For the best answers to these questions, it seems fair to go to those who have worked and are working in a "core" situation. The following statements are made by Mary Beth Wackwitz and Lucille Lurry of Prince George's County, Maryland:

We feel at present we can point to the following:
1. Encouragement of the cooperative process at all levels of learning
2. Some evidences of changed behavior
3. More use of creative approach to teaching-learning situations
4. More emphasis upon "freeing" children to do critical thinking
5. More emphasis upon the method of intelligence
6. More emphasis upon individual worth
We have had enough success with the process of making art experience an integral part of the evolving core program to plan to further this development in all our schools next year.[11]

Some further considerations in core teaching involve the longer period of time in which to accomplish an art project, and the fact that in most instances the work is motivated by the "core" but is carried out in the art classes; often art periods are used for other developmental phases

---

[11] *Art Education Today,* 1951–52, New York, Teachers College, Columbia University, 1952, pp. 72–88.

140 of art, but pupils who choose may work on art in the core class.

The possible objections to such a pattern of art teaching were advanced above in the form of questions. But conversely, it should be stated that the spirit of core should determine whether the creative development of boys and girls is jeopardized or given wider opportunity and broader meaning.

CORRELATED TEACHING

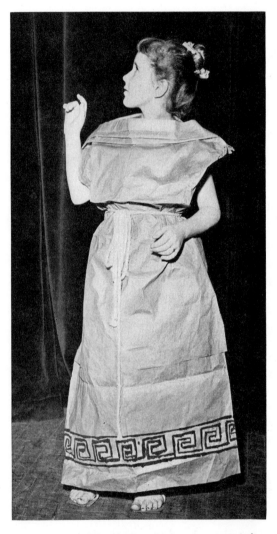

THE SELF IS REALIZED in many ways vital to art expression. Dramatization or "feeling the part" in plays and other situations may be a springboard to creative action in art (6th grade, Philadelphia, Pa.).

For a long time, a type of art teaching has been practiced which is referred to as "correlated." The intention of this method of working has been that whatever motivation or incentive the pupil needs can be and is often furnished by what he has learned or what he is studying in another subject field. As a matter of fact, art teachers who adhere to this particular approach make it their business to find out what is being studied by their pupils in history, science, mathematics, or other fields, and then proceed to plan the art work as an enrichment of those areas. While in many instances excellent results have been achieved, it is equally true that this has not always been the case. The chief objections leveled at this approach to the art program are these: (1) it is based on fictitious relationships, (2) it narrows the field of interest of a particular pupil, (3) art becomes a "servant" of other areas of study, and (4) it minimizes the developmental value of art expression and its significance in the pupil's life.

These criticisms, taken at face value, may appear as true; however, the only fair test of their validity would be to discover the motivating devices used by the teacher. If the teacher is a creative person and a wise counselor of boys and girls, he will remove all fictitious bridges and lead the pupil to see natural relationships. Then what has been learned and experienced in any other area may become the source of inspiration. It cannot be overemphasized that creative method and creative teaching are one and the same. Good method becomes ineffective at the hands of a poor teacher. A creative teacher, on the other hand, sees beyond the ephemeral and the obstructive and guides pupils so that they can utilize what is pertinent and discard what is trivial, irrelevant, and even inimical to their creative growth.

PSYCHOLOGICAL ASPECTS OF METHOD

What has been said thus far refers to prevailing practices, but even more significant are the psychological foundations upon which these practices rest. The nature of method is deeply rooted in what is known about young people and in the way one implements practices with human understanding. The remainder of this chapter is devoted to a consideration of some important means for the utilization of knowledge of child and adolescent psychology in guiding creative development.

MOTIVATION

The interests, attitudes, needs, and purposes of boys and girls at various age levels, as well as creative levels in relation to types of growth, are generally known by good teachers. Indeed, these characteristic elements are the foundations of the modern curriculum. They are guiding principles in the art of teaching and furnish the basis for all sound pupil guidance. But it will matter little whether one works in a core, integrated, or free-expression situation if the basic philosophy of those patterns is used only as a shibboleth while, at the same time, proper motivation is ignored.

Motivation may be defined and understood as the compelling or evocative approach used by teachers to lend *direction and purpose* to the pupils' natural desires to express themselves. This presumes that the teacher has identified himself with his pupils' active interests, values, goals, and abilities. A pupil who works mechanically, who fulfills the assignment, and who does all he is asked to do, but shows little spirit in the performance, is very likely motivated by extrinsic or outside forces. They suggest to him that unless he does what he is supposed to do he will fail, he will be disgraced, he will be punished. Such motives are mechanistic in nature and are foreign to creative expression. On the other hand, if a teacher has been able to guide a pupil to realize higher motives such as are induced by interest and curiosity or for the pleasure of achievement, then motivation is of the proper type. Prescott[12] says:

> A person is motivated to learn when he has the active attitude of desiring to learn. Everyone knows from common experience that the active desire to develop a given motor skill, to establish the easy recall of certain data, or to understand a given functional relationship, plays an important part in determining the speed and efficiency of the learning. Motivation influences directly the intensity of effort that a child will put forth to learn. It determines the single-mindedness, the unity of attention, that he is able to give to the task. It mediates the amount of fatigue or discomfort he is willing to undergo in the process of learning.[12]

There is a vast difference, then, between intrinsic and extrinsic motivation. The first involves a pupil's inborn tendency to adjust to the external world. In the classroom, such behavior is translated into self-assurance and self-direction, and usually establishes a pupil's worth as a person. Likewise, when self-determined goals of a wholesome nature are so reached, they lead pupils to adequate solutions of conflicts and hence to harmonious development.

Extrinsic motivation, on the other hand, such as rewards of a material kind, competition for gain, or even appeasement of the teacher, are detrimental to the personality of the pupil and generally result in mechanically performed tasks. However, not all extrinsic motivation is harmful; there are occasions when a good teacher feels that its application may result in positive reaction on the part of the pupil.

Motivation varies at different levels of growth mainly because experiences and interests differ. At the early elementary levels the desire to explore and to express are paramount. After pubescence these same in-

---

[12] Prescott, *op. cit.*, p. 162.

terests change to a strong desire to please, to become a member of the group, to win the affection and confidence of the opposite sex or of adults, including parents and teachers. In middle and late adolescence, social sensitivity is high. Boys and girls seek status, or a place in the world; prestige means a great deal to them; therefore, these desires should be regarded as good avenues for sound motivation.

Some Examples

1. An instance of good motivation is reported by a teacher as follows:

One day a group of fifth-graders noticed several cartons in the crafts corner of the room. The cartons seemed full. "What's in them?" asked one, then more questions and wondering on the part of several classmates. They came to the teacher, thus compelling him to make a game of the situation. Many guesses were made and eventually someone suggested: "Clay!" The excited group, pupils and teacher, discussed what they might do with clay. Someone mentioned Pioneer Days as a theme because they had been studying the pioneers. By the end of the week a large mural background had been painted, and arranged before it were modeled covered wagons, horses, some figures of men and women, a pioneer settlement, and a number of other pertinent items.

What happened, exactly? Simply this: a wise teacher recognized a spontaneous interest (motivation) on the part of pupils, decided to make the most of it, and so organized the group that all participated in one way or another. All profited by the experience, and an effective educational adventure was concluded.

2. A teacher in a sixth grade asked the children if they had many friends outside of school. Who are these friends? What do they look like? What do they do? Wouldn't it be fun to make a booklet containing drawings of their friends? One pupil suggested that a brief story about the friend might be on one page and a drawing or painting on the opposite page. The children arrived at a practical size for the booklets and discussed how to make booklets in various ways. Many pupils already had ideas for the cover; the teacher made suggestions in the form of questions to start some of the other children thinking. The teacher concluded by suggesting to pupils that many people would be looking at these booklets and that everyone surely would want to do them as attractively as they could. The class would choose the booklet with the

best covers and drawings for the display case in the school hall following the classroom exhibit.

3. A child mentioned living on a farm. The teacher asked how many had ever been to a farm, or had seen farm animals. As hands went up, the teacher asked what kinds of animals they had seen on the farm and what they liked most about the farm. Pupils suggested that they draw some of the things they had seen on the farm and some of the things they did there. Johnny had lived on a farm and had milked a real, live cow. Johnny needed no further motivation; he was ready and eager to draw what he had experienced. Suzie had never visited a farm, but she had seen farm animals in the fields. What animal did she think was the most interesting? She wanted to draw that animal. Andy thought the barn and the silo were the most interesting things on a farm, so he drew the silo as he saw it.

3. A certain school has set aside one hour of the day when children who wish to do so may come to the art center for a "fun" period. The children usually come in, choose their own materials, have their own ideas, and go to work automatically. The teacher in charge noted very early that those who come neither seek nor welcome suggestions or approval from her. There is only one rule in the art center at that time, namely, that everyone will return things where they belong and leave the room in good order. The teacher reports that many of the results achieved are of high caliber, although a good deal of work is finished and disposed of by the children as an indication that they have tried whatever they wished and are satisfied with the experience. Many children are "regulars"; others come and go. This is an example of intrinsic motivation. It indicates that the pure satisfaction of a desire to paint or model or accomplish something above and beyond the classroom requirements can and does serve a purpose. Abuse of the practice could, however, result in purposeless and aimless activity.

STIMULATION

Stimulation differs from motivation in that the known interests, purposes, and goals that rest deep in the pupil's conscious or unconscious being need to be aroused. The creative forces are dormant and need to be awakened to the point where the child recognizes the impulse and is ready for action. Here the teacher plays her usual role, that of guide and counselor. Through informal talks, the use of visual and other aids, available exhibits of various types, examination of a specific source, and whatever else seems feasible and within the scope of the task, the teacher guides the pupil toward a realization of his own interests and goals.

Stimulating devices and their use, like motivation, must of necessity vary with grade level, capacity for achievement, and creative type. The treatment, the language, and the scope of topics suggested for art expression should be at the pupil's level. The same topics, having assumed heightened meanings, may be just as suitable at a higher level. The type of stimulation, therefore, must be suited to the mental and creative level of the pupil; in other words, it must be understood by pupils in order to arouse, quicken, or even challenge them, if that be the case.

Incentives are often used as stimulating devices, although they must be cautiously selected and handled. Altogether too many popular forms of incentives are of the wrong sort: money prizes, medals, ribbons, and the like. What is to be gained by the child through such incentives but false pride, a notion that he has arrived, that he is superior to his class-

SHARING in work, ideas, and responsibility is best achieved through group undertakings. Through them, the development of the individual is assured while the need for coöperation is made evident (8th grade, Stratford, Conn.; *below*, Senior High School, Oklahoma City, Okla.).

mates? Contests and competitions by far and large fall in the category to be carefully scrutinized.[13] The following examples of good incentives were contributed by a teacher in service:

1. The Distributive Education students of the high school study about display and advertising techniques. Their interest in merchandising is very high; therefore, I thought it wise to capitalize upon this interest by actually setting up a situation in which they could apply their knowledge of methods of selling to arousing school spirit, or to some phase of school life for which they have a feeling. The best of a series of designs created by them would be displayed in the foyer for the inspection of all students. Later, the class would determine which piece should be developed as a display for the window of a store operated by a patron of the school. The enthusiasm and the results were most gratifying.

2. The industrial-arts boys usually feel socially inferior. The idea somehow persists in their minds that because they do not dress up every day and do not have as many academic studies as other students, they do not have "prestige." Since there are numerous ticket sales throughout the year, I suggested that the boys design and construct a booth of their own. This would definitely identify their group. The booth was constructed and attracted a good deal of attention in the foyer. It further served as an excellent base of operations for the shop boys for the ticket sale. Comments were generous and pointed up the fact that they had gained the admiration and approval of their own classmates and of the faculty. A sense of pride had been gained by the "shop boys."

3. There is a large number of students in my school who wish to work in art but can do so only for one hour a week. Many of them are also interested in athletics and others in nonathletic activities. They feel that they do not like to spend that hour making posters or fulfilling other specific assignments; this would take away from them the only hour they have to spend in art class. But since activities must be advertised, to solve the problem I organized an Art Service Squad. Its membership is advertised as being "exclusive." Many more students than I expected indicated that they would be interested in the type of work to be accomplished by this club: helping teachers prepare campaign charts, activity posters, dance decorations, and publicity for various school affairs. In talking to students I sensed that they were seeking the prestige that membership in the Squad would bring. An added incentive was the privilege of using study periods to do art-club work in addition to the regularly scheduled time. The Art Service Squad has proved to be a real incentive for these young people because they can produce art in a way they enjoy most.

---

[13] See the National Art Education Association's statement on this point.

The ultimate end of education is to help people grow into effective persons, capable of solving life problems with a maximum of equanimity. Therefore, education must strive to develop within the person those resources, qualities, and balances which may be called up when facing issues. This suggests that children's outlooks are a central concern of all education and a major task of teaching. An individual's behavior may be compared to a woven piece: there is a warp and a weft, there are innumerable threads running in opposite directions, yet in the process of weaving they interlock; they become one and form a *whole*, or a pattern. Experiences of various types, materials of many sorts, learnings gained in many ways, participation in group enterprises, and other educational means need to be utilized to make more effective the teaching-learning situation. All these efforts are employed in order to develop, through appeal to diverse personal interests and capacities, a resourceful, self-reliant individual.

It is in the process of unifying learnings, sensing relationships and meanings, that integration occurs. Thus it is evident that, although a teacher's function is to provide the right atmosphere and to stimulate learning in a manner that will permit integration to take place, it is the *learner* who must be integrated and unified. When unification occurs, the learner's view of life is one of confident growth in the direction of potential maturity.

Integrative Teaching

In education, this concept gained prominence over 35 years ago. Art educators became seriously aware of it in the thirties, and since then it has had advocates and opponents. In practice, it has been used successfully in many instances, inadequately in others.

The meaning of integration in the teaching of art involves the totality of the creative experience. It must be accepted that all learning can be creative and that all forces—economic, social, religious, political, aesthetic, geographic, and climatic—are affective elements. It follows that a learner's reactions are evoked and affected, directly and indirectly, by these same forces. The pupils' awareness of the forces just named and of the interactions among them becomes the vital spring of creative activity. In the process, the learner identifies himself with the total environment and the experience is a complete response. When this occurs, integrated behavior may result.

In practice, the method means more than the stimulation of art expression. It involves examination, selection, analysis, and much learning in a number of related fields, but particularly those which have immediate bearing upon art activities suggested by the broader topic under consideration.

Integrative teaching calls for broad planning. Unit planning is often associated with this method of teaching.

Advocates of the method properly claim that much more than art is learned: meanings, social intentions, group values, and, of course, personal reaction and individual expression. Critics of the method contend that the paraphernalia involved in the process often minimize and obscure the specific end of art expression.

Whatever the case, it is the spirit of integration that matters. If the ends of art education are in terms of development, no controversy need exist. If its purposes were proficiency and academic standards, no other method would do as well as directed teaching.

The chief question is: How is integration induced? The answer is certainly not to be found in fictitious combinations of subject matter, nor by arbitrarily superimposing one area of learning upon another. Integration of concepts occurs only when the meanings and relationships, let us say, of an event in life or history are felt by a pupil in such a way that he is ready to translate his feelings into a mural decoration, a drawing, a painting, or a piece of sculpture. Or when the meanings of the situation are so clearly related to a pupil's personal experiences that he is impelled to express himself through art.

It is a demonstrated fact that the desire toward integration is characteristic of all living organisms. It is as natural as breathing. However, if the wrong educational instruments are applied or if environmental forces begin to play havoc with the various facets of the individual's tendency of growth, then the harmonious wholeness for which he was intended is jeopardized.

Enriched curriculums, meaningful experiences, proper motivation, and above all skillful guidance in the use of resources are some avenues toward integration, both individual and social.

The art program can and should strive to help pupils develop whole-somely. With proper caution, a good teacher can provide, through art education, a varied array of experiences: some will be aesthetic, some mental, some emotional, and some perceptual. This variety has been advocated for a long time as a basic condition of a well-balanced cur-riculum (see Chapter 2).

Thus, integration, as a method or as an educational ideal, becomes the cornerstone of the educational structure and the chief aim of art in the classroom. The various forms of art, its skills and technics, are then re-garded as tools through which growth is facilitated rather than ends in themselves.

THE ART OF QUESTIONING

Some attention might be given to questioning as an educational method. If it is possible to agree at this point that art education is an evocative process, one through which the teacher brings out of pupils what is within them, then it is conceivable that pupil growth is best achieved through self-evaluation, self-motivation, and self-criticism on the part of boys and girls themselves. A misconception seems to prevail, namely, that the teacher does not "help" the pupil by making specific suggestions, or by giving information or suggesting tools or technics. It has been pointed out that there are situations when such help, *if needed* by the pupil to enable him to take the next step, is educationally de-fensible. However, by far and large, the specific help given by teachers should be in terms of stimulation and general suggestions, and these in the form of questions.

Socrates, one of the world's greatest philosophers and teachers, is said to have propounded more questions than to have given answers. It was his "method" of teaching, his way of stimulating thinking, perceiving, and acting on the part of his disciples. He envisioned self-education as a quest, a search, an adventure. Modern education must be of the same nature and bent.

When pupils ask questions, the best teacher counters with questions. "Is the color too dull or too brilliant?" "Is this your own conception?" "How do you feel about the composition?" "What is it you cannot draw?" "Have you ever experienced a situation like this?" "Have you tried some other way?" "What seems to be wrong?" "Have you looked care-

150 fully at some paintings recently?" "How can you accomplish what you have in mind?" "Do you really see what your drawing indicates?"

The question, of course, must deal with the subject on hand; it must be in the pupil's language and suitable to his level of comprehension. It must stimulate further thinking—feeling—perceiving—doing. If it fails to do these things, it is a poor question, lacking in evocative power and in effectiveness.

Lastly, the spirit and inflection of the question must be such as to encourage and not irk; it must lead to self-improvement and self-analysis. Only then will a teacher's questions stimulate growth.

GROUP PROCESSES

Competent teachers have used group processes for a long time. This approach to educational situations has received additional impetus during the last few years. It bids fair to become even more effective as a method of evoking pupil expression and reaction as it is better understood, refined, and not abused.

Helen Parkhurst,[14] a pioneer in progressive education, has demonstrated again and again how simple it is to get young people to pour out their hearts and thoughts to the right teacher. This pouring-out process mirrors their interests, their ideas, their feelings, and their emotions. Actually, young people have ideas about art, art teachers, and art teaching. If heeded, the art program may benefit not only so far as pupils with ability are concerned but will also make a legion of adherent from among those whose chief interest is the appreciation or consumption of art.

Michaelis and Grim point out to young teachers that "Group discussions, sharing, planning, doing and evaluating are significant activities in all areas of the curriculum. Group-action skills are essential in clubs, social activities and Student Government. Creative group work is fre-

---

[14] *This is Art Education,* 1952 Yearbook, Kutztown, Pa., National Art Education Association, 1952.

USE OF ENVIRONMENT, immediate or somewhat remote but accessible, stimulates creative work and gives reality to children's activities. A story, literature, history, and the sciences are valuable as stimulation (*above,* 3rd grade, Tucson, Ariz.; *below,* Senior High School, Baltimore, Md.).

quently planned and developed in connection with expression in art, music and language."[15]

While this phase of method is unquestionably the better way through which the individual identifies himself with the group and helps develop goals and values, it is also of inestimable value in bringing out what each individual may have to contribute. In this bringing-out process the individual has opportunity to express the self which in turn is essential to the establishment of every pupil as an entity.

The art laboratory, or any classroom for that matter, can furnish the proper climate in which human values, personal or social, may be developed. The informality of the art class or the art laboratory is naturally conducive to best results in the use of group processes.

There are several major types of processes. They can only be pointed out here, but it is hoped that all persons who teach art will delve into the subject as a personal venture.

1. *Informal Group Sharing.* This is the simplest and most natural of the group technics. The teacher and the pupils freely tell each other of their problems, of ideas they have, of interests, hopes, and even worries. It is a sympathetic and a mutually appreciated exchange of what is spontaneous and uppermost in the mind. In art education, boys and girls have been known to make suggestions for topics, for solving technical problems, and for pointing out faults and good points in a work of art produced by themselves or by a member of the group. Such sharing in art education might follow the showing of a movie, or the return from a field trip; it may concern an exhibition that has been visited, or it may deal with proposed new activities. Through this informality every pupil is encouraged to express himself; everyone learns to respect the points of view and the problems of other pupils. As a motivating device for genuine, fresh, spontaneous work, group sharing has infinite possibilities.

2. *Group Discussion.* This type of technic differs from informal sharing in that a definite direction or problem is established and the discussion is held to the point as nearly as possible. Generally, group discussions are intended to pool ideas and to find solutions to a common problem. The teacher is an interested bystander to whom pupils look for assurance

---

[15] John Michaelis and Paul Grim, *The Student Teacher in Elementary Education,* New York, Prentice-Hall, 1953, Chapter VII.

that their facts, opinions, suggestions, and solutions are correct and feasible.

However, there is need for flexibility in group discussion, especially depending on the case and purpose of the discussion itself. Younger pupils can and do respond naturally to informal group discussions in which they recognize a leader or chairman. Through repeated experiences, they are able to arrive at tentative conclusions. Older children, while continuing with group discussions, enjoy the lecture, which may be presented by one pupil to whom they later direct questions. In art education the demonstration as well as the lecture may be profitable. In the demonstration, one pupil, or perhaps two, may go through the steps of a process or may actually produce something fresh, and then open the way for questions and answers. The various forms of group discussion serve as very effective means of discovering special abilities, interests, and qualities of leadership.

3. *The Symposium.* Another way of turning the classroom into a community of interest is the symposium. As a method, it is most effective from the intermediate grades and upward. The talents of several pupils may be utilized here, either in discussion or evaluation or demonstration. It calls for careful preplanning by the group, but the efforts are well rewarded if they succeed in getting questions from the class.

4. *The Panel Discussion.* This differs somewhat from the symposium in that a chairman and several pupils discuss a topic decided upon and each member contributes as he feels that he can. The chairman sees to it that all have a fair chance. Eventually, he invites questions from the class and, at the right point, makes a summary statement of what has been presented and points out the conclusions reached, if that is the case.

5. *The Forum Dialogue* is another worth-while means of emphasizing to a class certain goals and values already agreed upon, or certain principles that have been stressed. In this case, only two pupils participate by asking and answering questions. The method requires very meticulous preparation and accuracy; therefore, it is not advisable to use it in grades below the junior high school.

The last three technics may be used quite successfully in art education to reach group conclusions concerning teamwork, such as in planning murals, or the art features of the school annual, or the decorations for the annual prom, or to develop certain generally desirable art concepts dealing with good taste and general appreciation.

In a certain senior high school, the symposium and the panel methods were used as the springboard for a unit on "Art in Daily Life." The pupils involved explored for the class the many ways in which art touches living. They used visual materials to make their points clear and reached some general conclusions that were acceptable to all. Following the discussion, pupils decided either singly or in small groups to develop certain art activities.

The most significant aspects of method involved in group processes are these: leadership is discovered and developed, every member of the group has an opportunity to express himself, a variety of talents may be utilized, and followership is accepted voluntarily by the majority of the group. The latter is true because values and goals were reached democratically and by action of a group of peers.

SUMMARY

The purpose of this chapter has been to point out the nature and scope of educational method as distinguished from classroom routines. The claims of most of the methods employed in art education have been analyzed with particular reference to their impact on the individual pupil, on the group, and in relation to democratic social living. Certain elements of educational method have been identified through definition and by example, both for practical purposes as well as to clarify meanings. Although not all known practices have been subjected to scrutiny, it should be remembered that good teachers everywhere evolve successful procedures based on the nature of art expression, on the realization of the needs of young people, and on the belief that the chief purpose of education in a democracy is maximum development for each individual.

Implicit in the nature of method, there is the idea that it is not fixed. Rather, it is flexible, broad, and constantly evolving. In the last analysis, method begins and ends with each individual pupil.

Finally, the value of sound educational method should be considered uppermost by all teachers since the pupil's behavior and its manifesta-

tions in the form of art expression, or of taste, are largely dependent
upon it.

For Discussion and Activity

1. What is involved in the term *method?* How does its educational meaning differ from "routine"?
2. Do you agree that method begins with the child? If so, how could you diversify your method in a classroom with, let us say, forty children?
3. What is your concept of creative teaching; how does it differ from the noncreative type? Illustrate by contrasting examples.
4. Reëxamine the major foundational elements of educational method, then discuss one of the facets in an effort to relate its meaning to the art of teaching. This may be done for each of the elements.
5. Stage a debate on the question "Children cannot create unless they are taught systematically and directly to master basic technics."
6. Select an area that is of interest to most boys and girls, such as games, practices, or trips, and develop a plan of teaching based on one of the teaching methods discussed in this chapter. Submit it to the group for discussion. Does the plan account for foundations of good method?
7. Arrange for a planned visit to a school and observe how the teacher motivates pupils; what types of stimulation are used; what types of questions are asked the children. Make careful judgments of how good teachers use these psychological means to achieve satisfying results.
8. Scan the literature of education and from it abstract examples of good motivation. Translate these in terms of art education.
9. Select an area of activity suitable to a specific grade level and develop a plan of presentation in which some forms of group processes are used. Be as specific as if you were the teacher of that particular group.
10. As you review the principal methods analyzed in this chapter, what appears to be the major emphasis? Can you justify that emphasis?

For Further Reading

Bayles, Ernest E., *Experiments with Reflective Teaching*, Lawrence, Kan., University of Kansas Studies in Education, 1956, Vol. 6, No. 3.

Cane, Florence, *The Artist in Each of Us*, New York, Pantheon Books, 1951, pp. 41–153.

Gaitskell, Charles D. and Margaret R., *Art Education in the Kindergarten*, Peoria, Charles H. Bennett Company, 1952, Chapters V, VI.

156   Gaitskell, Charles D. and Margaret R., *Art Education During Adolescence,* New York, Harcourt, Brace and Company, 1954, Chapter III.

Hoffner, Dan, "Exposition of Method," *Art Education,* November, 1951.

Lowenfeld, Viktor, *Creative and Mental Growth,* rev. ed., New York, The Macmillan Company, 1952, Chapter VII.

McDonald, Rosabel, *Art as Education,* New York, Henry Holt and Company, 1941, Chapter IV.

Prescott, Daniel, *Emotions and the Educative Process,* Washington, D.C., American Council on Education, 1938, pp. 234–242, 288–290.

Read, Herbert, *Education Through Art,* New York, Pantheon Books, 1949, Chapters VI, VII.

Schultz, Harold, and Shores, Harlan, *Art in the Elementary School,* Urbana, University of Illinois Press, 1948, Chapter III.

Ziegfeld, Edwin (ed.), *Education and Art, A Symposium,* Paris, UNESCO, 1953, Section III.

EXPERIENCE AND CREATIVE DEVELOPMENT

> We recur to our basic principle: experience is a matter of the interaction of organism with environment, an environment that is human as well as physical, that includes the materials of tradition and institutions as well as local surroundings.
>
> John Dewey,
> *Art as Experience*

EXPERIENCE AS A BASIC FACTOR

THE GOALS OF DEMOCRATIC SOCIETY AND THE ENDS OF CONTEMPORARY art education can be achieved only if teaching and learning are weaned from traditional schemes and from all those procedures that have proved inimical to creative development. To gain an insight into better ways, certain newer concepts need to be appraised. If in the light of analysis they are found worthy, they should be implemented for educational action. However, the reader is warned that there are also some older concepts which only need to be reinterpreted and understood in terms of present needs to become effective means of education.

Experiencing is one of the oldest and most fundamental educational concepts. It is so vital, in fact, that it has been considered and has been given much attention at various periods throughout the history of education. Its latest revival was given added clarity and impetus by John Dewey, and today it is being rediscovered as one of the most powerful single factors in the teaching-learning situation. It would seem that it is especially valuable in the field of creative education.

Art, particularly when it is understood as being integral with all education, must be realistic as well as idealistic in its approach and in its organization. One might, therefore, ask how children learn best or, in this context, what will evoke from them the most satisfying artistic expression. The essence of this discussion is to point up the fact that experience in and through things and situations is essential as the true source from which children draw ideas and concepts which later manifest themselves in the creative unfolding of each individual.

EXPERIENCE IN THE HISTORY OF EDUCATION

The earliest forms of education, those found in primitive societies as well as the common aspects of preparing children for successful participation in the family and in the communal life of our own time, are based not so much on abstract concepts as they are on experience. But as individuals mature, it is both logical and necessary to expect that the building of concepts should find its proper place in the scheme of living and of education because the ability to generalize on experience increases with age, maturation, and learning.

As one looks back on the history of education in the western world, it becomes evident that with the advancing of time verbalization became increasingly entrenched as a mode of communication—so much so that Erasmus, the Dutch scholar of the Renaissance, was compelled to cry out against it. The crusade which he began eventually enlisted nearly all the chief figures of succeeding generations: Comenius, Rousseau, Pestalozzi, and Froebel. Those men invariably advocated experience with and in those media which today are referred to as sensory aids. The famous *Orbis Pictus* of Comenius is one of the earliest attempts to visualize the meaning of words. Dewey and many other contemporary educational philosophers have spoken insistently for experience in contrast to sheer verbalism.

MAN AND ENVIRONMENT

These are brief historical references to the importance of a method which gives the education of the senses a permanent value. But to the method there must be added a crucial fact, namely, that the subject matter of art may be expressed in two simple words: *man* and *environment*. When due consideration is given to the endless relationships suggested by these words, the significance of experience becomes self-evident. In those relationships are bound up all the activities, longings, successes, and failures of mankind. They are the basis of peace, war, worship, economic efficiency, social well-being, and all else that makes history, whether of individuals, of nations, or of entire cultures.

EXPERIENCE REDEFINED

In an attempt to define the term *experience* as it is used in education, perhaps no sounder authority could be cited than Dewey. He says:

The nature of experience can be understood only by noting that it includes an active and a passive element peculiarly combined. On the active hand, experience is trying—a meaning which is made explicit in the connected term experiment. On the passive, it is undergoing. When we experience something we act upon it, we do something with it; then we suffer or undergo the consequences. We do something to the thing and then it does something to us in return: such is the peculiar combination. The connection of these two phases of experience measures the fruitfulness or value of the experience. Mere activity does not constitute experience. It is dispersive, centrifugal, dissipating. Experience as trying involves change, but change is meaningless transition unless it is consciously connected with the return wave of consequences which flow from it. When an activity is continued into the undergoing of consequences, when the change made by action is reflected back into a change made in us, the mere flux is loaded with significance. We learn something. It is not experience when a child merely sticks his finger into a flame; it is experience when the movement is connected with the pain which he undergoes in consequence. Henceforth the sticking of the finger into flame means a burn. Being burned is a mere physical change, like the burning of a stick of wood, if it is not perceived as a consequence of some other action.[1]

Here, then, teachers have a yardstick by which to measure the effectiveness of whatever experiences they plan for boys and girls. Experiences are not merely enrichments which are imposed on an otherwise traditional way of teaching. When such is the case, teachers and pupils lose out because no learning takes place. Furthermore, Dewey speaks about a "change" made in the undergoing of the experience. What

---

[1] John Dewey, *Democracy and Education*, New York, The Macmillan Company, 1938, p. 163.

EDUCATIONAL JOURNEYS give all pupils firsthand experience with things and situations. To touch, to handle, to use, to feel something, will make subsequent art expression meaningful and "real" (*above*, 1st grade, Laboratory School, State Teachers College, Kutztown, Pa.; *below*, 6th grade, Seattle, Wash.).

change? Ultimately, *insight* into the relationships between doing and undergoing, results in more satisfying or changed outlooks. The satisfaction of having conquered a situation or having solved an aesthetic problem through what was learned in the experiencing becomes permanent learning. Furthermore, true experiencing means the sensing of relationships which give rise to new conceptualizations and the gaining of insights. All this, through activation, becomes part of a learner's mental equipment with which to attack art problems or problems in other fields of activity.

In his penetrating analysis Ziegfeld puts it this way: "All of life is experience; it may be varied or monotonous, scattered and diffused or intense, pleasurable or repugnant; but whatever the characteristics of the specific experiences in a lifetime may be, it is certain that, from the first breath to the last, all living is experiencing."[2]

The use, direct or indirect, of any experience depends on the degree of consciousness of the individual, and on the purposive direction that he is able to give his experiences when he recognizes them as such. One of the functions of education is to make individuals sensitive to the meanings of experiences. In the converse sense, education uses experience as motivation or as stimulus in the process of attaining for the individual a satisfactory relationship between that individual and his environment. Dewey clarifies the universality of experience when he states that "Experience occurs continuously because the interaction of live creature and environing conditions is involved in the very process of living."[3]

What is generally meant by experience? In the simplest possible terms it may be said that it is a matter of firsthand contact, whether physical or emotional. It is an intimate relationship between man and the things he contemplates, or sees, or does. It is a oneness of which the individual is an integral part or concerning which he has become fully sensitive. The importance and meaning attached to what is often called self-identification point up clearly that a relationship, intimately felt, is at the core of motivation and at the basis of individual development in art as well as in other learning activities. The story is related that Turner, the English water-colorist, had himself tied to the mast of a ship in

[2] Ernest Ziegfeld, *Art in the College Program of General Education*, New York, Teachers College, Columbia University, 1953, p. 66.

[3] John Dewey, *Art as Experience*, New York, Minton Balch and Company, 1934, p. 35.

order that he might feel the force of the wind and the power of the lashing waves. He wanted to experience the terror and the agony of a man swaying to and fro between the two extremes of eternity. His whole point was that in order to express in painting that particular type of inward feeling, he must go through it; he must see it and feel it himself.

There is no intention here to indicate that all experiences must be agonizing, although some may be. What is inferred is, rather, that experiences to be educationally effective must be real for each individual. In practice, controlled experiences are selected in such a manner as to ensure that even though all pupils are not affected in the same manner or to the same degree, all of them will gain sufficiently to be stimulated.

Dewey[4] further clarifies the meaning of experience by indicating that it is true and valuable only as it represents a completed act; that it has a beginning and a fulfillment. The educational validity of an experience, therefore, would seem to depend on whether the person has had an experience and not merely a distraction, or an amusing interlude, or has satisfied a whim. In Dewey's own words: "Experience in this vital sense is defined as those situations and episodes that we spontaneously refer to as 'real experiences'; those things of which we say in recalling them 'that was an experience.'"[5] When this occurs, the doing and undergoing of the experience have their own aesthetic qualities that distinguish them from nonaesthetic experiences, which are ephemeral and inconclusive. The timeliness and the worth of an experience are readily sensed by pupils if these elements are present. In that case, they give it spontaneous acceptance and generally ensure its success.

A concept that should be understood is that an experience has form; that is to say, it is an integrated whole upon which effectiveness depends. In schematic terms an experience would take a form like this:

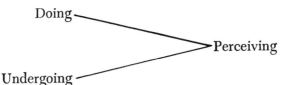

---

[4] *Ibid.*, p. 35.
[5] *Ibid.*, p. 36.

Doing does not merely refer to the immediate physical action such as may occur even in ordinary occurrences. It refers to *all the related events which cause the individual to undergo or have an experience.* Undergoing is the sense feeling, the physical action or inaction, the mental and emotional reaction or control. The result of having undergone an experience is then a new perception: mental, emotional, or physical.

What are the inferences of all this in terms of educational practice? Chiefly, that in considering experiences for young people, in planning and carrying them out, the teacher should ensure that all pupils are capable of undergoing the experiences. It means that teachers need to evaluate their plans to ascertain total validity. In other words, it is important to see that the proposal has qualities that promise worth-while outcomes. In order that this issue may be clarified, it may be well to look at some of the major categories of experience and thus be better able to judge the affective role that each of them may play in education.

TYPES OF EXPERIENCE

Generally speaking, one thinks of experience in terms of the senses first: seeing, tasting, touching, hearing, smelling, and manipulating. There is, however, a level of undergoing which is characterized by the higher processes such as are involved in thinking, organizing, classifying, and the like. In the second group many of the sensory experiences become a part of the total process. It must always be remembered that experience is an integrated and unified event and never a series of isolated items in human action. Therefore, all components of an experience have significance in relation to ultimate perception. In fact, all types of doing-undergoing are necessary to achieve what is generally called a *rich* experience.

For practical purposes it may be worth while to examine some differentiations that may lead to a clearer and more realistic understanding of experience above and beyond its theoretical meanings. In general one speaks of direct, contrived, and vicarious experiences. These are discussed hereafter.

DIRECT EXPERIENCE

Direct experiences are those associated with the senses: smell, taste, touch, sight, sound. Dale refers to them as the "unabridged version of life itself—tangible experiences, which we commonly refer to as 'something you can get your fingers on; something you can sink your teeth into.' "[6] The distinguishing mark of direct experience is the actual participation of the individual in the total act. The experience is suggested by a need; the individual recognizes the need, responds to it first by mental planning, then executes the plan and surveys the results. He has identified himself with the totality of the experience and is, therefore, completely responsible for its outcome.

In art education direct experience implies finding out for oneself with a minimum of guidance. It may mean that teachers make provision so that children, impelled by their own needs for expression, will discover how clay responds to manipulation, how water color mingles, how the brush works, how hard is the stone. Or the pupil experiences the rhythm or lack of it in the lines and forms he has put down, or recognizes the beauty of the grain in a piece of wood, or senses the "feel" of the textured cloth. It is when these things have been experienced directly, purposefully, that the child recognizes the same elements in works of art produced by classmates or by acknowledged artists. The sense of awareness, which slowly dawns as children grow, is stimulated by contact and experiment. And as growth and development take their natural course, children are able to move from the reality of the contact to abstract thinking.

The importance of direct experience at the elementary-school level should be obvious. The wonders of the environment, the control of the body, the relationships to be established, in fact the business of living as a whole, constitute one real experience after another. In late elementary grades and in the junior high school the sense of awareness is on the increase and the adventures of living and learning demand even more complete undergoing or "finding out," "trying out," "having fun" with real things. The senior high school pupil at work on more serious pursuits in the shop, in the science laboratory, and in the art studio now

---

[6] Edgar Dale, *Audio-Visual Methods in Teaching*, New York, The Dryden Press, 1946, p. 38.

seeks even broader, more direct experience through challenging experiments, varied organization, and more adequate technics.

To be more explicit, it may be appropriate to refer again to the everyday areas of living as sources of experiences, all of them rich and valid. The home, the school, the community, religion, play, festivals, and similar activities, when properly organized on the basis of the interests, the age levels of children, and in relation to other subject fields of the curriculum, usually furnish experiences which may evoke art expression.

It has been intimated elsewhere that there are many who believe that art education has a sphere of its own; then again, there are those who believe that logical correlation is a legitimate activity. Elementary teachers in particular may engage in natural correlation with profit for the child as artist and for the child as a normal, growing, learning being. It should be emphasized that it does not matter quite so much whether one thinks in terms of correlated art or whether the child is free to draw from his real experiences, since he is still dealing, as a human being, with his environment. Subject matter which has recently engaged a pupil's attention and interest, let us say from the fields of literature, the sciences, history, or geography, may be very stimulating indeed. Often it gives rise to art expression of a correlated type which draws on both direct and vicarious experience.

CONTRIVED EXPERIENCE

A class of sixth-grade children was working feverishly on "models" of their community. Upon inquiry it became evident that several committees had been diligently at work for nearly a week studying their home town to learn all the good things about it as well as some features that needed improvement. Some questions brought out the fact that it was clear to them that they could not remake their town over night. Yet they were agreed that in time some changes could be made. One young designer said: "We are making our dream town." There was excitement in the classroom and obvious desire to see which group would produce the best model. The streets were wide and landscaped, schools were located conveniently, church spires dotted the plot, factories had been placed together near the railroad station, and there were abundant play areas here and there. Most of the children were constructively occupied with one task or another and each group seemed to be purposefully active.

The wise teacher had set up a situation in which many types of experience were going on: thinking, visualizing, doing, and directing. In terms of activity, these would involve choosing, eliminating, evaluating, and otherwise implementing the experience. The children were using a large variety of materials and varied tools. Some were painting, others were cutting cardboard models, while others were attending to apparently necessary chores. What was the purpose? The teacher explained that the work was part of a unit on the community and that the original suggestion had been made by one of the children and had been accepted by the group as a whole. The ultimate purposes were citizenship education, awareness of community needs, and the stimulation of desire for better surroundings.

Making a "model" or using a model in lieu of the real thing is a contrived experience from which, depending on the effectiveness of the planning, boys and girls generalize and build concepts. In time, the activation of all experiences furnishes the basis for adequate expression.

Dramatization, demonstrations by pupils and teachers, exhibits, still pictures, motion pictures, recordings, and other media discussed in Chapter 6 are, basically, means of providing contrived experiences.

VICARIOUS EXPERIENCE

Imagination and originality are important in all forms of art; their development is a central function of creative education. These qualities are the distinguishing marks of the musician, the poet, the novelist, the painter, the sculptor, and the industrial designer. As a matter of fact, they are the characteristics of all those upon whom the world looks for the improvement of the environment and for a richer life. They are people with fertile minds and active imagination; they are dreamers as well as doers.

Beyond natural endowment, upon what does the imagination feed? How does it grow? The things which pass before the physical senses and the mind have a profound impact upon an individual's immediate and future action. Maier, reporting on the project concerned with the Genetic Studies in Artistic Capacity, states that the researchers concluded that *"perceptual facility, creative imagination and aesthetic judgment* refer more directly to learning."[7] This is in distinction to hereditary traits which contribute to artistic capacity. The "learning" which children acquire as they read, as they witness motion pictures, as they observe illustrations in books, and as they see paintings in museums has a profound effect on their imagination. What they see and hear on television, on the stage, and on the radio may be added to the list of active forces. These, when coupled to personal experiences and as they are associated with movements, actions, and persons, form the background upon which individuals automatically base their imaginative work. The changes in imagination that all teachers and parents observe as children reach maturer stages of reasoning are significant in that they are changes in the *character* of their imaginative thinking. The difference between child's play and fancy and serious imaginative thinking is a matter of maturity of experience. Basically, imagination grows as contacts with the environment become richer. It is also interesting to note from Lowenfeld's[8] study of the blind that the power to create "from within" is a reality. Partial impressions of all types can stimulate the imagination; therefore, the nonphysical and indirect experiences should be encouraged to a degree consistent with the child's level of growth and his mental health. Natalie Cole's example of the child who says: "I closed my eyes and seen an angel and then I made one like I seen"[9] is indicative that the dream, the inner vision, the fancy, needs encouragement, guidance, and in some cases careful protection.

PLANNING EDUCATIONAL EXPERIENCE

To put it simply, the affective role of experience, or its educational value, lies in the fact that it stirs the individual. Here again, to quote Ziegfeld: "Only in the rarest cases is the creative product born full-fledged in the mind of the creator. It comes to full life through a painful process of experimentation, trials, errors, and new trials."[10]

---

[7] Norman Maier, "Research in the Psychology of Art," in National Society for the Study of Education, Fortieth Yearbook, *Art in American Life and Education,* Bloomington, Ill., Public School Publishing Company, 1941, p. 339.

[8] Viktor Lowenfeld, *Creative and Mental Growth,* New York, The Macmillan Company, 1952, p. 251.

[9] See p. 112.

[10] Ziegfeld, *op. cit.,* p. 80.

The true worth of experiencing, then, rests on the dependable insights and stimulations that come to the aid of the creator as he reconstructs his experiences and gives them tangible form in painting, carving, or building.

Therefore, whatever the type of experience, it is important to inquire into the calculated effect that it will have upon the growth of children and what its impact will be on their subsequent expressions.

Experiences, it has been pointed out, vary not only in type but in emphasis. There are, for example, those experiences which utilize bodily action, such as the rhythm of the dance, the playing of certain games, or the handling of certain tools and materials. Whenever physical or sensory experiences are planned, it may be expected that the pain-pleasure effect will evoke creative action. But there are also emotional and spiritual responses or experiences, such as accompany listening to music or poetry, or the singing of stirring songs or melancholy chants. These affect the "spirit" of the child and, in turn, give rise to creative work of a keenly felt nature. Furthermore, it is not uncommon to have emotional experiences through contemplation, simply by beholding a work of art such as Michelangelo's *Pietà* or El Greco's *Christ with the Cross* or Meštrović's *Archangel Gabriel*. Religion has long utilized this particular role of experience; in gen-

PARTICIPATION fosters growth and understanding. Discussing, arranging, and selecting are experiences in problem solving. They make real such abstract ideas as "principles," "elements," and "composition" (*above*, Elementary School, Richmond, Va.; *below*, 5th grade, Kansas City, Mo.).

eral, it is an effective method for the development of genuine appreciation.

Experiences may be pleasant or unpleasant, satisfying or frustrating. Some will arouse sympathetic response, others anger. Some will affect each individual within a group differently; others may affect entire groups in a like manner. It remains, however, that the affective role of all experiences is a sound basis for the stimulation of drawing, painting, carving, and other forms of creative pursuits. Within the wide range of human action and reaction children, even more than adults, find the myriad facets of life exemplified and are profoundly affected by them even if at the moment there may be a lack of outward signs or tangible evidences.

IMPORTANCE OF GOOD PLANNING

The teacher may say: "Touch it—does it feel rough or smooth?" or "Have you ever seen a more beautiful tree?" or "Let's listen quietly." These are examples of spontaneous invitations to experience something new or unrealized up to that moment. These are the instinctive and un-planned ways of good teaching which occur every day in may class-rooms.

But the chief problem is for teachers to know how to plan extensive experiences for their classes. In a real sense, to provide worth-while ex-periences is as difficult as to stimulate properly. Careful planning, there-fore, cannot be overestimated, nor can the validity of experiences be given too much attention. The teacher must make quite certain that what he has planned will have its calculated effect even when account-ing for the limitations and differences among the children. A first ques-tion may be concerned with the purpose of what is planned. To engage haphazardly in what may be called an experiment, or to visit a special place, or to present a dramatization may result in waste of time and dissipation of energies. The purpose must be clear to the pupils and to the teacher. Furthermore, the validity of the experience can and should be given attention beforehand: Will pupils find the experience interest-ing? Is it adapted to the level of the children concerned? Will the ex-perience be rich enough to evoke creative action? Perhaps some illus-trations of categories of experience will clarify the approach to the problem of selecting and carrying out activities that may prove educationally worth while. Detailed examples are found in the chapters dealing with the operational programs in the elementary school, the junior high school, and the senior high school.

CATEGORIES OF EXPERIENCE

There are many possible categories of experience, but for conciseness only the following will be analyzed: experiences that center around the self, around materials and tools, around the life of appreciation, around independent work, around experimentation or problem solving, and around social values.

1. EXPERIENCES CENTERING AROUND THE SELF

The child, it is agreed, is egocentric for a long period of time. He thinks of himself, he thinks of what is his own, he thinks of his immediate family, of his pets, his toys, his games, and his clothes. Often as he plays he talks, even though alone, as if he were conversing with a real person. Actually, he is imagining, and vividly. At the earliest stages of school life it is "I," "my," "mine," and "me" that spell out the interests of the child. Whether one thinks of activities related to play, to family life, or to the child himself, these are the experiences which the child recognizes as his own, and therefore he responds to them willingly and effectively. As the child grows, the interest in self does not disappear. He eventually adds other experiences and other people to his sphere of concern, but self-interest remains preëminent, in one form or another, throughout life.

2. EXPERIENCES CENTERING AROUND MATERIALS AND TOOLS

One of the chief characteristics of all young people is that they need to act. To act means to be a party to, to be involved in and with, to be using something, to be definitely related to the ongoing activity. There is a time-honored dictum to the effect that one learns best by doing. The child learns what happens when colors run together, not by being told, but by being permitted to paint freely one color next to the other. He learns that certain materials are hard and that some are soft by handling them; he learns that clay responds to the pressure of his hands and fingers by manipulating clay or other plastic materials. As the child becomes older and the use of simple tools comes into play, he learns how these tools are to be used in order that he may accomplish the things that he wishes to accomplish. This is a gradual process, but the desire to master tools and materials continues unabated to and through-out manhood. As the child grows and improves in physical coördination, he learns to handle the brush, the knife, the needle, the hammer, and other simple tools more effectively. The motivation is inherent in the accomplishment of his goals: cutting, carving, painting, building, and the rest. It will be remembered at this point that the Bauhaus ideas, stressed by Moholy-Nagy and detailed elsewhere in this work, center exactly on tools and materials.

3. EXPERIENCES CENTERING AROUND THE LIFE OF ENJOYMENT AND APPRECIATION

Since the tremendous importance of individual freedom and personal growth has been stressed, it seems appropriate at this point to indicate that the child needs experiences that generate genuine enjoyment or appreciation of his own work and of the work of others. The child, at all levels, must be guided to see that all individuals, young or old, have a responsibility in the process of interaction, in their relationships to their fellows. The thinking here concerns the effort to see merits and to accept the work of others; it also means respect for the things that others own. This sense of respect for what belongs to others, of admiring what others accomplish, and of admitting their excellence is crucial in democratic social living. "What are some fine things we see in Betty's painting?" "Anne is wearing a beautiful dress today" "John has brought his new toy to school to share it with us." When evaluation of the work of the class is in progress, children should be guided to see the fine idea, the beauty of the color, the interesting interpretation, in the work of their classmates. This is the type of guidance that eventually leads to the enjoyment of masterworks in painting, sculpture, architecture, and crafts.

4. EXPERIENCES CENTERING AROUND INDEPENDENT WORK

The insistence upon and the demonstrated significance of freedom must always be paired with responsibility. It is important to under-stand that freedom can only be exercised by realizing that it is achieved not as an open field but by following the laws governing it. People are free to the extent to which they accept the natural limitations and ad-

ACTUAL DOING, at all levels, utilizes prior experiences, information, and observation. The development of technical facility and taste is closely related to learning through doing (*above*, Baltimore City College (H.S.), Md.; *below*, Shenley High School, Pittsburgh, Pa.).

vantages of the surroundings. In life, those persons are most free who observe the laws of society. There comes a time in the life of every typical child when he must be set to the task of working independently, by himself, without associates or teacher to help him. Through this type of experience he will learn to free himself by solving the problem and by controlling materials and ideas. He will then realize that he can be successful, that he can accomplish all this, on his own. The therapy which accompanies the achievement is a very potent factor in growth as well as in the banishment of certain frustrations.

5. EXPERIENCES CENTERING AROUND EXPERIMENTATION OR PROBLEM SOLVING

Most typical children are extremely curious. As they ask questions they grow. What causes the rainbow; what makes the flowers rise out of the earth? These and other similar phenomena are of intense interest to them. It is natural for human beings to be inquisitive. Socrates discovered this fact long ago and developed the art of questioning as a method which he bequeathed to humanity and to modern education. It is the spirit of inquiry, of wanting to know, of desiring to find out, that needs nurturing at all divisions of the educational system in order to achieve the highest level of development and of crea- tive achievement. One may say without fear of contradiction that the more inquisitive the mind, the more highly creative are the potentialities of the individual. Often, therefore, art experiences should be of an experi- mental nature, of the type that will send the pupil on a search for an- swers. There was a time in art education when many technics were learned, as one learns a poem, by a succession of steps. Teachers today find that children and youth invent technics, combine interesting media, and originate arrangements, thus contributing to their own development and to art in general. The sense of adventure that stimulates science is just as valid in art. In fact, the scientific discovery and the work of art issue from the same source and are motivated by the same drive.

Some purists in art education may claim to believe in growth and de- velopment through art, but would accomplish the task by eliminating all restraints, all suggestions, and even guidance. The fallacy inherent in the laissez-faire school of thought is that it is unrealistic. Quite re- cently, a plea was made by Ulich[11] to the effect that pain, failure, and discomfort are as much a part of life as pleasure and success, and that good citizenship as well as the development of leadership profit most by experiencing both types of feeling. Under the fallacious laissez-faire aegis, children are more likely to grow into extremely individualistic personalities. Children naturally tend to do those things which please them most and to avoid those things which are either unpleasant or present obstacles. Therefore, experiences based on problems to be solved have very significant values in personality development. Simple prob- lems such as "How shall we arrange the clippings on the bulletin board?" or "What colors would be most appropriate for this particular situation?" or "Is this design suitable to the function of this object?" are examples of fairly simple yet basic problem-solving experiences. In the final analy- sis life as a whole is made up of constant solving of problems. Some are simple and some complex, but all demand critical judgment and a sense of adequacy. When children move into adolescence and later into adult- hood, they will face life unafraid if they have learned to solve problems and resolve issues.

---

[11] Robert Ulich, "Leadership and Education," *The Educational Forum*, March, 1955, pp. 261–269.

6. EXPERIENCES CENTERING AROUND SOCIAL VALUES

Some experiences are the outgrowth of play and of natural relationships with other children. It has been claimed, for example, that the highest value, outside of the artistic worth of a mural painting or other group projects, is that children learn to share. They share ideas, share space, learn to value someone else's opinion, learn to express themselves honestly, and learn to be at once polite and coöperative. These social virtues are not learned overnight; furthermore, their practice has a relationship to the development of integrity and honesty in the individual as a child, and are carried over as he becomes an adult. Invariably, the qualities of honesty and integrity are reflected in the work that children produce in those classrooms where social values are practiced and appreciated. It is obvious that community interrelationships and enterprises will yield abundant material on which to plan experiences of this sort.

Thus one may pause and ask again: What kind of experiences are best suited to the creative development of boys and girls in the schools? The question may be answered best in terms of those stimulating activities that are vital, meaningful, and appropriate to the child's psychological and chronological level. Wise selection of experiences, avoidance of stereotypes, variety, and child participation in planning are points to be considered at all times. Ultimately, the expressive power of children develops best under the guidance of kindly yet realistic teachers. Such teachers understand young people; they realize that the world is full of new adventures for children to experience, and that the need is to provide a wide array of opportunities in order that full growth and development may flourish. Edgar Dale's words seem an appropriate summary to this matter: "The use of a wide variety of teaching aids in the school enables education to be more concrete and, therefore, to build better abstractions. Intelligent, well-grounded abstractions are impossible without rich, meaningful, concrete experiences. And well-organized concepts and generalizations enable us to manage new concrete experiences with increased skill."[12]

In concluding, it should be made clear that experiences cannot be

---

[12] Dale, *op. cit.*, p. 36.

isolated; that a boundary line cannot be placed around them. Experiences are more in the nature of the ripple caused by a pebble thrown upon the waters: the little circle that is created widens, moves farther and farther, and then seems to become a part of infinity. It is only for convenience that categories have been suggested. Otherwise, neither the teacher nor the child will ever know, precisely, the effect and extent of an experience. Its true impact has the power to transmute, to recall, to stimulate, and to evoke expression not once, nor only immediately, but again and again. This is the reason why experiencing is here advocated as a larger aspect of creative education.

SUMMARY

Experience, it has been pointed out, is the most significant single element for the stimulation of creative activity. As such it should be the basis of all motivation. Nor can an experience be had in unrelated doses; it is begun, it is undergone in all its phases, and then perhaps it is evaluated for its worth.

To have *an* experience means to have undergone the mental, emotional, conceptual, and physical involvements of a situation. In creative work, all phases of the undergoing usually evoke action; and when such is the case, the doing is part of the total experience. Man, with all his faculties as a human being, as well as his total environment, becomes involved in the act of experiencing. Moreover, imagination and what is generally called originality, as well as other emotional reactions, are stimulated in the process and contribute to it.

Verbalization, although significant in some respects, can be overdone at the expense of actual or contrived contacts with the things discussed, or of the vicarious experiences through which human beings may profit more directly and permanently.

The impact of an experience differs with each individual, but it may be assumed that under normal conditions most typical learners react largely according to a pattern. In learning and in creating, one moves quite naturally from the experience to generalization and eventually to abstraction. For example, experience with design precedes understanding of the principles involved.

The affective role of experience is far-reaching, but it is dependent on the wisdom of choice, on the clarity of purpose, and on the validity of what is planned for learners to experience. Mere activity is not worth while in and of itself.

Broadly speaking, experience centers may focus on the self, on materials and tools, on appreciation and enjoyment, on individualized activity, on experimentation or problem solving, and on social values. It is obvious that the individual is involved in all of them, but for the purpose of classification it is possible to isolate activities that are chiefly concerned with the person undergoing them.

The importance of well-planned and well-carried-out teacher-pupil experiences is central to motivation. Even the process of planning is an invaluable experience which teaches and establishes relationships, and reinforces the value of coöperation and the need for assuming a proper share of responsibility for task ahead. Above all, experience should be regarded as the fountainhead from which may spring worth-while activities. In the present context, such activities are the creative expression of children.

For Discussion and Activity

1. From the history of education or from literature dealing with method discover as many evidences as possible that indicate how *experiencing* has been used as a means of teaching.
2. What are some experiences you recall having had as a child? List them and analyze them as best as you can. Do you know of others who had similar experiences?
3. Apply Dewey's interpretation of the "completed" experience to those mentioned in answer to the question above. How do they fare?
4. Observe a good teacher at work and note the types of experiences he provides for his class. Make judicious evaluations of them.
5. How do you relate the affective role of experience to art activities in the elementary school, the junior high school, the senior high school? Submit your thinking to evaluation by your associates.
6. What criteria seem important in affording *direct* experiences for young children? What for older children?
7. What are the important factors to be considered in planning worth-while experiences for children? Discuss each factor with reference to a specific experience.
8. Having a specific age group in mind, make lists of art experiences with

reference to each of the following: the self, materials and tools, appreciation, independent work, experimentation or problem solving, and social values.

9. Debate the proposition: "Experiences based on complete reality are the most effective for all children." Note the arguments for and against the proposition.

10. Since the creation of art is itself a type of doing-undergoing-perceiving, what is the role of other types of experiences in art education?

For Further Reading

Abbihl, Gertrude M., "Art Education and Spiritual Values," *Art Education,* February, 1955.

Cane, Florence, *The Artist in Each of Us,* New York, Pantheon Books, 1951, Chapter VII.

de Francesco, I. L., "Experience as Basis for Creative Growth," in *This Is Art Education,* 1952 Yearbook, Pa., Kutztown, National Art Education Association, 1952, pp. 127–137.

Dewey, John, *Art as Experience,* New York: Minton, Balch and Company, 1934. This is a basic book which should be read by all teachers of art. For minimum reading: Chapters I, II, III, XI, XIV.

Erdt, Margaret, *Teaching Art in the Elementary School,* New York, Rinehart and Company, 1955, Chapter II.

Long Beach Public Schools, *Secondary School Art Curriculum Guide,* Long Beach, Calif., 1955.

Nahm, Milton C., *Aesthetic Experience and Its Presuppositions,* New York, Harper & Brothers, 1946, Chapters X, XII, XIII.

Ziegfeld, Edwin (ed.), *Education and Art, A Symposium,* Paris, UNESCO, 1953, Section II, pp. 33–38.

Ziegfeld, Ernest, *Art in the College Program of General Education,* New York, Teachers College, Columbia University, 1953, Chapters IV, V.

RESOURCES IN ART EDUCATION

> The use of these materials calls for more than a mastery
> of the mechanics and for more than an understanding of
> their power as teaching techniques. The teacher must also
> have a sense of proportion. She must be clear about her
> purposes and their relative values.
>
> Edgar Dale,
> *Audio-Visual Methods in Teaching*

THE NATURE OF RESOURCES

Art education has moved from a stage of stereotyped activities
and a fixed, year-after-year program into one of vital concern for the
growth and development of boys and girls. The newer emphasis often
finds the art teacher at a loss to know just how to vitalize her program
for the most effective achievement of the major objective. The answer
is to be found in the realization of existing wider horizons.

When one speaks of self-identification he has someone in mind; it is
the pupil or pupils with whom he is concerned at the time. The suggestion that as they grow children become increasingly aware of their
surroundings or environment may be interpreted to mean a correspondingly greater interest in the home, the school, the neighborhood, the
family, the children of the immediate vicinity, friends, the things the
children possess, the games they play, and all the items that together
affect their living. As children grow, and their environment becomes
larger, one thinks of the community in a broader sense: the town, its
stores, churches, people other than the family, perhaps the town nearby,

or the not-too-distant big city. Eventually, one thinks of the state, its history, historic spots, products, industries, scenic beauty, economic and cultural resources. Later on the nation becomes a significant concept, and today, more than ever before, the nations of the world and their people have become the concern of all.

ENVIRONMENTAL RESOURCES

Two facts, then, emerge clearly as one thinks of the individual and his identification with the self and with surroundings. In the first place, identification is personal and grows with the child's physical and mental development. In the second place, and in the same ratio, the world of the child slowly but surely expands into the universe. The universe, be it near or far, is peopled with human beings who are alive, who do things, see things, possess things, create, sing, play, suffer, and rejoice. As people, they have a history, traditions, customs, aspirations, and religions; briefly, they represent a culture. Then there is the physical

RESOURCES ARE MANY and varied. As children play with their toys, admire them, or show their friends the colors, the shapes, and the purposes of the gifts from Santa, they may include them in their drawings and paintings (Kindergarten, Laboratory School, State Teachers College, Kutztown, Pa.).

world, with its immense variety and constant wonder, which again is apprehended by the child in ever-increasing tempo, through the physical senses as well as through the development of perception.

All this, when translated in terms of resources for the education of children and youth, implies experiences, contacts, the establishment of relationships, new learnings, assimilation, and, eventually, action. Action takes the form of expression in the arts, and mastery of subject matter in other areas. Concurrently, the pupil establishes personal and group relationships: goals, values, and ultimately integration of his own being. In general, therefore, one may think of resources as either human or physical.

HUMAN RESOURCES

A consideration of human resources must, obviously, begin with the child and his teacher. Their rapport, common understandings, and friendship are sure foundations upon which to build. But then there are people at home, in school, and in the town. There are other teachers, the principal, and the art coördinator. In fact, there are people all about who are very interesting and who do things in various ways. What do they mean to the child? What is their job? If one visits the store, the post office, the factory, an industrial plant, or a newspaper, he may ask: What do people do? How are they dressed for work? What does the machinery look like? What is the process? What is the value of the product in terms of personal and social good? Could children sketch from "real" people in action? Would a mural depicting a process be interesting? Could children model in clay some of the folks they have seen at work?

Of course, there are special people, such as the postman, the policeman, the fireman, the bank clerk, the store clerk, the janitor of the school, the doctor, the dentist, the school nurse, and many many others. Could the class paint panels showing the professions or trades in which it is interested? Could a visit to the local shoe factory be the basis of a class discussion and then of some creative work? But the child, as a person, does interesting things at play, at work, in school, in church, at home. How can these experiences be utilized in the classroom?

Human resources, when viewed in the broader sense, mean better understanding between pupil and teacher, a realization of the dependence of people on one another, and a utilization of all human activities as the sources of inspiration for creative work. (See Chapters 8, 9, 10.)

Further consideration of human resources at once suggests an area of interest which has become very real within the last few years. That is the peoples of the world outside the child's own country. It is true that Mexico and the American Indian have been rather abused in the development of units and in related art activities. But there is more to the world than just the two groups mentioned. Children are made aware of many nationalities through motion pictures, magazines, and the well-illustrated books they use in various courses in school.

There are very few communities in this country that are completely homogeneous in so far as national extraction is concerned. Could the children be made aware of the fact that there are many national groups in their town? Do they have special holidays? Do they have special dances, costumes, artifacts, and other interesting things that, perhaps, have been handed down for several generations? Would these interesting items make a fine display? Could the design qualities of many handcraft objects be studied? Could the children write stories or perhaps a play, or make a wall decoration depicting the people of their very own community? Could some parents be invited to the school to show and talk about some of the fine customs and crafts of their land of origin?

MODELS, ARTIFACTS, pictures, and other sensory aids, when properly used, are effective means of teaching. In art education, they may serve to activate knowledge and stimulate creative activity (Campus Junior High School, State Teachers College, Kutztown, Pa.).

The values to be derived from the activities suggested are not unlike the values that UNESCO is seeking: understanding, appreciation, friendship, and the feeling of mutual interdependence and mutual trust.

A college class was discussing this very question not long ago, and after a realization of the many possibilities for art education it organized into groups for activities that would exemplify the present implications.

One group created large decorative panels for a cafeteria. The subject of each panel was a large stylized figure of a typical worker in a foreign country from which a particular type of food comes: coffee from Brazil, spices from India, exotic fruits from Africa, and so on. Another group chose to do a large plaster frieze showing peoples from a number of foreign nations in the typical context of their surroundings.

The children in an elementary school are planning, as these words are written, a "Musical Journey" in which they will be attired in the costumes and sing the songs of Holland, Switzerland, France, and Alaska together with songs that recall the growth of America.

Boys and girls in junior and senior high schools are deeply concerned with social and racial problems and are very receptive to a suggestion that they research and study people of other lands. Perhaps such research, wisely guided, may stimulate artistic expression of a fresh and meaningful type.

HISTORIC RESOURCES

A few years ago, the school district of Philadelphia embarked on a very ambitious program of art appreciation in which the human as well as the material resources of the community were utilized to the fullest degree. Bookbinder[1] describes in detail how the work was organized and points out its thrilling possibilities. The result was a series of "pageants" combining the visual arts, music, games, people, historic events, public buildings, and impersonation of prominent figures; in short, all manner of resources. One of the productions involved Independence Hall, the Liberty Bell, the Philadelphia Museum, the old Customs House, a historic church, City Hall, and many other landmarks. But people were portrayed as well as things. Their lives and works were dramatized in such a manner that the total result was a work of art in which the human and historical resources of the city were combined into a grand panorama. There is no hamlet in the nation that does not have a history, interesting spots, and people of significance. The Philadelphia story can be duplicated again and again to give vitality to the work in art, increase the appreciation of history, and foster the development of broader understandings and social meanings.

---

[1] Jack Bookbinder, "The Growth of an Idea," *Art Education*, October, 1949.

Another aspect of communal life that involves human and material resources may be found in community agencies devoted to the general welfare: Boy Scouts, Girl Scouts, recreation organizations, Y.M.C.A., Y.W.C.A., Y.M.H.A., museums, libraries, historical societies, and many other similarly organized groups. These represent vital resources that can stimulate art expression.

EDUCATIONAL JOURNEYS

One of the most profitable and exciting ways of teaching and learning and actually "seeing" and sensing the world, its people, their activities and the results of their activities, is by actually visiting places of interest that are judged to yield material for art expression. In art education the field trip can serve two purposes. The first may be to observe firsthand, to examine, to become acquainted with people, places, objects, and the rest. This alone would be worth while in that it adds to the knowledge and appreciation of the pupils and becomes a reservoir from which the individual will draw at the proper time. The second purpose may be actually to work in art, on the spot, as may be the case on visiting the zoo, the farm, or the market place. In either instance, the value rests on the experiences, the contacts, and the new knowledge acquired by the children.

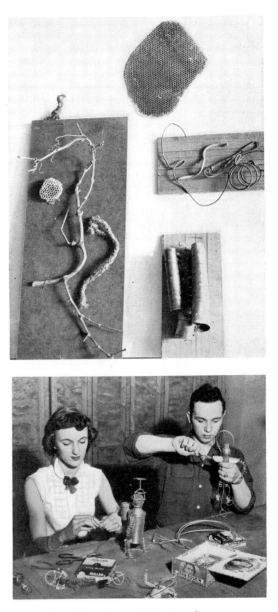

NATURE'S STOREHOUSE and the immediate environment furnish materials from which imaginative design may be developed (4th grade, Seattle, Wash.). "Discarded" and inexpensive materials often teach the meaning of form, texture, and other elements. The tools used in designing add to the experience (Senior High School, Atlanta, Ga.).

How significant it is to plan well and to carry out the plan of an educational journey may seem obvious, yet the cautions suggested by Dale[2] may be worthy of mention: unclear purposes, poor planning of details, the problem of accidents, covering too much ground, inadequate plans for food and rest periods, failure to see the trip on the way as educational, being too schoolteacherish on the trip, failure to keep records of the trip, inadequate follow-up, failure to check on what was learned, and failure to make broad preparation.

When teachers and pupils plan together and are clear in their purposes for the journey, much can be gained.

It may be asserted that what is suggested here is not a new approach. That is true in one respect. However, it points out that art education needs to make use of technics already well known to elementary and secondary teachers in other fields. It reëmphasizes that art cannot be evoked from a vacuum; that the days are past when still life and plaster casts and all-over patterns could occupy boys and girls for long periods of time, and profitably.

Local museums and art galleries, the county or parish historical societies, private collections, art shops, department stores, the farm, the zoo, the industrial plant, and the many other places of interest that are to be found in every locality should be utilized in the art program to give it vitality and meaning.

SENSORY AIDS

The field of sensory aids involves such a vast array of resources and such a large amount of materials that it is almost imperative to select wisely. The more-popular forms are motion pictures, slides, mounted and unmounted pictures, reproductions of works of art of many categories, film slides, models, actual objects, process charts, process sample collections, and recorded music or other auditory media.

The sources of these valuable aids are almost as numerous as the aids themselves, yet it is important that teachers and pupils develop a sense of awareness for them. The agencies of government, local, state, and national, are not used as much as they could be. Museums and art galleries

---

[2] Edgar Dale, *Audio-Visual Methods in Teaching*, New York, The Dryden Press, 1948, pp. 151–154.

have a great variety of services available, industry is ever ready to help, many schools often make provision for the purchase of audio-visional materials, and teacher-education institutions, generally, provide such help to their service areas. The resourceful teacher, with the help of pupils, can often develop a local collection of a variety of aids at practically the cost of mailing a few requests to the proper sources. The same is true of those aids that may be had on a loan basis. Furthermore, many collections of stimulating materials may be made by pupils and teachers, and with proper handling these may last for a reasonably long time. Among the latter are slides, photographs, models, and small collections on specific subjects.

Radio and TV

Education in general and art education in particular have not yet made the most effective use of radio or of television in the classroom, nor have they utilized the by-products of these two means of communication to an appreciable extent. Perhaps this is explainable, to a degree, since the availability of these media is still far from being adequate. There are at the moment 13 educational stations on the air, 13 under construction, and about 100 now in the planning stage. The American Council on Education, the Fund for Adult Education, the Ford Foundation, the Joint Committee on Educational Television, and the National Citizens Committee for Educational Television are among the larger groups attempting to develop this newer field. Millions of dollars are being expended annually toward a goal that may soon be realized, namely, television in every classroom, or nearly so. Nor should one forget the educational programs now on the air and sponsored by commercial stations; they have made a distinct contribution to the education of children.

The objectionable aspects of television and radio have been too frequently aired to warrant repetition here. On the other hand, if television and radio can be harnessed so as to serve educational purposes during school time, and perhaps beyond, under able and competent sponsorship, the children of the nation are bound to benefit from these media.

Art educators in Philadelphia, Pittsburgh, Buffalo, New York, Detroit, Cleveland, San Francisco, and other cities have given ample evidence of the fact that, under proper guidance and with adequate preparation, radio and television can be used effectively. What has been done thus

WORKS OF ART in the form of well-framed, good reproductions are an asset to any school system. Museum visits, whenever possible, will add the thrill of seeing originals. Children's appreciation as well as their knowledge of art are fostered by exposure to worth-while examples (elementary grades, Tucson, Ariz.).

far has "sold" art to millions of parents. It has attempted to teach art, in a broad sense, with children participating or without them, and it has broadened the scope of popular appreciation of art.

One fact that merits mention is that educational television in art has demonstrated that sound programs may be produced in contrast to the "tricky" and shoddy presentations of "how to do it" which have been sponsored by commercial interests.

The opportunities along this line are widening and it may serve art education well if teachers are alert to the tremendous possibilities ahead.

Nature's Resources

Aside from the sensory aids mentioned, there is another reservoir of great value seldom used by teachers, namely, nature itself. This aspect goes beyond mere collecting and may involve the actual manipulation of the materials of nature for the creation of new objects or finding new uses for them. For example, the first step may be the expansion of the awareness of boys and girls to their immediate surroundings. The seasons of the year, as they recur, may well be used by teachers and pupils to appreciate the fact that they live in a world of color: the rich colors of the leaves in fall, their restful green variety in spring, the mellowness of summer, and the subtle hues of winter. Flowers, leaves, birds, rocks, twigs, and animals of all sorts offer limitless opportunities to see colors, to feel textures, to sense the movement of the lines in growing things, and to appreciate the moods of nature. Beyond the aesthetic awareness to the phenomena of the seasons, many elements from nature may be used in the creation of original designs, or in the actual making of texture pictures, stabiles, and a host of other forms of expression that will challenge the imagination and stimulate the sense of design. The common clay from the nearby hill, colors derived from leaves and berries, the cornhusks, the gnarled tree branch, or the graceful twig are but a few items that may quicken an appreciation for the world of nature that surrounds boys and girls everywhere.

Creating Sensory Aids

Art education deals mainly with visual products. In a manner of speaking it is visual education in the best sense. Therefore, it is conceivable that teachers of art should be in a position to produce sensory aids of quality. By enlisting the help of pupils the task becomes less burdensome for teachers in service. A few examples may show how this may be accomplished.

An elementary-school art coördinator asked the children in the schools of her jurisdiction if they would find out from their parents whether they received the Book-of-the-Month-Club announcements. The community is a fairly large one and the coördinator had hoped for reasonable success in her project. In a brief time, she was deluged not only with current and old copies of the Book-of-the-Month-Club reports but with other magazines of high caliber. The plan was to enlist the aid of the classroom teachers and of the children in clipping and mounting the color reproductions of the covers and to arrange them in as many sets as possible to serve a variety of purposes. The coördinator was able to develop the following sets of reproductions: children, animals, landscapes, flowers, and portraits. The sets were attractively matted and are now serving as a circulating picture library. A junior-high-school teacher discovered the intense interest of a pupil in graphic arts. Teacher and pupil planned, researched, accumulated, selected, and eventually mounted examples of processes as well as of finished products in etching, dry point, block printing, monoprints, serigraphs, engravings, line drawing, and many more. That collection is now being used as an *exhibition* as well as a reference portfolio for pupils interested in that area of art.

EXHIBITIONS IN GENERAL

Educational exhibitions have been used for a long time by good teachers to point up ideas and to extend meanings beyond verbalism. Not all persons gain full understanding when the sole medium is the word. Many people are visual-minded and they seize upon ideas rather quickly if confronted by pictures, objects, diagrams, and similar vehicles of communication. But while art exhibitions fulfill the educational function indicated above, they can do much more. The nature of the art exhibit demands that it be so conceived, so selected, so arranged, and so focused as to result in a work of art in itself.

Not long ago, the art staff of a teachers college,[3] realizing the importance of this subject, prepared a service bulletin dealing with it. What is suggested here is a résumé of that more extended presentation.

Exhibitions are important. In the first place they are important in art education because they motivate creative activity on the part of pupils who enjoy seeing, not only their own work, but the work of other pupils and of maturer artists. Exhibits communicate ideas and stimulate individual thinking. The technics employed by others may well be the stimulus for individual experimentation. Furthermore, exhibitions may serve as opportunities for the evaluation of a pupil's own work by stimulating self-evaluation and self-criticism.

Exhibitions speak to school groups and to the community. They often explain, more clearly than words, the total school program, the art pro-

[3] The Kutztown Bulletin, *The Exhibition*, Kutztown, Pa., State Teachers College, 1953.

gram, the relationships of educational experiences to daily living, and many other professional aims not easily clarified by other means. Art exhibitions may also elevate the general taste of the school and of the community by suggesting personal and communal aesthetic improvement by means of contrasts and comparisons.

Space surrounds us. It is precisely because space is all about us that all one needs do is to search briefly for unused wall areas. Eyesores may be transformed into beauty spots; simply built screens placed in corners may result in attractive exhibit areas, or if placed in front of unused doorways these may be turned into exhibition windows. Existing cabinets, blackboards, and bulletin boards in the art room should be utilized as constant points of stimulation.

Exhibits should attract. Obviously, this is one of their chief functions; therefore, the design of exhibitions, even if they are temporary ones, should consider the area to be used. Are they accessible to the largest number of persons? Do they have good visual possibilities? Do they afford good circulation? A center of interest should be established and the law of variation of textures, dark and light, and colors should be observed

HUMAN RESOURCES. Visits to the studios of local artists and craftsmen, such as Bill Freyes, the creator of Major Hoople, add to the pupils' interest in art. At the proper levels, talks and demonstrations from unusual people are stimulating (public schools, Tucson, Ariz.).

because variety intrigues. Ropes, yarns, burlap, monk's cloth, metals, and woods varying in shape and texture will enhance exhibitions, furnish eye appeal, and act as means of unifying exhibitions.

The question of when to exhibit is one that must be determined by the individual teacher. If he has vision and can sense the needs of his classes, of the school, and of the community, he may be rewarded in many ways.

EFFECTIVE USE OF RESOURCES

Perhaps the many aids mentioned so far are not altogether new to teachers of experience. Somewhere along the line they have heard of them, or may have seen them used, or have read about them. But they may have wondered just how a particular teacher was able to obtain fine work from his pupils, or what his method was, his approach, or his teaching technic. Perhaps one of the answers may be found in his effective use of sensory aids as stimulants.

Sensory aids are so called because they help in the effort of promoting pupil growth and development through seeing, hearing, handling, using, and otherwise experiencing various elements. Yet it is a well-known fact that teachers and students can and often do abuse, rather than use, these resources. Resources should not be regarded as gadgets and sideshows, but rather as integral parts of the motivation-stimulation process in teaching. They should be varied from time to time for effectiveness; repetition soon loses its power of attraction and pupils may begin to regard sensory aids as entertainment. For this reason, as well as to establish sound criteria for the effective use of resources, it may be well to seek answers to the following questions: Are the particular resources timely and purposeful? Are they within the understanding of the pupils? Are they effective as stimulants? Do they represent the best available, from the point of view of aesthetic quality? Will they evoke creative action?

RESOURCES WITH A PURPOSE

The first criterion is that whatever is used as a sensory aid should have a purpose: to arouse interest, to clear up a point, to extend understanding, to exemplify, to stimulate. Unless the purpose for showing a motion picture is clear, both to the teacher and to the pupils, the entire effort may be a waste of time. Pupils may be entertained for a little while, but no worthy results may be expected. Merely to be up to date educationally is a poor reason for using sensory aids. On the other hand, one might point to the high-school teacher who decided to show her pupils the film dealing with the sculpture of Alexander Calder to stimulate the imagination of her class prior to an experience in creating mobiles. The class had previously discussed the principles involved and had been shown a mobile made by the teacher. But now the work of a master was calculated to establish respect for the craft and also to see how he proceeded. The showing of the film was both timely and purposeful.

RESOURCES SUITABLE TO LEVEL OF GROWTH

The extreme care with which curriculum resources should be selected includes their suitability to the level of growth of the pupils and to their mental, emotional and creative abilities to utilize the material. Is the language simple enough?, are the examples well chosen?, are the technics easily understood? These are possible questions the teacher should ask herself prior to deciding on a selection.

STIMULATION

Resources used to expand learning must not only be chosen with a purpose and be adapted to the learners' level of development, but must be effective as stimulants. Effective stimulants are those that excite the imagination to the point that one idea acts as a germ for many more ideas. The caution that must be taken is that they should not generate stereotypes; that they are not imitated, and thus

RADIO AND TELEVISION are relatively new media which are making their impact upon the education of all pupils. Presentation of art programs, or reception of them in the classroom, is a stimulating experience when properly planned and adapted to the children's level of growth (Laboratory School, Illinois State Normal University, Normal, Ill.).

defeat the original intent. Suggesting too much may result in uniform responses. As a case in point, one is reminded of the teacher who attempts to stimulate pupils through the use of recorded music, but who interprets the rhythm and the mood for the class rather than simply suggesting that the children listen for the rhythm, try to discover the mood, and draw or paint as they are inspired.

QUALITY

Since this consideration deals primarily with art, although the criterion holds true for every area of education, it is imperative that the resources used have aesthetic qualities. Good color reproductions, well-chosen film slides, well-mounted visual materials, carefully selected examples of manufactured objects, well-arranged exhibits on the bulletin boards, attractive display cases, and other similar common resources act as silent teachers and exemplify good taste and good working habits.

EXPRESSION

Finally, in so far as art education is concerned, resources should evoke creative response on the part of pupils in addition to activating knowledge, exemplifying technics, or whatever other sound purposes may be served. Recently a group of art education students were shown the film *Conspiracy in Kyoto*. The beauty of the calligraphic drawings, the sensitiveness of line, and the charm of the details were a source of real aesthetic delight. However, students not only talked about the film for a long time but their subsequent work was obviously affected by it, because it had the power to inspire.

Even though brief, this discussion should suffice to point out the worth of resources. They are stimulants, or *aids*, in enriching the experiences of pupils, in making art expression more meaningful for them, and in making teaching the pleasant and rewarding task that it ought to be.

SUMMARY

By inference as well as by direct statement, it has been indicated that the subject matter of art expression is comprised within two simple words *man* and *environment*. This is true at all levels of creative development, even though the interpretation of the two words obviously differs at various stages of growth and at various levels of experience. If this fact is clear, then it must follow that one of the functions of education in art, or in other areas, is to achieve understanding, to appreciate, to use, and otherwise to treat man and environment as the natural sources of inspiration and as springboards for creative action.

The human equation is the most important; environmental resources and forces follow. Human beings are interesting to other human beings whether they are at play, at work, or at worship. What they do, how they do it, what results from their endeavor, all these things seem to interest people. In fact, throughout the history of man they have been the subject matter of art.

Nature, or environment, is so versatile and so engaging that it too has a large place in the creations of man. The majesty of mountains, the beauty of the sunset, the fertile plain, the flowers of the field, birds and beasts, and all else that attracts the senses are first causes in man's experience. Young people should be made aware of them through firsthand contacts.

As man celebrates, plays, and records, these manifestations also become part of the environment and part of the inspiration. In addition, man shapes and combines the materials of nature to his own purposes, to create new comforts and new forms in response to his needs. The results are the new art forms of every age.

The art program can make use of all these educational means to stimulate creative thinking and creative action in the classroom. Reproductions of works of art, artifacts, slides, motion pictures, models, collections of significant materials, are only a few of many resources available to or that can be created by teachers and pupils. Educational journeys and the planning of exhibitions, if properly planned, can add measurably to the experiences of pupils. Radio and television are new media which promise a great deal in the near future.

Finally, the very materials of the surroundings may be utilized to create new arrangements, new technics, and new uses. This is the substance of the present chapter.

For Discussion and Activity

1. Make a survey of your home community. What are its historic landmarks, its natural resources, its general plan, its principal architectural styles? How could these be utilized in an art-education program? Detail.
2. Exhibitions are good stimulants. Make a study of available exhibitions of free or inexpensive materials that could be used by art teachers. Obtain all details: size, purpose, level suitability, repositories, and other pertinent data. Share with your associates.
3. Reproductions of good paintings, architecture, sculpture, and industrial products are easily assembled if one's purpose is clear and strong enough. Make a collection of one of the subejcts indicated, then exchange with your associates. This may become the nucleus of inexpensive resource materials.
4. Junior-high-school children are expecially interested in vocations. Plan an

introductory lesson to be followed by art activities dealing with the world of work. Include in your plan several types of sensory aids.

5. If you were faced with the task of preparing a program for a school assembly, how would you utilize community resources? Be specific and detailed in the answer.

6. If possible, secure from your library a short film, such as *The Loon's Necklace* or *Gaston et Martin*. After viewing the film decide for what grade level it would be suitable and what next steps you might take to utilize it as a springboard for art activities.

7. Gather a variety of materials from your surroundings and create whatever your imagination suggests. How could such materials be used in the classroom? At what level? Submit your product to an evaluation by your associates.

8. What are the public or semipublic agencies in or near your home community where you may secure sensory aids? List and describe.

9. How do you evaluate audio-visual materials? Discuss and demonstrate the evaluation process.

10. What are the values of educational journeys? Discuss in detail and with examples.

For Further Reading

Bookbinder, Jack, "The Growth of an Idea," *Art Education*, October, 1949.

Bridgewater, Mavis, "Exhibitions with a Purpose," *Art Education*, February, 1950.

Burton, William H., *The Guidance of Learning Activities*, New York, Appleton-Century-Crofts, 1944, Chapter XXI.

Chapin, Barbara M., "A Creative Heritage Lives Through Sharing," *Art Education*, February, 1954.

Clapp, Elsie R., *The Use of Resources in Education*, New York, Harper & Brothers, 1952, Chapters I, II.

Conant, Howard, "Creative Art Activities in a Viewer-Participation Type Television Program," *Art Education*, January, 1953.

Dodge, Hannah, "Art as Visual Education," *The Art Education Bulletin*, May, 1950.

Eastern Arts Association, Ninth Yearbook, *Sources and Resources in Art Education*, Kutztown, Pa., the Association, 1954.

Gaitskell, Charles D. and Margaret R., *Art Education During Adolescence*, New York, Harcourt, Brace and Company, 1954, Chapter IV.

Shultz, Harold, and Shores, Harlan, *Art in the Elementary School*, Urbana, University of Illinois Press, 1948.

Winslow, Leon L., *Art in Elementary Education*, New York, McGraw-Hill Book Company, 1942, Chapter IX.

Ziegfeld, Edwin (ed.), Education and Art, A Symposium, Paris, UNESCO, 1953, Section III, pp. 65–74.

EVALUATION IN AND THROUGH
ART

> The child is constantly changing. As he develops new feelings and attitudes, new habits and skills, and new knowledges and understandings, these form his behavior pattern. Interest, success, and satisfaction are essential factors in determining the direction of growth. Behavior change is one evidence of the growth that has taken place within the child.
>
> Edith Henry,
> *Evaluation of Children's Growth*
> *Through Art*

HUMAN BEHAVIOR

THIS CHAPTER IS CONCERNED WITH EVALUATION OF HUMAN BEHAVIOR AS seen through art. But in order that the importance of evaluation through art may be properly understood and given adequate attention, it is proper first to look into the meaning of the term itself.

Evaluation, as used in this discussion, is closely related to appraisal of development. It includes informal and intuitive judgments of the pupil's progress, as well as the aspect of valuing or of determining what is desirable and good for the pupil. Only to a limited degree does the term refer to measurement or testing as those terms are used in connection with so-called standardized tests or tests of aptitude.

Logically, it may be asked why the definition is limited. The chief reason is that as yet, in the field of art education, testing and measuring scales have not proved valid for the task. There have been attempts to measure art ability or to test "appreciation" in art, but by far and large the instruments have fallen into disrepute. However, recent interest in evaluation through art is a sign of a felt need for adequate means of appraising the endowment as well as the progress made by pupils. It is hoped that the combined genius of the psychologist, the aesthetician, and the educator may develop valid, objective instruments for use in art education.

But before proceeding to see how evaluation in art can help in the improvement of pupils' outlooks, it is important to establish the character of what one wishes to evaluate. To do this, several terms are clarified hereafter.

HUMAN BEHAVIOR DEFINED

Education is chiefly concerned with human behavior, and its aims may be either to improve behavior or to change it in one way or another. People, it is commonly said, "behave" well or badly, properly or improperly, and so on. Children, youth, and adults play, work, rest, sleep, and perform all manner of things in all manner of ways. Whatever the case, each individual behaves in a way suitable to him; it is within his nature to act as he does. This indicates that there are psychological reasons why people are what they are. In teaching, those reasons become very significant if the goals of education are to be achieved. Therefore, within the limits of this discussion, it may be profitable to inquire further into the nature of behavior.

One way of defining behavior is to assume that for every action or response there is a stimulus. In simple situations this is clear, but when reactions become involved, and most of them are, the matter becomes a chain of reactions or a rather complex series. Most psychologists refer to such complex stimulus-response situations as behavior. Actually, there are two prevalent theories of behavior, the *stumulus-response* theory and the *goal-insight* theory. The stimulus-response theory relies largely on the stimulus, considers the environment a dominant influence in the initiation of action, and views learning as dependent on previous action. In general, this point of view almost denies the possibility of original or independent action in human behavior.

By contrast, the goal-insight theory magnifies the organism which is continually seeking expression. Action involves all the functions of the organism, and the environment is considered a shaping and coöperative agent rather than an initiating one. Interestingly enough, the organic unity of creative expression (see Chapter 1) is perfectly matched by this second theory.

Some further light on the behavior of humans is gained by studying their growth pattern as well as their general development. What do these terms imply?

GROWTH, DEVELOPMENT, AND MATURATION

Growth, to begin with, is a measurable quantity. One may measure size, height, weight. However, not only physical but mental, emotional, creative, aesthetic, and perceptual growth may be also measured by reference to a previous level. Growth of any phase of human behavior is only one part of the larger process which is referred to as development. Normal growth proceeds according to an established rate; accelerated growth is in advance of the established norm; slow growth proceeds at a lower rate than the norm. Growth is dependent on several factors for its well-being: on nurture or food, on hormone secretions, on heredity, and on use, or exercise. These facts are based almost entirely on biological grounds, yet they make the meaning clear and indicate relationship to teaching and to evaluation.

Development indicates the observed changes in the shape, functions, and degrees of coördination of the human being. The nervous system acts as the coördinating or integrating agent; when normal growth is taking place, the whole organism does all the things that normal beings are expected to do.

Maturation means readiness to act. It involves all the growth and development needed at a given level to perform any unlearned behavior, or readiness before any learned behavior can take place. For example, a child needs to be able to hold a crayon or a brush before he may be expected to perform in a certain manner or with a degree of quality. Motor control, or coördination, is involved in this case.

The significance of all this with respect to evaluation is that growth and development are intimately related to human behavior and to whatever causes its manifestations. The intrinsic motivations or goals, the capacity for growth, and the potential development of an individual are other aspects that suggest why children, young people, or adults behave as they do. Furthermore, total behavior is bound up with the learning process: skills, emotions, feelings, habits, understandings, goals, and values. As each of these is considered in its relationship to performance or behavior, a truer picture of a pupil is possible. Therefore, the crux of the argument in this chapter will be that those who evaluate must have on hand more than the end results of teaching. The latter are important, but they are not the *whole* pupil.

It may now be stated unequivocally that the purpose of evaluation in art, even though by means differing from traditional ones, is to gather and analyze all the knowledge that it is possible to gather about the behavior, the growth, and the development of individuals in order that such knowledge may be used in their best interest, individually or collectively.

GENERAL AIMS OF EVALUATION

Important though knowledge may be, simply to gather data about individuals will not solve any problem. On the other hand, when certain general objectives for a program of evaluation have been formulated, it is possible to use that knowledge with profit for the teacher as well as for the pupil. Some possible aims of a program of evaluation are these: (1) to predict the degree of achievement in art; (2) to measure progress or growth in concepts, manipulation and control of materials, and adequacy of expression; (3) to differentiate and certificate pupils; (4) to diagnose learning difficulties, mental, physical, emotional, creative, aesthetic; (5) to diagnose defects in teaching procedures; (6) to determine possible remedial technics and the aims of subsequent teaching-learning situations so that they may help pupils in need.

In practice, evaluation is tied up with grading, reporting, and promotions. The manner in which these matters are handled are closely related to the objectives that a school system, or a teacher, or education in general sets up as its goals. For example, if the purpose of an evaluation is to measure the effect of training in a specific skill or to measure the mastery of a technic or a process, as might be the case in art education, the problem is considerably narrowed down. Then it is possible to measure individual achievement on the basis of scales or masterworks or other comparative instruments, either available or locally designed for the specific task. If, on the other hand, the purpose of an evaluation is to measure the effect of education upon an individual in terms of behavior or of growth in one or many directions, including creative and aesthetic, the problem is decidedly a different one.

The thesis maintained so far assigns to art the cultivation of the senses, the education of the emotions, of innate vision, and of the intellect through creative experiences and action.

For that reason a Relational Theory was suggested in an earlier chapter. When reflected in the teaching-learning situation, that theory underscores the organic unity which is characteristic of creative experience in art, or in other fields for that matter. Edman's[1] view of art as education indicates that deliberately to "teach" art may result in mere pedantry. The true purpose of teaching is to disclose, to present, or to point out the qualities of the environment which the senses make available to man. There are forms, colors, and lines to see, sounds to hear, nuances to discover, and words to be moved by. This shows the value of teaching not necessarily, or always, by logic, argument, or fact, but by exposure. Exposure to painting, design, sculpture, music, and other art forms becomes an experience which may be calculated to have responses in the form of art expression or in terms of appreciation. These are forms of behavior.

Regarding education of the emotions, it should be remembered that they are at the basis of all behavior. And since education is concerned with changes in behavior, art must assume its proper share of the task. Mere performance, no matter how perfect, is only a partial answer to the education of man. Therefore, insistence on creative activity, as distinguished from ordinary activity, is a logical one, because the former represents an organic process. Barkan describes creative experience in these words: "Its elements include the related human functions of seeing, perceiving, reacting, organizing, and acting. An individual sees something; he perceives its meaning; he reacts to it; he organizes his functions in relation to it; he acts in terms of it."[2]

A differentiation in types of education is logical because individuals differ. Because of its nature, art suggests a type of evaluation of growth

[1] Erwin Edman, "Education Through Art," in *Art Education Today, 1951–52*, New York, Teachers College, Columbia University, 1952, pp. 11–17.

[2] Manuel Barkan, *A Foundation for Art Education*, New York, The Ronald Press Company, 1955, p. 55.

in tune with its nature and media. By way of contrast, the traditional subjects and views of education stressed the learning of a conglomeration of information and skills; creative education, on the other hand, strives for harmonization of the individual. The activities of creative experiences have residues in the form of a painting, drawing, modeling, design, or whatever is within the scope of the experience. Furthermore, as in all creative education, art must strive for growing control of elements and materials, of knowledges that give new meanings and directions, and, finally, of new concepts. When these functions of art education are understood, it is possible to proceed to an examination of systems of appraisal and of necessary instruments for the evaluation of growth through art.

GRADES, GRADING, AND REPORTING

The traditional and still prevalent way of evaluating the attainments of pupils in the schools is by means of grades. These are either numerical or are translated into alphabetic symbols. Generally, it is reasoned that if a pupil does the most outstanding work in a subject such as English, history, or science, according to standards set by the school, he is awarded a grade of 100 or as close to that percentage as he achieves. In alphabetical symbol, the pupil who achieves such a grade is considered an "A" pupil. At the other end of the scale one finds the pupil who does the poorest work; he is an "F" or failing student. Between the extremes are the "B", "C," and "D" students.

DUBIOUS VALIDITY OF GRADES

Obviously, the basic questions that arise are these: What is the meaning of 100 or "A," and so on down to "F" or whatever the lowest percentage equivalent may be? Does the standard upon which a grade or symbol is based remain constant for all teachers and all pupils? Are the same standards and grades equivalent in all schools and in all systems? Even when there is reasonable evidence that the standards in a given school are fairly uniform, is the pupil measured against his classmates or in relation to his own capacities in a given field? And lastly, are the grades thus assigned true measures of the individual's achievement in relation to his *Gestalt* or pattern of growth?

Of course, there are many more questions needing adequate answers

if the awarding of grades as described above is to be accorded any validity. The debate concerning the obvious inadequacy of percentage or
letter grades has been going on for several decades. It continues even
now, and unquestionably will be carried on at the local level of school
systems for a long time to come. Among the chief reasons for the continuance of the debate are, first, education as a whole is still subject-mat-
ter-centered, even though it gives lip service to pupil development; second, because parents still insist on knowing what their children are
achieving in subject-matter fields; third, because institutions of higher
education still demand grades as the objective evidence upon which
they either admit or reject those who seek entrance to colleges, universities, and professional schools.

But it seems proper to go beyond the obvious inadequacies of prevalent systems of grading and to point out some of the more serious dangers inherent in them, especially in regard to their emotional effect on
boys and girls. Olson states that "The marking system may be emphasized to the extent that it constitutes a major frustration in the lives of
many children."[3] The inference is that failure, in contrast to success, is a
poor basis for stimulating growth. Failure encourages tensions, poorer
performance in subsequent work, and poorer social and personal adjustment. A further point often advanced is that competitive work encourages dishonesty. Marks also have an undesirable effect on pupils capable
of high achievement in that priggishness sets up additional undesirable
attitudes which eventually harm children as they grow up. Their attitude toward school, parent-teacher relationships, public-administration
relationship, all are strained by the emotional reactions that traditional
grading systems invariably cause.

TRANSITIONAL METHODS

A sense of realism suggests that as long as education is unable to resolve the problem entirely, certain transitional methods must be employed. Olson and other educators have suggested that for administrative purposes, to satisfy parents, to transmit grades to other schools, and
to certify students to colleges and universities, grades be recorded, but

---

[3] Willard C. Olson, *Child Development*, Boston, D. C. Heath Company, 1949, p. 312.

not publicized in any way. In the meantime, pupil-progress reports should go to the child and to parents.

It is heartening to note that as the battle of the grades continues, a number of methods of appraisal of the growth and development of boys and girls are being developed, tried out, and, in some communities, actually established.

Among the newer methods of evaluating pupil progress in school, the *anecdotal report* seems to hold promise. As it is refined and as the public accepts its intentions, this instrument may become more useful and more widely used. Another system of reporting is the *conference method*. The latter method suggests that the parents of a child come to the school, meet the child's teachers, and be given a verbal report, supported by records, on his growth and his behavior. But the time element, problems of personalities, and the unwillingness of many parents to come to the school are among the obstacles involved in administering this scheme successfully. However, small yet advanced communities are able to implement the plan; it is quite difficult in larger communities where heterogeneous populations live.

The fact remains that if the broader ends of the education of children are to be attained, better and more effective means of appraisal and of reporting must be found. Perhaps the solution rests in the coöperative development of such means by parents-teachers-administrators. When such coöperation is effected, common understandings may be reached and better mental health ensured for children, parents, and educators.

With this as a background, the next task is to attempt a review of broader concepts for the adequate use of evaluation of development.

THE SIGNIFICANCE OF EVALUATION

The two major human elements involved in the teaching-learning situation are the teacher and the pupil. How well they are getting along, each in his proper role, and how effectively the teaching-learning process is functioning, can be reasonably determined if adequate time, adequate data, and adequately defined purposes are available.

Evaluation may be defined as the process of determining not only the amount but also the quality of growth and development that have taken place or are taking place in the pupil. At the same time, as a matter of self-evaluation, and even gratification, it may indicate the extent and the quality of success attained by the teacher in achieving clearly defined goals with respect to pupils. In this context, the chief concern is to discover how best to evaluate pupil growth through art.

SIGNIFICANCE FOR TEACHERS AND PARENTS

The importance attached to the process of evaluation and its technics in recent years may be largely attributed to a realization of the new significance of education in the development of children. Mere testing for achievement or for mastery of subject matter is, at best, a partial approach to the problem of growth; certainly it is not the most significant aspect of it.

There are other aspects of development which are revealed through procedures devised especially for the purpose of diagnosis. In general, one thinks of pupils as growing mentally, physically, socially, aesthetically, and creatively. Unless all facets are kept in mind, parents and teachers will gain only a side view of the boy or girl in question. Furthermore, it should be remembered that the various phases of growth, even though differing in character, often bear a relationship to one another. For this reason it is important to appraise and compare all phases in order to have an adequate picture. Only thus will teachers and parents be in a position to guide pupils to achieve the utmost wholesomeness desired for them. It must be concluded, therefore, that the chief aim of evaluation is *diagnosis*. Later, the evaluator may proceed to employ corrective measures, special instruction, and special guidance. The technics available for the redirection or general improvement of teaching or of learning may then be expected to be effective, since the many-faceted aspects of development are considered. By the same reasoning, any appraisal of pupils that is based on partial data is bound to be biased. Under such circumstances, whatever measures are taken are likely to be detrimental to the total development of the pupils.

SIGNIFICANCE FOR PUPILS

Evaluation has another aspect. It concerns pupils directly because most coöperative technics involve them in the process of diagnosis and total evaluation. How, then, do these technics affect the pupils? When pupils are asked to look over their own work in the light of explanations which a teacher has offered, or to furnish answers to some of the elements of the work before them, or to give frank reactions to certain situations or things, they are likely to compare, examine, and react in terms of their own capacities and experiences. Actually, these activities become self-examination. Self-examination may lead to self-criticism and to self-redirection. It is conceivable that self-examination may lead to greater confidence in one's own judgments and reactions, and consequently to one's growth. There are technics which involve pupils in the evaluation of their art products or activities; these will be discussed later in the chapter. However, it should be clear that evaluation involves pupils very actively.

VALUE FOR ADMINISTRATORS

Evaluation of specific aspects or of growth, in general, when based on criteria that are wisely chosen and properly validated and implemented, may furnish the administrator with pertinent data for the improvement of teaching, teachers, and pupils.

Whether the administrator thinks of the evaluation of an entire school program or of one subject field, this basic fact holds. The superintendent, the principal, or the art consultant may wish to know how satisfactorily the entire program is moving. Or they may wish to know how each phase of the program is affecting pupil behavior. Whatever the case, it will involve improvements, changes in direction, changes in method, varied groupings, and other devices. These devices are designed to bring about maximum benefits for pupils and teachers. Invariably, questions are raised by parents, public, and teachers about what happens in schools. Answers may be readily furnished when sufficient evidences can be produced and when the procedures are clarified. This is equally true of the results of evaluation and of their interpretation.

EVALUATION OF THE WHOLE CHILD

It has been intimated all along that growth is a simultaneous process. Its various manifestations have been referred to as mental, emotional, social, physical, aesthetic, and creative.

But it is important to understand how the present discussion of evaluation is related to the true ends of education. While a child's growth shows a pattern, its various manifestations are not necessarily equivalent. This means that a child may exhibit a certain degree of social maturity, but that same degree is not matched by his creative development. The reverse could be true. Therefore, in any type of evaluation it is the totality of what the manifestations show that should lead the teacher or parent to reach even a temporary conclusion. Periodic appraisals, over a reasonable length of time, could result in a general conclusion and a plan of guidance.

This reiteration of the function of evaluation leads directly to some definitions of the various elements of growth. They are not all-inclusive, yet they should furnish a basic understanding for initial use and further study.

DEFINING MENTAL GROWTH

The popular understanding of mental equipment and capacity for growth is that these traits are demonstrated by the pupil's ability to master "fundamental" learnings. This is largely true of conventional content subjects in the curriculum. A review of tests in those subjects makes this assertion evident. But a further evidence, or even a different type of evidence, of mental ability is shown by the learner's response to situations which arise from conditions of environment, or his ability to cope with problems differing from "fundamental" learning.

In art education, this same mental alertness is shown by the child artist in his awareness of differences, changes, details, and unusual aspects of a situation, and it is generally shown in his work. Another evidence of mental capacity is shown in art by the child's ability to understand and to solve problems inherent in the creative process. In a real sense, the act of creation begins with a conceptualization of a situation, it is followed by analysis, and only then is it given embodiment through the media and the elements at the disposal of the creator. A high degree of conceptualization indicates high mental ability. It may or may not match creative or other types of ability, but it is a good index of high potential in a broad sense.

Knowledge is of little use to the child if he does not relate it to subsequent pursuits or to art activities. In art, knowledge supplies the differentiations among objects, relationships in space, size, and form. Perception or creative insight does the rest. The typical child includes new elements in his art work to the degree that he utilizes, retains, and increases his knowledge. His subsequent growth is clearly seen in the de-

CHILDREN DIFFER WIDELY in native capacity and in those traits that constitute intelligence. In addition, children within the same intelligence category differ among themselves in special abilities. The drawings reproduced below come from the Drawing a Man Test, which is a part of the Metropolitan Readiness Test, Form R. All come from first grade, all have had one year in kindergarten, and their age is the usual one for the grade. Children 1 and 2 were given a general rating of *superior;* yet in the drawing test, the first child rated an A while the second rated a C. Child 3 was ranked as a *high normal,* yet he ranked an A on the drawing scale. In the second row, children 4 and 5 were ranked as *low normal;* but in drawing, child 4 rated a D while child 5 rated an E. But child 6, who was rated as *poor risk,* did better in the drawing test than child 5. Evaluation must, therefore, proceed on an individual basis because each child is a distinct personality.

velopment of his symbols for man and environment and in the larger outlooks on life.

One fact that may seem contradictory at first is that not all bright pupils will be first-rate young artists. This is due to a disparity in the growth pattern. In general, however, intelligence and ability to create show a high degree of correlation. The Goodenough Draw a Man Test, which is usually administered to first-graders, will prove this to be true, as indicated in the illustration on page 207.

Further evidence of mental ability may be seen in certain processes in art, particularly the crafts. These involve coördination, intelligence, and inventive ability. Even though some mentally slow children seem to do well in the crafts, it must be noted that superior children do considerably better. This suggests that a caution to be exercised in evaluating child growth is not to confuse the elements of the pattern of growth. Each element has its own value and place. Therefore, it is important to relate the various aspects of mental ability in order to determine the growth attained by a child. From the standpoint of teaching, his performance may indicate that he needs confidence more than additional guidance in art activity; or that he needs encouragement, or stimulation of his intellectual and other capacities.

DEFINING EMOTIONAL GROWTH

Emotional growth may be defined as a constantly rising rate of adjustment evidenced by an individual. Specifically, the evidences are in terms of confidence, normal freedom within the environment, conceptual development, flexibility, deepened perception, and obvious enjoyment of an undertaking.

In Chapter 1 an attempt was made to clarify the nature of art and the function of the emotions. At this point, the concern is with evidences of emotional progress.

It is not claimed that art alone brings about emotional balance; nor can it be assumed that art activity is the only way of inducing emotional growth and behavior change. However, by its very nature art lends itself admirably as a means of release and fulfillment. In no other area can an individual be as free as when he is given opportunity to create. Tensions, emotional strain, bottled-up feelings, all these find release through art activities. The therapy of art has been discussed elsewhere, yet a restatement of its efficacy cannot be avoided here.

But beyond release, if unhampered, the process of creating offers the child a means of adjustment. He chooses, he decides, he compares, he solves problems. In all these experiences he exercises the faculty of judgment and finds pleasure in asserting it. Often he identifies himself with his work in a positive manner.

A well-adjusted pupil is usually buoyant and reflects that buoyancy in his work. There is wholesomeness in his expression and evidence of enjoyment and inner satisfaction in the use of color, line, and form.

The pent-up energies of young people tend to make them tense and irritable. Art makes use of those energies in a positive manner. It is also evident that a well-adjusted child shows variety and flexibility in ideas and in ways of expressing them. Usually he seeks new experiences and is confident in undertaking them.

By contrast, the maladjusted are retiring, fearful, unwilling to undertake new experiences. They feel comfortable in the protective shell they have built around themselves. Stereotyped expression, meaningless repetition of subjects and technics, and, usually, objective work are indications of emotional strain.

The degree to which children and youth identify themselves with their work and the freedom which they show in the handling of the materials of art are a fair measure of emotional well-being. As they grow physically, in abilities, and in knowledge, they should also grow in confidence and satisfaction in their creative work.

DEFINING SOCIAL GROWTH

It should be very apparent to teachers that social adequacy is one of the chief ends of education. The most brilliant child, the most capable, the most intelligent, will not succeed as a human being unless his behavior fits him to take his place among his peers. His role may be one of leadership or one of intelligent and coöperative followership.

Social intelligence, as it grows, gives the pupil increased ability to cope with the demands and the problems that arise in school life and in all of life. This point of view has been stressed throughout these pages. It is here repeated in order to clarify the function of evaluation as a means of measuring and guiding this type of growth. The ultimate end is the best development of each individual.

Precisely, what are some forms of changed behavior that indicate social growth? For the sake of clarity the following presentation may help:

EVIDENCES OF SOCIAL GROWTH

Original Tendency	Changed Behavior
1. Egocentric, self-centered	Thinks of and about *others;* identifies himself with others
2. Aloof, "lone wolf"	Seeks to work and play with others
3. Independent	Accepts help, suggestions, and advice of others
4. Self-satisfied	Seeks self-improvement through self-criticism and that of others
5. Antagonistic	Friendly, coöperative, participating
6. Likes own work only	Appreciates work of others; accepts points of view of others also
7. Plays alone	Plays with group; contributes to group enterprise
8. Resents criticism	Accepts suggestions; profits by criticism; tries to improve
9. Selfish	Shares ideas; lends a hand; works harmoniously; participates
10. Snobbish	Likes others; is friendly; shares his pride
11. Unwilling to "serve"	Willingly assumes proper share of responsibility; goes a second mile
12. Domineering	Learns to follow; learns to share and coöperate; learns to take turns

DEFINING PHYSICAL GROWTH

Manipulation has been emphasized because it is through handling that children develop the necessary coördination and muscular control. The crayon is not unlike a spoon one gives a child at a very early age. Both are tools to be mastered through practice. Later, other tools, materials, and technics are added by parent and teacher or are sought out by children as their needs increase. A physically sound child learns to control tools and materials within a reasonable time and with sufficient success. When normal facility is lacking, the child is not functioning properly from a physical standpoint.

Balancing the body, swinging the arms, or playing games that call for certain types of dexterity are physical necessities that a healthy child learns to master. To these simple examples many other and more complex ones may be added.

But in art education, it is not only the control over tools and materials that matters. It is the reflection of the physical self in the art work, the total identification of the child artist in what he produces. The rhythm of the body, the eventual realization of its parts and their use, and the keenness of the sense of touch find their way in the work of the child. In fact, the ability to use all his senses in relation to his work is an example of normal perception. A physically sound person will sense texture, space relationship, balance of areas, and other equally important elements. Often, as stimulation, many teachers encourage children to enjoy some physical activity as tuning up for art activities. These, of course, must be well chosen and must be within control.

Briefly, then, it is safe to state that in evaluating a child's work his physical health is an index to consider. On the other hand, art activity encourages the development of proper functions of the body and thus aids in promoting coördination, perception, and sensitivity.

DEFINING AESTHETIC GROWTH

In the discussion of the aims of democratic education, it was brought out that the ideal citizen needs much more than a knowledge of traditional subject matter. Extension of the culture of a nation calls for aesthetic education as well, and growth of art in the schools is evidence that the wisdom of the people has awakened to this need. Therefore, art education itself has become concerned less with art production as such, and more with art as it functions in the life of the individual. Response to the beautiful, or its appreciation whether in nature or in objects created by man, is a legitimate province of education and particularly of art education.

Simply as a convenient way of differentiating between two desirable ends of education, the term aesthetics here refers to the appreciational aspects of art. The creative aspect will be discussed in terms of the drawing, the painting, the modeled piece, or some other work produced by a pupil.

The two aspects, creation and appreciation, are not separate reactions in actuality. The child artist chooses the colors, shapes, textures, lines, and forms he employs to express himself. This very choice, if adequte for him, is an aesthetic experience involving both aspects of the experience. It is clear then that a function of guidance in art education is to encourage choosing, comparing, contrasting, and interpreting.

EVALUATION MEANS more than grading. It means appraising the kind and extent of growth taking place in a pupil. For pupils, it may imply enjoyment and selection with a degree of understanding and may involve a child's own creation or that of other children. Awareness of qualities in works of art leads to self-improvement and to the development of taste (public schools, Tucson, Ariz.).

For the sake of clarity, it may be said that *appreciation* is the active consumership of art. It involves repulsion or attraction to one object rather than to another. In a technical sense, it means passing judgment upon a work or a situation. After the judgment follows warmth of feeling for or against, and enjoyment of or revulsion from, the object. In any case, appreciation depends on several factors. It depends on what the observer brings to the work of art by way of cognitive equipment, technical knowledge of aesthetic principles, familiarity with similar works of art, and, lastly, on what is called *intuition*. The last term automatically refers back to the kind of education to which the individual has been exposed.

The life of appreciation includes small things as well as big things. Children may now be discussing their own work or that of classmates, but shortly they will be enjoying, discussing, or studying the works of mature artists. Whatever the case, this type of experience is one which involves the senses, the emotions, the mind, and even the intuitive powers.

This type of growth is best aided by frequent exposures to various modes of art. In the classroom, self-evaluation or the "telling" period, or the question, is its best ally. Again, for the sake of clarity some specific examples of aesthetic growth are listed as starting points:

1. Spontaneous reaction to colors in a painting, in nature, in one's own work.
2. Evident pleasure in rhythms of form, line, texture, color, whether in their use or enjoyment.
3. Spontaneous sense of organization in drawing, painting, modeling, or other work. Recognition of organization in the work of others.
4. Sensitiveness to situations and "meanings" in general, and in art works in particular.
5. Ability to analyze or tell the why of certain moods, feelings, and situations.
6. Awareness of many possibilities in the use of color, texture, form, and line; self-improvement, as induced by analysis.

In evaluating the aesthetic growth of an individual child, the question is to what degree, how often, does the child show some of the reactions mentioned?

DEFINING CREATIVE GROWTH

The two significant words in this connection seem to be *creative* and *growth*. The latter indicates that a step forward has been taken; that new behavior has been evidenced. In education, growth indicates progress. When the terms are used in conjunction, they mean that the conceptual powers of the pupil are adequately and progressively expressed through the art form, with growing control over materials, through processes, and with evidence of deepened insights and broadened outlooks.

At the conclusion of the chapters dealing with art in the elementary, junior, and senior high school, there appear summaries of the major art expectancies for each level. In a sense those expectancies, if fulfilled, represent normal growth.

But for the purpose of illustrating the present concern, a number of self-evident indices of creativity are listed. Creativity and virtuosity must not be confused, nevertheless. Growth must mean measureable improvement from early childhood through youth in the full use of the creative impulse.

The evidences of creative growth that are suggested below should be watched for in evaluating creative development. Some are natural, progressive improvement in *handling* materials and tools; natural, progressive development of the *symbols* of representation (see stages of creative development); evidence of the use of *freedom* in expressing ideas and in solving problems; sustained interest in *experimentation* with ideas, tools, materials, and eventually with technics; evidence of sustained *independence* in the use of ideas, technics, and tools; evidence of *originality* in ideas, organization, combination of materials, and use of tools and technics; evidence of *uninhibited* yet inoffensive behavior; evidence of *coherence* and adequacy in the current creative experience.

When these indices of growth, and others, are evident in the work of children, at the proper level of maturity, normal creative growth is taking place. But more than that, integration of the child or youth is taking place. The degree to which these characteristics of growth are taking place determines the needed guidance, the redirection, and the next advance for each individual child.

BASIC PRINCIPLES IN EVALUATION

The deep concern that has recently developed in growth rather than in mere fact learning or technic mastery has led to the search for valid principles to aid in the evaluation of gorwth. It seems important that broadly accepted procedures and principles be understood if evaluation is to bear the desired results. The literature of art education is rather sterile on this point for the simple reason that for a long period of time technical qualities were the chief interest rather than the behavioral effects of art experiences. Lately, some serious efforts have been made in the new direction by people in the art field. These are discussed fully later in this chapter. At this point, the principles of evaluative technics used in other fields of education may be examined with profit. Subsequently, they may be adapted to the evaluation of art activities.

Michaelis and Grim have proposed the following principles for guiding an evaluation program:

1. Evaluation should be based upon a particular set of objectives.
2. Evaluation of all major aspects of child growth and development is necessary.
3. Evaluation should make significant contributions toward the improvement of the school program.
4. Evaluation must be carefully planned and should provide for a continuous program of appraisal.
5. Evaluation should stress the importance of the cooperative participation of all individuals involved in the learning process.
6. Evaluation necessitates the use of many devices and techniques for collecting data about pupil progress.
7. Evaluation requires adequate recording of data about pupils and careful interpretation of these data.
8. Evaluation should stress the importance of group work in a variety of school situations.
9. Evaluation encourages teacher research, experimentation and growth.[4]

MAJOR CONSIDERATIONS

Even a cursory glance at the above principles will indicate the importance of a clear point of view, or of knowing what the purpose of the evaluation is. The objectives must be crystal clear. In the second place, it seems paramount that not one facet of growth but *all* possible facets revealed by a child's activities be taken into account in order to reach a fair conclusion as to his progress or lack of it. Third, it seems reasonable that evaluation of child growth is not an end in itself but a means for improving the individual pupil and the total school program. Only thus will all children profit by the changes in procedure or other ameliorations which may be suggested by the process of evaluation.

The futility of any type of appraisal must be obvious if only spasmodic attempts are made. Evaluation, to be effective, must be an integral part of the whole task of teaching. It should be a continuing enterprise that will eventually have gathered enough evidence to be of genuine worth to teachers, parents, administrators, and to the children themselves.

---

[4] John V. Michaelis and Paul Grim, *The Student Teacher in the Elementary School,* New York, Prentice-Hall, 1953, p. 345.

216 Careful planning and systematic review are a part of an effective program.

Parents, teachers, and all others who are directly involved in the process of evaluation, including physicians and psychologists—in fact, all persons who can contribute to the total picture—should be *partners* in every sense. Coöperation is the key word in the evaluative venture.

It stands to reason that many devices and many instruments are needed to gather information and to make records of the many phases of growth. Although these are material elements, they are, nevertheless, essential and in need of continual improvement.

Evaluation for whom? Generally, one thinks of this process as being intended for the good of children. That is true; nevertheless, it is also true that as teachers engage in an evaluation program, the nature of their task, the problems involved, the multiplicity of aspects of develop-

CHILDREN EVALUATE their work and describe their experiences when given opportunity. Self-confidence and esteem are thus built up. These are vital to further expression in art (Campus Elementary School, State Teachers College, Kutztown, Pa.).

ment, and other professional problems are clarified. This clarification and the possible further research suggested by the process of evaluation are extremely worth while as stimulants for the growth of the teacher as well as of the pupil.

ADAPTATION TO ART EDUCATION

How do the above general principles apply to evaluation in art education? This is of real concern. If each of the basic principles is elaborated upon in terms of art activities, it should be possible to arrive at a point of view and a set of procedures adaptable to the field of art.

1. *Evaluation should be based upon a particular set of objectives.* First of all, the purpose of what is being evaluated should be very clear. Is it achievement in the application of art principles? Is it achievement in technics? Is it creativity and originality? Is it spontaneity in the use of color or design? Is it an attempt to determine how the creative or aesthetic aspects of growth are being achieved? Is it social adjustment? Is the concern with the pattern of development or with specifics? Is it the product or the process? In evaluation, the broad objectives must be clear as well as pertinent, not only to the art teacher but to all general classroom teachers who teach art. A program fails or succeeds depending on whether the entire school or the whole system has a common understanding of the purposes of the program. Therefore, it is imperative that the particular objectives be agreed upon by general consent. Then it must follow that the basic purposes will guide all persons involved and become the unifying thread in the activities, units, practices, and technics used in every classroom. This task is not an easy one, but it can be accomplished.

Some ways of achieving unanimity have been described in Chapter 16. Unequivocally, the broad objectives of art education for our time center about the creative unfolding of each pupil personality; the specific objectives were detailed in the first two chapters. As pupils grow from one level or stage to the next, the specific aims and expectancies also change. Therefore, the objectives must be suitably adapted and the method of stimulation for satisfying fulfillment must be diversified for each level. Nevertheless, basic to the entire program is the pupil's individual development. As the objectives are clarified and understood by all teachers, evaluation will proceed with intelligence and a measure of confidence in its worth.

2. *Evaluation of all major aspects of child growth and development is necessary.* If we believe that a pupil is to be given opportunity to develop to the very optimum of his potentialities, it is difficult to justify any evaluation 'that takes into account only one facet of his growth pattern. Logically, it seems imperative that all phases of growth mentioned heretofore be considered simultaneously if an accurate picture of the pupil is desired. Art educators must recognize, through the pupil's work in art, the various facets of growth, and must account for them in the total estimate.[5] On the other hand, the specific types of development implicit in the art experience itself may be revealing. John is very adept with three-dimensional materials but weak in graphic expression; Mary has a marked sense of design but lacks in color perception; Samuel is slow and methodical but gets there eventually; Susan is as lively as her color mingling; Bill cannot do much in art but is a born leader and organizer. These are a few of the diversities such as one encounters in the art laboratory. How may one evaluate these various individuals? The principle cited above offers the answers: one must account for as many facets of each individual pupil as it is possible and guidance must do the rest.

3. *Evaluation should make significant contributions toward the improvement of the school program.* An experienced teacher of art was approached by her superintendent on what he felt was a very important new assignment. He told the teacher how highly she was regarded by her associates and her superiors, then proceeded to describe the dire situation in a school located "on the other side of the tracks." The teacher knew very well what the situation was and braced herself for the superintendent's next statement: "Would you be willing to leave Northeast, go to that school next year, and see what you can do to raise its tone?" The teacher agreed to try.

The children at the school in question were considered of "low" mentality. The neighborhood was "notorious"; the art teachers in the school remained a year or two and then asked for transfers. The principal was

---

[5] Viktor Lowenfeld, *Creative and Mental Growth*, rev. ed., New York, The Macmillan Company, 1952. (See evaluation charts at ends of chapters.)

a strong, kindly man, by now used to the situation and willing to try anything. The art teacher knew that she must have the coöperation of all associates and that art must pervade the school if it was to accomplish any good. She set out to give the whole school "tone." These are some things she did: placed pupils' work in the halls; organized work teams to paint murals for some of the classrooms; organized an "Assembly Crew" that set the stage and worked on lighting each week; lastly, she placed a large supply of art materials in each classroom for those who wished to use them. All this was done with the willing coöperation of the teaching staff. By the end of the first semester, she was ready to work more intensively with pupils. Several "campaigns" were organized by the children themselves but stimulated by her. Some. of the slogans adopted were: "Let's Keep Our School Clean"; "Look Your Best, It Pays"; "Are You Antisocial?" and so on. Posters, illustrations, three-dimensional displays, classroom discussions, and other germane activities were carried on in all classrooms to accomplish the objective. The tangible school-wide improvements were the evident personal growth of the pupils, happier teachers, pride in self and the school, and increased interest in learning and in the coöperative solution of social problems.

4. *Evaluation must be carefully planned and must provide for continuous appraisal.* In art education, single marks have little significance due to the fluctuation of growth that a pupil may exhibit from one art experience to another. It is, therefore, of utmost importance that the plan and the devices for a continuous program of pupil growth be carefully thought out, well in advance. The program of evaluation should not be static. Rather it should consist of a continuous improvement of the technics and instruments of evaluation. The types of records that are needed, the facets of growth that should be recorded, how often the recording should be done, and the use that will be made of the records are questions that should stimulate the teacher's own thinking on this important phase of child development through art. Some instruments and technics will be discussed farther on in this chapter. For the present, it seems essential to reiterate the importance of planning ahead, carefully and in long-range fashion.

5. *Evaluation should be the result of coöperation on the part of all those concerned with the process of a pupil's growth.* This principle is significant since it means that the job of evaluating is not done by one

person, the art teacher, let us say. It must involve the pupil himself, the principal, the parents, and the other teachers. Each has a specific role, appropriate to his place in the school program. Parents can learn a great deal about their children from teachers, but the reverse is also true. Home-room teachers have opportunity to observe pupils in a situation differing from the art laboratory or another classroom; therefore, they have special contributions to make. Teachers of subjects other than art can furnish details on behavior and learning abilities which may be of value to the art teacher, and vice versa. The principal has a school-wide view of the problem of growth; therefore, his observations are of decided worth. Finally, the pupil himself, when approached correctly, will reveal himself as no one else could. It is the pooling of data that results into a truer picture, rather than a pupil's attitude or ability in any one subject or situation.

6. *Evaluation necessitates the use of many devices and technics for collecting data about pupil progress.* Some time ago, the National Art Education Association undertook the development of a study on evaluation through art. The conduct of the study, the technics used, and some of the devices employed were reported in *Art Education*, the Journal of the N.A.E.A. Some of the technics and devices suggested in that study are these:

a. The open question (interview, conversation)
b. The simple questionaire
c. Tape recordings of discussions
d. Anecdotal records of observed situations
e. The individual folder (for each pupil)
f. Individual pupil record sheet
g. The "Center" Chart (area of pupil interest: crayon, paint, clay, etc.)
h. Self-evaluation chart
i. Class folder (what can be expected of most pupils?)
j. Photographs and slides of pupil's work[6]

Most of the devices and technics suggested above may appear quite simple and understandable, yet in the actual development of them, and more particularly in their actual use, many questions will arise.

Before attempting to develop evaluative devices or to use them, the

[6] Edith M. Henry, "Evaluation of Children's Growth Through Art Experiences," *Art Education*, May, 1953.

teacher will do well to rethink some of the significant aspects of growth, the major objectives of art education for the various levels, and especially to have a clear purpose for the immediate evaluation and the particular instrument. What are some of the evidences of growth along social, mental, creative, emotional lines? Each pupil will exhibit such growth in terms of changed behavior, general attitude, willingness to work with others, earnestness in his own creative work and even in the quality and maturity of his art work. The art teacher, in coöperation with others, may feel the need of changing, adding, or eliminating certain items in order to improve the instrument for more effective use. On pages 227 and 228 some evaluation instruments are suggested. They were designed and used by teachers in the field. They should be studied carefully in terms of specific situations and then only should they be adapted.

It is of major significance to remember that behavior is the most important index of growth. How a pupil changes, how he learns to adjust, how articulate he becomes with art materials, and how his interest grows in expressing himself through art are a few examples of the meaning of behavior. A very important fact is that art education deals mainly with visual expression. Therefore, while mindful of other manifestations of growth, the art teacher is chiefly concerned with the effect of the art experience on the pupil. The total effect may be seen either in the process or in the tangible art product.

Generally speaking, in the evaluation of satisfactory growth through art, a teacher will need to consider the social, mental, and personal behavior as well as the aesthetic and creative growth of the pupil. Such evaluations must be in terms of the level and stage appropriate to the pupil and in relation to his known endowment and prior experience. The degree to which certain elements are evident in a child's work is indicative of growth. Henry's listing of evidences useful in evaluation may be studied with profit:

a. Confidence in ability to express one's self visually
b. Interest in expressing ideas and feelings in visual form
c. Awareness of the environment and power of observation
d. Power to interpret everyday experiences
e. Inventiveness in the areas of ideas and materials
f. Ease and satisfaction in using a variety of tools and materials
g. Sensitivity to the need for beauty and ability to create it

    h. Understanding and appreciation of the contributions of other peoples
    i. Resourcefulness in leisure time activities
    j. Ability to use art experiences to relieve emotional tension
    k. Ability to work in a problem situation
    l. Ability to co-operate in group activity
    m. Individuality in expression and appreciation of individuality in the work of others
    n. Power to produce unity and to give meaning through the organization of line, form, color and texture
    o. Ability to choose ideas, materials, techniques and design in terms of the child's purpose[7]

It should be noted that in the above listing, development is interpreted in its many-sided aspects and not simply in terms of the art product. This fact brings to the fore the necessity of thinking of art *as education.* The relational point of view advocated at the beginning suggests that the three elements of art experience need to be upgraded as pupils move from level to level in the elementary and the junior and senior high school. Serious deviation from the norm for each grade or level may then be easily spotted.

The actual recording of data becomes more meaningful if the symbols employed are clear to the user. A self-evaluation chart, for instance, is most effective if the pupils actually do the phrasing of the questions or statements. On the other hand, if the data are intended for administrative or teachers' use, a code or symbol may be best.

7. *Evaluation requires adequate recording and careful interpretation of data about pupils.* The newness of evaluation in general, and the great desire for adequate evaluation in art education, have caused many teachers to leap at conclusions. Often, unfounded and certainly not warranted deductions have been reached by merely looking at or even studying one piece of work by a pupil. The fallacy of psychoanalizing boys and girls on the basis of such limited data is not only professional quackery but an extremely dangerous practice. Careful interpretation demands consistent and sufficient data on the child's art and other achievements. Close and abundantly documented observation of the pupil in a variety of situations, a study of his total pattern of behavior, and, finally, the unbiased points of view of teachers other than the art

---

[7] *Ibid.,* p. 6.

teacher are essentials. Careful interpretation of art data, when seen in the light of other pertinent facts, may lead the art teacher to a correct diagnosis of the case. Only then, it may be possible to arrive at a clearer understanding of the child, to improve behavior, and to enrich his experiences in art.

8. *Social adjustment.* Thus far the discussion has centered on the individual pupil's achievement in or enjoyment of art. It is equally important that teachers observe, record, compare, and analyze data concerning his relationships to the group. Coöperation, participation, sharing, constructive leadership, and intelligent followership are significant personal qualifications in a democratic school community. Indeed, it cannot be stressed too strongly that evaluation must take into account evidences of behavior changes that reflect adequate social living. This aspect of development is, in a real sense, a part of the relational approach to art education.

9. *Evaluation encourages research, experimentation, and progress.* Lastly, although most significantly, the teacher of art must look upon evaluation as a professional venture in which he is taking an active part and from which he will benefit abundantly. The returns in satisfaction and the thrill of achievement are difficult to measure. Yet no one will contest the fact that the teacher who seeks to find better ways of understanding pupils and is alert to refined means toward that understanding, is a growing teacher. Such a teacher is a fit guide of young people who eagerly search for their place in school and society. Art education needs greater devotion to research and experimentation; through them it will improve the quality of living as well as the quality of art. Evaluation takes on added meaning when the teacher asks himself to what degree he is improving, to what extent he is successful in guiding boys and girls, and what problems seem to face him with recurrence. In Chapter 14 a number of suggestions for self-evaluation as well as a self-improvement profile have been provided. They should be of interest to art teachers and consultants either for personal use or for discussion with groups of teachers in service. Young persons preparing to become teachers of art or consultants may study the material to discover personal weaknesses and strengths in the light of professional expectancies. In the final analysis it will be to their advantage to know themselves before launching on a career. In practice, teachers will

find that most school systems use some methods of evaluating new entrants into the profession. Whatever their form or whatever the procedures employed, they will be recognized in the instruments of appraisal discussed in Chapter 14.

PUPIL-CENTERED EVALUATION

SELF-APPRAISAL FOR SELF-IMPROVEMENT

The modern school is one in which learning and behavior changes are the most significant purposes. Teaching, important though it is, is auxiliary to the major purposes. It is for these reasons that the school places the setting, the atmosphere, and the tools at the disposal of the learner. Evaluation, or more properly self-evaluation, is a part of the process of growing and learning.

It was indicated a while ago that the pupil has a stake in the process under discussion. His stake is in the form of taking stock of his accomplishments, of his weaknesses, of his recognition of aesthetic and expressive qualities in his work, and even of the appraisal of the satisfaction he has experienced in the production of a drawing, a painting, or a craft object. In the exercise of self-evaluation the pupil identifies himself anew with his creation. In so doing he relives his success, his struggle, and his pleasure or displeasure. The development of honesty, the cultivation of taste, and the incentive to better oneself are broad aspirations in education. A pupil should be free to say: "I might have done better"; or "That's my drawing, I think it is good, and I enjoyed doing it"; or "I had a bit of trouble in cutting this block but I learned a lot." When this type of honesty can be practiced, the proper growth of a child is aided tangibly.

The method of self-appraisal is then to be commended as a means of developing the basic qualities desired in the good citizen as well as in the creative artist: respect for truth, honesty, integrity.

Simply as suggestions which may be amplified at will or adapted as desired, three evaluation forms are presented in this connection. The first is a Pupil's Self-Evaluation Form, the second is a Teacher's Single-Center Record, and the third is a Teacher's Multiple-Center Record. These and similar instruments, when consistently used, may form the basis for a long-term record of the growth and development of pupils.

If anecdotal records, a file of samples of work, and general information are added, it should be possible for the art teacher better to guide the progress of a pupil.

THE JURY SYSTEM

If there is any merit in the contention that art education holds potentials for the development of individual as well as for the achievement of social goals and values, the jury system of evaluation is a valid one. In practice, this method may be implemented in various ways; some of them are discussed hereafter.

It was the author's custom when teaching in a senior high school to invite small groups of students to assist him in arriving at a grade value to be assigned to the work produced by various classes. The teacher usually reviewed the broad considerations to be kept in mind, such as the expression of the idea, compositional qualities, inventiveness, and adequacy of technic. The "jury" was then asked if there were questions, and if such was the case further explanations were given. Eventually the work to be appraised was arranged before the jury. To listen to eager young people discuss the merits of one piece of work as compared to another, the qualities of color, the presence or lack of inventiveness, problems of organization and originality

A JURY OF ART EDUCATORS, who understand the meaning and range of children's expression, may undertake the evaluation of children's output for research purposes or for other plausible reasons (Scholastic Art Awards Jury, Kanahwa County, W. Va.).

of ideas, is one of the most rewarding experiences of teaching. They worked seriously, argued vehemently, and arrived at a consensus of opinion in true democratic fashion. But even more significant is the fact that as they evaluated the work of others they were deepening their own insight, enhancing their personal taste, and developing their ability to discuss art intelligently and fairly. What else were they gaining? Many would come back to class on the following day with a vigor and a purpose such as the teacher had not seen before.

The groups, usually three to five, were rotated so that over a period of a year a fairly large number had had the experience. Several excellent pupils became volunteer "jurors" and participated more frequently.

But what about the grades? The school demanded grades; therefore, grades were assigned. In truth, it must be stated that pupils received more impartial treatment and a fairer appraisal at the hands of their peers than they might have at the hand of the teacher, because the jury represented a consensus of opinions rather than one point of view.

The same system is in vogue in a teachers' college where art teachers are prepared. In that situation, the use of the system is even more significant than in a public school. The reason is that the student jurors not only practice the ways of democracy and of fairness but also realize the value of properly analyzing and appraising creative work. They have a foretaste of what it is hoped they may do a few years hence with their own pupils in the public schools.

It should not be assumed that all the work of all students is appraised by other students. Oftener, student jurors join the art staff in the evaluation process. Always, the staff as a whole appraises all work as a jury. The system has much to recommend it as a practice at all levels of education.

FUTURE ART TEACHERS evaluate the work of classmates prior to an exhibition. They are aware that variety in concept, technic, and subject matter are desirable aspects of self-expression. They often join the art staff in the weekly jury sessions (State Teachers College, Kutztown, Pa.).

CLASS-DISCUSSION SYSTEM

The real value of criticism and of guidance in developmental activities must be measured by the effect that such criticism and guidance have in the subsequent experiences of those whose work is being appraised. A method that has been found extremely worth while is that of class discussion. In the campus school of a teacher-education institution, at regular intervals teacher and pupils engage in such evaluations with profit for all. Questions and voluntary answers, as well as debate, bring out appreciations, criticisms, and suggested improvements. The atmosphere of critical awareness is soon established and a sense of sharing becomes the dominant spirit.

Again, what about grades if such are required? The teacher is placed in a better position to establish a grade value for a piece of work when unbiased, spontaneous, and fresh minds have reacted to each expression in the spirit of mutual respect.

Finally, any approach that admits of group critical thinking and consensus of opinions in contrast to the single judgment by an adult, valid though the latter may be, is a superior approach. It brings out details and information which will have values greater than the setting of a grade when such information is used judiciously. As a means of guiding the pupil concerned toward further development, whether in art or simply as a person, the jury system or the discussion have no rivals.

PUPIL'S SELF-EVALUATION FORM

Pupil's Name_____   Date_____

Grade_____

	Very Good	Good	Fair	Poor	Reasons I Think So
I think my picture is					
I think my linoleum cut is					
I think my illustration is					
I think my modeling is					
I think my weaving is					

A chart such as the one above could be mimeographed and given to each pupil. He should understand its purpose and its use. When he has exhausted the possibilities of each art activity which he has undertaken, he evaluates his own work and returns the record sheet to the teacher. In the column marked "Reasons," he may put down why he thinks the work has been so rated by himself. But he may also give reasons for his lack of success, problems he has encountered, needs he feels, and other valuable data which may be useful in further guidance by the teacher.

TEACHER'S SINGLE-CENTER RECORD

Grade_____   Teacher_____   School Year_____

Pupil's Name	Date	Center	Success	Comments
1. John	5/10/56	Clay		
2. William				
3. Joycelyn				
4.				

A card such as the above may serve to record several pupils' progress when a group is working in a common or single center. Children who show persistence in one center may need to be guided into another, depending on their success in the single center of activity. The card is one of several types of records that the teacher may use.

TEACHER'S MULTIPLE-CENTER RECORD

Grade_____   Teacher_____   School Year_____

Name	Date	Center	Date	Center	Date	Center	Comment
Charles							
Nancy							
Geary							

A form similar to the one above could serve to record a pupil's growth as he progresses from one art experience to the next. It could reveal a number of things: Does the pupil stick to one mode of expression? Does he stay with the same medium? If so, is it because he is successful in it, or is it because he has been unable to find a new interest? Does he always work next to the same person or does he change occasionally?, etc.

SUMMARY

The objectives of art education will, in the final analysis, determine what the teacher of art should look for in an evaluation. It has been stressed that *art as education* is concerned with the best development of the pupil with particular emphasis on the creative aspects.

It should have been made clear that grades or other types of marks are not valid as indexes of a child's growth. More is needed to present the proper picture of the *whole* pupil. Certain systems of evaluation place greater emphasis on the social, mental, creative, aesthetic, and personal traits evidenced in the art laboratory than they do on the art product itself. The values of the product in terms of control of medium and aesthetic qualities are not denied; they are considered as part of the pattern of growth of the child.

Certain basic principles of evaluation have been suggested. These encompass the whole process of development: the child, the purposes of education, the total school program, and social living. Obviously, the principles are concerned with the manner of gathering data, and with their interpretation and their use in pupil guidance. These data are also valuable in informing parents and in the administrative organization of the school.

It has been emphasized that evaluation also involves the teacher's personal estimate of his own success in the guidance of boys and girls through art experiences. The sum and substance of the process of evaluation is contained in one word, *guidance*.

For Discussion and Activity

1. Adopt a child from your neighborhood or from the laboratory school and develop instruments for the evaluation of his growth over a semester. At the end of the semester report your findings to your group.

2. If it is true that the *total growth* pattern of a pupil is a proper index to his development, what are some types of growth you would look for? How many of these are recognizable in his art work? How conclusive would your observation be if based on the last-mentioned evidence? Discuss in detail.

3. What use would you make of evaluation records in conference with parents or administrators? How many types of records would you need to feel confident? Discuss in detail.

4. Discuss the merits and the shortcomings of each of the technics mentioned on page 228. Which do you prefer, and why?

5. Discuss the meaning of each of Henry's evidences of growth listed on page 220. Observe children in a classroom, by prior arrangement, and examine their work as a check-up. Report your observations to your group.

6. What traits expressed in the art situation are indicative of satisfactory social adjustment in third grade, seventh grade, twelfth grade?

7. What values are there in a program of evaluation from the standpoint of the art teacher or the general classroom teacher? Discuss or debate these values.

8. If you were asked by your principal to set up a program of evaluation through art in the schools under your supervision, how would you proceed? What instruments would you require? What general understandings would you feel are necessary?

9. If you are teaching, or student-teaching, develop a self-evaluation scheme for the use of your pupils. At the end of a week, compare their statements and judgments of their own work with your opinion and evaluation of each pupil. Do you find honesty and sincerity in them? How can the pupils' own statements help you in guiding their further growth?

10. Do you believe that art work by pupils should be graded? Discuss the question and its alternatives.

For Further Reading

Commission on the Secondary School Curriculum, *The Visual Arts in General Education*, New York, D. Appleton-Century Company, 1940, Chapter IV.

Fitzgerald, Lola Hinson, "Evaluation in Art," *Art Education*, January, 1953.

Henry, Edith M., "Evaluation of Children's Growth Through Art Expression," *Art Education*, May, 1953.

Little, Sidney W., "No Grade," *Art Education*, October, 1949.

Lowenfeld, Viktor, *Creative and Mental Growth*, rev. ed., New York, The Macmillan Company, 1952, pp. 20–45.

Prescott, Daniel, *Emotion and the Educative Process*, Washington, D.C., American Council on Education, 1938, Chapter X.

Spears, Harold, *Improving the Supervision of Instruction,* New York, Prentice-Hall, 1953, Chapter XXI.

Stratemeyer, Florence, and others, *Developing a Curriculum for Modern Living,* New York, Teachers College, Columbia University, 1947.

Wood, Ben, and Haefner, Ralph, *Measuring and Guiding Individual Growth,* New York, Silver Burdett Company, 1948.

Wrightstone, J. W., "Trends in Evaluation," *Educational Leadership,* November, 1950.

PART III

THE PROGRAM
IN ACTION

ART IN THE ELEMENTARY SCHOOL

> Two generations ago nobody dreamt that every child is a born artist, which does not mean that every child should or could become an artist. The discovery of Child Art is parallel with, or perhaps a consequence of the discovery of the child as a human being with his own personality and his own particular laws.
>
> Wilhelm Viola,
> *Child Art*

THE MEANING OF ART ACTIVITY FOR CHILDREN

THE LONGING OF LIFE

WHAT IS REFERRED TO AS ART IN THIS CONTEXT IS A VISIBLE EMBODIMENT of the urgent and insistent impulse to say, to express, and possibly give form to a thought, an idea, or a feeling that stirs deeply within the individual.

Perhaps there is no better way of beginning this consideration than by pondering the words of the mystic poet Kahlil Gibran:

YOUR CHILDREN

. . . Your children are not your children.
They are the sons and daughters of Life's longing
   for itself,
They come through you but not from you.
And though they are with you yet they belong not to you.
You may give them your love but not your thoughts,

235

For they have their own thoughts.
You may house their bodies but not their souls,
For their souls dwell in the house of tomorrow,
    which you cannot visit, not even in your dreams.
You may strive to be like them, but seek not to make
    them like you. . . .
For life goes not backward nor tarries with yesterday.[1]

The child, at this moment, is in the early stages of the elementary school. He has already experienced hunger, thirst, fear, assurance, loneliness, joy, or sadness. Perhaps he has heard quarrelsome words or felt the warmth of parental love and respect. He may have come from a bleak home or from one where order and cleanliness dwell. He may have experienced the beauty of the song or he may never have dared to lift his voice at the sight of a bird. He may have expressed some of these things or none of them. But he has lived and watched and stored up feelings, thoughts, and unheeded questions. He is a thinking and feeling being. In him are all the potentialities of success, failure, fame, or oblivion. He is the future artist or simply the good citizen. In that child life has implanted the seeds of growth for teachers and parents to nurture with care and with understanding until the day of flowering.

By the time the child comes to school he has not only experienced but has wondered much. He has learned many things, some through his own effort, some by example, and some through precept. He has done many things willingly and some unwillingly. He has come to realize that he lives in an environment which is sometimes free and friendly and other times coercing and unfriendly.

He has learned to satisfy physical wants by accepting what is provided by parents and other older people. But meantime his very own experiences have taught him to solve simple problems as they have arisen, by adapting himself to conditions as he found them.

The child, however, is more than a biological entity. He is compounded of emotions and feelings that are not as evident as the color of his hair, his sparkling blue eyes, or his well-built body. Feelings, emotions, and thoughts are the things that make him "tick." They are the personality that is, and is to be, his basic character, the true ego.

---

[1] Reprinted from *The Prophet* by Kahlil Gibran with permission of the publisher, Alfred A. Knopf, Inc. Copyright 1923 by Kahlil Gibran; renewal copyright 1951 by Administrators C.T.A. of Kahlil Gibran Estate, and Mary G. Gibran.

It is because of the desires and compulsions of these feelings, emotions, and thoughts that he behaves as he does. He may be responsive to guidance or may regard the slightest interference with suspicion and fear. He may be quick or slow, vivacious or sullen. His moods, reactions, and general attitudes may be the result of inner reconciliation as he relates them to his experience with things, people, and surroundings. But now all of him, as he is, appears in the average classroom.

THE RIGHT ATMOSPHERE

Is the classroom a place where he finds a warm atmosphere and an understanding teacher? Will the longing of life to express itself be assuaged, repressed, circumscribed, or free? Is the classroom regimented and inflexible or is it designed for children who have so much to ask of life? Does the teacher pride herself in her "discipline" or in guided self-control? Is there evidence of self-expression and self-assurance on the part of children? In short, will the powerful drives within the children find release or frustration?

The function of education is to satisfy these longings, and the task can only be accomplished as children learn to relate themselves to new experiences. Each child is not the only child, or one child among a few; each is a member of a group. There are 25, perhaps 30 or more, boys and girls in the classroom, but only one teacher. This is a problem to be reckoned with. The teacher, gently, convincingly, and with much understanding, assumes her place *in loco parentis* and faces the task of assuring that everyone has a place and everyone will have the opportunity to grow and develop in a conducive atmosphere in which freedom is consistent with order and self-expression is consistent with the right of the group.

The task is not a simple one, but a resourceful teacher has sturdy allies in the children's endowments and in the tools of education. One fact remains paramount: the early years at school are formative years. This is the time when "Life's longing for itself" must be understood, satisfied, and guided by sympathetic teachers and parents.

ART AS A DEVELOPMENTAL ACTIVITY

The universality of the art impulse is affirmed by history, by psychology, and by observation. It manifests itself very early in the life of the individual, and in various ways. Plato and other philosophers before and after him have placed a great deal of weight on the arts in the education of children. Modern psychology and psychiatry acknowledge the art impulse and credit it as a therapeutic in the alleviation of mental and emotional disorders.[2] Educators recognize its value not only as the source of genuine expression but as a measure of child growth.

In the study of current trends in art education, it was indicated that although prevalent points of view in art education differ in their emphases, they are all agreed on the assumption that the function of art as education includes the cultivation of the senses, the encouragement of creative self-expression, the development of insights and concepts, and the harmonization of the individual with the environment. These functions, when seen as a whole, should affect the pupils' outlooks on life.

The dance, music, gymnastics, and dramatization, in addition to the visual arts, are some of the aesthetic forms that manifest themselves early in childhood. They should all receive utmost consideration. In fact, any one of the arts may be the natural and chief mode of expression for a particular child. All art forms are evident in the play activities of children, and the natural tendency of each individual eventually transmutes play into art. But in many instances the pleasurable and sensuous feelings experienced by the performer or by the spectator are sufficient in themselves. On other occasions they act as motivating agents for further creative expression. Therefore, in motivating children, all forms of art may be used to evoke response.

SPECIFIC VALUES OF THE VISUAL ARTS

The main concern of this discussion is with the visual arts: drawing, painting, modeling, building, and a host of other activities too obvious to require specific mention at this point. The inquiry, therefore, will tend to determine what the specific meanings of visual art activities are for children. Educators are agreed on the proposition that the visual arts are excellent means of expression and that they are most effective vehicles for child growth and development. In support of this general agreement, the reader's attention is called to the several points made and analyzed hereafter.

---

[2] Margaret Naumburg, *Schizophrenic Art: Its Meaning in Psychotherapy,* New York, Grune and Stratton, 1950.

1. *Expression in visual form is a tangible evidence of creative growth.* **239**
When a child has produced a drawing or a painting, has modeled in
clay, has conceived a design, or has made a mobile, he may stand in
contemplation of his achievement. The result of his experience is not
evanescent in the physical sense. It is there to be seen, to be admired, to
be judged, and to be handled. This tangible evidence of the creative
activity which the child has undergone may be, and often is, the end of
an experience. However, it may also serve as stimulus for the next experience, or it may become the basis for self-criticism and self-improvement. The child's visual achievement is an excellent source for individual
and group appreciation through discussion and telling. "Why do we like
the colors?" "Which of the shapes or lines make us feel like dancing?"
"Why does the man have such short [or long] arms?," and so on. In such
appraisals the experience is re-created and concepts are often clarified.

When the work of art is taken home to mother, her understanding and
subsequent approval may further build the child's self-confidence and
give him the assurance he so much needs. Contrariwise, the unapprecia-
tive reactions of unsympathetic adults, and this includes parents and
teachers, may damage the child's pride, weaken his feeling of security,
and destroy his confidence. Therefore, the very nature of visual art compels teachers to evaluate carefully and to avoid overemphasizing the
product to the exclusion of other phases of the creative act itself.

2. *The visual arts combine the basic aesthetic elements common to all
the arts: rhythm, color, form, and texture.* The materials with which the
child works at a given time matter little. What matters is that they are
suitable for the expression of the ideas he has chosen to explore. Typical
pupils respond to the varied qualities of a medium in a number of ways
natural to them. It is not uncommon to hear a child sing, chant, or hum
to the tempo created by the movement of his arm as he draws the
rhythmic lines or as he blends the colors in his painting. Cane,[3] it will be
recalled, used chanting and the rhythmic movements of the body as
preparatory to visual experiencing. The writer realized this fact anew
recently when he was privileged to see an unrehearsed although regularly
scheduled activity period for children at the University of Wisconsin
Laboratory School. The spontaneous dramatization of stories and poems

---

[3] Florence Cane, *The Artist in Each of Us,* New York, Pantheon Books, 1951.

with or without musical backgrounds, with or without dance accompaniments, was used by children as a prelude to vital art activities. The results seemed fascinating. And why not? In an atmosphere of freedom, the motivating arts on this occasion acted as auxiliaries to visual expression. The point could well be advanced that even if no visual results had been obtained, the creative and aesthetic needs of the children had been served. And it is precisely this unitary and complementary nature of the arts that may furnish classroom teachers with an answer to the problem of "what to do with Johnnie" who, presumably, does not express himself well in the visual arts. On the other hand, observation indicates that, oftener than not, stimulation gives rise to creative action of one type or another.

3. *Visual arts have the power of individualizing.* It has been reiterated again and again that differences are significant in education. In art education, individual variations should be capitalized upon rather than regarded as stumbling blocks on the road to growth. At the same time, it should be evident that the particular endowment and the sensitivities of a child may lie in a variety of directions. Of particular significance is the fact that each child can, and generally does, paint, or draw, or model in his own way and according to his own insights. Compare, for example, the drawings of the same subject by three different children in the same grade: one is direct, firm, secure in strokes; the second is more delicate, almost poetic; the third is the picture of a struggle to perceive anything recognizable, although to the child it may be a definite object. Aside from aesthetic indications, it is important to realize that each child decided from *within* how he wanted to paint his idea. To be sure, on another occasion the mode and spirit could change, although the basic, characteristic qualities of his productions will probably be there for sometime to come, perhaps always.

Education for democratic living demands that teachers be concerned with the individuality of people, with their special gifts and their particular point of view. Therefore, individuation is to be encouraged rather than frowned upon. Can a child be identified as an individual in arithmetic, in spelling, and in most other "regular" subjects? Facts are facts, to be learned by drill; the other aspects of those subjects may take on a different mode. Creative expression, however, may truly be said to have many faces, and after the drills the child may write poetry or prose. In the visual arts it is the child's harmonious relationship to the environment and his deepened appreciation of it that set the limits of expression and subject matter. His artistic nature and his perceptive powers will determine his way and his style for a time.

4. *Visual arts lend themselves to a wide variety of expressions in relation to materials.* School budgets may or may not permit sufficient expenditures for the art program. Some administrators may or may not realize the "pound-foolish" economies they inflict on the arts. The teacher may often feel discouraged by the fact that the school district across the river spends a reasonable amount of money for art materials while she is confined to a few basic items: paper, pencils, crayons, and little more. Such a situation is by no means defended, but at the same time it must be stated that it need not bog down the art program if the teacher is a resourceful person.

Art expression may be achieved in many ways and through many materials and tools. In fact, the relation of materials and tools to adequate modes of expression is a desirable fact to establish early. What can be done with wood, local clay, plaster, string, odds and ends, yarn, cloth, and many similar media? The teacher should think of the possible explorations and the inventiveness that such materials will induce because of their limitations as well as their potentialities. Conceptual development and problem solving are involved in such explorations; therefore, they are very effective.

Children need to be challenged. By using a variety of media and materials suitable for visual expression, children who differ from the typical may find their particular way and gift. Choosing shapes, textures, and colors to make a mobile may be just as satisfying as an attempt to paint a picture that just will not be painted. To create rhythms by rolling and twisting a string dipped in color may be more satisfying than a forced attempt to shape clay into prescribed form, or to produce design motifs based on a traditional formula.

Variety of experiences is a fundamental concept that should encourage teachers of elementary-school children. At the same time, the need for a balanced program should be recognized. If variety is accepted, the differences in endowment and inclination, so prevalent at the early stages of development, will be safeguarded. Some children paint or draw quite freely; others model with equal satisfaction and ease; others naturally build or design. The evidences of growth are there, regardless of the materials chosen. But there is one caution in this regard: materials and tools should be understood as means to the end, not as ends in themselves. This holds true for color, design, drawing, and other phases of art.

ART AS A SOCIALIZING ACTIVITY

Important though art is as a developmental activity in the cultivation of the senses and of expression, it is also valuable for the stimulation of those social qualities deemed essential for the child as a member of a group, now and later in life.

During the preschool years coöperation and planning are not easily obtained, due to the egocentricity of the children involved, because of lack of experiences with other children, because of age and other differences. However, by the time children reach the elementary grades they should be made aware of the importance of coöperating in group activities. The idea of planning together, of deciding together, of solving problems as a group, and similar technics are both feasible and desirable. For instance, the play situations, the backgrounds for dramatizations, the bulletin-board displays, and the party-table decoration and arrangement are real problems that should be solved coöperatively. It is in the process of solving these real-life problems that children learn give-and-take, to accept a better idea, and to allocate and accept responsibilities. The carry-over effect of such valuable experiences is not to be minimized or thought of as not being art. They are an art if they develop harmonious relationships, if they stimulate imaginative solutions, or if they give children the sense of satisfaction that comes to all individuals when they have dealt successfully with a problem.

Teacher-Pupil Planning

As children grow chronologically, mentally, emotionally, and physically, the need of planning together increases in importance. If the ends of democratic living are to be served, art must make its contribution by encouraging boys and girls to practice the ways of democracy. "How can we share the work?" "Who can do this part best?" "Where do I fit into the picture?" "How and where can we find the information we need?" These questions are typical of those that will arise when children are made to feel that they are working as a group and not as individuals. The social living situation must not be fictitious, but rather it must grow out of needs. It must involve problems that challenge, but which are not beyond the ability level of the group; it must envision success for each child as well as for the group.

A fact that should be recognized is that children, particularly beyond the third grade, are quite capable of planning under guidance. Especially when they are involved in the situation from the planning stage, they develop pride in carrying out *their* plans to a happy conclusion. It is at the early stages of teacher-pupil planning that group goals and common values have their beginning. On these goals and values children sincerely base the selection of activities, choice of leaders, division of labor, and other responsibilities for each member of the group.

The teacher's purposes for group activities will naturally vary from time to time, yet there are certain definite outcomes which are deemed

A HEALTHY PERSONALITY is often revealed through freedom, boldness, and sense of observation of the child artist. That freedom is the priceless quality to foster and preserve in all classrooms. Even simple occurrences are experiences for children; therefore, they are suitable subject matter for expression ("A Rainy Day," 1st grade, Baltimore, Md.).

desirable in all education; these should be constantly sought. In addition to social values children should be led to a realization of art values through appraisals of the results of their activities, either as a group or by individuals within the group. "How satisfied are we with what we have accomplished?" "Are our colors pleasing?" "Is our room improved by the new arrangement?" "Is it a brighter and happier place in which to play and learn?" "Should we invite other grades to see what we have done?" "How can we further improve?"

Thus, it is possible, particularly beyond the second grade, to plan activities that develop an increasing amount of art awareness and of generalized democratic concepts at one and the same time.

Social values are of various types. There are values that relate to the individual and to his immediate group; then there are those which relate to the school, to the community, to the state, to the nation, and to the world. School subjects other than art concern themselves with these broader relationships largely through the social studies and the language arts. Therefore, the question is: How can art activities make their contribution? Sharing ideas, working together for the good of all, leadership in activities, willing followership, courtesy toward members of the group, and other desirable traits can and must be developed early. Art experiences, when planned coöperatively by teachers and pupils, and when conducted under conditions which include guidance and proper stimulation, help to develop these traits and others which center around the understanding and appreciation of the larger community and of democratic society. Whatever objections one may have to the correlation of art with other interests, it will be difficult to demonstrate that any harm is done to the creative development of children by stimulating their thinking and guiding their action along lines such as "One World," or "This Is My Town," or "My Native State." Murals, illustrated maps, three-dimensional wall decorations, models of buildings, and other germane activities are valid as creative experiences when they grow naturally out of well-planned units in social living. Such art activities call for reflective thinking on the problem, inventiveness, good design, imaginative solutions, and require manipulative skills of tools and materials commensurate with the grade and maturity levels of elementary-school children.

Art and Children's Taste

The literature of education has long insisted on the importance of developing very early the creative potentialities of children. This is best done before children acquire inhibitions or sensitivity to adult criticism. As they grow older, feelings of inadequacy may become persistent. For the same reason, elementary art programs should make early and continued provisions for developing good taste. Appreciation cannot be taught, in the narrow sense, any more than creation of art can be taught. But the implication remains that experiences such as choosing, arranging, and organizing are experiences which lead to sound taste. A third grade is given the opportunity of selecting color reproductions of paint-ings for the classroom walls; another group is given the task of arranging materials on a bulletin board; a third group is asked to choose materials for drapes in the classroom. These problems are not "doing" problems in the general sense. They are problems which involve color relations, subject-matter choice, and design consciousness. Early elementary-school years are hardly the place when formal principles are discussed and taught directly. And yet, through experiences such as have been named, children will be exercising design and color judgments which are real and which lead to the practice and development of good taste. Shultz and Shores refer to this particular phase of art education as that of making "carefully considered choices."[4] But these experiences need not be confined to those named above. Flower arrangements, "sharing" peri-ods when children discuss recently acquired toys and other gifts, dis-cussion of the pictures in the story book during the story hour, visiting people at work, the museum trip whenever possible, and, of course, the evaluation of the children's own creations are additional activities that will help in the growth of appreciation. The value of these experiences is of inestimable worth in the life of each child: in the home, the com-munity, and the school. The common dictum "Art is a way of life" becomes a reality as elementary-school teachers nurture the emotional reactions of children with respect to considered choices in a real, rather than a too hypothetical, sense. The enrichment of life by actual planning and purposing with the children is much more tenable than the assump-tion that appreciation and values are by-products of painting or drawing activities. For some pupils the latter may be true; for the many it must be planned.

PSYCHOLOGICAL FACTORS AFFECTING THE PROGRAM

It has been inferred that the creative impulse and its modes of ex-pression are psychological phenomena. It has also been stressed that the function of the teacher is to guide children with understanding, so that full and unimpeded development may take place. If teachers are to fulfill their role adequately, they must focus attention on certain basic

[4] Harold Shultz and Harlan Shores, *Art in the Elementary School*, Urbana, University of Illinois, School of Education, Bureau of Research and Services, Bulletin 1948, p. 55.

246   yet simple aspects of growth. Among these are age-grade level, normal growth at those levels, creative stages and types, social maturity, typical physical and emotional characteristics at certain levels, and the needs of children within certain age and maturity groups. It is also of great importance that teachers relate the meaning of these facets of growth to each individual child so that the theoretical and the practical may find harmony rather than disparity.

LEVELS OF GROWTH   *Psych.*

Since children differ considerably among themselves, especially with regard to rate and kind of growth, it must be assumed that each child is a particular problem. This is a fact which cannot be overemphasized. But the present organization of the schools suggests that teachers must face the task realistically and think in terms of classes of children within the same age-grade groups. Psychological findings indicate that "average" children within a given age-grade level exhibit similar characteristics and similar needs, and follow a reasonably similar growth pattern. Therefore, in practice it should be possible to keep in mind likely deviations and proceed with the knowledge of levels of growth and types of artistic personality. When these are understood, classroom problems and teaching may be handled on the basis of those factors that are recognized as common to most children. Such a procedure results in economy of time and energy for the teacher, and exceptional individuals may then be given attention commensurate with their needs.

For convenience of reference as well as for practical classroom purposes, the major characteristics, major interests, significant needs, and the usual responses of children from kindergarten through the sixth grade have been abstracted from the literature of education and psychology and have been organized into three tables. They appear in this chapter and are designated as follows: Table 1, preschool, kindergarten, and grade 1; Table 2, grades 1, 2, and 3; Table 3, grades 4, 5, and 6 (See pp. 250, 256, 260). In each case the higher grade level represents the reasonable limit of the developmental period.

A careful study of each table should serve as a reminder of what is essential for teachers to realize with regard to each group.

In a more general way, it may be well to study each level from several points of view. In so doing, these important facts should emerge: (1)

Growth is quantitative and qualitative; (2) Growth is continuous; (3) Growth is individual with every child; (4) Growth is modifiable through proper education and environment.

Because growth is not a fixed process, it is incumbent on all teachers who teach art to watch for changes and to adjust the child's program to the changes as they occur *in him.* By way of example, Millard says:

DRAMATIC EVENTS are experienced by every child as he grows up. A fire, a parade, and similar happenings make a deep impression on him. Those impressions, especially with younger children, involve wonder, and sometimes, concern. Children are eager to "tell" how they see them or feel about them ("The Fire," 1st grade, Toronto, Canada).

"Within a given child there may be a range of growth-ages, at a given time, of more than seven years. At twelve years of age, a seventh grade girl may be eight years old in height. Specific achievement ages for reading, arithmetic or other studies may also appear at the extremes."[5]

A not-uncommon observation is that a child may be very precocious in art expression and slow in other studies. Vice versa, he may be advanced in arithmetic age, let us say, or in social-studies age, but very

---

[5] Cecil V. Millard, *Child Growth and Development in the Elementary School Years,* Boston, D. C. Heath and Company, 1951, p. 17.

248   slow in art. This is true in spite of the fact that both Goodenough's and Gaitskell's[6] experiments point out that there is positive correlation between general intelligence and creative ability. The cycle and the pattern of a child's growth must be observed, understood, and coped with in such a manner that he will not be discouraged, lose self-confidence and happiness, and miss ultimate integration. The fact also indicates that teachers should expect differences; and while they should be thrilled at the discovery of superior talent, they should not be discouraged at the temporary lack of creative expression *at a given time*. Readiness is recognized in the more formal subjects. Obviously, there is a readiness, an acceleration, and a point of normal maturation in creative development as well.

STAGES OF CREATIVE DEVELOPMENT[7]

It has been stated that for the elementary level, at least, there are a number of approaches that shed much light on *how* to help children develop. Among those approaches were mentioned free expression, play, conceptualization, appreciation, and purposive action. But these will remain simply as terms, or as empty words, until they are put to the test in the actual conduct of a classroom program of creative education.

The first age group of concern to elementary teachers is the preschool and kindergarten group. In most public-school situations the boys and girls involved would be in nursery school and kindergarten. Table 12, page 572, is an attempt to relate the approximate periods of growth to similarly approximate stages of creative development from early childhood through adolescence for typical pupils. Although the present chapter deals only with the elementary-school level, it may be worth while to refer to and study that diagram. It should clarify the concept that growth is continuous and that it varies from child to child.

The level referred to by psychologists as that of early childhood, as well as its many facets, are variously detailed by educational writers. There is, however, agreement on the essential characteristics of these

---

[6] Charles D. and Margaret R. Gaitskell, *Art Education in the Kindergarten*, Peoria, Charles A. Burnett Co., Inc., 1952.

[7] Detailed descriptions of all intermediate stages are presented in Herbert Read, *Education Through Art*, New York, Pantheon Books, 1949, Chapter V.

children. What follows is an attempt to bring out the meaning of the characteristics of that level in terms of growth through art.

The Manipulative Stage

This early phase of artistic development occurs during the ages of 2 to 5, although some writers fix its span as lasting only from 2 to 4 years of age. Because of the interest in nursery schools and kindergartens, it may be profitable to examine this stage of development as an introduction to the early elementary grades. Quite appropriately, Millard says: "The activity of children with paints and crayons before three years of age is mainly of *scribbling*, exploratory nature. At three or four years of age children are usually delighted when given the opportunity to create a riot of color on a large sheet of paper. At this time, they are also ready to express some initiative in design and pattern. Such concepts usually take shape in the making and is not until the child is four or five years of age that he can project a design and carry it out."[8]

The importance of giving young children early opportunities to manipulate with arms, hands, and fingers is that such activities will permit basic physical skills to develop at a normal rate. Delay in offering these opportunities will slow down the child's rate of learning basic skills in the kindergarten and the early elementary grades. This implies that while children in the early childhood years rely a good deal on manipulation and are concerned with muscular control and movement, the works they produce have more than one kind of significance. They supply a physical need as well as a creative outlet. The scribblings of a child thus involve the self in "body and soul," as it were. The vast importance of the scribble is not to be underestimated, but rather it is to be encouraged, watched, and guided.

Learning to control the movements of his shoulder, arm, and hand, and to master them, is closely related to the child's total development and to his social adjustment. This is true not only at this but at all levels of growth. In the case of art education it is extremely important for teachers to realize that the kinesthetic experiences involved in scribbling satisfy the whole child and, therefore, encourage further practice. Satis-

---

[8] Millard, *op. cit.*, p. 110.

TABLE 1. A Child Goes Forth: Manipulative and Presymbolic Stage (Preschool, Kindergarten, and First Grade)

Chief Characteristics	Major Interests	Significant Needs	Usual Responses
1. Differences among children are wide	1. The self is most important	1. Guidance of a "mother" sort	1. Varied response as children vary among themselves
2. Fear of the unusual	2. Possessiveness: "I" and "my"	2. Love of parents and teacher	2. Interested in all new experiences
3. Motor activity predominates	3. Parents, later on brothers, sisters, neighbor children	3. Freedom under patient guidance	3. Fearful at first; later develop confidence
4. Attempt to relate art to reality; grows with individual	4. Pets and toys	4. Assurance that someone is watching	4. Eager to do and act largely through play
5. Self-identification is strong; ego predominates	5. Teachers, schoolmates, and playmates	5. Encouragement by parents, teachers, and older people	5. Enthusiastic; generally ready to respond
6. Frequent change of symbols; motion and sound	6. The world about them is an ever new experience: pleasing, surprising, sometimes frightening	6. Praise when due	6. Imaginative answers, stories, activities
7. Proportion is in relation to significance to the self	7. Games	7. Firmness of guidance with clarity	7. Spontaneous responses
8. Color choices to please the self	8. Art of any type	8. Confidence in themselves as they move, play, and accomplish	8. Stereotyped tendencies
9. Noisy, vigorous, alert	9. Singing rhymes		9. React quickly to environmental stimuli as new experiences
10. Clear purpose of own activities	10. Rhythmic activities (dance, band)		10. Oblivious of adult world and concepts
11. Symbols become more definite as child grows	11. Dramatics (make-believe)		11. Conclusions are reached in a child's manner, but definitely
12. Relationship to environment grows with the individual	12. Stories about children, animals, and things		
13. Realization of space is gradual	13. Making things, manipulation		
14. Realization of physical body is gradual but certain			
15. Naming of symbol may occur as early as kindergarten			

factory practice eventually brings about a mastery which is reflected in healthy emotional growth. In turn, the emotions play a prominent role in the development of creative unfolding. Again, to quote Millard:

"Creative impulses are almost entirely associated with motor activity. As the child becomes adult, he may do creative work without any accompanying motor activity. The young child, however, *thinks and creates with movements*."[9]

As the child grows, the kinesthetic enjoyment undoubtedly continues in some form. But from the creative point of view, it is the visual realization of what he has scribbled that interests him. He moves from uncontrolled scribbles to purposive scribbles: up-and-down, circular, and mixed line movements. In due time the child will make known his purpose by naming his work.

The caution at this point is that teachers should be careful not to discourage the child by asking thoughtless questions, such as "Is it a train?" or "Is that a baby carriage?" The child may use the same symbol for a number of things and may also change its meaning to suit the mood or inclination at a given time.

Fortunately, the vivid imagination of children finds new topics and adequate technics when they feel the

THE IMMEDIATE ENVIRONMENT, its activities and character, furnish children abundant stimulation for drawing, painting, design, and other creative experiences. As children grow, control of medium increases, problems of technic are solved, and knowledge expands. Observation becomes keener and expression has its full sway ("The Street Near My School," 6th grade, Pittsburgh, Pa.).

need, when they are encouraged, and when they are free to venture. Another caution that should govern teachers is that forcing expression to

---

[9] *Ibid.*, pp. 113–114; italics are the author's.

gratify adult overzealousness is just as harmful as imposing standards or ideas, or asking destructive questions.

But children at this level do more than draw. They engage freely in other art activities; these will follow the same growth tendencies until they reach the peak for the level. Work in clay and the use of color are among them. Clay may be introduced early, but color because of its strong appeal is a distracting medium which may interfere with and minimize the kinesthetic development.

It is obvious that in working with clay, the breaking up, pounding, flattening, and other possible ways of shaping it will, in a relatively brief time, give way to spontaneous expressions of elemental form concepts. Because clay, plastiline, or other similar materials call for motor activity, they should be introduced early.

Color, on the other hand, will have a new and different interest after motor control has been achieved. It will be used by the child not so much to represent a visual relationship to objects as for its very own natural appeal.

The child's growth at this level may be evaluated in its many phases. The thoughtful teacher should keep a file of the work of each child and at reasonable intervals attempt an evaluation of growth on the basis of the work, on observations of the child, on his changed behavior, his play activities, his work habits, his physical controls, and his general temperament. Play, discovery, and control are the key words at this level of growth. Children are on their way, naturally, if they are normally active, if they respond to gentle yet firm guidance, and if they scribble or draw or pound the clay and seem happy in so doing.

Presymbolic Stage

This phase of artistic unfolding is still in large part within the manipulative stage of development. It involves children in the kindergarten and first grade. However, some children in nursery school may already have reached this stage, and some children in the second grade may remain at this creative level and others will go beyond it. Flexibility of the art program is necessary if children are to be helped to grow at their own natural rate.

By this time most children have arrived at progressive, manipulative and visual control. "People" or "me" find their way into their drawings and paintings. Drawings are largely based on circles or ovals for heads and bodies, while horizontal and vertical lines stand for legs and arms. Seldom are all parts of the body present, although especially precocious children may have fairly complete symbols for "me" or "ball" or "boy." The *naming* of the object is worthy of special attention when it occurs at this level because of its various implications in evaluating the growth of the child who produces the named drawings.

An interesting study, which involved nearly 9000 children of kindergarten age, was made in the Province of Ontario, Canada, by Charles and Margaret Gaitskell,[10] who refer to this stage as that of *manipulation*. A pertinent statement made by the authors supports the observation just made to the effect that this stage varies in span. The experimenters observed that the duration of the manipulative stage varies for individual children. A number of factors appear to govern the length of time in which a child remains at this stage. These include the nature of the medium with which the child works, the extent of his experience with the medium, and the appeal which the medium may have for him. A review of the experiment reveals several facts which seem especially significant to mention here:

1. Chief interest is in materials.
2. Discovery of resemblance in his work encourages the child to give his work form, or to finish a product.
3. Regression from symbol to presymbol occurs in many instances. Persistence of this fact calls for remedial attention.
4. Preliminary work in color lacks variety; with experience the child produces works of marked aesthetic quality.
5. Nonobjective paintings are not infrequent.
6. About 54 percent of the cases studied show the human figure as first to appear.
7. Growth in expression develops following the mastery of symbols; foldover, x-ray, and series pictures occur in many instances.
8. Aesthetic qualities are at first wanting; later the work becomes better composed and shows unity. A "center of interest" seems to appear early by making one symbol large; children also unify by means of rhythms and strive for balance.
9. As children develop creatively, they seek out more details and relationships to environment.

---

[10] Charles D. and Margaret Gaitskell, *op. cit.*

In general, this stage is a prelude to the growing and much clearer concept of man and environment. As the child's knowledge grows and his experiences broaden, he achieves more satisfying and more definite symbols. For the time being, he generally expresses these concepts through what may be called geometric or abstract lines. These are substitutes and are valid only as transitional means.

Sky, background, foreground, middle ground, and other space relationships begin to be noticed by most children at this level. Drawings or paintings will often show a number of objects arranged over the entire paper, and the child may be ready to "tell" what they mean to him. However, his works are not "composed" in an adult sense; the concern of the child is emotional and nonrealistic. This explains why his abstractions are often amazing. This is true whether the child is drawing, painting, or modeling.

The most important educational need at this stage is to make abundant provision for experiences through which children may identify themselves with a situation. It is in this manner that knowledge and firsthand contacts contribute to subsequent growth. Psychology points out that this is the age of "I," "me," and "my," hence the nature of experiences should be in those terms and suited to that level of interest. As nearly as possible, activities should call for actual participation: handling, observing, putting together, taking apart, going somewhere, doing a chore, helping someone, such as teacher, mother, or father.

Symbolic Stage

The next developmental stage is the symbolic. Usually, it involves children in the second and third grades, although it should be kept in mind that a rigid line cannot be drawn. Therefore, some second-graders will have passed this stage, while some third-graders have not and may not do so until later. Regression of any marked degree or persistence of its characteristics into fourth grade calls for particular attention by the teacher.

Worth remembering at this point of growth is that environment and endowment have now played their part for some time. Beyond these, a number of influences have been exerted on the children, consciously or otherwise, by parents, teachers, and others.

In general this period is characterized by a keener concept of man and the world, man and things. The pupil begins to utilize his heightened instinctive powers, the knowledge he has accumulated, and the experiences he has undergone. He observes major changes in size, shape, direction, and often in relationships. The knowledge, physical skills, and coördination achieved by children so far, suggest to them that the inert symbols they have been using for "man" cannot act or accomplish anything. Therefore, children are inclined to bend and stretch legs or arms and to bend the body according to the action or position they have in mind. They begin to sense space relationships and with regularity make use of a base line, and sometimes two base lines. These are indications of abstract concepts of space as well as of a sense of relationship to and with surroundings.

Drawing, painting, modeling, and other forms of expression produced at this stage begin to acquire meaning. They are meaningful to the child in the sense that clear purposes may be observed. It is paramount that teachers and parents recognize such purposes. Having developed a graphic, although still diagrammatic, mode of expression, the child at this point is likely to use it often. He does so for the satisfaction he experiences at the accomplishment as well as for further mastery. But Goodenough[11] found that children at this stage actually have a wide variety of symbols. This fact should indicate to teachers that individuality and inventiveness are beginning to show forth and should be encouraged. Lowenfeld[12] calls attention to the deviations from the newly discovered symbols and points out that these deviations are significant, particularly the exaggerations of parts, omission of unimportant parts, and changes of symbols for the expression of emotionally important parts. These changes are meaningful because they may suggest experiences of a profound character; a fact not too common at this age level. A further meaning is that the changes suggest emotional influences which intimately identify the child with his personal attempt at full expression.

The changes or omissions referred to are indications of deep feelings or concerns. They reinforce the idea that children *will* draw or paint when they feel themselves in the situation. However, it is more common

---

[11] Florence L. Goodenough, "Children's Drawings," in *Handbook of Child Psychology,* Worcester, Clark University Press, 1931.

[12] Viktor Lowenfeld, *Creative and Mental Growth,* rev. ed., New York, The Macmillan Company, 1952, p. 110.

Table 2. A Child Grows Up: Symbolic Stage
(Grades 2, 3, and 4)

Chief Characteristics	Major Interests	Significant Needs	Usual Responses	Effective Stimulation
1. Buoyant, active, energetic; bodily movements more coördinated and conscious rhythm is sought for pleasure	1. People, particularly their schoolmates and playmates	1. Art needs are many; need help and counsel	1. Degree of independence felt	1. Self-motivation is on the ascent
2. Realization of the "adult" world and ways	2. Environment, particularly adjusting to it	2. How to adjust with little emotional disturbance	2. Choice of groups and friends; "gangs"	2. Group work and committee responsibility
3. Beginning of independence from teacher and parents	3. Skills sharpened to say what they wish to say adequately	3. How to fit in with others	3. Initiative shows itself on upgrade	3. Challenging standards (5–6)
4. Imagination not as active as formerly		4. More technical interest	4. Self-direction and confidence (6)	4. Competitive activity for its own worth
5. Sense of relationships of form and space			5. Inadequacy is felt, but as a problem to be met (6)	
6. More adequate sense of values, size, etc.			6. Emotions still very important	
7. Heightened sense of realism			7. Capable of sustained application to work (5–6)	
8. Emotional response is high			8. Self-organizing ability (5–6)	
9. Self-organization is rapid and enjoyed			9. Seeks company of own sex	
10. Critical faculties develop fast (6th grade)			10. Self-confidence	
11. Social growth is automatic (5–6)				
12. Sex consciousness (5–6)				

at this level for children to realize that inert symbols cannot tell what they feel. While they bend and stretch the body in search for action and while they draw the side view, simply to be sure, they retain an individual way of characterizing and of expressing feelings.

In addition to the highly individualized and diversified symbols mentioned thus far, children at this level realize direction and position in space. It is this realization that gives rise to folding-over and x-ray pictures. In the folding-over type of expression the child gives objects a position of significance rather than of perspective appearance. In the x-ray representations the outside-inside relationships are shown in the same picture. Often, in the same picture, several phases of one event are told; this is indicative of the thoroughness and completeness of thinking of the child artist. Space-time equivalences and concepts are often found in the work of old and new masters in painting. This is a fact which should encourage teachers when they discover this mode of expression in children, rather than cause them to think of it as peculiar.

CLASS TRIPS to places of interest are rich in possibilities for art expression: on the way, at the place, on the way home, interesting incidents that took place ("What I Saw on the Trip to the Bronx Zoo," 2nd grade, Livingston, N.J.).

The Meaning and Use of Color and Design. Mention has been made that color was at first used largely for its emotional meaning. It now gradually assumes significance in relation to objects. Formerly, the child evolved symbols and found success in expressing what he had in mind; now he discovers color symbols and relates them to the world about him. However, as in the case of graphic symbols, he will change color symbols as new experiences disclose to him that color changes exist in the environment: from one person to another, from one dress to another, from one flower to another, from one tree to another, and so on.

Design, or the creation of decorative motifs, follows the same mode of development as that for drawing or painting. It should be repeated that traditional formulas, "systems" for creating design, and other mechanical means are detrimental to the natural development of the child's innate sense of decoration. Good design will grow out of the same spontaneous, free spirit that was stressed in connection with drawing and color.

The feeling for rhythm and the urge for repetition are present within the child; all they need is encouragement. It has been pointed out that abstract concepts of form and space are inherent in the very nature of children's creative work; therefore, stimulation of the right sort will induce adequate expression. Direction, insistence on exactness, for evenness, for sameness of finish, and other adult concepts are likely to impede or retard rather than to help the child toward the achievement of his sense of design.

Three-Dimensional Experiences

Three-dimensional work, including clay, wood, cardboard, and other materials, must be given a place in the art program at this stage. The properties of the materials used will automatically serve to limit as well as to encourage the child. Encouragement will come from the fact that clay, for example, is pliable and soft; that it can be pushed together or pulled apart. Through experience, the child will find that he does not need to make all components as one, as was the case when he drew or painted on paper. With clay he may add, take away, put things upright or lying down. In brief, he will find that the material permits flexibility. The restrictions of the medium, by the same token, are natural ones, inherent in the clay itself. Therefore, they are not disturbing to the child; rather, they show him that, like his symbols in drawing or in painting, the obstacles can be mastered. "How can I make things stay together?" "How can I shape them?" "How can I join them?" These are among natural problems he will want to solve.

What has been said for clay may be applied to most other three-dimensional materials. One fact of importance is that the child benefits greatly from such activities, particularly if he is not highly visual-minded but feels from within, kinesthetically. Actually, not enough provision is made for these meaningful experiences at this level in most classrooms.

In summing up this stage of development, it seems wise to do so in terms of cautions. These seem significant:

1. *Proportions* are important only emotionally, not as visual realities.
2. *Changes* of certain elements, such as emphasis on size, omissions, addi-

tions, or other deviations, are meaningful to the child and should be so accepted.

3. *Folding over,* x-ray, equivalences, time-space modes of expression are very natural when they occur normally; they should not be forced.

4. *Perspective* (adult concept) is practically nonexistent. It should not disturb teachers and, in turn, teachers should not force children to strive for what they do not yet sense.

5. *Color symbolism* slowly develops into color relationship to environment and objects.

6. *Design* is instinctive; it only needs encouragement and free play to develop.

7. *Three-dimensional* media appeal to different sense values and must be given a definite place in the program.

Stage of Inceptive Realism

At about the age of nine or ten, children embark on a series of realistic stages which represent the natural endeavor to create on a more mature plane. The first of these realistic developments is here referred to as *inceptive.* The child in the classroom may be seen blossoming forth. He is growing larger and taller, generally seeks friendships, associates with groups, and begins to evidence a degree of independence from teachers and other adults. If the child is what may be called average, or typical, he has reached the prepubertal stage in physiological development. He is beginning to function more and more as a self-motivated and a self-assertive being.

In artistic development he is ready to take new steps. He looks at the world and man with a certain amount of knowledge as well as with a certain degree of feeling. The child becomes more aware of the opposite sex as well as of differences in the surroundings. While all these are only preludes to greater and more significant changes later on, they nevertheless mark a milestone in the creative unfolding of the child.

The symbols he had so well established during the preceding stage no longer suffice for him to express completely thoughts and ideas. He sees details, notices character, and is conscious of action. He now realizes that boys and girls dress differently, boys have short hair, girls have long tresses or pigtails. These and other realistic discoveries are new details to be incorporated in his work. From these types of awareness one might conclude that preadolescents are fully capable of representing visual realism. Such is not the case generally, although some preadoles-

TABLE 3. A Child's World Grows Larger: Stages of Inceptive and Analytical Realism
(Grades 4, 5, and 6)

Chief Characteristics	Major Interests	Significant Needs	Usual Responses	Effective Stimulation
1. Physical and physiological growth and changes are very obvious	1. Broader interest in other people, in classmates; social concept involves others	1. Opportunity to do and make things	1. They enjoy doing things in an "organized" but not limiting way; design becomes meaningful	1. Repeated, though guided, experimentation with a wide array of material
2. A degree of independence from teachers and parents; can work on his own much better and longer	2. Slight interest in opposite sex because of new awareness of differences	2. Need for friends, clubs, "gangs"	2. Eagerness to participate in group experiences	2. Flexible program for individuals and groups to retain interest and to advance it
3. By the age of 10 most children have reached prepubertal stage	3. Action: people and animals doing things	3. New and more adequate symbols to express the larger world they now sense	3. Enjoy and express newly discovered phenomena, such as moods, feelings, color qualities	3. Posed model, self-portrait, portrait of favorite classmates
4. They see themselves as part of the environment	4. Imaginative situations in which they take part or in which they lead	4. Encouragement to continue to search for adequate ways of saying what they sense and how things look	4. Enthusiastic and co-operative because more able to accomplish	4. Short trips to see things in action: a house being built, traffic at a corner, a farm, an industry
5. Self-motivated to a degree; to some extent they are self-assertive	5. They wish to know the "why" of things and events, especially by 6th grade	5. Experimentation with the materials of art to find out, to arrive at answers	5. Acceptance of responsibilities for all types of projects	5. Memory drawing, painting, and modelling of things they have seen or participated in
6. A new consciousness of people and environment; knowledges have accumulated	6. Dramatic events such as fire, storm, parades, and similar events capture their interest	6. The early sense of realism finds expression in textures, forms, direction of line	6. Proud of self and school	6. Committee organiza-
7. They are more free to ask questions about many things, including art				
8. Awareness of sex difference is				

tion of class for leadership development and for intelligent followership

7. Rewards of a nonmaterial nature, such as praise when due; recognition for accomplishments

8. Self-evaluation of work

9. Discussion technics

7. Need to develop own technics to express feeling, mood and appearance: dark and light, distance, perspective, and details

8. Broadened experiences in personal and group relations and in terms of new knowledges and technics

a gradual development

9. They begin to feel dissatisfied with their accomplishments; seek improvements

10. General awareness suggests details, general character, and action in people, animals, objects

11. In art and other creative fields children see more, sense more, and relate themselves to the world

12. Children are imaginative and like to express themselves in that manner

13. Sensitivity to color, line, form, and other elements is manifest in their work and in their social contacts

14. Because of the wide range in endowment it is possible to find great variety in their creative achievements

15. Older children tend to be neater in appearance; like to be attractive

16. They are increasingly more observant as they reach 6th grade

262 cents may be capable of so doing. It is wiser to conclude that pupils face new, and to them serious, problems. Now they need even more understanding and guidance than before. Children have reached a stage of inceptive or beginning realism. They see more, sense more, know more, and yet are not fully capable of expressing visual realities. They are aware, however, that mere symbols are not adequate.

As preadolescents overcome the new difficulties, physical, emotional, and creative, they begin to show interest in perspective appearance and replace folding over. They realize that people, houses, and trees are not just anchored to a base line, but that they are related to space and ground in such a way that trees grow from the earth and rise to the sky. Many boys and girls at this level also realize and strive to see a picture as composed of planes; that there is a background, a middle ground, and a foreground. They also sense that certain objects, because of their position, overlap other objects and will, therefore, be seen only partially. But not all children will reach this level of understanding at the same time.

SELF-IDENTIFICATION is often recognizable in the spirit and in the characteristics of the work of children. Games, acting a part, or even imagining oneself as a character, human or animal, should be utilized in the stimulation of art activities ("Animals We Made Ourselves In," Saturday class, Pennsylvania State University, University Park, Pa.).

The pupils' reaction to and acquaintance with color at this point have meaningful possibilities. Colors will be recognized as qualities of light rather than simply as names or as classifications on a chart or on a color wheel. Color feeling, color mood, and color symbolism are the essential experiences pupils need and seek at this time. For example, it is possible to motivate a class to be aware of the beauty of the day by asking it to observe the color on buildings, on the ground, on shrubs, and on trees. "How does the sun affect objects?" "How does a sunny day differ from a rainy day?" It is possible to evoke feelings and real knowledge of color by having pupils examine an appropriate color print and by asking them to describe the color *qualities* they see. Such terms as dull, bright, happy, warm, cold, will come to the fore and assume a meaning that children transpose in their own paintings or other art experiences.

The following is an example of a situation which occurred to the writer. The night before the occurrence a group of children witnessed the play *Seven Old Ladies from Lavender Town*. It was produced by a group of their own classmates. The writer asked a simple question: "How did you like the play?" The responses were both exciting and revealing. The children reacted in subjective terms with reference to the colors of the costumes, the scenery, and the stage lighting. The Seven Old Ladies looked drab and dull, according to the children, but they liked the play so much when the ladies were changed, by magic, into the seven young wives who looked so bright and cheerful.

Thus it is obvious that while color has meaning at this stage, it is not of scientific or visual significance. This indicates that it is advantageous to capitalize on this natural tendency toward color. Through it, it is possible to stress the observation of color qualities, stimulate emotional reactions to color and light, and develop an appreciation of color symbolism and color moods. The use or making of color wheels and charts is of dubious value.

The Meaning of Design. Pattern, or surface decoration, to be more exact, also takes on new meaning at this stage of development for several reasons, and especially because design offers an avenue of expression closely related to the child's desire to decorate himself. This is true particularly on the part of girls; in the case of boys, teachers will note a closer observation and apparent approval of pattern as it appears on girls' dresses, on the wallpaper at home, and on other decorative features in their surroundings in general. It is the natural development of the child's powers of observation and of his greater awareness of the details about him. Therefore, design deserves proper attention and ample opportunity at this time.

The most important caution for teachers in this connection is to avoid teaching "principles" and "elements" of design, as such. These are intellectual schemes which have been developed over the years by creative minds and are recognized in the works of mature craftsmen. The child is an artist and a craftsman, but in the sense that he works spontaneously and with originality. The child is not an artist in the same sense as one speaks of an accomplished painter or a finished craftsman. His achievements will come in due time if the innate and unspoiled feeling for design are not crushed by adult rules and systems. Rhythm, balance, emphasis, unity, and the rest are felt by children and will invariably be expressed if given unhindered opportunity.

This being the last stage of development for children of elementary-school years, it may be appropriate to make a general statement to the effect that formal teaching of any sort is not only futile but actually thwarting. The best teaching focuses on children rather than on formalized production.

How should the child experience design at this stage? Natalie Cole gave the children paper plates to decorate; but only after they had been properly motivated, only after discussions of eventful situations in the children's lives. Then they were ready to create designs of genuine worth. The plates are round; therefore, instinctively children will follow the round form and realize that what they are doing is decorating a plate, that what they are doing has a purpose or function, namely, to make the plate attractive. When this occurs, one is assured that children are designing *consciously*.

What is true of shapes is also true of the materials with which the child designs. A few simple design experiments may lead to further search and development. Leaf, rubber, sponge, or potato printing, as well as block printing and stenciling, are often used as experimental media. Without preconceived formulas the child is encouraged to cut his design from the material, to experiment with a printing medium, and then to apply the created motif to whatever he chooses. The idea of application at this level is quite important since it gives the experience a "real" purpose. Notebook covers, curtains for the classroom windows, or gift desk pads are but a few possibilities.

What is the nature of the created motifs? Many children will rely on geometric shapes; however, there is no evidence that children will not create imaginative shapes or forms inspired by real things or objects. They will and should design as they feel without interference. The tendency which lies within the child should be controlled only by the requirement of the materials he uses.

Three-Dimensional Experiences. The natural feeling for design that has been discussed is, in a sense, basic to the idea of designing with three-dimensional materials. Children delight at getting the "feel" of cord, wire, thin-gauge metal, clay, plaster, thin wood, and a vast array of other possible materials. The emotional reaction to color, texture, and design typical of children at this level of growth is also evident in three-dimensional work. New forms will be created and the imagination will suggest combinations of materials and textural relationships heretofore not experienced. Mobiles, stabiles, and texture pictures may be added to the usual activities in the field of form design. Thus the child's creative horizons broaden just as his knowledge in other directions has broadened. Appreciation of the form created in relation to its possible uses is a desirable goal. For example, in working on simple pottery forms the teacher may reasonably ask whether the object would hold many or few flowers, tall or short flowers. Or whether the object would look well on a table, and whether it looks topheavy or is too broad at the base. In other instances it is plausible to ask whether the object is intended for pure decorative enjoyment, as in the case of a stabile or a free form or a mobile. The questions which have been asked may lead children to think in terms of function or to consider the requirements of sheer decoration.

A special word should be said regarding the use of clay as a modeling medium. Children at this level do not realize as yet the distinction between modeling and sculpture. This being the case, it is quite proper to give them the opportunity to express themselves in clay for the pure joy of creating. The result may be the expression of a single thought, such as "I kneel to pray" or "I am the batter" or "I salute the flag." Then again the expression may be the child's contribution to the diorama on local history. The last instance is an example of autonomous coöperation in terms of a contribution to a group project. Technic as such is of minor importance except as it helps the child to express himself adequately. The true significance of modeling lies in pure expression in a medium not too frequently used. Through modeling it may be feasible to recognize those children for whom this medium is the best means of expression.

To sum up, the significant role of three-dimensional experiences at this level suggests the following important points:

1. Three-dimensional design tends to establish the relationship between materials and objects.
2. The sense of form in relation to use is reinforced or awakened.
3. The creation of new shapes, combinations of textures, and other similar adventures stimulate the imagination.
4. Formal principles (proportion, rhythm, emphasis, and others) are experienced informally and instinctively.
5. The use of various materials opens up new avenues of expression and may lead to the appreciation of contemporary design.

Stage of Analytical Realism

This is the second phase of the child's realistic cycle. It occurs at approximately the sixth-grade level, although it may appear before that time and in many instances as late as the end of the seventh grade. This period of a child's life is perhaps the most crucial one because it represents the time when he moves from childhood to adolescence.

The reason for including this stage in a consideration of the elementary program is to alert elementary teachers as well as special art teachers to the fact that the physiological changes that are taking place in the child are likely to alter his artistic endeavors.

The term *analytical realism* is used here to indicate the heightened awareness of children between the ages of 11 and 13. Psychologists point out that this is the period of reasoning, of attempting to find causes, or to analyze facts and situations in the activities of life as well as in the environment.

The many ways in which the analytical powers of a child begin to function are based on a keener sense of observation. Whereas until recently he noticed only main characteristics in people and things, he now observes details. Folds in clothes; changing effects of color on objects; character of the major anatomical components of the body, such as joints; and changes in the appearance of figures according to differing action are some new interests. Also significant are perception of space and perspective appearance.

IMAGINATIVE WORK can be genuine if properly motivated. Storytelling, seeing a play adapted to the level of the children, listening to music or poetry, often inspire children to paint or draw (puppeteers, 4th grade, Oklahoma City, Okla.).

The seriousness of this intermediate stage is that it may mislead. While all the technical terms in the paragraph above represent new optical discoveries on the part of the child, they are not signals for teachers to work with vengeance toward adult realism. The child still has much growing up to do. He should not be prodded along the lines of scientific perspective, color science, and the rest. He should be guided to make further discoveries for himself, naturally, and through experience and observation.

Recognition of Perceptual Types. The importance of this stage of development is further emphasized by the fact that it represents a bridge. It is the bridge to adolescence. More than that, it is the bridge to a more permanent identification of the child with his type of perception. The careful teacher may ask himself the question: "What is the perceptual leaning of this pupil?"[13] In general, the visual and the haptic are emphasized as the two extremes. But it must be clear that there are many other possible types of perception. A. Barclay-Russell, the English psychologist, as well as Read and others have pointed out the importance of identifying the child's mode of seeing for purposes of guidance. Barclay-Russell[14] names these types: architectural, classical, decorative, dramatic, emotional, haptic, impressionist, intellectual, lyrical, mystic, romantic, simple, storytelling, two-dimensional. These are descriptive terms which point to possible leaning; however, it is possible for the same individual to move from one type to another, depending on intervening experiences and subsequent growth.

The significance for classroom purposes seems to be that there are children who *see* and others who *feel*. Some are extroverts and some introverts, perceptually speaking. Another way of saying it is that some children are interested in appearance, while others are interested in the meaning of what is before them. If this central fact is borne in mind, then all of the in-between types may be recognized.

Proper stimulation, which is the secret of good teaching, must be based on what the teachers recognize in the child. The tremendous importance of this transitional stage is a challenge to all teachers. Difficult as adolescence is, its attendant discouragements can be lessened, indeed removed, by careful and sympathetic guidance on the part of broad-visioned teachers.

The Place of Technic. If the critical nature of this stage has been properly understood, then it must follow that a distinction may now be made between expression as such and artistic refinement on the part of the child. The specific reference here is to what, or how much, value to place on the finished products of a child artist. The answer is found in the natural and progressive stages of growth and development thus far described. As a child moves from one stage to the next, one notes greater awareness of the environment, wider concern with man and his activities, increasingly conscious identification of the child artist with his creations, functioning of accumulated knowledge, and development of

---

[13] Lowenfeld refers to the nonvisual type as *haptic*.

[14] A. Barclay-Russell, "Art and the Adolescent," in Edwin Ziegfeld (ed.), *Education and Art, A Symposium*, Paris, UNESCO, pp. 46–49.

critical faculties. What do these facets of growth indicate? First of all, they indicate that there is rhythm in the creative growth of children. The rhythm does not occur at specified times for all, but it does occur when nurtured in freedom and through guidance. In the second place, the progressive development indicates that as concepts grow and as technics are developed by children to satisfy each particular creative stage, the child seeks a natural adequacy and a natural satisfaction from his creation. Briefly, as the child grows and develops he attaches greater significance to *his product*. He sets standards of achievement adequate to his mode and his concepts, but no longer does he find satisfaction in the infantile scribble or the geometric symbol of a few years ago.

To minimize finish, or technic, at this stage of development is to assume a laissez-faire position which is inimical to creative unfolding. To overemphasize these is equally detrimental. Table 5, page 294, is an attempt to indicate the growing significance of subject matter, of technics, and of final product.

SELECTION OF ART ACTIVITIES

THEORY MUST BECOME MEANINGFUL

In the preceding chapters an endeavor was made to present those educational aspects of philosophy, psychology, and method that appear to be the very minimum essentials for a beginning in the understanding of the nature, place, and function of art as education. The child, his nature and development in general, and particularly as a creative being, were also considered.

But even if universal understanding of all the educational implications of the task of developing children's creative powers could be assumed, those very understandings would be of little value until translated into a practicable scheme of operation for the classroom. It is with this thought in mind that the remainder of this chapter has been prepared. Reference to Table 13, page 587, may be of some assistance in understanding how art activities may be selected and upgraded to meet the needs of growing children.

Most normal children are self-motivated. They act and think until external forces place barriers before them. These barriers are often placed before them, unwittingly, by adult requirements and adult thinking with regard to what children ought to do, what they should achieve, what technics they ought to use, and what ideas they should accept. It is at this point that classroom teachers and art teachers need to reconcile theory with practice. What is the meaning of experience? Are children different? Are standards of achievement uniform for all? How important is technical mastery at the elementary-school level? Do children have ideas of their own? What is the level of growth and what is the perceptive type of each child?

These are significant questions which teachers must answer in the best professional light. Then there will be little danger that the creative unfolding of children can be seriously impeded. But even more significant would seem to be a reiteration of what purposes art is to serve. Self-expression, admittedly, is the desirable end. Yet all self-expression, unguided and devoid of conceptual meaning, may not give a work the quality which is required for a certain level of growth. Furthermore, unless proper motivation has cleared for the child the purpose behind his expression, no thinking will take place. Finally, what appreciations will come out of the expression? Regardless of its specific form, increased appreciation is another desirable end to be borne in mind.

Some Criteria

For practical purposes it may be worth while to translate the broad suggestion made above into simple criteria which may be used as yardsticks in the selection of activities for the classroom. When properly applied, these criteria may pretty well determine the effectiveness of the art experiences. The criteria proposed are these:

1. Is the projected activity within the experience level of the children?
2. Does the proposed activity permit sufficient variety of interpretations to satisfy each child's inner vision?
3. Are the materials and tools of expression suited to the manipulative and mental levels of the children?
4. Will the proposed activity lead to further self-development of the children?
5. Is the objective of the proposed activity worth while in terms of healthy mental growth for the children?
6. What stimulations will best evoke expression on the part of children?

Critical examination of the six criteria shows that art activities in a classroom cannot be reduced to mere busy work if they are to be of real value as developmental opportunities for pupils. It should also be evident that while the teacher must always endeavor to anticipate the needs of an entire class, she must also be mindful of the particular needs of each member of the group. Again, it seems clear that even though a single art activity may, in and of itself, be a complete experience, it should also act as a link to the subsequent experiences and further development of each pupil.

The Source of Ideas

Children have ideas. They have ideas about things, situations, places, people, and events. They also have vivid imaginations and are capable of reaching conclusions that would hardly occur to inhibited adults. However, the sources of their ideas are, by far and large, not unknown to good teachers and wise parents, even though children often amaze adults with their interpretations, concepts, and insights.

Life is as real for children as it is for adults. The difference lies in the degree of experience, the clarity of inner vision, and the uninhibited manner of expressing ideas and visions. In other words, life itself—the everyday occurrences, the work, the play, the festivals, the occasional event, or the seasonal sports—is "subject matter" from which children derive interest and by which they are motivated to draw, paint, model, or otherwise express themselves and thereby broaden their knowledge and outlooks on life.

FEELING FOR DESIGN in children is as strong as that for picturemaking; progress follows the same natural unfolding. Printing methods are one way of developing a sense of design; often, the spontaneous design created by a child may be turned into a block print or other application (printing with assorted shapes, 4th grade, Kansas City, Mo.).

But, in addition, there is the vast area of knowledge which unfolds before children as they read for pleasure, as they study, and as they see motion pictures and television. As knowledge becomes active, children find in it other sources of inspiration for creative expression. When children learn, there is less separation between the realities and experiences of life and active knowledge. Children discover that these intermingle and complement each other. This is one reason why some children show greater maturity than others even though they may be of the same age and in the same grade in school.

The Child as Artist

Above all other considerations, however, there is the fact that the child is an artist. A vast amount of evidence has been accumulated to establish the creative autonomy of children. Their imagination and their innate compulsion to express what they feel, as they feel or see, are powerful sources of ideas. These sources, above all others, need encouragement, careful guidance, and sympathetic understanding.

The child as artist is not to be confused with the adult as artist. This human attribute should be understood in its proper role and should be permitted to function in the development of the child. The child as artist may not always be concerned with the visual illustration of an idea or an event. There are times when he may merely wish to paint or design. He may even take pleasure in pure abstract ordering of shapes and colors and lines, whether with two- or three-dimensional media. Although persistence in this type of expression may well justify inquiry on the part of teachers and parents when it occurs spontaneously and as an event, it should not be a disturbing factor. All this points to the fact that ideas are not furnished by the teacher, but by the child. The teacher stimulates, guides, sets the stage, and makes purposeful activity possible. Purposeful activity will always help in the development of new concepts and in the acquisition of new knowledges and appreciations.

SOME ACTIVITY AREAS

There are many ways of organizing classes for purposeful art activity. Some of the possible interest areas are suggested hereafter. However, it must be emphasized again that the best way of selecting art activities will always involve the pupil and the teacher.

In studying the interest areas that follow, it seems important to bear in mind that each listing is merely an indication of what may be done. Each list could be extended many times by the children themselves, and certainly by teachers who understand children because they have had experience with them.

General Categories

There are some general categories of activities that, properly presented, will evoke response on the part of most children. These are founded on basic urges and general appeal to all human beings. They are natural springboards that set the creative impulse into motion because they are based on the play, the work, the ideas, and even the dreams of children. Simply as a beginning, the following may be explored:

1. Everyday occurrences
2. Holidays and holy days
3. Unusual events
4. Things one likes best
5. Things one likes least
6. Chores to be done at home
7. Animals and pets
8. Games that children play
9. Stories children know
10. Trips to interesting places
11. Acting a part or character
12. People children know
13. Family
14. Neighborhood friends
15. Things children can make
16. Dreams and wishes of children
17. The larger community and the state
18. People at work
19. Happenings that bring praise or blame
20. First experiences
21. Motion picture and television characters and stories
22. Imaginary situations
23. Situations that bring surprise
24. Handling new or unusual materials
25. Contemplation and observation
26. School campaigns
27. Community enterprises
28. Helping other people
29. Religious life and customs
30. Ideals of our nation

It should be observed that the thirty categories are stated broadly, because in practice they would suggest a wide variety of meanings. For instance, if the teacher were to ask a third-grade class to name one thing each member likes to do best, there might be as many ideas as there are children in the group. This would hold true for any of the categories listed.

Specific Interest Subjects

A second point to note is that each item in each category could lend itself to many modes of expression: drawing, painting, modeling, crafts, and others.

It is also true that while a particular variant in each category could become the personal interpretation of each child, in his chosen medium and mode, it is conceivable that group work might also result. It will depend on the direction that the class or the teacher, or both, feels or wishes to give to the thematic category.

An additional observation is that any category can become, through group agreement and teacher guidance, the beginning of a *unit* from which a large variety of modes of expression, technics, group organization, and utilization of many media may result. This is an advantage on which the teacher should capitalize since it will give the widest scope, afford the utmost in individuation, and permit each child to function in his own best role. The following breakdown of the broader categories will illustrate the point.

Everyday Occurrences

1. Getting ready for school
2. Eating breakfast (lunch, dinner)
3. Feeding my cat (dog, or other pet)
4. I brush my teeth
5. I comb my hair
6. Putting on my shoes
7. Putting on my skates
8. I ride my bike
9. Saying my prayers
10. Going to the store

Things I See (or Have Seen)

1. On the way to school
2. On the playground
3. On a shopping trip
4. On my way home
5. On the bus
6. From the schoolroom window
7. On the farm
8. At the grocery
9. In church
10. From my yard

Animals I Know

1. My dog
2. My cat
3. My pony
4. My rooster
5. My rabbit
6. My brother's horse
7. The squirrel in the park
8. My turtle
9. My duck
10. Sister's pet chicken

Games We Play (for Younger Children)

1. Hopscotch
2. Jumping rope
3. Farmer in the Dell
4. Did You Ever See a Lassie?
5. Around the Mulberry Bush
6. Cat-and-Rat
7. Duck-Duck Goose
8. Little Sallie Saucer
9. Bulebird, Bluebird
10. Stop-and-Start (Red Light)

Games We Play (for Older Children)

1. Baseball
2. Volleyball
3. Badminton
4. Soccer
5. Dodgeball
6. Chinese ball
7. Shuttle relays
8. Three-deep (running-dodging)
9. Basketball

Trips to Take

1. To the firehouse
2. To the farm
3. To the big town
4. To the dairy
5. To the bakery
6. To the police station
7. To the post office
8. To the factory
9. To the museum
10. Into the woods and fields

Unusual Events

1. A fire
2. A serious accident
3. A wedding
4. A storm
5. The rainbow
6. A sunset
7. A sunrise
8. The first snow
9. A new baby in the family
10. The first trip

Chores at Home

1. Raking the leaves
2. Carrying in the groceries
3. Bringing in the milk
4. Sweeping my room
5. Drying the dishes
6. Making my bed
7. Working in the garden
8. Putting away my toys
9. Feeding my pet
10. Setting the table

Drawing Portraits

1. Myself
2. My family
3. My older brother
4. My little sister
5. My mother
6. My grandfather
7. My pet
8. My teacher
9. My best friend

Things I Like to Do

1. I like to read
2. I like to draw and paint
3. I like to dress my doll
4. I like to ride my bicycle
5. I like to visit
6. I like to walk in the garden
7. I like to go to dancing class
8. I like to work with clay
9. I like to sing
10. I like to play house

What I Saw at the Circus

1. Animals I saw
2. Clowns and funny people
3. The peanut man
4. The ice-cream man
5. The rides
6. The band
7. The man on the trapeze
8. The ringmaster
9. The acrobat
10. Eating candy apples and candy cotton

Easter

1. My sister in her new Easter bonnet
2. My brother in his new Easter suit
3. I dreamed about Easter presents
4. We make Easter gifts for mother
5. What Easter means to me
6. We put designs on Easter eggs
7. We make Easter baskets
8. A picture of my bunny
9. The egg hunt
10. The Easter-egg tree

Halloween

1. The Halloween parade
2. Myself dressed up as a pirate
3. My sister in costume
4. Charles dressed as a clown
5. Our float in the parade
6. The Halloween party
7. Games we play at the party
8. We make Halloween lanterns
9. We make our own masks
10. A ghost story (to be told and illustrated)

Thanksgiving

1. Mother cooking dinner
2. We all gather around the table
3. In church on Thanksgiving Day
4. At a football game Thanksgiving Day
5. A Thanksgiving story
6. My idea of the first Thanksgiving
7. When Pilgrims came to America
8. We go to a farm for the Thanksgiving turkey
9. A Thanksgiving song or poem
10. Famous Indians
11. What Thanksgiving means to me

Christmas

1. Decorating the Christmas tree
2. Carrying the Christmas tree home
3. Making decorations for the tree
4. Hanging the Christmas stocking
5. What I dreamed on Christmas Eve
6. A Christmas party
7. Going to church on Christmas Eve
8. Exchanging Christmas gifts
9. The toys I got at Christmas time
10. I make a Christmas gift for mother
11. What Christmas means to me

ORGANIZATION OF ACTIVITIES

THE UNIT OF ACTIVITY

Many classroom teachers, art teachers, and art coördinators find great value in the unit of experience in art. Particularly, those coördinators whose itinerary does not permit them to visit the classrooms as frequently as they would like, find the unit approach administratively worth while and educationally sound.

What is a *unit* of work? Briefly stated, a unit of work is the organized effort on the part of children and teacher (or art coördinator) to relate the subject matter of art, the development of necessary experiences, and the skills adequate to a particular level around important interests, topics, or problems.

The advantages of unit planning are many. Flexibility, adaptability to individual abilities, and concentration on felt interest are among them. In fact, a good unit is planned by teachers and children to fit the specific situation which originally suggested it. But there is no single pattern for a unit of experience and it may be carried out in various ways. The conditioning factors are these: the children's interests, the teacher's response to their interests, and the resources available for carrying them out.

Unit organization does not limit children's opportunities. Rather, it

CREATING WITH MATERIALS appeals to most children. Care should be taken that difficulties of handling will not injure or overpower the children. Otherwise, interesting results are obtainable. The process is of greater significance than the product in the primary grades; standards should be raised as children reach fifth and sixth grade (firebrick carving, 6th grade, Alliance, Ohio).

increases them because, although all may participate in a common experience, each may share in accordance with his ability, interest, and past contact with similar situations. Gifted children can enrich the entire enterprise through many types of contributions, whereas the more-limited children learn by participation in those activities which have meaning and value for them. Therefore, although all children become contributors to the common experience, each child works at his own level.

Types of Units in Art

Since the chief concern here is with art activities, only two types of units are briefly discussed: the art resource unit and the correlated unit.

The resource unit, as the name indicates, has its own reason for being. It originates from suggestions made by the pupils under the guidance of the teacher and is composed of a large variety of activities, experiences, experiments, committee work, individual research, and group concerns. As a matter of fact, it utilizes all those technics and procedures that are deemed necessary by the children to solve the problems they encounter as they work toward the larger goal of the unit, or that are deemed essential by the teacher by way of stimulation.

This type or organization will necessarily involve a large variety of materials and usually includes drawing, painting, modeling, model making, carving, building, and many others. On the other hand, and particularly at the early elementary-school level, the children's active knowledges, their abilities to manipulate materials, and their experiences will naturally limit the extent of the unit. The interest span, as demonstrated by the children themselves, should suggest the extent and breadth of the unit.

By way of example, a subject or activity area may be chosen from the suggestions on pages 275–276; more specifically, the subject "chores we do at home." Proper stimulation would first of all entail a listing of the chores that children perform at home; grouping of children who perform similar tasks may be the next step; then the children may decide whether they wish to draw, paint, model, or do other types of creative work. The larger aspects of the unit may now be discussed with the entire class. How can we utilize each contribution? Do we need to make models? Where will each contribution be placed when finished? What materials do we need? Who will be responsible for each group? How could we share with other children in the school when the unit is completed? These are some of the basic problems to be resolved.

The organizational phase of the unit should be brought under reasonable working control as soon as possible in order that the enthusiasm may not wane. From this point on, the teacher-pupil relationship resumes the usual role: questions, guidance, help, and suggestions whenever needed and warranted.

One phase of the art resource unit that needs special attention is with respect to the child who exhausts his energy and enthusiasm rather soon. In such instances, the unit approach is quite helpful because the many things to be done will, under guidance, point out to the child that he may now try something else that will be different from his first contribution but very useful in the total enterprise.

At the completion of the unit its true worth will be its evaluation by the class or group. Not only the satisfaction of having accomplished the task but the individual contributions and the total visual effect are rewards that will elicit self-improvement, self-assurance, self-esteem, and even motivation for future art experiences.

The correlated art unit represents a very common way of working with children. Elsewhere it has been pointed out that the correlation of art with other subject-matter areas is not only feasible but actually desirable. However, certain conditions must obtain if this type of organization is to be effective. The conditions are these:

1. Art expression must be the natural outcome of related learnings and an integral part of the unit.
2. Art is not to serve ulterior purposes, but must remain as the expression of the pupils and a result of the activation of knowledge derived from the related fields.
3. The aesthetic qualities of the art work must be upheld and not forced in order to suit alien motives such as derivative illustrations.

When classroom teachers develop a genuine respect for art, particularly along the lines suggested above, they will find art teachers and coördinators ready to coöperate and children eager to work. The serious implication in related art expression, therefore, is that it cannot be chosen at random or improvised. It is planned by teachers and pupils, coöperatively.

It is fallacious, for instance, for teachers to decide in a matter-of-fact fashion that China or India or the belabored Mexico is a subject to work on, and suggest to the children that they should "create" on such themes. The results are bound to be stereotyped, inartistic, and purposeless

TABLE 4. A Unit in Social Living. Unit Subject: Our Neighborhood
(Grades 2 or 3, Teacher-Pupil Planned)

1. Origin (P-T)[a]	2. Objectives (P)[a]	3. Organization (P-T)[a]	4. Things We Could Do in Art (P)[a]	5. Things We Could Do in Language and Music (P)[a]	6. Culmination and Evaluation (P)[a]
A. Teacher-pupil discussion leads to what children would like to study and to a choice of topic(s); this may result in the unit subject	A. To help us understand our neighborhood better	A. We make up our groups	A. We could make a map of our town and children of each neighborhood could fill in their part	A. We could write about our own neighborhood	A. Are we satisfied with our result?
	B. To learn how we can be good neighbors	B. We choose our leaders (volunteers)	B. We could make paintings and drawings of buildings, yards, flowers, and people in the neighborhood	B. We could make poems about people in our neighborhood	B. What have we learned about our neighborhood?
B. Selection of objectives by children and teacher through discussion (see col. 2)	C. To learn about important things and people in our neighborhood	C. We need to find out about our neighborhood: a. Children from each group describe their neighborhood b. Trips are planned if necessary c. Records are kept by leader for each group	C. We could model in clay people who work or carve them in soap	C. We could write some music to sing our poems to	C. What have we learned in art, in music, and in language arts?
C. Selection of activities by children and teacher; guidance needed in selection based on ability and choice of children, but *all* have a part (see cols. 4 and 5)	D. To see what a good neighborhood we have	D. We decide what we want to do and how we want to make things (see cols. 4 and 5)	D. We could make small houses and churches and the school, using boxes and cardboard, and could paint them for our map	D. We could write a play about our neighborhood and act it for the school	D. What are some of the best things we did and why do we think so?
	E. To decide how we can have a better, cleaner neighborhood		E. We could make a big book with drawings of our neighborhood		E. What are some things we couldn't do so well, and why?
	F. To notice the pretty things in our neighborhood, such as gardens,				F. How could we improve what we have done?
					G. What is each of us

churches, the
countryside, and
other things

E. We get our mate-
rials from the
leaders and the
teacher

F. Each day we put
away our materials

F. We could make big
models of important
buildings in our neigh-
borhood

G. We could make some
small-garden designs by
looking at the ones in
our neighborhood

H. We could make pic-
tures of a block party
and other things that
happen in our neigh-
borhood

I. We could make a
frieze of our whole
town with separate pic-
tures from each neigh-
borhood

most pleased
about?

H. What are some
things we could do
next that have
come out of this
unit?

---

a P and T refer to pupil, or teacher, or both, as indicated in the column.

282 because they are not felt, either artistically or intellectually, by the pupils.

On the other hand, when the classroom teacher permits the art activities related to an ongoing unit to be selected by the pupils who are

engaged in the development of the unit itself, the art expression may be adequate and justifiable. As in all good teaching, children should first be stimulated through suitable references, participation in discussions, allocation of responsibilities, planning exhibits, dramatization, and seeing slides or motion pictures related to the unit. Then the stimulation that comes from these varied sources and the utilization of old and newly acquired knowledge may result in worth-while art activities. But even under such conditions, the cautions mentioned a moment ago should prevail if true enrichment of related subject fields is the aim, and if art activities are to be valid.

The unit on page 280 was actually worked out in a typical classroom situation. It is offered as an example of the type of planning just discussed.

UNUSUAL PROCESSES capture the interest of older elementary pupils. Because they have grown in knowledges and in control over tools and materials, they are eager to explore new ways and more challenging pursuits (*above*, metal repoussé, 5th grade, Oklahoma City, Okla.; *below*, weaving with native and commercial materials, 5th grade, Seattle, Wash.).

MATERIALS AND TOOLS OF EXPRESSION

IMPORTANCE OF MEDIA

The importance of tools and materials, especially at the elementary level, is sometimes minimized on the pretext that the creativity of children may be hampered by directing their attention to the manipulation and handling of these means. It is true that overemphasis on such matters could result in unwarranted preoccupations. The necessity of understanding tools and media should be recognized for the value with respect to the relation of these means to the tasks to be accomplished and their appropriateness to the maturity levels of children. It is the school's obligation to provide adequate surroundings, including the means of expression, but when these are supplied it becomes the teacher's responsibility to guide children in the proper and adequate use of them. Through exploration of materials and tools, children learn about the possibilities of the materials, thus deriving greater pleasure from art activities and, perhaps, greater success.

The visual arts differ from most other types of expression in that they require materials of many types. There are many color media, several types of papers and boards, many types of modeling clays and doughs, and various kinds of drawing media; in the crafts there is an endless variety of usable materials. This same multiplicity is true of tools. There are modeling tools, cutting and carving tools, many types of brushes, and a number of adapted or improvised tools that respond variously to different handling and with different media.

Beyond the purely physical aspects of this problem there are educational considerations which cannot be overlooked. One of the chief advantages of experimentation with materials and tools is that children discover what materials will do and what they will not do, what effects are obtainable, and what limitations exist. In the case of some tools there is the important element of safety to be considered. Close guidance in the processes of handling and experimentation seems to be the way to cope with this aspect.

An especially helpful analysis of the problem, with regard to the grade placement of materials, has been done by the schools of Denver, Colorado,[15] and by several other systems.

SOME COMMON MEDIA

The following observations concerning materials are intended to assist art teachers and classroom teachers, but they are not to be considered as restrictive or final. Contact with children will ultimately indicate which tools and materials are most effective at certain grade levels.

---

[15] Denver, Colorado Public Schools, Department of Instruction, Bulletin No. XVI, 1951–52.

1. *Crayons.* Large crayons, wax or hard-pressed, permit the manipulative exercise and the development of muscular control needed by the children. Crayons are flexible in so far as their use is concerned because children may use the point, the side, and the end with as much pressure as is required in order to achieve whatever they wish. Large areas of flat color as well as details are possible.

2. *Powder Paint.* Sometimes this is referred to as cold-water paint. It may be mixed in various consistencies depending on the purpose, which ranges from ordinary painting activities to finger-painting. With this medium it is possible for children to paint in outline or solid areas, or to obtain interesting minglings. Long-handled brushes and a fairly thick consistency are generally advisable.

3. *Colored Chalk.* The nature of this medium suggests that its use is best deferred until the first or second grade. It has also been found that too many colors tend to distract the preschool and kindergarten child from the major purpose, namely, expression and manipulation. Interesting effects are possible by drawing on dampened paper and by using contrasting colors around rubbed (shaded) or flat areas of color. In the upper grades children will discover how to blend one color into another and then paint on the blended areas with brush and ink or opaque color. Pastels would naturally fall within this category, but they are too expensive for use in the elementary schools.

4. *Water Color.* For practical and economic reasons, water color is most effectively used from the third grade upward. At this level, the muscular control and the manipulation of a smaller brush are developed sufficiently to make the medium appealing rather than deterring. Washes, minglings, gradations, outlines around larger areas, all these will be discoveries that should thrill most children. Working on dry paper will reveal a certain crispness, whereas working on wet paper will result into unpredictable but thrilling effects. As children learn to use this medium, they will discover that painting with darker colors, or deeper values of the same color, on light washes can be a satisfying experience.

5. *Tempera* (or poster paint, as it is sometimes called) is opaque in contrast to water colors. While this is a somewhat expensive medium, children from the fifth grade on should have experience with it because it permits them to work quickly while their ideas are fresh. Tempera is relatively easy to control, and overpainting of details is feasible because

of its quick-drying quality. Paper of almost any type, as well as cardboards, may be used as painting surfaces.

6. *Clay.* It was inferred elsewhere that clay is a very significant medium because it is plastic and, therefore, permits the child to pull out, push in, add to, take away from, roll, squeeze, and otherwise manipulate the material. A measure of preplanning by the teacher will avoid the usual problems that arise in using clay. Many of the concepts that a child does not seem to be able to express with graphic media are often clarified for him through modeling.

At the primary level, modeling, much as all art activities, is intended to express ideas. Later, the useful aspects of the product emerge from the experiences. Modeling in the round is effective at all levels; modeling in relief, simple coil pottery, and ceramics are best deferred to the fourth grade and used from then on.

Decoration or just color is often added to the dry-clay work of younger children. Tempera paint or powder paint is used for this purpose and, when dry, shellac is brushed on as a preservative. At the upper elementary level, underglazes and transparent glazes may be introduced; firing completes the process.

7. *Plastiline.* There are various types of oil-base modeling materials which will give the children all the necessary experience. But these are not permanent in the sense that they may be taken home. Rather, after

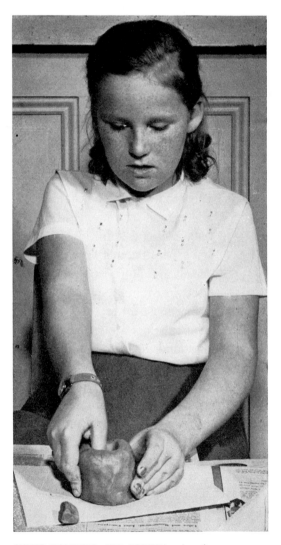

SIMPLE MODELING AND POTTERY, using the "thumb" or "coil" methods, have developmental and appreciational values that should not be overlooked in the elementary grades (3rd grade, Philadelphia, Pa.).

having been used for the pure joy of modeling, the plastiline is re-assembled, wrapped in wax paper, and placed in a metal container for future use.

In the upper elementary grades, plastiline may be used instead of clay to model pieces to be cast in plaster, or to make puppet heads to be covered with papier-mâché.

8. *Papier-Mâché.* Torn newspaper, newsprint, or discarded paper toweling, when adequately soaked and mixed with glue or paste to the consistency of clay, will produce an inexpensive modeling material. In the primary grades, it may be used as a substitute for clay since it is just as pliable and will harden. In the upper grades, paper strips or pulp, treated in the same manner, will be found useful to overlay crushed-paper forms, or to overlay on modeled clay masks to create the shell to be later painted. Another use of either the strips or the pulp is over the armature of an animal or figure made of folded newspaper to obtain the proper shape of the final product. In puppetry, the various parts of the puppet may be made from the pulp or strips.

9. *Doughs.* Additional modeling media that will harden and therefore have permanence are doughs made from sawdust and wallpaper paste, or salt and flour. The salt-flour dough has a crystalline effect and is often used in the upper grades to make relief maps or costume jewelry. The important fact is that the medium is inexpensive and easily obtained. The sawdust-and-paste dough has rather interesting texture and color and lends itself to modeling, directly or on an armature.

10. *Plaster and Soap.* The nature of plaster suggests that its use would be unwise below the third grade. Experimentally, it could be used earlier, and with profit for some pupils. Plaster of Paris is mixed with water. Its consistency depends on the purpose. If it is to be used to pour in a mold, it should be of the consistency of thick cream, allowed to set to whatever thickness is desired, and the excess poured out before re-moving the mold. For relief carving, the consistency could be slightly thicker than indicated above, poured into a cardboard boxtop of the size desired, and allowed to become thoroughly dry before any carving is done. Quite often a cylindrical, square, or rectangular block is desirable for carving in the round; the shape is achieved in the same manner as indicated for the boxtop. Precautions should be taken to protect the desks or tables when working with plaster. Carving knives, penknives, and

improvised instruments are necessary to work in this medium; thus the child learns not only to express himself in a not-too-familiar material but also that its dry and brittle nature calls for careful handling, for thinking before cutting, and for solving problems of form, texture, and volume in a way that will challenge him.

Soap as a medium has the advantage of accessibility, and it is not as "messy" as plaster. However, its softness when fresh offers little resistance to the knife or whatever tool may be used; therefore, the problems are, to a degree, similar to those encountered in handling plaster. Soap may be treated in relief or in the round; it can be handled in simplified planes or it can show details of texture. It may be used realistically or decoratively. Here again, the child determines his own purposes and consequently his mode of expression.

11. *Wood.* Scraps of wood from the industrial-arts department of the school system or from a local pattern shop may be turned into creative means for boys and girls of the elementary school. Imaginative birds, animals, and figures, as well as toys, can be assembled and glued by first- and second-grade children. Useful objects, such as gift boxes, sewing baskets, and many other articles, can be fashioned by older children under proper guidance. The manipulation of simple hand tools, such as a hammer, a crosscut saw, a plane, and a drill, is a skill that children need to master. While it is inadvisable to make extensive use of these tools before the second grade, from that point on most children will be able to handle them with some efficiency.

Soft woods, such as balsam and pine, may be used from third grade on for carving as well as for working in the round.

Toys and other wooden objects may be finished and, to a suitable and limited degree, decorated by using tempera or enamel paints.

12. *Weaving Materials.* Yarns, heavier threads, grasses, raffia, and reed are common weaving materials easily procured. Cloth makes a useful adjunct for sewing large stitches to create interesting surface effects or to appliqué design shapes of many types to a larger surface for such objects as decorative hangings and monograms.

For younger people in kindergarten and first grade, cutting shapes and sewing them on cloth will be good experiences in manipulation of the materials and threading the needle. In later grades, learning to cut and combine shapes and colors adds to the heightened interest. From third grade upward, weaving on cardboard looms, box looms, finger weaving, spool knitting, and other simple types of weaving will afford meaningful activities and may result in articles such as belts, change purses, mats, and other similarly worth while and interesting products.

Raffia over reed may result in attractive mats, baskets, and trays. Often reed is found useful in creating animal and figure armatures on which children can build with raffia. The natural color of the raffia may be retained or it may be decorated with suitable pigments.

13. *Thin-Gauge Metals.* Tin-can craft has been used successfully in the fifth and sixth grades. The fact that the material has certain inherent dangers makes it inadvisable in grades lower than those indicated. Tin snips, pliers, steel wool, and wooden mallets are the necessary tools for cutting and shaping flat forms, or bending the material into a variety of designs suitable to the child's ideas. Soldering of parts may be a necessary process in addition to shaping and cutting

Thin-gauge tooling copper is available commercially, and it may be used not only as indicated above but for the creation of repoussé plaques. These may be developed with textural effects as desired, tooled, or stamped with original motifs created by pupils for the purpose. Class emblems, coats of arms, monogrammed plaques, and decorative motifs make interesting gift items or items for personal use.

14. *Decorative Print Making.* A common method of introducing print making is to ask young children to take a small piece of thin wood broken from a larger stick, dip it in color, and then press it on paper, or make some rhythmic movement on paper several times. The result is not only interesting but revealing to children. They soon discover that many materials can be used effectively to create patterns. Carrot printing and potato printing are very common media. From third grade upward, children are quite capable of cutting irregular indentations at the end of a piece of doweling or soft wood to make their own design. A semihard eraser or a piece of kneaded eraser, shaped at will and handled carefully, will produce interesting effects.

Children from middle grades upward enjoy and profit from making monoprints. A monoprint is easily made by arranging twine, leaves, and other flat materials on a piece of glass or wood or metal which has first been rolled with a coat of color; a clean sheet of paper is next placed on the arrangement created, and rolled with a clean brayer or a rolling pin. When lifted, the paper will show interesting results which can be improved upon and diversified with each monoprint. Rubber inner tubing, battleship linoleum, and mounted linoleum blocks are commonly used to make greeting cards, bookplates, purely decorative designs, or motifs to be applied to cloth or whatever the child's purpose may suggest.

15. *Assorted Materials.* It has been found by many teachers that working with a variety of materials, generally referred to as discarded materials, often gives rise to original and interesting arrangements. These serve as springboards for further creative ventures on the part of children. Buttons, earrings, wire mesh, cord, cork, pipe cleaners, broken bits from mirrors, costume jewelry, patches of textured cloth, and other similar materials, in themselves considered of no further use, when properly manipulated and arranged in effective relationships may result in attractive wall decorations, table favors, or items of personal adornment.

The greater value of all these ventures is that children learn to establish relationships of lines, colors, shapes, and textures which eventually lead to more significant aesthetic experiences.

SOME IMPORTANT CAUTIONS

CREATION VERSUS DEVICES

Harold Fink,[16] an eminent American physician and psychologist, states quite emphatically that the first ten years are by far the most important in anyone's life. This truth has been confirmed in various ways throughout this work. Yet it deserves repetition and continued stress.

The crucial years will leave their stamp upon a child's future, not only in so far as creativeness is concerned, but upon his total growth. Courage, freedom, assurance, individuality, and other highly prized characteristics of the successful citizen are involved in what happens early in life, and particularly in the elementary school.

Over the years certain damaging practices have appeared under the guise of educational aids. Among these are certain workbooks, coloring books, pattern books, holiday project books, camp or playground crafts

---

[16] Harold Fink, *Release from Nervous Tension,* New York, Simon and Schuster, 1943, Chapter XII.

290   kits and instruction manuals, and the now infamous paint-by-number sets. The irreparable harm that these devices inflict on artistic growth has been suspected for a long time; but only recently have sufficient evidences been developed to point out to teachers and counselors the real dangers inherent in these "aids."

Teachers of art cannot, morally speaking, sanction such practices. Among the latest studies that indicate what happens to creative growth when workbook influences are introduced, Heilman's[17] makes it evident

CORRELATED ACTIVITIES, if properly motivated and carefully guided, will produce worth-while results. In the self-contained classroom, there are many opportunities for children to realize how valuable art is in all phases of life and education (paper construction of medieval castle, 6th grade, Richmond, Va.).

[17] Horace F. Heilman, *An Experimental Study of the Effect of Workbooks on the Creative Drawing of Second Grade Children,* doctoral dissertation, University Park, Pennsylvania State University, 1954.

that regression, stereotypes, reliance on "crutches," and other harmful effects soon take their toll. Patterns, ready-made posters to be colored, and "idea" books have similar ill effects on children. To wean them from these "aids" is a very difficult task if not an altogether impossible one.

Closely related to workbooks and patterns is the tolerance of, and even direct permission for, copying or tracing pictures, designs, models, and other materials of a seemingly useful nature in the classroom. It is obvious that not only bad habits but outright dishonesty is being encouraged when children are permitted to copy or trace work which they have not originated. No amount of rationalization on the part of parents or teachers will alter the harmful effects of such practices. Elizabeth Harrison puts it this way: "Any original effort, however crude, is of more value than the neatest copy of a 'grown-up' drawing."[18] And, it is even worse when children are permitted to copy or trace bad drawings or other visual materials by inferior artists.

However, classroom teachers may ask: What is there to replace these very convenient and time-hallowed devices? Actually, there is but one answer: *Let the child create!* Children only need opportunity and encouragement to work in art. Administratively, it is just as defensible for a principal to find children busy creating as it is for him to find them filling in, or adding to, as is the case in workbooks and other devices. Enlightened administrators and specialists in arithmetic, the language arts, and other fields are becoming aware of the fallacy of devices and of the superiority of methods that evoke thinking and original doing on the part of the child.

CONTESTS AND COMPETITIONS

A second scourge inflicted upon children by well-meaning but uninformed people is that of contests and competitions. While this practice has many negative angles for all levels of the public schools, it is most dangerous at the elementary-school level because of the impressionable nature of the children. The National Art Education Association and the Committee on Art Education have considered this problem on various

---

[18] Elizabeth Harrison, *Self Expression Through Art,* Toronto, W. J. Gage and Company, 1951, Part Four, p. 57.

occasions. Their findings and recommendations indicate that teachers need to be extremely cautious in accepting participation in such activities. The sum and substance of the objections may be epitomized in these terms: work involved in competition is usually imposed; is irrelevant to children's interests; relies on forced technics for the sake of prizes; places a premium on cleverness rather than on creation; gives winners a false notion of their true abilities and losers a sense of futility and frustration. Is a prize worth all this?

There are many instances, however, in which children should be made responsible for producing art work for worthy causes and fine ideals. These public-relations situations and community-related enterprises have social values that cannot be overlooked. The antagonism which teachers must develop is in regard to becoming "poster factories" and "favor mills" at the cost of developmental and artistic activities.

SUMMARY

With rare exceptions, all children draw or manipulate materials in answer to the impulse to create and to express themselves. From scribble and casual manipulation to purposive drawing or diagram, and from the latter to realistic representational attempts or sophisticated abstraction, are matters of gradual maturation. With the development of perception and of physical control over materials, within the bounds of the natural endowment of each individual child, there is an evident normal increase in ability to express himself more adequately. The importance of guiding a child in the process of growth rather than of imposing upon him adult standards is, therefore, the most crucial fact which must be realized by parents and teachers.

The freshness and spontaneity of child art are not only to be prized for their genuineness and for their potentials, but are to be valued also as indexes of the child's mode of growth in various directions: physical, mental, social, aesthetic, and creative.

A child's world is to be appraised and considered in its own right. As a child develops, he acquires new skills, new knowledges, new insights into the total environment, and, eventually, awareness of the adult world. This is part of the process of growing. It may be marred by dictation and by overzealousness for adult ways and knowledge on the part of parents and teachers. Such practices may result in arresting the proper course of development and in setting up emotional disturbances.

The atmosphere of the home and of the school should be one in which normal growth may take place. Kindness, positive guidance, and encouragement are the keys to the situation. This does not imply a laissez-faire attitude on the part of adults, but rather a sympathetic understanding.

Psychology and education have identified, to a reasonable degree, the stages of growth and of creative development. These should be understood and utilized by teachers and parents for the effective planning of the activities of children. In art education the special emphasis should be on children's experiences, on imaginative creation, on growing control over materials, on the activation of knowledge as it is acquired, and on the understanding of children as individuals.

Classroom practices in art can utilize all these emphases by wise planning and by the recognition of children as artists in a variety of areas.

The socializing aspects of art activities are extremely valuable at the elementary-school level, where children move from an egocentric position to one in which group recognition and group values become meaningful.

In the total development of the child through art, it must be recognized that wide differences exist in abilities, controls, modes of working, and types of perception. Therefore, these differences should become factors along which a child's personality is guided.

Materials and tools for the art program should be ample and varied to ensure that each child will find his own way of expression. In practice, this is not a difficult matter when the right teacher and proper understanding exist.

The elementary-school years are crucial ones. In planning for and with children, it is essential that honest approaches and developmental activities be used in preference to stereotyped means and extraneous devices. Te latter will hamper future development.

Above all, it is significant to point out again that art is for all children and that the potentialities of each must be fully developed. Only thus is the social obligation of art education adequately met.

TABLE 5.　General Growth Expectancies in Art for the Elementary School

		Grade Level						
		K	1	2	3	4	5	6
Development of the Symbols	Children scribble or manipulate materials in uncontrolled, later in controlled, fashion. Scribbles and forms represent what and how children *feel*, to some degree what they *know*, and how things *appear* to them. They are searching for adequate symbols and forms.	X	X	X				
	Symbols for house, tree, people appear early: circle for head, longitudinal line for arms and legs. Striking similarity of symbols for same objects among all children. Same symbol may be used for several objects: the circle is for head, sun, wheel. Facial parts are similar for people and animals.	X	X					
	Logical appearance rather than visual is common.	X	X	X	X			
	Gradual change of symbol by addition of parts.	X	X	X				
	Development of personalized symbol for objects.	X	X	X				
	Symbols characterized by "geometric" appearance.				X	X		
	Geometric symbol insufficient; new symbol shows interest in parts of the body, joints, folds. Inception of realistic appearance.					X	X	X
	Awareness and knowledge of self and others spur quest for more adequate representation. Analytical realism is evident in work of children. Attention to creative type is important.						X	X
Manipulation and Control	Very important for young children. It represents *play* and pleasure, also gain in control and what materials will or will not do. Color, line, form, texture are used at first without meaning. With older children it becomes adventure and experiment.	X	X	X	X	X	X	X
	Controlled arrangement of line, form, color, texture should occur by first grade. Pattern or "design" feeling should be manifest by first grade and grow with each grade.		X	X	X	X	X	X
	Imagination suggests that designs can have meaning: "my dream," "a parade," etc.			X	X	X	X	X
	Organized arrangements of line, form, color, textures result in "designs." Experimentation with several media is desirable. Moods and feelings are interpreted; dance rhythms and music aid in imaginative conceptions.				X	X	X	X
	By varying materials, such as crayon, water color, chalk, children from third grade upward develop personal modes of expression. This is a necessity by fourth and fifth grade, when control and manipulation are con-					X	X	X

		Grade Level
		K 1 2 3 4 5 6

		K	1	2	3	4	5	6
	sciously purposeful and interest in subject and product are keener.							
	Ability to name and use primary colors and color schemes.	X	X					
	Ability to name, mix, and use secondary and intermediate colors.				X	X	X	X
	Ability to handle clay or a substitute to make thumb pieces and objects by adding and taking away clay; later to shape animals, people, and objects.	X	X	X	X	X	X	X
	Ability to use a variety of materials—weaving, block printing, papier-mâché, various color media, and several simple tools—increases with interest and manipulative ability.							
Meaning	Scribbles and forms are created at random without apparent meaning. Children usually tell "stories" from their scribbles; different stories are told from the same scribble or form. Change in symbol by added details.	X	X					
	Naming of symbol usually occurs by end of kindergarten or by first grade.	X	X					
	Overlapping of forms may occur; when it does, it represents superior perception. Later it is used more frequently by more children.			X	X	X	X	X
	Inside-outside appearance of a house, and simultaneous happenings in the same drawing, may be looked for in first grade. The extent of what children see and draw is indicative of growth from grade to grade.			X	X	X		
	Characteristics and details in animals, people, objects, buildings observed and used more extensively as children develop.				X	X	X	X
	Action of people or animals is noticed; position of body is attempted. In the fifth and sixth grades this becomes even more significant: joints, folds, action line.				X	X	X	X
	Contrasts of dark and light become common to show form.				X	X	X	
	Shading appears in the work of some children to gain round or solid appearance. The concept of form or solidity grows steadily through the sixth grade.				X	X	X	X
	Interpretation of mood and feeling is a reflection of growing personalities from fourth grade upward, and should be encouraged.					X	X	X
	Sensitiveness to line, form, color, and texture may be expected from fifth grade or in varying degrees. It increases in significance by sixth grade. Varied materials aid this phase of development.						X	X

295

		Grade Level						
		K	1	2	3	4	5	6
Gradual Changes	Gradual change in relative completeness and characteristics of people, animals, and objects should be expected as children grow in knowledge of the environment. To the head and legs are added a body, arms, fingers, and a double line for arms and legs. The extent and rapidity of changes is an index of growth.	X	X	X	X	X	X	X
	Logical approach continues, but symbols for some objects begin to change with greater knowledge of structure and details.		X	X	X	X	X	X
	Awareness of picture plane is constantly growing so that parts are often off by the edges of the paper; relation between ground and sky is realized and represented.			X	X	X	X	X
	Conscious planning is shown by the selection and placement of objects. Perspective appearance in planning indicates greater maturity.				X	X	X	X
	Upsurge of interest in representation of characteristics of people, animals, situations. Observation of real things and memory drawings are stimulating.				X	X	X	X
	Children realize that they are part of environment. Their work shows their relation to space. Earth and sky become separate identities.					X	X	X
	Observation becomes keener with each grade. Posed model and actual environment develop observation and skills.					X	X	X
Space and Form Concepts	Objects are at first placed on paper at random; in clay the objects are arranged without particular order.	X						
	By first grade things are related to space by a ground line; the sky is a strip of color at the top of paper; by the end of first grade a second base line may appear to indicate near and far. So far there is no concept of a vantage point: above or below or at eye level. Several views are logical to the child. This may continue into fourth grade.		X	X	X	X		
	Picture plane may be realized by the second grade when, unconsciously, there may be a foreground, middleground and background in painting. The concept continues to grow.			X	X	X	X	X
	Two base lines may appear by the second grade as evidence of growth. Placing of objects in zones, one above another, suggests objects near and far. They may be of same size; some children begin to place things in front or back of each other.			X	X	X	X	X

296

		Grade Level						
		K	1	2	3	4	5	6
	By third grade, children may continue to use ground lines, but sky or background are extended to the top of the drawing. Space division of ground is more varied. Several ground lines may appear. Objects are usually drawn in front view.				X	X	X	X
	Vertical objects on horizontal plane often represented as lying down when several base lines are used.				X	X		
	The ground line is transformed into a horizon line; objects are suggested in distance by overlapping. Some children begin to make distant objects smaller. Some disregard the horizon line, but make objects higher and smaller on the picture plane; details in foreground; use of dark and light appears in fourth grade.				X	X	X	X
	Perspective appearance may be used by few pupils, but not by all. It is a gradual development from third grade on.				X	X	X	X
	Overlapping of planes to suggest distance becomes more general. This may appear in third grade, but certainly by the fourth.					X	X	X
	Fifth-graders may persist in drawing objects from several points of view in the same picture. However, they begin to notice that lines on receding planes appear to come together; that the eye level rises or lowers as their position changes; that lines slant down if plane is above eye level or up if plane is below eye level.						X	X
	Dark and light (shading) to show things near and far, sensitive use of color for conscious emotional effect, and the development of "individual" technic and a sense of form cumulate by sixth grade.						X	X
Proportions	This concept is foreign to young children; *importance* determines size. Exaggeration of head, hands, feet, or other parts of drawing indicates emotional importance. Omission of parts or details means lack of importance for the child.	X	X	X				
	Closer relations to reality, detail, and color. Develop by end of first grade and increase in a normal way.		X	X	X	X	X	X
	Proportion and action are noticed by few fourth-graders, become important in fifth grade, and continue to interest older children.					X	X	X

297

For Discussion and Activity

1. On what grounds can it be claimed that art education is the rightful heritage of every child? What psychological evidences and what social factors bolster this contention?
2. If the child is to be permitted to create unhindered by adult influences, what is the function of the classroom teacher or of the art teacher? Answer in detail and cite authority.
3. What special functions are served by the visual arts that cannot be served through other means of education?
4. Since children differ widely among themselves in rate and quality of growth, how can the elementary teacher differentiate her art program?
5. If you believe that a pattern of growth is evident in all children, what particular directions of growth would you look for in evaluating a child's progress through art?
6. What meanings can be attached to the omission of certain details or emphasis of certain other details in a child's drawing?
7. What value do you attach to the general characteristics of so-called average children? How does a knowledge of these aid the teacher? How are these same characteristics reflected in the art curriculum?
8. To what extent and under what conditions do you feel that the correlation of art with other learnings is defensible? Present arguments for and against this approach to art activities. Do the same for the unit of teaching.
9. What is subject matter in art? What is its source? How is it implemented for stimulation in the classroom?
10. What arguments for or against contests and competitions can you advance? A debate on this subject might be quite revealing.

For Further Reading

Alschuler, Rose H., and Hattwick, La Berta W., *Painting and Personality,* Chicago, University of Chicago Press, 1947, Part I, Chapters 6, 7, 8.

Bannon, Laura, *Mind Your Child's Art,* New York, Pellegrinin and Cudahy, 1952. The entire book is 62 pp.

Burrows, Alvina Treut, *Teaching Children in the Middle Years,* Boston, D.C. Heath and Company, 1952, Chapters I, II, III, and XII.

Cane, Florence, *The Artist in Each of Us,* New York, Pantheon Books, 1951, Chapter XV.

Cole, Natalie R., *The Arts in the Classroom,* New York, The John Day Company, 1942, Chapters I, II, and III.

Gaitskell, Charles D. and Margaret R., *Art Education in the Kindergarten,* Peoria, Charles H. Bennett Company, 1952, Chapters II, III.

Keiler, Manfred L., *Art in the Classroom*, Lincoln, University of Nebraska Press, 1951. The book is intended as a practical help in determining art activities of children and methods of stimulation.

Lowenfeld, Viktor, *Creative and Mental Growth*, rev. ed., New York, The Macmillan Company, 1952, Chapter I.

Mathias, Margaret, *Art in the Elementary School*, New York, Charles Scribner's Sons, 1929, Chapters I, II, V, VII.

Mendelowitz, Daniel, *Children Are Artists*, Stanford, Stanford University Press, 1953, Chapters I–V.

Pearson, Ralph, *The New Art Education*, New York, Harper & Brothers, 1941, Chapters I–II.

Shultz, Harold, and Shores, Harlan, *Art in the Elementary Schools*, Urbana, University of Illinois Press, 1948, Chapters I, IV.

Winslow, Leon L., *Art in Elementary Education*, New York, McGraw-Hill Book Company, 1942, Chapters I, II.

ART EDUCATION IN THE JUNIOR HIGH SCHOOL

> The changes occurring at this time enhance rather than diminish the student's ability. Feelings deepen, minds awaken; a great new hunger and thirst for life, understanding, experience, and expression take place. The desire and need to create are there; the fault lies rather in the quality of the teaching.
>
> Florence Cane,
> *The Artist in Each of Us*

THE JUNIOR HIGH SCHOOL PUPIL

THE PROBLEM OF ADOLESCENCE

THE COMPLAINT IS GENERALLY MADE THAT ADOLESCENTS ARE A DIFFICULT group to teach, a difficult group to lead, a difficult group to understand. It is all very true. But therein lie major challenges to a master teacher. What are the causes that make young people of this age group act, react, and feel as they do? Additional challenges are corollaries and may also be stated in the form of questions. How can teachers find the best possible means of helping adolescents grow through their anxious years? How can teachers guide so that pupils may achieve their best desires? How can these young people be led to see clearly and act confidently upon personal and social problems? How can their learning and experiencing be guided so that doubts may be dispelled, self-esteem built up, wholesome relationships established, and reintegration achieved?

The seriousness of the problems of adolescence is widely admitted, but rather superficial attention is given to it in practice. This makes it imperative that the plight of the young people involved and the critical nature of this period in their lives be reiterated and reconsidered again and again.

The Function of Art Experience

Art teachers have a particularly significant role to play in seeking answers to the questions propounded above. Together with teachers in other creative fields, they can offer adolescents those means of expression that will assuage the difficulties encountered by pupils. But even more, art can put to immediate use, in a positive manner, the urges and the energies so typical of this group. Perchance, through self-expression they may be led to self-discovery, self-esteem, and self-adjustment. If this can be accomplished to any appreciable degree, the behavior changes that will have taken place will justify whatever efforts have been made in that direction. Indeed, as the Gaitskells point out, if art teachers can engage the attention of young adolescents to take part in a well-planned program, a degree of stability may be established.[1]

However, to bring out only what is there, on the surface or even somewhat below it, is to demean the true power of art. The years represented by the junior high school are critical in terms of the future of a pupil. The subsequent development of his attitudes, indeed, of his outlook on life, is also involved. Therefore, art should present a challenge to juniorhigh-school boys and girls as well as a pleasant path toward growth. The prevalent attitude of assuming that this is the period of decline in artistic output should be taken to mean that stimulation must be sharpened and purposive education must replace the more expressive mode. If art is the powerful urge that it is held to be, surely the need is to discover the motivations of pupils and then build a program to match them. Understanding of adolescent problems should not be construed as slackening of effort to educate pupils. Art activities are of many types; some come closer to what is real in life, in terms of practicality and of utility.

---

[1] Charles D. and Margaret R. Gaitskell, *Art Education During Adolescence*, New York, Harcourt, Brace and Company, 1954, p. 5.

302   Perhaps in such activities teachers may discover the needed "bridge" to the time of creative renascence of junior-high-school boys and girls.

In the course of this discussion, many activities will be suggested; many of them will be found useful as problem solving or reflective learning. They may have less glamour as "art," but may constitute the bridge referred to a moment ago.

The Critical Years

Generally speaking, boys and girls within our concern at this level of growth are in the seventh, eighth, and ninth grades in school and are between the chronological ages of 11 and 14. In some sections of the country, the practice has been to extend junior high school to include tenth grade. These young people are no longer children, for they are too big for that; but neither are they adults, much as they wish to be. They are somewhere between those two categories and feel very uncomfortable in their situation. Perhaps no group of pupils will show as much variation and as many differences among its members. Even though their chronological ages may be nearly the same, some are big and some are small, some are short and some are tall; some undergo the physical and emotional changes of adolescence early and some late. Yet they may all be perfectly normal, each in his own being.

Furthermore, it is generally agreed that there is much more than physiological change to make these years difficult ones for the pupils. There are, in addition, the social concerns of youth, the problem of values, and the establishment of selfhood. For these reasons, it is neither simple nor practical to set down specifics that will apply to all junior-high-school pupils equally. For a broad understanding of the situation, however, the general statements which follow are indicative of the crisis which all adolescents are undergoing in varying degrees. The general statements also infer that these children need not only wide and sympathetic understanding but also definite help in their struggle to overcome their problems.

General Characteristics of Adolescents

In general, the following characteristics may be noticed by most teachers:

1. *Physical.* The bodily development of adolescents is spasmodic although rapid, constantly changing, and therefore causing the appearance of self-consciousness and some awkwardness.

2. *Social.* Adolescents strive for acceptance and work diligently, in their own way, for the approval of members of their group. They resent adult authority, parental or otherwise, and are prone to want to rebel and to cut loose. Yet they follow the cultural pattern of their families with some normality.

3. *Emotional.* They are very unstable. They have not yet mastered self-control and self-discipline, yet they long for independent action. They are aware of injustices, inequalities, and differences, but are not yet able to resolve these fundamental relationships. Most junior-high-school children feel insecure, yet they are idealistic and tend to be overly critical of themselves and of others.

4. *Creative.* Junior-high-school pupils are at the point where sharpened vision and accumulated knowledge of the immediate environment make them keenly aware of the world and of things as they are. Throughout elementary school, "free" expression has been accepted as valid by teachers and by themselves. But the new sense of visual realism, which is partially natural and partially induced by observation of the work of adults, leads them to the conclusion that they cannot express themselves adequately with regard to the technical perfection they see in the work of adults or in featured works of art in general. This is the chief reason for the prevalent discouragement and the apparent lack of interest in art that teachers find at this level.

5. *Mental.* The acceleration of physical growth and the utilization of various types of knowledge make junior-high-school pupils inquiring persons. They are eager to learn, to explore, to experiment, to "find out" for themselves; their curiosity operates to their advantage because almost any lead will send them seeking for more experience. This eagerness, coupled to the dissatisfaction with their knowledge of and ability in art processes and technics, is one of the clues to what teachers might do by way of motivation and stimulation to offset dissatisfaction and build self-confidence.

Table 6 is a summary of what has been presented up to this point. It also indicates how some of the needs of junior-high-school children may be met.

TABLE 6. Adolescents Are That Way
(Grades 6–9)

Chief Characteristics	Major Interests	Significant Needs	Usual Responses	Effective Stimulation
1. Very enthusiastic 2. Feel "frustrated" 3. Resentful of authority 4. Zest for "reform" 5. Adventurous 6. Physical changes rapid 7. Energetic, even pugnacious 8. Lacking self-confidence 9. Self-assertive 10. Tendency toward realism 11. Interested in opposite sex 12. Critical awareness high 13. Strong desire to "belong" 14. Attention-span wavers 15. Seeking approval of group 16. Argumentative 17. Wavering creative powers, attitudes, interests 18. Desire to "grow up" 19. Idealistic	*Themselves:* Explore own capacities Discover own personality Discover own special talents Make the most of own appearance Aware of physical self *Contemporaries:* Their needs and desires Their social life Making friends Planning together Working together Playing together Participating in group activity (clubs, gangs, parties) *Their Families:* Relationship to siblings Share in family work Proper place in social life of family Realization of parental authority Give and take at home *Vocations:* Admire some adults Think of home, marriage, and a position Study of requirements in terms of own ability	1. Self-confidence 2. Heterosexual adjustment 3. Coördination and control: mental, physical, emotional 4. Independence of action 5. Recognition by own group 6. Adult treatment 7. Responsibility 8. Sense of belonging: family, club, church 9. Social acceptance 10. Guidance in choice of vocation, curriculum, personal action	1. Coöperation 2. Eagerness to plan 3. Acceptance of leadership within group 4. Flexibility to adjust to role in group 5. Aim to please 6. Interest in vocations 7. Acceptance of responsibility	1. Exploratory vocational experiences 2. Allow to plan own program and activities with guidance 3. Provision of opportunity for strong aptitudes 4. Discussion groups 5. Confidential and personal conferences 6. Opportunity to meet opposite sex socially 7. Self-evaluation 8. Setting up personal goals 9. School journeys, camping, short trips 10. School campaigns, group and community projects 11. Use of varied expression and media 12. Praise and encouragement

Administratively, most school systems today operate on what is known as the 6–3–3 plan, although, as indicated, they may operate on the 6–4–2 plan. This simply means that after six years of elementary education, boys and girls progress to a three-year school, which, in theory, acts as a bridge between elementary school and senior high school. There are, however, school systems which still operate on the 8–4 plan; this plan makes elementary schooling eight years in length and secondary school-

GUIDANCE is a most essential part of teaching in the junior high school. Career conferences, teacher-pupil planning, personal interviews, and individualized programming are desirable means of helping younger adolescents discover their proper role (Career Conference, Campus Junior High School, State Teachers College, Kutztown, Pa.).

ing four years. These facts should be uppermost in the minds of teachers because, assuming that the reasons for establishing the junior high school are basically sound, then it becomes necessary for teachers of art to think differently of pupils in seventh, eighth, and ninth grades than they would of pupils in the six years of elementary school, irrespective of the administrative organization of the school.

On the other hand, it would be a fallacy of the first order to interpret any of the administrative setups indicated above as meaning that each of the three stages of school life are absolute and unalterable stopping points. The education of boys and girls, much as their total growth pattern, is most effective and best understood as a continuum. Indeed, a glance at the actual enrollment of any junior high school will show overlapping of both chronological age and grade sequence. This is indicative of the fact that children develop at various paces and often without regard to grade-age placement. Therefore, to abandon completely, or even partially, the philosophy of freedom and the acceptance of personal expression at the end of any period of schooling might well be disastrous for the pupils concerned and for art education.

Bridging the gap between childhood and adolescence is not an easy task. Actually, many seventh-graders may still be in the throes of early adolescence and, therefore, undue pressures and lack of understanding, added to the newness of the school situation, may have lasting, harmful effects.

Educational Implications

It is best to think of the junior high school in terms of the biological and psychological characteristics enumerated at the beginning of this chapter. In a sense, they were and remain the basic reasons for the establishment of such an institution. Up to the sixth grade, it is reasonably feasible to deal with the growth and development of pupils within one administrative organization. But beyond that level, the many-faceted and more complex pattern of growth of the older pupils makes it clear that preadolescents and early adolescents need a different type of organization, special guidance, and a flexible curriculum. Their educational needs and physical growth as well as their social outlooks and personal problems demand an institutional organization that is geared to this difficult time of life. Furthermore, the equipment and the atmosphere of the elementary school, as compared to the almost "grown-up" situation of the senior high school, have suggested an easier and less-abrupt transitional period in which early adolescents may gradually adjust to the more serious ways and pursuits of secondary education.

A keyword in junior high school education is *guidance;* another may be *harmonization.* As one ponders the characteristics of these boys and girls, it becomes evident that merely bringing out what is within them will not suffice. They need help in harmonizing with the environment, and in relating what they learn and what they express to the world as well as to the self.

Table 6 is an attempt to picture a typical junior-high-school pupil. Its study may help teachers in the formulation of art programs adequate to meet the needs of pupils and thus help them to grow creatively and as socialized human beings.

The problems of the junior high school have lately received further attention by the United States Office of Education. One of its recent publications[2] points up many of the issues already broached in this chapter and makes definite suggestions for the successful handling of the task. The report is based on an analysis of 76 schools in 23 states.

All boys and girls in the junior-high-school group need a sense of security, worth, and responsibility, according to the study. They want love or affection from adults; they seek it both from their parents and from their teachers. The common needs of all seventh- and eighth-grade children, as reported by the United States Office of Education, are these:

1. Environmental conditions to maintain healthy, growing bodies.
2. Individualized program of activity and rest to nurture health and growth in every child.
3. Program of health services, practices, and instruction to secure for each individual optimum health, protection from disease and accident, and correction of defects, and to educate children in the care of their bodies.
4. Conditions to enable children to gain the affection and friendship of those upon whom they depend for the sense of security and worth and to develop the attitudes and skills which are fundamental to a sense of security.
5. A school program to meet the needs of each child, aiming ultimately at self-guidance or independence.
6. Curriculum opportunity to help each child grow continuously in basic academic skills, understandings, powers of expression, emotional resources, and working with others.

School administrators and teachers are urged to bring the parents into the school program. Reports and conferences are commonly used as a means of helping parents keep in touch with their child's progress and of helping both the parents and teachers better to understand the child.

---

[2] United States Department of Health, Education, and Welfare, *Educating Children in Grades Seven and Eight*, Washington, D.C., Office of Education, Bulletin 1954, No. 10.

In several schools conferences are held once a month on released time, usually provided by closing schools for two half-days or a whole day. One school provides for mothers who work out of the home to come after they have finished work. Teachers go to the homes when parents cannot be reached by these plans.

Most of the schools send home periodic reports on personality growth and scholarship achievements. One school finds it very helpful for the parent and teacher to sit down together to fill out a report for the child concerned. Other schools are substituting conferences for written reports.

IMPORTANT CONSIDERATIONS

In view of the educational problems facing both teachers and pupils at this level of growth, it would seem wise to focus attention on certain important considerations that may establish rapport between pupils and teachers and ensure an adequate measure of success in the artistic unfolding of the pupils. Among the crucial points to be considered are these: (1) the need for guidance, (2) the need for proper stimulation, (3) the need for producing satisfying products, (4) the need for personal harmonization with the group, (5) the need for significant activity, and (6) the need for social integration. Each of these major needs is discussed hereafter.

THE NEED FOR GUIDANCE

Although the necessity of providing guidance for young people is not confined to junior-high-school years, its role at this particular level of education is deemed paramount. It should be established that the purpose of guidance is to lead learners to make wise decisions in regard to a problem. The teacher, as counselor, does not impose a point of view, but questions, suggests, and stimulates thinking.

The uncertainties that arise with physical growth, the anxieties brought about by physiological changes, the emotional imbalance caused by social restraints in general, by parents, teachers, and the school, add up to a very uncomfortable existence for these young people. The results of this unhappy situation manifest themselves in several ways. Antagonistic attitudes toward adults, rules made by adults and adult institutions, are common at this level. The formation of groups referred to as "gangs" is another manifestation; but boys dislike girls and vice versa, hence the rise of "cliques" along the lines of sex. The desire for independence and for personal or group decisions is very strong. Actually, the antagonisms of these young people are symptoms of almost opposite needs: understanding, friendship, and personal acceptance. They strive for attention by whatever means seem plausible. Girls gradually become clothes-conscious and like social affairs such as dancing and parties; boys prefer sports and camping.

The latest rise in juvenile delinquency demonstrates again that the peak of conflict among gangs is between the ages of 10 to 11. The need, therefore, is for wide participation in guidance by all teachers; this is amplified by Gutekunst thus: "The program of guidance should take place in the administration as well as in the curriculum of the school."[3] Truly this is the period of *Sturm und Drang* and lasting adjustment depends on the seriousness of the guidance program.

It is not inferred that art can or should solve this problem alone. It is affirmed, however, that purposeful and creative outlets, such as the many activities involved in visual arts, can be implemented in an attempt to find some solutions to this vast problem.

Directed teaching was decried for its negative effects. A pupil needs to do his own thinking, choose his own materials, and reach his own conclusions; then only is he expressing himself fully. Furthermore, art is not merely self-expression; it is self-expression with a quality. It follows then that the function of guidance, or of teaching, is a quest for qualitative behavior.

Positive guidance differs from dictation in that it leads the pupil to see better ways and other meanings. It has the power of widening the horizons of a pupil, of broadening his outlooks and extending his insights. Guidance of the proper sort is a means at the disposal of teachers for the achievement of *quality* in thinking and, consequently, in expression. As guidance through art opens wider the horizons, other problems and issues, personal or social, are more likely to be appraised and handled in the same reflective manner.

---

[3] Josef Gutekunst, *A Guidance Program for a Four-Year Junior High School,* Master's thesis, Bethlehem, Pa., Lehigh University, 1949, p. 1.

310   THE NEED FOR PROPER STIMULATION

The meanings of stimulation and its varied types were discussed in Chapter 4. A brief review of that material may be of help toward a better understanding of its applications to the junior-high-school art program.

Most teachers of art have experienced the situation to which Lowenfeld refers emphatically: "This period in which the youth has neither an unconscious childish nor a conscious approach of self-expression is marked by a very profound crisis which sometimes shakes the whole self-confidence."[4] It has already been indicated that many pupils stop doing creative work at this period, and to offset this condition it is essential that art people recognize the crisis for the devastating force that it is.

It is usually agreed that, having identified the problem, its solution is not an unattainable goal. Perhaps a restatement of the problem in terms of its manifestations may prove worth while. First of all, it must be

---

[4] Viktor Lowenfeld, *Creative and Mental Growth*, New York, The Macmillan Company, 1952, p. 230.

SOCIAL SITUATIONS that have meaning for the pupil find ready response and coöperation from adolescents. Planning for school parties, decorating the cafeteria, creating a setting for a dance in the gymnasium, are types of significant activity. They often act as stimulants for other art activities (painting a Mural in the cafeteria, Junior High School, West Reading, Pa.).

realized that individuals are different, and, as already indicated, they differ in many ways from each other. But now a major variance appears, namely, the type of creativity. This fact should not surprise art teachers, since they are acquainted with the fact that differences among mature artists are vividly attested by the history of art, while differences among children are sustained by experience and research. Specifically, in art education one must distinguish between the *impressionistic* and the *expressionistic* types. Pupils of the first type are largely visual-minded; they absorb what comes within their sphere of experience through the physical senses. In the case of the visual arts, this type focuses attention first on appearance and general character, later on details of form, color, dark and light, and the finer nuances that together make the art object. Obviously, pupils who are visual-minded are also largely objective in their approach to art, be it creation or appreciation.

The expressionistic type is subjective in character and in approach. He reacts more readily to kinesthetic impressions, relies on touch and muscular sensations, and places value not so much on appearance as on feeling. Furthermore, personal identification with the work is generally obvious, since the expressionist takes part in the shaping of the creative work itself.

It follows that if the differentiation of creative types is recognized, the teacher-pupil relationship is likely to become a wholesome one rather than one of antagonisms. A teacher should make every effort to point out that a work of art differs from a work of nature and, therefore, any technical dissatisfaction that the pupil may feel regarding his work has no valid foundation. The teacher will also guide the pupil in the direction in which he inclines and will use every appropriate means to praise and to encourage.

Stimulation, then, will not be of a formal type but suited to the personal needs of the pupil, to his method of working, and to his inclination. This does not preclude certain disciplines which are calculated to challenge the pupil to self-appraisal and, ultimately, to self-improvement.

Whatever the case, it should be understood that these types are not mutually exclusive; therefore, it must be borne in mind that each pupil responds differently, and that stimulation must vary. This necessity does not exclude those broad types of stimulation that are found effective for group action and the setting up of group values.

THE NEED FOR PRODUCING SATISFYING PRODUCTS

Because the junior-high-school pupil has reached an intellectual capacity of consequence, the aesthetic elements and the true values of his work come under his very critical scrutiny. As he observes the work of his peers, of adults, and of artists, he reaches conclusions that are often the basis of his discouragement and loss of interest and self-esteem. Barclay-Russell goes to the heart of the problem when he says: "As the child grows into adolescence, the consciously intellectual, logical and critical faculties develop very quickly. As a result his natural reaction, encouraged by current educational belief, is to reject all standards which do not conform to a logical approach. Painting and drawing which are not photographically accurate in representation not only offend his ideas of art itself but tend to destroy the structure of confidence he is being encouraged to build upon purely intellectual conceptions of life and standards of judgement."[5]

It would be a serious misunderstanding of the philosophy of creative expression to continue, at this level, a tolerant attitude toward indifferent expression, shoddy, poorly designed, and badly executed works of art. As a matter of fact, constant upgrading of the quality of the work produced by children at any grade level is justified. The only limitation is the creative power of the individual pupil. Certainly, beginning with the seventh grade and on through the twelfth, the importance of the product is coequal with that of the art process.

The strong urge of adolescents to paint or draw or carve in such a way that the final product will look "real" is natural. Teachers should understand it for what it is and cope with it. This feeling is partly based upon pupils' observations of works by old masters and contemporary artists, and partly on prevalent taste, which runs in the direction of what is erroneously called realistic. Nevertheless, it poses a serious problem.

However, the readiness of most adolescents to intellectualize and their willingness to reason are characteristics which should be utilized by teachers. Pupils are ready to see, by comparison, that many familiar subjects by recognized masters are achieved differently. They will see that one mode is just as "real" as another; that one may contain more "feeling"

---

[5] A. Barclay-Russell, "Art and the Adolescent," in Edwin Ziegfeld (ed.), *Education and Art, A Symposium*, Paris, UNESCO, 1953, p. 46.

while another may strive for surface appearance. Class discussions on topics such as suggested above may dispel the notion that there is only one way of painting, carving, or modeling.

The same method of comparison, examination, and debate will show early adolescents that not all great artists produced works in the same technic, or conveyed the same feeling, but rather that each was expressing *himself*. Good reproductions or slides will help clarify the issues, so that when pupils look at their own work, or the work of their classmates, they will not be disturbed or unfavorably impressed but will accept them as *personal* expressions, as sincere statements of what the person sees and feels.

An elaboration of this approach to establish a sense of adequacy as well as an understanding of art may not only be helpful to the pupil who is concerned with producing art. It may also attract a pupil whose abilities are in other directions but who may be interested in art from a consumer point of view. Gauguin will be remembered for the patterns he created in his work, Van Gogh for his intensity of color and depth of feeling, Rouault because of his luminous color and the strong stained-glass delineation. Better still may be a comparison of similar subjects, such as *Madonna and Child* by various artists.

By these methods, and others equally convincing, junior-high-school pupils may realize that they are not inferior, incapable, and futile, but that they are individuals of worth, with their own way of saying what they feel or see, and that their contribution has validity as personal idiom. It is also likely that in time pupils may identify themselves with masters, modern or old, classical or contemporary, who belong to their particular creative type: visual, haptic, lyrical, or other. When that happens and teacher or classmates point it out, the pupils concerned will feel more adequate. Furthermore, if their work wins the approbation of others, students have a taste of the self-confidence and self-esteem which they so much need and seek.

Another problem is: How can teachers best exemplify integrity, truth, honesty, and other personal and social qualities that these young people strive to attain? A product, to rise to the quality that makes it art, must be an honest expression in terms of the concepts, treatment of materials, composition, and whatever other considerations may be involved. Imitations of the ideas of others and the camouflaging of ma-

314   terials with colors or surface ornamentation are two common classroom problems. A pupil can be made to see that the textures and the natural color of materials should be exploited rather than hidden, and that the composition should be his very own. When such positive guidance is offered, pupils may be led to see the relationship of honesty in expression, in design, in composition, and the rest to other situations in life. This is frequently done in the study of the novel or other types of literary art. Boys and girls observe and sense the presence or absence of the qualities of honesty and integrity in the words, works, and attitudes of adults. Another example might be the insistence that there are standards of excellence for each individual, and that neither teacher nor pupil should be satisfied until full expectation is reached.

Here are some questions to ponder: Are the activities challenging? Are standards of workmanship high enough? Have personal goals been established? Do pupils respect their own work? Are the results of such aesthetic excellence as to evoke genuine appreciation in the pupil artist, his classmates, his parents, and his friends?

THE NEED FOR PERSONAL HARMONIZATION WITH THE GROUP

One of the chief claims of art is that it is a means of self-discovery and of subsequent self-identification with environment. The work of psychologists such as Naumburg[6] and others have pointed out how potent a factor art can be in affecting the reintegration of people. Even though art teachers are neither psychologists nor psychiatrists by training, they have observed the therapy of art for a long time. Therefore, under typical conditions they need only utilize the arts to help pupils achieve a measure of personal and social adjustment.

A typical junior-high-school class will represent most of the degrees of emotional variations which are observed among so-called normal groups. The situation suggests that teachers should recognize pupil characteristics such as were listed in the early part of this chapter, and make conscious efforts toward the achievement of the larger objectives of education.

Although the significance of personal worth needs to be emphasized,

---

[6] Margaret Naumburg, *Schizophrenic Art: Its Meaning in Psychotherapy*, New York, Grune and Stratton, 1950.

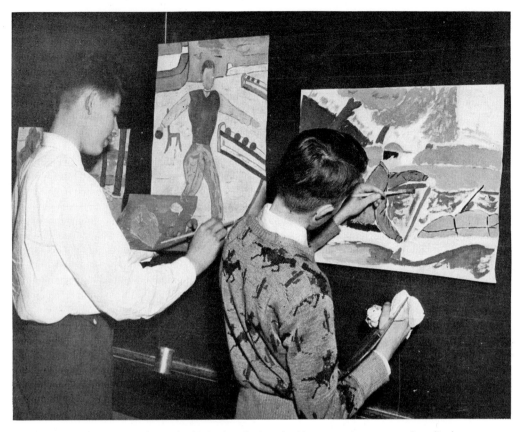

ADOLESCENT INTERESTS are a basic criterion in the selection of subject matter in contrast to formalized, teacher-planned activities. Pupils should be participants in the selection of activities in order to keep interests alive and to promote genuine growth (picturemaking, Maurice Cody School, Toronto, Canada).

it is equally important that individual pupils learn to identify themselves with the group. In the arts, therefore, personal expression and group undertakings are a balance that must be sought as teacher and pupils plan single activities, units, the work of an entire semester, or for the year. It is through guided contacts and socialized experiences that junior-high-school boys and girls find many of the answers to their perplexing problems.

THE NEED FOR SIGNIFICANT ACTIVITY

Unless pupils recognize that the activities in which they engage have personal meaning or social worth, their interest is likely to lag. It is in this particular respect that many of the activities of traditional art programs fail.

Not long ago, a simple questionnaire was submitted to the eighth-graders of a junior high school for the purpose of discovering what they thought about art classes. Following are some of the negative statements taken from the unsigned returns:

> I hate to make all-over patterns. We make them every year.
> Who cares about color wheels? I don't.
> Everything we make is on paper and it's never real.
> I like to work with clay, but the teacher says it's messy.
> When I paint something the way I think, I don't like the teacher correcting it all the time the way she wants it.

On the positive side there were many excellent statements that point out why young people like art. Among them:

> I feel moody sometimes and I paint the sky just the way I feel, and then it's all over.
> When I put the monogram on my jacket, it looked pretty good. Then I put monograms on the other kids' jackets.
> The reason I like art is because you can use it in so many ways at home, in the club, and I even made a picture for church school.
> When I saw my drawing in the school paper I felt good. Everybody said it was good.

A comparison of the two sets of statements raises questions concerning the validity of some art activities. At the same time it attests to the effectiveness of much that is being accomplished by understanding teachers.

Teacher-pupil planning, it was pointed out, is a method of achieving satisfying results because implicit in the method there is willing acceptance by the pupil. Even more, there is understanding, a feeling of the worth-whileness of the activities involved, and, finally, there is the feeling of shared responsibility. But beyond the spirit of the approach, it is likely that what the pupil has suggested has meaning for *him*.

THE NEED FOR SOCIAL INTEGRATION

Group activities are calculated to guide pupils in their effort to develop coöperation, a sense of the worth of individual contributions to the group, mutual respect, the development of acceptable social behavior, and the making of friendships. At the junior-high-school level, understanding of and acceptance by the opposite sex need definite

guidance. It would appear that art activities and the less-traditional atmosphere of the art laboratory, by bringing together boys and girls to
make decisions, to discuss, to share and compare, should be of particular
value.

However, social coöperation means more than sociability and good
manners. It means understanding of social problems, of mores, of institutions, of rights and responsibilities, and of the democratic pattern
of living. The concern of adolescents along these lines is a well-established
fact. Therefore, it is important that art education should assume its
proper role in this area. Art is a medium through which judgments, values,
and purposes can be realized by the very act of creating or by the development of appreciations for the elements of specific situations. Some ways
in which art activities can be organized to help solve some of these needs
are presented later on in this chapter.

GENERAL SCOPE OF THE ART PROGRAM

It has been shown that the complicated nature of the adolescent makes
it difficult for teachers to cope with the problem. Nevertheless, an art
curriculum can be implemented in such a manner that its contents and
spirit may be of help to pupils beyond the art product itself. Dangers to
be avoided are a matter-of-fact attitude, or an unsuited and stereotyped
program of the preplanned and teacher-dominated type. The needs
suggest an individualized approach to art experiences through which
positive guidance can accomplish the most for each pupil.

There are many excellent course-of-study guides at state levels, and
many more at the local level. Such materials are worthy of careful
study because they represent coöperative efforts and, generally, sound
thinking. However, the preparation and implementation of any program
is, in the final analysis, in the hands of the teacher. Thus he becomes
the key to the situation, and unless he is conversant and sympathetic
with the basic needs of junior-high-school pupils he cannot deal with
the problem with the sense of security that he seeks for his pupils.

BROAD DIRECTIONS

Consonant with what has been presented thus far regarding the nature
of the junior-high-school pupil, some broad directions for an art program

are proposed simply as a framework upon which to base classroom activities.

As each broad direction is developed, it should become apparent, in terms of the psychology of adolescence, that the program must recognize these significant elements: deepened understandings of art and of life; extended appreciation of art as it functions in experience; and widened powers of perception. All these will be evidenced in broadened concepts and outlooks as well as in improved skills in handling of materials.

The Directions Defined

1. *Art activities should provide for the continuous development of each individual pupil.* This direction calls attention to two significant factors. The first is the need for continuity in the belief that freedom and creative development are integral. What was believed wholesome for children in the elementary school continues to be true of slightly older brothers and sisters. But the teacher must make the transition with the pupils, and art experiences must be arrived at through teacher-pupil understanding of the problems involved. The second factor points up the significance of each pupil as an individual, endowed as no one else in the entire class. He brings whatever talents, whatever experience, and whatever shortcomings he has inherited or acquired. As a person he has his own contributions to make and his own way of expressing himself. These two factors are tremendously important in determining to what degree the adolescent will realize his worth and feel that he has a place in the sun.

How will his work be evaluated? Can he be guided into art activities in which he can taste a measure of success? How can he be helped to adjust to and improve his own level? How can he be helped to contribute to his group?

2. *Art activities should develop assurance, pride, and confidence in each pupil.* This is to say that the art activities of the junior high school should develop in each individual assurance, pride, and confidence in self and others. What has been inferred earlier concerning the insecurity and lack of confidence evidenced at this level indicates that adult overcritical attitudes toward what pupils achieve seldom build up and often tear down the confidence of early adolescents. Reference has been made to the fact that this is the period when a creative slump occurs. This is

largely due to dissatisfaction brought about by the sharpened critical awareness on the part of boys and girls. By contrast, it should be emphasized that creativity and the use of the imagination are at their height at this same time of life. Obviously, then, here is where masterful guidance, proper motivation, and stimulation will play their largest role. Encouragement, suggestions, and practical examples of solutions to art problems encountered will build up the confidence and the respect for the self that pupils need.

Wise decisions in the selection and execution of art experiences should assume a major role in the pupil-teacher relationship. The chief task of the teacher now is to ensure a measure of success for each pupil, to build faith in his own abilities, and to develop wholesome self-criticism which may lead to self-improvement.

3. *Art activities should encourage each pupil to search for the technics that will facilitate expression.* This is in line with the increased awareness and sense of reasoning characteristic of this age group. It is a direction that leads into somewhat controversial ground, and yet it is so important that its proper understanding may determine the further success or failure of pupil and teacher. The tendency to switch from schematic and geometric symbols to visual realism, which seems to satisfy the critical awareness of early adolescence, raises the question of technics, of more mature modes of expression, and of aesthetic qualities. In general, teachers have been prone to follow their own artistic bent and the traditionally accepted ways of painting, drawing, and modeling. If expression is to mean what its definition implies, "to bring out," the pupil must be given the latitude he needs in order to express himself as he feels. The *realism* referred to here, and which is characteristic of pupils at this level of growth, does not mean "photographic" or "imitative" of nature. It means sharpened visual conceptualization; and if that is the natural mode of the pupil, it is acceptable and deserves the teacher's approval and nurturing. How this can be accomplished without handing down a technic is to realize the true role of the teacher, namely, a guide and counselor.

The urgent need, at this level, is to discover how problems can be solved so that they may result in works of art satisfying to the creator. Therefore, the teacher must be conscious of the need and send the pupil on a search for technical solutions through experimentation and observa-

tion. While the function of the teacher is to evoke ideas and concepts, he is also duty bound to guide the pupil in arriving at successful ways of handling technics, controlling of materials and the aesthetic means of line, color, form, texture, mass, and all the rest. Works of modern as well as of old masters will serve admirably for purposes of analysis, for their possibilities in increasing appreciation, and as examples of how technical problems have been solved by other artists.

The physical and emotional changes through which adolescents are passing are accompanied by conceptual changes as well. No longer will the productions of childhood satisfy. Pupils are now painfully but surely acquiring the status and outlook of young adults. Therefore, they will be satisfied only with results that exhibit the characteristics of maturity, even though subject matter may be of their own time and interests. The product as well as the process are now of equal significance.

The teacher's fear of suggesting too much, of interfering with the natural growth of pupils, and of imposing adult standards may be over-emphasized. Actually, this attitude results in a passive kind of school-keeping that is neither teaching nor guidance. Ultimately, it causes pupils to fall into a period of regression from which they may never re-cover. Junior-high-school boys and girls need to be actively guided to-ward the solution of their problems so that they may face the crisis of adolescence with vigor and assurance.

4. *Art activities should stimulate each pupil to solve creative and aesthetic problems*, with full regard for his personal mode of expression, his social relationships, and his responsibilities. The important point here is that the teacher should make clear to the pupil that he is regarded as a person. As such he may exercise his right to freedom within the limita-tions of the environment. Erikson, in emphasizing the need for a sense of identity, says:

As is well known, adolescence is a period of storm and stress for many young people, a period in which the previous certainties are questioned and previous continuities no longer relied upon. Physiological changes and rapid physical growth provide the somatic base for the turmoil and indecision. It

THE CRAFTS offer many opportunities to explore various materials and ensure a well-balanced program for the junior high school. The wavering character of the pupil suggests that through many activities he may discover himself, appraise his abilities, and strive toward adjustment (*above*, clay modeling, 9th grade, Pittsburgh, Pa.; *below*, hand-loom weaving, 8th grade, Shelby, N.C.).

may be that cultural factors also play a part, for it has been observed that adolescence is less upsetting in some societies than in others.

The central problem of the period is the establishment of a sense of identity. The identity the adolescent seeks to clarify is who he is, what his role in society is to be. Is he a child or is he an adult? Does he have it in him to be some day a husband and father? What is he to be as a worker and an earner of money? Can he feel self-confident in spite of the fact that his race or religion or national background makes him a person some people look down upon? Over all, will he be a success or a failure? By reason of these questions adolescents are sometimes morbidly preoccupied with how they appear in the eyes of others as compared with their own conception of themselves, and with. how they can make the roles and skills learned earlier jibe with what is currently in style.[7]

A way for teachers to convey this feeling to pupils is first of all to abandon conventional procedures, old formulae, repetitious exercises to be done in a specified manner, rigid controls over technic, and other stifling procedures. These allow very little originality of approach or development of ideas, and have the tendency to belittle the pupil. This statement does not contradict what was maintained a moment ago; indeed it reinforces the previous direction in terms of supplying what is needed without imposing what is not wanted. Therefore, not all water-color painting need be "wet" or all "dry"; not all oil painting must of necessity be smooth; some of it is rough in texture, as when applied with the palette knife. Not all pottery need conform to Greek forms. These matters should be decided on a personal basis by the pupil rather than by the teacher. If the junior-high-school pupil is to develop a sense of identity, he is to be encouraged to develop his own style and his own controls over materials. Having achieved these, he should be made aware of his accomplishments and urged to further growth.

After having identified himself as a creative person, the pupil needs to be oriented toward the realization that he belongs to a group, be they boys, girls, or boys and girls. Moreover, he must be made conscious that he has responsibilities toward the group, the school, and the community. Many art experiences offer opportunities for personal identification and at the same time contribute to group solidarity. Leadership,

---

[7] Erik Erikson, *A Healthy Personality for Every Child*, Raleigh, Health Publication Institute, Inc., 1951, pp. 8–25.

coöperation, contacts, exchange of point of view, friendships, and other wholesome aspects of personality development may be achieved while working together. But, when this is true, it is also true that personal self-

expression is controlled and subordinated to the goals of the group. Group enterprises, such as assembly programs and community-improvement projects, are activities that contribute, in a real way, to solutions of the larger problems of personal and social relationships. They develop the general sense of adequacy, proper relationship between sexes, suitable language and demeanor, personal appearance, and emotional balance in general.

5. *Art activities should utilize the personal endowment and experiences of pupils, their widened interests, and their desire for a larger sphere of activity in many aspects of living.* The need that is pointed up in this direction is for art activities that have meaning in the life of a junior-high-school pupil. The significance of experience as a motivating force and as a means of evoking genuine art has been discussed elsewhere in this book; therefore, for the moment it may be assumed that experience is essential to worthy expression. The teacher may wish to ponder these questions: What are the experiences of most adolescents? What are their chief interests? What are their attitudes and ideals? If these questions can be answered with a modicum of understanding, then the art pro-

DRAWING AND PAINTING are popular with junior-high-school students, especially if through them pupils can identify themselves, indicate what they would like to be, or refer to classmates they admire (*above*, self-portrait, 9th grade, Allentown, Pa.; *below*, "Meet Me at the Fountain," 8th grade, Toronto, Canada).

grams may be designed to be of help to the boys and girls concerned.

Entertainment such as TV, motion pictures, and radio seems to occupy a great deal of the time of the pupils under consideration. These passive types of entertainment furnish the adolescent something akin to escape. They satisfy, they consume time pleasantly, they place the spectator in the role of hero, they usually end up happily or successfully, and they glamorize characters and situations. The "make-believe" seems to attract, simply because young adolescents are struggling to establish an ideal self. What is it they wish to be, and like whom? Guidance in the choice of programs may aid in preventing the escapism involved in any type of passive recreation and perhaps channel the interest in positive behavior.

Junior-high-school pupils like attractive clothes because they glamorize; they strive for the approval of their peers, enjoy their company, and seek their affection. These desires may also be channeled into positive behavior.

The inference to be drawn is that the right sort of an art program can also engage the interests of these young people. Early adolescents enjoy art activities that deal with the heroic, that spell success, that supply the feeling of adequacy, and that make them feel that they are treated as young adults who can assume responsibility and carry out commitments. In a general sense, solving the art needs of the school, of the community, and of the self may be avenues toward the solution of this particular phase of the problem of adolescence.

SUGGESTED IMPLEMENTATION OF THE PROGRAM

If the purpose of art education were training in the traditional art skills, the art teacher's task, being delimited, would be a simple one. But because several educational purposes of concern to all pupils must be served, only a broad and flexible guide may accomplish the desirable ends. The scope of the suggestions offered hereafter is to indicate how the broad directions suggested may be put to work. But they are not to be construed as an outline to be followed, except in principle.

INDIVIDUAL ACTIVITIES AND GROUP CONTRIBUTIONS

1. *Block cutting and printing* of subjects of individual choice, such as sports, holidays, holy days, club activities, camping, parties, and others

that denote action and participation. These individual works may be used as illustrations in school publications, to develop a design for drapery in the school cafeteria or the classroom, to make a school calendar, to develop a wall hanging for the entrance hall of the school, girls may apply the block print to material to be made into articles of wear or use in the home.

2. *Individual illustrations* of school activities, such as a dance, a party, the play, the game, the carnival. These individual works may well be combined into a frieze to decorate classrooms or main hall for a period of time, or they may become integral parts of posters to advertise the next dance, the party, or the game to townspeople and to the student body.

3. *Individual drawings* of the important buildings of the community, such as the town hall, the post office, the junior high school, the elementary school, the bank, the department store, the churches, and other structures of communal significance. These individual efforts may be combined into an album totaled "This Is Our Town," the drawings may constitute an exhibit in a store window in town, they may be developed into stylized stage settings as background for the annual play, or they may be reproduced as inserts in the school annual.

4. *Designing with assorted materials.* The likely results of this activity will be multifarious: imaginative animals, figures, birds, insects, and other forms. They may be used as table or desk ornaments, as lapel decorations for girls, as table favors, and for other useful purposes. Singly, they afford an opportunity to create from assorted materials unified and unique designs; as a group project they may serve as gifts to patients in hospitals for the holidays; they may be used as favors for P.T.A. or other school-group gatherings; they may be sold to raise funds for the school band, the school newspaper, or other plausible causes.

5. *Clay modeling* of figures: running, carrying books, playing an instrument, kicking the ball, wrestling, dancing, singing, praying, skating, reading, lounging, and other suitable poses. These individual efforts may be grouped for exhibitions; or may be grouped according to categories, such as "sports" or "the arts," and exhibited to promote participation in these activities; some may be cast for reproduction and sold to raise funds for worthy causes, or to purchase original works for the school.

ACTIVITIES CENTERING AROUND VOCATIONS

1. *Drawings and paintings* that deal with the subject "What I Want to Become." These will vary with each pupil and should lead to self-expression motivated by the real or transient interests of the youths. Some typical suggestions may be these:

At the barber (how he is dressed, tools he uses, atmosphere of shop)
At the bank (general appearance of locale, people at windows)
At the dentist (how he is dressed, tools he uses, reception room)
On the farm (farm machinery, animals, farmer at work)
At the office (any office, equipment, atmosphere)
At the milliner (the window, the interior, displays)
At the dressmaker (the window, the counter displays, special equipment)

2. *Model making* of vocational situations, including workers in action, made to scale. The subjects will be most varied, but for the sake of concreteness a few examples are listed:

Plowing the fields (power machinery, animals, people at work, the landscape)
At the lathe (man working, the machinery, type of atmosphere)
The artist at work (a studio interior, objects displayed, general atmosphere)
The bank teller (a portrait sketch, or a more general composition)
The airport (the general atmosphere, type of buildings, types of services)
The family garage (the workbench, various tools on wall)
The auto-repair shop (variety of machinery for special purposes, men at work)

3. *Decorative friezes and murals* dealing with the world's work. These activities may be developed into the more popular form of mural, or may be developed as large linoleum carvings which are later highlighted with color, or they may become the basis for plaster carvings or decorative medallions. Examples of suitable subjects are:

Gasoline—from the earth to your car
From grain to bread
Episodes from the lives of great scientists
The story of food, or clothing, or iron, or steel
Men of medicine or men of science
Public-service occupations
Careers in religious work

ACTIVITIES DEALING WITH SOCIAL LIVING

These may be done in many forms, such as painting, modeling, commercial art, three-dimensional displays, or decorative settings. Some subjects for stimulation may be:

Decorating the gym for the senior dance

Designing and making my Halloween costume and mask

Portrait of my partner at the Valentine party (painting or modeling)

"Come to the School Fair" (this could be conceived as a hall display with figures in action made in a variety of ways)

"If You Care How You Look" (this may be conceived as a series of posters dealing with posture, dress, hair styles, proper dress, proper manners, how to apply rouge and lipstick, and many other personal-social problems of concern to young people of this age group)

Mural or frieze or linoleum-block prints stimulated by the subject "We Are All Brothers," or "Of One Blood," or "The Freedoms We Cherish"

Designing with materials for the purpose of creating attractive, simple, but unusual party favors may be utilized in this activity. Texture pictures or decorations may also be developed in this manner.

ACTIVITIES DEALING WITH PERSONAL NEEDS

These activities will naturally range from pure self-expression to down-to-earth needs such as "How do I paint a monogram on my jacket?" The need for flexibility, consistent with growth, is obvious in this connection. It would seem futile to suggest experiences, but it may be of value to list some of the personal needs of boys and girls in junior high school:

Self-expression through preferred art media
Problems relating to personal appearance
Problems relating to one's home
Problems relating to one's art activities out of school
Problems relating to personal art activities in school

ACTIVITIES REQUIRING PARTICIPATION OF ENTIRE CLASS FOR SUCCESS

The need for association, for the development of coöperation and the sense of responsibility for the success of the whole group, and for experiencing the give-and-take of life under normal and healthy auspices make activities of this type especially desirable. Some suggestions may open the way to the vast number of possibilities.

Putting on a class play. The obvious requirements in this case call for organization of a stage crew, a costuming committee, a properties committee, a poster committee, a staging committee, and many others.

Patron's Day. This is variously handled and variously called in different parts of the country, but usually involves the organization of an entire class for ultimate success. Some activities involved might be the arrangement of the art exhibition, designing and producing the invitation, making attractive and meaningful signs to guide visitors, making favors and other decorations if a social hour is called for, and, finally, arranging for group demonstrations of art activities.

Planning and executing decorations for the class dance. There are many instances in which the otherwise bleak gymnasium is transformed into a South Sea island, a pirates' ship, or some other exotic locale. The need for such decorations can evoke really genuine art interest and may lead to other forms of expression of more serious types.

The school assembly. Many junior high schools assign to each class, department, or section the development of an assembly program. The art department could well utilize the energies and varied types of creative expression available in a class or section. There are the writers, the set designers, the actors, the costumers, the directors, the managers, all of them in the art classes. Everyone has a creative contribution to make to the success of the group. Additional types of experiences are simply listed below.

EXPERIENCES ENCOURAGING EXPLORATION OF UNTRIED MODES OF EXPRESSION

Instinctive pattern and rhythms developed into symbols of individual interests

Minglings developed into landscapes, suggesting moods, or stage sets for school plays and puppet shows

Finding interesting free forms in clay, wire, or rolled paper from which containers of various types may be created

Making use of unusual materials for traditional purposes, such as newspaper, screening, glass or rope for posters, murals, costumes, or masks

Painting with cotton, rolled paper, leather, feathers, grasses, etc., instead of brushes

Modeling with sand, snow, paper pulp

Trying some "resist" effects with crayon and water color, tie dye, wax on cloth, float oil paint on water, etch on copper or pewter

EXPERIENCES IN APPRECIATION

Evaluation of each pupil's work as a group experience

Discussion of trip to a museum, pooling sketches and visualization of a use for them

Giving individual illustrated reports on the most attractive home, shop window, factory, gas station in town

Holding a popularity vote to select pictures for the school from a loan exhibition of reproductions

Asking local artist to exhibit and discuss his work; planning the questions the group will ask about materials, processes, how he designs and markets his products

Visits to other school art exhibitions; have pupils demonstrate and talk about their work

FURTHER ASPECTS OF CURRICULUM PLANNING

The foregoing illustrations were intended to point up art experiences directly related to the needs and interests of junior-high-school pupils. However, it should not be assumed that what has been suggested is either inclusive or final in character. Indeed, the needs and interests of young people differ so widely that even the generally observed needs and interests that have been mentioned are altered by the conditions prevailing in specific situations. The social life of the community, its cultural climate, its provisions for young people, the religious and moral tone of the people, and other social and economic factors of necessity condition young people and, to a degree, are reflected in the art program and other phases of education. Therefore, attention may be called to certain other aspects of curriculum planning.

AREAS OF LIVING

As an approach to the art curriculum of the junior high school, areas of living rest on a very defensible basis. Industrial and agricultural localities are particularly sensitive to the fact that sooner or later their children will be assimilated in the life stream of the community and share in its work, its play, its worship, and its civic activities. By the same token, the boys and girls themselves are aware of the environmental forces. In reality, part of their struggle is to find out how they may fit into the pattern of adulthood as they see it about them.

Generally, the following areas of living may yield sufficient suggestions for art activities that will find response and creative action on the part of most pupils:

1. *Work:* trades, professions, services, labor
2. *Leisure:* hobbies, avocations, interests
3. *Industry:* designing, production, manufacture, processing
4. *Commerce:* distribution, advertising, purchasing, selling, display

5. *Citizenship:* government (local, state, national), participation, duties, rights, improvements
6. *Home:* making a home, building a home, furnishing a home, family life
7. *Worship:* moral and spiritual values, religion, church and temple, stained glass, music, religious art, ecclesiastical crafts
8. *Communication:* the spoken word, the written word, radio, TV, drama, visual arts, travel, transportation (sea, land, air)

It can be readily seen that the material suggested following each caption can be expanded and varied as determined by the actual interests and need of each pupil or of an entire group. Personal choice of subject, mode, and medium can be determined by individual pupils, and teacher-pupil planning can assume its proper role in the determination of activity areas. It is also clear that guidance opportunities must be gauged, in each instance, to attain maximum development for each student.

LEARNING THE LANGUAGE OF ART

By now it should have been made evident that, although it is essential to creative unfolding, freedom must be protected through positive guidance and coöperative planning. Contrariwise, it is possible, through lack of anticipation and planning, to restrict the freedom a teacher seeks for pupils. Therefore, it seems appropriate to give some attention to the meaning and function of art elements and principles. Principles and elements, especially at the junior-high-school level, can become the very means of articulation that pupils need in order to express themselves clearly and adequately.

Unfortunately, even today it is still common to find situations where principles and elements of art are taught in completely unrelated fashion. When this is done, the language of art becomes a set of rules, purfunctory exercises, and deadening formulas. It should be stated clearly, then, that art principles and elements, while important, are not ends in themselves but means through which art expression may be facilitated and may become intelligent communication. Baziotes, Kandinsky, and Picasso speak as intelligently as Raphael, although their use of elements and principles is different in each case: some is visual realism and some is abstraction.

The paramount question seems to be: How can these aesthetic means be taught so that pupils will understand them as dynamics of expression?

The answer will vary with each teacher and will be affected by his experience, background, and resourcefulness. Nevertheless, an attempt is made here to point a direction toward possible answers.

Color, line, mass, texture, form, and space are living elements in nature and in the art of past and present. The qualities, properties, dimensions, and variations of the elements, therefore, are best understood at this level when *seen* in good color reproductions, in good black and white, in photographs, and generally in most materials which abound in magazines. But most elements are best understood by examination of actual examples and by making use of them in spontaneous design and experimentation. Textures are felt, while color is experienced; line movement is best understood through observation in forms of nature and in art. Form is perceived not only visually but in the handling of clay, wood, plaster, metal and other three-dimensional materials, or it is experienced while developing a painting. Space is sensed in its relational presence in the class-

TECHNICS interest junior-high-school pupils. Especially as they progress toward ninth grade, they find mastery of several graphic media challenging and may discover the medium in which they can succeed. Creative types are often revealed through such variety (pen-and-ink and wash, Audubon Junior High School, Cleveland, Ohio; "Construction Work," water color, 8th grade, Baltimore, Md.; dry point on celluloid, 8th grade, Easton, Pa.).

CHURCH   by Joan L. Flagler

room or in an arrangement on the bulletin board or in the exhibition case. It is experience that teaches.

All this leads to serious consideration of the demonstration on the part of teachers and pupils, or the method of discussion, or the impromptu class discussion of materials on hand, or an evaluation of the work produced by pupils. In fact, discussion and evaluation are necessary supplements to experience. If, in addition to the suggested approaches to the problem, the class and the teacher can visit museums or other local exhibitions, or plan other educational journeys, the matter of appreciation as well as of improved performance will be gradually solved for each pupil to the extent of his endowment and sensitivity.

What has been said concerning the teaching of art elements is equally true of the teaching of principles. But greater emphasis needs to be placed on experiencing principles, since they are not only or always seen, but are perceived and felt in an abstract sense. Some further implications of a practical approach to the language of art will be pointed out presently.

ART AND THE CORE CURRICULUM

The nature and scope of the core curriculum itself were discussed in Chapter 3. A reiteration at this point is intended to focus attention on its operational aspects in the junior high school, where it is widely used today.

The characteristics of children in grades seven, eight, and nine, which is the prevalent pattern, would seem to warrant an organization of art activities around the common needs and interests of the pupils during this period of growth. Interests and needs are thus utilized in behalf of the pupils who seek to discover their personal abilities and interests through exploration. It is in this search that pupils achieve their particular mode of adjustment and learn the value of self-improvement.

Basically, the claims of core teaching may be identified with similar recent claims in general education. When these aims are adequately pursued, art becomes an essential element in core teaching, and, other things being equal, art teachers should welcome participation in the broad activities which give rise to meaningful art expression.

In his discussion of typical art activities in core situations, Ziegfeld[8]

---

[8] Edwin Ziegfeld, "Art and the Secondary Program," in *Art Education Today, 1951–52,* New York, Teachers College, Columbia University, 1952, p. 27.

points out that they have very great value for several reasons: they bring art to a large number of students; they involve more teachers in art education; they grow out of more general interests; and they demonstrate that art has a basic relationship to wide spheres of human concerns, such as family, community, world understanding, sociological and technological developments, freedom, and the spiritual and moral welfare of man.

The arguments against core teaching, in so far as art is concerned, are chiefly based on the fear that art may become the "servant" of other fields. That the situation has its dangers is true, yet one is prompted to ask whether art education in the junior high school is concerned with developing a "special" field or with the growth of children. The dangers attributed to core are minimized when one realizes that many teachers, for want of actual situations, have set up hypothetical conditions in order to elicit expression from pupils. The truth seems to rest on the active interest and wholehearted participation of the art teacher in the planning, the group conferences, the evaluations, and the other activities necessary in core teaching.

LETTERING AND POSTERS which deal with school or community appeal to adolescents. Junior-high-school pupils are concerned with such problems from an ideological and personal point of view (fire-prevention poster in tempera, Addison Junior High School, Cleveland, Ohio).

Since core is a newer approach to the teaching of art in general education, it is likely that experience alone, over a period of years, may furnish the proof either for its claims or for the fears of some art educators.

For practical purposes it may be profitable to examine a tentative outline (Table 7) produced coöperatively by the "core" teachers of a junior high school.[9] From such examination it may be possible to determine how

---

[9] The Campus Junior High School, State Teachers College, Kutztown, Pennsylvania.

TABLE 7. "How We Live Together Democratically": An Outline for the Integration of Social Studies, Geography, and Science with Coöperative Action from Other Subject Fields

Contributions of Subject-Matter Fields		
Closely Integrated Concepts: Social Studies, Geography, and Science	Contributory Activities:	
	English	Art
(Representative samples of concepts in this area)	A. Background for students	1. Games we play (illustrations any medium: water color, crayons, etc.)[a]
1. There are rules for every game	1. Organization of a group	
2. The Greeks established the Olympic Games	2. Rules for discussion—parliamentary procedure	2. Mural—"The Olympic Games" (groups of children contribute)[b]
3. Regulations are necessary for social living	3. Talking and helping others to talk	3,4. Three-dimensional studies—"Growth of Democracy" (shadow-box effect using cut-cardboard construction, painted)[b]
4. The Greeks established an early form of pure democracy	4. Using books for reports (library unit)	
5. The geography of Greece contributed to the organization of democratic government	5. Making reports—story "The Marathon Runner" (Kieran)	5. Design for a map of Greece (showing important monuments: cultural, religious, and governmental centers)[b]
6. Greek scientists had a large measure of freedom to investigate natural laws (Aristotle, Plato, Archimedes, etc.)		6. Paper sculpture—"The Philosophers" (armatures, paper, and paste)[c]
7. Roman government was a republican type in contrast to Greek democracy		7. Class booklet (illustrations of contrast between Greek society and contemporary life)[b]
8. The geography of the Mediterranean area influenced Roman law and government		8. Table model of Rome (showing architectural styles of the time)[c]
9. Roman science was an extension of Greek natural philosophy, but was more practical		9. Cut-paper display (bulletin-board arrangement showing Roman scientific developments)[c]
10. During the Dark Ages, repression of rights and lack of scientific advancement went hand in hand		10. Papier-mâché figures (showing costumes of the Middle Ages)[a]
11. The Renaissance and the accompanying invention of printing stimu-		11. Design for textile print (using linoleum blocks

TABLE 7. "How We Live Together Democratically (*Continued*)

Contributions of Subject-Matter Fields

Closely Integrated Concepts: Social Studies, Geography, and Science	Contributory Activities: English	Art
lated a revival of interest in the natural rights of man		to exemplify movable type of Gutenberg)[a]
12. The processes involved in printing depend on important scientific principles		12. Silk-screen design and print (cover for the junior-high-school yearbook)[b]
13. The Magna Charta, an important document in the history of freedom, guaranteed certain rights to English noblemen		13. Pen and ink drawings (illustrating rights guaranteed by the Magna Charta)[a]
14. The Mayflower Compact and the deliberations of the Virginia House of Burgesses were early examples of democratic action in the New World	Poem "Courtship of Miles Standish" Story "Pine Tree Shillings" (Hawthorne)	14. Puppet show enacting the Mayflower Compact[c]
15. Vast time-distance from an autocratic government in the motherland was one factor which made possible early American experiments in democracy		15,16. Mural illustrating progress in transportation[b]
16. Inventions which shortened time-distance have made One World of the New and Old Worlds		
17. The American Revolution was a triumph of the philosophy of the Natural Rights of Man	"Paul Revere's Ride" (Longfellow) "Grandmother's Story of the Battle of Bunker Hill" (Holmes)	17. Design ceramic title utilizing "Natural Rights of Man" as theme[a]
18. A German invention, the Pennsylvania rifle, and the brave men who handled it were important factors in the War of Independence		
19. Yankee and Pennsylvania craftsmen and inventors were given new freedom for experimen-	Stories "Beneath the Saddle"	19. Prepare an exhibition showing illustrations or actual early inventions[c]

TABLE 7. "How We Live Together Democratically (*Continued*)

Contributions of Subject-Matter Fields

Closely Integrated Concepts: Social Studies, Geography, and Science	Contributory Activities: English	Art

tation as a result of the American Revolution

20. Geographical peculiarities of the North American continent fostered a new emphasis on individual freedom

21. We are the beneficiaries of a great heritage of freedom. It is our responsibility to maintain and extend it

22. Social democracy is a natural extension of governmental democracy

23. Modern science enjoys, in democratic societies, unprecedented freedom to experiment and to develop principles and processes for the benefit of society as a whole

24. In totalitarian societies science is hampered by governmental and ideological restrictions

25. Recent efforts to restrict freedom of choice, speech, and scientific experimentation must be resisted if our democracy is to survive

26. Modern methods of communication and transportation have revolutionized certain geographical concepts, such as those dealing with mapmaking, distance, natural resources, etc.

"Into the Shakes"
"Lost in the Apple Cave"
"Johnny Appleseed"
"In the Wilderness"

Poetry
"The Flag Goes By" (Bennett)
"America" (Smith)
"Star-Spangled Banner" (Key)
"America for Me" (Van Dyke)

20. Tempera posters depicting phases of individual freedom[a]

21. Plan assembly program, using slides on architectural design, showing early and modern ideas in contrast[c]

22. Sketches of interior and exterior (typical homes for average incomes common in our democracy)[a]

23. Experimenting with color minglings, decorative paper, or finger paint to be used as book cover[a]

24. Exacting drawings involving perspective or different areas to illustrate restrictive nature of some art experiences[a]

25. Outdoor sketching and painting involving modifications and showing freedom on the part of the pupil[a]

26. Design and painting of mural to illustrate old and modern modes of communication[b]

[a] Individual activity.
[b] Initiated individually, developed as group.
[c] Group work.

and to what extent art can fit into the "core" scheme. In studying the outline of proposed activities, it may be well to ask whether the art experiences are valid or not; whether they show proper balance between graphic and three-dimensional work; whether they provide for individual effort as well as for group participation and contacts; and whether they are limiting in terms of media and related processes.

It should be borne in mind that in the program under examination, as in all core programs, all seventh-grade children were involved. The talented in art and those with meager endowment, those who had an interest in the unit as well as those who had no positive interest, boys as well as girls, all needed to be organized and stimulated for creative action.

In a core situation the pupils gather a great deal of related information, do some research, and often engage in a fair amount of experimentation prior to undertaking any art activity. It is hardly logical to discount the totality of those experiences as being irrelevant to creative outcomes.

Typical junior-high-school boys and girls have a high degree of critical awareness. Theirs is a questioning age. If it is possible to reach them and to help them develop as they should, the approach may be judged successful. If growth can be aided by way of core, or the integrated program, or by way of an independently organized program in art, the chief purposes of education will have been fulfilled.

The merits of core teaching as well as its defects should be assessed on the basis of experimental evidence rather than on prejudicial grounds. Perhaps the best approach for the doubting mind is to visit core situations and discuss its possibilities with art coördinators and teachers who have learned through experience.

THE BALANCED PROGRAM

One last qualification with regard to the spirit of the art program, regardless of its organizational form, is that it should have balance. Much recent literature in the field of art education has concerned itself with drawing and painting. Nearly all the reported experimental studies have dealt exclusively with graphic manifestations of creative expression. Furthermore, they have drawn conclusions which, even though applicable to the subjects covered by the studies, have nevertheless been generalized in their implications. Obviously, such erroneous use of data has not strengthened art as a developmental area in education; in fact it may have done harm.

Art education for *all* the children of *all* the people involves more than painting. Indeed, any discussion of the legitimate place of art in the curriculum, of its developmental and therapeutic claims, or of its function as a leisure-time pursuit must admit of many forms.

Particularly as concerns the junior high school, it should be observed that most children become absorbed in the "making" of things. It may be due to a larger assurance of success and, therefore, of satisfaction in accomplishment through the crafts. It is for this reason that the activities suggested in the preceding pages have not neglected experiences in three-dimensional design.

An examination of the available data on the staggering number of dropouts from school during and at the end of the junior high school is convincing evidence that retention may be improved if education as a whole, and art education, during the early adolescent years can be conceived more broadly. Only then will it reach the larger numbers, be they capable of painting or not. Another fact worth noting is that often the boys or girls whose interests have waned because of inability in graphic expression find themselves through experiences with wood, leather, jewelry, weaving, carving, and other art forms. Finally, if art education is to function in the lives of junior-high-school pupils, its offerings must be as wide as the avowed sympathies for these young people who are groping to find themselves.

INTERACTION BETWEEN THEORY AND PRACTICE

There is slight newness claimed for the art activities suggested; teachers of experience have known of them for a long time. The chief reason for their inclusion is that they may serve as starting points for adequate organization. The true value of art activities is realized only if implemented, not perfunctorily, but in the light of their affective power in the creative development of pupils.

No amount of theorizing will ever produce integrated lives. Sound conceptualization, appreciation, reflective thinking, perceptual growth, and other aspects of creativity are desirable ends which may be achieved only as teachers plan to help pupils resolve intrapersonal conflicts and other problems which may otherwise cause discord in living and learning.

Therefore, the plea made in Chapter 4 regarding the necessity for interaction between theory and practice, and the importance of having a clear concept of method and a clear purpose in teaching, are reëmphasized at this point.

SUMMARY

In this chapter an attempt has been made to show the critical nature of the junior-high-school years. The problems of early adolescence arise from the fact that pupils are on their way toward maturity in a number of ways. Therefore, many conflicts and perplexities arise. Above all, pupils need guidance.

The characteristics of early and middle adolescence reveal that each child is a study in contrasts. He may be a grown-up in some ways, and in other ways he is still a child; he is growing rapidly in his physical body, and that very fact makes him appear somewhat uncoördinated; or he may appear almost an adult, yet his emotions may indicate inner conflict. But such conflict can be resolved through sympathetic help on the part of teachers so that pupils learn to solve their problems and gain new outlooks.

The importance of understanding early and middle adolescents is paramount because for many pupils the junior high school is the end of formal education. Retention of these pupils in school can be measurably helped through sympathy, constructive guidance in meaningful activities, and a discovery of pupil tendencies.

In art education, graphic expression seems to subside for awhile; a balanced program which includes working with materials as well as picture making may afford a measure of success for the pupil and, consequently, an adjustment to the conditions of growth. The ninth grade appears to be the turning point. At that age, those who are successful in the crisis continue to show harmonization and progress normally. Some fall by the wayside, are unhappy, and constitute the continuing problem for the school and for parents.

The characteristics of a good junior-high-school program show balance of activities, variety of media, experimentation in technics, increased attention to the product, and the encouragement of a personal style.

TABLE 8.   General Creative Expectancies in the Junior High School

		Grades		
		7	8	9

The Graphic Symbol This period of growth is notably one of apparent contradictions and regression. Wide variety in success and rate of growth must be expected. Low ebb falls at ninth-grade level, but ninth grade is also a high point of resurgence. The symbol reflects the child artist and his reactions to his environment. Insecurity is chief obstacle. Fluctuation is typical.

Growth in knowledge and general awareness in contrast to disparity in ability are noted as pupils advance from seventh to ninth grade. Experimentation continues, however, even if not successful. X X X

"Realism" of a sort displaces intuitive drawing and causes dissatisfaction until the new and personal symbol is found. X X X

Portrait, still life, and landscape become important art interests. X X

Major problems are perspective, foreshortening, proportions, and composition. In middle adolescence many overcome these difficulties and begin to develop personal styles. X X

Recourse to simplification or "stylization" is common during early adolescence. Composition and design are almost completely ignored. Later adolescents often overcome these problems satisfactorily. X X

Manipulation and Control
Materials and Tools Pupils are capable of using a variety of materials and tools for conscious experimentation. This ability continues to grow as pupils mature. X X X

Physical control and coördination have reached a reasonable level. Pupils are able to use small tools for cutting, carving, sawing, weaving, etc. Small power tools may be used under guidance. X X X

Art Elements and Principles Color media are handled with a fair degree of ease. Pupils are able to control medium for gradation, flat areas, textural, and other effects. Control reaches a high degree by ninth grade. X X X

Line, form, texture, area, and dark and light begin to be used with increased purpose and control. Physical control permits thick, thin, wide, narrow, large, small, and other visual or manipulative qualities. X X X

340

		Grades		
		7	8	9
Design	Surface decoration, creation of motifs, cease to be accidental and become controlled toward significance. Designing with materials becomes easier and more enjoyable with physical growth.	X	X	X
Processes and Technics	Growth in control accentuates desire to "know how"; processes interest junior-high-school pupils. Mastery of ways of accomplishing things increases. Printing processes, the creation of technics, combining materials, are welcome challenges.		X	X
Product	Ability to control materials and tools is accompanied by desire to produce more "real" things. Construction, appearance, organization, and even utility come to the fore as pupils advance from grade to grade. Ability to conceive ideas, to organize, to see details and differences, is at a high peak and should be encouraged.	X	X	X
Growth of Meaning Materials and Tools	Increased physical ability aids pupils to express various meanings. Tools and materials become important in the achievement of desired results. Variety is desirable.		X	X
Art Elements and Principles	The significance of color is at first largely for realistic rendering. In design, its meaning is largely subjective.		X	X
	Interest in theater, costume, commercial design, and crafts brings about symbolic and decorative use of color.		X	X
	Line, form, color, texture, area, and dark and light assume meaning: action, "feel," space, distance, and mood. Greater control permits the use of elements in purposeful ways and to express ideas. Balance, rhythm, transition, and unity acquire meaning and are used to convey thoughts.	X	X	X
Design	Three- and two-dimensional design gain in significance as pupils realize their application; they are "real" in the sense of purpose. The vocational, exploratory thinking of pupils is reflected in the work. Crafts are enjoyed because they have a function.	X	X	X
Processes and Techniques	Ability to mix materials, to handle tools, to follow through a process, is enhanced by curiosity and exploratory desires. Pupils "find out," invent, create own technics to achieve something. Block printing, stenciling, celluloid etching, crayon resist technics, and problems in modeling and painting are challenging because they lead to mastery. Middle adolescents tend to mimic the technics of known	X	X	X

TABLE 8. General Creative Expectancies in the Junior High School (*Continued*)

		Grades		
		7	8	9
	artists; this fact needs careful guidance and encouragement of personal expression.			
Product	Junior-high-school pupils require a reason for doing and making. The product becomes increasingly important to them. Guiding according to inclination and interest will result in confidence, self-respect, and satisfaction. They set high standards for themselves.		X	X
Understanding Space and Form	Seventh-grade pupils are not obviously concerned with space and form in composition. By the end of eighth grade and surely by ninth grade some will show keen awareness of plane and form and grow measurably from that point on. Overlapping, variety of shapes, and dark and light become meaningful. Perspective, proportions, and the use of art elements are consciously used to gain desired effects by ninth grade and upward. Teachers should encourage "expressionistic" modes in order to encourage the solution of these problems which hold the interests of pupils.		X	X
Change of Concepts Social Life	As confidence is regained and problems of growth are solved, pupils widen their artistic concepts, technically and in terms of subject matter. Seventh-graders continue to be interested in themselves, family, and a few friends. As the circle widens, young adolescents become interested in social aspects of living and in adventure. Music and poetry are often used as springboards for interpreting art forms.		X	X
Community	Community problems, social issues, and vocations appear as subject interest of late eighth-graders and most of those in the ninth grade and upward. Differentiation in subjects selected by boys and girls is noted.		X	X
Art in General	Abstract design and art problems for their own sake begin to interest pupils of ninth grade and beyond because of relationships to uses in industrial or commercial purposes. Vocation is uppermost in their mind.			X
Vocation	New sense of self, interest in school and community, encourage some forms of commercial design and lettering. Campaigns, slogans, club activities are good motivations.		X	X
	Humor appeals to boys from eighth grade upward, as seen in interest in cartooning or other forms of exaggeration. Later, this interest may turn to serious interpretations of new-found truths in contrast to legend.		X	X

These characteristics would be true of a traditional organization, in a unit approach, or in any modification of the core pattern.

The summary of normal expectancies for the junior-high-school level points up the major fluctuations in creative unfolding. The most important task of the teacher would seem to be the guidance of pupils in learning to recognize their problems, and guidance in finding ways of solving problems to the end that outlooks may be improved and a degree of harmonization achieved.

For Discussion and Activity

1. Make an inventory of the causes that affect the behavior of junior-high-school pupils and in the light of the findings suggest ways of alleviating the situation as it may exist in the classroom. Discuss this problem with your group.
2. By arrangement, visit a junior-high-school class for the purpose of observing (1) the general attitude of pupils, and (2) the classroom teacher's handling of situations as they arise. Discuss with your group what you have observed.
3. From the literature available in the curriculum laboratory or in the general library discover what activities and what approaches are suggested for meeting the needs listed on pages 308–316.
4. As a general project, develop an art-curriculum guide for a junior high school embracing grades seven, eight, and nine and a total population of 1000 students. Check your curriculum guide with the directions discussed on pages 318–323.
5. How do you interpret the general decline of interest in art at the junior-high-school level? What causes it? Is it unavoidable? Discuss ways in which the situation may be improved.
6. How would you teach art principles and elements in the junior high school? Make specific recommendations and submit them to group analysis.
7. What place should the crafts have in the junior high school? Discuss the subject from the standpoint of the nature of the adolescent.
8. What are the arguments for and against a "core" program in the junior high school? Is it detrimental to the art program? Debate the question and attempt to summarize the issues.
9. In view of the nature of the junior-high-school pupil, his needs, and his problems, to what extent should technics be emphasized in art?
10. What proposals can you make to ensure that the general knowledge and appreciation of art are effective at this level of education? Pool the ideas of the entire group and examine critically.

For Further Reading

Burley, Josephine, "Should We Examine Our Secondary Art Programs?" *Art Education*, February, 1955.

Cane, Florence, *The Artist in Each of Us*, New York, Pantheon Books, 1951, Chapter XVII.

Commission on Secondary School Curriculum, *The Visual Arts in General Education*, New York, D. Appleton-Century Company, 1940, Chapter II.

Gaitskell, Charles D. and Margaret R., *Art Education During Adolescence*, New York, Harcourt, Brace and Company, 1954, Chapters VI, VII.

Hausman, Jerome, "Art in Junior High School," in *Art Education Today, 1951–52*, New York, Teachers College, Columbia University, 1952, pp. 64–71.

Mendelowitz, Daniel, *Children Are Artists*, Stanford, Calif., Stanford University Press, 1953, Chapter VI.

Rannells, Edward W., *Art Education in the Junior High School*, Lexington, University of Kentucky, College of Education, 1946, Chapters I, II, IV, V.

Winslow, Leon L., *The Integrated School Art Program*, rev. ed., New York, McGraw-Hill Book Company, 1949, Chapter VI.

Ziegfeld, Edwin (ed.), *Education and Art, A Symposium*, Paris, UNESCO, 1953, Section II, pp. 46–49.

CHAPTER 10

ART EDUCATION IN THE SENIOR
HIGH SCHOOL

> Because the crisis of adolescence is connected with bod-
> ily, as well as with emotional changes, we deal here with a
> complex crisis in which body, emotions, and mind have to
> adjust to a new situation. Indeed, we can, therefore, say
> that this is an *important period of decision* in human de-
> velopment.
>
> Viktor Lowenfeld,
> *Creative and Mental Growth*

THE AMERICAN HIGH SCHOOL

EVOLUTION AND GROWTH

IN THE PREVALENT PATTERN OF SECONDARY EDUCATION, EXCEPT FOR THE
variations noted at the beginning of the previous chapter, the senior high
school includes the tenth, eleventh, and twelfth years of schooling. In
general, boys and girls of this age group are in the full swing of adolescence. Many of them are in late adolescence, a few have reached maturity,
and, of course, some linger in their maturation. Normally, these youths
are between the ages of 15 and 18, although variations may be found
even in this chronological span.

The senior-high-school population has grown tremendously since its
introduction in the scheme of American public education. The statistics
on this point are revealing and have definite implications for education
in general and for art education. They will be noted in the development
of this chapter.

The steady rise of the birth rate that began in the early forties and continues upward, is now making itself felt at this level of education. It follows that a continuing expansion of the high school must be anticipated and that plans need to be made to meet the larger enrollments and educational demands. The statistics on this condition are offered in Table 9.

TABLE 9. High-School Enrollment Projected to 1966–1967, Grades Nine Through Twelve

1929–30	4,740,000	1956–57	7,144,885
1939–40	7,059,000	1957–58	7,665,416
1945–46	6,187,000	1958–59	8,020,043
1947–48	6,255,000	1959–60	8,222,915
1949–50	6,379,000	1960–61	8,617,388
1950–51	6,493,000	1961–62	9,226,125
1951–52	6,518,000	1962–63	9,821,158
1952–53	6,619,000	1963–64	10,483,446
1953–54	6,291,834	1964–65	10,734,443
1954–55	6,478,431	1965–66	10,750,217
1955–56	6,734,261	1966–67	10,979,044

SOURCE: Basic data from United States Office of Education.

EDUCATION FOR ALL AMERICAN YOUTH

Population growth is but one phase of the problem. Other equally important aspects arise from the changing character of the secondary school. The broadening of its scope and the widening of its services to youth and to the nation have resulted from new social and economic needs.

It should be realized that the secondary-school population was at first a very select one. Over the years it has slowly grown to include all youths who care to avail themselves of an education beyond the elementary grades. This extension of opportunity is, of course, in tune with the principle of universality inherent in American education which was discussed in the first chapter of this book. However, with the extension of opportunity there has also followed a widening of the scope and the inevitable alteration of the nature of the American high school. It is no longer an institution for the preparation of an elite to enter college or some other professional school. Today it is an institution that seeks to meet the varied needs of young people who wish to enter fields such as commerce, industrial arts, homemaking, and vocational agriculture. For many it is simply general citizenship education, and for a smaller but growing group it serves as preparatory to college entrance. In other words, the high school of today is a far cry from the Latin Grammar School of Boston in 1635, or of the first public high school of 1821.

The Changing Curriculum

Just as the types of curriculums have gradually become numerous, so have the course offerings. Each curriculum has its own major and minor emphases; therefore, the originally narrow range of subjects has become very wide. Through administrative adjustments most courses are made available to all pupils who can profit by them within the time limitations and the scope of the curricula chosen by pupils.

Another interesting development has taken place simultaneously. Colleges and universities that previously held to time-honored admission requirements have broadened their pattern, although scholarship is still the basis for admission. In addition, most colleges have retained the traditional liberal-arts curriculum but have ventured into vocational preparation. In consequence, more young men and women are enabled to go to college to prepare for their life careers. Thus, the broadening of senior-high-school offerings to meet the varied needs of a fast-growing population, as well as a higher appreciation of education, have been followed by parallel broadening of college programs. It may be said quite definitely that today it is possible, for anyone who so desires and is able to meet the flexible admissions requirements, to secure a college education. As a matter of fact, the extension of the senior high school by a two-year period, referred to as the junior college, is becoming a common expansion of public education, although there are at present a fair number of private institutions of this type. In many parts of the country it is the accepted pattern. The junior college serves, in general, two purposes: the first may be terminal preparation for skilled service in some phase of work; the second is general education for subsequent advanced study in a senior college and eventually in professional schools. Usually, local needs determine the direction of the junior college.

THE IDEA OF GENERAL EDUCATION

This brief statement on the evolution and growth of the senior high school furnishes an overview of a vastly expanded educational opportunity for youth. It makes it clear that the nature of the educational program has also changed. Its character and its functions have been directed toward the new socioeconomic needs of the American people and of youth in particular.

Modern living as a whole, modern technology, the growth of communities, the rise in the birth rate, the highly diversified fields of labor, as well as the demands for newer services, are reflected in higher standards of living. This fact indicates the necessity for the further enlightenment essential in an evolving democratic social order and has suggested a higher level of education for all. At the same time, the improving working conditions of people, the broadening interests which result from greater leisure, and economic well-being, are evidenced in an increased desire and a keener appreciation for extended education.

The changing character of American life was early sensed in education. Long ago, under the leadership of former President Harper and later under the militant guidance of President Hutchins, the University of Chicago embarked on an educational adventure that had repercussions all over the nation. In time, and more particularly during the last decade, the movement known as general education has occupied a central position in curriculum thinking. At the secondary-school level, it found ready allies because of the social and economic conditions referred to above, as well as in the matured sensitiveness of school administrators who were conversant with local thinking and local conditions.

A great deal has been written and said concerning general education. Much debate has ensued with regard to its meaning, its scope, its extent, and its administration. This healthy concern will undoubtedly continue for sometime to come. Meanwhile, a liberalized public education is answering the needs of the people at the local level.

For purposes of clarity, general education is here defined as that body of knowledges, those areas of culture, and those experiences which should become the possession of all citizens for the attainment of the aims of a democratic society. To realize the further implications of the term *general,* it is important to contrast it with the term *particular* or *special.* All individuals need certain specific knowledges and training to become skilled laborers, technicians, or professional workers. But general education is desired for all, even though a part of basic preparation goes above and beyond it. The common concerns of all people center around work, family life, the community, worship, and leisure. These in turn give rise to the ideals, the values, and the aspirations of all men. Granting that man needs specific training to earn his daily bread, it must be borne in mind that he desperately needs a general education which will enrich his daily life and make it bearable in the face of the standardization, the regimentation, and the automation of present civilization.

Purposes of the Senior High School

Another aspect of general education stresses the cultural achievements of the present and of the past. These, properly understood, are the basis of current progress and a stimulus for future advance. The preservation and extension of the cultural heritage of the nation thus become a significant function of public education, especially at the secondary-school level.

The purposes of the modern senior high school would seem to be these:

1. To continue the program of education of every youth in those fields and subjects chosen by them by reason of prevocational interests, personal abilities, and felt ideals or goals.
2. To furnish a broad base of general education for all youth, regardless of special, subsequent preparation, to achieve the desirable enrichment of life for all citizens of a democracy.
3. To provide those areas of education which have specific meaning in terms of later preparation for the fields of work chosen by individual pupils.
4. To offer opportunities, curricular and cocurricular, so that all youth may learn, exercise, and master the ways of democracy.

Integration as Major Aim

Since the senior-high-school years represent the last opportunity in formal education on the part of millions of American youths, it is obvious that the central aim of all education must find its fulfillment at this point.

Reflected in the four purposes of the senior high school listed above, one finds the major aim to be the integrated personalities of young people. Concepts, knowledges, technics, and appreciations, whether through activities or the more formal classroom procedures, are merged into the single purpose: wholeness of thinking and action. The meaning of integration and the evolution of concepts in American education, including parallel development in art education, have been fully discussed in

Chapter 4. The frequent references to these two points should serve as reminders to the teacher or the student of art education that the ultimate task is not the teaching of subject matter but of growing young people.

Specifically, what is it that is to be integrated? At this level of schooling, young men and women have a pretty clear idea of what they want from life; their development is approaching complete maturity. Therefore, it is reasonable for teachers to expect that pupils be socially and mentally sensitive to problems. These may be problems other than art, yet through art an approach can and should be made to aid this sensing. By now, it is also true that young people have gained a good deal of knowledge and concepts, and therefore should have a fluency of ideas even at the hypothetical level. Problems of housing, for instance, will involve more than a *house;* they will involve the sociological concepts of human beings, the need for refining surroundings, sanitary, recreational, and cultural facilities. When students are not just making a model of a house but have thought out the problem as a whole, then they are capable of handling ideas at the integrative level. But, more than that, they should be guided into making careful analyses of possible solutions to the problems and eventually reach a synthesis of what they find. Originality, or capacity to create, will then suggest what can be adapted and what may be modified for a successful solution of the problem.

What has been said about housing as a problem can be applied to other areas of art activity. The point is that *just making things has little value.* When concepts enter the picture, approximately as described, integrative or reflective teaching-learning takes place and both teacher and pupil will have gained. The activities suggested on pages 372–378 may be treated in this manner, although the chief purpose of the suggestions is to indicate that art experiences may be geared to fulfill purposes that focus either on the individual or on other educational goals. Yet the method of achieving the goal is what matters most.

THE STATUS OF ART EDUCATION IN HIGH SCHOOLS

DISPARITY BETWEEN PHILOSOPHY AND PRACTICE

From what has been stated so far concerning the growth, prevalent point of view, and purposes of secondary education at the upper levels,

A DIVERSIFIED PROGRAM is advisable in senior high school. Later adolescents think seriously about vocation, marriage, and life in general but their needs and aspirations differ widely. A diversified program is also better administered in elective classes (Senior High School, Reading, Pa.).

one might anticipate that art education is a well-established area in senior high schools. Such is not the case. Therefore, art educators and secondary-school administrators still have a gigantic task before them.

Much lip service is given to the meaning of creative activities in senior high schools, especially by secondary educators. The changing emphases in senior-high-school programs, the popular demand for art at the adult level, and the insistence that education must seek to integrate are signs that raise the hope that what is being accomplished at the elementary-school levels and even at the junior-high-school levels may presently manifest itself in the senior high schools and in the public junior colleges. A survey of art programs today, however, discloses that most small high schools do not offer art. In medium-sized school systems, art is offered on an elective basis. In large schools, the elective system also prevails,

352   although certain high schools have more elaborate offerings that range from the elective system to fully accredited "major" curriculums.[1] The overall picture, nevertheless, indicates that the vast majority of senior-high-school pupils are denied any appreciable art opportunity beyond the junior-high-school years.

An even more serious situation prevails with regard to the elective scheme where it exists. Most high schools, large or small, permit students to elect art if it fits into their schedule, or during free or study periods. This procedure generates two inimical situations: the first is that barely 10 percent[2] of high-school students can avail themselves of art offerings; the second, and more serious, is that in any given period the art teacher may be faced with a group of students ranging from the tenth to the twelfth year. Some pupils come with prior experience in art, some with little background, and some without experience since elementary school, or at best not since the eighth or ninth grade.

Even though art has the virtue of individualizing, and even though subject-matter sequence as such has little validity in art, it nevertheless remains that the art teacher is faced with an extremely complex situation. Grade and age differences, the naturally wide range in individual growth and potentiality, the usual problems inherent in heterogeneous groups, and the necessity of providing a variety of materials and equipment required by the diversity of pupil interests—all these present a bewildering condition. It is to the credit of high-school teachers of art that much is accomplished in spite of these handicaps. Yet it is morally and professionally unwise for art educators to continue to close their eyes to the situation.

Inferences from American Education

It should be understood that what is stated above refers to the general situation. There are hundreds of high schools where enlightened and sincerely interested administrators, together with professionally minded art teachers, have solved many of the problems cited. As a result, most

[1] Baltimore, Newark, and New York City are among them.
[2] Edwin Ziegfeld, "Art in the Secondary Program," in *Art Education Today, 1951–52,* New York, Teachers College, Columbia University, 1952, p. 21.

art educators speak and write from the better vantage point in the hope
that secondary-school administrators everywhere may accomplish as
much in their local situations.

But in order that the art teacher or consultant may improve the physical
as well as the developmental situation, it is important to marshal the
most valid points of view available.

What are the inferences of education for all American youth? Of the
changing concepts and purposes of the senior high school? What is the
function of art education in the preservation and extension of the culture? What is the function of art education in a democratic social order?
Finally, one may ask, what is the meaning of art education for the individual citizen?

It will be recognized that the answers to the questions just advanced
are not simply academic; they are inherent in the character of American education as a whole. In a sense, these issues were considered as
axiomatic at the very outset (see Chapter 1). However, they are reconsidered here in order to focus attention on the senior-high-school art
program.

ART FOR ALL AMERICAN YOUTH

If the validity of the principle of universality of opportunity in education is to be upheld, it is difficult to deny to senior-high-school youths
who desire it the opportunity to develop their talents or to enrich their
lives through art. Those who select to pursue commercial subjects or
industrial arts, homemaking, or other fields are generally given ample
opportunity. All concerned with the education of youth in a constantly
changing society and amidst increasingly improved standards of living
cannot fail to see the ramifications of art in the myriad facets of life. To
serve all youth compels the secondary educator and administrator to
reëxamine the functions of the institution in terms of the society which
supports it. It is for this reason that the claims of art education for young
people of this level are briefly restated hereafter and commented upon.
The effort is, unequivocally, to point out wherein the average senior high
school fails to serve *all*. Later on, a similar effort is made to find ways and
methods of organization for the attainment of the principle of universality
of opportunity in so far as art education is concerned.

How Art Serves Youth

From the standpoint of vocational worth alone, art offers unlimited possibilities. Therefore, for practical reasons art should not need justification. A study of art careers[3] reveals the many vocations which art opens up to young people who are prepared to enter them. But the avocational aspects of art are even more impressive. If secondary education truly seeks to enrich life, to provide for worthy leisure, to promote emotional harmony, and to aid in personal adjustment, then it cannot deny boys and girls of this age level creative experiences as well as the sheer opportunity to enjoy art.

A review of the purposes of the senior high school indicates that it is a continuing program through which individuals seek to achieve their goals by self-discovery and self-improvement. The large number of children who emerge from the struggle of early adolescence with ability in art and a genuine appreciation of it are totally deprived of these benefits to themselves and society whenever further provision for creative activities are minimized. Conversely, continuation and enhancement of such opportunities may lead many to find themselves, and will actually function as a way toward the general education envisioned for all citizens. Higher standards of taste, of the level of living, for consumership, and of intelligent membership in communal life are the likely by-products of creative experiencing.

A further look at the purposes of the senior high school indicates that beyond curriculum offerings there are many cocurricular activities which automatically and continually involve art. Among these are the school assembly, dramatic productions, Patron's Day, school campaigns, and many other similar school-wide enterprises. When these activities are capitalized upon, they involve large numbers of pupils in the implementation and in the final outcome. However, if the senior high school is to have these enrichments, it goes without saying that an art program is assumed. The stronger the program and the wider the opportunities for youth to participate in it, the more successful will be the school-wide activities.

A fact of major significance is that American culture cannot advance

---

[3] Elizabeth McCousland, *Careers in the Arts—Fine and Applied,* New York, The John Day Company, 1950.

unless the schools seek out the talented in all fields: science, commerce, and the arts. But the concern of this discussion is with art; therefore, it seems proper to stress the necessity of recognizing the talented in art at the senior-high-school level. It is largely from the high schools that youths with marked abilities will go into the fields of art teaching, painting, sculpture, architecture, industrial design, and the many forms of commercial art. Furthermore, there is hardly an institution of higher education today, whether an art school, college, or university, that does not require an acceptable high-school record as prerequisite for admission. This is sufficient reason for providing art experience, as well as other experiences, for those who will enter the liberal professions. The culture of the nation and its advancement in many directions make it incumbent upon the public high school to make adequate provision for such furtherance through the creative education of youths.

Recent developments in education and, obviously, in art recognize the developmental factors inherent in certain educational experiences. It is an uncontested fact that art activities hold vast potentialities for individual growth. In addition, democracy believes in equal educational opportunity for all, although equal opportunity does not mean equal education but, rather, education by which an individual may profit. At this level, the tendencies, abilities, and preferences of students are pretty well delineated; therefore, those who can profit most through an art education should be given full opportunity.

If the philosophy of American education and of its socioeconomic beliefs are to be fully achieved, the arguments advanced point to the necessity of well-planned art programs at the senior-high-school level, which is the threshold to active citizenship.

CONSIDERATIONS AFFECTING THE ORGANIZATION OF ART PROGRAMS

PSYCHOLOGICAL FACTORS

By inference and by direct statement it has been contended that art education at the high-school level is both the birthright of every youth and a practical way of meeting the needs of society. Indeed, the high-school years are the fruitful years, the decisive years in young people's lives. Life to the high-school student is a serious undertaking. It means

356 vocation, family, citizenship, and a "place in the sun" in which individual worth and personal contribution count.

It is because of this youthful earnestness and sincerity of purpose that art education at this level must, likewise, be purposeful, appealing, and rewarding in terms of the present and of the immediate future. However, to plan with pupils of senior-high-school age calls for an understanding of their needs, characteristics, hopes, and capacities.

Nature of Late Adolescence

Not long ago, a group of art-education students were charged with the task of ascertaining from the literature of psychology as well as from firsthand observation what characteristics are typical of most high-school boys and girls. After much research and discussion they arrived at the list which follows. The list, they agreed, is not necessarily complete, nor is it applicable to all young people, but it is important as a general index to their nature. Most high-school students, they discovered, are:

1. Physically strong and active
2. Capable of emotional stability
3. Independent and self-assured
4. Endowed with highly creative powers
5. Experimentally minded
6. Self-motivated and self-assured
7. Capable of sustained concentration
8. Fond of precise and scientific work
9. Capable of adjusting to situations
10. Capable of careful planning
11. Interested in adult activities
12. Capable of intelligent cooperation
13. Aware of themselves as human entities
14. Idealistic about life and work[4]

When he considers the above listing of characteristics and those which might be added in the light of the highly heterogeneous nature of the senior-high-school population, the art teacher is at once aware of the tremendous opportunities ahead, and of the problems as well. The many references made regarding individual differences, and those relating to

---

[4] Art Education at Work, *An Art Program for Secondary Schools,* Kutztown, Pa., State Teachers College, 1951, p. 12.

vocational, avocational, and general citizenship needs, further enhance the possibilities and the dangers involved in working with high-school pupils.

The Stage of Creative Renascence

Psychologically, the senior-high-school pupil has emerged from the crisis of adolescence either as victor or as vanquished. In the crisis, he has either lost or gained a great deal of confidence in himself and others. He may have given up his creative attempts or may have gained new vigor and new vision. In either instance, however, he is a new creature. He is almost an adult, who must be treated as such and from whom much should be expected, with due consideration for his personality, which is by now fairly well established.

Creatively, this is the stage of renascence. Those boys and girls with high endowment, having successfully gone through their natural cycle of development, may be identified as the "gifted" in each class. But there are many who are still growing and still groping and will soon find their proper place. All youths that may be classified as typical, with the usual exceptions, can perform acceptably in some form of art, with satisfying results, from their point of view at least.

Interest in vocations and the concern with life as a productive venture

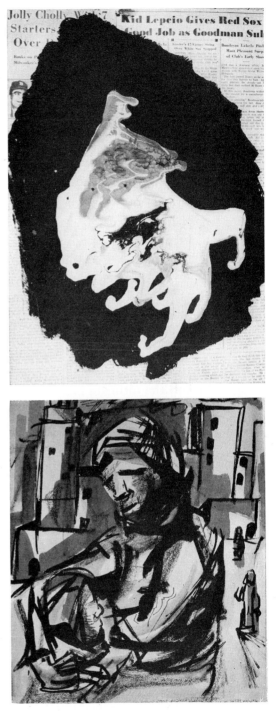

EXPERIMENTAL APPROACHES are desirable at the senior-high-school level in view of the accumulated knowledge, the experiences, and the technical facility that many students have achieved (above, experimental painting, 10th grade, Rio Vista, Calif.; below, portrait from life, Lincoln High School, Cleveland, Ohio).

may suggest to these youths the many art fields in which they may wish to engage: commercial art, fine arts, industrial design, costume and fashion design, the crafts, the theater arts, and other forms requiring an art background. For others, art should serve as the emotional stabilizer, the life-enriching element that, directly or indirectly, contributes to a firm moral and spiritual basis for abundant living.

Creative renascence will manifest itself in many ways. Some ways may appear unrelated to a narrow interpretation of what constitutes art, but need to be nurtured and guided nevertheless. For example, the boy who has a high interest in art but little ability in performance may be a genius as organizer and leader. The girl whose sole interest is the feminine tendency toward costume design may be capable of holding together a group and seeing through a project in school dramatics which involves costuming and make-up. Boys and girls who may not be highly original as painters may be efficient members of a stage crew that is responsible for producing the scenery. The ramifications of the renascence are indeed too many to enumerate. However, the wise teacher will discover, guide, nurture what is there, and bring it to full fruition as a contribution toward the ultimate integration of each individual.

NEED OF DIFFERENTIATION

All the facets of the late-adolescent personality (see Table 10) suggest possible curriculum directions that may be implemented if the needs of young people are to be met in spite of the many obstacles mentioned elsewhere. The obstacles themselves, as suggested at the beginning of the chapter, may well be regarded as challenges.

The teacher will realize at once that a uniform pattern for all pupils will not be effective. If anything, uniformity leads to the establishment of forms of imposed discipline, so inimical to creative experience. The heterogeneity of the pupils, on the other hand, suggest grouping by interest, grouping by prior art experience, or grouping on the basis of demonstrated ability. Such a situation will give the teacher an opportunity to put to work the idea of reflective teaching which was advocated in the discussion of method.

Grouping by interest will facilitate teaching through reduction of the problems of equipment and materials as well as by providing the teacher with time in which to focus attention on the real issue of teaching: con-

TABLE 10. Youth Faces Forward (Senior High School)
(Middle Adolescence to Adulthood)

Chief Characteristics	Major Interests	Significant Needs	Usual Responses	Effective Stimulation
1. Conscious control	1. Himself as an adult	1. Emotional security	1. Highly objective or subjective art response according to type	1. Self-motivation
2. Physical buoyancy and energy	2. Adults and their society	2. Adult acceptance		2. Art vocations
3. Analytical attitude toward life and art	3. Opposite sex	3. Responsibility	2. Coöperative	3. Community and school as a "work-shop"
4. Critical judgment is high and growing	4. Processes and technics	4. Confidence of adults (teachers, parents)	3. Accepts challenges	4. Life situations as subject matter
5. Emotional stability of marked degree	5. Emotional security	5. Attraction of opposite sex	4. Self-assured	
6. Consciousness of own abilities, interests, and limitations	6. Vocations	6. Challenging situations	5. Independent	
7. Perception has developed almost to full capacity	7. Life and its relationships	7. Wholesome attitude toward self and own work	6. Adjusts to situation	
8. Resourcefulness	8. Logical planning and execution	8. Experimentation	7. Idealistic toward life	
9. Individuality		9. Freedom to act, to decide		
10. Creative development high				

cepts, insights, and significant appreciations which may be the outcomes of a single experience area at one time. This type of grouping suggests physical arrangement of the studio into work areas; these may contribute to efficiency and may lead to fuller creative development. Many of the high-school buildings being erected today provide for such areas. In one school the all-purpose art laboratory is thoughtfully divided in half: one part of the laboratory is designed for painting, drawing, and other graphic activities; the other is equitably divided into metal, clay, and weaving and textile areas. Flexibility of arrangement to include other crafts, such as leather, papier-mâché, and basketry, demonstrates its distinct advantages over a "general" laboratory. But important though this compartmentalization is, it is even more important to stress that the idea of differentiation is recognized as an essential for the best development of an individual or of like-minded groups.

One of the most important aspects, often overlooked in the idea of differentiation by interest grouping, is its socializing effects. The meaning here is not to be misunderstood for its popular connotations. The procedure results in exchange of ideas, comparisons, mutual help in the solution of problems, learning by seeing and experimenting, and, above all, in group self-control. From the standpoint of democratic living, these results of the procedure are eminently desirable types of social living which should be fostered whenever possible. Actually, they are a chief cornerstone of the educational structure.

Teacher-Pupil Planning

A second direction that grows out of the needs of late adolescents is teacher-pupil planning. The virtues of this form of curriculum development have been touched upon elsewhere and its values in the growth of the pupil have been inferred throughout. In the present context, it should be related to the artistic unfolding of the individual pupil, whether gifted, otherwise atypical, or falling in the category of average. Even though several pupils may be working in the same interest center, it is conceivable that specific guidance will vary with each pupil in that group. At the same time, it is also conceivable that pupils with definite desires and corresponding abilities may wish to plan ahead, or more comprehensively. In such instances it is advisable to discuss the problem involved, set up hypotheses, explore the possibilities, analyze them, and then proceed. In any case, the teacher is there to stimulate pupils in a manner that will produce a complete experience and one that will have involved reflective thinking.

Units of work, correlated activities, single experiences, group projects, personal contributions to group undertakings—all these are types of teacher-pupil planning in which each pupil's tendencies, needs, and aspirations may be fulfilled. The realities of the average high-school art laboratory and the scheduling problems referred to some time ago are not here minimized or overlooked. Yet, in spite of them, art teachers must continue to find ways of overcoming them and thus successfully solve those physical problems.

In a democratic society, preplanned, predigested, and preconceived programs are antagonistic to wholehearted personal or group participation. On the other hand, coöperative planning, digesting, and conceptualization become educative in the highest sense. Active and effective participation in social and communal life presupposes that the ways of democracy have been a continuous learning process from childhood to adulthood. Art activities, especially those that arise from human relationships and needs, seem to offer tremendous possibilities for coöperative learning. In turn, this practice is a prelude to creative participation in the life of the community.

Effective Stimulation

Of all the elements of method, not one is more significant at this level of growth than stimulation. The meanings and types of this central element in all good teaching have been stressed a number of times in this work. Yet it seems important to reiterate them and to relate them to the art expressions of senior-high-school students.

Not only are these pupils young adults who are eager to practice adult ways and receive adult consideration. They have also reached a high level of knowledge, and have achieved a sense of relationship and an ability to reason that cannot be overlooked. Stimulation at this level, therefore, is by far and large intrinsic in nature. Pupils know what they want, what they need, what they can or cannot do. They have fairly definite ideas about life, people, society, and their own aspirations with respect to all these.

Good stimulation will proceed largely on the basis of answers to *why,*

362 *what, how, when, where.* The art of questioning, properly employed, will bring out of pupils the answers to their art problems. On the other hand, successful stimulation presupposes that the teacher-pupil relationship is a complete and satisfying one.

By way of example: Is the proposed art experience meaningful to the pupil? Does he realize its potentialities and its problems? Does he sense the values of the experience to himself or to others? Does he understand the possible ways of handling the aspects of technic involved? Is the art experience significant to him in terms of his present interests and future ramifications? The questions, obviously, could continue indefinitely. The important point for teachers is a realization that good stimulation and motivation depend on the convictions which they arouse in the pupil. When the pupil has adequately answered his own questions, the way for creative action has been opened.

Lastly, on this point, it seems proper to epitomize by saying that coöperative planning is a way of evoking reactions, and that good motivation is a way of making purposes clear, for pupils as well as for teachers.

SUGGESTED ORGANIZATION OF THE PROGRAM

IMPORTANCE OF A REALISTIC APPROACH

The facts cited with regard to the present status of art education in the majority of American high schools and the problems that confront art teachers are realities that cannot be brushed aside. The ideal situation is a noble and desirable goal toward which all art educators must continually aspire and for which they must be willing to expend time, energy, and study.

However, the best-prepared teachers, the best-intentioned individuals, and the soundest plans will fail, thwart, and perhaps damage the steady progress of art education if a measure of realism is wanting. Administrative problems, finances, physical conditions, and above all the point of view of those who administer the program at the local level are some of the problems that must be faced. By facing them squarely, by working coöperatively, by constantly educating associates in other areas of education as well as parents and public, by persistent efforts along all these lines, art education at the high-school level will come nearer the ideal of the profession.

The general situation being as described, what are some ways of setting up an art program that will be of the utmost worth for boys and girls in the senior high school and, at the same time, point toward the ideal? What follows is in the nature of suggestions which may be interpreted and adapted to local situations, or as starting points.

Desirable Outcomes for All Pupils

It should be repeated that if the general aims of the American high school are to be properly implemented, it is obvious that certain basic provisions must be made for *all* youth. Art in the senior high school should be organized so that its inclusion in the total school program may touch the lives of all young people. To do so effectively, the program should be based on defensible grounds and on socially desirable goals. These goals are self-evident in the purposes of the senior high school as well as in the nature of the high-school pupil. For practical purposes the outcomes of the general organization and, therefore, the criteria for the selection of activities of an art program may be visualized in this manner:

1. For the individual	*Maximum growth and development* (Mental, creative, aesthetic, emotional, social, and physical)
2. For effective social living	*Intelligent participation* (Skills, knowledge, discrimination, ability to plan, ability to coöperate)
3. For moral and spiritual growth	*Emotional harmony and sensitivity* (Values, goals, appreciations, integrity, resourcefulness)
4. For occupations	*Knowledge and proficiency* (Skills, technics, processes, concepts)
5. For leisure	*Buoyancy, versatility, resourcefulness* (Ability to do, appreciations, sound mental health, inner resources)

General Art for All

On page 366 two possible ways of organizing the art program are proposed. Unquestionably there are other ways; therefore, those suggested may serve as points of departure. The two plans indicate what is considered minimal for all, what is desirable for most pupils, and what should be provided for those who possess a high degree of ability and

364   interest in creative work. Viewed from another angle, both plans incorporate the five desirable outcomes. These should prevail in any scheme of organization if art education is to permeate life and living at the senior-high-school level and in later social contacts. An examination of the meanings implicit in the desirable outcomes will reveal the magnitude of the task as well as its feasibility when a modicum of organization is effected.

A general art course required of all students in the senior high school would result in heightened appreciation, sounder standards of taste, deepened interests, and the possible identification of those who should be guided into professional fields of art. General art would, furthermore, promote the growth of those personal qualities that education desires for all citizens. The home, the community, business, industry, religion, recreation, and the moral and spiritual resources needed by man are spheres of living that touch all youths. Properly organized, those areas could form a basis for general art activities.

MATURE ART EXPRESSION is often encountered in senior high school. For some, art will be a vocation; for many, an avocation; for all, a way of understanding themselves and the world (*above,* water color, Senior High School, Seattle, Wash.; *below,* soapstone sculpture, Roosevelt Senior High School, Seattle, Wash.).

The Art-Elective Area

It has been indicated that the current practice in senior high schools is to permit those students who so desire to elect art. But even if one were to agree with such a situation, its actual operation defeats the purpose. As stated previously, if a pupil wishes to elect art he may do so whenever a "vacant" period appears on his otherwise predetermined schedule. As a result, the art teacher finds himself with groups of young people who in addition to being different as individuals are also heterogeneous in their prior experience in art, grade, and maturity level.

The major fallacy of an elective system without prior or recent contact with art is that it makes the program only partially effective. Furthermore, it tends to demean art and to convey the notion that art has no standards. Worst of all, it continues the erroneous idea that because the art teacher works with individual pupils there is no need for continuity in the field. That notion is a remnant of the days when art educators were attempting to "sell" art to administrators and public. In their zeal, they established a precedent that would be unthinkable in music or in any of the academic fields. Growth of art interest in the schools suggests that the administration of art must be given new consideration. The present acceptance of the situation does not account for the dispersion of energy on the part of the teacher, the heightened emotional complications of an already diversified program, and the fact that what was intended as an opportunity for pupils is turned into a frustrating experience, especially for those students who need more guidance than is possible under the circumstances.

Ideally, general art should precede as the common ground for all. Then the elective area would function more adequately for pupils and more satisfactorily for teachers. Can this be done? The answer rests largely with enlightened administrators and resourceful art teachers who are willing to demonstrate the feasibility and worth of a more logical plan.

An encouraging example of how the present situation may be corrected is best illustrated by what was accomplished in one high school. The principal was approached by the art teacher with the suggestion that before the closing of school a survey be made through the homerooms to discover how many boys and girls planned to elect art the following fall. When the number of pupils so inclined was discovered, the principal planned the art schedule so that all pupils of the same grade who wished to elect art were scheduled for it together. Pupils who did not decide to elect art until fall were scheduled in the old manner, but within two years the problem of heterogeneous scheduling was reduced to a minimum.

However, even where conditions are favorable, it is important to consider the scope of the elective area for achievement of desirable goals.

A POSSIBLE ORGANIZATION OF THE ART PROGRAM IN HIGH SCHOOLS

PLAN A

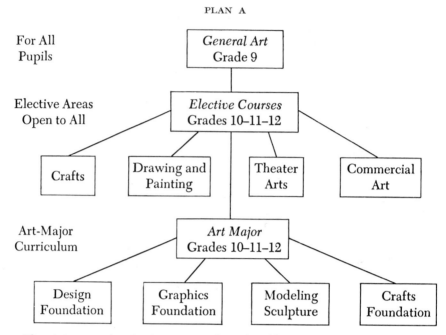

Plan A is comprehensive in nature and is adaptable to situations in most large or middle-sized schools which combine the ninth year with the senior high school. A continuity of interest and of the program is feasible under these circumstances. The interests of all are served through general art, the further interests of some through the elective area, and those of talented pupils through the art-major curriculum.

PLAN B

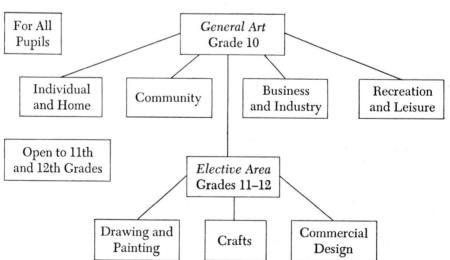

This type of organization represents a minimum offering in small high schools where the number of pupils and the teacher man power are limited. Here, art for daily living is stressed for all in the tenth grade. The elective area should permit all pupils who so choose to develop their gifts and deepen their appreciation through broad areas.

Bearing in mind the art interest, the increased abilities, and the creative tendencies of pupils concerned, elective art activities should be sufficiently broad to include a number of basic aspects. Reference to the proposed schemes of organization will show that in the more comprehensive Plan A the following interest centers are suggested: crafts, drawing and painting, theater arts, and commercial art. Even a minor breakdown of each center will yield a vast array of possible art experiences. A balanced program, personal interest of pupils, and the needs of the school and the community will serve as guiding principles in the determination of experiences that may be undertaken most effectively for the development of the pupils involved. Plan B assumes that physical facilities as well as pupil enrollment suggest a less-elaborate program with these interest centers listed: drawing and painting, the crafts, and commercial design. Here again, the possible variations within each center are innumerable. In both proposals differentiation and interest grouping are possible within each broad field of the visual arts.

THE MAJOR ART CURRICULUM

Several recent studies dealing with general education and with secondary education point out quite forcefully the fallacy of a high degree of specialization at the secondary-school level. In addition to the educational reasons for such a position, there are the implications of socioeconomic changes that have taken place within the last quarter-century. Altogether these changes have brought about greater leisure for all, thus deferring the necessity of young people going to work at an early age. Furthermore, there is at present a heightened social consciousness of the value of normal development for all youth and a recognition of the fact that a broad general education is a more effective basis for later development. The suggestion of a major art sequence in high school is, therefore, not only a means of extending the art program but a way of meeting newer social needs and of saving talent.

Breadth and Depth

What, then, should be the nature of the art-curriculum major? It should first of all make provision for education in the communication arts, such as written and spoken English and literature. Then it should offer the basic sciences and social studies. Beyond these broad elements of general

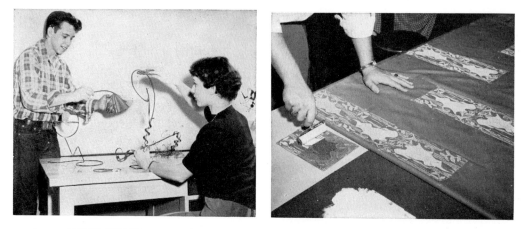

DESIGN APPEALS to many who are not interested in painting or the graphic arts. An effective program should include work in a variety of crafts. The processes involved in them, as well as the end product, are satisfying experiences for many adolescents (*left*, designing with wire and thin-gauge metal, Westport High School, Kansas City, Mo.; *right*, block printing on material, Jefferson High School, Richmond, Va.).

education the visual arts would constitute the major field of interest. The art field itself should have a general-art basis in the first year so that pupils may appraise their own strengths and weaknesses as well as their preferences. In the second year, two or three art areas could be explored. The third year's work would be a deepening of the pupil's own interest in a field in which he hopes to specialize further as he enters college or university or art school. Reference to Plan A, page 366 may suggest ways of adapting the program in harmony with local conditions. Therefore, when the idea of a complete curriculum in art in the senior high school is advanced, its intentions should be clear to the pupils who seem interested. They should understand that they should relate their desires to the necessary breadth and depth of the major sequence.

Dangers of Specialization

The aim of such a curriculum should not be specialization in art. Its scope and content should have as their chief purpose the saving of talent, the development of the superior,[5] and the continuation of creative opportunities for those boys and girls who evidence exceptional gifts. Nor should such an aim be regarded as a luxury. That is an obsolete notion that belongs to the era of the "ivory tower" type of art and art education.

---

[5] Educational Policies Commission, *Education of the Gifted*, Washington, National Education Association, 1950, pp. 13–31.

The intellectual and creative assets of the nation are dependent on what is done with the intellectual and cultural potentialities of youth.

By the same reasoning that commercial education, industrial arts, home economics, and agricultural curriculums have been introduced in the pattern of the modern high school, so should a major art curriculum find its proper place in the scheme of public secondary education. Aside from its developmental phase and its intensely personal aspects, a curriculum in art in the high school should be recognized for its virtue as the reservoir from which architects, painters, sculptors, illustrators, commercial designers, industrial designers, and teachers of art will come. These are but classifications; when otherwise expressed, they encompass hundreds of art fields that supply the basic human needs of all citizens. The realistic bases for establishing a major curriculum would be that a sufficient number of pupils can be interested in its offerings; the physical equipment and materials can be provided; and able teachers can be made available to do an adequate piece of educational work.

Guidance Is a Constant

Having stated unequivocally that specialization is not the function of art in senior high school, but rather a deepening of interests and a broadening of them, it may now be affirmed just as clearly that guidance remains the constant function of the art teacher. Guidance is here used in its broadest sense. It should include personalized help in creative development, advice in course selection and in terms of future vocation, and, lastly, counseling in social adjustment. Is the pupil sufficiently endowed to succeed in a particular art field? Does he understand the nature of the required further preparation? Is he financially, physically, and mentally able to undertake such further preparation? What are the opportunities in the field of his choice? These are but a few of the fundamental questions that must be answered by the pupil himself under the kindly direction of the art teacher. And this is not only true of pupils who aspire to an art vocation but of all young people who may come within the influence of the art teacher. Special abilities are often discovered in unlikely individuals; on the other hand, many misguided students undergo preparation beyond high school only to find that a field is crowded, that competition is too keen, that another vocation would have offered greater security and mental health.

SELECTION OF SUBJECT MATTER AND AREAS OF ART EXPERIENCE

SIGNIFICANCE OF THE ACTIVITIES

One of the difficult problems for the senior-high-school art teacher seems to be the selection of what is generally referred to as subject matter.

There exists an unfortunate tendency to mimic the art school, college, and university requirements and procedures. That is a poor criterion because at the post-high-school level the art activities are directed toward an already-announced purpose, namely, the vocational intention of the student. Such intention is not clear during high school, or at least it is deferred until the end. The criteria for the selection of art activities at this level are well summarized in Prescott's[6] qualifications of all experiences. These are viewed by him in terms of pupil needs: psychological, social, and integrative. Reference to the statement of aims proposed on page 363 suggests that the selection of subject matter is directly related to the individual (pupil), his social living, his many-sided pattern of growth, possible occupations, and the enrichments of life. These aspects of human development have been elaborated upon. They furnish a clue to the vastness of possible activities that may be utilized in experiencing art. In general, the art teacher needs only to be reminded that, in reality, the subject matter of art is embodied in all the relationships of the pupil with his environment.

AREAS OF LIVING

For purposes of exemplification, one might consider ways of organizing curriculum materials so that teacher-pupil planning may proceed with a degree of ease and assurance. The areas of living which are common to all men have been found to be effective sources from which experiences may be developed, not only in art, but in all education. Problems that revolve around the home, the community, work, worship, play, communication, and transportation are not only of concern to all individuals but have definite relationships to social groups, particularly when they are faced reflectively. The fact that all these relationships

---

[6] Daniel Prescott, *Emotion and the Educative Process,* Washington, American Council on Education, 1938, Chapter III.

and situations may be expressed, plastically or graphically, by each pupil in his own way and in his own idiom further enhances their value as springboards for artistic action. The seriousness of life as viewed by youths, their desire for adult status, and their general concerns at this level of growth suggest the almost universal quality of these areas and hence their ultimate effectiveness as *real interests*, intrinsically motivated. They only need stimulation of a reflective sort to be set in motion for creative action in the art laboratory.

The significance and versatility of this point of view are perhaps best illustrated through an examination of course-of-study guides prepared by committees from the field and published under the auspices of state departments of education. The Pennsylvania *Course of Study in Art Education*,[7] for example, suggests that there are general areas of experience and specific areas of experience. Upon further examination, one finds that the general areas include understanding of peoples and their cultures, both past and present; the home, the school, the community, clothing, industry, commerce, and nature. Each area is first studied from the point of view of human needs and then in

[7] Pennsylvania State Department of Public Instruction, Bulletin 262, Harrisburg, 1951, pp. 25–88.

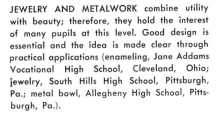

JEWELRY AND METALWORK combine utility with beauty; therefore, they hold the interest of many pupils at this level. Good design is essential and the idea is made clear through practical applications (enameling, Jane Addams Vocational High School, Cleveland, Ohio; jewelry, South Hills High School, Pittsburgh, Pa.; metal bowl, Allegheny High School, Pittsburgh, Pa.).

terms of the understanding of art content which manifests itself through expression evoked by such understandings.

Other phases suggested by the *Course of Study* involve art elements, organization, and expression. Here again, reference is first made to the meanings in terms of human needs, then in terms of understandings of art content through discussion, exhibitions, research, and, eventually, expression.

The specific art areas suggested are the art of the book and the magazine, theater arts, architecture, ceramics, drawing, graphic arts, leather, metal painting, photography, plastics, sculpture, textiles, and wood. Obviously, the contention of the course of study referred to is that an understanding of human needs and their varied manifestations is essential to art expression. For the senior-high-school level the approach seems logical because the maturity of the pupil demands an intelligent basis for action.

What follows is a concrete example of a possible way of organizing curriculum material in line with the thinking advanced in this chapter.

A HIGH-SCHOOL ART CURRICULUM BASED ON AREAS OF LIVING

A. For the Individual (Maximum Growth and Development)

Drawing and Painting (various media and personal technics)
At the dance; at the game; the school cafeteria; the art room; the grocery-store window; portrait of my friend John; planning and execution of a mural suitable for the school library (in collaboration with two classmates)

Surface Design (various media and personal technics)
Block-print design for drapes in my room; pattern design for my notebook; silk-screen poster to advertise the basketball game; stenciled design applied to a scarf; a decorative composition to be used as a wall decoration for home

Three-Dimensional Design
Carving a fork and spoon from wood and elaborate on the handle; using several materials create a table decoration; design, make, and decorate a key case or simple wallet; create a simple clay figure to be glazed and fired; using plastics, make a simple jewelry box; build a T-D loom and weave enough material to make a purse

Graphic Arts

Make a dry-point portrait of your best friend; from local scene create a white-line block print; compose and execute a blockprint of a community public building for use in the school annual; design a letterhead for your school and submit it to the principal for approval and possible use; in collaboration with other members of your class make a series of silk-screen posters advertising the school operetta

Architecture

Study styles of architecture prevalent in your community, then design a home, both interior and exterior, for a family the size of your own; take what is considered a poor part of the community and create a plan for its improvement; make a series of pen-and-ink sketches of public buildings in your town; design, in three dimensions, a proposed community center for your town

Sculpture and Modeling

Model a portrait of your brother or sister; make a plaque with the school seal as the motif, then cast it to have a number of them; secure a piece of native stone and after careful planning carve an animal; using wood, carve a profile self-portrait in bas-relief

Pottery and Ceramics

Experiment with clay to produce original shapes suggested by pressing the clay in your hand; make a small vase by merely pressing the clay with your thumbs; study good classical design in pottery, then make a ten-plate, hand-built piece of pottery; create a figure of a ball player in action, make a mold, cast, glaze, and fire

Theater Crafts

From color minglings plan simple, imaginative settings for a play of your choice; make a mask of some favorite character or type; plan and costume a pantomime; plan a mask recital for the school assembly; experiment with colored light on pigment; plan multiple effects on backgrounds by changes of colored light

B. FOR HOME, SCHOOL, AND COMMUNITY (Intelligent Participation and Consumership)

Drawing and Painting (various media)

At the picnic, the parade; a historical landmark in our town; Sunday on Pine Street; in collaboration with classmates, plan and execute a mural about local industries for a public building

Surface Design (various media)

Stencil draperies for the Y-Teen Room; embroider a large sampler of community activities; silk-screen posters for community clean-up week; block-print a wall decoration using local buildings

Three-Dimensional Design (assorted materials)

A well-planned town (three-dimensional maps); winter table decorations for the Children's Home; construct a Christmas scene for your tree yard at home; design and make an ornamental pin for a gift; plan and construct a large paper-sculpture display for Education Week; design and make a weathervane for your garage

Graphic Arts

Block-print a calendar, using local scenes; letter and frame a literary selection for your home; make an etching of your favorite local landscape; make a two-color block print of a community landmark

Architecture

Make a model showing how your own bedroom might be redecorated; be a style detective for the public buildings of your town; make a model of a recreation house for your local park; show how your lawn or plantings might further improve the appearance of your home

Sculpture and Modeling

Carve an ornamental garden piece from a log; model an ornament for a desk at home; whittle; make a series of plaster reliefs of school athletics

Pottery and Ceramics

Design a study lamp; make a mold of the lamp; duplicate it; make a lamp base; decorate tiles to be inserted around sink in art room at school

Theater Crafts

Design and make marionettes for a play about local history or a local problem; make designs for costumes for a play read in English class; plan and execute decorative reredos for the school stage to be used in connection with holy day programs; choose your favorite local character and make a mask of him

C. For Occupations (Related Information, Skills, Technical Proficiency)

Drawing and Painting (all media)

Drawings and paintings of several figures representative of several occupations or professions; portrait sketches of workers in local industries; paintings and drawings of factories, plants, shops, etc.; drawings and paintings of school personnel: the janitor, the bus driver, the fireman, the cook, etc.

Surface Design

Create motifs based on labor, industry, and the professions, to be used in shops; plan and execute wall hangings using "the air age" as motif

Three-Dimensional Design

Study processes of manufacturing: glass, steel, textiles, plastics, etc., and make visual presentations of them; hammer a copper dish, create an appropriate design, and etch it; design and make a simple ring for self or a member of the family; design and make a pin using silver and copper

Graphic Arts

Etchings, lithographs, block prints, and silk screens based on industry, commerce, labor; safety posters for use in shops; trade marks for industrial products; package design for various products; counter-display designs

Architecture

Models of industrial plants; design murals for a plant cafeteria or recreation room; study of modern architecture: Larkin Laboratories, RCA, and others

Sculpture and Modeling

Model free-standing figures of workers; carve a plaster relief panel, using industrial subject; study methods of casting in bronze and other metals; design and execute a mosaic mural, using specific occupation

Pottery and Ceramics

Study the processes of preparing glazes, clays, casting methods for industrial production, etc.; create free-form pieces of ceramic pottery; make molds for complete dinner service and produce the same

Theater Crafts

Study work of modern stage designers; observe the various styles of stage design; plan the working drawings and an elevation for a play; plan a convertible unit setting, using a limited number of screens. Adapt it to possible settings for community play, local-talent hour

D. For Moral and Spiritual Growth (Emotional Responsiveness and Sound Values)

Drawing and Painting (all media)

Drawings and paintings of local churches; original illustrations for basic ethical concepts; holidays and holy days as subject for inspiration; the freedoms; brotherhood, world citizenship

376   *Surface Design* (various technics and media)

Design and execution of window decorations in the mode of stained glass for school use; designs for holiday greeting cards, silk-screened, block-printed, stenciled, etc.; creation of designs for decorative papers according to seasons

Three-Dimensional Design

Tooled leather cover for religious book; leather bookmark with symbols; repoussé in thin metal for wall plaque, using religious motif; carved bookends, using symbols related to ethical life; create a wood carving, using Biblical or moral theme

Graphic Arts

Create and cut a block to be used as a greeting card for Christmas or Easter; make a dry point on celluloid, using such themes as faith, hope, charity, helpfulness, sorrow, etc.; make a silk-screen poster advertising the school's cantata, or the Thanksgiving Assembly, using appropriate symbols and design; create an etching on a theme such as "Singing Angels" or "The Helpful Hand" or "My Brother's Keeper" or a similar subject

Architecture

Study first, then make a scale model of local place of worship; plan your own design and create a model for a community church; make a well-designed chart showing the development of ecclesiastical architecture from the early Christian era to the present

Sculpture and Modeling

Model in clay any Biblical character you favor; from wood carve a low-relief interpretation of such themes as brotherhood, peace, coöperation, etc.; plan and execute a mosaic decoration, using a theme as indicated above; make a series of plaques, using symbols related to ethical and spiritual values

Pottery and Ceramics

Study the work of Eric Gill and of the Renaissance ceramists della Robbia, then plan a series of activities that may include the making of candle holders, figurines of religious characters, wall plaques, carved plaster (round and relief), flower containers

Theater Crafts

Make a set model for a Christmas or Easter play or pageant, such as "Why the Chimes Rang"; prepare the setting, design, and prepare a background for choir recital; study meaning of "line" in theater design and plan an imaginative setting for "A Cathedral," "Aspiration," etc.

E. For Recreation (A Buoyant and Versatile Personality)

Drawing and Painting

From posed models draw and/or paint a boxer, a baseball player, a basketball player; paint or draw a portrait of the best boy athlete or girl athlete in the school; from experience and memory compose several figures in action illustrating games, parties, dances, etc.; paint a self-portrait, "Myself Reading a Book," or "Listening to Music"

Surface Design

Study the methods of batik, then compose figures in action (hockey, tennis, etc.) to be done in batik as a wall hanging; prepare and execute a series of block prints in two colors on various forms of recreation for use as inserts in the school yearbook; create the design motifs for stenciled material to be made into a skirt or dress, the motifs being various activities like dancing, swimming, tennis, etc.; plan and execute a pictorial map with figures and other related items to show location of recreational spots in the state

Three-Dimensional Design

Design and execute a carved-linoleum wall decoration on sport or a specific game or other recreational activity; from carved plaster develop a low-relief decoration on the subject "The Skaters" or "The Bathers" or other recreational activity; model in papier-mâché couples dancing, skating, players tackling one another, and similar combinations; using several materials, design subjects similar to the above

Graphic Arts

Study the technic of making lithographs on zinc plates, then, using a subject such as "The Football Game" or "The Senior Prom" or "The Cafeteria" or similar subjects, develop a lithograph. Plan a silk-screen poster with figures in action to advertise the sports, dances, and other all-school functions; design and execute a two- or three-color block print to be used as illustration on poster advertising the operetta or class play or Christmas Assembly; make etchings or dry points of school athletes in action

Architecture

Develop a plan for a youth recreation center for your community; plan a garden for one of the courts in your school; make a scale model of the interior of a clubhouse for Scouts or Campfire Girls or other youth group; make a scale model of a complete camp site to be used by an art colony during the summer and by local groups during the rest of the year

Sculpture and Modeling

From the imagination, model "The Singer," "The Wrestlers," "The Dancer," etc.; using a block of plaster, carve subjects of your own choosing but dealing with a recreational activity similar to the above; prepare, cast, glaze, and fire a group of figures in action but related, as in a game or other recreational activity, such as reading for pleasure, listening to recordings, looking at television, etc.; create the design and execute the reliefs for a series of medals or plaques to be presented to top athletes and other activity leaders in your school

Pottery and Ceramics

Study Greek, Oriental, and modern forms of pottery, then develop your own design for "trophy" vases to be inscribed and presented much as the cups of commercial houses are presented. Study the work of modern ceramists and from your own experience create, cast, glaze, and fire figures in typical poses of certain games or other recreational activities; create your own forms in pottery and decorate them (sgraffito, slip decoration, underglaze decoration) with motifs typical of recreational pursuits; design, cast, glaze, and fire medallions for wall decoration in one's room, subject matter may deal with recreational subjects

Theater Crafts

Study examples of period costume, then create your own designs for costumes to be worn by principals in the school operetta; design costumes for a school Halloween Ball; design and construct a model for a background that could be used for a giant pep rally; design, construct, and paint a scale setting for the senior-class play; create a design for the setting of the Spring Dance, May Pageant, or a similar event.[8]

It is not claimed that what has been presented above is a perfect scheme of organization. It is only one way of attacking the problem. However, an analysis of the material may point out its chief characteristics, and its validity may then be appraised in relation to the function of art education for the senior high school.

First, it will be noted that all activities are suggested by the personal and social needs of pupils. Second, the specific activities take into account various types of art expression. Third, the experiences suggested include two- and three-dimensional areas in order to provide for various abilities and inclinations. Finally, the suggestions are grouped on the basis of the outcomes desired for all pupils (see page 363).

---

[8] Art Education At Work, 1951, *An Art Program for Secondary Schools,* Kutztown, Pa., The Kutztown Bulletin, State Teachers College, pp. 13–21.

GENERAL GROWTH EXPECTANCIES

If boys and girls emerge successfully from the fluctuating, uncertain, and rather difficult early teens, they may be considered as having grown normally. When such is the case, they will probably progress in art much as they do in other subject fields; specifically, they will show continued improvement in relation to their endowment. Those whose interest leads them to continue in art, or to elect the subject with regularity, may be expected to master matters of technics and processes to the extent demanded by their artistic needs and personal tendencies. Among those who survive, as it were, there will be the artists, the art teachers, the designers of tomorrow.

Table 8, page 340, may be used by teachers as a point of reference to determine how well and to what degree senior-high-school pupils overcome the problems that faced them only a year or two ago.

By tenth grade, most adolescents have arrived at a mode of expression which is judged satisfactory. The graphic symbol may be a highly personal one, exhibiting characteristics of an individual style. The imagination and the inventive powers of pupils should be discoverable to a reasonable degree. There will be expressionists, naturalists, and abstractionists among them.

GRAPHIC PROCESSES, because of their almost scientific nature, have special appeal for many students; for the talented pupil they hold even more fascination. Dry point, etching, lithography, block printing, and other types should find their place in the art program (lithograph, Senior High School, Allentown, Pa.).

Manipulation of tools and materials required in three-dimensional work should exhibit growing control, versatility, and skill. Most technical matters, such as proportions, perspective, space concept, form, and the rest, should be handled reasonably well by the eleventh grade. These solutions to the problems of expression do not necessarily conform to traditional standards; they are plausible solutions to the manner and mode in which the pupil chooses to work.

At this level, the creative type becomes very clear: poetic, haptic, architectural, or other. The teacher should strive to stimulate growth along the direction that seems natural for the pupil.

Composition and design, as well as meanings, are pretty well established by the eleventh year. Skillful teaching at this level of growth should recognize and promote the individualized nature of the work of the student by encouraging experimentation and research toward further achievement.

Interest is at a high point of significance and every effort should be made to maintain it by setting up standards. However, many forms of art should be experienced by the pupil so that he may see the broader aspects of the field. This indicates that growth in skill should not be confused with narrow specialism, a tendency that needs watching even by those who are considered to be good teachers. The ever-present danger is to become too narrow, whether in teaching or in learning. The further education of the pupil may then be looked upon as a period of culmination and of the full flowering of the artistic renascence which marks this age-grade span of life.

SUMMARY

The American high school is an almost indigenous product. Although there were academies in this country prior to the founding of the first American high school in Boston in 1821, they were intended for those who could afford to pay the cost. Development of the high school, on the contrary, and its expansion are truly an answer to the demands of society and the fulfillment of a deep-rooted belief that all the children of all the people should have a free secondary education if they can profit by it.

As the senior high school has grown in popularity, its curriculum has also been expanded. To the original college-preparatory function there have been added many other curricula, such as industrial arts, homemaking, commercial education, general citizenship, agricultural education, and, in a few instances, an art curriculum. Some larger cities have an entire high school devoted to the arts.

The upward extension of educational opportunity for American youth now includes the junior college in many localities, and in others technical institutes are being organized.

But in addition to popular demands for a senior-high-school education, its expansion today is due to the general increase in population. It is estimated that by 1967 the pupil population of the senior high schools will be nearly eleven million as compared to the present enrollment of seven million students. The problem confronting the nation in this respect is not only one of space and equipment but one of further reviewing curricular offerings. Yet, acute as these problems are, the chief one seems to be that of manning the school. But the equal rise in college enrollments may, in part, resolve the situation.

Art in the senior high school is considered part of the general education of all youth; its inclusion in the program is consistent with the overall point of view in education. However, current provisions and facilities for art instruction at this level are inadequate and not in line with what school administrators claim to believe.

Progress is nevertheless being made. It remains for art educators to have a clear comprehension of their task and an understanding of the problems faced by public education. Art education at the senior-high-school level presents a challenge in that it should serve all youth and, at the same time, discover and nurture those whose talents should be guided into art occupations and professions. But of equal importance is to extend the cultural frontiers and to elevate the general taste.

The teaching of art at the senior-high-school level requires teachers whose general education, professional preparation, and technical background are adequate to the task. An understanding of youth and its needs, command of basic art fields, and a thorough belief in the philosophy of the senior high school as an institution are essential for success.

Concerning the program, it is essential that art should reach more than the present meager number of pupils. General art for all, elective opportunities for those who express interest, and, whenever warranted, a major sequence should be developed.

The modern art program for high schools cannot be based on timeworn academic tradition or on a stereotyped, synthetic approach. It must be conceived as an extension of the foundations laid in the elementary school and in the junior high school. It must develop individuality, creative power, and technical achievement commensurate with the needs of each pupil.

The use of those educational techniques that best exemplify freedom, coöperation, and realization of individual and social values must be given prior consideration, to the end that the youth of the nation may find their proper role as citizens of a democracy.

For Discussion and Activity

1. What is the inference of the growing high-school population for art education at that level? List the specific problems raised by the situation and discuss each of them to discover possible ways of meeting the challenge.
2. Why is the senior-high-school period referred to as that of artistic renascence? What psychological factors affect the art production of youth during that period?
3. What factors would determine the establishment of a major sequence or of an art curriculum at the high-school level? How would you justify such a proposal to your principal?
4. Make a survey of practices in the administration of the art program in the senior high schools of a nearby county or parish, then analyze the findings. If warranted, suggest ways of improving the conditions.
5. Review the purposes of the modern high school and relate the possible contributions that an art program can make to those purposes.
6. Visit the local high school or the high school from which you were graduated and by prior arrangement with the art teacher interview several students to ascertain their reactions to the art program. Report your conversations with these pupils to your group with a view to interpreting the thinking of young people regarding method, subject matter, and related aspects of the art activities.
7. Develop a tentative art-curriculum guide for a suburban senior high school of 600 pupils. Assuming that 15 percent elect art each year, what specific goals would you set for such a program? What experiences would be common for all students and at what point would you differentiate the activities? To what extent would graphic, three-dimensional, and appreciational activities find their place in the scheme?
8. Justify the place of technics as a reasonable aim of teaching at the high-school level. Either side of the argument may be presented for discussion by your associates.
9. In the selection of subject matter and areas of experience in art how does the principle of teacher-pupil planning operate? Answer with specific rather than general terms.
10. Since the average high school offers only a general art program, how can the teacher satisfy the vocational, the avocational, and the more personal creative needs of students?

For Further Reading

Cane, Florence, *The Artist In Each Of Us,* New York, Pantheon Books, 1951, Chapter XVIII.

Gaitskell, Charles D. and Margaret R., *Art Education During Adolescence,* New York, Harcourt, Brace and Company, 1954, Chapters I, II.

Kainz, Louise C., and Riley, Olive L., *Exploring Art,* New York, Harcourt, Brace and Company, 1951, Chapter I. The book is especially useful in arriving at a broad concept of subject matter for junior and senior high schools.

Landis, Paul H., *Adolescence and Youth—The Process of Maturing,* New York, McGraw-Hill Book Company, 1945, Chapters I, II, XVIII, XIV.

Lowenfeld, Viktor, *Creative and Mental Growth,* rev. ed., New York, The Macmillan Company, 1952, Chapter VII.

McDonald, Rosabel, *Art as Education,* New York, Henry Holt and Company, 1941, Chapters VI–VIII.

Mendelowitz, Daniel, *Children Are Artists,* Stanford, Calif., Stanford University Press, 1953, Chapter VII.

Seidman, Jerome M. (ed.), *The Adolescent—A Book of Readings,* New York, The Dryden Press, 1953, Part II, "Growth and Development"; Part VI, "Understanding and Helping the Adolescent."

Ziegfeld, Edwin (ed.), *Education and Art, A Symposium,* Paris, UNESCO, 1953, Section II, pp. 50–52.

Ziegfeld, Edwin, "Art and the Secondary Program," in *Art Education Today, 1951–52,* New York, Teachers College, Columbia University, 1952, pp. 19–30.

ART AND THE EXCEPTIONAL CHILD

> Looked at from the standpoint of the welfare of society,
> it should be clear that failure to make adequate educa-
> tional provisions for handicapped persons contributes, on
> the one hand, to an increase in the ranks of the socially
> and economically incompetent and, consequently, to social
> liabilities. On the other hand, if individuals of superior ca-
> pacities are to make the contributions of which they are
> capable, their abilities must be developed to the greatest
> possible extent.
>
> Karl C. Garrison,
> *The Psychology of Exceptional Children*

THE PROBLEM OF DIFFERENCES

THE INCLUSION OF A CHAPTER DEALING WITH THE EXCEPTIONAL CHILD IN A
work that is mainly concerned with art as it functions in the average
classroom situation should not convey the notion that the problem of the
exceptional is in any way covered adequately. The intent is merely to
call attention to an area of education that sorely needs the services and
the beneficence of creative activity. Those who find in this brief presentation sufficient challenge may be rewarded by a realization that art
teachers have some contributions to make to this unusual and extensive
field.

The literature of psychology and of education have, for a long time,
stressed the significant role that differences play in the development of

all children. These sources indicate the need for an awareness of differences on the part of teachers and parents in order that they may better guide child growth and development. Teachers and parents have heeded the advice only to the extent that surface attention is given to the problem as it affects those children who may be termed typical. But when differences are of a marked character and children are obvious deviates, the situation presents innumerable obstacles, and therefore it is not always adequately attacked. In fact, it remains one of the serious problems with which the school and the home still must cope.

The purpose of the first part of this chapter is to present an overview of the problem and, to a degree, of the probable values of art experiences for those exceptional pupils who are termed handicapped. The second part will deal with the gifted child and his needs.

The detection of differences, whether they be slight or of a marked degree, is an essential first step in all education because the determination of the rate of growth, success in learning, and change or lack of change in the behavior of a pupil can be handled adequately only over a period of time and with a knowledge of the extent to which pupils differ from the accepted norm. It is no less important to realize significant differences in children if teacher and parent are to understand the manifestations of tendencies, of developed interests, and of the growth of aptitudes. As pointed out elsewhere, the evaluation of the growth of any child, whether through art expression or in a more general sense, may be said to be valid only when it relies on the availability and adequacy of data on the kind and extent of differences in the many-faceted growth of an individual child in relation to others.

But, important though it is to realize ordinary differences among normal children, it is of critical significance to be fully aware of certain wider deviations that exist among many children. These are not always easily detected, and even when discovered little can be done regarding them in the typical classroom situation. Therefore, the identification of the exceptional will call attention to the need for special services.

DEFINING THE EXCEPTIONAL CHILD

The exceptional child may be defined as one "who deviates from the normal child physically, mentally, emotionally, or socially to such an extent that specialized services are essential to provide an adequate educational program."[1]

One may properly ask whether the problem is so widespread as to call for special consideration. Martens[2] furnishes the answer in unequivocal terms in the figures that follow:

TABLE 11.   Estimated Percentage and Number of Exceptional Children in the United States, 5 to 19 Years Old

Exceptional Children	Estimated Percentage	Estimated Number
Blind and partially seeing	0.2	67,208
Deaf and hard of hearing	1.5	504,060
Crippled	1.0	336,040
Delicate (of lowered vitality)	1.5	504,060
Speech defective	1.5	504,060
Mentally retarded	2.0	672,080
Epileptic	0.2	67,208
Mentally gifted	2.0	672,080
Behavior problems	2.5	840,100
Approximate total (estimate)	12.4	4,166,896

A closer scrutiny of the statistics suggests that even if the estimated percentage of 12.4 remained constant since the data were gathered, it would be a sufficiently alarming situation. But as one considers the steady rise of the birth rate during the last decade, if the percentage were the same, the total number of children needing special education has obviously increased to a bewildering figure. The responsibility of education in school and home toward the children concerned has, obviously, assumed larger proportions than ever before.

For the sake of clarity, as well as for a realization of the extent of the problem, it may be worth while to list the major categories involved in the term *exceptional children.* Baker[3] indicates the following: the blind,

---

[1] *School Life,* March, 1947, p. 7.

[2] Elsie H. Martens, *Needs of Exceptional Children,* Leaflet No. 74, Washington, U.S. Office of Education, 1944, p. 4.

[3] Harry J. Baker, *Introduction to the Exceptional Child,* New York, The Macmillan Company, 1944.

the partially seeing, the defective-sighted; those with defective hearing, the hard-of-hearing, the deaf; those with defective speech; those with orthopedic handicaps; those with disorders of physical growth; those with lowered vitality; and a multitude who have miscellaneous physical conditions that deviate from the normal. To these, of course, must be added the slow learner, the mentally subnormal, and the feeble-minded. Nor can one forget the thousands of children who suffer from neurological and psychogenic diseases such as epilepsy and other psychotic conditions.

But among those children classified as exceptional there is another group whose plight is just as great even though its deviation is in the opposite direction. The reference here is to the rapid learner and to the gifted. This category is of special interest to art teachers and is, therefore, treated separately later in this chapter.

DESIRABLE ATTITUDE TOWARD THE HANDICAPPED

Classroom teachers, and art personnel in particular, are inclined to be sympathetic toward the children under discussion, but they may feel inadequate to handle them. Therefore, they assume that the task is for specialists. In general, it is true that special preparation is required to administer the treatment needed by such deviates if any appreciable amount of good is to be accomplished. Yet in most communities the problem is still untouched, and unless those who teach, as well as parents, assume a positive attitude and develop the will to do what is within their power, thousands of children will grow into adulthood without help of any sort and become the charges of society.

The problem that all handicapped children face is one of major adjustment. Somehow a positive compensation for their condition must be found, and unless it is found through correction, help, and sympathy, they will tend to isolate themselves from the environment. It is this separation, the harsh realization of being considerably different from most other children, that causes further social maladjustment, mental disturbance, and emotional imbalance. Added to the original plight of a handicapped child, these further complications amplify his problems and, consequently, those of society.

Minor problems of hearing, minor problems of sight, certain minor emotional deviations, and even many minor physical handicaps can be handled by most observant teachers and parents on the same basis as most minor social maladjustments are handled. But when the problems assume larger proportions, the psychologist, the psychiatrist, and the physician must enter the scene. The plea at this point, however, is that teachers should be alert to the condition and, whenever feasible, act in the best interest of the child concerned.

CONTRIBUTION OF ART

The purpose of calling attention to this area, long neglected in art education and little better implemented in education generally, is to point up the possibilities of the arts as helpful instruments. Workers in this phase of education require specialized training, suitable facilities, and adequate financial support. These are not yet available in adequate amounts at either the local, state, or national levels. Nevertheless, it should be mentioned that there are many quasi-public, some private, and a number of state-supported institutions established for the purpose of caring for serious deviates. Societies for the prevention and correction of major physical impairments have existed for some time. New groups continue to be founded as public consciousness is aroused to the realization that the condition is much more widespread than was suspected.

At the proper point the general literature on the subject of exceptional children will be surveyed. For the moment it should be stated that a fair amount of experimental work has been done by physicians, psychologists, psychiatrists, physiotherapists, and by some educators, who have largely acted as collaborators. But the magnitude of the problem is such that only the surface has been touched, thus leaving a vast field of endeavor in which the combined genius of a variety of personnel, including art teachers, may engage for years to come.

THE ROLE OF THE EXPERT

It is not to be assumed even for one moment that an art teacher, regardless of how well prepared he may be to do an acceptable piece of work with typical children, is sufficiently skilled to handle exceptional cases of an advanced nature. That is the role reserved for an expert.

Psychologists, psychiatrists, and other specialized personnel are being attached to school systems because of their particular preparation. Their advice, their help, their counsel and direction, should always be sought by the art teacher or coördinator. When the case suggests it, unquestionably the specialist will know how to proceed and, if warranted, where the case may be institutionalized for adequate diagnosis and treatment.

Closely related to this situation is the dangerous pastime in which teachers of art have lately engaged because of a serious misunderstanding in the use of evaluation of child art. The situation has reached the proportions of malpractice of psychology. Some teachers have read all manner of supposed symptoms into children's work. This nefarious practice has caused unfounded reports to reach parents and teachers, has subjected children to unnecessary emotional hardship, and has wasted the energies of other teachers and administrators.

It can not be stated too strongly, therefore, that art teachers should refrain from tampering with a field which is foreign to them. An expert is the person to call when cases warrant it.

MENTAL AND EMOTIONAL THERAPY

The contribution that art can make to relieve mental and emotional conditions caused by various deviations is just beginning to be understood and to be used. A number of studies are now available which show how art can function in mental, emotional, social, and physical rehabilitation. Until such time as art personnel particularly interested in this area of education can be adequately prepared, the scope of this discussion can only serve the humble purpose of keeping the problem before the minds of educators, parents, and teachers. Some recommendations on the use of art with certain types of exceptional children will be made as this presentation develops. First it is important to realize that there are numberless general benefits to be derived from a study of the handicapped pupil which seem sufficiently important to be pointed out.

VALUE OF STUDYING EXCEPTIONAL CHILDREN

The value of studying problems that center around exceptional children lies in the fact that the technics and the methods employed by experts may indicate to those who work in normal situations and with normal pupils certain improvements in methods and technics. In the second place, the results obtained by specialists who work with institutional cases may indicate certain abnormal trends which may be detected

390   in children of the average classroom. Third, such a study should awaken teachers to a realization of the vastness of the situation and the possibilities inherent in art expression as a means of alleviating it.

It should be said, furthermore, that a consideration of the problems of exceptional children may serve to reinforce the beliefs that art educators

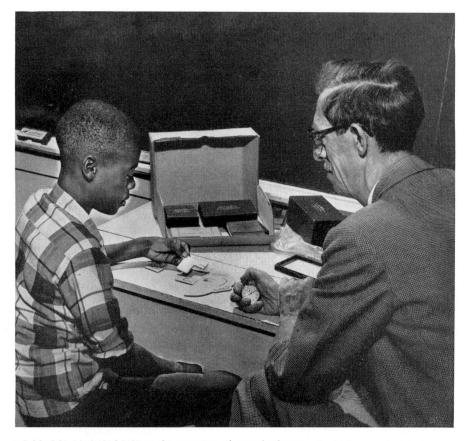

THE SCHOOL PSYCHOLOGIST or the supervisor of special education should be consulted in the case of all seriously atypical children. Their diagnosis and the suggestions of activities that may help the children concerned should serve as guidance (School District, Reading, Pa.).

hold with regard to the function of art as a developmental activity and with regard to its broad therapeutic value. If freedom of expression offers release to the normal child, and if the normal child's world and mind are revealed through art expression, is it not a perfect vehicle through which the troubled minds and the blocked emotions of exceptional boys and girls may reveal themselves? Is it not conceivable that art expression may furnish the key to the causes of some of the difficulties and hence to the treatment that exceptional children require?

One of the latest claims of art education is that through evaluation it can aid in child growth and development. In Chapter 8 it was contended that many facets of growth may be revealed by a child's artistic productions if sufficient samples are made available. In relation to the problem on hand, the sampling of art work may indicate those mental, social, and emotional forces at work to prevent full expression, or to cause certain types of art production or certain abnormal tendencies.

THE DUAL FUNCTION OF ART

It may be easily seen, therefore, that the role of art activities in the education and the redirection of exceptional children is a dual one: that of diagnosis and that of therapy.

It has been indicated why it would be presumptuous to assume that anyone untrained in the field of psychology, psychotherapy, and physical therapy could undertake difficult cases. But it is not out of place to re-affirm the belief that art is a potent instrument in the analysis and amelioration of social maladjustments and some emotional disorders. Actually, art has made distinct contributions to physical and mental therapy. One of the most illuminating examples comes from the scientifically planned and skillfully handled experiments of Margaret Naumburg. She writes encouragingly of the ample evidences which show how the art productions of schizophrenics, which begin with fragmented or divided forms, under guidance eventually become satisfying nonschizophrenic types of art. She states: "Questions are sometimes asked by certain artists, teachers of art or occupational therapists, as to how such dramatic improvement could occur in the expression of mental patients when they have received no formal art training. Sometimes it is difficult to convince such people that an outpouring of unconscious material during the process of therapy can become the basis of artistic as well as personal integration."[4]

But a child need not be an advanced schizophrenic before proper

[4] Margaret Naumburg, *Schizophrenic Art: Its Meaning in Psychotherapy*, New York, Grune and Stratton, 1950, p. 37.

attention is paid to him. There are many children in typical classrooms who may profit by special attention, and who through the healing power of art may be aided toward a healthier mental, emotional, and social behavior. The problem is actually one concerned with the intensity and the consistency of the application of art to help the child discover himself. It is a problem of activating whatever skills, knowledges, attitudes, and aptitudes he may possess. Then the child is placed in a position of confidence and of self-reliance which, in turn, may permit him to find and establish his place and role in the normal situation. Many children classified as slow learners or of low mentality have often amazed teachers and parents by their accomplishments when "treated" by competent and sympathetic teachers in proper surroundings and with facilities suitable for the task.

It should be evident at this point that the releasing, revealing, and healing effects of art should be utilized by teachers if only to bring about a modicum of harmony in the lives of those individuals who are in any way afflicted. This is particularly true and feasible in the case of exceptional children with minor difficulties.

Even with this meager background of the problem under discussion, it should be possible to examine those types of maladjustment and impairment that seem to warrant the special attention and active interest of art teachers.

What can be done for those afflicted by various degrees of sight deficiencies? Can art be of help to children with hearing and speech defects? What can be done for those of low mental capacity? In a limited way, some answers to these questions are proposed in the paragraphs that follow.

TYPES OF HANDICAPS

THE PROBLEM OF VISION

The weak-sighted, the partially sighted, and the blind naturally present three different aspects of the problem; but since they are three degrees of the same abnormality, they are considered simultaneously first, and in some detail later.

Art teachers have at their command materials and processes which, when used with children within this broad category, may help those so afflicted to develop that inner vision and those mental resources that will, in a measure at least compensate for lack of optical vision.

The weak-sighted represent a group that may be found in the classroom. A weak-sighted child may be unable to perceive and, therefore, to draw or paint the details, the colors, tones, and values, or even the entire objects in the surroundings that are clearly visible to normal-sighted children. In a relative sense, his lot is one that can be improved by developing in him certain habits, such as observation at closer range, drawing larger, or using stronger colors and more decided contrasts. If the teacher is able to discover haptic tendencies, these should be fostered and encouraged because they will absorb many of the problems the child would have to face if he were visual-minded. The likelihood is that such a child would fare better if he could be encouraged to express himself three-dimensionally, although this may be contingent on factors of age and general development.

It is now a well-accepted fact that weak-sighted persons can be prepared for vocations; therefore, if the child's mental health and emotional stability can be bolstered in the early years, the problems of adjustment will be at a minimum and the proper compensations will have been supplied for later development.

The Partially Sighted

The partially sighted present a serious situation, but it is a matter of degree when compared to the weak-sighted. In such circumstances, the procedures suggested for the weak-sighted need only to be analyzed and adapted for use with this group. Although, in general, the practices suggested will be equally as effective, greater importance might be given to modeling, carving, and other three-dimensional activities. The major compensation will be found in the use of the sense of touch, which, incidentally, is the least-cultivated physical sense even among normal people. Through touch, the general configuration of objects, the variations of textures, the relationships of sizes and proportions, may be sensed by the child if in his mental reaction he deems them important.

The matter of drawing and painting, obviously, is more difficult to handle; but through guidance and the cultivation of the sense of touch, as indicated above, it may be possible to lead the child to express himself even in a graphic manner.

Involvements of general intelligence, of willingness to coöperate, and the teacher's resourcefulness and patience are, necessarily, important ones. It may not be amiss to refer once more to the possibility of developing innate haptic tendencies of children, because when this is done it will matter very little what color, proportions, and details a drawing or painting will have. The essential fact is that a child so impaired will have at his disposal a medium of expression. His creations may even lead to further analysis of his thinking and feeling and thus permit even greater opportunity to bring about needed social and emotional adjustments.

The Totally Blind

The totally blind are generally institutionalized and are under the care of workers whose professional training ensures a type of education that leads to useful citizenship. But the tragedy of blindness is not the concern of only those individuals who have chosen to work with persons so afflicted. Garrison, who has studied the problem thoroughly, places the responsibility on many. He says: "Parents, educators, public health officials, nurses, social workers, industrialists, and illuminating engineers have important responsibilities so far as concerns the conservation of vision and the care of the eyes."[5]

What can art teachers do in this instance? It has already been suggested that three-dimensional work is not beyond the ability of blind persons. Nor should one confuse a physical disability with the possible keenness of mind that a blind person may possess. Blind persons have been known to work in science, in mathematics, and in other equally difficult fields. But the reverse of the picture may be just as true, namely, that a highly gifted child may have very poor vision. Terman[6] and others, in a study of the mental and physical traits of gifted children, found that 20 percent of the gifted and 16 percent of the control group had subnormal vision. The point to bear in mind is that there is no direct relationship between the two conditions and that each case must be treated on its own merits.

---

[5] Karl C. Garrison, *The Psychology of Exceptional Children,* New York, The Ronald Press Company, 1950, p. 300.

[6] Lewis M. Terman and others, *Genetic Studies of Genius,* Vol. I, *Mental and Physical Traits of a Thousand Gifted Children,* Stanford, Calif., Stanford University Press, 1925, p. 26.

Art teachers who are so inclined may study the work accomplished by such people as Berthold Lowenfeld, B. McLeod, and others.[7] The publications of the National Society for the Prevention of Blindness will also be very informative.

Suffice it to say that in so far as art teachers may be called upon to work with the blind, the chief vehicle with which they may work is the kinesthetic sense. Kinesthetic sensations and the temporal sequence of processes seem to develop to a high degree in the blind, perhaps as positive compensation. Whatever the case, these appear to be effective points of emphasis through which art can make substantial contributions. The role of imagery should not be stressed, especially with the congenitally blind; with those who were sighted and became blind, the possibility is present but not to a predictable extent. In either instance the issue should not be forced, because the dangers of possible discouragement would nullify whatever wholesome effects might be obtained by the use of three-dimensional and other tactile experiences.

THE MENTALLY RETARDED

Most children with I.Q.'s of between 55 and 85 or 90 are considered as of low intellectual capacity. These are the retarded and the backward children who are in need of special education if eventually they are to assume a useful role in society and develop self-respect.

A great deal of study has been devoted to the problem of the mentally retarded, and a large volume of evidence is available to indicate their deficiencies and also the possible areas in which they may achieve a measure of success. It is in terms of the possible success and the general amelioration of the lot of the mentally retarded that the following considerations are advanced.

Performance Ability

Although it cannot be assumed that mechanical ability is a common characteristic of subnormal children, it is interesting to note from studies that it is in this area of performance that such children come nearest the norm for their age when compared to average children of the same

---

[7] For additional sources, see "For Further Reading" at the end of the chapter.

age. The experiments conducted by Cruickshank[8] show that a retarded child falls considerably below an average child whenever concepts of *abstract thinking* are required. On the other hand, a retarded child achieves almost as well as a normal child in problems of a *concrete* nature. Other studies corroborate Cruickshank's findings and lead to the generalization reached by Robson to the effect that the retarded child "can work with actual things and sometimes with models, though he cannot deal with maps and plans. He may be quick at grasping spatial relations, but only in connection with concrete things."[9]

The studies mentioned above and the general observation of children assigned to special classes for the retarded indicate that it is possible, for the patient and understanding classroom teacher and the teacher of art, to offer some means of expression that may induce a measure of social adjustment and general mental health for the children in this category.

The art activities suggested here obviously will need to be in the area of things and materials. Three-dimensional work in woods and clay, simple weaving, leathercraft, simple toymaking, and many other similar undertakings are quite within the ability of such pupils. The handling of the tools required in the performance of various tasks, as well as the therapeutics inherent in the manipulation of materials, may furnish the much-needed sense of adequacy and accomplishment.

What standards of achievement should be sought under these circumstances? It seems wise to conclude that, as in the case of normal children, each individual pupil will achieve according to his capacity. The teacher's role, even here, is one of guidance, of stimulation, and of encouragement.

In large communities where provisions are made for the mentally retarded, an art coördinator may have opportunity to study conditions and offer constructive suggestions for a program in the handcrafts, and for the upgrading of the activities as children improve. In many schools where no provision is made for the handling of such children, classroom

---

[8] William M. Cruickshank, "Arithmetic Ability of Mentally Retarded Children: II, Understanding Arithmetic Processes," *Journal of Education Research*, December, 1948, pp. 279–288.

[9] G. M. Robson, "Social Factors in Mental Retardation," *British Journal of Psychology*, 1931, pp. 22, 133.

teachers and the art coördinator may collaborate in the development of plans and suitable activities for the mentally retarded and slow learners either within the school day or after school, or even in Saturday classes.

Of real significance is the fact that teachers of art should recognize in these children a challenge to be met and a professional service to be

THE HANDICRAFTS and some types of two-dimensional art work are used effectively with the handicapped. The activities are chosen with due regard to the physical impairment. Children of low mentality are also able to profit by arts and crafts experiences. In all instances, the results are a source of pride for the pupil and a step toward his social competence (public schools, Easton, Pa.).

rendered. The social value of this service can only be measured in terms of the relative harmony and, consequently, the relative happiness that may be brought into the lives of the children.

CHILDREN WITH OTHER PHYSICAL DEFICIENCIES

The condition of children with serious speech deficiencies, the hard of hearing, the deaf, and the mute is, of course, one to be faced. From the standpoint of experiencing art, the problem may not appear as too serious since it is possible to communicate with such pupils in other ways than through the spoken word. Thus art has its role to play even in the lives of these children. Tests by Pintner[10] and later tests by Pintner and Lev,[11] as well as many others, indicate that the intelligence and the manipulative abilities of children so impaired, when compared to the intelligence and manipulative ability of similar groups of children who are not afflicted, do not differ materially. This does not mean that no problem exists. It means that whatever conditions are manifest are significant enough to cause mental and emotional disturbances which eventually widen the deviation from normal living. Herein lies the problem for the educational worker. Social and emotional adjustments of such children must be sought.

The totally deaf and the mute, who must be institutionalized in order that they may be educated for useful citizenship, will benefit by the advantages of the arts and crafts much as normal boys and girls do, and much more. The emotional strain of being different needs the compensatory satisfaction of being able to create. This is in itself a healing and a heightening of the personality of the afflicted individual. Actually, a new language comes to their aid and the feelings of inferiority are minimized. Clair James, who works with the deaf, says: "The art studio serves many purposes for the deaf student. There are the therapeutic values in developing motor coördination and manipulative skills to which she is particularly adept if guided. Also it is an agent for relief of frustrations which are so prevalent in late adolescence."[12]

It is evident that the problem of teaching art to the deaf or to the mute becomes one of approach. When a suitable method of communication has been established and the teacher is conversant with the emotional problems of such children, it is likely that their work in art may be of a quality equal to that of normal children. In many instances it may even possess greater intensity and meaning because of the new-found avenue of communication.

---

[10] Rudolph Pintner, "An Adjustment Test with Normal and Hard of Hearing Children," *Journal of Genetic Psychology*, 1940, 8, pp. 380–381.

[11] Rudolph Pintner and Joseph Lev, "The Intelligence of Hard of Hearing School Children," *Pedagogical Seminar and Journal of Genetic Psychology*, 1939, 55, pp. 31–48.

[12] Clair G. James, "Art and the Adolescent Deaf Girl," *School Arts*, March, 1955, p. 22.

GIFTED CHILDREN

Discovery and training of leaders, of those whose intelligence, creative talents, or specialized skills are of value to the social group, has always been one of the concerns of man.

In various ways and by different methods, from primitive society to the present, attempts have been made to provide the proper kind of education for the gifted. But each age and each culture has had its own criterion of what constitutes superiority.

NEED FOR EARLY IDENTIFICATION

Primitive society identified, very early, the boys who seemed to give promise of leadership and, usually upon reaching adolescence, introduced them to the rigors of training, the mysteries of the ritual, and eventually to the individual adventure that marked them either as future leaders or forever excluded them from such role. The Age of Reason in Europe placed greatest emphasis on intellectual superiority and the Renaissance gave support to and was interested chiefly in the intellectual capacity of men of science, men of letters, artists, diplomats, military strategists, and business leaders.[13]

Until quite recently, the English system of secondary education and the subsequent higher education were designed primarily to prepare leaders for service to the Crown's far-flung empire. The highly selective systems of education in France, Italy, and Germany until a few decades ago were intended for a similar purpose. In fact, most education beyond elementary school, in nearly all countries of the world, was intended for the purpose of training for leadership of one sort or another.

The American idea of a secondary education and beyond, for all who wish to avail themselves of it, is both recent and unique. As democratic thought has spread to other countries, similar patterns have been partially adopted.

But it should be evident that as the opportunities for extended education have become more widespread and larger numbers of boys and girls have entered the secondary school, it has become more difficult to

---

[13] Will Durant, *The Renaissance*, New York, Simon and Schuster, 1953. The entire volume is a revelation of the abundance of talent which the new humanism brought to light and utilized.

devote proper attention to those with superior gifts. Paul Witty states very succinctly the plight of the gifted child in these words: "Since the bright child usually conformed to school routine, he was generally permitted to drift through school with his superior abilities unrecognized and unchallenged."[14] It seems, therefore, that in spite of the fact that the necessity of identifying leaders has always been recognized, for a variety of reasons, systematic and adequate provisions for the purpose have never been undertaken on a meaningful scale.

In so far as modern endeavors are concerned, it is safe to say that not until the latter part of the nineteenth century was a serious study of the problem made. Galton's *Hereditary Genius*, which was published in 1869, is credited with arousing considerable interest in the problem of individual differences and, indirectly, influenced the thinking of educators in the direction of the present concern.

Some cities, such as Elizabeth, New Jersey, and St. Louis, Missouri, made early provisions for the accelerated promotion of bright pupils. In these cities, and later in Santa Barbara, California; Cleveland, Ohio; and Rochester, New York, enriched and individualized instruction was practiced as early as 1900. Homogeneous grouping and the "multiple track" plan were being tried in several localities in the early 1920's.

THE LITERATURE OF THE FIELD

A clearer picture of the effort made in behalf of the gifted child may be gained by even a brief mention of some major studies dealing with the problem. Galton's work, which has already been mentioned, is perhaps the cornerstone of the movement, while Terman's[15] study, published in 1925, is the most monumental piece of work of its type done in this country. It gave impetus to the study of the gifted by American educators and has been a source of authority in dealing with this aspect of education. In 1930, the White House Conference on Child Health and Protection resulted in the volume *The Handicapped and the Gifted*. It focused on the handicapped, although it called attention to the seriousness of the problem of the gifted. That report indicated that at the time there were slightly over one million gifted children in the nation, but

---

[14] Paul Witty (ed.), *The Gifted Child*, Boston, D. C. Heath and Company, 1951, p. 2.
[15] Terman and others, *op. cit.*

that only four thousand of them were receiving some special attention. In the same year, Lamson[16] made a scientific study of the situation and outlined significant steps toward the solution of the problem. In 1935 Merle Sumption[17] reported on the work with gifted children in Cleveland and Cohen[18] accounted for similar projects in New York City. These studies have a great deal to offer in the way of methods of organization and practices. Marten's[19] study, which followed some years later, is both authoritative and practical since it indicates specifically how the problem of the gifted may be tackled in schools of various sizes. The National Education Association made a distinct contribution toward the solution of the problem in its research bulletin *High School Methods with Superior Children.*[20] Among recent studies, the most helpful to teachers is Terman and Oden's[21] follow-up study of the original experiment. The findings of this last study are tremendously significant in that they establish with living proof many of the earlier assumptions. Leta Hollingsworth's[22] contributions to this area of education are of inestimable worth; in fact, they are regarded as foundational by experts in this area of child study.

THE AMERICAN ASSOCIATION FOR GIFTED CHILDREN

The achievements and continued interest in the movement today are due, in large part, to the support given to it by the American Association for Gifted Children. The work of this organization consists of stimulation of research, distribution of pertinent literature, production of studies such as *The Gifted Child,*[23] and similar worth-while projects.

---

[16] Edna Lamson, *A Study of Young Gifted Children in Senior High School,* Teachers College Contributions to Education, No. 424, New York, Teachers College, Columbia University, 1930.

[17] Merle R. Sumption, *Three Hundred Gifted Children,* Yonkers, N.Y., Wald Book Company, 1941.

[18] Helen L. Cohen and Nancy Coryell, (eds.), *Educating Superior Students,* New York, American Book Company, 1935.

[19] Elise H. Marten, *Curriculum Adjustment for Gifted Children,* Bulletin 1946, No. 1, Washington, D.C., U.S. Office of Education, 1946.

[20] Research Bulletin, Vol. XIX, No. 4, Washington, D.C., National Education Association, 1941.

[21] Lewis M. Terman and Melita H. Oden, *Genetic Studies of Genius,* Vol IV, *The Gifted Child Grows Up,* Stanford, Calif., Stanford University Press, 1947.

[22] Leta Hollingsworth, *Children Above 180 I.Q.* (ed. Harry L. Hollingsworth), Yonkers, World Book Company, 1942.

[23] Witty, *op. cit.* It is an example of the fine work of the association.

The importance of the organization can be readily appraised as one considers the tremendous waste of talent all about. The National Education Association, through its Educational Policies Commission, has spoken for the entire profession by calling attention to the much-needed work to be done in this area if the nation is to remain strong and free. The Association's most recent work in this area, *Education of the Gifted*, speaks eloquently of the task which faces the schools in this regard.

SOCIAL ADJUSTMENT OF THE GIFTED

It is quite likely that the intellectual position of the gifted may give rise to misunderstandings with respect to their serious need for adjusting to the social group. Talent, high intelligence, marked special aptitudes, and other attributes of the children in the category under discussion bring with them sharp maladjustments. These may be partially minimized if special programs and special guidance are given such children; however, it seems important to indicate here that highly gifted children present a somewhat ambiguous situation.

The children are superior, yet they may develop feelings of inferiority because they are singled out. They are highly adequate in one way or another, yet they may develop feelings of inadequacy in relation to the larger group because they are above the group. They are intelligent, so that it could be assumed that they can resolve social situations easily; yet often they become "lone wolves," feel isolated, and show a craving for friendship. Their superiority, in one way or another, should make them confident, yet often they show lack of self-confidence.

There are many reasons for this peculiar situation and common ones may be easily spotted by classroom teachers, including art teachers. They are elaborated upon simply as a help in their general understanding. If, when identified, gifted children are placed in a special environment, the very fact may give rise in some of them to a dislike of being different. To be different, and to realize it, is an uncomfortable situation to be in and often causes the child to want to be like others, like many of his friends. This may cause difficulties that need to be overcome.

A second reason for maladjustment is that the gifted often realize what they wish to be and what their ambitions are. These wishes and ambitions may be in the very opposite direction indicated by their intelligence or special abilities. Herein lies a likely conflict between parents

THE GIFTED CHILD is also an exceptional case. He needs opportunities beyond those of the typical classroom. Special classes for such children are often organized by museums, art schools, and school districts (*above*, plasticine, rhino, wrestling match, and bear, age 9–11 group, Worcester Art Museum, Worcester, Mass.; *below*, "City Common," poster paint on paper, age 15, Worcester Art Museum, Worcester, Mass.).

and children, or between teachers and children. The conflict must be resolved if at all possible or the entire effort of making provision for these children is wasted.

A third reason for maladjustment originates with adults, the very adults who would like to see the gifted adequately educated. But adults, be they parents or teachers, succumb to enticements, exhibitionism, exploitation, and pressures. Public performances for their own sake, competitions, auditions, contests, and similar activities, often disturb the gifted child to the point where he becomes a problem within a problem.

Another cause of maladjustment may be the inadequacy of the regular instruction, or even of the special instruction, and the guidance that is being furnished. The ordinary curriculum of any typical school is boresome to the gifted child. Therefore, in self-defense, or even in defiance, he invents ways and schemes that make of him a deviate in the opposite direction. Here again, it may be worth reiterating the importance of identifying the gifted as early as possible and then of challenging them adequately, consistently, and expertly.

GUIDANCE ONE ANSWER

One answer to this very important phase of education is guidance. But, not guidance in the generally accepted sense. These are special children, hence they require *special guidance*. The function of the expert must be definitely recognized in connection with this problem. The best authority available; the most-competent instruction, such as reflective teaching, which will be challenging to each one; the most understanding teaching—these are essential needs of superior children, of the talented, and of those with marked special abilities. Strang makes it very clear when she says: "The optimum development of the gifted child requires attention to his emotional and social life as well as to his intellectual needs."[24] It is obvious then that efforts in the direction of saving the gifted, and resources spent in attempting to bring out their gifts, will not avail if the emotional life and the social growth of the children are not developed simultaneously with their gifts.

---

[24] Ruth Strang, "Mental Hygiene of Gifted Children," in Witty, *op. cit.,* p. 137.

All the possible financial support and all the facilities for carrying on the work in art for the gifted child will be of little worth if teachers adequate to the task are not in direct charge of the program.

One may safely say that only gifted teachers should attempt to teach gifted children. Even if it could be taken for granted that well-prepared teachers of art were available, guiding exceptionally talented pupils is in itself a special task. The teacher of the gifted should be a truly creative person in every sense of the word, but in addition he should be well grounded in psychology and in the nature and method of creative education. He should be fully aware of the import of the special assignment; lastly, he should be a dynamic, growing person who can recognize growth in those whom he teaches.

In what respects, then, is the teacher just described different from the ideal teacher described in Chapter 14? The answer would seem to be that the teacher of the gifted is all that a good teacher ought to be, but even beyond possessing adequate technical and professional skills. He is a person of unusual insights, of exceptional resources, and of wide understandings. Individuals such as Minnie Levenson of the Worcester Museum, Thomas Munro of Cleveland, and Florence Cane, formerly at New York University, are the type of teacher that gifted children need and deserve.

THE TALENTED IN ART

A NEGLECTED AREA

Thus far the consideration has dealt with the gifted in general. It has been so because unless teachers and parents realize the broader aspects of the problem, it is not likely that they will be sympathetic toward the talented in art, with whom the balance of this discussion will deal.

That superior talent in art has manifested itself in thousands of individuals in all ages and in all cultures is attested by the history of art. The public admiration for works of art by masters of the past and of the present is a living testimony of how highly genius is prized. The fact that much talent seems available at the present time may be explained by several facts: greater opportunity for expression has been made possible, the schools have become interested in art as a phase of development, and art teaching as an educational field has grown to respectable stature. People's taste for things artistic has been raised by the work of a number of agencies, and a subsequent demand for the products of artists has resulted; lastly, scientific studies of exceptional children, and of art abilities in particular, have given fresh vigor to the search and cultivation of talent.

All this suggests that the need for identifying creative individuals and of nurturing the gifts with which they are endowed is both clear and immediate. It is an obvious need because it is intimately related to the general responsibility of education to provide for the fullest development of the individual so endowed; it is unmistakable from the standpoint of the demands of society; and it is plain in terms of the historic responsibility of education to preserve as well as to extend the cultural heritage.

The problem of the gifted in art is of immediate concern to all those who deal with children if the recent acceptance of art expression as a means of education is to be strengthened. In this country at least, tremendous strides have been made in art at the elementary-school level, somewhat less gratifying progress is noted at the secondary level, and lately some hopeful advances may be seen at the art-school and college levels. But it is doubtful that many who would achieve eminence in art are identified sufficiently early. It is equally doubtful that under present circumstances adequate and continued provision is made for those who appear to be potential creators.

Art teachers and coördinators must become more sensitive to this situation and by all plausible means should develop suitable opportunities for the relatively few children who give promise of unusual development.

AVAILABLE RESEARCH

Contrary to general opinion and in spite of the fact that the mass of art teachers may not always be aware of the fact, there exists a substantial body of scientific data to guide teachers and parents who may be confronted with the problem under discussion. The fields of aesthetics, of appreciation and judgment, of skills and abilities, of emotions as they relate to art, of perception, of specialized aptitudes in the ele-

ments of art—all these have been subjected to experimentation by psychologists, aestheticians, and by some art educators. The bibliography
developed by Faulkner[25] several years ago was impressive even at the
time and has increased considerably. It should prove a real stimulus to
those whose interests may lead them to serious research in this phase of
art education. Munro,[26] on the other hand, provides not only original
studies, but surveys the entire field of psychology and creative expression
and offers significant, critical evaluations of the work of others. Meier,[27]
a psychologist interested in aesthetics, and coauthor of the Meier-Sea-
shore Art Judgment Test, is concerned with the psychological aspects
of art. The present ascendancy of the psychological approach to educational problems gives studies of the gifted a heightened value. Of particular significance in the identification of superior children in art is
Meier's "Factors in Artistic Aptitude."[28]

Goodenough's[20] work is of special importance and Cane's[30] earlier
work with the gifted is both scientific and inspirational. As a source,
The Measurement of Artistic Abilities by Kinter[31] is eminently worth-
while.

In general, it will be found that the *Journal of Applied Psychology,
Psychological Monographs,* the *Journal of Psychology,* and related publications often report on current research and on completed experiments.
The mass of materials such as has been indicated above is becoming
available more and more in English. In the past a great deal of research
in art was available only in foreign publications. The present situation
should encourage wider reading and application of scientific research in
the work of the art teacher and particularly in the area of art talent.

[25] Ray Faulkner, "Research in Art and Art Education," in *Art in American Life and
Education,* Fortieth Yearbook, National Society for the Study of Education, Bloomington,
Ill., Public School Publishing Company, 1941.

[26] *Ibid.,* Chapters XXI, XXII, XXIII.

[27] *Ibid.,* Chapter XXVI.

[28] Norman C. Meier, "Factors in Artistic Aptitude: Final Summary of a Ten Year Study
of a Special Ability," *Psychological Monographs,* 51, 1939, pp. 140–158.

[29] Florence L. Goodenough, "Children's Drawings," in *A Handbook of Child Psychology,*
Worcester, Clark University Press, 1931, pp. 480–514.

[30] Florence Cane, "The Gifted Child in Art," *Journal of Educational Sociology,* October,
1936, pp. 67–73.

[31] M. Kinter, *The Measurement of Artistic Abilities: A Summary of Scientific Studies in
the Field of Graphic Arts,* New York, Psychological Corporation, 1933.

THE TASK OF THE SCHOOL

Having surveyed, broadly, the nature of the problem, it now seems appropriate to discuss what the schools may be able to do in regard to it.

One of the frequently repeated statements in the literature of art

education is that school art does not claim to prepare young people for professional careers in the arts, but that it hopes to develop and nurture the creative spark so that, eventually, it may be brought to full fruition by those agencies prepared so to do. On the other hand, the present discussion seems to stress the necessity of doing more than the usual art program would imply. This is true to the extent that the highly talented are a special concern. The reference here is to the over-and-beyond provisions that might be made for those children who evidence not only deep interest but continued application and unusual powers of perception in graphic or in three-dimensional expression. The old adage that "genius will out" is hardly to be taken as scientific evidence. Even the occasional success of those who are referred to as "untaught," or "primitives," is quite rare. Unless op-

EXPERT INSTRUCTION, conducive atmosphere, and sympathetic guidance can do much to develop the talents of young people. Summer classes for such children are sometimes organized by colleges, museums, and school districts (summer workshop for high-school students, State Teachers College, New Paltz, N.Y.).

portunity is provided, a gifted child may never be identified and his gifts will be forever lost. Therefore, the classroom teacher, or the art teacher who is sympathetic and alert to the problem, should consider it his privilege to discover an exceptional child. The next steps are the problem of coördinators and administrators.

RESPONSIBILITY OF THE ART COÖRDINATOR

When art teachers, and particularly coördinators, have recognized the implications of the situation presented in the foregoing statements, they will realize their responsibility for implementing a program of special opportunities for talented children.

The superintendent of schools or the person in immediate charge of the educational program for the system should be consulted and his support for the program secured. If the program is to be financed by public funds, it will become his responsibility to procure the adequate budgetary allowance. If, on the other hand, the financing of the project is to be the responsibility of a community group, such as the Junior League or the local woman's club, it is equally important for the coördinator to have the consent and professional support of the chief school administrator. When the initial approval and financial support have been secured, the art consultant or teacher may proceed to make detailed plans.

As a first step, it is suggested that the art coördinator make a careful survey to ascertain the number of children judged as gifted by the classroom teachers in those grades or school levels in which the program is to be initiated. Since it has been intimated that unless talented children are identified early a number of forces will submerge them, it may be advisable to begin such a program with children of the elementary school. As opportunities develop, it should involve older children up to and including those in the senior high school.

It may be assumed by some that children in junior and senior high schools are properly cared for since they are taught by specially trained, competent art teachers. A study of the pupil loads carried by such teachers, the scheduling problems that obtain at the secondary level, and the multifarious other activities for which art teachers are responsible should convince anyone of the impracticability of the situation to help solve the problem of the gifted pupil. This may not be the case in large school systems where major art sequences have been established and where the teacher may have opportunities to offer special guidance to boys and girls of promise.

TYPES OF PROGRAMS FOR THE GIFTED

As a general criterion it is advisable to begin with the elementary school and gradually extend the program to include older children.

When the coördinator has surveyed the problem with regard to numbers and has determined on a course of action, he may wish to contact

410   the parents of the children involved to ascertain their coöperation and wishes as well as inform them on specific details.

Opportunity Classes

A possible course to follow at the outset may be to establish "opportunity" classes for the talented at centrally located school buildings where sympathetic and able teachers assigned to the work may meet with the children. This may be done during regular school days in some situations; in other instances such classes may meet immediately after the close of the school day. In large elementary centers there may be a sufficiently large number of such children to warrant setting up an art laboratory where the children may report at specified hours.

Saturday Classes

In some localities special Saturday classes for the gifted are conducted in conveniently located buildings. These special classes afford greater freedom of operation because only those children who have been identified will be in attendance in the building. In these classes the teachers involved are assured a measure of autonomy and freedom from the restraints of regular school situations and routines. But most important in this case is the degree of homogeneity of interest and, in a sense, of the abilities of the children to be taught.

When age factors and group sizes have been considered and adequate arrangements have been made, the teacher is ready to undertake the important task. Now the problem resolves itself in the skillful stimulation of interests that are genuine and abilities that await to be called forth.

Museum Classes

One of the best opportunities to give talented children special guidance in creative activities beyond the more restricted possibilities suggested so far may be found in local or nearby museums. When such institutions are reasonably accessible and rapport has been established with their education departments, it should not be difficult to initiate classes for gifted children. A number of excellent examples in which the schools and the museums coöperate and give joint support to such activities are to be found in Reading, Pennsylvania; Toledo, Ohio; Providence, Rhode Island; Philadelphia, Pennsylvania; Worcester, Massachusetts; and many

others. Low[32] indicates that the educational divisions of many such institutions are not only ready but eager to coöperate.

The significant work done with exceptional children by Levenson at
Worcester, by Munro in Cleveland,
and by Jantzen in Philadelphia is not
only a testimony to the excellent opportunities available but an evidence
of the soundness of the educational
philosophy which prevails among educational personnel in museums. A re-

---

[32] Theodore Low, *The Educational Philoso-
phy and Practice of Art Museums in the United
States*, New York, Teachers College, Columbia
University, 1948.

CHALLENGING MEDIA represent new ventures for the gifted. Various technics offer new problems to be
solved; therefore, they are excellent means of stimulation for the talented (*above*, scratchboard composition, Jane Addams High School, Cleveland, Ohio; *below*, Boston Boys' Club, Boston, Mass.).

cent development which indicates an awareness of the problem is the establishment of children's museums. The Brooklyn Children's Museum is an example of such an enterprise. The children's classes sponsored by the Museum of Modern Art in New York are further evidence that such institutions are alert to the problem and willing to find a solution to it.

But it will be said, and justifiably so, that too many communities are far removed from museums and, therefore, cannot avail themselves of their services. There are other means and other ways: Maud Ellsworth[33] found the answer in Lawrence, Kansas, by challenging the community while offering her own services. In Reading, Pennsylvania, the Berks County Art Alliance has established Saturday children's classes which are taught by members of the Alliance; a teachers college conducted free classes for gifted children for a number of years. These are but a few of many instances which show how art coördinators and teachers have surmounted obstacles in order to give talented boys and girls an opportunity to develop fully those gifts that enrich the life of the child and, in the long run, of the total culture.

SUMMARY

In this chapter, the problem of all those children referred to as exceptional has been considered as a situation to be realized as being very real. The function of art education as an ameliorating factor has been pointed out to reinforce the general value and the healing qualities of art experience in connection with some of the major classifications of exceptional children.

There is little doubt that art can be used to alleviate emotional and mental illness; there is also ample evidence that art is used both to diagnose and cure some mental conditions through self-revelation on the part of the patient and his rediscovery of the self from which he has been alienated.

Certain possible methods of using art with the blind, the maladjusted, the hard of hearing, and the mute have been advanced only as beginnings in what may eventually become a branch of art teaching in and of itself.

---

[33] Maud Ellsworth, "The Children's Summer Studio," *School Arts*, 1947, pp. 303–305.

The important fact is that art teachers and coördinators should be at least aware of the abnormal conditions of many children, and, rather than disregard their plight, teachers may study their case and act in their behalf.

It has been made clear that this is a vast and difficult problem and that only experts such as psychologists, psychiatrists, physicians, and others with specialized training should diagnose and further handle difficult cases.

But the term exceptional child includes the boy or girl with above-normal intellect, or those children with marked abilities in one field or another. The talented child in art is of special concern to art teachers and coördinators; therefore, particular attention has been devoted to his lot.

A number of suggestions have been made regarding enriched art programs for the gifted in art: special classes, afternoon and Saturday classes, museum instruction, and special curricular adjustments. These are possibilities that must be appraised at the local level since they involve additional teachers, additional financing, and additional materials.

In spite of the obstacles that seem to stand in the way of solving this vast problem adequately, some progress is being made from year to year. As more teachers become aware of the problem and are willing to spend themselves in its solution, more thousands of boys and girls may be helped toward a happier existence.

This is an area which art education has hardly explored. It may be several decades before any tangible work will be done in it. However, if the profession becomes aware of the possibilities for service inherent in the area, then the healing quality of art may be extended even to those whose lot in life is less than a happy one.

For Discussion and Activity

1. For a realization of the extent of the problem of the exceptional child make a survey of your immediate community or county. What agencies deal with the problem? How many children are involved? What are some of the solutions employed? What phases of the whole problem are untouched? Share your finds with your class or group.
2. If possible, identify children who are specially gifted in art and who are

attending the local schools or the laboratory school of your college. Make a study of one or two such children and devise a simple program that may help them for one semester. Watch their progress in art, their general emotional reaction, and other aspects of growth worthy of note. Write up their case studies and share them with your associates.

3. Follow the procedure outlined for the gifted child (Question 2, above), but apply it to a handicapped child from the school or community.

4. Visit, as individuals or as a group, a school for exceptional children located within reasonable distance. Report on the nature of the school, its program, its problems, its successes, failures, and any other aspects that will clarify the problem. How is art used with the children in the school? How might art be used?

5. What are the principal reasons for insisting that the gifted in art should be given additional opportunities beyond those possible within the regular school program? Discuss these reasons and develop a plan which might be acceptable to the superintendent in a moderate-sized school system.

6. If the Supervisor of Special Education were to ask you to develop an art program for weak-sighted children who are to be taught in classes especially suited to them, what would your program include? Prepare a general outline of activities and justify it before your group. What equipment and what materials would your program involve?

7. As art coördinator you may discover the need for a class for gifted children of elementary-school age. How will you proceed to develop the program? Discuss with your group such matters as time, place, transportation, teacher time, finances, and other pertinent items.

8. If your school system should organize a special program for mentally retarded children, would you be ready to suggest art activities for such children? What would be the nature of the activities? What facts or statistical data could you use in support of your selection of activities?

9. From the literature of art education discover what tests are available and what experiments have been conducted to measure or to determine art aptitude or ability. What are the findings? What do they indicate? What local means are there for teachers to determine talent in art?

10. Make a survey of nearby communities to ascertain what is being done in junior and senior high schools to care for children with special talent in art. What do the findings show?

For Further Reading

Baker, Harry J., *Introduction to Exceptional Children,* New York, The Macmillan Company, 1944, Chapters III, V, XVII, XVIII.

Beckman, Albert S., "A Study of Social Background and Art Aptitude of Superior Negro Children," *Journal of Applied Psychology*, December, 1942, pp. 777–784.

Cane, Florence, "The Gifted Child in Art," *Journal of Educational Sociology*, October 1936, pp. 65–108.

Garrison, Karl C., *The Psychology of Exceptional Children*, rev. ed., New York, The Ronald Press Company, 1950, Chapters I, IV, VI, X–XII, XIX.

Heck, Arch O., *The Education of Exceptional Children*, New York: McGraw-Hill Book Company, 1940, Chapters XII, XVII, XXIII, XXIX.

Lowenfeld, Berthold, "Research in the Education of the Blind," *Journal of Educational Research*, April, 1947, pp. 583–589.

Marten, Elise H., *Teachers' Problems with Exceptional Children*, Vol. II, *Gifted Children*, Pamphlet No. 41, Washington, D.C., U.S. Office of Education, 1941.

Terman, Lewis M., and others. *Genetic Studies of Genius*, Vol. I, *Mental and Physical Traits of a Thousand Gifted Children*, Stanford, Calif., Stanford University Press, 1925.

White House Conference, *Special Education: The Handicapped and the Gifted*, New York, Century Company, 1931, pp. 537–550.

Wilbur, L., *Vocations for the Visually Handicapped*, New York, American Foundation for the Blind, 1937.

Witty, Paul A., *A Study of One Hundred Gifted Children*, Lawrence, University of Kansas, Bulletin of Education, Vol. II, No. 7, 1930.

Witty, Paul A. (ed.), *The Gifted Child*, Boston, D. C. Heath and Company, 1951, Chapters I, II, VI, VII, XII.

CREATIVE ADULTS

> Our first and most important task, therefore, is to arouse
> in people an awareness of the aesthetic values and of the
> potentialities of creative activity in terms of human devel-
> opment and human satisfaction.
>
> Ernest Ziegfeld,
> *Art in the College Program of*
> *General Education*

A NEW FRONTIER IN ART EDUCATION

THE MEANING OF LIFELONG LEARNING

Recently, a new department has affiliated with the national education Association, namely, the Department of Public School Adult Education. The fact in itself might be taken as a matter of course. However,
it has great significance because it indicates the sizable extent of the
participation by the public schools in this newer phase of educational
service. It also points to implications for art education.

A second interesting fact is that placement officers in colleges and
universities report that more and more young teachers are being employed to work not only with the children in the public schools but with
adults as well.

These two developments indicate that teachers of arts and crafts need
to be made aware of this area of public education and that, as nearly as
possible, they must be educated, or reëducated, to render service in adult
education. The intent of this chapter is to present an overview of the
problems, the challenges, and the opportunities of this new frontier.

The entire problem has assumed a magnitude that requires special study; but for initial purposes, only what seems essential is presented. The public-school aspects are emphasized only because of their pertinence in the framework of this volume.

In his definition of adult education, Lyman Bryson,[1] one of the earlier writers on this subject, makes an important distinction in regard to types of adult education. It seems appropriate to indicate that distinction even in this brief consideration. Bryson distinguishes between educational activities for adults which are dictated by *urgency* and those which are suggested by *importance*. In general, whatever is done for adults as a matter of safeguard, or to correct a local situation, or to forestall a likely personal or social calamity falls in the category of the urgent. On the other hand, whatever organized educational efforts are made in response to the natural, deep-seated desires and longings of adults may be considered important.

The distinction between the two terms is significant from the standpoint of creative education. In a materialistic world, it is imperative to make provision for the yearnings, the innate urges, and the compelling wish to express oneself at all age levels. In this respect, adults are like children: they wish to grow, to find themselves, and to express themselves in a variety of ways suitable to them. When seen in this light and with regard to art as experience, adult education as a whole becomes a tremendously important factor in the enrichment of life. Such enrichment becomes the fountainhead that feeds the moral and spiritual energies of the individual and sustains him as he meets the problems of existence.

It should be said that the gains made by art education in the schools have found a correspondingly strong appeal among older citizens. Parents, relatives, and neighbors have become art-conscious through the activities of children. Evidences of this fact are revealed by the impressive consumption of art of all types by an ever-expanding public. Museums have been organized in a large number of communities all over the nation; public lectures and forums reach the millions; amateur art organizations flourish; noncredit art courses are made available by extension divisions of colleges, universities, and similar agencies. The public schools and

---

[1] Lyman Bryson, "What We Mean by Adult Education," in Mary L. Ely (ed.), *Handbook of Adult Education in the United States*, New York, Teachers College, Columbia University, 1948, pp. 1–6.

other local organizations are opening their doors during late-afternoon and evening hours to offer adults opportunities in the arts. Ziegfeld's[2] report of the situation in New York State is both revealing and encouraging. It is a challenge to art education of the next quarter-century. Truly, art education for adults is a new professional frontier. Its promise of expansion is bright and its potential effects on richer living for thousands of people are beyond ordinary imagination.

NATURE AND SCOPE OF ADULT EDUCATION

In a sense, the problem of lifelong learning is not a new educational venture. Indeed, it is an old ideal, traceable throughout the development of earlier civilizations. Bryson, writing on the subject, indicates that the great teachers of the ages, teachers such as Buddha, Socrates, and Christ, addressed themselves to the mature minds of their day, thus continuing the learning process beyond whatever schooling may have existed at the time. There are evidences throughout the history of mankind of the need for and the willingness to continue learning beyond youth. The ritual and the council of primitive society, the medieval crafts guilds, and the thousands of contemporary, voluntary organizations which minister to adults are some of the evidences. In fact, the mature mind realizes even more deeply than the youth that lifelong learning is an inevitable process if man is to cope successfully with the problems of living. The mounting complexities of each succeeding historic age have made this fact very clear to the people.

On the other hand, adult education, as the term is used today and in its present form of organization, is relatively new. Its claims to public and private support have never been stronger. The pressures and the changes of modern life, when added to the desire of many to continue to learn, have caused this newer phase of education to receive the attention and the backing of civic, religious, philanthropic, industrial, and governmental bodies of citizens.

PRESENT STATUS

Adult education takes within its fold all persons above the age of 18, or all those for whom compulsory education has ended. The Council of

---

[2] Edwin Ziegfeld, *New Frontiers and Responsibilities in Art Education*, Sixth Yearbook, Kutztown, Pa., National Art Education Association, 1955, pp. 37–52.

National Organizations of the Adult Education Association reports the following categories: (1) younger ages; 18 to 30 years of age; (2) middle ages, 30 to 55 years of age; and (3) older ages, 55 years of age and over.[3] The groupings suggest the breadth and scope of the program. They also suggest the extent of the organizational structure that has developed for meeting effectively the needs of the groups represented. When looked at from the standpoint of the actual numbers of people reached by all organizations at work in this area, the figures are staggering. La Salle reports: "By the end of the current school year some three million adults in this country will have participated in classes, discussion groups, forums, work-shops, lectures, and social-recreational groups promoted and supported, wholly or in part, by public schools."[4]

But because art education for adults may also involve teachers in the work of groups outside the sphere of the public schools, it is important that the broader aspects of the situation be studied as well. The Council of National Organizations of the Adult Education Association[5] actually estimates that 72,000,000 adults are enrolled in all types of groupings. These range from "audiences" and college groupings to small workshops and classes. What the figures indicate is simply that the task is a vast one and that the number and variety of required instructional personnel are just as impressive.

ORGANIZATIONAL STRUCTURE

The organizational structure of this sphere of interest has assumed formidable proportions. The report of the Council referred to above shows that in a fact-finding project of recent date 148 national organizations working with adults were invited to submit information. Of these, 126 responded, and 113 of them were actually participating in the Council's program. The Council further states that it is impossible to ascertain how many organizations and groups actually exist and carry on some sort of program for adults. What seems definite is that there are many more than responded to the Council's inquiry.

[3] Council of National Organizations, Adult Education Association, *Adult Education: A Directory of National Organizations*, New York, Association Press, 1954, p. 12.

[4] Loy B. La Salle, "Public-School Adult Education," *Journal of the National Education Association*, February, 1955, p. 85.

[5] Council of National Organizations, *op. cit.*, p. 10.

VARIETY OF INTERESTS is likely to be evident in the typical arts and crafts program for adults. Personal problems and aspirations must be a chief concern of the teacher of adults (adult class in the arts, public schools, Kutztown, Pa.).

A further study of the organizational structure of the various groups within the Adult Education Association indicates that they vary a great deal with regard to geographic interest. Twenty-two organizations operate on local, state, and regional levels; 33 organizations have national, regional, and state units; 17 organizations have one unit below the national level; other groups operate only on the national level. These data suggest the complexity of the problem and also the necessity for variation because of the nature of the services or participation required.

With regard to types of services and programs, adult education presents one of the most diversified pictures of any organized group of citizens. The services and activities range from public and governmental affairs to higher education, recreation, hobbies, leadership training, skills training, study groups, workshops, and classes in an infinite variety of subjects including the arts and crafts. In addition, there are several thousands of adults enrolled in classes for foreign-born, elementary education, physical education, and the practical arts which, in the judgment of the Council, are not reported on adequately.

It is natural that the vast number of participants, the variety of interests, and the many types of organizations and services should reflect an equally large diversity of means of communication, differentiated policies, numerous publications, and a vast staff of workers numbering nearly 22,000 persons.

DEVELOPMENT OF GOALS

Sound as the reasons may have been for the earlier development of adult-education programs of various sorts, most of them were temporary in character. Prior to World War I the program attempted to cope with current emergencies. Once solved, many programs quite naturally passed from the scene to give way to new needs. It may be useful here to recall the point of view expressed by Bryson in his introduction to the *Handbook of Adult Education in the United States.*[6] Much of what was done in the early days of the program was considered urgent at the time. On the other hand, much of what constitutes adult education today is considered not only an important task but a continuing and an enlarging one. Its goals have been refined, and even though they are not in any sense stated in final terms they nevertheless reflect years of history and experience with the larger issues inherent in the growing population of a young nation.

Briefly, the objectives of current adult education are these: (1) vocational efficiency, (2) economic understanding, (3) civic participation and responsibility, (4) better human relations and community improvement, (5) group interests, (6) personal growth and self-realization.[7] It is from these areas that the senior citizen who has the opportunity of further education may formulate his goals and from which the teacher may develop plans for the enhancement of the life of out-of-school men and women.

Interestingly enough, one finds recorded in the six areas for adult education an echo and a reaffirmation of the very bases on which the entire art-education program for the schools has been postulated. The individual, the social group, the community, occupations, human relations, and self-discovery and self-realization are all a part of the continuing and expanding role of education for democratic associational life. This is a point worth remembering when teaching adults. Indeed, the goals of adults are continuing ones; the deep-seated motivations

---

[6] Bryson, *op. cit.*, pp. 3–6.
[7] *Ibid.*, p. 7.

422 are not unlike those of the adolescent who seeks his place in the world. The major differences are the age of the learner and his accumulated experiences. The desire to grow is just as strong.

THE MEANING OF ART FOR ADULTS

The values and, therefore, the meanings of creative education for adults are not the result of mere theorizing or of the wishful thinking of overzealous art educators. They are supported by the experimental evidences furnished by thorough and sympathetic studies of adults and by the recorded observations of thousands of cases in the process of reintegration.

Hughes Mearns[8] has recorded his studies and reported his experiences with adults in what is now a classic work. Many others have made statistical recordings of the participation, sustained interests, and permanent benefits received by adults in the process of reëducation. Some of these data have been presented; further reading in the literature of this phase of education will furnish additional evidence of the effectiveness of the venture.

But aside from statistical or experimental evidences, one needs only to observe the spontaneous response of out-of-school people to almost any form of further education: evening schools, clubs, radio and television, forums, extension classes, conferences, book and magazine clubs, public lectures, and myriad other offerings too obvious to require mention. This widespread interest bespeaks the fact that out-of-school people respond as they do because of a need which becomes all too clear as they become involved in the realities of everyday living.

THE SOCIAL AND CULTURAL PATTERN

Workers in shops and fields, clerks, professional men and women, businessmen, executives, housewives, and all others who are otherwise engaged in the world's work seem to respond to post-school activities as sources of relief and release. The humdrum, the mechanical, the monotonous, even sordid, day-after-day occupations seem to stimulate the need for antidotes which rebuild and give new meaning to existence. Yet

---

[8] Hughes Mearns, *The Creative Adult*, New York, Doubleday & Company, 1940.

the arts cannot be conceived only as therapeutics; their functions in adult education may be many. These are described and appraised hereafter.

The most powerful cause that compels adults to turn to the arts for regeneration is to be found in the pattern of contemporary social and cultural life. Even a brief examination of the present condition of man throws a great deal of light on those forces that make it imperative for all education, and creative education especially, to offer adults outlets that will lead them to a restoration of human dignity and self-esteem.

It is evident that a new challenge is facing the arts, and it is also evident that this area is becoming a major concern of education. Therefore, those engaged in the arts need not only to be alerted to the opportunities but to be conversant with the problems, the approaches, and the media required by this new field. The competition of other areas of education, traditional attitudes toward art, and the tenor of the times are lions in the way. By recognizing them for what they are, it may be possible to meet them intelligently and successfully.

A MATERIALISTIC SOCIETY

There is today a widespread notion to the effect that science will cure all the ills of mankind; that science is the surest answer to all the problems of man. The unscientific character of such a notion is evident, yet the popular mind has generally accepted it. The machine and automation, which are results of the applications of science, seem to be the controlling forces of the times. Values and standards which actually belong to the realm of the aesthetic and the spiritual are, instead, calculated largely on a materialistic basis. This fact is all the more reason why it is essential to counter with the arts and to establish a balance between the material and the spiritual. It is more nearly true to conclude that science must be harnessed to serve man. Science also proves conclusively that man has a mind but that he also has emotions and motivations which are of entirely different character.

A second danger to a balanced and rich life is inherent in present-day technology and the inevitable standardization in the processes of production, of consumption, in fact of all life. These mechanistic forces have robbed man of the individuality that he once enjoyed. Originality and self-expression are nearly impossible in the affairs of men. Instead, conformity and routine are the accepted mode. Adults who must earn a living for themselves and their families cannot overlook the sources that furnish them bread. Thus, unwillingly, they accept the attendant evils.

On the other hand, the very fact that individuals must live in a world of machines and of conformity makes it imperative that they be given outlets for release, and that they be acquainted with modes of expression which are not dependent on mechanistic requirements. Man does not live by bread alone. He also lives by his dreams, by participation in creative activity, emotional satisfactions, and spiritual insights. These are the ends of creative experience which are made possible through the arts, the crafts, and germane activities.

A third challenge in contemporary life is the direct outcome of increased leisure. The machine is both a blessing and curse to man. It is a blessing in that it has lifted his burdens and has improved his standards of living; it is a curse in that it has released time. The social responsibility of professional art education is one of presenting a program that will not only absorb the excess of time but utilize it for the reorientation of adult citizens. Such reorientation should be in terms of new outlooks for the individual, of reflection on the changes that have taken place within a lifetime, and should lead to a renewing of concepts in the light of new knowledges. Through new experiences, the teacher should stimulate the adult learner toward the reorientation of a life in which work, play, and creation become the elements of a new pattern of culture.

A further problem in modern society seems to stem from a traditional reverence for what is considered practical, or useful. Indeed, as pointed out in Chapter 13, the very distinction between "fine" arts and the crafts is a holdover from the erroneous thinking of post-Renaissance days. But the matter goes deeper than that. Somehow, the worship of what is practical and the cult of the scientific have brought about a disregard and a minimizing of some of the most powerful forces in life. It has been demonstrated elsewhere in this book that the emotional and the expressive forces are just as practical and just as essential. Art cannot be viewed only as adornment, an affair of idle moments, or as something apart from the more earthy aspects of living. Fortunately, there is dawning a new realization of the meaning of the emotions and of the aesthetic elements in life. The gains made by education at all levels of schooling are beginning to restore the arts to their rightful place. The further hope is that through the education of adults a new valuation of creative pursuits may result.

Generally speaking, older citizens approach the arts with a dual set of feelings: tradition and popular notions on the one hand and personal desire for freedom from inhibitions on the other. If it is possible to demonstrate to them the practicality of art experience, not only as a means of release, but as a way toward self-discovery and expression, the obstacles may be overcome.

Ziegfeld sums up his hopes for a realignment of art, individual, and society in these words: "Properly conceived, the awakening of aesthetic awareness can and should play an important part in the reconstruction of our culture."[9] The statement clearly reveals the true aim and meaning of art in the field of adult education. How the task may be accomplished, the means and methods of accomplishing it, are briefly presented below.

TEACHING OF ADULTS

IMPORTANCE OF INDIVIDUALITY

From the standpoint of teachers and teaching, the crucial question seems to be: how can the individual adult be reached when he accepts the opportunities offered him? Of course, there is no patent answer. Yet from the experiences of those who have worked with adults it should be possible to find some clues. The success or failure of the program hinges on the understanding of the individual and on a sympathetic approach to his problems and his aspirations.

Simply to transplant the well-planned, ideally conceived, and logically structured art program that may have been organized for young people in the public schools could easily defeat the entire venture. This failure would affect both the program and the adult who comes with high hopes and expectations.

This statement is not a denial of the proper planning advocated for younger pupils. What is meant here is that a different type of planning is necessary with adults because the motivations and the maturation levels are different.

Uppermost in the mind of the teacher must be the inalterable fact that

---

[9] Ernest Ziegfeld, *Art in the College Program of General Education*, New York, Teachers College, Columbia University, 1953, Chapter VI.

each adult comes with a purpose of his own. Each comes with a personal concept of art, with special needs, with a particular mental and artistic endowment, and with a social background which differs from anyone else's.

MODELING, POTTERY, AND CERAMICS have a special fascination for many older citizens who seek the "practical" in art. The creation of original forms as well as original molds should be stressed (*above*, ceramics class for adults, public schools, Hazleton, Pa.; *below*, U.S. Military Academy, West Point, N.Y.).

Actual contact with adult teaching may clarify some of these points. An evening-school class in arts and crafts met for the first time. The teacher, to familiarize himself with each individual in the group, passed out cards and asked for the usual information: name, address, type of art interest, prior experience with art, work engaged in, and formal education. He then asked each person to turn to the other side of the card and explain, briefly, why he had chosen to enroll in art and what he hoped the experience would do for him. Some of the findings of this simple procedure should be of interest and point up the importance of the facts gathered through it.

The age range showed that there were people in the group as old as 62 and as young as 17. The formal education ranged from seventh grade to college graduation. Prior experience with art revealed that one man of 26 had had considerable training in art in a German school of industrial design. Most members of the group had had some public-school art contact and the rest had no formal experience whatsoever. The type of work engaged in by members of the group was extremely varied: housewives, draftsmen, steelworkers, a store clerk, a secretary, and many, many others.

The reverse of the card was most important and most revealing. A lady, a minister's wife, well educated, having reared her family was now eager to develop her own interests. She had read the works of Roerich, had visited his museum in New York, and was intensely concerned with the spiritual aspects of art. A younger member of the group wanted to learn Sho'Card Writing and start his own business; someone had told him he could make a good living at it; he felt he had a talent for it. The art-trained young man from Germany wanted further instruction, and was interested in experimenting with media with which he was not acquainted, for the fun and pleasure of creating. Most women were concerned with applied design; they wanted to "make things" for the home, friends, and themselves. A medical man just wanted to paint. A mechanic revealed that he wanted to go to art school when he was young, but that his parents thought he ought to go to work; here was his opportunity.

The significance of individuation in adult education is clearly shown by the composition of the group described. It is also clear that it is erroneous to formalize instruction, or to disregard the personal goals of each person involved. The first session, therefore, was devoted to a discussion of the importance of the person in art; of the need for integrity, of the fact that creating a picture and thinking creatively are not different things after all, and that art is closely related to each individual's life.

Subsequent meetings revolved around personalized programs. As time went on and persons became acquainted and group interest began to develop, it was possible to organize interest centers. Actually, groups began to form spontaneously as students observed one another at work. In this way, personal guidance within interest centers became a natural way of handling the class and the program evolved on its own momentum.

The situation just reported is not unusual. It is very much like what exists in most medium-sized and suburban communities. This is not only true of programs supported by the public schools but of those supported by Y.M.C.A.'s and similar organizations. In larger communities, specialized programs are available. However, they are the exception rather than the rule when adult education is seen in its nation-wide role. Nevertheless, specialized programs will be touched upon in due time. But what of reorientation? The discussion of self-discovery and cultural reawakening

428 that follows points out what happened to the thinking, the tastes, and the life outlooks of the cases referred to.

SELF-DISCOVERY

In working with senior citizens, it must be remembered that they have had many and varied experiences. They know the true meaning of work, of hardships, of success and failure. They have experienced anxieties, happiness, and sorrows. They are not like children, except in their desire to express, in some way, their thoughts and ideas. But fear of the world, moral and social inhibitions, have accumulated over the years. Traditional points of view and socially imposed restraints have been at work for a long time; these are negative forces which tend to submerge the real personality of the average adult. And the few who seem fairly positive about what they wish to accomplish often delimit their new desires and their approach in line with what seems to be currently approved by society.

The first task of the teacher, therefore, is to lead the adult to rid himself of such conditioning factors. This is not an easy matter, nor is it accomplished in haste. Nevertheless, until the individual willingly discards some of the notions that hold back genuine expression, and in their place substitutes new concepts, it will be impossible for him to achieve the very thing he wishes to accomplish—a different outlook on life.

The role of the teacher, particularly in a democratic society, is not so much one of teaching art. It is one of liberating the adult from fears and inhibitions concerning art, the self, and society. This may be done through the encouragement of whatever types of expression are natural to the individual, of saying through art whatever needs to be said. Furthermore, if self-revelation is one of the great needs of adults and one of the chief functions of the sympathetic teacher, then it may be hoped that through these, reorientation may be achieved.

Self-rediscovery of a genuine type is then the sum and substance of any program of adult education. In the arts, it is not the caliber of the work that is produced as much as the miracle that it is produced at all, at that point in life. To discover for oneself new abilities, whether limited or superior, to walk in fresh paths of self-expression, and to feel that life is a never-ending adventure may give adults a brighter outlook and inward self-sufficiency. Improvement in the direction of quality will come as a matter of experience.

CULTURAL REAWAKENING

It should be remembered that adults who come to be reëducated do so on their own. For them there is no legal requirement; it is a personal answer to the need of keeping intellectually alive and culturally abreast of the times. Theirs is a hunger that must be satisfied.

In a way, the adult who seeks the opportunities of further growth is experiencing a reawakening of the senses and a rebirth of the self. If this is true, it must follow that the program in the arts must see in the reawakening an indication of its principal objective rather than a preconceived plan. There is little room in such a program for a teacher or a point of view which leans and directs in one direction and one only. The point of view must be discovered in each individual to be educated. For example, the minister's wife, to whom reference was made above, began by painting "pretty pictures." She had a definite idea of what she wanted from the outset. In fact, during the first year she painted specifically to decorate her dining room and her living room, to show her friends "what she could do." But the following year, by choice, she began to analyze her own paintings with a sense of healthy dissatisfaction and with a determination to achieve something she felt but could not yet conquer. Today she exhibits with local and regional groups. She attends the openings of new exhibitions in New York and Philadelphia and speaks with feeling and intelligence about contemporary art. What does her case indicate? It indicates that a new set of values, a changed point of view, a new desire to do differently, a new appreciation of the meaning of art, have been the outcomes of her search.

EVOLUTION OF METHOD

The interesting development in the case of the minister's wife is typical of the cultural reawakening and reintegration of many individuals. Her case shows plainly that arbitrary teaching and standards might have defeated the whole situation.

A second case in point is a young man in his thirties. He came to night school to get "pointers," as he put it, on woodcarving. He had

430 carved, or rather copied, some old Pennsylvania-German butter molds. He seemed to have feeling for wood and the mechanical ability to master the materials. Teacher and pupil learned much from each other in the venture. Slowly, by seeing examples of the work of contemporary sculptors, he became intensely interested in their work and their technics. For awhile, he stopped carving and read a great deal. He examined every available reproduction in the school library. Eventually, he announced to the teacher that he was through copying butter molds and

WEAVING AND TEXTILE DESIGN are not only interesting to many adults but may lead them to profitable hobbies (exhibitions of hand weaves by Mrs. Dorothy Sherry, Allentown, Pa.).

wanted to try his hand at something of his own. He began all over: drawing first, some plasticine modeling next, and, lastly, woodcarving again, but of his own design.

The reorientation of this man was possible only because his enthusiasm and his point of view were accepted as valid, for him, from the beginning. His subsequent development was a matter of guidance and kindly stimulation. But again, what did actually happen to him? Obviously, new concepts had replaced the old: a new appreciation of carving, a new understanding of integrity, a new sense of the worth of himself.

The method emphasized by the teacher in this case was not of a ready-made type, since there is no formula available. The method was suited to the case even though the foundations of good method were known to the teacher. Here was an older person with fixed ideas and outlooks; here was a man, such as may be encountered in many adult classes, who was sure of what he wanted. The teacher simply made him feel accepted, identified himself with the problem of the pupil, and slowly guided him to realize that his motives were fine but that the approach might be modified. Through such positive guidance the pupil was led to "see" other ways, to gain new knowledges of the craft, to tackle the problem on a creative basis, and thus to achieve true satisfaction through original thinking and a personal technique.

The obvious conclusion, with regard to all methods, and particularly with adults, must be that method is dynamic, that it changes from pupil to pupil, according to the type of guidance needed.

It was pointed out in Chapter 4 that it is important to begin with the child. It is equally true that in teaching adults one must accept them as they are, and where they are, artistically. From then on, the teacher's efforts will be in the direction of lifting the individual to the plane where he ought to be.

Once again one is inclined to refer to the impressive discoveries of renewed personalities and reawakened talents reported by such master teachers as Hughes Mearns[10] and Florence Cane.[11] They both give detailed accounts of how men and women past middle age made new beginnings through art. Indeed, the experiences of all who have taught adults would make interesting recitals of reclaimed lives.

AWAKENING OF TALENT

Aside from the worthy use of leisure and the therapy that art experiences may bring, there is the very significant possibility that talents which have been dormant for a long time may be brought to the surface.

There are altogether too many reasons why in the past, and even now,

---

[10] Mearns, *op. cit.*, Chapters VI, VII.
[11] Florence Cane, *The Artist in Each of Us*, New York, Pantheon Books, 1951, Chapters XX–XXIII.

many young people are forced to abandon their interest in art. Among these are the specific educational requirements of certain curriculums which prohibit talented young people from taking advantage of art while in high school. Then again, many are forced to discontinue their education to go to work; others who complete the senior high school may lack the financial resources necessary to enroll in art schools or colleges where they might advance their art education and make it a career. Many such persons eventually find their way into adult programs and blossom forth as painters, sculptors, potters, jewelers, or designers in one medium or another. Some of them achieve real stature in time. Mearns records such cases as examples of what he calls "unguessed gifts." There are indeed many who possess unguessed gifts among those who attend arts and crafts classes. For them the adult program may be the vehicle to a wider opportunity in creative fields, and even new careers.

The creative unfolding of adults, when assured of sympathetic understanding, can be very dramatic for the many reasons suggested elsewhere: broader experience, greater definiteness of goal, and deeper feeling for accomplishment. These add up to a motivation that is seldom matched among young people in the schools.

VOCATIONAL REDIRECTION

What has been discussed so far might lead to the conclusion that lifelong learning programs are therapeutic or even recreational, but little more. Such is not the case.

There are certain practical aspects of the education or reëducation of adults in arts and crafts that should not be overlooked. Many institutions of learning are especially designed for out-of-school people of all ages who are seeking new ways of making a satisfying livelihood. Such persons are eager to retrain themselves to achieve new goals. Indeed, it is not uncommon to find individuals who begin in the rather heterogeneous groupings which exist in public-school adult programs and move on to specialized schools. In those instances, the guidance function of the art teacher and the nature of the art program should focus on the specific aims of the individual. Rehabilitation and redirection of an immediate type can mean the further happiness of the students concerned.

Courses in specific crafts, sign writing, stage and costume design, and others that might be requested by students who have vocational intentions should constitute the offerings of the program of retraining. Evidences of this type of practical education offered to adults are many. While adequate data are not available to permit a definitive statement of the situation, talks with teachers of adult classes seem to bear out the fact.

Small shops where leather, jewelry, pottery, ceramics products, and weaving are created for public consumption may be found in many localities. A random survey made by the author in a three-county area disclosed that 90 percent of the places visited were operated by individuals who received the early stimulus in an adult class in arts and crafts.

Personal contact with a number of persons trained in evening schools reveals that they found employment in stained-glass studios, commercial advertising agencies, and as window decorators in stores. A number of them set up shops for sign and card writing. All this following their preparation in adult art classes.

SUGGESTIONS FOR PUBLIC-SCHOOL PROGRAMS

The social and cultural reasons why adults are interested in arts and crafts have been touched upon in the preceding pages. To those broader reasons there should be added the equally varied goals and abilities of the individuals who show such interests. When they are considered, it becomes clear that the approach to and the content of the program must, of necessity, be just as varied. On the other hand, a realistic view of problems encountered by teachers with regard to space, equipment, and physical energy must also be considered. The suggestions which follow are intended to help teachers of adults face the problem efficiently, with satisfaction for themselves and with profit for the learners. The suggestions are offered only as starting points which may be broadened or adapted according to local needs and resources.

THE WORKSHOP PLAN

Because the interest areas may be many and because usually only one person may be available to teach, the workshop plan is the most effective for small school districts. The regional or area high school may be assumed as the focal point of the program where adults will meet. The art laboratory is one which lends itself well to diversified activities such as painting and other graphic arts as well as the crafts. Under the circumstances, a general plan such as the following may prove helpful:

434

1. Make an inventory of interest areas, then group people accordingly.
2. Furnish each interest group with appropriate visual materials to examine and enjoy while groups are being organized.
3. Begin working with the interest group requiring the least amount of stimulation to get under way, then proceed to the next group, until all of them are purposefully engaged.
4. At this point focus attention on individuals to help them solve specific problems in design, technics, or even personal matters.

The procedure indicated suggests that the personal interest of each individual must not be allowed to wane. It further implies that as quickly as possible each person should begin experiencing the art form he has

METALWORK AND JEWELRY appeal because of their personalized interest and use. Sound design is especially important in these areas because aesthetic values are generally sought in such items (adult classes, public schools, Hazleton, Pa.).

chosen. Above all, the procedure indicates that an attempt to teach all members of the class at the same time is futile and contrary to the principle of individuation which must prevail in adult education in the arts. This does not preclude the fact that on occasions the teacher may wish to share with all members of the class an experience or other helpful information which deals either with art in a broad sense or with administrative matters.

Progress in a workshop type of organization rests completely with each participant. The degree of ability, the dexterity, the speed, the intensity of interest, in short, all the elements that make each person different from his associates, are given full play. On the other hand, the teacher must determine the amount and kind of guidance needed by each learner. All in all, a diversified program seems to be the best answer to adult development because it is in harmony with the nature of creative activity and with the psychological basis of development.

THE SPECIALIZED APPROACH

In school systems where several teachers may be employed to conduct the adult program in arts and crafts, a degree of specialization in offerings may be feasible. In larger communities the situation permits the further advantage of choosing among several localities and several activities. Under such circumstances, the director of art education in collaboration with the director of adult education may select those schools and those teachers best suited for the special features of the program. Regarding the offerings, the greatest advantage seems to be that the teacher in charge has only one area of art to consider and consequently may go deeper and farther into any craft.

On the other hand, he will have within one class several degrees of proficiency, that is to say, the beginner, the more-advanced student, and perhaps some who have had considerable experience in the interest area. It may appear superfluous, yet it must be repeated here, that even under such circumstances the principle of individuation and the particular background and bent of the learner must be considered seriously. Even though this may be a specialized program, the learners are different as persons. Actually, this point of view is even more significant in the specialized program since the adult may concentrate and, therefore, develop to a finer degree the specialty he has chosen to explore or to master.

The interest areas to be offered are usually determined by the demands. Sometimes, past experience may suggest what courses ought to be offered. Usually classes in painting, drawing, graphic arts, commercial art, modeling, pottery and ceramics, jewelry making, and weaving seem to be popular with many adults.

GENERAL EDUCATION

In some localities, courses in art history and appreciation are very popular. While these courses are of a cultural nature, if the temper of the community demands them, the art teacher should not shrink from them. A broader knowledge on the part of the people and a sounder taste will lessen the cultural lag that exists between artist and layman. The idea of art as general culture has already been advocated as part of the preparation of young people. But intelligent participation in the activities of life, wiser consumership, and greater enjoyment of the arts certainly hold true for adults. Actually, this aspect is even more significant as part of lifelong learning because the adult is the voter, the taxpayer, the policy maker, and the civic leader. The cultural fabric of American society, democracy itself, and the extension of this important segment of our total culture depend on the level of understanding and upon the sympathy with which people view the arts.

Many are the intelligent adults who ask themselves: What is modern art? What is back of modern design? Why do tastes change? What forces and principles underlie the art expression of various epochs? What of American art itself? But then there are many who seem concerned with the possibilities of home planning and furnishing, with landscape gardening, and even with community planning or improvement. Surely these are interest areas that will broaden the intelligence and the tastes of all peoples and cannot be overlooked either as special treatments or in the general teaching of adults.

A survey of local conditions and demands may be the best method of discovering the needs and possibilities for broadening the horizons of older citizens. On the other hand, the vision of school authorities and of art personnel must be such as to sense opportunities as they present themselves for the enrichment of adult programs through art.

STANDARDS OF ACHIEVEMENT

In order that the true ends of adult education may be adequately achieved, it is important that certain standards of work and accomplishment be set up. Such standards must be valid in relation to the social task and defensible with respect to those who are taught. While such standards cannot be inflexible, they must nevertheless be determined, if only as desirable goals for teachers as well as for pupils.

A fair amount of the output of adults enrolled in arts and crafts classes is admirable, but the larger proportion seems to be of dubious aesthetic value. It is this general observation that raises the question of standards.

The general effort to popularize the arts with adults and the eagerness of teachers to fill their classes seem to account for the lowering of values, aesthetic or personal. How erroneous such a practice is may be demonstrated by the number of dropouts from courses. However, the greater loss is in the direction of good taste.

UNPRODUCTIVITY OF LAISSEZ FAIRE

A study of this problem indicates that the question of standards is tied up with the type of teaching that is done. At least two general tendencies prevail in teaching adults. These are not unlike similar tendencies in the teaching of young people in the schools. The first inclination is exemplified by the teacher who believes that as long as adults are kept busy and seem to be entertained by what is provided for them, it will all contribute to their enrichment regardless of standards. Such thinking has resulted in copies of paintings or photographs, in traced or otherwise adapted design motifs, mechanically superimposed on leather or pottery or jewelry. In many instances adults have proudly shown pieces of ceramics or pottery which were the mere result of commercial molds and transferred ornamentation. It seems hardly necessary to point out

HIGH STANDARDS of workmanship commensurate with the potential abilities of adults must be set up and maintained to challenge senior citizens (Pennsylvania Guild of Craftsmen, Lehigh Chapter, Allentown, Pa.).

how false such teaching is and how unfairly the adult is being treated. The very fact that adults come to arts and crafts classes is an indication that they are eager to learn. The creative potential, whatever it may be, should be properly appraised and guided so that honesty of expression and a growing sensitivity for good design will become the true standard of their performance. Can adults learn to create their own molds? Can they create their own compositions for painting and other graphic modes of expression? These are academic questions which, in a sense, have already been answered in preceding chapters.

But an even more serious consideration which must be kept in mind is the fact that adults cannot be misled for long. A craftsman, for example, who is required to produce goods that meet the standards set by his company will not be chided by false encouragement and dishonest practice. He will soon know, therefore, the worth of what he produces in the arts and crafts class, as well as the worth of the teaching he receives.

Freedom of expression, individuality, the release inherent in creative work, all these deny copying, patterns, short-cut methods, and, above all, dishonest procedures.

DANGER OF FORMALISM

The second inclination in working with adults is characterized by the teacher who may be classified as a formalist. He knows his craft and has high standards. He believes in technical proficiency and directs his pupils along a preconceived pattern. Those who can follow him from the outset may survive; others will drop by the wayside, disillusioned and discouraged. This type of teaching fails the very purpose of adult education because the high hopes and the aspirations of the pupils are destroyed even before they have had an opportunity to reveal themselves. The only situation in which such teaching may have a place is in specialized courses which have set prerequisites or equivalent experience. Certainly, formalism is not in the spirit which should prevail in most adult programs sponsored by the public schools of most communities.

The nature of creative activity and the psychological maturity of most adults should be seriously considered by the teacher who earnestly seeks to fill the gaps in the lives of those who come eagerly searching for new sources of personal enrichment.

THE RELATIONAL POINT OF VIEW

It will be remembered that in Chapter 3 the author proposed a *relational theory*. It should be applicable to the problem of standards. The process of creation on the part of an adult is all important because it is through the experience that he gains new perspective on life. In creating he replenishes his spiritual resources and realizes again that he is a worthwhile being. Whatever he produces must be a satisfying visualization of his intention. He must feel that the object created has a value, artistically and otherwise, to him as the creator and, perhaps, to his social group.

The three elements of the theory imply that in setting standards for the work of adults the teacher must begin with the individual's capacities and his past contacts with art, and allow these full play. Second, as the adult grows in ability to express himself and to handle the necessary media, more should be expected of him in terms of mastery of process and product. Third, through self-evaluation and through appraisal by the teacher and others in the group, the individual must be challenged to seek adequate aesthetic values in his productions as works of art. Ultimately, he should feel that he is "a workman that needeth not to be ashamed" but rather proud to possess what he has wrought.

SUMMARY

Statistics and observation indicate that lifelong learning is a vast field with a future that bids fair to becoming an even more significant area of education. Adults, that is to say, all out-of-school persons beyond the age of 18, are taking serious advantage of the many opportunities open to them. For some it means further education, for others vocational reorientation, for many civic intelligence, and for a vast number the pure enrichment of life.

The arts and crafts have a special appeal for a sizable number of adults. Classes for such people seem to be very popular all over the nation. Agencies of all types are set up to provide the opportunities: private, religious, federally supported, state-supported, and locally supported. Nation-wide organizations, the American Association for Adult Education and, more recently the Public School Adult Education Association, integrate, as far as it is possible, the work of thousands of local, state, and regional groups.

The reasons for the popularity of the movement, especially in the arts, are many, but unquestionably the urge to create is preëminent. Through creative activity adults hope to replenish those spiritual resources that are heavily taxed in the workaday world. Materialism, automation, mass production, and standardized living give rise to the desire within each person to establish his own identity. Through art it is possible to achieve such reintegration.

The problems confronting art teachers who teach adults are many. Adults have experienced the world; they have definite purposes and are eager to accomplish. On the other hand, they have set ideas; they feel the impact of tradition and are somewhat timid. These are the assets and the liabilities with which they come to evening classes or late-afternoon classes.

Should art teachers assume a formalistic attitude in their teaching? This could well defeat the purposes of the adult-education movement and of each individual within it. Should the teacher merely entertain his pupils? Such a course would likewise defeat the scope of the program.

The answer to the dilemma is not a difficult one if the teacher believes that art expression is a matter of self-discovery and that each individual has motivations of his own. Growth is a never-ending human quality; it is certainly alive in those persons who continue to search for ways through which they may improve their lives and broaden their horizons.

Individuation, variety of experiences, exposure to fine examples of art of many types, self-evaluation procedures, all these are keys to successful teaching. They are just as valid with adults as they are with children.

The quality of the products of adults should be commensurate with their endowment and growth. In general, it will be obvious that adults seek mature types of accomplishment. Shoddy products will hardly justify the processes with adults, certainly not for long. The task of the teacher, therefore, remains one of guiding and stimulating the adult whose dormant talents may be reawakened, and of moving him to higher levels of accomplishment with each new experience. It is through such teaching that the entire cultural tone of the nation may be raised. Actual experience in the arts will tend to enrich the lives of participants, open new fields of endeavor for some, and surely broaden the public's appreciation for the work of artists and designers.

For Discussion and Activity

1. Make a complete survey of the adult-education opportunities available in your immediate community, indicating the nature of the opportunities, how

they are supported, how they are patronized, budgetary provisions made for them, staffing, housing, and other aspects. Share your findings with your associates.

2. If you were the art coördinator of a community in which you felt there was a need for arts and crafts opportunities for adults, how would you proceed to establish a program? Submit your plan to a discussion group of your associates.

3. Visit a class in arts and crafts for adults by prior arrangement with the teacher. What is the atmosphere like? What activities are being undertaken? What are some problems adults seem to encounter? Make a report to your associates and compare your findings with theirs.

4. "Since most adults have had many experiences with problems of everyday living, they should be expected to do mature work in whatever form of art they choose." Do you agree with this statement? Do you disagree with it? What is a proper attitude in this regard?

5. Following the reading of this chapter and additional literature, propose several methods or procedures you would use in teaching adults. Submit these to a jury of your associates.

6. To what extent would you diversify the program of an adult group if your class was the only one offered in arts and crafts? How would you proceed to determine interest centers? How could the entire group profit by the work of individual members?

7. "Because adults must see results, it is necessary to permit them to use various devices such as copied motifs and ready-made molds for pottery or modeling." Defend this position if you believe it is sound. Otherwise, give all the arguments for the negative.

8. Prepare an outline of the contents, methods, and resources you would use if you were to teach an art-appreciation course for adults. Discuss the prospectus with your associates.

9. Assuming that you were teaching an "advanced" group of adults in painting or modeling, what standards of achievement would you set up for your class? What point of view would you stress? What technics would you advocate? Discuss your ideas before your classmates.

10. Under what circumstances would you advise your administrative superior to establish adult classes of a specialized nature, such as pottery, modeling, weaving, jewelry making, and others? What resources would such a plan involve?

For Further Reading

Bryson, Lyman, *Adult Education*, New York, American Book Company, 1939, Chapters III, IV, X.

442 Cane, Florence, *The Artist in Each of Us,* New York, Pantheon Book, 1951, Chapters XX–XXIII.

Clapp, Elsie R., *The Use of Resource in Education,* New York, Harper & Brothers, 1952, Part II, Chapter II.

Ely, Mary L. (ed.), *Handbook of Adult Education in the United States,* New York, Teachers College, Columbia University, 1948. This is a source book which should be consulted thoroughly while studying the problems of adult education.

Logan, Frederick M., *Growth of Art in American Education,* New York, Harper & Brothers, 1955, Chapter VIII.

Mearns, Hughes, *The Creative Adult,* New York, Doubleday & Company, 1940.

Mossman, Lois, *The Activity Concept,* New York, The Macmillan Company, 1939, Chapter IX.

Ziegfeld, Edwin (ed.), *Education and Art, A Symposium,* Paris, UNESCO, 1953, Section VI, pp. 93–99.

Ziegfeld, Ernest, *Art in the College Program of General Education,* New York, Teachers College, Columbia University, 1953, Chapters IV–VI.

THE CRAFTS AS EDUCATION

It is not a soul, 'tis not a body that we are training up,
but a man, and we ought not to divide him.

Montaigne

A NEEDED EMPHASIS

EVEN THOUGH MANY REFERENCES TO THE CRAFTS HAVE BEEN MADE AND their values for the various levels of the schools have been noted at several points throughout this book, there are two principal reasons for the writing of this chapter. The first reason is to highlight the crafts as significant aspects of the well-balanced school art program. The second is to point up certain artistic considerations that must prevail if the crafts as educational ends are to rise to the quality of fine art.

THE INDEX OF AMERICAN DESIGN

During the years of the last depression, a very ambitious program was undertaken by the federal government known as the WPA or Works Projects Administration. It included in its activities the reproduction, in graphic form, of a large variety of folk crafts wrought in America from the earliest days of colonization. The resulting collection is now housed in the National Gallery of Art for reference as well as for inspiration to contemporary designers.

The importance of the *Index of American Design* is not merely historical. In a larger sense, it shows how the many crafts in wood, clay, tin, iron, stone, glass, thread, and sometimes combinations of these are direct answers to human needs. They are also examples of forthright

444 workmanship, of regard for materials, and of ability to utilize available resources to best advantage. Furthermore, they show a definite relationship between design, materials, and the use to be made of the crafts article.

An industrial civilization, even more than earlier cultures, needs individuals who, in the spirit of the pioneer, will create with materials for the needs and in the materials of their own time. The machine, when it comes into play for mass production, will at least have been directed by a creative mind and skillful hand.

Several studies have made it clear, however, that one of the major shortcomings of current art-education programs all over the nation is the insufficient attention given to the crafts and to three-dimensional design in general. Progress has been made more recently, but the extent of the effort and the quality of the product indicate that greater emphasis and deeper concern need to be given to this phase of education.

Ziegfeld's[1] study of course requirements in the education of teachers of art revealed that by far the largest amount of the art preparation was concerned with two-dimensional experiences, expression, and media. A parallel study by the present writer[2] confirmed Ziegfeld's findings and, on that basis, recommended the strengthening of three-dimensional design experiences in the preparation of teachers in order to effect a corresponding strength in the art program of the public schools.

It seems quite clear, from the data reported by the studies mentioned as well as from field observation, that the lack of proper interest in the crafts derives from two sources. These are briefly elaborated upon hereafter.

LAG IN TEACHER EDUCATION

The specially prepared teacher or coördinator of art is, obviously, the key to the situation. The major reason for the prevalent lack of experiences and of better standards for crafts derives, without question, from a weakness in the preparation of teachers of art. This is equally true of the prepa-

---

[1] Edwin Ziegfeld and Walter Hager, "Course Requirements in Fifty Institutions," in National Society for the Study of Education, Fortieth Yearbook, *Art in American Life and Education*, Bloomington, Ill., Public School Publishing Company, 1941, p. 741.

[2] I. L. de Francesco, *The Preparation of Teachers and Supervisors of Art*, doctoral dissertation, New York University, 1942.

ration of general classroom teachers. The natural outcomes of such a condition may be seen in the meager results of the classrooms.

It is true that three-dimensional experiences are often included in correlated units and occasionally as independent activities. But in general, the fear of the materials involved, the "messiness" caused by certain processes, and the lack of proper background in the design qualities required seem to prevent a wider and more serious employment of the crafts as education.

Strangely enough, the crafts are utilized rather extensively with children of low mentality, in therapeutic programs, and in the industrial-arts shop. The effectiveness of crafts with these groups is not denied. However, it seems both anomalous and unsound to confine designing with materials only to those children. Normal boys and girls, and especially those with a superior sense of design, could not only profit much by crafts experiences but might also be directed to use their talents in vocational channels following their formal education.

With regard to teacher-education programs, it will suffice to reiterate the fact that traditional curricula can only produce traditional teachers whose vision is limited by antiquated methods, a minimum of materials, stereotyped techniques, and a narrow concept regarding the wider nature and sphere of art experiences.

ERRONEOUS MEANING OF "FINE" ARTS

The second cause that hampers an adequate program in three-dimensional design is deep-seated. It is a part of the false reverence for the so-called "fine" arts as distinguished from the "minor" arts, or the crafts. This unfortunate and persistent late-Renaissance notion has tended to set up a highly arbitrary division in the field of art and, consequently, in art education.

Sensing the attitude current in his own day, Emerson wrote: "Beauty must come back to the useful arts and the distinction between the fine and applied arts be forgotten. If history were truly told, if life were nobly spent, it would be no longer easy or possible to distinguish the one from the other."

Much quibbling and hairsplitting have already attended this futile dispute. For the benefit of those who teach art in the schools of today, it

STITCHERY, SIMPLE WEAVING, and related processes offer boys and girls opportunity to integrate design and materials. The color choices, the decorative effect of the design as it develops, and the necessary control of the materials are worth-while experiences for the craftman, young or old (*above*, 5th grade, public schools, Kansas City, Mo.; *below*, 3rd grade, public schools, Tucson, Ariz.).

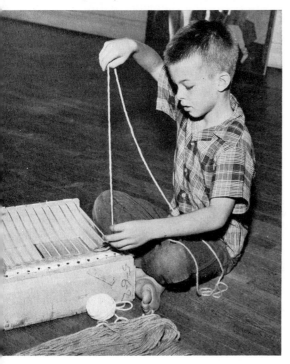

should only be concluded that the distinction alluded to has no place in a philosophy of art education for a democratic society. Nor is the point of view defensible on psychological grounds, as must have been gathered from previous chapters.

The term "fine" connotes quality, not kind, of art. Indeed, a beautifully wrought piece of pottery may be of fine aesthetic quality; at the same time, a badly structured painting or drawing, in spite of the difference in category or in the medium used, fails to achieve the standard of a "fine" piece of work.

To clarify the issue at hand, it may be well to examine the values inherent in the area of three-dimensional design from several points of view. These are, first, its value as a fundamental mode of expression; second, its educational and social worth; third, the basic aesthetic principles involved in its creation.

CRAFTS AS A BASIC MODE OF EXPRESSION

ANTIQUITY OF CRAFTS

When the primitive potter shaped the clay found in the neighborhood of his cave into a receptacle, he was converting the raw material of nature into a useful object. When he bent a limb from the nearby tree into a bow suitable for hunting, he was creating an implement that was essential to the continuance of his life. When he sharpened stone against stone, giving shape to each according to a purpose, he was fulfilling a need dictated by the urgencies of living. When the primitives wove grasses and twigs either into cloth or into baskets, they were again creating for use and by means of available materials. It is in that manner that certain crafts were perpetuated and in time assumed traditional character. It is also true that implements were created in the same way and stimulated by the same motivation, utility.

In each instance, the primitive craftsman was a true creator. In each case he was shaping the raw materials of the environment to his own purposes. In a sense he was engaging in an experience to control the physical world.

Yet there are abundant evidences to indicate that early man recognized more than utilitarian or material wants. He was an emotional being with capacity for appreciation and sensitivity, to respond to beauty in terms of line, form, pattern, and color. His utensils and weapons, while primarily shaped to fulfill a specific function were, in addition, embellished with details that made them attractive and meaningful in the ritual or in the amenities of the communal life of his group.[3]

The tradition of utility and beauty was highly developed by the Egyptians and the Greeks. By the time of the Renaissance the crafts guilds had developed standards of excellence in the crafts as well as outstanding craftsmen such as Cellini.

Unfortunately, by the end of the nineteenth century the handicrafts had fallen to a fairly low estate, though not lower than the standards of industrial products turned out by the newly invented machine. William Morris, the noted English writer and designer, rendered great service by undertaking the revival of the crafts. With his pen he called attention once more to those fundamental principles which had been characteristic of honest handicrafts for many centuries. He made it clear that "The wares which we make are made because they are needed; nothing can be made except for genuine use; therefore, no inferior goods are made. It is each man's business to make his own work pleasanter and pleasanter, which tends toward raising the standards of excellence, as no man enjoys

---

[3] Ruth Benedict, *Patterns of Culture,* New York: Houghton Mifflin Company, 1934, pp. 34–35.

448   turning out work which is not a credit to him."[4] It should be pointed out, however, that Morris may have erred in turning his back entirely on the machine or in failing to recognize its possibilities. The man of the twentieth century has had to accept the machine and has found, in some measure, ways of controlling its products through better design.

REVIVAL IN AMERICA

In America the revival of the handicrafts received great stimulus through the international expositions held in this country during the past eighty years. These, in turn, gave impetus to research and to renewed interest in regional crafts traditions. The expositions kindled an interest in industrial design by demonstrating to American business and industry that good craftsmanship had survived in many countries. Even the crafts of remote and obscure parts of the world pointed out that much could be learned from simple cultures with regard to the appearance and to the function of products. The expositions also made it clear that the United States, being the world's leading industrial nation, must not remain in the position of having to import designers, but rather that it should train its own craftsmen.

Massachusetts, New Hampshire, Vermont, Connecticut, South Carolina, Tennessee, and Pennsylvania are but a few of the states in which the handicrafts have been well reëstablished by subsidies from the state or through independently supported programs. Some states employ directors, whose job it is to improve the design, encourage the output, and find markets for the products of woodcarvers, potters, weavers, silversmiths, and other craftsmen. Nearly twenty states have organized crafts guilds. In turn these have local chapters at geographically strategic spots within each state. Many prominent craftsmen and good designers exhibit annually at crafts fairs, which, in many cases, are "juried" exhibitions. A number of craftsmen have achieved such excellence that their work may now be found in exclusive shops in New York, Chicago, San Francisco, and other important centers.

These interests have found response on the part of educational institutions, so that today many of the major art schools and universities

---

[4] William Morris, *News From Nowhere,* 1895 (available only at the Library of Congress).

have established industrial-design departments as well as courses intended to develop appreciation through basic experiences as part of general education and in art-teacher education programs. Among the recently established centers for the development of superior craftsmenship is the American School for Craftsmen at the Rochester Institute of Technology. On the other hand, industry itself has developed or has endowed clinics for designers as well as design departments within its own structure.

It is interesting to note that in 1948 the Canadian government, by an order in council, established the National Industrial Committee with

EXPLORATION OF MATERIALS, such as wood, reed, thin metal, and others, leads children to realize the limitations as well as the advantages of these media. In turn, such discoveries point the way toward honest workmanship (Kimberton Farms Schools, Phoenixville, Pa.).

the specific recommendation that the committee promote greater use of Canadian talent in the designing of all types of consumer goods. By 1953, in view of the increasing importance of its functions, that committee became the National Industrial Design Council. The personnel of the Council includes educators, manufacturers, retailers, research workers, and consumers. A small brochure published recently presents in attractive form the aims, the accomplishments, and the hopes of the organization. It appears that the main objective is that of "encouraging better design of Canadian products in everything you use, from a teakettle to a chair."[5]

In the United States, while there is no institution subsidized by the federal government, there are a number of organizations, including museums and industrial concerns, which sponsor sound modern design on the same broad base as the Canadian Council. The Society of Industrial Designers, which receives its impetus from Loewy, Dreyfus, Teague, Reineche, Stevens, McCobb, and other equally well-known designers, exerts a powerful influence on American industrial design.

INSPIRATION FROM NATIVE CRAFTS

The sustained interest in the crafts has also been aided by considerable research conducted among the various ethnic groups throughout the world. The results of such research are extremely valuable when properly used, because they present a wealth of material for reference in designing products suitable to the present age and present needs.[6] Specifically, one may look for inspiration to the simple artistry of the Negro sculptor, to the handsome leather and metal crafts of the Spaniards, or to the bold design of the southern Germans. To these may be added the woodcraft of the southern Highlanders, the simple but direct woodwork of the Swedes, the gay embroidery of the Slavic people, and the delicate lace of the Italians. Perhaps overworked but still capable of fresh interpretation are the pottery and metalwork of the American Indian and, farther to the south, the virtually untouched sources of inspiration offered by the work of the Aztecs, the Mayas, and the Incas.

As one studies the handiwork of these people he discovers that they, like the earliest groups in civilization, appreciate and use the common resources about them: grasses, husks, seeds, bark, pods, berries, wood, stone, metal, clay, and many others. These are but a few of nature's

---

[5] *The Story Behind the Design Centre,* Stratford, Ont., National Industrial Design Council, 1953.

[6] *Unesco Courier* for the last several years has been profusely illustrated with photographs of the native arts and crafts of many countries of the world.

mediums available to nearly everyone. Many beautiful as well as useful objects may be created with seemingly humble materials. The great need is to stimulate the use of the imagination, an understanding and an appreciation of the immediate environment, and a sound feeling for design qualities.

EDUCATIONAL AND SOCIAL VALUES

Designing with materials has distinct contributions to make to the social objectives of all education. The possible variety of end products in addition to the necessary processes permit nearly every individual to utilize handwork either for a market or purely for personal satisfaction. There is fascination about shaping materials into objects and in working out processes. They invariably induce the pleasure which accompanies mastery over problems or personal achievement. Surely the boys and girls in the schools of the nation should not be deprived of that joy.

EMOTIONAL AND MENTAL THERAPY

The recency of the Second World War and the role played by crafts programs in camps, hospitals, and on the home front make it unnecessary to repeat what has been reported fully in various publications. The record stands, nevertheless, as a witness to the effectiveness of crafts as means of individual and group therapy.

It is important to note that the term therapy needs to be interpreted more broadly than it usually is. Personal and group mental health is a much-to-be desired condition in an era of rapid movement, of tensions, of quick changes in economic and social outlooks, and of population shifts. Mental health, when used in its broader connotation, indicates a state of reasonable emotional balance. It implies a feeling of security and, in general, a flexibility that permits adjustment. To be able to engage in any creative pursuit and thus replenish the depleted reservoir of emotional, mental, and spiritual energies is a mark of health. Whatever by-products craft activities may generate are in addition to the very important function of regeneration. Even prior to the last war and the realization of the value of crafts in hospitals and camps, industry was already making wide use of the crafts. Industrial hazards are just as great as those incurred in a war.

Currently, the arts and crafts program of the armed services is being strengthened and extended. Hundreds of art teachers and craft specialists are sought for employment in order to make the crafts available to the men and women in camps, both at home and abroad. The whole purpose is to aid individuals by maintaining morale and mental health at a high level.

USE BY SOCIAL AGENCIES

The crafts offer one of the answers to programing for out-of-school youth. The problem is a real one from the standpoint of the young people themselves and from that of parents and society. The frightening current rate of juvenile delinquency is partially due to lack of proper motivation to engage in worth-while activities. During the days of the last depression a sharp rise in juvenile delinquency was also noted. At that time, the schools were thrown wide open during the evening hours and many crafts courses were made available. These proved very popular with young people. Community agencies, such as Y.M.C.A.'s, Y.W.C.A.'s, Y.M.H.A.'s, and other similar organizations, engaged in parallel programs for young people during the day. Strangely enough, the arts, which are usually curtailed during periods of economic distress, attracted so many and proved to be such invaluable assets that they were strengthened and extended on a more-permanent basis.

Summer camps and playgrounds are making increased use of the crafts to teach and to foster the interests of young and old. One of the more encouraging signs, in public recreation and in camping, is the gradual rise in the standard of work that is produced. This is largely due to an awareness of the true meaning of self-expression and to the fact that more and more adequately prepared persons are being employed to conduct the programs. The traditional "kits" for leatherwork, and other similar gadgetry, are vanishing. In their place honest, creative effort is being introduced. This is a further evidence of the value of crafts in the raising of popular taste. In such experiencing there is bound to be an increase in interest on the part of people in the development of their abilities, the desire to express themselves in worth-while ways during the hours of leisure, and to gain personal satisfaction and appreciations.

For adults who are looking ahead to the well-earned pleasure of retirement, or for those older individuals who wish to enrich their lives through

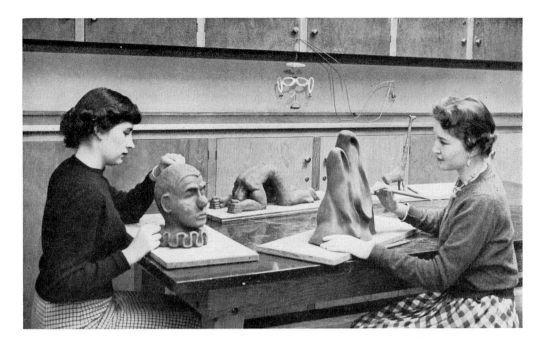

creative activities, the crafts have been a real boon. The fact is attested by the preponderance of classes in leatherwork, jewelry, woodcarving, metalry, and similar activities in the evening-school enrollments of both large and small communities. This statement is not intended to compare or to promote the crafts over other forms of art. Rather, it is a positive

MODELING AND POTTERING (*above*, modeling, Tucson, Ariz.; *below*, pottery, Millville, N.J.).

statement of the obvious appeal of three-dimensional expression to young and old alike and a singling out of some of the more obvious values of crafts for people.

There are, in addition, values of a less tangible but equally important nature. One of the problems which faces an industrial civilization is inherent in industrial progress itself, namely, the ever-present need of preparing the market for new and better products. In this connection one is reminded of the dictum "It takes an endless amount of history to make a little tradition." Taste is like that. Through the crafts, properly guided, boys and girls will gain appreciation and understanding of the products of their time. In addition, they may develop their powers as

454   designers and, eventually, may go beyond the stages of appreciation and personal satisfaction into worth-while vocations.

EDUCATION IN THINGS

Perhaps no better argument could be advanced for a serious reconsideration of the crafts as education than the one presented by Herbert Read in his address "Education in Things."[7] His cue admittedly came from Eric Gill, the English sculptor and writer, who deplored the fact that, in general, there is "book education," "games education," but a lack of "education in things."

Nearly all human beings possess things, some make things, all use things, enjoy seeing things. If leisure is interpreted not as a passive way of using up time but as an active way of utilizing it, then the crafts, any craft worthy of the name, will be a healthy pursuit for the body and for the spirit of the individual. Read concludes in this manner: "When what we do is the exercise of human skill and imagination in *every* department of human work, then the distinction between work and play, between art and industry, between vocation and recreation, between games and poetry—all these false distinctions disappear. Man becomes a whole man and his way of life a continual celebration of his strength and imagination."[8]

IMPORTANCE OF GOOD DESIGN

There is a commonly held notion that it is easier to achieve in the crafts than in graphic modes of expression such as drawing, painting, and allied forms of art. It is a carryover from the false belief described at the beginning of this chapter. The crafts are not "minor" arts, as they are sometimes described. From an educational viewpoint, they afford almost endless possibilities for personal enrichment. This virtue gives them a universality of appeal which should not be confused with the ordinary. It should also be remembered that a well-designed piece of ceramics or jewelry is but a step removed from a masterpiece produced by the Oriental craftsman, by the Greeks, or by an Albers. Modern crafts by

---

[7] Herbert Read, "Education in Things," in *Art, the Balance Wheel in Education,* Yearbook, Eastern Arts Association, Kutztown, Pa., 1948, pp. 10–25.

[8] *Ibid.,* p. 25.

contemporary artists, such as Albers, Odorfer, and others of similar standing, are truly works of fine art. They are originally conceived, they are structured on the basis of sound aesthetic principles, and they are functional. In the final analysis these are the qualities of all fine art.

Assuming that the rightful place and the proper values of crafts are recognized, what further considerations will help teachers and pupils to engage in them with satisfaction? In a summary way, the problem in teaching or in practicing the crafts resolves itself in the word *relationships*. These relationships are based on the fact that one deals with education to form.

Education to form is dependent on the relation of material, of function, of technic, of decoration, and finally between the expression and the form. A slight expansion of these relationships should make their meaning clear.

RELATION OF FORM TO MATERIALS

First among the concepts that underlie good design in the crafts is the relation of form to material. The qualities of each material should be exploited to the utmost. Meantime, no medium should be forced beyond its inherent possibilities. Clay, lacking tensile strength, should not be made to look like or function like metal; work in wood should make use of the grain and texture of that material; metal, being pliable, may be bent, twisted, or flattened. It is a mark of good craftsmanship to employ only those decorative treatments that become one with the material rather than an ornament for its surface. For instance, the decorative elements of a Greek vase are congruous with its form and enhance it by the sensitive disposition of the motifs. Utilizing the textural possibilities of a surface may relieve monotony without altering the form, the character of the material, or the object. The current mode of doing more with the material itself than with surface decoration is an endeavor to retain the integrity of the material.

RELATION OF STRUCTURE TO FUNCTION

The second basic concept is the relation between structure and function. The fulfillment of this requirement is dependent on the understanding of function. The term "design" means order; and unless the structure is related to its purpose, the object will tend to be of the sou-

456   venir type. In the classroom, unless proper guidance is furnished, the activity may become purposeless play and busy work. This may hold little more than the advantage of experimentation.

The Greek formula, "That is most beautiful which is most useful," has found its counterpart in the current phrase, "Form follows function." Combining, shaping, and bending materials into a form is only the beginning of the process of creation. When the craftsman deliberately handles materials for a purposeful end, his craft reaches fulfillment. For example, there are a number of technics that might be used in making a bracelet: one may etch a design upon the metal, or pierce the metal, or superimpose metal upon metal, and so on. The choice of a technic is conditioned by the desired result, by the originality of the designer, and by the suitability of the technic to the final form.

GOOD DESIGN is not only functional, but original in concept and aesthetically appealing (Peabody High School, Pittsburgh, Pa.).

In addition to sound structural principles, work in the crafts needs define motivation. A well-executed painting may be regarded as an object of beauty even by those with meager technical background. To be able to express himself through painting is considered a mark of achievement by the artist himself and by his audience. In the crafts the motivation must be just as strong and just as significant. But since one deals with actual materials rather than with an illusion, it must be stated in slightly different terms. Briefly, a design must result in a functional product which exhibits mastery of techniques and of structure, and a clear purpose.

MEANINGS FOR THE CLASSROOM

Any art teacher fails his pupils whenever he allows them to ignore the primary purpose of design. Good design is not accidental. It is founded on at least these types of activity: first, study and research; second, original and spontaneous visualization of an experimental nature in the best sense; third, a planned approach to the design for a specific purpose. These activities presuppose significant and well-understood prior experimentation with materials.

At no time should patterns, copied designs, imitative ornamentation, and other common stereotypes be permitted to interfere with the originality of the pupil. In planning crafts activities, teachers and pupils should be aware from the outset of the nature and potentialities of the materials; they should be able to visualize the end product and carry it out with fullest integrity.

THE LIVING PRINCIPLE

A product, it has already been pointed out, must exhibit a relative mastery of technic. One of the shortcomings of much craftswork is its shoddy appearance. This can be overcome by agreeing on proper standards of workmanship in the classroom. Technique, it must be repeated, is not an end in itself but a means to the end. However, unless the work proves emotionally and aesthetically stimulating to the pupil, a most important objective of the activity is lost. It is an established fact that when pupils have reached the junior- or senior-high-school level, they are ready for and seek to understand principles and elements of design. Through the crafts one finds a perfect vehicle for the concrete visualization of otherwise abstract terms. Actually, in the transition from the idea to the product, the pupil grasps the true significance and universality of principles and elements. Balance, or lack of it, becomes an obvious quality in the ceramic or metal piece. Variations of textures and patterns are tactile and visual realities in weaving or leathercraft. Form, line, the interplay of dark and light, and the resulting planes are visually realized or kinesthetically sensed in a three-dimensional or relief carving. It usually follows that the more-abstract concepts and the subtleties found in mature work are eventually understood. Careful handling of tools and material, a sense of pride in the work itself, and sensitivity to important details and finish are other developments that lead to growth in skills. The age and maturation level of pupils will suggest the degree of mastery to be expected, but it is always true that desirable work habits and

458   adequate finish are essential throughout the art program. Only then will each pupil achieve according to his capacity.

SOME INTEREST CENTERS

In the chapters dealing with various school levels it was stated that the art program should exhibit balance between the amount of time devoted to graphic activities and the time allotted to three-dimensional experiences. In the crafts, if students are given opportunity for choice, their natural interests and capacities will largely determine the activities they wish to undertake. When the unit plan of teaching is in operation, or when art is an outgrowth of a core situation, students and teachers will suggest a number of three-dimensional experiences related to the broad scope of the work in progress.

General school subjects, such as the social studies, geography, and even mathematics and science, are often vitalized and clarified through a variety of crafts activities. When the relationship is a natural one and not an imposition upon expression, the results may be worth while not only as clarifiers but also as art. For instance, if students in the social studies are concerned with a historic period, the members of the class could logically undertake the preparation of models to clarify styles of architecture, clothing, transportation, and other aspects of that period. Such activities afford opportunities to design in clay, paper, cardboard, plaster, and other suitable materials. In one school a series of figures modeled in papier-mâché and costumed with historical accuracy resulted in a delightful, permanent school display. Under similar conditions a group of students might plan the activities for an entire unit or for any cultural era. Pottery making, modeling, model building, jewelry, masks, repoussé, carved-linoleum plaques, wood and plaster carving, bookmaking and binding, and a host of three-dimensional activities will suggest themselves as students and teachers plan and work together.

SERVING CONTEMPORARY INTERESTS

While historical eras lend themselves admirably to expression in crafts, the present and the self indicate even more possibilities. A group of students may be interested in the theater; here they will find suggestions and inspiration for varied and challenging ideas, such as puppets, stage settings, furniture, furnishings, properties, and masks. The experimentation and the individuality which such undertakings involve in terms of scaling, construction, decoration, and arrangement will result in worthwhile creative experiences which have meaning in terms of pupil interests.

The problem of housing, which looms so large at the present time, affords a tremendous challenge for three-dimensional work. Such experiences can go beyond the making of models for modern housing. The planning of interiors, landscaping, the designing of entire blocks, and an awareness of other community needs may be some specific outcomes of a general interest. When properly stimulated, pupils who can create with materials may realize their own larger artistic possibilities while giving vent to personal interests.

SATISFYING INDIVIDUAL NEEDS

Crafts for personal and home use have advantages and disadvantages; these must be evaluated in terms of the abilities of the pupil and in relation to the total art program. Quite often it is through satisfaction of a very personal need that pupils discover their interests and vocational as well as avocational leanings. When ability and personal desire are com-

ENAMELING, JEWELRY, and other crafts demand a high degree of skill, knowledge of the media involved, and careful planning (Vocational School for Girls, Cleveland, Ohio).

bined, motivation of a high character is present. Many pupils, so motivated, have eventually gone to specialized schools for further preparation in the field of design for industry.

It has been intimated that in a highly industrialized age the identification, guidance, and encouragement of talented young people for the productive fields of design seem to be legitimate aims of art education. The schools must meet their obligation to society by making available to boys and girls all forms of creative activity in order that they may wisely choose those best suited to their temperaments and abilities. As Hilpert[9] points out, the obligation changes with each generation; and if art education is to function in its proper role, it must recognize the needs of contemporary society. Adequate attention to crafts will fill an existing gap in the art education of many adolescents who are not inclined toward painting. The diversified experiences will make such individuals happier for having learned to use with profit their chief physical tools, their hands.

PROCESS AND PRODUCT

Once again, one is reminded of the recurring debate in art education: What stress should be placed on the process and what value should be placed on the finished product? The soundest position would seem to be contained in the Relational Theory proposed in Chapter 3. It has been made abundantly clear that experimentation, control of materials, coordination of the body, and freedom of expression are of primary significance in guiding younger people. But there is also the obligation to set up standards of quality adequate to the age and development level of the pupil. Actually, and sometimes sooner than one expects, in the natural unfolding of their creative faculties, boys and girls "put away childish things" and begin to speak and act as men and women. At that time, they need to experience more than "self-expression." Pupils ask themselves questions regarding the worth of the expression as an object of art and about the value of the object to someone.

The best criterion to determine when the importance of the process ends and emphasis shifts to the product is the rate and kind of growth of the pupil himself. As individuals grow, they attempt to produce more satisfying products. With growth in manipulation, three-dimensional work takes on added meaning. It is also true that as boys and girls achieve critical awareness they seek standards that will justify the activities in which they engage. While individuality must always be preserved, guidance in achieving the standards of which the child is capable is a definite responsibility of the teacher, the parent, and the school as a whole.

---

[9] Robert S. Hilpert, "Trends in Art Education," in National Society for the Study of Education, Fortieth Yearbook, *Art in American Life and Education*, Bloomington, Ill., Public School Publishing Company, 1941, p. 452.

Craft experiences are justifiable and desirable at all levels of growth. The limitations are mainly physical ones. The good teacher is aware of them and has learned to overcome them. It is true that clay is "messy," and it is equally true that plaster of Paris causes "dirt." Yet many teachers have found ways of solving these problems because they believe that

the discomforts are not sufficient reason for depriving pupils of experiences that induce proper development and awaken sensitivity to materials and to design.

Children in the primary grades are capable of doing many simple crafts. These form the basis on which they build later on. By the sixth grade and in junior high school the crafts have special meaning because at those points of growth many children feel dissatisfied with their graphic output. While it cannot be stated with absolute certainty, empirical data show that a large number of them are likely to succeed in crafts of a wide variety. It is important that they create their own. It is equally important that they learn the proper technics and the processes involved in the materials they are using. At this stage the teacher's function assumes the

CHALLENGING PROCESSES, such as designing, casting, jiggering, and glazing, require high standards of workmanship for ultimate success (work of two senior-high-school pupils, Peabody High School, Pittsburgh, Pa.).

form of guiding spirit: one that nurtures appreciation, encourages honest craftsmanship, and stimulates the development of those abilities that may eventuate in good design.

At the senior-high-school level the need is for a strengthening of the exploratory function of art education as well as for increased meaning in the results obtained through creative activity. Because the crafts are, to a degree, utilitarian in character, the teacher must strive for an adequate degree of performance, and relation of form to function.

Life is real to late adolescents; they see man and the world in a truer light. Therefore, fine jewelry, leatherwork, wood and stone carving, original weaving, well-designed pottery and ceramics, metalwork of quality, and many other products can be created by these youths under expert teaching and the stimulus of high standards.

In concluding this brief consideration of the importance of crafts as education in things, it seems proper to repeat that the crafts can and do have special significance vocationally, in avocations, and for individual satisfaction or for the sheer joy of being able to say "This is my own," "I made it."

SUMMARY

The scope of this chapter has been to call special attention to a field of creative education which still needs to be properly developed in the schools. Some of the reasons for the lack of emphasis in the crafts are that materials create debris; materials and tools need special storage and care; many art teachers and most classroom teachers feel inadequate to do the work. Lastly, the concept of "fine" arts as distinct from the crafts has continued an erroneous notion.

On the positive side, or from the standpoint of pupil development, the chief reasons for the inclusion of the crafts in the art program are these: manipulation, such as is involved in the crafts needs to be encouraged; the crafts are a primary mode of expression, quite natural for many pupils at all levels; the crafts have vocational and avocational potentialities because of their material nature, in addition to aesthetic satisfaction; the crafts, being a form of industrial design, should be fostered for the economic welfare of the nation.

It has been stressed that the essential qualities of good crafts, such as relation of design to form, function, and materials, should be preëminent in the teaching of crafts above and beyond their educational significance. This is especially true as children gradually develop critical awareness from the early grades, and increasingly so in junior and senior high school.

The worth of crafts experiences in mental and emotional health, as socializing activities, and as vehicles for the development of good taste, are all too evident to need bolstering.

The teaching of crafts calls for sympathy and sensitivity on the part of the teacher. But of particular importance is the recognition that the individual creator need not fit into a preconceived pattern. Rather, each student should be guided to explore, experiment, and identify his own powers through the activity. Meantime, the wise teacher guides and supports every effort in the direction of good design and sound craftsmanship.

For Discussion and Activity

1. Do you believe that the so-called fine arts and the crafts should be considered as separate departments in the average-sized school system? Advance arguments for your position and submit them to a jury of your group.
2. Prepare an outline which will clearly show the events, the influences, and the contemporary forces which have aided the current revival of the crafts in this country.
3. From the literature of education and of the education of exceptional individuals, gather pertinent facts concerning the use of the crafts as corrective aids and for diagnostic purposes.
4. What do historical evidences indicate regarding the place of crafts in earlier societies? How do these evidences fit into the scheme of contemporary life?
5. What aesthetic principles are necessary for a piece of craftswork to rise to the level of a fine work of art? What implications do the same principles hold for the teaching of three-dimensional design?
6. At what level of the public schools should crafts be introduced? Make a listing of crafts activities, suggest their grade placement, and justify such placement on psychological grounds.
7. If you were teaching adults in the crafts, what would be some of your problems? How could you overcome them?
8. What values may be ascribed to crafts activities with regard to both the vocational and the avocational interests of young people? Prepare a chart showing a number of crafts in the first column, the vocational applications in the second, and the avocational possibilities in the third.
9. Do some research to ascertain the number and names of organizations concerned with crafts of all sorts in this country, e.g., the Society of Industrial Designers, and similar groups.
10. Outline a year's work in crafts for the tenth grade, a similar outline for boys enrolled in the industrial-arts curriculum of a senior high school, and do the same for girls enrolled in the same grade of the home-economics curriculum. Submit them for the criticism of your group.

464   **For Further Reading**

Cane, Florence, *The Artist in Each of Us*, New York, Pantheon Books, 1951, Chapters IV, XIV.

Czurles, Stanley, "What About Crafts?" *The Art Education Bulletin*, November, 1951.

Gaitskell, Charles D. and Margaret R., *Art Education During Adolescence*, New York, Harcourt, Brace and Company, 1954, Chapters V, VII.

Kainz, Louise, and Riley, Olive, *Exploring Art*, New York, Harcourt, Brace and Company, 1951, Chapters XI, XIII, XIV.

Lundy, Kenneth, "Handcrafts Are Important in Life," *The Art Education Bulletin*, March, 1951.

McDonald, Rosabel, *Art as Education*, New York, Henry Holt and Company, 1941, Chapters IX–XI.

PART IV
ADMINISTRATION OF THE PROGRAM

14

THE TEACHER AND ART

> Teaching is a social service profession. It is almost impossible to prove that any one profession is of more value to society than another, but you can be sure that no other career offers a worker a greater opportunity to benefit others.
>
> Lawrence D. Haskew,
> *This Is Teaching*

SOCIAL SIGNIFICANCE OF TEACHING

ANY IMPORTANT CONSIDERATION OF THE PROBLEMS AFFECTING ART EDucation must of necessity involve an understanding of the role of the teacher. This is true because the preparation, personality, philosophy, general aptitude, and attitude of the teacher comprise the most significant elements of the teaching-learning situation. The growth and development of children, of youth, and of adults, ultimately rest on the teacher.

It is extremely important for those who teach or who are preparing to enter the field to have a clear concept of what their personal and educational equipment ought to be in order that they may happily and successfully continue in or begin this professional career. Self-motivation, self-appraisal, self-direction, self-improvement, and self-adjustment are the ends sought through art education for children. How much more important are these ends for teachers?

On the portal of an eastern teachers college are engraved the words "Who Dares to Teach Must Never Cease to Learn." The fullness of the meaning of these words may only be realized as teachers themselves, aware of their professional inheritance, are willing and able to move forward with the progress of education as a whole. Art teachers, and all those who teach boys and girls through art, have an even more daring task before them because they deal with a less tangible, less "organized," and less rooted field of human development. To this should be added the many traditional barriers to be scaled owing to the confusion between art practice and art as education.

In this chapter the preparation, the role, the qualifications, the responsibilities, and the overall point of view of the good teacher are presented. The not-too-distant tomorrow will make even these proposals inadequate. Therefore, the vigilance inferred by the words engraved in stone on the portals of the teachers college must be a continuing one if each generation is to be served by teachers adequate to their own time.

THE MAGNITUDE OF THE TASK

In Chapter 1 it was made clear that American education is, in many respects, unique. That same uniqueness, including all its characteristics, is intimately interwoven with the beliefs which give special significance to the democratic way of life. It has also been reiterated in previous statements that individual development as well as associational life and group values are equally important goals of education.

The magnitude of the task of teaching, therefore, is at once bewildering and challenging. In a philosophy of education such as has been outlined, it should not be difficult to recognize the prominent place and the social significance of the teacher. Ultimately, the success of American education is contingent upon the work of the teacher. Its structure will either stand as a monument to democratic social ideals or it will crumble. It will depend on the faith, the personal qualities, and the professional equipment of its teachers. The making of the good citizen, the cultivation of taste, the acquisition of knowledge, the development of personality, and the unhampered growth of creative powers—all these are idealistic as well as practical objectives. They will be attained only if teachers bend their energies and lend their genius to the task.

But if the importance of teachers and of teaching seems fraught with social responsibilities unmatched in the ranks of public service, it is so because society commits in their hands the plastic lives of millions of children. These children are the citizens, the consumers, the creators of the immediate future. Actually, that future is being shaped in the classrooms of the nation today.

The slow economic advances made by the profession in the last few years indicate that society has not yet expressed itself fully, or tangibly, concerning its debt to the teacher. Public praise and occasional recognition have not been altogether wanting, but somehow the services of the teacher have been taken for granted. However, the press, the radio, professional and lay publications, parent-teacher groups, and other institutions have become increasingly aware of the key position that teachers hold, and, therefore, of the social respect and material rewards to which they are entitled.

PERSONAL AND PROFESSIONAL REWARDS

Those who are preparing to teach and those who are already in the field have every reason to believe in their calling and in the crucial nature of their work. The social rewards of teaching are clear even in the apparent restrictions placed upon teachers in certain communities. It is because society values the character and the worth of its teachers that taboos have been in vogue. These are slowly but surely disappearing and are being replaced, by teachers themselves, with examplary human conduct in activities of a more normal and more universal acceptance.

A great deal has been said and written concerning the economic status of the teacher. As a result, much-needed improvements in salaries and working conditions are now prevalent and promise to continue the upward trend. Conversely, teachers cannot overlook the permanent nature of their work, following adequate preparation and the meeting of certification standards. Nor can they overlook the widespread state systems of retirement with reasonable and improving annuities. The fact that most teachers, if they wish, can enjoy a deserved summer holiday for travel, relaxation, creative pursuits, or other occupations is an item that should not be minimized.

But when the material advantages and the social prestige of teaching have been summed up, there remain certain factors that overshadow all these. William Lyon Phelps of Yale wrote these lines:

I do not know that I could make entirely clear to an outsider the pleasure I have in teaching. I would rather earn my living teaching than in any other way. In my mind, teaching is not merely a life work, a profession, an occupation, a struggle; it is a passion. I love to teach. I love to teach as a painter loves to paint, as a musician loves to play, as a singer loves to sing, as a strong man rejoices to win a race. Teaching is an art—an art so great and so difficult to

THE TEACHER'S MAJOR CONCERN IS WITH CHILDREN: their nature, their way of thinking and of expressing themselves. Subject matter is the means through which children say what they feel. The identification of the teacher with the needs of pupils must be emphasized in art-teacher education (above, State Teachers College, Kutztown, Pa.; below, State Teachers College, Indiana, Pa.).

master that a man or woman can spend a long life at it, without realizing much more than his limitations and mistakes, and his distance from the ideal. But the main aim of my happy days has been to become a good teacher, just as every architect wishes to become a good architect, and every professional poet strives toward perfection.[1]

To guide children, to see them grow into manhood and womanhood, to see their creative powers develop, to look into the future and see the successful worker or professional man, are rewards of teaching which can neither be bought nor sold for a price. They are a part of the creative drama of life itself, and the teacher partakes in the unfolding of its children.

BEYOND THE CLASSROOM

HUMAN RELATIONS

The various facets of this subject are amply developed in Chapter 15. However, because a sufficiently large number of art people are engaged for the sole purpose of classroom teaching, it seems proper to advance, even at this point, some pertinent matters that may affect the success of such teachers.

Paramount among the relationships of any teacher is his daily contact with coworkers. Experience shows that the respect one gains, the friendships one establishes, and the coöperation one is able to give as well as receive from associates have a profound effect on the mental health of the teacher. Furthermore, the attitude toward teaching as a career and the regard that one develops for the profession are highly related to human relations on the job.

The inevitable contacts that arise through many nonteaching yet essential duties, such as work on faculty committees, homeroom and guidance conferences, overall planning of the cocurricular program, and other types of meetings, of necessity will bring the art teacher in frequent touch with associates. It is obvious that the art teacher will want to accept these contacts and duties wholeheartedly and contribute to them in the highest possible measure. There was a time, not too far in the background, when the art teacher took pride in being different, and

---

[1] William Lyon Phelps, *Autobiography,* New York, Oxford University Press, 1939, p. 307.

472 special. That worn-out notion, wherever it exists, usually confirms a traditional point of view that works to the detriment of the art teacher and of the art program.

The cultivation of good human relations involves the willingness to coöperate in matters of general concern, the sharing of ideas with co-workers, and the consideration of the point of view of others. Also of importance is the recognition of human personality and respect for it. Professionally, this implies open-mindedness as well as genuine interest in others.

Relations with supervisors, special personnel, the principal, and the departmental chairman do not differ, materially, from those enumerated in connection with associates. Relations toward those in administrative positions are broader and their scope is wider, but they center around the idea of mutual respect, coöperation, and the open mind.

AUDIO-VISUAL AIDS of a broad variety must be familiar to teachers if they are to be adequately prepared to use these resources with their pupils (State University Teachers College, Buffalo, N.Y.).

PUPIL GUIDANCE

To be sure, all teaching and all activities related to work with children are guidance. In the present context, however, the interest is with those informal but frequent contacts that the art teacher will want to establish with pupils, on a plane that differs from classroom and scheduled activities. The vast amount of good that is accomplished for pupils when they are met on a personal basis rather than in the classroom, free though the latter may be, is incalculable. But it goes deeper than that. It is through such friendly and informal interest that certain pupils are reached and directed or redirected, as the case may suggest.

At the elementary-school level, this type of teacher-pupil relationship is a widely accepted procedure on the assumption that children need constant help and friendly guidance. In the junior high school, where planned guidance is recognized as central to the total program, the informal relationship referred to here can and should be used in connection with cocurricular activities: when setting the stage for the assembly or the play, in the art club, at the meeting of the hall patrol, and whenever teachers and pupils meet as persons and not as classes.

Senior-high-school youths not only enjoy the adult approach to personal guidance but actually seek it. At that level, the art teacher should capitalize on the vocational interests of the individual pupil and on his art abilities, which are by now pretty well defined. While a high type of specialization is of dubious value in high school, the art teacher has the obligation of discovering the talented and of guiding them into those art careers most suited to them. Teaching as a career should be especially called to the attention of intelligent and capable young people who possess the qualifications necessary for the field. Teachers of art may wish to make use of available aptitude tests in order to avoid purely personal judgments in the process of directing high-school pupils into art careers.

SPONSORSHIP OF ACTIVITIES

Reference has already been made to the many associative activities performed by art teachers. Another reminder in this connection is that art services and the extension of art activities into the varied phases of school life are, for many hundreds of pupils, the only evidence they will ever have that art pervades all segments in life. It is also possible that those pupils who have a slight desire to learn more and experience more art may be encouraged. For the art teacher such activities are a further demonstration of the value of art in human relations.

PROFESSIONAL GROWTH

The busy life of the art teacher may sometimes leave a very narrow margin of time for personal creative work, for professional reading, or for participation in the activities of professional art groups. To offset the disastrous consequences of falling into a rut, art teachers must make every possible effort to continue their professional education even beyond that required for the master's degree, either in art education or in fine arts. It is inconceivable that any person can remain in the field and not feel the need of occasional contacts with members of the profession. Such contacts are provided through the regional art associations, the state art associations, the National Art Education Association, and county or local groups. In addition, teachers colleges and universities that are alert to their proper functions conduct annual or occasional art conferences. Teachers should use all these avenues to retain contacts, to make new ones, and to keep professionally alert.

At the local level, especially in large school systems, it should be possible to join groups of fellow art teachers who are interested in developments in the field and in creative work. By whatever means, it is imperative that those who teach art should continue to grow, lest they become sterile and ineffective as guides of boys and girls. Some specifics on this particular point will be proposed as this chapter develops.

ART TEACHERS FOR OUR TIME

HISTORICAL NOTE

Little over eighty years have elasped since art-teacher preparation of a sort was begun in America. Progress in the professional approach to this problem seems to have lagged for a number of reasons. Some of them are discussed in this chapter, but progress at various points is also noted.

The early teachers of art in America were trained in England.[1] In fact, the first person to be employed for that specific purpose was Walter Smith, master of the Art School at Leeds, England. He was brought to this country to organize art instruction in Massachusetts, and later, in 1873, to establish the Massachusetts School of Art. Smith also acted as supervisor of drawing for the State of Massachusetts and for the city of Boston.

However, it is to be noted that Rembrandt Peale was giving free lessons in Philadelphia as far back as 1840; as early as 1852, Professor Breinerd was giving gratuitous instruction in the city of Cleveland;

---

[1] Royal B. Farnum, *Present Status of Drawing and Art in the Elementary and Secondary Schools of the United States,* Washington, D.C., Bureau of Education, Bulletin 1914, No. 13, p. 18.

and in 1870, the city of Syracuse had established teacher training classes in drawing in one of its high schools.

THE LAG IN TEACHER EDUCATION

An overview of the historic past indicates that the chief problem in art-teacher preparation seems to have been the lack of realization that change is the most constant element in life and in education. In his book *American Life and the School Curriculum*[2] Rugg strikes the keynote to the kind of teacher education needed in our time. The sum and substance of his argument is to the effect that the goal of all our education should be a man fit to live in the modern world. None of the ideal types of earlier cultures will serve the society of the twentieth century: neither the Greek scholar-philosopher nor the Chinese student-statesman, neither the medieval gentleman nor the aggressive businessman of the earlier industrial epoch. None of these is sufficient, for this is the modern day and only modern man can live it successfully.

To understand the lag in art-teacher education it is necessary to account for the power of tradition in American art. An index is furnished by observing the quick succession of

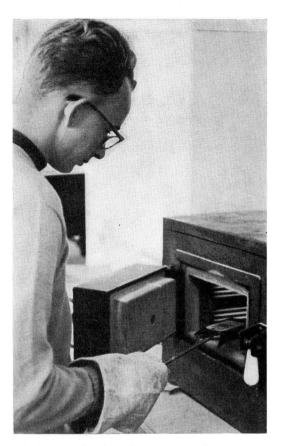

PROCESSES AND TECHNICS are important in the education of art teachers. Development of a large variety of them ensures resourcefulness and richness of background in the classroom. Meantime, aesthetic standards of workmanship are established (*above*, Long Beach State College, Long Beach, Calif.; *below*, State Teachers College, Kutztown, Pa.).

[2] Harold Rugg, *American Life and the School Curriculum,* New York, Ginn and Company, 1936.

the founding of schools of "fine arts" in this country during the nineteenth century. These art schools were intended for the training of producing artists and designers for industry. But they became a natural reservoir of persons who, for various reasons, ventured into teaching, primarily because of the lack of persons professionally prepared for the latter task.

Accurate records are not available concerning the type of training received by those persons. As a matter of fact, until the recent past, catalogues of art schools, even where a department of teacher education had been established for some time, carried hardly more than a general listing of courses. One of the oldest art schools in America, in response to a fairly recent inquiry, replied: "the closest we come to preparing for teaching is to equip our people so that they occasionally find employment in junior colleges or private schools." Nevertheless, until thirty years ago most art teachers were trained in the typical art schools of the time. Within the next few years, however, colleges and universities established art departments, even though offerings and staff were not unlike those of the art schools. Whitford was able to say with a degree of certainty in 1929 that "practically all the state universities and larger colleges provide training for art teachers."[3] Subsequent improvement in the type of curriculums offered and even in the preparation of the teaching staffs is impressive. Yet, in the main, the problem of art-teacher preparation continued to be a serious concern for some time.

The situation as it exists today is not the lack of schools to prepare teachers of art; rather, it is the vast number of them in the field, variously equipped to prepare persons who can meet the demands of a contemporary program of art education. Arthur Dow, as early as 1900, warned that "unless the professional people have recognized the necessity for general culture in art, and have thoroughly studied the conditions, the probability is that they will offer only a modification of what we will call Academic teaching."[4] This has been the case in large measure, and art education has not advanced equally with other fields of teacher education.

[3] William G. Whitford, *An Introduction to Art Education*, New York, D. Appleton and Company, 1929, p. 17.

[4] Arthur Wesley Dow, *Theory and Practice of Teaching Art*, New York, Teachers College, Columbia University, p. 2.

THE NEW CONSCIOUSNESS

By 1920 a new concept of the task of art teaching was dawning. Two factors were making their impact: increased interest in art education on a national scale, and the scientific movement in education in general, as noted in Chapter 2. The first of these forces created an unprecedented demand for teachers of art for the nation's schools; the second stimulated an inquiry within the ranks of art education itself. To cope with the new interest several agencies set to work: the teachers colleges, many of them with specially designed curriculums for the professional preparation of art teachers; the creation of the Federated Council on Art Education in 1925; active interest in art on the part of general educators; and the emergence of art-education departments in many colleges and universities in contradistinction to "fine arts" departments.

At long last the importance of the teaching of art to children was being recognized. But as indicated elsewhere, practice lags far behind principle, and art-teacher preparation, in general, still was not harnessing its program to meet the contemporary concepts of art as education. The findings of the Commonwealth Teacher Training Study,[5] as well as a somewhat later study by Hurwitz[6] which deals with the many tasks performed by teachers of art, called the attention of art educators to the importance of a preparation beyond courses in education and in technical skills.

The shift from technical subject-matter instruction to a broad concept of teaching was clearly enunciated in the late thirties by leading art educators. They pointed out that while it is essential that the art teacher receive suitable instruction in color, design, representation, art history, and appreciation, it is equally important that he should be instructed in the organization and administration of art education in the schools. The latter part of the statement indicates a function performed by a large percentage of art teachers, but for which, even today, little provision is made during preparation. The reference is to the function of coördination.

---

[5] W. W. Charters and D. Waples, *The Commonwealth Teacher Training Study*, Chicago, University of Chicago Press, 1929.

[6] Elizabeth Hurwitz, *A Syllabus for Student Teaching in Art for Institutions Preparing Teachers of Art*, doctoral dissertation, New York, New York University, 1949, pp. 106–109.

Enlightened art educators and leaders from the larger field of professional education have felt that for too long only lip service has been given to the entire problem and that actual preparation lags behind theory. D'Amico, as late as 1938, pictured the art teacher thus: "Let us build a picture of the so-called average teacher of art. We find him an isolated specialist, concerned with art and little else. He is a technician, not a craftsman or a creator. His techniques belong to a period in art which has already passed. These may include water color methods, poster devices, pencil rendering or charcoal technique."[7] With reference to institutions preparing teachers of art today, the same writer pointed out that "most schools still train the art teacher along technical lines."[8]

However, some progress has been made, even though much more needs to be done. Evidences of improved teacher education are to be found in good schools. There are proofs that experiences are replacing art "projects," and it is equally clear that art education is more and more concerned with a developmental program. Problems of the school and of the community, individual needs and interests, are becoming the basis for the activities advocated. The growth of the pupil, his taste in the things he uses, wears, and creates, as well as his general appreciation, are considered more significant than formalized exercises neatly mounted and ready for exhibition.

Even though the implications that art as education holds for teachers have been already advanced and discussed in several previous chapters, it is well to reiterate them at this point. They are summarized by the Commission on Secondary School Curriculum of the Progressive Education Association thus:

1. The art teacher should have respect for personality.
2. The art teacher must be highly sensitive to art and to life about him.
3. The art teacher must possess imagination and originality.
4. The art teacher should possess emotional security and self-confidence.
5. The art teacher should be friendly toward and able to work well with all types of persons.

---

[7] Victor E. D'Amico, *Problems in Teacher Training*, New York, Eastern States Association of Professional Schools for Teachers, 1938, p. 141.

[8] *Ibid.*, p. 142.

6. The art teacher must be sympathetic with youth.

7. The art teacher must have the desire to grow.[9]

The statements which follow are further indications of the earnestness with which solutions are being suggested by professional art educators. Glace says emphatically: "On the positive side it is imperative that we who are art educators keep firmly in mind *that we are first and foremost educators.* Undue stress upon art itself would mean the loss of opportunity for wielding art as an instrument effective in the functioning of democratic institutions. It is essential then that we use our subject field to promote the social growth of our pupils rather than to retard it by an undue emphasis on pure art problems."[10]

Johnson,[11] discussing the training of tomorrow's art teacher, points to a lack of unity in programs currently offered and pleads for a pattern in which not subject matter or semester hour of credit is the criterion of accomplishment but rather unified, "whole," integrated experiences. The same writer points out that the world in which tomorrow's children will live will be "complex, and shall we say, a devastatingly industralized, coöperative social order calling for a cumulative effect of continued interaction with the art environment." Hence, the art teacher must continually take cognizance of these facts. Johnson further contends that if one were thinking of artists, it would be fair to ask for more "art" classes; but that since the problem refers to teachers of art, the emphasis must be placed upon a broad background, coupled to and concurrent with a study of the emotions, contact with children, and creative pursuits.

Gerhart suggests these as the ends and means of art education which teachers should ponder:

1. Art has achieved a definite place in education today as a means of fostering worthwhile individual interests leading to creative originality and the development of right personality characterization.
2. The recognition of art as a socializing agent is an influence to be considered in offering guidance to the prospective art teachers.

---

[9] *The Visual Arts in General Education,* Commission on the Secondary School Curriculum, Progressive Education Association, New York, D. Appleton-Century Company, 1940, pp. 128–37.

[10] *Department of Art Education Bulletin,* Washington, D.C., National Education Association, 1940, p. 184.

[11] *Department of Art Education Bulletin,* Washington, D.C., National Education Association, 1939, pp. 147–153.

THE ARTIST-TEACHER, as a person, needs the satisfaction and the confidence that come with the mastery of some phase of art. Drawing, painting, crafts, sculpture, and the graphic arts are essential areas that must be explored (*above*, Pennsylvania State University, University Park, Pa.; *right*, State Normal University, Normal, Ill.).

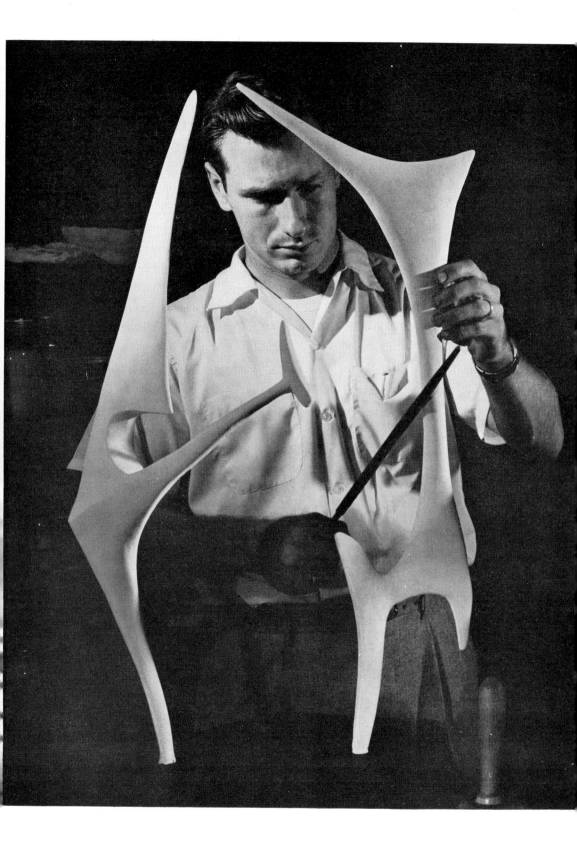

482 3. The use of art to further ideals in a democracy.

4. The tendency of art to follow the greatest impulse and so to reveal the trends of the times, demands a flexible structure in building a course.

To meet these demands, the education of the art teacher must be adjusted so as to include a workable educational philosophy, an operative knowledge of skills and techniques, an appreciation of art's place in the life of the time and acquaintance with the culture of past epochs and of the present.[12]

Mish[13] suggests that the modern art teacher, to do an effective job, must be acquainted with such diverse means as manipulation of varied materials, trips, demonstrations, moving pictures, talks, the radio, and exhibits.

The art teacher, according to Schultz,[14] when thought of in terms of the goals of genuine education, cannot become isolated in the studio from the rest of the school; just as art in the world at large functions in relation to the rest of life, so it must within the school. Clark[15] believes that the art teacher needs a broad understanding of the development and function of creativeness in the personality of the student; needs to teach individuals rather than subject matter, primarily. The pupil must be seen as a whole and in relation to his environment.

RESPONSIBILITIES OF THE TEACHER

The foregoing statements describe the type of teacher needed today. The statements also imply that redirection of thinking is essential, both on the part of teachers in service and in teacher education. The experienced teacher of art must accept the fact that tradition alone is a poor substitute for educational vision. He must also accept the fact that a great deal of knowledge from the fields of psychology, biology, and education is now available and must be put to work on behalf of boys and girls. In fact, one of the most salutary signs on the horizon is that art educators are more and more taking advantage of progress in education in general. By evaluating and adapting the successful outcomes of experimentation and of psychological findings to the media

---

[12] *Ibid.*, pp. 162–163.

[13] *Department of Art Education Bulletin,* Washington, D.C., National Education Association, 1940, p. 164.

[14] *Ibid.*, p. 292.

[15] *Ibid.*, p. 295.

and objectives of art education, the quality of art work by children is improved and the total education of children enhanced.

Specifically, what principles may help art teachers of today fulfill their role most effectively in line with recent concepts of art as education? The suggestions that will follow are perhaps not all-inclusive, yet they may form a basis for reorientation or self-appraisal on the part of teachers.

The laissez-faire attitude prevalent a few years ago and the confusing effect of the multifarious points of view discussed in Chapter 3 have somehow conveyed the notion that the teacher's best policy is one of "hands off." How erroenous this notion is has been discussed elsewhere; therefore, the thinking will now center on some of the positive functions of the art teacher in the administration of the program in the classroom.

It should be noted that for each of the six areas of a teacher's function the term *obligation* is used. This is not by accident, but by choice. The term has been chosen because, in accepting a position in the nation's schools, a teacher is thereby vested with certain rights, prerogatives, and authority, in the sense of competence. But at the same time, he also accepts certain responsibilities or obligations. There are obligations toward the profession in general, toward the community which employs him, the state, and above all toward the children who are to be educated. Throughout these pages, a sincere effort has been made to relate all considerations to a democratic philosophy of art and of education. Implicit in the acceptance of such a point of view one must recognize privileges as well as responsibilities.

The role of the teacher, in consequence of what has been said, may be expressed and commented upon in terms of professional duty.

1. *The art teacher has an obligation with respect to a tenable philosophy of art education for his time.* This is the responsibility of keeping professionally alive. Analyzing, assimilating, putting to use new knowledges and facts which are made available in educational literature, through professional meetings, or personally selected readings, are ways of keeping abreast of the times. The history of education, as a whole, shows that its progress has been evolutionary in character and that change and flux have been the rule rather then the exception. The preparation of art teachers has undergone and is undergoing tremendous

THEATER ARTS, POTTERY, MODELING, AND JEWELRY are among design experiences needed by teachers of art. Later contacts with young people at various levels of the schools will demand a knowledge of these phases of design (*above* and *center*, Pratt Institute, Brooklyn, N.Y.; *below* State Teachers College, Kutztown, Pa.).

changes. For example, the emphasis on the technical aspects of preparation, so prominent years ago, is not questioned. However, regardless of past preparation, a teacher who understands and accepts this obligation must strive to adapt his professional background and bring it to focus on the current objectives of the field. The objectives of art education for today are founded on the "Basic Premises" proposed and analyzed on pages 23–56; further detailed statements on the evolution of objectives in art education were discussed in Chapter 2. These sections may be reviewed with profit. Actually, when a teacher is out of tune with the times he ceases to grow and his effectiveness as a guide of children is arrested. Yet it should be said that an honest point of view is not questioned; it is only when tradition and inertia become the arguments for an outmoded philosophy that the teacher clearly disavows his first obligation.

2. *The art teacher has an obligation with respect to a knowledge of the educational and psychological implications of method, growth, and behavior.* The vast amount of progress made in the art of teaching is unquestionably due to refinements of method, to experimentation, and to the utilization of knowledges discovered in the educational process itself. The findings of psychology indicate that

children progress according to certain levels and stages of growth. When recognized, such knowledge will help teachers understand pupils and, therefore, do a better piece of work in the classroom. The psychology of the emotions, of the meaning and function of the senses and, therefore, of sensory education, the nature and meaning of the creative impulse and of creative activity, and the significance of experience—all these are matters with which teachers for the schools of today need to be conversant if they are to discharge their obligation fully. Human behavior, its measurement, and desirable changes are more than words in the professional literature; they are fundamental to all education and have special significance in art because art is more than doing and making. It has been pointed out that concepts, insights, appreciations, and then action are links in the creative act. How and why children react as they do under certain conditions or stimuli are matters of behavior. Actually, a teacher's method is bound up with his understanding of human behavior. Method can cause either antagonisms or sympathies or passiveness on the part of children. Dynamic method implies understanding of human beings and of what impels them to act as they do. The success or failure of the teacher is closely correlated to his awareness of these basic knowledges. Hence, continuing self-education in these areas seems a professional imperative.

3. *The art teacher has an obligation with respect to the physical working conditions and the educational climate of the art laboratory or classroom.* This particular point may at first appear very obvious. But as one reflects upon it, it will be evident that it involves much more than having seats and desks properly lined up or that the windowshades are pulled to the same length. Working conditions for art require that a certain amount of free movement be physically possible as well as educationally permissible. A reasonable variety of materials and tools for expression should be where children may avail themselves of them, because only then can they make choices, experiment, and eventually set themselves to the serious pursuit of creating a painting, or modeling, or whatever may seem appropriate at the time.

But the appearance of the classroom also teaches. What children see, the things with which they are surrounded, whatever may be observed, heard, or touched, are effective and affective means of teaching and learning. Without straining, it may be said that the physical appearance of the classroom may determine the general attitude of children, even with regard to order as opposed to lack of it.

Restrictions on ideas or movement are inhibiting, whereas a well-organized working arrangement, with pupils participating in the decisions, will eliminate many problems: social, personal, and creative. Above all, the teacher's positive attitude toward and respect for children's ideas and suggestions will encourage creative thinking in many ways.

4. *The art teacher has an obligation with respect to evaluation of pupil growth.* An entire chapter has been devoted to the importance, meaning, and functions of evaluation, because it is closely associated with the appraisal of pupil growth. The ultimate purpose of all education is to aid the learner in the process of growth. Art is one of the phases of education for the attainment of that goal; therefore, it is incumbent upon the teacher to discover the potentialities of pupils, to diagnose their needs, determine what is best for each of them, and focus the method and the content of experiences in appropriate directions.

It is obvious that the professional teacher, from a purely personal angle, will want to know how well and how much his pupils are achieving in relation to their potentialities. Parents and administrators are also interested in what education in the arts is accomplishing in the area of behavior. There are technics, instruments, and ways of discovering and interpreting the development of pupils. These instruments are at the disposal of teachers. When such are not available, the resourceful teacher may develop his own if he is conversant with the literature of behavior measurement.

Creative activity, it has been indicated, is an organic process which includes, but does not separate: creator-creation-object. The creative experience is a *whole* in which one of these facets may now play a major and now a minor role, yet all three are always organically tied together. Process and product, therefore, are given equal recognition at the proper levels of pupil development.

The literature on the meaning and measurement of human behavior is ample. The art teacher needs only to become familiar with its many aspects, possibilities, and adaptations to the art field. Progress in art as education may well depend on the wisdom of art teachers to experiment and ultimately to develop instruments for the adequate evaluation of creative and aesthetic growth and changes in behavior.

EXPERIMENTATION develops a broad range of purposes and processes. It becomes a means toward creative expression for the teacher and will suggest many adaptations to classroom activities (State Teachers College, Edinboro, Pa.).

5. *The art teacher has an obligation with respect to curriculum development.* Particularly when the art teacher in question is the only person especially trained in art, his function with respect to the curriculum is heightened. When he is one of several individuals concerned with the program, he has a definite share in determination of objectives, in implementation, and in evaluation of the total area. Therefore, whether alone or in collaboration with associates and the coördinator, the art teacher must be concerned with what is taught, how it is taught, what are reasonable expectancies, and how to facilitate expression from a physical as well as an educational standpoint.

The nature and affective role of experience, levels of growth, interests, motivation, stimulation, and evaluation are among the aspects of educational means that the teacher may call upon in visualizing the program at one level of schooling or another. These various foundational elements have been discussed elsewhere in this text. They are mentioned again to establish the point that a mere list of activities for children "to do" will not suffice. Actually, this is not what is expected of the art teacher; rather, it is expected that a clear and broad road be charted which will intimately involve pupils in planning. The charting should be flexible, adaptable, and in harmony with the principle that individual pupils, their interests and abilities, differ. Finally, the charting should envision desirable growth expectancies at various levels.

There is a further aspect of curriculum planning which needs special attention, namely, the relations of art to the total curriculum of the school. This is a significant point and on it may hinge the success or failure of art education. Abundant examples across the nation indicate that this relation and rapport are crucial, particularly at the elementary-school level. At the same time, the teacher is cautioned to safeguard the developmental aspects of the art experience.

6. *The art teacher has an obligation with respect to personal experimentation and research.* Books on art education have been and will continue to be written; special research and experimentation is being carried on in graduate schools, the results disseminated, and reports on successful ventures in teaching are verbally reported at professional meetings. These are some of the ways in which progress in the field is stimulated. However, by far the most effective way of improving the teaching-learning process in the classroom is to have teachers themselves engage in personal research and experimentation. Experiments in methods, in teaching technics, in ways of evaluating, ways of stimulating, or comparative studies of situations, are but a few suggestions of what teachers may do at their own base of operation to improve their own teaching and the growth of the pupils in their care. But there are other residues of such worth-while activities on the part of teachers. Their findings, if disseminated, may benefit the profession as a whole.

The monotony that results in going through the same routine year after year is detrimental to the mental health of the teacher. Often it is the basis of that discontent which leads to professional atrophy.

The alert mind, the mind that searches for new and better ways, is rewarded by the satisfaction of achievement in the classroom and the improvement of the art of teaching in general.

IMPLICATIONS FOR ALL TEACHERS

It may appear that so far the burden of this chapter has been directed to the special teacher of art. While that has been the intent, directions and points of view have been indicated which have meaning for *all* teachers who teach art. Indeed, the obligations just discussed can become realities only through continued awareness of changes in concepts, methods, and objectives in art education on the part of consultants, art teachers, and classroom teachers.

Experience is the greatest of teachers. Unquestionably, those who have served the profession for some time and have participated in professional activities may have discovered, through practice, many of the significant points raised. However, it is because of the greater wisdom that comes with experience that teachers in service will want

TOOLS AND MATERIALS are essential in the three-dimensional design expression. Their proper handling and care are an integral part of the education of art teachers (State University Teachers College, New Paltz, N.Y.).

to evaluate, periodically, their own effectiveness. What could possibly come from such a reëxamination? These are some hoped-for outcomes:

1. Self-evaluation (How good a teacher am I?)
2. Self-criticism (Why do my pupils act and react as they do?)

3. Self-improvement (How may I improve my method of teaching?)
    4. Self-direction (Where and how may I find better ways of teaching?)

A good deal of attention is devoted to these questions in Chapter 15. In it, the supervisory program, particularly that portion that deals with the in-service education of teachers, is detailed. From that discussion, it should be clear to teachers that the greatest hope lies in *self-motivated* growth, improvement, criticism, and direction. When the teacher feels impelled to inquire, to evaluate his own work in the classroom, and to seek better ways, real growth occurs. And when it occurs, its effects are evidenced in the development of the boys and girls with whom the teacher has contacts.

The reader will find a Self-Evaluation Scale on pages 498–503. It is an adaptation of an instrument used to evaluate the work of student teachers.[16] It has been used to help future teachers realize how much is involved in the process of guiding children. It has often been administered for self-appraisal by the novices. At the same time, it is believed to be an effective reminder and a good gauge that may be used with profit even by teachers of experience.

CHALLENGE TO ART-TEACHER EDUCATION

Because this book is addressed to those who are preparing to teach art as well as to teachers in service, it seems proper to devote a minimum of attention to art-teacher preparation. In the final analysis the best outlook is a forward one. What redirection is needed in teacher preparation? What minimum knowledge should be demanded? What contacts and other experiences seem of value? Finally, what basic philosophy should inspire the future art teacher in order that he may be a worthy member of the profession, even though lacking in teaching experience?

In harmony with all that has preceded thus far, it would appear that the pattern of art-teacher education for the immediate future might take on the form described by the five directions suggested hereafter.

1. *The art teacher should possess a background of general education and culture comparable to that of teachers of other fields.* To be effective, the art teacher must envision the totality of his work. A sound foundation

---

[16] The Laboratory Schools, State Teachers College, Kutztown, Pennsylvania.

in English and American language and literature, as well as in world literature, would represent minimum requirements in the language arts. To imply that any teacher should possess a broad general education hardly calls for apology.

Preparation in the field of social studies is equally as important, if not more so. If creative activity is considered part and parcel of living, as suggested by the newer aims of art education, then the art teacher must be conversant with developments in the world in which he lives. He must realize that human needs are founded on social, economic, and historic conditions. A rich background will not only be a cultural asset, but will actually serve as a tool which will enable the art teacher to see life as a series of relationships, of causes and effects, of human experiences, aspirations, and achievements. With such a background he should be better able to see the organic relationships of art to life. In consequence he should also be a better guide of children and of youth.

The nature and method of the sciences, aside from cultural values, offer practical assistance to the teacher of art. The biological basis of education, particularly with regard to those aspects that deal with child growth and development, is sufficient reason for teachers to become informed in psychology and education. Beyond these larger aspects, there are the direct relationships of science to color, light, and sound as they apply to design, painting, and the theater arts; of nature in general to design in its myriad applications; and of chemistry to the graphic processes, ceramics, and sculpture.

The kinship of the visual arts to the dance, music, and drama are so abundant and so rich in integrative possibilities that the art teacher for the schools of our time should explore their possibilities as stimulating agents.

The value of a wide background is attested to by the judgment of teachers in service.[17] It is likewise implied in the nature and meaning of integration, and it is suggested by the activities of an associative type generally performed or supervised by teachers of art. Actually, it is implicit in the fact that teachers of art are members of a learned profession.

---

[17] de Francesco, *An Evaluation of Curricula for the Preparation of Teachers of Art, op. cit.*, p. 156.

The length, breadth, and depth of general education should be limited only by the individual's capacity to undertake varied experiences and by the limitations of time.

2. *The art teacher should possess a professional education that will make him adequately conversant with problems and practices in education, psychology, and method, both in the field of art and of education in general.* Art education has evolved in such a manner that today one thinks of it as a means to a larger end, namely, individual development.

Mere facility in art does not ensure that its possessor is a good teacher. Education, psychology, and method have contributions to make to the ultimate success of the teaching-learning situation. Above all, an understanding of the nature of the individuals to be taught is paramount.

The art teacher for the modern school cannot be looked upon merely as an artist in the popular sense, nor merely as a teacher in the traditional sense. He must be an *artist-teacher,* one whose knowledge of children and youth and whose sympathies for them are deep and broad. He must be a person whose professional equipment goes far beyond a mere bag of tricks, erroneously called methods. His method must evolve from a clear concept and a deep understanding of the creative impulse, how it is nurtured and guided toward full development. The artist-teacher is one who possesses a knowledge of art and of education, and above all of the art of teaching, itself founded on the best contributions of psychology and educational practice.

The diversified activities of the modern school suggest that the artist-teacher must develop keen sensitivity in many directions and a broad knowledge of the means of education. This is a phase of the art teacher's preparation which has often been minimized, as is shown by studies.[18] Lastly, the laboratory school should be the center around which the professional phases of preparation revolve. True professionalization of education and the application of psychological principles seem to suggest this position.

3. *The art teacher should possess a competence in the area of the arts commensurate with his needs as a teacher and as an individual, and in harmony with art education as conceived today.* The art teacher's chief function in the schools of today is to stimulate the creative growth of

---

[18] *Ibid.,* pp. 162 ff.

children. Formulas, schemes, devices, and other types of preconceived gadgetry imply directed and, therefore, ineffective teaching. Instead, his technical preparation should be oriented in the direction of conceptual thinking, development of insights and wholesome outlooks, through the medium of art.

The current objectives of art as education, the nature of the demands made upon the art teacher, his professional contacts, and his needs as an individual would indicate that narrow preparation will hardly fit him for the profession. Even through technical courses he should recognize the organic pattern: creator-creation-society.

The art teacher should be master of his subject in the same sense that teachers of English, science, or languages are masters of their subject fields. Therefore, the art background of the teacher, while commensurate with the teaching task to be done, should be aimed at the educational ends to be achieved. These are basic understanding of the function of art experience, the psychology of growth and development, and the function of art *as education* for complete living.

Teacher preparation in this area should furnish art skills and knowledges necessary to render adequate service at the elementary and secondary levels. A reasonable elective area could serve to advance the personal interests of the teacher as a person.

4. *The art teacher's chief interests should focus on the education of children and youth through art activities so that their creative urges and their personal, social, and emotional needs may be properly nurtured.* One of the major recommendations of the National Survey of the Education of Teachers is to the effect that "the task of educating teachers should not be minimized in order to realize outcomes unrelated to those implied in a professional institution."[19] The significance of the recommendation is that the objectives of an art-teacher-preparing institution must be crystal clear. Preparing persons who eventually are neither teachers nor producing artists is detrimental to the individual who is being educated and to the children who eventually come under his influence.

The methods of study and of teaching in the preparation of teachers

---

[19] *National Survey of the Education of Teachers,* Washington, D.C., U.S. Office of Education, Vol. III, p. 42.

of art should be a constituent part of the curriculum. Professionalization of art subject matter must be vital, while the degree of technical achievement should be limited only by the creative powers of the student being educated for the profession.

When the objectives of institutions preparing art teachers are clear, it is hardly conceivable that any part of the preparation can be separated from its ultimate purpose. Constant evaluation of their own work, or of children's work, as well as of educational conditions necessary in the production of works of art, is the way through which teachers may develop proper approaches to the education of young people.

5. *The art teacher must seek contacts and activities sufficiently broad to ensure a well-balanced personality.* The plan of selection and recruitment adopted by many art-teacher-preparing institutions is unquestionably of first importance. However, backgrounds and inclinations differ; therefore, there is need of providing facilities and opportunities for a wide range of contacts and experiences of a type less formal than is possible in classroom or studio.

The activities usually performed by teachers in service and the practices in the schools of our time should be the criteria for determining the extent and character of the provision to be made during the preservice period. Guidance, not only in subject-matter selection but also in the selection of activities of a cultural and professional nature, should be considered part of the total preparation.

The effective teacher is not only grounded in subject matter and in professional techniques. He constantly grows in interests and outlooks outside the narrow sphere of his particular area. The extent to which teachers avail themselves of enriching experiences is of serious concern because not only proper length and depth, but proper breadth is important in the education of those "who dare to teach."

ART TEACHING AND GENERAL CLASSROOM TEACHERS

SIGNIFICANT CONTRIBUTIONS

More and more, the art education of children in the elementary schools is becoming the responsibility of general classroom teachers. There are those who deplore the fact, unmindful of the tremendous contribution made by such teachers to the overall program of art education. Elementary teachers, by far and large, are sincere in their purpose, willing to learn, and, generally, better informed in the aspects of child growth than most other teachers. These facts alone offset the fears and misgivings generated by an unfortunate parochialism in art education. Wise supervision, as will be pointed out in Chapter 15, has already accomplished much in the reorientation of the general classroom teacher toward a sound art program. As art coördinators themselves learn to value what general classroom teachers can accomplish because of their day-long closeness to young people, in that measure will the worth of such teachers increase.

INADEQUACY OF PRESERVICE PREPARATION

General education has become an accepted factor in all types of preparation, particularly at the college and professional-school level. Art education should be, basically, a part of the cultural background of all people; even more so in the preparation of all workers in fields of professional education. Ziegfeld[20] has admirably presented the case for and the method in art experiences in general education at the college level. In the case of general classroom teachers, regardless of the level of service for which they prepare, the arts admittedly are an indispensable phase of their education. Especially, it should not be difficult for teacher-education institutions to see the heightened significance of art experiences, as well as of appreciation, in the program of those who plan to enter elementary education. The elementary-school years represent the crucial span of life for all children: the citizens, the consumers, and perhaps the creators of the immediate future. Contemporary educational practice has, therefore, recognized the value of offering creative opportunities to children, both as related activity and as creative experience. The significant position of the elementary teacher, therefore, is too obvious to call for further comment.

But in effect, how adequate is the current preparation of elementary teachers to guide art activities in the self-contained classroom or in any other pattern? A recent survey of certification requirements made by the author reveals that the national median requirement in art for cer-

---

[20] Ernest Ziegfeld, *Art in the College Program of General Education,* New York, Teachers College, Columbia University, 1953.

tification in the elementary field is 3.7 semester hours. The requirement includes art appreciation, art laboratory, and method. However, while this median requirement does not obtain in all states, in several others enlightened educational leaders have realized the importance of art as a means of education and have set their requirement to not less than six semester hours. In a few instances, the art requirement is as high as 12 semester hours. In two of the states, elective possibilities permit an elementary teacher to obtain a "minor" of 18 semester hours in art education.

SUGGESTED IMPROVEMENTS

The data point to at least three major needs: first, more art opportunities must be made available to elementary teachers in service; second, art educators and state certification officers need to be more realistic in regard to the present and future needs of elementary teachers while in training; third, teacher-preparing institutions need to be aware of the situation and amplify their offerings through field courses, workshops, and electives for elementary teachers in service.

The first of these needs is perhaps best satisfied through workshops and other types of aid offered at the local level under the direction of the art consultant. This phase of the consultant's responsibility is fully discussed in Chapter 15. The second need may be better satisfied, through proper approach, by state art associations, the regional art associations, and the National Art Education Association in coöperation with state departments of education. The third need rests on the vision of teachers' colleges and other institutions preparing elementary teachers. The importance of the task indicates that art coördinators must be generous and that leaders in art education must concentrate more on the functional needs of the field and less on esoteric problems and issues. Lastly, all those who are concerned with art as education must strive to ease the minds of elementary teachers, guide them sympathetically, and allay their fears. The overall imperative at this level of education is to focus on developing the child, rather than on "teaching" art.

SUMMARY

The importance of the teacher as a guide of children and as the interpreter of the philosophy of the art program indicates that his preparation must have several dimensions: length, breadth, and depth. Progress has been made in the determination of the why, what, how, and how much of the entire program of teacher education.

The personality of the teacher, his understanding of the psychology of children and youth and of foundations of method, seem to be of first importance. But the teacher of art must also understand the function of his field and the aims and purposes of its particular contributions to the total education of the child. It is likewise significant that man and environment, which constitute the subject matter of art activities and experiences, be properly understood; the latter calls for a broad general education.

Teachers of art are not unlike teachers of other subject fields. They share in all the activities of the school and the community. Therefore, experience in and understanding of the cocurricular program of the modern school should be part of the teacher's preparation. In addition, such educational technics as evaluation, curriculum planning, public relations, and many others should be experienced while preparing for the total task of teaching.

As teacher education evolves, therefore, art teachers in service, as well as general classroom teachers who are concerned with art, must recognize as important the basic elements that obtain in more recent preparation. They should keep abreast of newer technics and newer points of view in order to continue to do effective work with children.

In the final analysis teachers must evaluate their own professional equipment and growth in relation to the realities of the task they perform daily. True growth in service is best measured by the degree of self-motivation on the part of teachers. And when they are aware of their own needs as professional workers, children invariably benefit.

The general classroom teacher, even though not highly specialized in art, can do and does an extremely important job of guiding children in their development through art. The specially prepared art teacher or coördinator has the responsibility to help classroom teachers understand art as a developmental activity as well as to demonstrate for teachers those methods and technics that will permit them to do a more adequate piece of work in art as education.

It has been contended that in order to achieve the unique goals inherent in democratic education and the professional advancement of art as education, the dissemination of research findings and the achievement of a synthesis are of prime importance. The magnitude of the task is indeed bewildering, yet the opportunities are unmatched in the entire history of educational progress.

SELF-EVALUATION SCALE FOR ART TEACHERS

To those who wish to attempt a self-evaluation, it is suggested that they first give sufficient study to each of the twenty items; later, they may wish to transfer these *honest* opinions of themselves to the last form, which is a "profile." Then it may be possible to ask oneself: What are my strengths and my weaknesses? And again: How may I improve my professional status so that I may be more effective in guiding children toward complete development? (The numerical ratings are in ascending order: 1 = lowest, 5 = highest.)

I. PERSONAL QUALIFICATIONS

Appearance ("My appearance is . . .")

_____ 1. Careless, untidy
_____ 2. Extreme, inappropriate
_____ 3. Satisfactory, neat
_____ 4. Pleasing, appropriate
_____ 5. Unusually well groomed

Poise ("My emotional poise shows . . .")

_____ 1. Nervousness, excitement
_____ 2. Self-consciousness, tenseness
_____ 3. Self-control under most situations
_____ 4. Calm, atmosphere of confidence
_____ 5. Confidence, dignity, social competence by example

Voice ("My voice is . . .")

_____ 1. Indistinct, monotonous
_____ 2. Irritating, weak
_____ 3. Clear, agreeable
_____ 4. Distinct, flexible
_____ 5. Fluent, pleasing

Coöperation ("My professional attitude reflects . . .")

_____ 1. Hostility toward work of school, negligence
_____ 2. Irresponsibility, spasmodic action

_____ 3. Harmony with others, average dependability
_____ 4. Willing coöperation, reliability, "going a second mile"
_____ 5. Search for opportunity to aid program, reliability even in emergency

Sympathy for Children ("My attitude reflects . . .")

_____ 1. Ignorance of child's point of view
_____ 2. Indifference toward interests of children
_____ 3. Friendliness, slight use of child psychology
_____ 4. Interest in needs and aspirations of children
_____ 5. Guidance of activities for fullest child development

Initiative ("My work and attitude show that I am [or do] . . .")

_____ 1. Lazy, physically weak, mentally sluggish
_____ 2. Do minimum, spasmodic, offer no suggestions
_____ 3. Do required work well, planning with variations
_____ 4. Methodical, careful in planning, energetic
_____ 5. Dynamic, enthusiastic, original planning

Leadership (Reactions from children and associates indicate that I [or I
    am] . . .")

_____ 1. Ineffective
_____ 2. Follow, rather than lead
_____ 3. Effective under encouragement
_____ 4. Accept responsibility, secure coöperation
_____ 5. Tactful, gracious, commanding respect

Adaptability ("Reactions indicate that I . . .")

_____ 1. Cannot adjust to children's age and individuality
_____ 2. Adjust with difficulty
_____ 3. React with some interest to new contacts and situations
_____ 4. Adjust myself to most situations with intelligence
_____ 5. Enthusiastically seek opportunity to meet new situations

Professional Attitude ("I feel that I [or I have] . . .")

_____ 1. Apathy toward work, routine attitude toward teaching
_____ 2. Seldom read, seldom contribute to discussions, vaguely relate art ex-
    periences
_____ 3. Read minimum, use tried plans, apply same to life situations
_____ 4. Read professional literature with understanding, continually relate art
    to growth
_____ 5. Experimental attitude, base work on newer approach in art educa-
    tion, conscious feeling of the relation of art to child growth

Reaction to Criticism ("I feel that I . . .")

_____ 1. Ignore advice
_____ 2. Resent criticism as personal

_____ 3. Accept criticism and try to improve
_____ 4. Use self-criticism, act upon suggestions
_____ 5. Seek advice, continuous self-improvement

Mastery of Subject Matter ("I am conscious that I [or I am] . . .")

_____ 1. Lack skills, too highly specialized to realize children's needs
_____ 2. Able in art fields, fair, poor, average
_____ 3. Sufficiently in command of skills and appreciations needed in art education
_____ 4. Skillful in most techniques, understand their applications
_____ 5. Adequate in all skills, broad in appreciation

II. Professional Performance

Planning ("I believe that generally I show [or I am] . . .")

_____ 1. Lack of consciousness of objectives, impractical
_____ 2. Perfunctoriness of manner
_____ 3. Good planning and carry out units well, sense of "tie-up" with previous experiences, allowance for choice of activities
_____ 4. Efficiency in most respects, purposefulness, breadth
_____ 5. Maximum efficiency; planning that guides, not limits, activities; interest that something definite be achieved by the activity

Pupil Needs ("My teaching indicates that I [or I am] . . .")

_____ 1. Seldom consider the understandings, interests, and level of skills of pupils
_____ 2. Use routine experiences and activities
_____ 3. Conceive needs of majority of pupils; slightly conscious of individual differences
_____ 4. Vary activities to suit individual differences
_____ 5. Determine subject matter and stimulation based on needs of group or of individuals

Ability to Motivate ("Results and comments suggest that I . . .")

_____ 1. Do not have necessary information to motivate
_____ 2. Have and use some information, have slight child understanding
_____ 3. Explain clearly and adequately
_____ 4. Seek opportunity to clear emotional difficulties, anticipate possible problems
_____ 5. Thoroughly emphasize purposes and functions of art experience

Pupil Participation in Activities ("I feel that I . . .")

_____ 1. Direct activities without regard to pupil interest, do little thinking, secure meager and frustrating results
_____ 2. Give some attention to pupils' contributions, do much of the thinking for the children

___ 3. Interest majority of pupils, use pupils' contributions, accomplish purposes
___ 4. Secure general participation, guide rather than direct
___ 5. Am able to secure interested and participation of all, guide while pupils lead

Pupil Growth ("I believe that I . . .")

___ 1. Allow growth and interests to deteriorate, ignore or am indifferent to pupil difficulties
___ 2. Plan experiences to meet most needs, sense some growth, solve some problems for children
___ 3. Encourage self-improvement, self-criticism, appreciations
___ 4. Definitely strive for development of pupils, foresee and prevent discouraging situations
___ 5. Strive for improvement in all, challenge the most talented as well as the weakest

Use of Resources ("I believe that I . . .")

___ 1. Seldom use sensory aids, allow pupils to depend on books and magazines for ideas
___ 2. Choose materials poorly, use sensory aids pointlessly
___ 3. Use sensory materials on occasions, demonstrate on occasion
___ 4. Often use sensory aids to interest and inform group
___ 5. Choose materials that inspire and enrich, demonstrate frequently and well for stimulation

Management ("I believe that my classroom shows . . .")

___ 1. Poor handling of materials and equipment, waste of time and energy, ignorance of children's needs and abilities
___ 2. Ineffectiveness in details, slight attention to room and equipment
___ 3. Definite appreciation for materials and equipment, inspiring appearance, orderliness consistent with type of activity
___ 4. Materials and equipment are effectively used with a measure of freedom to choose
___ 5. Coöperation and efficiency, inspires good work

Communication ("I feel that I . . .")

___ 1. Fail to express ideas clearly, make occasional grammatical errors
___ 2. Express ideas vaguely, uninterestingly; do not correct errors
___ 3. Use average vocabulary, am understood by class
___ 4. Put ideas clearly, use art vocabulary consistently
___ 5. Express ideas accurately, concisely, interestingly; employ and teach art vocabulary

The Art-Teacher Profile
(See page 498)

	1	2	3	4	5	
						1. Appearance
						2. Poise
						3. Voice
						4. Coöperation
						5. Sympathy for Children
						6. Initiative
						7. Leadership
						8. Adaptability
						9. Professional Attitude
						10. Reaction to Criticism
						11. Mastery of Subject Matter
						12. Planning
						13. Pupil Needs
						14. Ability to Motivate
						15. Pupil Participation
						16. Pupil Growth
						17. Use of Resources
						18. Management
						19. Communication
						20. Climate

Climate ("I believe my classes show . . .")

_____ 1. Frequent antagonism, lack of self-control
_____ 2. Order, control
_____ 3. Routine, order when undisturbed and when supervised
_____ 4. Coöperation in routine, measure of freedom
_____ 5. Greatest amount of freedom consistent with type of work, understand self-control and self-direction

For Discussion and Activity

1. Justify in specific terms the statement that any consideration of the teaching-learning situation ultimately involves the teacher.
2. What are the rewards and what are the responsibilities of the profession of teaching? To what extent are material rewards being achieved? What do you, individually, consider the highest reward of teaching as a career?
3. Cite some of the causes that seem to have retarded progress in art-teacher education and relate them to other educational situations occurring during the same period.
4. Make a list of the characteristics of the good art teacher: personal, professional, and social. Discuss their implications in terms of the task of teaching.
5. Study the Art-Teacher Profile on page 502. How adequately are you being prepared to undertake the many activities suggested? By a similar analysis of the professional and of the general education areas, determine the degree of adequacy of those areas.
6. Read again the section of this chapter dealing with the proposed type of preparation for art teachers. Do you agree with these proposals? If not, what are your counterproposals?
7. If you believe that children profit most through self-evaluation, does the same principle apply to the teacher? Using the Self-Evaluation Scale provided in this chapter, determine your professional stature.
8. Should teachers participate in the life of the school and of the community? If you believe they should, develop the argument for it. If you have reservations on the matter, present the argument for your position.
9. How high on the scale of values do you place human relations? Present the arguments for your belief. What is involved in professional relationships beyond classroom teaching?
10. What value do you attach to personal research? How does it contribute to the success of the teacher? How can it contribute to progress in the profession?

For Further Reading

Commission on Secondary School Curriculum, *The Visual Arts in General Education*, New York, D. Appleton-Century Company, 1940, Chapter V.

Evenden, E. S. (ed.), *Teachers for Our Times*, Washington, D.C., American Council on Education, 1944, Chapters III, IV.

Gould, George, and Yoakam, Gerald, *The Teacher and His Work*, New York, The Ronald Press Company, 1947, Chapters I–IV.

Hoover, F. Louis, "Improving the Education of Art Teachers," *Art Education*, April, 1950.

Hoover, F. Louis, "Who Are the Teachers of Art?" *Art Education*, February, 1949.

Kilpatrick, William (ed.), *The Teacher and Society*, First Yearbook, John Dewey Society, New York, D. Appleton-Century Company, 1937, Chapters IV, V, IX, X, XII.

McDonald, Rosabel, *Art as Education*, New York, Henry Holt and Company, 1941, Chapter V.

Maul, Ray C., "Art Teachers for the Future," *Art Education*, May, 1954.

National Commission on Teacher Education, *Teaching—A First Line of Defense*, Washington, D.C., National Education Association, 1951. The report points up the newer significance of teaching.

Rugg, Harold, and Brooks, Marian, *The Teacher in School and Society*, New York, World Book Company, 1950, Chapters I, III, XV, XVII.

Spears, Harold, *Improving the Supervision of Instruction*, New York, Prentice-Hall, 1953, Chapter XX.

Winslow, Leon L., *Art in. Elementary Education*, New York, McGraw-Hill Book Company, 1942, Chapter III.

Ziegfeld, Edwin (ed.), *Education and Art, A Symposium*, Paris, UNESCO, 1953, Section V.

Zirbes, Laura, *Teachers for Today's Schools*, Washington, Association for Supervision and Curriculum Development, 1951, pp. 26–27.

SUPERVISION OF ART EDUCATION

The purpose of supervision is to facilitate learning by improving the conditions that affect it. This is not accomplished by the mere provision of personnel bearing titles denoting staff service to teachers. This is but the starting point.

Harold Spears,
Improving the Supervision of Instruction

NEEDED DEFINITIONS

In ART EDUCATION THERE IS WIDESPREAD MISUNDERSTANDING OR AT LEAST misinterpretation of the term "supervision" and consequently of the term "supervisor." The newer terms, "coördinator" and "consultant," have, so far, only added to the confusion.

The meanings of the terms and of the functions assigned to them are, in reality, related to the legal definition of the position. Specifically, if a person is employed for more than one-half of the time as a teacher who is fully functioning in the classroom, he is a teacher. If he devotes more than one-half of the time as a coördinator of art education, actually guiding the program, he is, legally a supervisor, or a consultant, whichever term is employed locally. From this standpoint alone, the art person involved should know exactly for what purpose he is employed and inquire about the legal status of the position and its financial remuneration.

But even more significant is the professional status of the person involved. The functions and responsibilities of the total art program, the

506   development of a basic philosophy, and its general implementation require a great deal of time, energy, coöperative planning, and a pattern of organization. The classroom art teacher, by whatever name he is called, can hardly devote his energies and talents to supervisory duties and at the same time hope to accomplish a satisfactory piece of educational work in the classroom. It seems imperative that this problem be given due consideration by those in authority if the best interests of art education are to be served.

TYPES OF SUPERVISORY POSITIONS

The tremendous development of art education in the schools of America is, of course, paralleled by similar advances in other areas of so-called special education, including music, the industrial arts, home economics, guidance counseling, and other newer phases of educational service. Growth in the number of persons employed to administer the program in art, as well as the growth of art in educational significance, naturally requires a fairly complex administrative organization. Depending a great deal on the size of the school system, several types of positions in art education have developed. Their broad aim is the same: a larger opportunity and a sounder art education for all the children in the nation's schools. The functions of these positions, however, differ according to their relationship to the chief administrative school officer. A description of some typical situations may clarify the problem.

The Art Director

Large city systems usually employ a director of art, who, in turn, has a staff of supervisors, especially prepared to work at one or more levels, namely, the elementary, the junior high school, or the senior high school. The number of such persons obviously depends on the size of the district and on the total school population. The art director is responsible to the superintendent of schools or to an assistant superintendent, or to a director of instruction. In brief, the art director, in so far as art education is concerned, is the first link in the chain of authority and responsibility. It is his duty to represent art education in the best possible sense, to convey its claims, to secure maximum financial support for it, and to ensure for art education the highest professional respect. He must be a statistician and must be conversant with the psychological aspects of development. He must be able to write professionally, to speak intelligently, especially for his area of education, and he must assume leadership in the major public-relations aspects of art education. He must understand and practice democratic principles of administration, employ group dynamics and be thoroughly familiar with curriculum thinking. He must translate these abilities into positive leadership in art-curriculum planning through his special assistants, special teachers of art, elementary teachers, principals, and sometimes directly with parents and the public at large.

The Art Supervisor

Smaller systems usually employ one person as a general supervisor for the entire art program. Such a person performs all the major functions ascribed to the art director, but in addition has frequent and direct contacts with principals, with art teachers in secondary schools, and with elementary teachers. He is the direct line to the superintendent of schools and is the thread that coördinates the entire art staff and program. There are many more persons employed in this capacity than there are art directors. But it is not uncommon to find in medium-sized school systems two persons employed in similar capacities, one devoting his time to elementary art education and the other to secondary art education. In either case, it is quite likely that one of the persons, because of seniority or other plausible reasons, is regarded as the supervisor and the other as the assistant. In that case, the assistant collaborates in administrative details, while the supervisor is the liason person with the chief school officer.

The Art Coördinator

It has already been suggested that in recent years the term coördinator has been substituted for the term supervisor. However, the newer term has not displaced either the supervisor or the director of art education. The new term has come into use more particularly because art education has somewhat advanced from its position as a special subject to a fundamental one, integral with the total education of all children at all levels. Formerly, the specially prepared person made the rounds of classrooms and "taught" art. The newer concept, widely accepted, assumes that in the elementary school the classroom teacher is the art teacher.

508   That she may need assistance, guidance, and in-service training is all too true. Such will be the case until elementary-teacher-education programs realize the necessity of extending the art preparation of the elementary teacher beyond its present limited scope. Therefore, the new task of the art coördinator is to secure the direct, willing, and sincere coöperation of all elementary teachers. He must sympathetically realize their limitations, magnify their strengths as teachers of children, convey to them the developmental values of creative activities, and as often as practicable help their in-service growth, especially in art.

The newer term, coördinator or consultant, whichever may be used in a particular locality, does not absolve the chief representative of art education in a school system from any of the tasks performed by such a person from the time the supervisory position was created. Rather, the new term adds to his many responsibilities the supreme task of welding, by educational means, a new pattern which includes all elementary teachers as coworkers.

STATE AND COUNTY SUPERVISION

At the present moment, there are but ten states in the entire nation sufficiently aware of the magnitude of the task of art coördination as to employ state directors of art. Here again, it is worth noting that the terminology embodied in school laws determines whether he is a chief, a state supervisor, or a state director of art education.

Regardless of the terminology, the major aims and functions of the position are these:

1. To advance art education at the highest state educational level by advocating its inclusion in all grades and types of public schools.
2. To develop, through coöperative effort, a flexible yet inclusive curriculum guide as a frame of reference for the entire state.
3. To represent, ably and intelligently, the claims of art education as part of all education and to secure for it financial support, legal status, and educational respect.
4. To lead, initiate, and coöperate in all types of art or general education groups whose aims are to improve and extend art as education.
5. To speak for, write about, and conduct research in the field of art education so that its benefits may be extended to all, its methods refined, and its program enriched.

In a large sense, state direction is the source to which all teachers in the field should look with confidence for leadership in the philosophy and practice of art education, curriculum planning, and educational statesmanship.

County or parish supervision has been making headway within the last decade. The importance of this type of coördination can only be appraised as one realizes the geographical extent of some areas and the large number of small school systems within their boundaries. In a county or parish there may be as many as twenty or thirty school units with as many local art teachers, or persons who teach part of the time and coördinate the balance of the time. To establish relationships, to share points of view, to exchange ideas, to develop curriculum materials, and to gather other resources that could be made available to all systems are the chief problems of the county supervisor. In all other respects his work is not unlike the work of a city or large-town coördinator. The difference lies in the geographic area that he must serve. County and area superintendents who are aware of the benefits of a central place for meetings, of the advantages of a central art-curriculum laboratory, of a center for sensory aids for the art program, and of the tremendous advantages that such a step can bring to the creative education of boys and girls are usually ready to accept this type of organization. Its benefits to rural and suburban communities are yet to be realized.

It should be reiterated that terminology should not be a hindrance to the essential accomplishments of the task of coördinating art education. The broad characteristics of the diverse types of positions have been sketched thus far. The larger implications affecting all types of democratic coördination will now be described in some detail.

BROAD IMPLICATIONS OF DEMOCRATIC SUPERVISION

LEADERSHIP

The idea of supervision thus far presented can only imply one thing, namely, that the art supervisor is a person capable of leading others to see fully and completely the aims and purposes of art activities as an integral part of general education.

The professional leadership of the art coördinator will manifest itself in a number of ways. He is first of all a *guide*. A guide is one who leads the way, points to the dangers and thus avoids stumbling blocks, and at the same time is careful to show the bright spots along the journey. He does all this with the assurance that comes from having experienced the road before. He is a *helper*, who, by virtue of larger experiences and more extensive preparation, can foresee the effectiveness, or lack of it, in a projected art program. He is ready to promote or to redirect such plans in order that the desired goals may be achieved. He is a *counselor* who inspires, one who stimulates self-criticism and careful evaluation of plans and results in the light of the best thinking in educational theory and practice. Above all, he is a democratic leader.

Such leadership implies that the coördinator is capable of recognizing the true worth of his associates in art education. It means that he can allow for differences of opinion and independence of thought, and along the line discover and make clear the coalition that can be obtained by working and thinking together.

COÖPERATION

It should be clear to teachers and coördinators of art that they are working for a common end. That end is the enrichment of the lives of boys and girls in order that American life and society, in the present and in the immediate future, may be fuller and more satisfying. The following statement by the Department of Supervisors and Directors of Instruction seems appropriate: "All supervisory agents work toward common ends. This implies that common ends have been determined through the refinement that comes only with the conflict of minds."[1]

The "conflict of minds" refers to the give-and-take that a good supervisor will permit, to the sifting of ideas and arguments, to the clarification of issues and terminology, to the definition of the philosophy, and other similar issues. Through such "conflicts" common ends are recognized and agreed upon. Whatever has not been agreed upon is held in abeyance until such time as situations demonstrate what is the right position to take.

---

[1] Department of Supervisors and Directors of Instruction, National Education Association, Third Yearbook, *Current Problems of Supervisors*, New York, Teachers College, Columbia University, 1930, p. 8.

The coördinator who is capable of coöperating even when conflicts **511** arise will soon earn the right to the leadership to which he is called.

CREATIVE OVERVIEW

A distinguished professor of education, explaining to a class the meaning of supervision, asked for the privilege of using a homely breakdown of the word. Said he: "The word is really a compound of two fine attributes: the first, *super,* refers to a high quality or high degree of something; the second, *vision,* refers to the wisdom and long-range view of the thing talked about." Supervision or coördination is a term that indicates not merely educational rank but a high degree of educational statesmanship.

Creative supervision is capable of finding the strengths in every teacher and of emphasizing them while overlooking any weakness that may exist. It encourages originality and self-expression in the teacher, just as every teacher of art encourages initiative and self-transcendence in the child. It is aware of the fact that there is no fixed pattern of doing any one thing, but that there are many ways of achieving the goals of art education.

Sound supervision strives to clear the tracks, as it were, by providing the right environment and by developing situations in which teachers can do their best work. It thinks in terms of physical environment as a necessary means to the attainment of educational goals. It strives to keep alive in the art teacher the creative impulse both in teaching and in personal work.

OBJECTIVITY

There has slowly grown a notion, now prevalent in art education, to the effect that art, being a matter of self-expression, should not, or cannot, be measured, tested, checked. Without overemphasizing the issue, it should be stated quite unequivocally that the end products of art education, at the levels where the product becomes significant, can and should be measured, compared, and tested. It should also be clear that teachers and coördinators, from their knowledge of aesthetic standards, should be in a position to establish, by proper procedures, for themselves and for all those working with children, the importance of good design, good composition, and the like. Sound administration suggests

512   that the proper interpretation of standards may in time raise the tone and quality of the entire system. Indirectly, insistence on design quality is a valuable aid in the improvement of teachers and teaching.

Supervision, to be successful, must be objective and not personal. It should work on evidences and not on fancy. It should never be on the defensive; all this can only be done with facts on hand. In the final

PUBLIC RELATIONS is one of the concerns of the art consultant. Television, radio, and newspapers are effective means of explaining the art program to the public (public schools, Tucson, Ariz.).

analysis, the art coördinator will want proof of his own achievements; the proof is yielded, among other possible means, by the evidences of the creative growth of the pupils. The purposes, methods, and technics of evaluation were discussed in Chapter 7. At this point it should be reiterated that it is of primary significance to art education. The good coördinator will use it as the means of stimulating the thinking of the classroom teacher, thus improving classroom performance and, inevitably, the quality of the art expressions of boys and girls.

COÖRDINATION

One of the primary objectives of supervision is to coördinate, to establish an effective articulation of the various facets of the total work of teaching so that normal child growth may result. The successful coördinator should be certain that teachers are thoroughly familiar with the tools of the profession. State and local guides, the significant literature of the field, sources of materials, the nature of method, technics of evaluation, are educational procedures that contribute to the achievement of ultimate objectives. But because it is through the proper use of professional tools that instruction advances, it is imperative that the effective art coördinator should always be on the alert to seek the improvement of those tools.

Coördination, however, refers to more than tools. It refers principally to the basic philosophy underlying the principles and practices of teaching art. Principles poorly interpreted or badly practiced will result in weak child-guidance. When properly interpreted, methods and procedures become living forces in the stimulation of the creative impulses of children and youth. What follows is a very comprehensive statement on the business of coördination and administration of art. Its study should throw light on the problem as a whole.

What We Believe About the Supervision of Art Education

The supervision of art education should:

1. Encourage art as an organized body of aesthetic experience coördinate with other major curriculum areas and growing out of the experiences of the entire educational program, a creative entity which suffuses with its freedom and emotional release the entire curriculum.

2. Operate whenever a process calls forth in visual expression the attempt to satisfy a need, aiming to maintain a balance between individual and social consciousness on the part of the pupil.

3. Recognize that progress in art education is realized in the expression of the hopes, the ideals and the aspirations of our own homes, schools, and communities, of our own times, and of our own lives.

4. Make clear to those involved, that art is an important means of interpreting and expressing ideas and feelings, through which all school subject areas become more meaningful, and the life of the pupil richer.

5. Be a coöperative activity based upon responsibility shared by teachers

and supervisor working together, enabling both to be mutually helpful, sincere and impartial.

6. Encourage in teachers independence of thought and initiative which will render them increasingly confident and self-reliant in their work.
7. Concern itself with the development of personality, through recognizing the worth of the individual and his capacity for growth.
8. Provide opportunities for all to engage in enjoyable, meaningful, informational experiences as well as in those involving the use of materials.
9. Inculcate, on the part of teachers and pupils, a love of the beautiful in all man-made things, clarifying understandings and promoting good taste.
10. Emphasize participation in creative activities which challenge ability to assume responsibility, to plan, to carry through, and to evaluate results of the art program.
11. Constitute a flexible program resulting in constructive practical help for the teacher, stimulating continuous professional development and self-appraisal.[2]

PATTERNS OF TEACHING AND SUPERVISION

A recent survey by the author discloses that currently several patterns are followed in the teaching of art. They are discussed at this point because the patterns suggest various roles for the art coördinator.

THE ITINERANT ART TEACHER

The first of these, and the most prevalent, is the pattern in which the so-called art supervisor actually is an itinerant art teacher. He comes to each room in each of the schools to teach art on an average of once a week and then trusts that the classroom teacher will carry on what he has motivated and begun. In addition, there is the hope that the classroom teacher will use art as a correlating medium with English, the social studies, arithmetic, geography, and other fields, or whenever the children or the teacher feel the need of using art to clarify and amplify meanings.

---

[2] The statement is based largely on Frederick G. Bonser, "My Art Creed," in *Art and Industry in Education,* New York, Teachers College, Columbia University, 1912; Will Grant Chambers, "Art Creed," in Margaret F. S. Glace, *Art in the Integrated Program,* The Maryland Institute, Baltimore, Md., 1934; and William H. Lemmel, "The Superintendent's Philosophy of Supervision," an address to the Baltimore Supervisors' Workshop, June 7, 1949. It is used here by permission of the Baltimore, Maryland, Schools, Division of Art Education.

How unsatisfactory this procedure is, especially with regard to art expression as a developmental medium, can be readily seen. Under this pattern, the classroom teacher takes little interest in art; as a matter of fact, it is generally charged that when the itinerant art coördinator arrives, the classroom teacher leaves the room or attends to other chores. Of course, this is not true of better classroom teachers. Whatever the case, it is obvious that the specially prepared teacher, who assumes the usual 25 to 28 periods per week, will have neither time nor energy left for coördination of any sort at the end of her scheduled teaching routine.

An amelioration of this situation is attempted through the use of a manual, a guide, or a course of study, usually prepared by the coördinator and followed by classroom teachers between visits. It seems hardly necessary to dwell on the sterility of such a pattern in so far as pupil growth and teacher improvement are concerned. However, it is important to point out that the inevitable results of the pattern are stereotyped and lifeless. They have little in common with creative expression.

THE SPECIAL ART TEACHER

A second pattern of administration of the art program, less prevalent because more costly, is one in which a special art teacher is employed in each building to do all the art teaching. It is assumed that art, so administered, affords the children all the advantages of a well-qualified person, technically and professionally able to nurture their creative development to the fullest. There are several major fallacies inherent in this pattern. The first is that since it is necessary to have fixed art periods, motivation must be completely extrinsic, and much stimulation fictitious, because the time element precludes adequate understanding and real experiencing on the part of the children. The second weakness lies in the direction of planning, which of necessity must be done by the art teacher only. Third, the essence of art lessons is likely to tend toward technical compartmentalization: color, design, drawing, and other areas for their own sake. This is done by the art teacher to ensure that children have a wide variety of experiences and that they may gradually build up a body of knowledges in the art area. It should also be recognized that this pattern exonerates the classroom teacher from any meaningful interest and participation in the art program, except as she may realize its value in correlation with other subjects or as an aid in special programs. This pattern is often popular among elementary teachers because it lightens their burden. But what of child growth, and what of integration of personality?

THE ART CONSULTANT

A third pattern, and one that promises to accomplish the most good for children, for classroom teachers, and for art education, is one in which the special teacher becomes a consultant. The functions of the consultant are best described by a term used in isolated situations: the helping teacher. In this type of administration the curriculum guide has been planned coöperatively by teachers and specialist. The activities are suggested with children in mind, and while the classroom teacher is responsible for the program, the consultant is on hand to help when help is wanted and needed. Furthermore, the coördinator teaches for demonstration purposes whenever deemed necessary or desirable, and with the aid of classroom teachers plans future activities, evaluates children's growth, gives personal or group help to teachers, and is responsible for the larger implementation of the program. Usually, the consultant follows a schedule of visits to buildings and grades; teachers know where he may be located if needs arise for consultation, and together they plan for conferences, workshops, exhibitions, and otherwise make arrangements for group or individual collaboration.

Unquestionably, the latter pattern is the most effective, even though it places heavier responsibilities on the consultant. However, even at the present moment, this pattern shows weaknesses; but they are of the type that time will obviate. Some of the weaknesses are enumerated hereafter. In the first place, in the average school district it is difficult for the consultant to work as effectively as he would like because of lack of time to cover the ground. Second, the art preparation of elementary teachers being insufficient, many feel inadequate and afraid of art; yet time for workshops seems wanting. In general, little provision is made by administrators for the implementation of a program of human relations and of in-service education by the consultant in behalf of the classroom teacher.

Nevertheless, inherent in the pattern are the widest potentialities. Among them are that the services of a specially prepared person may be utilized to the fullest; all teachers may share in the planning; with proper staffing and coöperation a program for maximum child development may be developed; and finally, the in-service growth of teachers may be realized.

SUPERVISION AND THE TEACHER

THE TEACHER AS A PERSON

The teacher, whether an elementary teacher or one especially prepared to teach art, is primarily and above all else a human being. As such he is endowed with certain capabilities, aptitudes, weaknesses, strengths, inclinations, points of view, biases, and convictions. But in addition he is a professionally prepared individual who, as an equal, is entitled to the same deferences and latitudes to which all other professional people are entitled.

If the larger implications of supervision discussed earlier in this chapter are fully accepted by the coördinator, there should be little difficulty in developing those understandings that are essential to the functioning of the program and to the establishment of friendly and coöperative relationships. To be specific: How well does the supervisor know the background and training of the teacher? How well are the strong tendencies and abilities of the teacher channeled to the advantage of the art-education program? How well does the supervisor understand the personal responsibilities of the teacher? How heavy is the teaching-activity load of the teacher? What is the emotional make-up of the teacher? Questions of this nature, properly answered, will furnish clues to the total personality with which the supervisor is dealing. Moreover, they become the guiding lines to follow toward the achievement of successful personal relationships. These, in turn, may affect the success of professional relationships.

There are, of course, certain cautions that the supervisor must observe: fairness in dealing with all teachers, proper sharing of responsibilities, equalization of teaching loads, and judicious use of initiative and leadership of the teaching corps.

NEED FOR UNDERSTANDING

Chief among the failures of many well-meaning supervisors is the assumption that teachers know just what is expected of them. It is assumed that they realize their respective roles, that they are fully aware of problems involved, and that they are always able to find successful solutions to problems. The truth is that most teachers are capable of understanding, but they are not ominiscient. In fact, they are very much like their professional supervisors: they need to be consulted. they need explanations, information, clearly defined objectives, personal help, personal assurance, praise, direction, and sometimes redirection.

It follows that the supervisor or coördinator must make every effort to know the teachers with whom he is to collaborate. Then only can he determine how much or how little individual help each one will need, how best to approach situations that may be irksome, how often and how much to praise, and how often criticism will be effective. Mature judgment suggests that personalities and peculiarities are never discussed or divulged. On the other hand, professional attitude need not be so narrowly construed as to preclude friendly social and personal relationships.

The larger understandings needed to achieve coöperative action are best obtained when all teachers are informed. Group action, group acceptance, and group sharing almost invariably bring about group solidarity and ensure the achievement of the common goals. The major understandings referred to here may include these: the evolving of a basic and commonly shared philosophy of art education, or the formulation of commonly accepted objectives, be they general or specific; acceptance of group-developed practices in the evaluation of child art and child growth; understanding of coöperatively devised procedures and forms for securing materials and equipment; individual responsibility for carrying out departmental public-relations projects; participation and/or collaboration in the implementation of in-service workshops, house organs, general bulletins, and the general organization of exhibitions. To these broad activities might be added many other teacher-supervisor activities that extend beyond classroom teaching. Unless there is a clear understanding of the purposes of these activities, of the responsibilities to be shared, of the needs to be served, and of the outcomes sought through them, teachers may well look upon them as mere busy work, or as chores that concern them little. The reverse is true; namely, that when teachers share in the planning, they are willing to share in the work, the responsibilities, and even the personal involvements that arise in the pursuit of the goals.

IN-SERVICE TRAINING

The current tendency to make the elementary teacher partially responsible for the teaching of art is a practice that may or may not prove beneficial to the creative growth of children. Success will depend largely on the attitude, somewhat on the aptitude, and, of course, on the recency

EXHIBITIONS may be designed to point up the functions of the arts in the lives of pupils. Parents and public understand visual presentations much better than words alone (Pima County Fair, Tucson, Ariz.).

of the preparation of the elementary teacher. The practice is not new in large cities, but it is a new problem in medium-sized and smaller communities, although there are small-school situations in which the special teacher of art introduces or originates the art activities and the classroom teacher carries them on to completion.

Under any condition, the person referred to as the art coördinator faces the serious problem of stimulating the professional growth of the classroom teacher. The problem is crucial because, in the long run, it involves the proper type of art experiences for boys and girls, and the right attitude toward art education on the part of elementary teachers.

Even the most ideal undergraduate preparation for an elementary-school teaching career is, at best, a foundation upon which each individual may build his professional future. The teachers' college or university has laid a solid basis consisting of essential art skills, general education, and professional education. In fact, in most instances it has exposed the future teacher to the operation of a classroom and to actual teaching under the tutelage of a master teacher. But it is safe to assume that all teachers, and young teachers in particular, need to be familiar with the general philosophy of a school system, the specific objectives of certain activities, and the particular procedures and details that are peculiar to a local teaching situation.

To be sure, the quality of preparation of the young teacher is usually revealed even at the time of the appointment. Nevertheless, the complexity of the details and the bridging of the gap between college or art school and actual teaching, fully independent of a master teacher, are often bewildering. It is the duty of the supervisor to make the transition a pleasant one, an experience that will confirm to the new teacher that he has entered upon a challenging and worth-while adventure.

It may be assumed from the foregoing that the young teacher is the major concern. This is true only to a degree. Other teachers, those who have served a few years or many years, are equally in need of constant help. If the philosophy of education and of art was stationary, once learned and once practiced, it might ensure continued success. But the evolving character of all education requires periodic refreshment, renewal of confidence, and a reappraisal of goals, points of view, activities, experiences, and method. Therefore, a well-planned program of in-service education for all teachers remains a major task of the art consultant.

Among common practices for the in-service education of teachers one finds grade-level meetings, optional workshops, curriculum-development committees, general meetings for the presentation and discussion of the broader aspects of child growth and development, and teachers' institutes where discussions are held under acknowledged professional leadership.

Another effective way of stimulating the growth of teachers is to encourage attendance and participation in art conferences offered by educational institutions within easy access, and the meetings of art-education associations of the state and area. Making available art-education literature, much of it free, in each building, and the exchange of exhibitions of children's work between buildings and between towns, will stimulate thinking, suggest evaluations, awaken the imagination, and encourage new activities on the part of teachers.

The in-service education of teachers of art may be further bolstered by enlisting the aid of the nearest teachers' college or university. Many school districts offer to pay tuition fees for teachers who avail themselves of extension courses. Oftener than not, teachers themselves are willing to spend time and money to improve in art education if the opportunity is presented. When the supervisor is of the right caliber and can meet academic qualifications, many colleges have employed him to offer needed courses locally, and have given teachers academic credit for the work done.

Finally, the resourceful and sensitive coördinator should readily discover the professional needs of his teachers and find proper means of organizing a meaningful program for their continued growth.

IMPORTANCE OF COÖPERATION

The professionally minded coördinator will want to know his teachers as thoroughly as possible. This involves a knowledge of the teacher's position in the community, her family relationships and responsibilities, her professional aspirations, and her economic status, in addition to those facets of cultural interests and outlooks mentioned elsewhere.

It should be made very clear that such knowledges are intended to guide the coördinator in making judgments and in reaching decisions which will affect the ultimate establishment of rapport. The gathering of these data should be accomplished without arousing suspicions, and the facts themselves should be held in strictest confidence.

Sympathetic understanding need not involve pity; at no time should the least deference for a teacher be obviously based on personal matters, but on a judicious evaluation of the circumstances. Criticism of a teacher, even when adverse, should be based on strictly professional grounds.

The coördinator should always be mindful of the fact that the success of the program, the happiness of children, and their normal creative development are intimately tied up with individual morale and with fitness to teach. The teacher is the crux of the entire teaching-learning situation. Teachers can either make an art program succeed or defeat its ends by their attitude toward the coördinator and toward art education. Even mediocre teachers, in so far as preparation is concerned, can be effective guides of children if their attitude is friendly toward the program.

Lastly, the total personality of the teacher needs to be studied by the coördinator in order to be able to appraise, guide, counsel, and otherwise direct the energies of the teacher toward the accomplishment of the task, the education of the child.

SUPERVISORY TECHNICS

In order to effect proper coördination of all the elements involved in the teaching-learning situation, the art supervisor makes use of a number of technics. Some of these are intended to bring about the chief under standings necessary to arrive at a commonly shared philosophy with regard to the function of art as education. Other technics are best suited to improve teaching performance, such as proper stimulation, teacher-pupil planning, the use of visual aids, and others. Some may direct attention to administrative details and others to help teachers in the use of materials and technics.

Not all technics are equally effective with all groups of teachers, nor are they equally effective to achieve all purposes. Therefore, it is well for the supervisor to determine which approach is best suited to a particular situation, at a given time, for a specific purpose, and for a particular group of teachers.

Experience and an understanding of human personality will, in the long run, suggest the wisdom of attacking overall problems in one manner or another. Nevertheless, as a basis for possible action, some promising technics will be reviewed.

THE INFORMATIONAL BULLETIN

The simplest approach to achieve group unanimity and general understanding is the informational bulletin. This may be either a brief or a more extended instrument through which the supervisor may alert, announce, inform, inspire, or guide his teachers. Brevity is generally considered a virtue; therefore, the length of the bulletin will be determined by the importance of and the necessity for details concerning the matters to be conveyed. Regularity of issue is also deemed significant; many teachers eagerly await the arrival of the right sort of bulletin. Perhaps an example will clarify several points. A young consultant, after discussion with the three principals with whom he worked and with the supervising principal, concluded that an informational bulletin would be a desirable contact with each teacher in the system. He also concluded from the discussion that the nature of the instrument would be a coöperative one; therefore, on his next visit to the teachers he broached the matter gently: "Would Miss Jones help by contributing a brief note on the outstanding activity just concluded by her grade?" "How often should the bulletin come out?" "What type of information would be desirable?"

The first issue of the *Coöp Teacher*[3] was an event. Teachers talked about it; children were proud to see their grade mentioned; interclassroom visitation soon became a regular part of school life to see what others were doing in art; teachers who had not contributed came forth with items for the next issue; suggestions for improvements were sent to the supervisor. In brief, the *Coöp* became an organ for solidarity, the exchange of ideas, and sharing in general. A recent review of this little house organ reveals the following captions: "What Children Are Doing in Grade Five," "Have You Seen?," "New Books on Art," "Meetings Worth Attending," "Have You Read?" Variations were introduced as time went on: brief quotations from authoritative sources, significant statements by children, a question box, and other desirable features.

It should be understood that the nature of such a bulletin, its frequency, contents, and format, must necessarily suit the local situation and the purposes it is to serve. Another point to be considered is that the supervisor cannot use the bulletin as his sole activity. Furthermore, no inference is here intended that a supervisor may hope to use the bulletin as a substitute for personal contact. Rather it is an interim visitor, a spark that keeps interests kindled.

---

[3] John G. Grossman, art supervisor, formerly in Millersburg, Pennsylvania, at present art supervisor in Bethlehem, Pennsylvania.

GROUP CONFERENCES

One of the serious problems facing professionally minded teachers and supervisors is the element of time. Time in which to do, to discuss, to plan, to evaluate, and otherwise attempt to improve the teaching-learning process. Therefore, in suggesting group conferences as a valuable technic, it is important to state that the first duty of the supervisor is to be mindful of the time element in the lives of teachers. The wise supervisor will discuss this problem with the administrators, attempt to develop a plan for such meetings, and be mindful of the location for such meetings, their frequency, and, above all, their value. It cannot be stated too strongly that such gatherings must (1) have a clear purpose, (2) be well planned, (3) be coöperatively designed, and (4) begin and end on time.

Experience has shown that unless the four points mentioned are observed, the ill will of teachers is usually forthcoming and all the good intentions of the coördinator are defeated, and that permanently. But experience has also shown that teachers will coöperate, will contribute, and will look forward to the next meeting with eagerness if the first experience has been profitable. The use of group dynamics in the planning and conduct of meetings is a democratic procedure that cannot be overemphasized. Teachers have ideas, questions, solutions, and suggestions to whatever problems may be raised. Therefore, the meeting should be *their* meeting at which time *they* help to resolve the issues.

Beyond these general considerations, if the size of the group warrants it, it may be best to hold grade-level meetings. The nature of the child, the nature of the problems, the suitability of experiences, the basis of method, and all other considerations are best clarified in terms of certain developmental levels. In this manner, it is possible to keep problems and solutions well defined and to maintain the teachers' interest at a high point. For example, if the size of the teaching corps makes it more convenient, it is wise to hold a meeting for teachers of preschool, kindergarten, and first grade; a separate meeting for teachers of grades two and three; a separate meeting for teachers of fourth, fifth, and sixth grades.

On the other hand, the energies of the supervisor, his time, and the size of the teaching corps may suggest other groupings. Whatever the case, meetings must be *meaningful*.

The possibilities of conferences are tremendous if one considers the fact that there may be but one art supervisor for the entire teaching staff of the school system. Simply as broad suggestions, the following topics gleaned from programs developed by supervisors in the field are here recorded:

1. The meaning of art expression of primary-grade children
2. The art expression of intermediate-grade children
3. How to motivate children for creative expression
4. Evaluation of child growth through art
5. The meaning of a balanced art program in the elementary school
6. Using materials appropriate to the developmental level of elementary children
7. Emotional development as shown by the art work of children
8. Natural correlation of art with other areas of learning
9. Teaching boys and girls to "see"
10. The use of community resources to motivate art expression in the junior high school

The effectiveness of either large or small group meetings may be enhanced in a number of ways. Following are some suggestions: the use of classroom teachers as discussants, provided they have been properly informed; making use of children's work as points for discussion, whether these are the originals or slides of the same; inviting and giving due recognition to questions from the group assembled; presenting a "tentative," concluding statement prepared by someone in the group; finally, making specific reference on how the various points discussed apply to the classroom situation to which the teachers will return the following day.

THE TEACHING DEMONSTRATION

The current point of view, which recognizes the classroom teacher as the art teacher, places an additional responsibility on the art coördinator with regard to the introduction of art activities to children. To be sure, the newer methodology has permeated the teaching of all elementary-school subjects; nevertheless the nature of creative expression, when coupled to the need for a more complete understanding of the child, does present added problems for the elementary teacher. To dispel fears and doubts about her ability to "teach" art, to give her tangible evidence that theory and practice in art education are not inconsistent with best practices in other areas of education, and to add status to the newer role of the art coördinator, demonstration teaching is desirable and, in many instances, necessary.

The coördinator who has become acquainted with the children, who knows the overall philosophy of the school system, who has made clear to the teachers her point of view in art education, should welcome the opportunity of working with children. This is best done in the natural or usual surroundings in which children normally work. Regardless of the physical situation, good or bad as it may be, here is the opportunity to work with children in the presence of the classroom teacher who spends the entire day in the same situation and with the same boys and girls.

The purposes of demonstration teaching may be many: simply to maintain contact with children, to develop a degree of professional camaraderie with teachers, to drive home an educational technic such as good stimulation or proper handling of materials, or to demonstrate the art of questioning as a vehicle for individualized expression. Independently of the major purposes, the teaching demonstration should be so prepared as to exemplify good teaching, sound method, and proper handling of the mechanical aspects of teaching. A discussion with the classroom teacher following the demonstration should be, as occasion demands, an evaluation of what occurred. Honesty and candor are among the most important characteristics of those who would lead others.

Demonstration teaching should be positive in spirit. Specifically, it should never suggest to Miss X that since she is weak, the coördinator will "show" her how it ought to be done. Caution in the selection of the grade to be taught, and therefore the teacher for whom the coördinator will demonstrate, is of major importance. Has the teacher asked for a demonstration? Is the time a suitable one for the coördinator to break into the routine of a classroom? Is the teacher receptive to the idea? These are but a few of many questions that might be asked before launching on demonstration teaching.

There is another type of teaching for demonstration which, if well implemented, may have a wholesome effect. The coördinator of a medium-sized eastern city has succeeded in convincing principals that a building demonstration will save time, help teachers, and ensure that all schools are adequately covered. The nonteaching employees of the school are made available for a 45-minute period to walk through the halls, enter each classroom, and see that all is well with the pupils while their teachers are gathered in the largest room of the building for a demonstration with children of a specific grade. General reports indicate that this method is effective.

By exercising all necessary cautions, by keeping the situation as normal as possible, and by having a clear purpose, demonstration teaching can become a strong instrument for welding all teachers who teach art into a harmonious group.

THE INDIVIDUAL CONFERENCE

It seems reasonable to restate that teachers, as individuals, differ greatly as to their innate potentialities. They also differ in preparation, outlook on life, and in their philosophy of education. When added up, these differences may at times create problems for the art coördinator. He must recognize them for what they are and decide on how best to help the individuals involved.

Before discussing the "problem" teacher, it is important to realize that personal conferences are not intended to be only correctives. They may, or should often, be in the nature of complimentary contacts with those teachers who seem to do a superior piece of work. It is also conceivable that through contact with the good teacher a leadership group may be identified. This is the group of persons on whom the coördinator may rely for support and guidance. Let it suffice to say, then, that while the purpose of the personal conference is usually calculated to help the teacher, it is quite possible that its purposes may be to receive help, to extend praise, to gain professional understanding, and to establish rapport.

However, the time element being very significant, the personal conference must be reserved for specific and significant reasons. The success of the personal conference will hinge on several factors: proper timing, proper approach, purposefulness, brevity, and objectivity.

Merely to pass by and exchange greetings should hardly be construed as having had a professional conference with a classroom teacher. The person to be visited should know in advance that the coördinator desires a conference; conversely, the coördinator should be informed in advance that a classroom teacher is desirous to have a conference. Many coördinators have designated a certain day, part of a day, or days for these personal contacts. This seems to be a fair arrangement; however, it need not preclude emergency calls from or to classroom teachers.

The object of the conference should be very clear. It would seem unfair to both parties to launch on a conversation dealing with a subject on which little thinking has been done. A purposeless visit not only consumes valuable time but is likely to result in an irksome situation because of emotional unpreparedness. A simple note will at most times suffice. The following form was designed for this purpose by a coördinator; it seems to fill the need and it is here reproduced as a suggestion.

SCHOOL DISTRICT OF HOMELAND

My dear M _____ :
    Is it convenient for you to have me come
to visit you for a conference on _____ at
_____ to discuss _____ ?
Date: _____
Please reply   J. W. Brown
                Art Coördinator

Proper approach implies many things. The coördinator and the teacher are professionally educated persons; therefore, the plane of the conference should be professional. Kindness, deference, and directness would seem to be essential in such meetings. The purpose of the coördinator should always be to help. The purpose of the teacher should be to receive such help and to clarify her problems. At times the discussion may be of broader scope; that is, it may deal with problems of evaluation, or with the gifted child or the subnormal individual in the class; in such instances the coördinator should be prepared to guide the teacher quite directly, although in terms that are general enough to allow the teacher the measure of freedom necessary to handle the situation.

Objectivity means that the coördinator and the teacher will discuss pertinent matters. Unwittingly, the purpose of a conference may be nullified by injecting into it totally irrelevant matters or prejudiced points of view. It may be wise for teachers and coördinators upon entering an office or classroom to ask themselves, and immediately to answer, the question: "What is my business here and now?" and then proceed to attend to it courteously, but directly.

Brevity, it is said, is the soul of wit. It is much more than wit in the lives of busy people such as teachers and coördinators. There is no implication in this statement to the effect that the parties concerned must hurry, scratch the surface of the problem, or rudely dispose of matters. The intent is that valuable time should be used with profit. If one conference does not settle the problems, then an additional appointment should be made, rather than upset a time schedule which may affect the personal life of the teacher, that of the coördinator, and perhaps involve children.

It cannot be stated too strongly that the personal conference is to be considered a two-way vehicle. The coördinator must keep in mind that human values are far more desirable than responses based on what is presumably expected by authority. The relation between teacher and coördinator and the manner of eliciting mutual respect have direct and lasting effects on the relationships between teachers and children.

THE WORKSHOP

Within the last decade the workshop, as an instrument for the improvement of teachers and teaching, has been perfected.

The meaning of the term *workshop* may be clarified if it is understood as a socialized, problem-solving educational experience, coöperatively organized and democratically conducted. It differs considerably from the formal classroom practices of colleges and universities in that it is relaxed, personalized, free, and broad in scope. Leaders, resource persons, consultants, and workers meet together to solve problems that are well defined by each participant. The outcomes are personal to the extent that each will receive in proportion to what he contributes. Characteristic of well-conducted workshops are the practices of sharing points of view, of examining data, of submitting ideas to group analysis, of comparing results, and of reaching conclusions coöperatively.

In art education a variety of procedures have been developed to give art workshops a special meaning and a realistic value. In the strictest educational sense, any group discussion or series of them, conducted in the spirit just described and dealing with major problems in art education, could and should result in an effective workshop. It should clarify meanings, point up directions, suggest ways, and in general broaden the horizons of the participants. However, discussion, examination, analysis, and conclusions reached by the group through the use not only of the word but of children's work, of pertinent visual or other sensory aids, would seem to be justified as a type of workshop for teachers of art.

Another version presupposes two phases: discussion and activity. Activity in this instance implies manipulation of art materials, use of

FURNITURE for art rooms must be adaptable to a variety of purposes. It is the responsibility of the co-ordinator to see that the working conditions are adequate, especially in junior and senior high schools (public schools, Toronto, Canada; Howard Dierlon, Supervisor and Designer).

technics, experimentation in design, and all else that may be involved in the creation of art in any form chosen by individual workers. Discussion may precede activity, but on the other hand it may follow it. In the latter case discussion serves as evaluation of the results, or as clarification of educational implications, grade placement, educational value, and significant aspects of creative activity. This type of workshop is extremely valuable for classroom teachers since it does not confine itself to the word, nor does it limit itself to the art object.

Another type of art workshop has developed from the obvious needs of elementary teachers for more experience with art as a tool for teaching children to understand processes, to solve technical problems, and incidentally to gain personal facility in creating, purely and simply as a satisfying experience. Parenthetically, the felt needs of teachers would indicate that teacher education in the area of art is not keeping pace with the newer concept that every classroom teacher is an art teacher. The popularity of art workshops with classroom teachers has pointed up the necessity of improving preparation in college and while in service.

This type of activity is planned by the coördinator as a first-aid measure. Oftener than not, professionally trained personnel in the employ of art-material concerns are imported to conduct the workshop. On occasion, the nearest teachers' college may offer such services either free or at minimum cost. In some instances the coördinator may have decided to conduct the workshop himself, or in collaboration with specially adept members of the teaching staff. The last approach is unquestionably the most worth while since it is directly related to local situations and is more likely to focus attention on those problems that will reflect immediately upon the work of the classroom. Its limitations, such as inbreeding of ideas and concepts, or an unwarranted satisfaction with what is being accomplished, may hinder the desired outcomes.

The coördinator who is sufficiently realistic will vary this phase of in-service improvement of teachers by alternating the type and personnel of the workshops so that the utmost good may be derived from them. Assuredly, the shift from the teaching of art by specialized personnel to a system in which all classroom teachers are active participants calls for larger vision and broader outlook. The workshop has proven its worth in supplying the needs indicated. Refinement of its technics should yield even more satisfying results in the future.

DISTRICT-WIDE EXHIBITIONS

Several of the supervisory means discussed thus far depend mainly upon the word to convey meanings, define goals, establish values, and reach desirable accords in order that art may function as a means of self-expression. Except for the workshops on technics and materials, the visual results of expression have been incidental, or at best have been used as auxiliary to the word.

But art expression is in itself the most eloquent and the clearest way to say: "This is what I mean," or "Compare this child's work to the other child's work," or "Notice the unhampered freedom in this work as contrasted to the rigidity of that," and so on. It would seem, therefore, that one of the most potent allies the coördinator may rely upon is children's work. These forms of expression lend themselves perfectly for comparison and for discussion, for pointing up similarities, differences, tendencies, modes of working, and whatever else is pertinent or important at the time.

Organized exhibitions of children's work at all levels, from all the schools within the system, representing as many children as space permits, and showing a variety of modes of expression, may prove to be a superior means toward the improvement of art instruction in the classroom. Exhibitions in general have been discussed in Chapter 6; therefore, in this instance the concern will be with those aspects that make exhibitions especially valuable in the improvement of teaching. Often, in connection with exhibitions, children have been asked to come and demonstrate, unaided and completely free.

It has become standard practice in a number of school systems to set apart a school building[4] or a large room in a building, adequately equipped for the purpose and centrally located, as an exhibition center. Here parents, teachers, and children may come at any time to study or just enjoy the creative efforts of boys and girls.

In order that these exhibitions may be effective as stimulants for teachers, certain conditions should obtain. They must be properly labeled as to grade and age level; they should incorporate brief but clear statements with regard to what each group of work shows with reference to mode of expression, type of experience that motivated it, use of medium, levels and types of growth evident in the work, and brief statements on the purpose of each form of art expression in relation to the child. Some items that this type of exhibition should avoid are these: name of the child artist, name of the teacher, name of the school, and any other data that may elicit unfair and unwarranted comparisons, or that may

---

[4] Scranton, Pennsylvania, has used this method for over a decade. Williamsport, Pennsylvania, is planning to establish such a center at this writing.

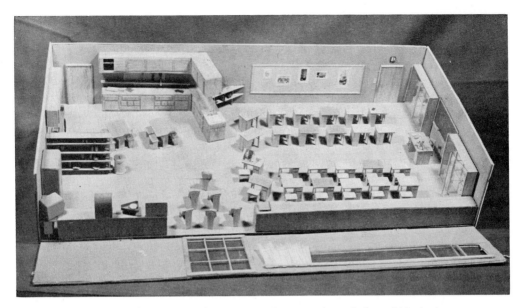

THE ART LABORATORY usually serves several purposes. Provisions must be made for activities in drawing, painting, and the crafts. Exhibition space and ample storage facilities are essential features that the coördinator will want to incorporate in specifications (designed by Student in art education, State Teachers College, Kutztown, Pa.).

set up unnecessary competition, false pride, or unwarranted adult criticisms.

When the exhibition is installed the coördinator may inform teachers that the system-wide exhibit is now ready; that it may be profitable for them to study it, and to send him comments, questions, or suggestions for future improvements. It may also be possible to schedule children and teachers of certain grade levels to visit the exhibition and to give them a "gallery talk," to answer questions, and to receive comments. Another approach might be to have a general gallery talk for teachers only, or for teachers and parents, by a competent person in the field of art education but from outside the system concerned. Such a person could be completely impersonal, objective, and constructive. Much good may be thus accomplished.

Exchange exhibitions of children's work, exhibitions circulated by colleges and universities, or those made available by art-education associations and by museums may be used very effectively by the coördinator to inspire his teachers, solidify his position, and ultimately to improve the entire art program.

THE CLINIC

Another most effective means of improving teaching performance and of establishing a desirable philosophy of art education on a system-wide scale is to hold clinics in which the work of children is evaluated objectively for the benefit of teachers. This method of evaluation will work best when organized on a grade-level plane so that the characteristics and expectancies in the growth of the children concerned may help establish reasonable bases for comparisons and contrasts.

The participants in the clinic are the teachers themselves. Each knows the individual child, his personality, his abilities, his peculiarities, his home background, and the many other facets that affect growth and development. The teachers also know under what condtions the work was done, what stimulations were used, what reactions were evident, what difficulties were encountered, and what successes were achieved. This technic of appraisal is soon learned, and the questions and answers that are certain to ensue will benefit each of the participants.

A number of cautions should guide the conduct of the clinic: respect for the child, respect for his background, and respect for the teacher under whom the work was done. In other terms, objectivity and an impersonal attitude are essential. A further caution to bear in mind in this connection, as well as in all methods of appraisal, is that *soothsaying* is not to be confused with *evaluation*. There has developed a tendency in the field to read in the work of children much that is without basis in fact. The true interpreter of a work of art is the artist himself. Outsiders, at best, may gain a little insight into the creative mode of a child. However, in each work there are sufficient visual evidences to guide the teacher in the unemotional appraisal of the way a child is growing. Such things as freedom or restraint, movement or lack of it, precision or buoyant disregard for it, dullness or brilliancy of color, realistic or expressionistic interpretation of subject, and other similar qualities are indexes that point to the direction of growth. It is only when the young artist has exhibited certain characteristics over a sufficiently long period of time that the teacher may make deductions, and these only on a general basis. Therefore, with due caution, the clinic may furnish clues on how and why children express themselves as they do. From the evidences, those who guide them may use the clues to advance creative development.

Another aspect of the clinic may be to focus attention on the desirable qualities shown by children's work. This may be done by the coördinator for the benefit of classroom teachers, or by teachers themselves within a building unit. The plan is easily implemented when a group of teachers agree to study the work of the children under their care and to exchange ideas on how the work was accomplished. The group evaluates the art of "nameless" young artists. What does the particular piece show? It may show vitality, freedom, imaginative interpretation, deliberateness, mastery of medium, sense of organization, inventiveness, restraint, delicacy, boldness, rhythmic quality, static quality, and other revealing characteristics. These characteristics will help teachers recognize the same tendencies in their own classes; even more significantly, they will point out how teachers may guide children in their further art experiences. In addition, it may be possible to ascertain to what degree the qualities in a child's work are indicative of his growth along other lines. Thus this form of appraisal serves a threefold purpose; it may tell the teacher how effectively she is working with children; it may be a diagnosis of her pupils' natural direction of growth, which the teacher may wish to nurture; and lastly, it may serve as stimulation to the clinicians to the extent that they may recognize their own need for improvement as teachers.

THE SUPERVISOR AS ADMINISTRATOR

STAFF RELATIONSHIPS

The art coördinator is one of a group of specially prepared personnel who, in addition to experience, has demonstrated leadership and possesses highly desirable personality characteristics which fits him for the responsibility of developing a field of education outside the traditional elementary or secondary area. In larger systems the last two named fields also employ supervisory personnel. In common with all other specially prepared individuals the art coördinator is a link in the administrative chain. He receives as well as gives support to his associates; exchanges ideas with them; shares in the overall planning of the district's program; assumes direct responsibility for those phases that involve art. Otherwise, he contributes to the formulation of general policies and plans that ultimately affect the entire system, but more particularly the teaching-learning situation in the classroom.

In these varied connections, he must work harmoniously with all his associates in matters of finances, research, the improvement of instruction, school-plant problems, selection and procurement of supplies and equipment, public relations, and many other activities calculated to support the general philosophy of the district to the best advantage of the children.

It is quite obvious that such large school systems as New York, Chicago, Philadelphia, Los Angeles, and others have developed complicated systems in which district superintendents and directors of divisions of instruction and administration precede, in the line of responsibility and authority, subject-matter directors in art, music, home economics, and others.

Medium-sized school systems, such as Baltimore, Pittsburgh, Kansas City, Denver, Milwaukee, and others of similar size, operate on a slightly less complex pattern; therefore, the line of responsibility and authority is briefer, or more direct, for personnel such as the art director. For practical purposes, it may be worth while to focus attention to less cumbersome systems, particularly to those that may be termed small school systems.

As indicated at the beginning of this chapter, the position of director or supervisor of art education assumes varied interpretations and, therefore, varied duties, varied authority, and varied relationships, depending on the size of the school system and the structure of the organization necessary under the circumstances.

The diagrams on page 537 show possible staff relationships in (A) medium-sized and (B) small school systems. A study of them should, at very least, shed light on the relative line position of the art director or supervisor and thus suggest a plausible sphere of responsibility as well as of opportunity for the continuous improvement of the art program.

The diagrams on page 538 are intended to show staff relationships and responsibilities as they operate in practice, and as they originate from the art supervisor or coördinator in (C) medium-sized and (D) small school systems. Here again, it should be clear that variations can and do exist in these relationships, depending on a number of local

A. GENERAL ORGANIZATION AND POSSIBLE STAFF RELATIONSHIPS IN MEDIUM-SIZED SCHOOL SYSTEMS

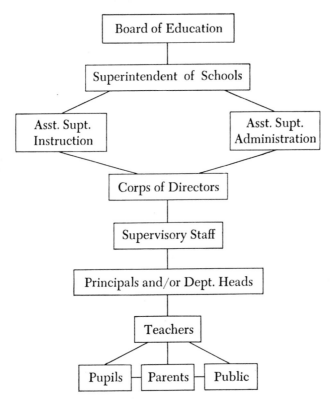

B. GENERAL ORGANIZATION AND POSSIBLE STAFF RELATIONSHIPS IN SMALL SCHOOL SYSTEMS

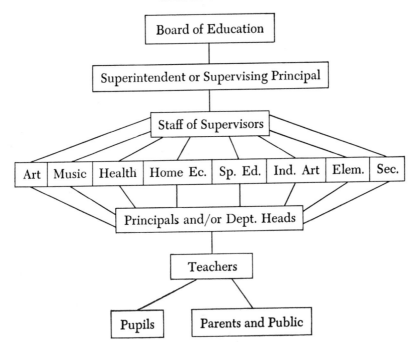

C. **Organization and Staff Relationships in Medium-Sized School Systems**

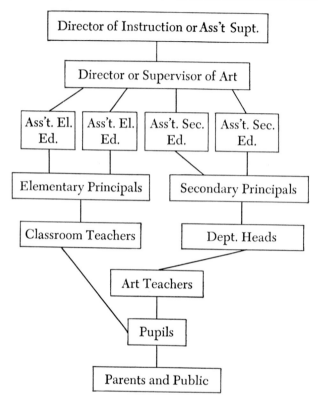

D. **Art Consultant's Relationships in Small School Systems**

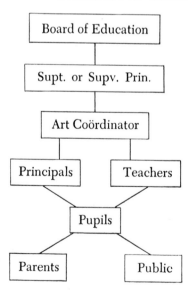

factors. The diagrams will only furnish a basis for the general understanding of the possibilities inherent in the position.

THE HUMAN EQUATION

Thus far only the mechanical relationships have been pointed out. Much more importance should be attached to those human qualities that truly spell the success or failure of the chief art administrator. The best plans, the soundest educational schemes, the most meticulous attention to theory and philosophy, will not guarantee that the program in art education will grow and that the pupils will be the beneficiaries. On the contrary, much attention to mechanics and little regard for the human equations involved in the work may be detrimental. The major purpose for which supervision and coördination are intended are these: the integration, the establishment of harmonious relationships, and the stabilization through art not only of pupils but of teachers as well.

With this caution properly underscored, it is possible to focus attention on those human qualities that may help to ensure the success of the program of coördination. Among the important qualifications of the right supervisor are these:

1. The ability to see the school program *as a whole*
2. The establishment of rapport with associates
3. Loyalty to associates and to those in chief positions of responsibility
4. Willingness to grow in service
5. Knowledge and practice of the dynamics of group action
6. A sense of efficiency
7. A feeling for democratic leadership

Brief elaborations of these seven cardinal qualifications may further clarify the magnitude and the worth of supervision.

The School Program as a Whole

It is important to realize that although the chief business of the art division is to promote and advance art as a developmental aspect of the education of all children, it is not its only function. In working with other staff members, there may arise innumerable occasions when the particular interests of art education must dove-tail, contribute to, even be subordinated to, the larger ideas under consideration. Again, under the same circumstances, it may be quite proper, but without overdoing the point, to indicate where art can make the most significant contribution to the total program.

Time allocation, coördination, budgetary provisions, public relations activities and other over-all policies are matters on which staff agreement is essential. The art coördinator who always insists on his point of view, who is always right, who is always "different," will soon find himself isolated. Isolation, in the sense implied in this connection, is the most detrimental single factor to the proper development of an art program. Contrary-wise it is the ability to work for the best interest of the entire school program that will redound to the best growth of art education, and consequently of the pupils.

Rapport

The logical corollary to what has been said above is proper understanding of rapport. Rapport means simply that the art supervisor is able to sense that his associates also have a task to perform, that they are anxious to do a professional piece of work, that they are well qualified for their assignment, and that they are individuals who also have feelings, ideas, strengths, and weaknesses, even as the art supervisor himself. In other words, rapport means a recognition of common ground. This implies that personal, social, and professional relationships should be at the finest level. An attitude that bespeaks friendship, coöperative spirit, mutual respect, and helpfulness is a human quality worth cultivating at all times. Informality consistent with the occasion, consultation on professional problems, and exchange of ideas will establish the type of human relations essential for the success of any team. Many art programs owe their expansion and success to the friendly attitude and eventual understanding of art education by those associates who work in the elementary and secondary fields. Unless the art consultant is personally able to establish successful human relations, the art program may not be eliminated but it will surely suffer.

Loyalty to Associates and Superiors

As a member of an educational team that is trained to see the whole problem of education, and as one who has been able to establish rapport among associates and superiors, the art coördinator needs one more ingredient to achieve complete group integration—loyalty to associates. Loyalty does not countenance gossip, open or *sub rosa* antagonism to a person or to an idea. Nor does it countenance habitual belittling of the point of view of associates or superiors. On the positive side, loyalty implies that at the proper time and place any disagreement, misunderstanding, erroneous report, or anything detrimental to anyone is openly, frankly, and objectively discussed and thereafter dismissed as a closed matter. Loyalty also implies that one will not withhold useful and positive information, ideas, or experiences that may improve the operation of any part of the program. Implicit in loyalty is also the possibility of unobtrusively encouraging and praising the accomplishments of any member of the staff. Finally, loyalty means understanding. Understanding of the burden of responsibility that an associate or superior may carry, and even understanding of certain human traits of which no being is wholly exempt. Loyalty is central to ethical conduct.

The Will to Grow

One of the most dangerous adversaries of personal development and of the development of the art program is the inability or the unwillingness of the art supervisor to realize that there is no end to professional growth. When one has achieved the chief position in the art-education scale of a school system, the responsibility of keeping abreast of new points of view, of recent literature, and of experimental studies, increases with each passing year. This is particularly true as one become acquainted with the mechanics of the position. It is important, at intervals, to refresh oneself, to look back as well as forward in order to gain or regain educational perspective.

Membership, attendance, and participation in the activities of professional art organizations as well as in those devoted to the broad aspects of education are imperatives. Occasional writing, the pursuit of some phase of art production, and participation in research are some ways of keeping mentally and professionally alert. If the consultant is to guide the work of others, it is necessary for him to grow in professional stature. Only thus will he take his proper place among his associates, gain and keep their respect, and be able to make significant contributions to education in his community.

Knowledge and Practice of Group Dynamics

The administrative staff meeting is an experience in democratic school control and an example of group action. If the supervisor of art expects loyalty, fair play, coöperation, and understanding from classroom teachers and from other art teachers who work under his leadership, it is fair to assume that in matters of policy and program determination he should give evidence of the same disposition. It has been pointed out that loyalty is a very significant quality; the stress at this point is on democratic procedures. Whatever the problem may be, it is best solved if a thorough understanding of the issues is achieved through debate, sharing of ideas, comparisons of experiences, and other means of group discussion. Goals and values are effective only in so far as they gain acceptance by those who are concerned. Group agreements having been reached, the goals and values are implemented for action. To be more specific, if the policy of a school system is accepted by the corps of supervisory personnel, obviously it would be professional heresy for the art coördinator to deviate from it or to completely disregard it. It is because of such slights that professional relationships are strained, sometimes to the detriment of the art supervisor as a person, and invariably to the detriment of the pupils in the classroom.

Compromise, give-and-take, and other democratic means of adjusting to general situations are not only plausible, but with due regard for others and with proper understanding, will solve problems peculiar to any area of education. But such solutions must always be found within the sphere of the democratic process and not on personal authority.

Democratic Leadership

To do one's work well, to maintain wholesome personal relationships, and to remain within the bounds of professional ethics is a plausible position to assume. However, progress in education as well as in other fields of endeavor involves much more. Leadership qualities that are not used, eventually atrophy. The chief school officer of the system not only welcomes but actually needs, from time to time, suggestions and feasible plans for the improvement of teaching, learning, public relations, business, and administrative procedures. There is no intimation in this statement that members of the supervisory corps should undertake to do the work of the superintendent or of the supervising principal. The intent is, rather, that when ideas and suggestions are solicited, those who have them should not withhold them. The further meaning is that whenever help is needed to implement ideas that come from sources other than one's own, it is a mark of leadership to offer assistance for possible solutions.

Of even greater importance is the willingness to undertake unsolicited educational experiments and to share the findings with the entire system. Such experimentation need not be of a revolutionary or dramatic nature. In any school system, large or small, whatever will facilitate learning and teaching is of value. Therefore, the art coördinator who initiates plans to find ways and means of accomplishing a task more efficiently, more adequately, with greater profit to pupils, teachers, or administrators, will have made a significant contribution.

Willingness to do more than the minimum, ability to organize, humble trail blazing, sensible management of resources, and the improvement of other professional services are marks of leadership. Such leadership usually has its own rewards. But often it is recognized by associates, by teachers in the classroom, and by those in chief positions of responsibility. To the extent that the art coördinator is a true leader, to that extent will the art program flourish and the personality of the consultant grow.

The Sense of Efficiency

A school system, be it small or large, is in a sense a business organization. Usually, taxpayers' money is being expended in order that children and youth within that system may be given the best education possible. The supervisory staff, under the direction of the chief school officer, are the administrators of the business of education. It follows that a measure of efficiency is expected of them.

Budgets, allocations, distribution of materials and supplies, and the selection and purchase of equipment, textbooks, and auxiliary teaching aids constitute the principal items involved in this function. There are time schedules to be observed if the business aspects of education are to be properly expedited. Therefore, one of the marks of a good coördinator is to accomplish his share of the work on time, and in proper form. Failure to comply with requests for certain types of information when needed, carelessness in the data themselves or in the manner in which they are delivered, invariably suggest lack of efficiency. Opinions by associates, classroom teachers, and superiors are thus formed, and unwittingly the art program and the art coördinator are either demeaned or praised.

Promptness, efficiency, accuracy, and common sense are qualities worthy of development by those who would lead.

SECURING SUPPORT FOR ART EDUCATION

One of the chief administrative duties of the art supervisor or coördinator is to secure adequate financial support for an effective program.

While art education has been accepted as an essential in the total school program, it is not uncommon to find that in many systems the financial support given to it is rather scant. On the other hand, there are as many school systems which regard art activities as being so worth while that the expenditures involved in the program are not questioned. Where good conditions prevail it is due largely to two factors: enlightened administration, on one hand, and effective art supervision, on the other. Contrariwise, where poor situations obtain they are the result of uninformed administration and laggard supervision. In the last analysis, the chief school administrator is occupied with overall problems and must rely on the advice and on the leadership of his staff. In substance, the implication is that the responsibility for adequate financial support rests with the person in charge of the art program.

The Budget

A good art program, well conceived, properly staffed, and properly housed, cannot function without adequate materials. Good equipment, and ample auxiliary aids such as slides, prints, films, projection equipment, funds for the rental of exhibits, and whatever else best practices suggest, should be made available. Whether these items are used with teachers or directly by teachers in the classrooms is of little import. What is important is the fact that if they are necessary they should be provided so that they may facilitate art experiences and other learnings.

On the basis of the knowledge that the supervisor has gained in conference with his immediate superiors, from the business officer of the school district, from past experience, and from the needs expressed by classroom teachers or art teachers, the supervisor should be in a position to determine the financial requirements of the art program.

Studies of per capita costs of various subject fields, with due consideration of their particular needs, may be a basis for the determination of what the art budget should be. Another criterion may be a study of the per capita costs of art programs in comparable communities; lastly, although very important, the educational ideals of the community in

SPECIALIZED EQUIPMENT for pottery, modeling, jewelry, leathercraft, and for working with a variety of materials must be provided if the art program is to be a balanced offering. Proper budgetary allowances must be secured for such equipment (public schools, Reading, Pa.).

which the supervisor works may serve as a gauge as to the extent of the budgetary requests.

The mechanics of preparing general requisitions, purchase forms, inventories, materials distribution sheets, and the like may seem trivial; yet one of the surest ways of receiving needed materials and equipment is to prepare requisitions in acceptable, intelligent, and prescribed manner. The art division will not then find itself without adequate provisions when these are requested by the schools. A tentative form is suggested on page 547. The form is only for study but it may serve for adaptation to local conditions and demands and may be extended for larger needs.

Supplies and Equipment

In the final analysis, it is the business sense of the art coördinator that often determines how much or how little is allocated to the art program. It should be borne in mind that taxation is the source of public-school finances; therefore, economy and efficiency must be considered. However, observation of general practices suggest that the overzealous supervisor, the one who proposes to "save," usually does so to the detriment of the pupil and of the program. With this caution before him, the supervisor should consider the needs of the children, the efficiency of the teacher, and the growth of the program before reaching a conclusion. A recent study by Foster[5] may be worthy of examination. The recommendations of that study are significant and could well form the basis for the formulation of the departmental budget. Art supply concerns often make available guides for determining the amounts of certain materials to be ordered for each child. These may be examined with profit, but they should not become the sole criteria for determining amounts or types of materials necessary.

In summary it must be reaffirmed that art expression requires certain material vehicles, certain tools, and certain conditions. Unless adequately provided for, art expression cannot function properly and will, in consequence, be limited in scope and sterile in effect.

---

[5] Elizabeth J. Foster, *Basic Costs per Pupil for an Effective Art Program in Grades One to Six*, doctoral thesis, Indiana University, 1952; also published by Related Arts Service, New York, N.Y.

SCHOOL DISTRICT OF GREENVALE

Greenvale, ⸺

Department of Art Education   John C. Doe, Coördinator

REQUISITION

Supplies and Equipment

Requisitioned by ⸺   School ⸺

Date ⸺

No. Units	Item(s)	Full Description	Name of Company	Cat. No.	Unit Cost	Total Cost

PHYSICAL IMPLEMENTATION OF THE PROGRAM

The last decade has seen a phenomenal development in school architecture. While all new schools have not been built equally as satisfactorily, there exists a general feeling that the school architect has emerged as a specialist in this field. The general improvement is due, in large measure, to the wisdom of educators who have insisted that school buildings be designed with the pupil in mind. Actually, a knowledge of the physical, emotional, social, and mental needs of children has played a large role in the development of the new architecture. The design and size of the furniture, the amount of light and sunshine admitted, color, play space, group-conference tables, proper heating and ventilation, adequate and accessible sanitary facilities, provision for the use of sensory aids, and special equipment for teaching and learning in a variety of subjects are the features incorporated in new school buildings.

The Self-Contained Classroom

Self-contained classrooms in elementary schools have emerged as partial solutions to several educational problems, chief among them integrated learning.

Because of the expansion of art as a developmental activity and as an integrating medium, and because the newer thinking makes the classroom teacher a participator in art education, the self-contained classroom, oftener than not, is the art laboratory. Therefore, its appointments, equipment, and general atmosphere become a part of the concern of the art coördinator in common with classroom teachers and other special-fields coördinators.

It follows also that the art coördinator has a definite responsibility in the planning of new schools and in the revamping of old ones. The simplest way of pointing out the essential minimum features that should be present in the self-contained classroom may be to ask a number of questions. Is the room ample? Is the furniture of proper size; is it movable? Is the room well lighted? Is running water available in the room? Has accessible and adequate storage space been provided for brushes, paints, crayons, and other art materials and equipment? Is there sufficient display space?

If the philosophy of integrated learning is not to be impeded, and if the self-contained classroom idea is to be effective, then the conditions suggested by the questions above should prevail.

The Art Center

The art-center idea has been implemented in some schools. The intention in such situations is that a room especially adapted for work in arts and crafts is made available to all teachers and pupils on a scheduled basis. The center, however, is also available for special group activities, such as the painting of scenery for a play, the painting of murals for the hall, and other extracurricular art services. Where that philosophy prevails, the center is used as the room where specific art instruction is given by a "special" art teacher on a scheduled basis. In such cases the children from various grades report to the art teacher. The merits of this

ELEMENTARY SCHOOLS designed along modern lines to meet modern needs should not omit proper facilities for an adequate art program (Penn's Creek Elementary School, Snyder County, Pa.).

arrangement can only be judged in the light of the educational philosophy of the local school system.

The present concern must necessarily consider the location and equipment of such a center. If it is to serve children and if it is to be the hub of special activities, its location should be on the first floor of the building. That location will facilitate the receiving of materials and equipment, and incidentally make the center a public-relations feature. With regard to facilities, the minimum items enumerated in connection with the self-contained classroom should be available, but on an ampler scale, since all the children will have their major art experiences in it.

The Secondary-School Studio

Secondary-school studios assume a more specialized role (see Chapters 9, 10) because art activities have also taken on a more mature function. Therefore, location and equipment call for serious consideration. Is the studio to be an all-purpose art laboratory? Is it to be a crafts studio? Is it to be a laboratory for painting and graphic experiences only? How many pupils will it accommodate?

Most secondary schools in average-sized school districts require a combination art laboratory in which arts and crafts may be experienced in reasonably spacious surroundings and with ample equipment. Such crafts as modeling, pottery, jewelry, leathercraft, theater craft, and work in wood and combined materials require running water, craft benches, electrical and gas outlets, hand tools, light power tools, potter's wheels, wedging blocks, casting boxes, and, of course, the many small tools for use in specialized crafts. Obviously, there is need for clay bins, ample storage and exhibition space, and either easels or drawing tables, or both. A reasonably comprehensive study of this problem has just been made in New York State.[6] It may be worthy of consideration.

Usually, in the combination arts and crafts laboratory the two sections are separated for convenience, to isolate the necessary noise that accompanies working with materials and tools, and to keep tools where they will be handiest for use. Especially in situations where only one teacher is in charge of the program, this seems an excellent solution. In addition, there are certain unitary advantages which are not always realized. For instance, a student creates a design, then with some guidance is able to carry it through to the finished product. As an experience this is educationally sound and should be encouraged.

In schools where two teachers are employed and two studios are available, it is possible to have one room equipped for the crafts and the other for graphic activities. This condition may create the problem of determining which teacher should teach one and which the other. However, in staffing such a school it is often possible to eliminate the problem by the wise selection of teachers on the basis of their major interest, aptitude, and experience. It may also be possible, by common agreement, to rotate teachers from one semester to another or from year to year.

In large schools where a number of teachers of art are employed, it is possible to offer specialized courses. The departmental organization in such schools solves the question of diversification quite effectively. Matters of equipment, tools, and other physical features do not present insurmountable problems if administrators and public feel that good use is made of these items.

From the foregoing it becomes rather apparent that, in a very real sense, the art coördinator is an administrative assistant to the superintendent or to the supervising principal. In this role, the coördinator must be able to secure the most for art education and at the same time exercise the best business acumen of which he is capable to retain and

---

[6] *Planning the Art Room for Secondary Schools,* Albany, University of the State of New York, State Education Department, 1954.

gradually extend the financial support needed to carry out a successful program.

ESTABLISHING GOOD PUBLIC RELATIONS

OPPORTUNITIES ABOUND

In many school systems someone on the superintendent's staff is charged with handling publicity and public relations. In that case, the art supervisor will only need to furnish information to the specially designated person in order to keep the art program before the public.

But in medium-sized school districts and certainly in small ones, the art coördinator must initiate, develop, and carry out his own public-relations program in keeping with the general policy of the district.

Why is a good public relations program important? The answer is probably made clearer by listing those purposes that a coördinator needs to achieve with a public composed of children, teachers, parents, and other taxpayers. These seem to be some principal items:

1. *To inform* parents and public about the purposes of art education.
2. *To create* interests on the part of parents and public in what their children are learning and how they are developing through art education.
3. *To develop* public taste and appreciation by familiarizing laymen with the varied activities of the program.
4. *To secure* public support for art education by presenting tangible evidences of what public investment is achieving.
5. *To expand* the sphere of art education by eliciting public favor for art in adult education and other forms of special education.
6. *To encourage* teachers and pupils by giving public recognition to their art achievements.

NEWSPAPER PUBLICITY

In order to accomplish the purposes listed, the coördinator has a vast number of resources at his command. He knows what is going on in various schools, and from this knowledge he may select what seems newsworthy at the time. He is informed on special school events in which art plays a prominent role and may choose to publicize it. He knows how well the students have done in the regional or national scholastic exhibition and may wish to feature the boys and girls who gained recognition. One of the teachers in the art department has distinguished herself in an exhibition or has appeared on an important program, and the coördinator may decide to use this as the occasion for publicizing the fact. Another art teacher has just published an article in a national publication and this may make good news; the art club of the junior high school has just completed a new set for the school stage, an accomplishment in which the public may be interested. The teacher on the senior-high-school faculty has been awarded a scholarship to continue his study at the state university, and surely this fact ought to be publicized. Actually, there is no end of opportunities to keep the art program before the public. One of the lesser used but very significant vehicles, especially in cosmopolitan communities, is the foreign-language newspaper; it should also be utilized.

The technics of newspaper publicity are soon learned. The coördinator should meet the editor or the person with whom he will deal thereafter, in order to establish good relationships, and to find out just how he prefers to receive the news releases and whether he has preferences regarding the photography related to the news. Photography of the right sort is important in this regard: featuring children and teachers at work, parents at an exhibition, a boy or girl painting or modeling, close-ups of well-chosen pieces of work on display with one or two persons looking on. These are examples of possible situations that will enhance the news story and call attention to the item.

Generally speaking, brief but well-worded releases are preferred by newspapers; names of people, especially local persons, make good news. It is important to realize that reporters rely on the coördinator for news once the proper relationship has been established. Promptness is also desirable because news is news when it happens, not a week or two afterward. Therefore, promptness in releasing it is appreciated.

DEMONSTRATIONS AND LECTURES

Most communities have a fair array of civic clubs, women's clubs, service clubs, and societies of various sorts. These groups are composed of people whose interest in the schools is very high. They are eager to hear about and see what is being accomplished in education.

With due regard to the time element involved, as well as to his personal energy, the art coördinator will do well to assume a number of speaking engagements each year to discuss before groups the purposes and accomplishments of art education in the schools. Demonstrations, with the aid of children or without the children, are very effective. Illustrated lectures are also highly successful to convey to the public how art affects life, how it helps children grow creatively and otherwise, how art develops the imagination, how it brings about adjustment. The selection of topics and the approach depend on the coördinator's abilities and the needs of the public. But the opportunity exists to develop good public relations in this fashion.

EXHIBITIONS

Reference has already been made to the recent widespread interest of parents and the public at large in the work of the schools. This interest should be utilized by the coördinator as a further way to fulfill the purposes of the public-relations program. By arranging periodic exhibitions of chil-

JUNIOR AND SENIOR HIGH SCHOOLS are designed to meet the needs of adolescents. The art laboratory is an essential feature; its location, size, and equipment must be carefully considered by the art coördinator and school authorities (Senior High School, Pine Grove, Pa.; Muhlenberg Bros., Architects).

dren's work it will be possible to convey to the public the directions of art education as well as to point up the particular facets of growth shown by current exhibitions. How to plan, label, arrange, and otherwise make the exhibition effective have been discussed at some length in Chapter 6 and further reference has been made on page 531 of this chapter. For special effectiveness as a public-relations agent, exhibitions should be of easy access. A centrally located school in town will attract more visitors than will a school at the edge of the community. Further utilization of exhibitions may be found in connection with P.T.A. gatherings, and in meeting rooms of social and service organizations. In any event, the work produced by pupils is by far the most tangible evidence of the accomplishments of art education. It should be used to inform, to interest, and to elicit the support of citizens.

PARENT PARTICIPATION

A recently developed public-relations vehicle is the planning of work sessions for parents. Often parents and children are grouped so that children become the guides of their elders. The latter not only enjoy the occasion but are impressed by a new realization of the opportunities their children have, and gain an insight in the pleasure and the value of the experiences offered by the schools of today. Often such beginnings have given rise to public demand for adult classes in arts and crafts.

SUMMARY

The general development of the art program in any community is largely dependent on the vision of the person in charge. The special art teacher, the art supervisor, the art coördinator, or the art consultant, whichever term is used, must understand his work as implying leadership, coöperation, broad vision, objectivity, and coördination.

The effective art coördinator should be familiar with the needs of the specially prepared as well as of the general classroom teachers. These needs differ according to the teaching pattern adopted for the art program. The specially prepared person who is an itinerant, helping teacher will need the coöperation and the good will of all classroom teachers. The coördinator or the consultant in larger systems not only needs coöperation, but he must sense the overall problems, sometimes transmit these to his staff, and, through them, attempt solutions on a democratic basis. At the same time, he will stimulate growth in service.

Above all else, it is of crucial importance that the person in charge of the art program think of himself as an engineer in human relations. Human relations begin with the teachers in the classroom. The teacher as a person, the understanding on the part of the teacher of the basic beliefs of art education, his personal growth through in-service training, and finally the sincere friendship that makes for rapport, are the essentials that spell success for the coördinator.

But rapport and friendship must be supported by practical and helpful aid in what is needed by special art teachers as well as by general classroom teachers. The coördinator should be familiar with those educational technics that have proven effective in other fields: the informational bulletin, the group conference, the teaching demonstration, the personal conference, the workshop, the clinic, the exhibition, the jury system of evaluation, and whatever other technics will be helpful to improve teachers and teaching.

The work of the coördinator, however, does not end with problems of human relations and the improvement of instruction. Indeed, his energy and time will often have to be shared with administrative responsibilities. In a reasonably sized school system, there will be good staff relationships to be developed and overall curriculum problems to be clarified above and beyond the art program. To do this effectively, the art coördinator must keep in mind certain ethical principles, such as loyalty to associates and superiors, respect for the personality and point of view of others, and a strong belief in democratic group action. But the coördinator also needs to assert his own personal leadership, and to accomplish this he must be willing to share, to do more than required, to do research, and to offer the findings to the group. A sense of efficiency is also essential to his success. Promptness, accuracy, and a sense of the value of time are the ingredients.

As an assistant in administration, the art consultant must secure maximum respect and support for art education. Sound business sense, as well as objective evidence, will help in this situation. Not least of his duties is to secure proper and adequate materials and physical means within which the art program may flourish. In attempting to implement the program's physical aspects the coördinator must keep in mind teachers, children, and the aims of the field. The elementary program, being basic, will need proper facilities; the secondary program being specialized in so far as teachers and process are concerned, the coördinator needs to be conversant with materials, tools, and equipment suited to art development at this level.

Finally, the coördinator, within the limitations of the policy effective in the school district, is responsible for the public relations and publicity of the art division. Newspapers, public lectures, demonstrations, exhibitions, and parent participation are some means at his disposal. The task of supervision is indeed for those who possess *super vision*.

For Discussion and Activity

1. Distinguish between the several existing types of supervisory positions and relate them to the kinds of school situation which they exemplify.
2. Make a survey of the county or parish in which you live in an attempt to determine the type of art service rendered by art personnel. Do existing patterns offer an effective type of art coördination to the communities they serve?

3. Organize a panel for the discussion of the broader implications of supervision. Secure a coördinator and a consultant from among the in-service art people of the nearby area.

4. Assuming that you are a coördinator, develop an outline of your activities for the year.

5. What is the place of the art teacher and of general classroom teachers in a scheme of supervision? Discuss their role, their activities, their professional importance.

6. Prepare a brief check list on the duties of a coördinator, on what he must consider basic to his philosophy, and on his various capacities in relation to the total program. After having secured the benefit of the criticisms of your group on the check list, send it to a selected number of supervisors in the field to elicit their reactions. Discuss the reactions with your group.

7. Indicate the advantages and the disadvantages of the supervisory technics discussed on page 522.

8. What are some of the characteristics of a good supervisor with respect to his administrative role? Select the characteristic you consider most important and present the argument for your selection.

9. Make a layout of what you consider an efficient self-contained classroom with special reference to art activities. Do the same for the art room of a junior high school, but in this instance determine location of special furniture and equipment.

10. Discuss the public-relations activities of the art consultant and indicate the effectiveness of each activity in relation to the group each hopes to reach.

For Further Reading

Browne, Sybil, "Beginning Art Teachers Appraise Themselves," *Art Education,* November, 1954.

Burton, William H., *The Guidance of Learning Activities,* New York, Appleton-Century-Crofts, 1944, Chapters III, IV.

Color Dynamics for Grade Schools, High Schools, Colleges, Pittsburgh, Pittsburgh Plate Glass Company.

Czurles, Stanley A., "Art Room Planning for Today," *School Arts,* February, 1953.

Dierlam, Howard C., "Toronto Designs Its Own Furniture," *School Arts,* February, 1954.

Gottfried, F. J., and Jones, Dorothy A., "A Comprehensive Arts and Crafts Center," *The Nation's Schools,* February, 1954.

Heilman, Horace F., "Improved Art Education Through Public Relations," 557
Art Education, November, 1952.

Kundis, Lawrence E., "Teacher Training Programs in Art Education," Art Education, November, 1954.

Milliette, Earl B., "The Public and Art Education," The Art Education Bulletin, March, 1948.

Norena, Glen K., "Facilities that Facilitate," School Arts, February, 1954.

Rilliet, V. Fouré, "Administrative and Teaching Aspects of a Successful Art Program," Art Education, October, 1952.

School Modernization, and the Classroom of Tomorrow, Toledo, Owens-Illinois Company.

Spears, Harold, Improving the Supervision of Instruction, New York, Prentice-Hall, 1953, Chapters I, II, VI–IX.

Ziegfeld, Edwin (ed.), Education and Art, A Symposium, Paris, UNESCO, 1953, Section IV.

SUPERVISION AND THE CURRICULUM

> . . . the value of a curriculum or any segment of it lies
> not in itself but in its service to the learner. What may be
> functional for one may not be for another; what may be
> functional at one time may not be at another; and what
> may be functional in one location may not be in another.
> Providing an effective program then becomes a matter of
> properly matching two variables, the curriculum and the
> learner.
>
> Harold Spears,
> *Improving the Supervision
> of Instruction*

A MAJOR CONCERN

IT HAS BEEN INFERRED THAT, REGARDLESS OF THE TERMINOLOGY EMPLOYED
in a school system and the complexity of its administrative organization,
the person in charge of the art program is responsible for its total development. Of all the duties of a coördinator, his chief concern is the curriculum. This educational function will involve, first of all, the establishment of an overall philosophy, the selection of principal aims for the entire
system, and the specific objectives for level subdivisions. Eventually,
the task will be to organize these elements into syllabuses or guides for
each division: elementary school, junior high school, senior high school,
and perhaps even the junior college and adult education.

The great significance of this function is inferred in the questions that follow. How can the responsibility be discharged so that the efforts involved in it may yield maximum understanding on the part of all administrators and teachers? What procedures should be employed with respect to the human relations that are sure to play a part? What are some of the problems of production? How effective will it be for pupil growth? These and other pertinent matters are considered in this chapter.

DEFINING THE ART CURRICULUM

The very mention of the word curriculum in connection with art education is likely to raise eyebrows as well as questions. Somehow the term has acquired the meaning of inflexibility. To many teachers and supervisors it has come to mean rigidly set-down requirements to be met, to others it infers a static outline, and to some it suggests dictated syllabuses to be slavishly followed week by week and year after year. The art curriculum is none of these, or it should not be.

The main source of misinterpretation of the term probably stems from traditional practices. Or it may be a lack of understanding of the basic philosophy of art education prevalent today. The art curriculum, if designed with proper appreciation of the contemporary point of view, will simply be an elaboration of the belief that the purpose of art experience in the total pattern of education is to contribute to growth and development. When the full meaning of growth and development is understood and accepted as valid, there should be little difficulty in visualizing the art curriculum. It would then be an interpretation of the broad concepts of art education in terms of experiences, activities, skills, knowledges, and appreciations which together contribute to the achievement of full growth for every child to the limits of his own potentialities.

The curriculum in art education is actually the teacher's compass. It indicates directions; it points toward the goal. At the same time it leads, by the best route, to destination. Perhaps it is this analogy that has given rise to the newer term *curriculum guide*.

A COMMONLY SHARED POINT OF VIEW

Several references have been made to the emergence of the self-contained classroom in the elementary field and to the problems raised by this relatively new development. To those problems must be added others which will confront the art teacher until such time as his talents and

560 preparation are fully utilized in a coördinating capacity rather than as an itinerant teacher.

The issue which comes to focus quite sharply in a consideration of the curriculum deals with the point of view and orientation of the art program. Specifically, how can the coördinator develop a sound, commonly shared understanding for the conduct of art activities in the elementary classroom? The greatest strides in art education have been

THE CHILD, his nature, endowment, needs at various levels of growth, and reasonable expectancies in development, are the true basis of the curriculum. Below a child admires her own creation. (1st grade, Kansas City, Mo.).

made at this level; yet it is here that the most difficult curriculum problems exist.

The general classroom teacher is accustomed to definite understandings on the scope of subject matter, on its various phases in relation to difficulty, and on levels of mastery of "fundamentals," let us say in arithmetic or in language. It follows that she will ask: What is subject matter in art expression? What are fundamentals? Is there a sequence? What standards of achievement may be set up? These are questions to which the coördinator or art teacher must give adequate answers if the program in art is to be endorsed and carried out successfully by elementary teachers.

At the secondary-school level, specially prepared teachers of art should already be conversant with the aims of the art program. The problem at this level is of a different nature. Seemingly, understandings should be easily reached, since admittedly there already exists a foundation of philosophy. Nevertheless, the issues of curriculum organization in secondary schools also call for serious consideration. The problems at this level arise from the diversity of preparation of teachers, from deeply rooted personal convictions, from educational inertia, and from contacts, or lack of them, with professional advances in the field. Therefore, at all levels, the coördinator who wishes to work democratically must seek a general agreement of those who will eventually implement the work in the classroom.

In a broad sense, professional aspects of curriculum development in art education do not differ materially from one level to the other. The procedures described hereafter could obtain for both general classroom teachers and special art teachers in junior and senior high schools.

GROUP DYNAMICS AND DEMOCRATIC ORGANIZATION

In the preceding chapter, the values of some aspects of group dynamics were described. Those technics are available to coördinators in the process of achieving a commonly shared point of view. In the present connection it may be repeated that one of the finest ways of ensuring the success of the art program is to work on a democratic, coöperative basis. Curriculum committees should be composed of classroom teachers, special art teachers, secondary and elementary supervisors, and, when-

562   ever possible, psychologists and guidance personnel. Under the general chairmanship of the art coördinator, these committees should formulate preliminary drafts, revise them as often as needed and practicable, and eventually proceed to design a tentative curriculum guide for those levels for which the committees are responsible.

Such a task cannot and should not be hurried. Due consideration should be given to all points of view. A harmony of opinions, based on best findings, should first be reached, and only then should outlines be drafted. Following group revisions and the eventual acceptance of an outline, it becomes the task of subcommittees to develop details and interpretations.

One of the most satisfactory ways for committees to begin coöperative curriculum planning is to gather and examine professional literature.

COÖPERATIVE CURRICULUM PLANNING, in which all concerned with child development take a part, results in understandings and wholesome relationships. Good teaching and effective learning are natural outcomes of such conditions (Kanahwa County Steering Committee for Art, Center School, Kanahwa County, W. Va.).

Literature on curriculum in general, on the art curriculum in particular, and existing curriculum guides deemed of worth should be made available to all committee members at a central point. It will be advantageous to analyze these sources carefully in order to gain direction,

to compare programs, and to reach conclusions with regard to a workable
format.[1]

These, then, are the mechanics of organization. What seems more significant is how groups or committees arrive at a basic philosophy that will undergird the program to be put into action in the classroom. This is the next concern of the present discussion.

DEVELOPING A CURRICULUM GUIDE

The guide should be the result of coöperative work on the part of those who will administer it. It takes the place of the fixed "course of study" of bygone days. Generally, it is produced in mimeographed or multigraphed form and assembled in a manner that will permit revisions of pages or entire sections to be easily inserted in place of older materials.

Such a document is most effective when widely distributed for use and when it is looked upon as an evolving tool in the hands of teachers. There are instances in which the local administration is in a position to have these interim documents printed; but what matters is that a curriculum guide, if it is to serve its true purpose and intent, must remain flexible, and its contents must always be improving.

Many guides provide space for notations by teachers, consultants, and administrators, either along the margins or at the end of each section or grade. The importance of these notations is paramount because they become valuable as the bases of further refinements.

FOUNDATIONS MUST BE BUILT

The first step in coöperative curriculum planning is to explore the pertinent knowledges and review the objectives of the field. From these there should emerge the essential elements of the philosophy that is to guide the program. There will be differences in points of view and, perhaps, not complete agreement on all details; yet that is part of the democratic way. Differences and points of view should be scrutinized

---

[1] Most regional art associations and the National Art Education Association have compiled lists of worth-while curriculum guides. These may be made available to local Committees.

and an eventual meeting of the minds should be reached. When this has occurred, the best interests of children will be served and the program will be built with them in mind.

To clarify meanings as well as to furnish an example of how curriculum building might proceed, the beliefs that have been expressed in this text are summarized. The intention is that such a review may serve as a point of reference; it is not suggested that it should be in any way adopted, except in spirit. Its best use may be as a beginning in the discussions that usually precede the organization of curriculum outlines or more comprehensive guides.

It will be noted that a basic philosophy with regard to the place and function of art in education is the first consideration. Next in significance is a statement of the specific values of art education to individuals and to the social group. Man and environment in all their connotations are then considered in terms of experiences that are *real* at various levels of maturation. Attention to creative types and personal inclinations as well as other differences among children obviously are to be kept in mind, as well as the necessity for differentiation and balance in the type of activities at all levels of growth. Finally, consideration is given to the suitability of activities to achieve maximum integration for pupils, relations to social living, and development of self-discovery and self-direction through evaluation. These are aspects which need to be understood by all teachers; therefore, they should be reflected in course-of-study guides or other curriculum materials.

THE BASIC PHILOSOPHY

The major concern of curriculum planners is with the philosophy of the program. In the light of the major beliefs presented here, art education must be considered as the birthright of all children and not the few; then it is feasible to lay a foundation for a program designed to evoke from *all* an art expression which is not only suitable to the individual but reflects his social setting. Such a view, obviously, must give primary importance to the development of expression, insights, concepts, appreciations, and outlooks in all pupils. So conceived, art education will not strive for esoteric ends, but for the optimum growth of each child to the extent of his abilities.

In the second place, curriculum planners need to realize that in the educational process as well as in the social setting, the individual must be considered paramount. Individual differences, tendencies, and gifts must be identified and coped with in order that art education may be fully effective in the development of pupils. The bright and the dull, the typical and the exceptional, the potential artist and the average citizen, are thus given that equality of opportunity which democratic society assures.

Third, a curriculum guide must suggest experiences which will involve all children in the solution of group problems. Whether the problem is the decoration of the primary party tables or the creation of murals for the senior high school, the involvements are there. Individual respon-

sibility to the group, coöperation, sharing of ideas, debating ideas and situations, will not only improve the art output by stimulating insights and reflective thinking but will also teach the ways of democracy. The meaning of freedom, the need for self-imposed limitations on one's own ideas and movements, the reaching of commonly shared points of view, and the achievement of social values and goals are thus encouraged. The curriculum guide needs to make clear to all teachers the inestimable value of group collaboration and its dynamics.

WHEN PARENTS AND CITIZENS are brought together with children and are invited to participate in experiencing art, they become interested not only in the program as a whole but in art itself (parent-child workshop, Livingston, N.J.).

Lastly, the basic philosophy of art education must give meaning to self-expression through practice. The curriculum guide should spell out the significance of freedom in terms of feasible situations within the classroom. For example, when every teacher believes that the concept "tree" can and does vary in its interpretation from one child to another, then the hectographed trees to be filled in will disappear. If self-expression includes freedom of choice in media and techniques, it is conceivable that water color, tempera, or chalks might be used by various pupils. The color effects, the structure, and the shapes that will result from the concept "tree" will then be seen as being varied, personalized, and differentiated. The example merely indicates that provisions for the exercise of freedom include the thinking of the teacher, the classroom climate, the variety of materials, and the acceptance of individual expression. Such a foundation represents a very fundamental outlook which must be commonly shared. Upon it, a child-concerned curriculum guide may be predicated.

FUNCTIONS OF ART EDUCATION

Next, the curriculum-guide committee should consider the special contributions which art can make to growth and development. Art alone cannot solve all problems of development, but because of its nature it can help measurably in several areas. The goal toward which education strives is the maximum development of each pupil. Yet for each level of development certain considerations are more important than others. Therefore, the curriculum guide should emphasize *what* aspects of development are best stressed at a given level. In general, it is crucial that the creative impulse, which is universal, be given constant opportunity for an unfolding consistent with abilities to manipulate, conceptualize, think, and perceive at every level.

The cultivation of the senses, the development of concepts, the acquisition of new knowledge, and the stimulation of insights are other facets of growth which need constant motivation. Texture, movement, shape, color are first "sensed" and then generalized upon. Therefore, at each step in the curriculum guide, the planners might indicate experiences from which children may develop perception and appreciation of these elements. Both two- and three-dimensional activities should be suggested to ensure that every creative type will find outlet.

It has been contended that art expression contributes greatly to the emotional growth of pupils. Hence it seems clear that curriculum guides should contain suggestions for the development of feelings. These may ultimately lead to harmonization with the environment. In general, such an accomplishment is facilitated when art activities are related to the needs of children, their deep concerns, even their dreams. The therapy of art, the sense of fulfillment, and the value of experience can then be calculated to help in the integration of the personality of the pupil. Integration is another way of saying that concepts, perceptions, and insights have been properly related by the pupil in his creation of a work of art.

All this implies that at each level of growth certain expectancies should be set up, not as inflexible goals, but rather as desirable outcomes.

ART AND SOCIAL LIVING

The curriculum guide should point up the very essential fact that art can make definite contributions to social living. Its effectiveness in this area is demonstrated by the history of mankind. Communal recreation, festivals, and other traditional activities attributed to cultural groups are compelling evidences of a deep-seated human need, namely, the need for association. The holidays and holy days, local and regional festivals, are extensions of the Greek Panathenaic procession so beautifully presented in the friezes of the Parthenon. The Colosseum was built for public use and for performances of public character. The miracle plays of the medieval church involved entire villages in their production. The present day has its own festivals, plays, and activities which the school may utilize for stimulation. The fact that the citizens of a democracy incline to play and work together, solve communal problems together, and share in responsibility as well as privileges, indicates the importance of preparing pupils to assume responsibilities of leadership or followership through school and community activities. School plays, dances, assemblies, publications, public meetings, and similar activities usually require art contributions. In many instances, the entire activity can be undertaken by an art group. Then there are many art activities which in themselves require group decisions and group coöperation, such as the planning and hanging of an exhibition, the planning and carrying out of an assembly devoted to art, the planning and execution of a three-dimensional display showing the development of architecture or other phases of art. These are a few of many possible examples of independent art activities that call for social relationships and a realization of interdependence.

Another aspect of this principle in curriculum building is implicit in the importance of developing a sense of identification with the social group. A very desirable attribute of art is that it can and does individualize. But no one lives unto himself; therefore, it is imperative that pupils be guided into group undertakings. They need to learn to assume their proper role in group enterprises and realize their responsibility in that area. Democracy itself, as interpreted in these pages, thrives when common concerns are solved by a community of effort. The curriculum guides should, therefore, suggest types of experiences and activities which will utilize individual contributions to class or school or community problems and projects. Central to this whole issue is the fact that young people in a democracy need to live democratically in order to understand and appreciate its meaning.

SUBJECT MATTER AND EXPERIENCES

Even a broad curriculum guide should suggest some areas of subject matter and experiences suitable at various levels. The guide should point up the fact that art subject matter or art ideas grow out of the daily experiences that boys and girls undergo: everyday experiences, unusual experiences, imaginative situations; these can all be stimulated for action. The necessity of clear conceptualization and reflective thinking on the part of pupils, and the value of creative solutions to problems, should be uppermost in setting up achievement expectancies. But the central point in this connection is that subject matter be related to experiencing, and of relating oneself to environment. In each of the chapters devoted to school levels there are suggestions for the selection of activities. They should be regarded only as springboards.

CREATIVE TYPES AND LEVELS OF DEVELOPMENT

When teachers accept the idea of individual development and the belief that art has the power to individualize, then it should not be difficult to conclude that each creative type must be acknowledged as valid. The several possible creative types have been discussed elsewhere; at this point a reminder should be sufficient. Those who plan curriculum materials have an obligation to make the fact clear to classroom teachers as well as to teachers with specialized preparation. Grade or level guides must recognize these important elements in the creative growth of boys and girls: creative development may differ in rate, may exhibit a particular perceptive type, may differ because of original capacity, and may be affected by environmental conditions.

A good curriculum guide should also make clear the stages of creative development so that expectancies for different ages, in different grades,

IN-SERVICE WORKSHOPS for classroom teachers are wholesome enterprises through which coördinators may help such teachers rid themselves of the fear of art, acquire new skills, and experience methods adaptable to the classroom (elementary teachers' workshop, Washington, Pa.).

and with different pupils will be properly recognized and the activities gauged accordingly. Furthermore, the guide should suggest that superior pupils need to be challenged beyond the expectancy level for a given grade or age. Otherwise such children become classroom problems.

DIFFERENTIATION AND BALANCE

Curriculum planners must see the whole problem and not parts of it. It is important that they emphasize the need for differentiation in types of experience, in media, and in approaches to creative problems. All children do not succeed in handling graphic media; but some of them may do better with three-dimensional materials. Some children have a sense of design in the abstract, while others may have a keen sense of color. To educate the whole child it is important to discover what his specific abilities are, what his preferences may be, what weaknesses he may have; and, through a varied program, guide him to learn to solve problems as well as enjoy success. This is not a plea for soft pedagogy;

570 rather it is an affirmation of the belief that even failure may help a child realize that he needs to work harder, more methodically and more assiduously, in order to succeed.

Furthermore, variation and balance are vital in sustaining interest, in broadening concepts, in utilizing new knowledge, and in gaining new insights. By exploring a variety of modes of expression and materials, pupils are guided to do some thinking. This ceases to be the case if they are always painting, or always building. Finally, balance and diversity are essential for the development of broad appreciations and emotional warmth for many types of art expression. These, then, are some considerations to be kept in mind in developing guides or other curriculum materials for the use of teachers.

EVALUATION AND INTEGRATION

The ultimate ends of art education are best served when pupils achieve a measure of harmony with the world about them as well as within them. Such harmony is the sum and substance of what is called *integration*. But how can teachers measure what has happened because of the art experience? What concepts have been clarified? What outlooks have been improved? To what extent has behavior been affected? These questions may be answered only if the purposes of art activities have been understood by teachers from the outset. Briefly, the general goals and the specific, if flexible, expectancies to be reached must be clearly stated. In a sense, they should be understood by teachers as well as by children, on different levels of understanding. Evaluation procedures, therefore, should be a part of the curriculum guide, whether stated broadly or in detail. Once again it must be said that self-motivation and self-development are the best yardsticks with which to evaluate the effectiveness of the art activities. For practical purposes, specific expectancies may be developed for each grade or level as indicated following Chapters 8, 9, and 10. Other approaches are equally plausible.

UNITY AND DIVERSITY

These two apparently contradictory qualities could well characterize a good curriculum guide. Unity in the basic philosophy is essential in order to ensure commonly shared meanings and goals. Diversity is desirable in the sense that a curriculum guide should not be a dictated document to be adhered to slavishly. If these two points can be held in mind constantly, curriculum committees will be rewarded by the general acceptance of their effort and by the willingness of teachers to suggest improvements for a continually evolving art curriculum.

DELIMITATIONS OF PERIODS OF GROWTH AND STAGES OF CREATIVE DEVELOPMENT

The varied nomenclature employed by writers to describe levels of growth and stages of creative development often prevents an adequate understanding of the nature of these tentative spans. What follows is an attempt to simplify the issue. Some cautions that should be kept in mind in developing curriculum materials are pointed out hereafter.

FLEXIBILITY OF GROWTH PERIODS

Periods of growth are extremely elastic. The true meaning of any span should be interpreted as indicating that most children grow in accordance with the norm, some grow faster, and some grow at a slower pace than is indicated by the limits suggested for each stage. This is true of all types of development. Chronological age, grade in school, and creative stages are not always parallel facets. It must be realized that the strong differences among children do not allow parallel or fixed growth spans. Any period should be interpreted broadly. Children who are growing according to the norm will be at the expected grade level at the expected age and may exhibit all the characteristics of the corresponding creative stage. Other children of the same age may be in the same grade; but their general growth may be below the norm, while their creative stage of development could, conceivably, be either typical or above or below the expectation. Teachers must evaluate the child's work for a considerable length of time before arriving at a fairly accurate picture of the growth pattern. This fact has been amply covered in Chapter 7.

CLARIFICATION OF TERMS

The diagram on page 572 has been designed as a frame of reference from which to work. For its effective use, the following definitions are offered in clarification of the terms as they are used in this text:

Periods of Growth	Ages	Creative Stages		Characteristics, Needs, Stimulation
Early Childhood	1			
	2	MANIPULATIVE STAGE 2-5 Yrs. of Age		See Table 1
	3			
	4			
	5	Kindergarten and 1st Grade		
Middle Childhood	6	PRESYMBOLIC STAGE 5-7 Yrs. of Age Grades 1-3		See Tables 1 and 2
	7			
	8	SYMBOLIC STAGE 7-9 Yrs. of Age Grades 3-5		See Table 2
	9			
Later Childhood (Prepubertal)	10	INCEPTIVE REALISM STAGE 9-11 Yrs. of Age Grades 5-7		See Table 2
	11			
	12	ANALYTICAL REALISM STAGE 11-13 Yrs. of Age Grades 7-9		See Table 6
	13			
Early Adolescence	14	PROJECTIVE REALISM STAGE 13-15 Yrs. of Age Grades 9-10		See Table 6
	15			
Later Adolescence	16			See Table 10
	17			
	18	RENASCENCE STAGE 15-20 Yrs. of Age Grades 10-12		
	19			
	20			
Youth				

APPROXIMATE PERIODS OF GROWTH AND STAGES OF CREATIVE DEVELOPMENT

The periods of growth have been adapted from W. C. Olson, *Child Development*, Boston, D. C. Heath and Company, 1949.

Creative stages of development are variously named by various writers. The present nomenclature is the author's responsibility. An attempt has been made to choose terms which refer to art. The importance of the stages and their meanings are elaborated upon in pages 573–575 of this chapter and in Chapters 8, 9, and 10.

Tables referred to are found on the following pages: Table 1, p. 250; Table 2, p. 256; Table 6, p. 304; and Table 10, p. 359.

Manipulative Stage (Ages 2–5)

From all standpoints the young child works to establish control over materials, over environment, and over self. Handling, grasping, holding, directing a tool or material are his chief preoccupations. Therefore, the activities of the child are characterized by his struggle to handle a spoon, a brush, a crayon, clay, a toy, or whatever his activity suggests. His art expressions are characterized by scribbles, first uncontrolled and then controlled. The handling of three-dimensional materials such as blocks or clay follows the same pattern. Improvements are noted as the manipulative powers increase. Some writers refer to this entire stage as that of *scribbling*.

Presymbolic Stage (Ages 5–7)

The child is still largely preoccupied with the establishment of control over materials and tools, and achieves a gradual measure of success. Very soon he is able to give the scribbling a semblance of the idea in his mind, even though adults fail to recognize it. A circle stands for the head, horizontal strokes for arms, and vertical ones for legs. The child usually names the object of his creation. These early successes satisfy his ego, but he continues to search and to strive for more effective means of telling what he knows and feels. Progress is very noticeable, although such progress may show marked differences in degree among different children. No specific formula has been as yet found by the child. For this reason this phase of early representation is referred to as the pre-symbolic stage.

Symbolic Stage (Ages 7–9)

A symbol stands for something: an idea, a person, a house, a tree, and so on. A symbol has a *form* which distinguishes it from other symbols that stand for other objects. Therefore, the form of one symbol differs from another. Normal children, having groped for more adequate expression of their ideas, by the age of 7, or before in many cases, should have achieved symbols that clearly relate to their concepts of a man and objects in the environment. These sets of symbols differ in details but not in kind among children. They are related to other aspects of their total development. Richer and more varied symbols represent richer and more varied experiences on the part of the child. A limited

EXHIBITIONS of children's work inform the community, inspire classroom teachers, and give children a feeling of confidence and pride. Good labeling helps to communicate the meaning and purpose of art education ("Art Is for All Children" exhibition, Atlanta, Ga.).

concept of form as well as of space is typical at this stage. The base-line concept is prevalent.

Stage of Inceptive Realism (Ages 9–11)

Symbols have been satisfactory up to now, but the child's sense of observation begins to sharpen his perception of the environment. This fact demands a more adequate mode of expression. His "geometric" symbols are too lifeless and do not lend themselves to the characterization desired. Therefore, art expression tends more and more toward the visual reality of the environment, or nature. Greater awareness of the physical self also inclines the child in the realistic direction. Relationship of parts to the whole as well as the character of parts becomes increasingly significant. Space concepts begin to sharpen; the base line is no longer sufficient nor is the sky merely overhead, but enveloping. Color is used not only for its emotional significance but in relation to the objects observed.

Stage of Analytical Realism (Ages 11–13)

The powers of observation which caused children to identify general characteristics of objects and environment through the duration of inceptive realism eventually reach an analytical stage. Color, form, space, texture, and plane are seen in terms of *changes* such as folds, dullness and brightness of color, or receding plane. This is a very important stage of development and calls for extreme care and understanding on the part of teachers. Artistic types[2] become very distinct at this point and guidance along the direction of the child's expressive mode is paramount.

Stage of Projective Realism (Ages 13–15)

This is the most critical period of development in life because the child, through much emotional and physical discomfort, passes from childhood into adolescence. Creatively, the crisis is just as great. It can be made an easy change or a harrowing experience with disastrous results. These are, normally, the junior-high-school years and represent a transitional stage of creative growth. Children now become objective in their artistic expression, highly critical of themselves, and aware of surroundings as never before. This stage is here referred to as that of projective realism because in seeing the work of adults, that of mature artists and the realism of nature, children are likely to attribute their temporary inability to create in a similar manner to these false standards. This is a time of crisis; therefore, wise teachers should encourage and bolster the confidence of children by guiding them along their lines of strength and creative types.

Stage of Renascence (Ages 14 and Upward)

Having surmounted the obstacles they met during the early adolescent years, youths find new strength and power. Those who were wisely guided through the stage of projective realism may emerge as the good art students. They are capable of almost-mature expression, are self-assured, confident, and reasonably well adjusted. The last year of junior high school and the senior-high-school years are productive periods for those who have successfully undergone the crisis. It is a time of general rebirth and especially of the creative powers of youth.

DESIGNING CURRICULUM MATERIALS

SCOPE AND SEQUENCE

When the "conflict of minds" has been resolved and basic common understandings have been reached, the general committee may wish

---

[2] See Herbert Read, *Education Through Art*, New York, Pantheon Books, 1949.

to submit to all those who are concerned with the art program a *scope-and-sequence* overview of the art curriculum. This instrument is found extremely valuable in many subject fields outside art education. Its merits are many: brevity of statements, ease of reference for detailed syllabuses, latitude of interpretation, coherence of organization, recognition of individual differences, and flexibility of standards for any point in child growth for purposes of evaluation.

The Portland, Oregon, schools, among other systems, have developed a Scope and Sequence Chart for art education, just as they have done for other areas of the curriculum. That document is here reproduced for the purpose of a brief analysis as well as for clarification.

TABLE 12. Art Education

Art Education is a body of knowledge, experience, tradition, and practice peculiar to itself, and also related to and a part of general education. It aims to satisfy an insistent urge, creative activity, and influence on society. The program in Art Education must serve the educational and cultural needs of the time. The art program must be significant, realistic, and alive. It must explore community and regional planning, industrial design, and contemporary culture. The program is a part of everyday living, a way of seeing and doing things through the graphic and constructive arts. These experiences give students an opportunity to express themselves, to solve problems, and to understand and appreciate their surroundings.

Kindergarten—Grades 1–2

Characteristics	Objectives
The child:	Satisfy innate urge to paint, model, and construct.
Concerned chiefly with nature of material.	Develop color knowledge.
Likes to scribble, smudge, and blotch.	Encourage good order in use of materials.
Sets his own goal.	Develop interest in working with others.
Works at own pace.	Learn self-direction.
Enjoys the sense of touch.	Learn to work freely.
Enjoys activity, not object itself.	
Enjoys plastic materials (malleable).	
Begins with abstract expressions.	

Likes big free movements.

Image later follows from excitements and stimulation.

Feeling later follows and stirs imagination.

Uses symbolic forms.

Desirable Experiences

Paints with big brushes and primary colors.

Models in clay, rolls, squeezes, pokes, etc.

Constructs with wood—simple furniture.

Prepares parent tea and program.

Makes murals.

Develops room attractiveness by arranging furniture; play corner, library, work area, bulletin boards, etc.

Plans projects.

Makes booklets for various occasions.

Shares ideas.

Takes field trips to zoo, stock show, farm, Art Museum, etc.

Has opportunities for development of personal taste and appreciation.

Evaluates own work and that of others.

Uses manuscript lettering for labels, booklets, and invitations.

Finger paints.

Makes doll clothes, aprons, costumes.

Works on committees to display care for materials, etc.

Materials and Tools

Tempera paints, pencils, chalk, crayon.

News print, finger paint paper, manila paper, construction paper.

Finger paint, large bristle brushes, cloth scraps, pairs of scissors, paste.

Wet clay, kiln, kiln furniture, slips, glaze, oil cloth.

Wood scraps, hammer, saw, nails, pliers, plane, file.

Buttons, yarn, sticks for printing.

Centralized collection of reference material.

Desired Outcomes

Understands relationships between different areas of living—within and without the school.

Is able to relate experiences to new learning.

Appreciates good order.

Develops muscular co-ordination through manual activity.

Likes to objectify on paper certain mental images.

Is able to follow simple directions.

Is able to work with some degree of order.

Is able to express ideas.

Uses care in use of materials and tools.

Appreciates developed skills.

Appreciates works of others.

Develops creative ability.

Enjoys sharing work with friends and family.

Respects rights of others.

Learns to communicate ideas to others.

Releases and stabilizes emotions.

Develops curiosity about the unusual.[a]

Grades 3–4–5

Characteristics

The child:

Desires opportunity for choice.

Wants art to explain and symbolize.

Works with added detail.

Shows muscular control.

Shows positive relationship of interest to knowledge.

Has special preference in materials.

Shows specific skills.

Desires prolonged activities.

Is often visual-minded.

Is subjective and emphasizes design, color, and person.

Is primarily interested in own work.

Objectives

Develop appreciation of community.

Encourage resourcefulness.

Develop individual interpretations in creative work.

Increase proficiency in the use of tools and mediums.

Develop appreciation of good grooming.

Relate art experiences to the larger area of living.

Desirable Experiences

Relate art to units (social studies, literature, and science).

Use basic forms in drawing.

Model in clay.

Plan group projects with dramatic interest.

Paint with varied color combinations.

---

[a] Possible outcomes.

Carve in wood, plaster, etc.

Make free forms in papier maché.

Present puppet shows—plays.

Make costumes, scenery, and properties.

Map a community.

Create murals of industries, transportation, etc.

Express space relationships.

Arrange objects to paint or draw.

Plan posters with use of lettering, color, and idea.

Keep room attractive and orderly.

Recognize good functional design—home-furnishings, buildings, utensils.

Make field trips to museums, industries, etc.

Work on complex construction.

Materials and Tools

Tempera paints, water colors, colored pencils, pencils, chalk, crayon, pen, and ink.

Newspaper, drawing paper, cardboard, construction paper, poster paper.

Bristle brushes. Camel hair brushes.

Wet clay, plaster of Paris kiln, kiln furniture, slips, glazes, oil cloth, stage tools, paste, boxes.

Textile paints, cloth, yarn, reed, raffia, looms.

Film, slides, current reference material.

Desired Outcomes

Is able to use art experience in all curriculum areas.

Is able to use various tools and materials.

Knows how to seek needed information.

Is able to plan projects.

Is able to follow directions and work in orderly manner.

Is able to use many materials in new ways.

Is able to apply knowledge to new ways of working.

Is able to show discriminating taste.

Develops appreciation of others' work.

Can release and stabilize emotions.

Learns to work with others.

Shows greater sensitivity in use of color.

Shows dissatisfaction in result of project.[a]

Reveals specific needs which teacher may develop.[a]

Is able to think beyond object level.[a]

Reveals differences in standards, feelings, imagination, etc.[a]

Shows varied degrees of individual abilities to integrate observing, thinking, and expressing.[a]

Characteristics

Student:

Sensitive to others' opinions.

Desires satisfactory expression of an idea.

Is increasingly conscious of his environment.

Desires to improve social behavior.

Has keen production interest.

Desires skills.

Willing to sacrifice on quality in order to achieve skill.

Desires a three-dimensional quality.

Expresses moods.

Shows ingenuity in work.

Expresses the spirit of the thing.

Objectives

An integrating force in the school curriculum.

An enrichment of all areas of learning.

A clarification of thinking.

An accumulation of knowledge.

Development of art appreciation and skills.

Development of personality.

Desirable Experiences

Paint and draw from imagination.

Design from nature.

Make pictorial maps.

Search for information regarding industrial design.

Design our City of the Future— showing functions, areas of living, commerce, recreation, industry, highways, and boulevards.

Build miniature interiors; stress comfort and harmony.

Model making of industrial machines, etc.

Enjoy classroom order and beauty.

Beautify school grounds.

Make working drawings.

Design to music.

Exhibit work.

Work together on projects.

Construct simple and effective scenes, costumes, stage properties for dramatic use.

Have Choice Day.

Evaluate art experiences.

Study beauty of crafts of various countries.

Materials and Tools

Paints (water colors, tempera, and oil).

Drawing paper, construction paper, and poster paper.

India ink.

Films, slides.

Photos.

Stencil cloth, textile paints, yarns, looms, kiln, clay, silk screen material, block processes.

Pens.
Assorted colored chalks and crayons.
Brushes.
Scrap materials.

Various color media, boxes, cardboard, reference material.
Bristol board, drawing board, T-square, rule.
Muslin, wallboard.

Desired Outcomes
Understands relationship of all areas of art study.
Understands environmental influence on art products.
Achieves good design—recognize good design.
Solves problems in a personal way.
Develops skills.
Develops creativity.
Learns to think through.
Understands and handles social situations.
Works in orderly manner.
Evaluates results.

Is able to use many media successfully.
Succeeds in dramatic plans.
Develops appreciation for order.
Achieves good social setting in classroom.
Appreciates home and apartment architecture.
Values are qualities in industrial design.
Sees with a "mental eye."
Releases tensions.[a]
Gains insight into interests, abilities, and personality traits, thereby affecting better guidance.[a]
Is sometimes hesitant to work for fear of criticism.[a]

High School 9–10–11–12

Characteristics
Art Appreciation: Desire to learn about are as expressed by different races and cultures. Desire for art expression and aesthetic understanding.
Art General: Desire to have a "successful experience" in drawing and painting. Desire for freedom, fun release, and relaxation which art affords. Desire to achieve understanding of the graphic arts.

Objectives
Art Appreciation: Enrich the student's appreciation of art in environment. Develop growth and enrichment of student's interests. Understand the way all people express themselves through their art.
Art General: Develop resourcefulness in creating with art forms. Develop discriminating attitudes, appreciations, and skills in drawing, painting, and sculp-

Art Commercial: Achieve proficiency in skills and techniques of mechanical and commercial work. Desire to participate in school activities through art communication.

Art Dress Design: Desire to improve personal appearance by developing taste and experience in selection of clothing. Interest in creative possibilities in the fashion fields.

Art Metal: Ability to socialize and co-operate in accepted activities. Achieve a realization of aesthetic values possessed in metal. Discovers various new experiences through school and personal experiments.

Art Crafts: Desire to develop manual dexterity with materials in combination with an *understanding of good design.* Desire to utilize *leis*ure time.

Desirable Experiences

Art Appreciation: An exploratory program which enables students to discover and analyze the basic principles of art. Creative ability in the general and constructive arts is stimulated.

Art General: A study of exploratory means of drawing and painting. Opportunities which give the student a broad study of the elements of design, the principles of art, and the role of art in daily living.

ture. Increase command of fundamental processes.

Art Commercial: Acquaint students with skills and techniques needed for professional use. Encourage related work in art to school and community needs.

Art Dress Design: Develop intelligent consumer buying. Develop good judgment and taste in personal appearance. Foster creative growth in areas of fashion design.

Art Metal: Increase proficiency in the use of tools and mediums. Develop ability to work with others in an orderly manner. Develop functional and creative possibilities in metal.

Art Crafts: Aid students to find new ways in expressing themselves. Foster profitable use of leisure time for vocational and avocational uses. Develop appreciation of creative and functional design.

design from the past and present.

Art Metal: Application of good creative design to metal. Development of proficiency and skill in use of tools, materials, and equipment. Stress the value in a balance of design to technique.

Art Crafts: Experiences in ceramics, sculpture, textiles, block printing, silk screening, stenciling, and weaving. Analyze form as it applies to function, empha-

Art Commercial: A study of the fundamentals of good lettering, poster design, packaging, cartooning, illustrating, and the vital parts they play in American advertising.

Art Dress Design: Exploratory design experiences in various media with regard to layout, construction of the human figure, and color harmony related to dress. Analysis of costume

size creative expression, design, and technical skill. Develop understanding of how art crafts contribute to daily living.

Material and Tools

Art Appreciation: Well equipped are laboratory. Standard fine arts tools, material, and equipment. Standard tools, materials, and equipment for crafts. Movies, slides, print collections, books, and reference materials.

Art General: Art laboratory well equipped with standard fine arts tools and materials. Art library containing reference material.

Art Commercial: Art studio equipped with standard fine arts tools, materials, and equipment, plus availability of silk screen, air brush, stencil, block printing and equipment.

Art Dress Design: Well equipped laboratory for fine art and crafts with materials for leather tooling, silk screening, block printing, ceramics, weaving, woodcarving, and dyeing.

Art Metal: Complete general metal arts laboratory equipment, plus materials required.

Art Crafts: Well equipped laboratory of commercial art tools, reference material with full coverage of period costuming.

Desired Outcomes

Art Appreciation: Develops importance and awareness of art in everyday life. Chooses art fields best suited to personal interest for further development by choice good work habits and flexible adjustment to changing problems of all people.

Art Dress Design: Improves individual selection of dress, personal appearance, and increases self-confidence. Fosters possibilities of professional pursuits. Directs better consumer buying.

Art Metal: Co-ordinates physical and mental powers. Encourages

High School 9–10–11–12 (*Continued*)

Art General: Works toward individual creativeness, confidence in self-expression. Achieves skills and knowledge to continue as a career or hobby. Understands historical and modern art.

Art Commercial: Understands purposes for consumer education in advertising. Develops lettering skills, sign painting, serigraphy, layout. Stimulates understanding of composition. Enriches life through understanding of good consumer buying.

appreciation of a standard of value. Increases creativeness. Builds toward vocation or avocation.

Art Crafts: Respects good design and craftsmanship. Develops skills. Enjoys home workshop.

Source: Portland Public Schools, Department of Curriculum and Instruction.

It should be noted that the chart represents a rather liberal approach to the problem of curriculum. It simply reminds the teacher that *the child* is the focal point of the art program. The typical characteristics at certain grade levels are the ever-present, all-important elements to be borne in mind. In addition, the document asks what art should do for the child at this particular level of growth. The answers are then stated in terms of the local objectives of art education. The document further points up the desirable experiences the child should have. These are broadly conceived, varied, and have supreme concern for the pupil and for his classmates. Suitable materials and tools through which the child expresses himself, and thus identifies himself with the experience, are enumerated. Lastly, the document states what may be the desirable outcomes of art experiences.

From the standpoint of evaluation alone, the document is of inestimable worth since it permits every teacher to appraise the growth of every child at any time and in many directions (Desired Outcomes). It also permits the teacher to check her own success in the light of the same outcomes. Finally, it permits the coördinator to note the degree to which the program is functioning in terms of child development.

A note of caution should be entered at this point with regard to any scope-and-sequence organization. It is this: its liberality and apparent simplicity should not be construed as an easily accomplished task. The truth is that the simpler the instrument appears in its final form, the more difficult it will be to design it. In other words, it must be a clear synthesis, or the distillation of the best thinking, after endless committee meetings and hours upon hours of work by groups and individuals. It must represent the resolving of the conflict of minds referred to previously. What subject matter, what activities, what tools, what objectives, what results? These questions, often asked by the general classroom teacher as well as by the special art teacher, must be answered, even if in terse form. From the general, the teacher must be enabled to work out satisfactory *specifics* suited to her particular situation. But a clear road has been chartered!

VARIETY OF INSTRUMENTS

The charting of the scope and sequence of the art program in terms of the nature, the characteristics, and the interests of pupils may be considered the only necessary instrument for the guidance of teachers. On the other hand, teachers and coördinators may decide to spell out, for each division of the school system, each of the major items in the chart. This has been done in many instances. When such is the case, further meetings of teachers, art coördinators, and general consultants may be necessary. But results will justify every effort in terms of better teaching and more effective learning.

A GUIDE BASED ON GROWTH RHYTHMS

Supervisors who have brought their teachers to a reasonable understanding of the purposes and values of art experience find ways of stimulating original and reflective teaching with a minimum of direction. An example of such stimulation is the chart on page 587.

In a general sense, what has been discussed in this and other chapters is exemplified in that diagram because it is another way of expressing what experiences are essential for children and youth at certain levels of growth. In that chart emphases are related to the developmental rhythm of typical pupils. The dotted line shows typical growth, plateaus of art interest, and, in a minor way, the increasing importance attached to the quality of the product as children grow and develop in a normal manner. With such a simple instrument on hand, classroom teachers or specially prepared teachers can evoke from pupils their own subject matter for visual interpretation. At the same time, growth and development are properly guided.

The present chart shows the rhythms for the entire period of schooling, but there is no reason why a detailed chart for a specific period of de-

SURROUNDINGS ALSO TEACH. Making use of pupils' work in offices and halls or where people congregate, is to place value on such creative efforts. Properly displayed, the work demonstrates to administrators, parents, teachers, and others what is meant by good taste. In addition, such a practice is a stimulus to young artists (school offices, Kansas City, Mo.).

velopment could not be designed. The instrument would then have distinct advantage for teachers of the grades concerned because much more could be stressed: specific skills, concepts, technics, and knowledges, both general and related to art. When several rhythm charts have been developed, it may be desirable to combine them into one instrument, similar to the Portland document.

Growth Rhythms and Suggested Emphases for Normal Creative Development[a]

Developmental Period	Stage	Age	School Level	Growth Rhythms and Suggested Emphases
Childhood — Early	Manipulative Stage	1–6 Years of Age	Preschool	Large muscular movements—Broad color areas—Unnamed and later named scribbling—Crayon or chalk effective—One color preferable—Freedom is important. Continue large muscular movement—The naming of objects occurs—Manipulative control increases—One color is best—Later several colors—Manipulative activities important—Encourage large brush movement—Encourage freedom and expression—Elastic program—Emphasize expression rather than production
Childhood — Middle	Presymbolic and Symbolic	6–10 Yrs. of Age	Elementary Gr. 1–3	Interest increases—Variety of experiences is profitable—Water-color control is increased—Exploration encouraged—Emphasis on process rather than on product—Continue encouragement of freedom of expression—Design may be introduced—Elastic program—Three-dimensional experiences are valuable for control and expression
Childhood — Later	Inceptive Realism	10–13 Yrs. of Age	School Gr. 4–6	Interest at high peak—Considerable proficiency—Design should be encouraged—Water color handled with assurance—Children find own technics—Variety intrigues—Concerns and dissatisfactions appear—Awareness of inability to do—Need for detail and finish—Begin emphasis on product—Crafts are enjoyed—Elastic program
Adolescence — Pre- and Early	Analytical and Projective Realism	13–15 Yrs. of Age	Jr. H.S. Gr. 7–9	Emotional expressiveness high—Originality should be encouraged—Distinguish between visual type and expressionistic type—Increase emphasis on product and technical proficiency—Critical awareness—Ability to reason increases—Designing with materials—Exploratory but realistic program needed—Encourage personal style
Adolescence — Middle	Artistic Renascence	15–18 Yrs. of Age	Sr. H.S. Gr. 10–12	Mental and emotional health paramount—Individualize program—Specially gifted need particular attention—Technics and materials highly significant—Product becomes very important
Adolescence — Late	Artistic Renascence	To 20 Yrs. of Age	Sr. H.S. Gr. 10–12	Mental and emotional health paramount—Individualize program—Specially gifted need particular attention—Technics and materials highly significant—Product becomes very important

[a] This chart should be read from the bottom up.

A GUIDE BASED ON CHILDREN'S NEEDS AND INTERESTS

Lastly, and by way of a further example, a very modest but different type of guide is presented. It was developed by student teachers and classroom teachers in the Campus Elementary School at Kutztown, Pennsylvania, State Teachers College. A study of the guide reveals that the pupil is of first concern. His interests, abilities, and normal experiences form the basis of the activities. It will be noted also that only suggestions are made, so that the novice in teaching or the general classroom teacher may proceed with some confidence but also with freedom to interpret and amplify. In this manner, it was found that teachers became accustomed to the basic point of view, that they realized the need for a flexible atmosphere, and that individuation is essential to a sound art education. In that school, a new guide is prepared each year by student teachers and classroom teachers under the guidance of the art coördinator.

On the other hand, larger school systems, mainly for administrative reasons, often produce elaborate and complete course-of-study guides.[3] These cover either the entire school range or each of its major divisions: elementary, junior high school, and senior high school. The advantages of such extensive ventures are many because all matters are detailed. The dangers are equally as great in the hands of teachers who rely on the word rather than on the spirit of the documents.

THE CAMPUS ELEMENTARY SCHOOL

State Teachers College, Kutztown, Pennsylvania

A GUIDE FOR PLANNING ART ACTIVITIES
In Grades K, 1, 2

I. WHY WE TEACH ART

Child growth and development are the important objectives of art education in the early primary grades. Psychology and education have shown that children learn best when their activities are based on their

---

[3] Pittsburgh, Pennsylvania; Long Beach, California; Denver, Colorado; New York City; and many other cities have developed excellent and very sound course-of-study guides.

interests, the things they know, and the deep-seated urge to express themselves. Art experiences should be selected to accomplish the following purposes:

1. To help them develop *creatively* (Through doing and appreciating)

    Communication of ideas
    Expression of feelings
    Freedom to express what they "see"

2. To help them achieve *coördination* (Over materials, tools, technics)

    Control over tools and material
    Experimentation
    Discovery of solutions

3. To help them develop *awareness* through art media and technics (Appreciation and "sensing")

    Color, form, texture
    Rhythm, balance
    Moods, feelings, sensations, relationships.
    Surroundings: nature, people, animals

4. To give them satisfying *experiences* (Carefully chosen for levels and personal capacity)

    Materials, tools
    Effective organization
    Meaningful activity
    Creative expression coupled with thinking
    Personal feelings and ideas tested

5. To guide them in the solutions of *problems* (Clear thinking, conceptualization, perception)

    Physical coördination in relation to material and technics
    Emotional release and improved outlooks through achievement, broadened concepts
    Social-group consciousness through working with others

II. WHAT INTERESTS YOUNG CHILDREN?

Interests reveal the real concerns and inner motivations of children. Interests give rise to urgent needs. These can be met in art by guiding children into meaningful experiences:

1. Themselves

    At play
    At work
    Ownership
    Home membership, worship

2. Their families

    Helping at home
    Parents: what they do, how they look
    Brothers and sisters
    The home
    The garden

3. Their playmates

Neighborhood friends
Games they play together
Visits next door
Sharing toys, book
Telling stories, make-believe stories

4. Their toys

Riding, sliding, pulling
Putting away toys (for neatness)
Being careful (for safety)
Sharing toys (for social living)

5. Their pets

My cat (plays with a ball)
My dog (jumps and runs)
My bunny (hops, hides, eats grass)
My pony

6. Their neighborhood

My yard, my garden
The street I live on
The store where mother buys food
The school I go to (or sister goes to)
The church-school where I go
The policeman, the mailman, the cab
driver

III. WAYS OF STIMULATING

Prior to initiating art activities, teachers and pupils talk about what they hope to do, how they hope to do it, what materials they will need, and similar important things. The most significant point to talk about is ideas the children are going to paint, carve, model, or make. Questions will reveal whether children's concepts are clear or false, whether any thinking is accompanying the doing, and to what extent the children see their problem. Well directed, all this can act as stimulation. Action is the last link in the creative experience. Some ways of stimulating for creative action are listed below:

1. Storytelling (by children, by the teacher, or both)
2. Dramatization (by children, by the teacher, or both)
3. Showing and talking about pictures of children (at play, work, in school, on the playground, in assembly)
4. Seeing works of art (with children or of children, of animals, toys)
5. Participation (in all activities enumerated above)
6. Experiencing materials (for fun, to "discover," to see what happens)
7. Playing games (How do we stand?, Who is the leader?, Who is running?, etc.)
8. Listening to music (Is it a lullaby? Is it soft, sweet, loud?)

IV. SOME ART ACTIVITIES FOR THE EARLY GRADES

A. *Children Love Color*

The concern being color, the teacher and children will want to see how much they know about it. Where do we see color? How many colors do we see in our room? What colors do we like best? What colors would we see on the farm (the barns, the fields, the machinery, the animals, the house, etc.)? A similar procedure may be followed for any subject of interest to the children, with color as the area around which the questions will revolve.

1. Making an easel painting (subject: imagination, memory, recent event, etc.)
2. Painting a portrait of mother, father, brother, etc.
3. On the farm
4. At the store
5. Mingling for fun
6. A sunset
7. Flowers are pretty
8. "Myself" all dressed up
9. I decorate my writing paper
10. A windy day

B. *Children Love Nature*

Nature is only a part of the child's environment, but it is an important part. He must learn to adapt himself to it, to use it to advantage, and to change it, if possible, in line with his needs. An appreciation of the beauty, the meaning, and the possibilities of nature will open up insights, stimulate sense perceptions, and, in a less tangible way, even contribute to the child's outlook upon life.

1. I draw the big tree near school
2. I draw the mountains and sky
3. I paint bright leaves
4. Snowflakes look like this
5. A picture of my cat (dog, bird, etc.)
6. My vegetable garden
7. Our cherry tree in bloom
8. The weather (it rains, it snows, a bright day, a dreary day)
9. I like spring (summer, fall, winter)

C. *Children Like to Make Things*

Because action is the final step in the creative process, manipulation assumes an important role in the education of children. Furthermore, there is the physical need of children to develop control, to master hands and body in order to accomplish what needs to be done:

holding a spoon, holding a crayon, holding a toy, holding a book, and so on in increasing complexity. Art can help children satisfy this need and at the same time develop in other directions. (Use wood, clay, yarn, papier-mâché, paper sculpture, cardboard boxes.)

1. Belts to wear
2. Kites to fly
3. Books to give
4. Printed curtains for our schoolroom
5. A clay dish for brother (thumb and coil)
6. Animal toys (for self, brother, sister)
7. Favors for special days
8. Costumes and scenery for class plays
9. Fancy hats for a party
10. Masks to wear on Halloween

D. *Children Are Interested in Other Children*

Human beings are also part of the environment. Obviously, children are interested in other children because of similar interests, similar play activities, and other similarities in growth. Because children are egocentric for a long time, it is important for them to think in terms of others. Art activities, which keep them constantly aware of others, will contribute to social living as well as to creative development.

1. A school trip (on the bus, at the farm, etc.)
2. Children of the neighborhood (the boy next door, etc.)
3. Children of other lands
4. Games at school (we play . . . , etc.)
5. Helping each other (crossing the street, getting on the bus)
6. Brothers and sisters (portraits or action)

E. *Children Are Interested in Food and Clothing*

Food and clothing—where they come from, how they are processed, how distributed, packaged, and then made available for consumption—are of interest to all human beings. For children these items have a special fascination quite outside the value of nutrition and comfort. The interest comes from the color, the pattern, the making and arranging of parts. Going to faraway places for foods, seeing dolls dressed in costumes of a foreign country, are types of experience. But then the interest in people involved in the situations mentioned increases knowledge, concepts, and outlooks, while the solution of creative problems further strengthens the insights of the child in the realm of art.

1. My new dress
2. How I dress on Halloween

3. We go to the farm (to the store, market, etc.)
4. The milkman helps me
5. This man brings eggs (bread, meat, etc.) to our house
6. The sheep give us wool for clothing
7. I dress my doll
8. I dress up like a fireman (policeman, farmer, groceryman)

VALIDITY OF INSTRUMENTS

For functional purposes, any convenient, efficient, and understandable way of charting the course of art education is defensible. But certain conditions must be met. Among the essential conditions that test the validity of instruments are these:

1. All concerned, including pupils, have participated in the undertaking.
2. The general philosophy is stressed through suggested methods and procedures which support it.
3. The learner is the focal point of suggested activities and experiences.
4. Freedom of interpretation and reflective thinking are ensured for pupils and teachers.
5. Evaluative criteria are furnished, as guidance, for the use of teachers and pupils.
6. The instrument is flexible and constantly evolving.

ACHIEVING SYNTHESIS

As a concluding word on the selection and organization of curriculum materials in art education, it should be stated that the term *coördination* summarizes and underscores all the implications of this crucial problem. Coördination means working together, functioning in harmony, and mutual adjustment. When all human elements are considered, the picture will include the child, the administrator, the teacher, and the parent.

Any type of organization of curriculum materials, honestly and intelligently done, will represent a synthesis in human relations and educational statesmanship. The freedom of children, teachers, and coördinators will be safeguarded by such endeavors. Meantime, child growth will at least have been given some thought, within the limitations of human knowledge and physical conditions.

SUMMARY

The art coördinator's work described in this chapter may appear to be a sizable task, as indeed it is. But the major concern of all persons engaged in teaching is the curriculum itself; for the coördinator it is particularly so. The development of children and youth is intimately bound up with the opportunities offered them, the methods that teachers use, and the understanding that permeates the program in action.

The value of curriculum planning is that the important aspects of teaching and learning referred to are clarified in the process of organization. When teachers, coördinators, psychologists, and level supervisors democratically arrive at commonly shared points of view, the same spirit will be operative in the classrooms.

The general classroom teacher is anxious to know in which direction to move and is particularly concerned with what are suitable experiences, and what she may reasonably expect of typical children. The curriculum guide is a foundation upon which coördinators and teachers may build with a degree of assurance.

There are many ways of designing functional curriculum guides, scope-and-sequence charts, grade-level guides, lessons, and units; therefore, the important requirement is that the instruments be effective and usable as guides in planning the detailed activities with the pupils themselves.

Particular attention should be given to stages of growth and development in planning art activities. These should be within the range of children's experiences, yet they should evoke the best from them, even challenge them. However, it is wise to remember that stages of growth and development are only guideposts; they are not fixed; certainly they do not apply equally to every child in a given group.

For Discussion and Activity

1. To what extent is the curriculum in art a responsibility of the chief art administrator? Discuss several approaches to the adequate development of the curriculum.
2. Make a survey of the curriculum-development practices in your county or parish. Discuss the findings with your associates in an effort to discern best ways.

3. As a group, attempt to develop a scope-and-sequence chart for the elementary grades, the junior-high-school grades, and the senior-high-school grades. What are the considerations you must first look into in each instance?

4. What is subject matter in art? Is there a sequential way of developing or teaching art? Discuss these points and substantiate statements from authoritative sources.

5. Assuming that you were the art coördinator in a middle-sized community, how would you proceed to reëvaluate the art program? Discuss each step in detail.

6. Make a careful study of a curriculum guide or similar material available in the curriculum library. Report to your group on the merits and the weaknesses of the material you have analyzed. Substantiate your statements.

7. What basic elements should underly curriculum building or revision? Discuss each major element in the light of your current study and of additional sources.

8. To what extent should curriculum guides and scope charts be followed? What deviations are plausible and under what conditions? Be specific in your statements.

9. As you study the Portland chart (pages 576–584), do you feel that classroom teachers are limited or free? Justify your statement in specific terms.

10. Of what value would be the advice of the school psychologist and the general supervisor in the organization or revision of the art curriculum? Specify the values.

For Further Reading

Barkan, Manuel, "Art and Human Values," *Art Education,* March, 1953.

Commission on the Secondary School Curriculum, Progressive Education Association, *The Visual Arts in General Education,* New York, D. Appleton-Century Company, 1940, Chapter III.

Howell, Alfred, "Basic Considerations in the School Art Program," *Art Education,* June, 1950.

Rios, John F., "Art Materials and Intergroup Relations," *Art Education,* December, 1948.

Spears, Harold, *Improving the Supervision of Instruction,* New York, Prentice-Hall, 1953, Chapter XVI.

Winslow, Leon L., *Art in Elementary Education,* New York, McGraw-Hill Book Company, 1942, Chapter X.

PROGRAMS OF PROMISE

> If the vision of the clearest and the farthest seeing can
> be conveyed to the multitudes who see less well, the stand-
> ard of human vision rises, and with it the level of mutual
> participation. We have a shared responsibility to enter into
> this process of shared experience at the highest capacity to
> which we can elevate our sensibilities.
>
> Richard Guggenheimer,
> *Sight and Insight*

A FOREWORD

SEVERAL REFERENCES HAVE BEEN MADE THROUGHOUT THIS WORK TO
the fact that theory and practice in art education, as in all education,
do not always show complete agreement. This is a natural condition,
but one that requires the constant and intelligent vigilance of all professional workers. Lag between the two elements must be reduced to a
minimum in order that the art program may be effective and that the
best growth and development of children may be sought and achieved.

One method of reducing the lag is to examine good practices, or those
practices that come nearest to the ideals set up by the profession. By
measuring or comparing local efforts with other good situations, the
art teacher or coördinator may realize that what may appear theoretical
is being applied and found worth while in many localities. It is also
likely that certain interpretations and certain aspects of method which
are being used locally by teachers and coördinators may find confirma-
tion in the practices examined. Young teachers whose experiences with

teaching and with children are limited, or those engaged in practice teaching, may find assurance and added help in the study of the procedure and beliefs of maturer art consultants. In a sense they may discover that what is generally referred to as the philosophy of art education is not simply *ideal* or *theoretical,* but workable, educationally feasible, and sound.

It is for these reasons that a number of art programs have been chosen, as examples of what a dynamic art program ought to be, from among many excellent situations existing across the nation. The individual accounts are honest reports of what is actually being accomplished. They include basic philosophy, hoped-for progress, cautions, successes, special achievements, and even limitations. From such field reports the novice or the experienced coördinator may gain new vision and renewed faith in a tenable point of view in art education and in the power of creative expression in the lives of children of all ages.

The examples of the work of children, of classroom conditions, of finished products, or of work in progress have, by far and large, come from the same promising situations reported upon. The purpose of such illustrations is to offer further stimulus to all teachers who teach art.

ALLIANCE, OHIO[1]

POINT OF VIEW

Art education should provide a continuous flow of experience for the child through which he learns to communicate his feelings, to satisfy his needs and desires for personal expression through a creative activity, to receive an aesthetic communication from others, to enjoy sensitively the creative efforts of individuals other than himself.

Art education should find its climax in the matured individual, who because of his experiences has well-developed perceptual powers, is critical of but can appreciate contemporary art, shows by his home, dress, and way of life that he is sensitive to good design. His "art roots" are of sufficient depth and strength that his interest and sensitivity continue to grow throughout his lifetime.

---

[1] Statement prepared by Henry W. Ray, Coördinator of Instruction.

ELEMENTARY ART EDUCATION

In the elementary school we accept a majority of the recommendations published during the last few years as a result of the findings of researchers in the field of child development.

In the lower elementary school we believe the child should have frequent unscheduled opportunities to give voice to his emotions, feelings, and reactions to his daily experiences through two- and three-dimensional media, with a maximum of adult (teacher) facilitation and encouragement and a minimum of teacher direction.

At the upper elementary level we increase the variety of materials and types of creative experience. The child is encouraged to invent, construct, design, and experiment. As his factual world and concept of community enlarge, as he becomes aware of his needs to become a coöperating member of a group society, art experiences provide the learning ground for realizing his maturing personality in a democratic direction.

THE SECONDARY SCHOOL

In the secondary school, technical tools are made available to the child to assist him in overcoming his obstacles to a satisfactory form of expression. He learns something of perspective, the figure, design techniques, and practical applications of these and other basic learnings. His exploration into the creative world now invades the world of adult interests and applications. He respects the materials of the arts. As an individual he accepts responsibility for a quality of workmanship and a completion of expression in keeping with his mental and intellectual years.

Finally, he chooses whether art is to be an avocation or is to provide his daily bread—and if he chooses the latter, he defines his advanced course of study with an intelligent, matured perception of art.

In our art education our teachers are free from directives on what and how to teach. As professional people they are encouraged to adapt and to experiment. Abundant materials are supplied with which to work. With their students our teachers can plan so that individual needs and interests can most easily be met. Small group meetings, held during the evening when time is most abundant, provide opportunities to exchange ideas, work with new media, and improve techniques of working with better-known materials. The latest in published research on art education is readily available.

ATLANTA, GEORGIA[2]

Our philosophy is founded on our belief that art is for all children at all levels as a part of general education because we believe that there is, indeed, an artist in each of us and that the urge for creative activity should not be denied but fostered for free growth through childhood to maturity. We believe, too, that the nature of society today—with its tensions and strains inherent in our mechanized existence—calls for more stress in education on all that makes us human.

We advocate art expression for all children, not for the sake of the products, satisfying as these may be, but for the sake of the child, his growth, his mental and emotional health, as he projects and proves himself as a person in his expanding environment. We believe that the importance of the art produced lies chiefly in the satisfaction and self-identification of the child with his product. Children's art is good art when it is uninhibited, expressive, and meaningful on the child's level; such art is characteristic rather than exceptional and is enjoyed by all who hold such values, but the significant contribution to education lies in the effect on the child as a growing, expressive personality.

We believe that the heart of the problem for educators is in understanding the role of art in child development at all levels. We need to hold this view in all our practices, hard as it may be to act consistently or wisely.

On the elementary level we believe that the classroom teacher should perform the major role in teaching art: the teacher who knows the child, his needs, his experiences, his pattern of growth, who understands group needs and interests. The classroom teacher works with a schedule of the blocks of time needed to plan, relate, and execute the desirable activities for an individual or for a group. Any good teacher, say, of reading, can be a good art teacher if she makes the effort to acquire the teaching skills and the art skills. The help of an art consultant should be available to all such teachers. Enrichment, know-how, encouragement

---

[2] Statement prepared by Katherine Comfort, Supervisor of Art.

for teachers to enjoy living more fully through freeing the artist in each teacher—these are essential services to the teacher which the art specialist should give.

On the high-school level our belief still holds that art is an important part of general education. However, under the present departmentalized plan, a special period for art and a trained art teacher are needed, although as far as possible the art program should be related to the total experience of the child. We recognize, too, the need for art-teacher guidance in the skills of art as the child grows toward adulthood.

Art is a required course for one semester in our eighth grade, with the specific objective of nourishing and guiding the creative art activities of all. The emphasis is on developing and maintaining confidence in one's own ideas and developing the skills to carry them out, as well as the development of greater sensitivity to the quality of art in works of other people, developing consumer taste, and possibly finding vocational as well as avocational interests in art.

Our program, grades 9 to 12, provides elective courses in painting, interior design, and general crafts, such as ceramics, textiles, weaving and woodcarving, jewelry, etc. At present, we offer no vocational courses in commercial preparation for a job in a specific field. We believe that a broad base for further training in art fields is formed by the experiences provided in the courses we now offer. We also provide the opportunity for students to explore the possibilities of careers in art.

Art education, based on the broad meaning of art and the values of the creative, is a force to be reckoned with in making a dynamic, democratic society by making dynamic creative personalities able to solve problems of personal adjustment in a complex modern world. We may hope to see man restored to his birthright as a human being in tune with nature and in control of the new world of scientific discovery.

SPECIAL PROBLEMS IN OUR ELEMENTARY ART PROGRAM

1. Need for a city-wide exhibit—every child a participant.
2. Elimination of competitiveness. No jury from outside the school.
3. Evaluation through the exhibition.

The response to our plan was truly overwhelming. In every section of the city, parents, teachers, children, administrators, all were enthusiastic and eager to repeat this highly rewarding project.

Next year we plan to have "evaluation clinics" for each area with teachers and consultants taking stock of the evidence as related to aims.

BALTIMORE, MARYLAND[3]

From the standpoint of administration, art in the school is regarded as coördinate with other studies. From the standpoints of content and method, however, art is somewhat, though not radically, different from the other subjects. It is concerned with the meeting of human needs through the transformation of materials into products, and with the appreciation of works of art.

The art-education program is concerned with developing human personalities and is, therefore, vitally tied up with the general education of the whole child, considering especially his emotional development. Art as a curriculum area should provide an emotional and creative outlet for individual expression, thus helping to integrate the personality of the child. Opportunities are afforded at all levels, which help all children to grow aesthetically, not just the talented few. The works of master artists, as expressions of past and present, are studied systematically by students, while their own art expressions result from vital experiences, both in and out of school. This program is related to the home, the school, and the community.

Because of this program the pupil gradually comes to acquire deeper understandings of art processes, skill in their performance, and taste, which implies the ability to judge and make wise selections. It appeals to differences among children in order to secure the interest and response of all.

Art activities are desirable to the extent that they accelerate the child's general growth and development. The purpose of instruction at the elementary-school level is to meet the general needs of all through the use of art materials, and to provide for aesthetic experiences through contemplative activities. The resultant art is often an index to the individual pupil's growth and development.

Social studies and elementary-school art have been so closely related that art has sometimes been regarded as a social study and thus absorbed by this area to the extent of losing its identity as a curriculum entity

---

[3] Statement prepared by Dr. Leon L. Winslow, Director of Art Education.

worthy in its own right. At certain times art should have no relationship to the social studies, but should grow out of science, the language arts, or some other curriculum area. At other times art should not relate to any other area but should exist merely as art, as science or reading and arithmetic most often exist *as such*. Children are all too infrequently given opportunity to participate in free art expression which in no way relates to any other curriculum subject, although its therapeutic values would seem to justify this on frequent occasions.

All handiwork with materials engaged in by elementary-school children should be elevated to the plane of art, and should be so considered by administrators and teachers. Even though attractive art products sometimes result from the interaction of various curriculum areas without any assistance from an art specialist, this should not imply that professional assistance in teaching art is either unnecessary or uncalled for.

Resource teachers of art are assigned to one or more elementary schools to help carry on the art program. This constitutes an outstanding and helpful addition to the art-education services. The chief function of this position is to assist the classroom teacher in carrying on and improving the quality of instruction in art, by working with the teacher in the classroom in any ways that may seen to be helpful to the teacher and the children, and by demonstrating procedures when this seems advisable; by helping develop in teachers an increased appreciation of the value of art to children; by establishing art as an integral part of the curriculum in the minds of faculty and parents; by challenging those teachers who already do good art work to do still better; by helping the teacher who lacks confidence in art to make an effective beginning and ultimately to succeed; by gathering art materials and information which may be needed, and guiding teachers in their proper uses; by strengthening the capacities of a school faculty for carrying on worth-while art activities to the point where all teachers will feel confident and capable in their teaching; and by assuming responsibility in school-wide activities such as an art club, exhibits, the preparation of scenery and costumes for school performances.

THE SECONDARY PROGRAM

In the junior high schools art is largely exploration and guidance for boys and girls with varying interests and abilities, but in the senior high schools pupils have the opportunity of electing a general art course, which acquaints them with the place that art occupies in the home and in the trades and industries. For those who wish to pursue the study further in the general senior high school, art-major courses are available. In grades 9 through 12 a sequence of courses leading to the high-school diploma is offered as the Art Curriculum, Baltimore's unique contribution to public-school art education, for the talented few. The art courses of this curriculum include general art, painting, sculpture, industrial art, commercial art, architecture, and theater art. It prepares the student who completes it successfully for entrance to college or art school. For those who wish to enter the vocational high school, there are courses in advertising art and sign painting, graphic arts, general design, and distributive education.

The Art Curriculum is one of six academic curriculums open to secondary-school students. It offers a cultural background that all can use and profit by; in it the student pursues art as a major subject six periods a week in the ninth grade, and ten periods a week in the tenth, eleventh, and twelfth grades. Some students who enroll will ultimately become producers of art, while others will enter the industrial or the mercantile fields, teach art, or work in an art museum or library.

The records made to date by Art Curriculum graduates in art school, college and university indicate that it is both sound and worth while. Since its inauguration in 1942, over 30 of its graduates are now engaged in advertising, drafting, or some other form of art occupation, while 92 are going on with their education. One of the charter graduates of the curriculum is now a candidate for the Ph. D. degree in a university. A number of others have earned the bachelor's and master's degree.

BOISE, IDAHO[4]

Art plays an important role in the daily lives of all people. Because it is so thought of, we give it an honored place in the daily program of the boys and girls in our Boise school system. Training and developing children to be better citizens for tomorrow is the school's business. Through the art program, we are giving opportunities for boys and girls to create in their own way. We encourage the pupils to experiment.

---

[4] Statement prepared by Paul C. Dalzell, Director of Art.

604   Working with many materials challenges the imagination and stimulates growth. We try to reach all the children through their needs and interest in what they see, hear, feel, and think.

IN THE ELEMENTARY SCHOOLS

In our elementary schools, teachers give opportunities for using many kinds of materials. This helps to create interest, and once that interest is developed, creativity is stimulated and individual growth begins.

Respect for one's own work as well as that of others is encouraged. Individual growth must be the ultimate aim of the school. Child art is not adult art and must not be evaluated on that basis.

Specific objectives for our elementary schools are growth through freedom of expression and creative thinking, developing personality through the needs of the child, developing an ability to evaluate.

IN THE JUNIOR AND SENIOR HIGH SCHOOLS

In our system, we have a junior and senior high school set-up. Due to crowded conditions in the senior high school, the tenth grade was moved back into our junior high schools. This has created several problems.

However, it is our feeling that the junior-high art should be very experimental, working with many materials in many ways. In other words the pupils are given the opportunities to explore many media and develop skills and techniques on their own level. Just having fun with crayon, pencil, or paint is most important. Keeping the "urge" to do something creative with that which is at hand is very important and of real value to the adolescent.

In the senior high we continue to give the students the opportunity to create and develop in their own way, at their own speed. Guidance in vocational and educational opportunities is offered. We try to develop an appreciation for all the arts as well as a better and more intelligent consumer of goods. All art students will not make their living through art, but all will find a real need for art in their daily living.

SPECIAL FEATURE

The art program in our elementary grades deserves special recognition. Teachers are constantly using art with other subject fields. Illustration in the primary grades is a must for a good reading program. An illustration of what the child experienced over the week end, on a trip to the lake or farm, affords opportunity for the child to draw or paint or mold out of clay that which interested him most. When these creations by children are finished they are hung about the room or placed on reading charts and evaluated before being taken home.

Number work is correlated with art in that the teacher may write on the board: "Draw four green trees or two red apples and one yellow apple." Color is introduced to an otherwise cold subject of figures.

Evaluation gives the child an opportunity to share his work with the class. Every child participates. In this way all children are made to feel that they belong to the group.

In the upper elementary grades, illustration continues to serve the child in his educational growth. Crafts help the child to develop muscular control and to keep an interest.

The art program in our elementary schools is one of great value. The real teacher helps the child grow and develop by giving him the opportunity to express himself in many ways during the normal school day.

HAZLETON, PENNSYLVANIA[5]

OVERALL PHILOSOPHY

The teachers of the Hazleton schools have a well-defined philosophy of art education; it embraces the elementary and secondary field and may be stated as follows:

1. To provide *all children* with an opportunity to enjoy and use art in their daily work and living experiences.
2. To develop the children's self-confidence in and through creative expression.
3. To promote individual and group activities for the development of social and democratic ideals so necessary to a free nation.
4. To provide for a wide range of experiences with media and materials that permit the children to attack their own problems and allow for individual differences in the interpretation of subject matter.
5. To encourage children to explore and experiment freely with new materials and media for creative expression.

---

[5] Statement prepared by Karl G. Wallen, Art Supervisor.

606   A COÖPERATIVE PROGRAM

The Board of Education, the Superintendent of Schools, principals, and teachers of the Hazleton Public Schools realize the importance of art as a definite aid in promoting the development of the children. It is only through the excellent coöperation of all concerned that the department is able to put into practice the overall philosophy of the art program.

SPECIAL FEATURES

Display Areas

All schools are equipped with display areas in individual rooms and a central display area in each of the school corridors, where a continuous display of the art work of all grades is shown from September to June. Teachers and pupils of the grade schools plan and hang the displays. A greater amount of art work, representing more children, can be exhibited through this method than the conventional once-a-year type of exhibition. It is the firm belief of this reporter that continuous exhibition of students' work, with proper publicity throughout the year, does more to keep art work before the public than the traditional once-a-year art exhibition.

Junior Art Gallery

With the coöperation of the public library, the Art Department installed display areas in the children's department of the library and established a Junior Art Gallery. Monthly exhibits of the work of grade-school children are shown in this gallery by the children's librarian.

ADULT ART EDUCATION—PUBLIC RELATIONS

The art department of the public schools sponsors an adult program that is designed to meet the cultural and recreational needs of the community. Classes for beginners and advanced students in the fields of painting, jewelry, enameling, ceramics, and ceramic sculpture are taught throughout the year. The public-relations value of this phase of the work is inestimable.

Hazleton Art League

The Hazleton Art League coöperates with our school art program in granting the use of its galleries and sponsoring displays of secondary students' work. The League is also instrumental in bringing painters and exhibitions of national importance to the students and general public. The Hazleton Art League also awards two medals each year to the outstanding senior art students in painting and in crafts.

IN-SERVICE EDUCATION OF TEACHERS

An in-service program permits teachers, by groups or grade levels, to meet and explore the varied art programs in the elementary and secondary fields.

All elementary schools close at 3:20 P.M., allowing grade teachers forty minutes each day to plan their work, exhibitions, and have conferences with parents and supervisors in the special fields. During this time provision is made to permit children to work on any phase of the school program.

JACKSON, MISSISSIPPI[6]

In the Jackson public schools, a system which includes 16 elementary schools, three junior high schools, and one senior high school, and approximately 450 teachers, we have attempted to develop each child as an individual with personal freedom and self-expression and with a sense of group interest and responsibility. This group participation, exemplified in projects such as mural painting and the making of clay tableaux, is an important factor in our program. Copy work and imitation are held to a minimum, and each child is encouraged to solve his or her own problems by creative thinking and experimentation.

The study of art masterpieces is a valuable part of the program. Our purpose in presenting fine-art reproductions in the elementary schools is to stimulate the child's interest in the meaning and significance of the works of art and to initiate an appreciation of the visual arts. Through picture study the child becomes familiar with the art elements—value, form, line, space, light, and color—in a very elementary way by observing these elements in the reproductions. An audio-visual library and projection equipment in each school aid in the enrichment of this phase of the program.

The evaluation of the child's progress within the program is not on

---

[6] Statement prepared by Mary Dell Burford, Elementary Art Supervisor.

the basis of his finished product but rather by his growth in art experiences, his enjoyment of the art period, and the development of taste and good selection in the choices he makes day after day.

In order to provide the classes with a variety of stimulating experiences, and to help the individual teacher in making up a particular program for her group, the art supervisor provides each teacher with a flexible program of tangible methods and techniques. These methods, all of which employ readily available materials, might include field trips, assigned topics, the use of real objects, pictures, natural phenomena, community and world events, music, and similar approaches. Naturally, every attempt is made to correlate the child's art program with his other school subjects.

Normally the art supervisor visits each classroom once each six weeks for observation and demonstrations. In order to give the teachers more help, scheduled conferences and voluntary clinics are held throughout the school year. The conferences are usually conducted by the teachers themselves. A typical conference was based on Elise Boylston's *Creative Expression with Crayons*. Several teachers on each grade level selected one of the crayon techniques suggested by Miss Boylston, taught this method to her students, and then showed examples of the selected crayon technique to the conference, explaining how she had made the presentation to her class. Attendance at these meetings has indicated a real interest on the part of the teachers, and a desire for additional help.

AT THE SECONDARY LEVEL

At the junior-high level, exploration is offered all pupils through a required general arts course with follow-up work of two additional courses in the fine-arts area; while at the senior high school three years of art are offered on an elective basis.

The general philosophy of art recognizes that the purpose of art in the school curriculum is to help develop in the individual a wholesome personality, stimulate creative thinking through imagination and observation, and encourage active participation in community affairs. The child should have continuous creative art experiences from the time he enters first grade through high school. The fulfillment of art education is realized when it fosters the proper relationship of an individual to his fellow man, to his surroundings, and to God. With a basic knowledge of art principles and techniques a foundation is laid upon which the child can make sound judgments and develop keen observations and appreciations of beauty in nature and man-made things. Creative expression should carry through the many facets of school and adult life.

KANAWHA COUNTY, WEST VIRGINIA[7]

Kanawha County is one of the largest and most complex county-unit systems in the United States. Over an area of 914 square miles there are in operation 269 schools taught and administered by 1903 principals and teachers who have under their control approximately 54,000 students. The county transports more than 20,000 children daily to consolidated schools on 102 buses which are owned and. operated by the county school system.

According to national recommendations, Kanawha County is short of supervisors. There is one superintendent, one administrative assistant, six assistant superintendents in charge of certain divisions, and eight supervisors of instruction—the supervisors of nutrition (hot lunch), audio-visual education, vocal music, instrumental music, industrial arts, rural education, and two employed as directors of instruction in the area—grades 1 through 12. These two directors were formerly supervisors of reading and art. Therefore, there is no supervisor of art, as such, for this large system. *The directors of instruction believe that reading and art should permeate all areas of instruction.* There are 23 art teachers in the secondary schools.

Good things in art are happening. Just as the classroom teacher should inspire the children and lend enthusiasm, so the supervisor (or director) should guide and help the teachers. She is on call and gives help when and where needed as far as time will permit.

The springboard for good art practices has been the Kanawha County Art Association. This started about six years ago with a group of teachers who expressed a desire to meet and work together. The supervisor called the meeting. Now this group is over 300 strong. Monthly meetings of an instructional nature are held. The group sponsors art workshops, with members volunteering to work with groups of fifty other teachers. It has been the practice to sponsor workshops given by commercial edu-

---

[7] Statement prepared by Gratia Bailey Groves, Director of Instruction.

cators and to close the year with a four-day spring workshop in which eight teachers each take one area of art instruction, with fifty teachers in each section. Teachers may attend one or all eight sections but must enroll in advance. In this way art in-service help has been given to at least 600 teachers each year and there is always a waiting list.

Another development this past year has been the forming of an Art In-Service Bureau. Twenty-three teachers, both elementary and secondary, have volunteered to go to other schools or community centers to hold workshop sessions with faculties and community workers. A seventh-grade printing class printed an explanatory folder. There is a separate sheet for each worker with his or her picture, educational qualifications, description of work he volunteers to do, etc. All principals have this folder and can call on these people for help.

There are five schools this year working as art-curriculum-center schools. These five schools have 56 teachers. They have developed a philosophy of art for these schools, also general and specific objectives, and are writing successful units showing the part that art played in the unit. They are likewise writing other successful art experiences. Next year these materials will be passed on to other schools which choose to work with the five original schools in the art curriculum. They will try out and add to this material or objectives in their own way. This curriculum work is going forward in 49 schools in the area of art, reading, health, language, science, mathematics, social studies, and music. Next year 58 more schools will be involved. Art is playing a big part in all areas of curriculum. For example, the schools working in the area of social studies find art indispensable for murals, charts, posters, picture maps, and three-dimensional construction.

A program of long standing in Kanawha County has been our *Musical Pictures* radio program. It is sponsored by the Junior League over station WGKV in Charleston. The purpose is to inspire creative art and creative writing through music. A Junior Radio Board of approximately twenty people includes Junior League members, principals, and teachers. They write their own scripts for broadcasts. Art and writing selected by the participating schools are displayed in an exhibit at the Diamond Department Store each year and are of much interest to the public.

The Scholastic Art Awards Exhibit is held each February. Many West Virginia students have been helped through scholarships. The growth in understanding of art concepts the past seven years has been evident from the work submitted. Scholastics has not been a goal in itself, but having work displayed has been a great inspiration for accomplishment in the regular art curriculum.

Regardless of one's situation, he can have promising art practices. Growth is slow but sure if he has the initiative to plan, to work, and to share; but above all he must help his teachers to develop an art philosophy which is their own and which is in keeping with the needs of our youth today.

KANSAS CITY, MISSOURI[8]

Art is more than making pictures and objects. It is more than enjoying the selected examples in museums and galleries.

Art is experience that touches every phase of life, experience with beauty—beauty of form, color, sound, rhythm, language, even of flavor and odor.

Response to art influences man intellectually, emotionally, spiritually. It influences the arrangement of his mantelpiece, the clothes he wears, the book he chooses, the fun and recreation he seeks, the kind of citizen he is, the ideals toward which he works.

Art is integrated with the cultural and social forces by which men live and die. It enriches and enhances life, making it worth the struggle.

Art, being tangible, sincere, and of the people, is a means of friendship and understanding between countries.

Art has a broad and integrated field and plays a vital role in democratic living. Thus, emphasis in our schools is placed on the development of sound thinking, sincere appreciation, creative effort, resourcefulness, and good taste in those areas of life in which the child is most likely to find his day-to-day living.

By art appreciation is meant knowledge of and response to both the fine and functional arts. Art appreciation is not apart from life itself but is integrated with daily living. When children place books neatly on a library table, pick up unsightly scraps, put together a pleasing flower arrangement, or discover that even surroundings at home can sometimes be made more attractive with a little thought and effort spent

---

[8] Statement prepared by Rosemary Beymer, Director of Art Education.

in the cause of orderliness and beauty, they show growth in art appreciation. To give the child experiences that will add to his knowledge and increase his enjoyment of art, the school takes care to:

1. See that the buildings and rooms are such that a child can grow in aesthetic responses.
2. Give him opportunity to participate in many kinds of art activities, because his appreciations have to be built upon a realistic and emotional basis.
3. Let him have firsthand experiences seeing, feeling, and discussing objects of art. These give enjoyment and build standards.
4. Teach enough simple art techniques to enable children to work with confidence.
5. Allow sincere, free response from children, emotionally as well as intellectually. Appeal to the eye is not a whole experience for a child; he has to bring emotion and language into the situation.

LIVINGSTON, NEW JERSEY[9]

ELEMENTARY SCHOOLS

We have always realized that if the scope of the program and if the art work is to progress, it must have the full coöperation of all the teachers, principals, and custodians.

We are particularly interested in providing for every child a large number of experiences with water colors, crayons, clay, paper, and other materials that call for manipulation and control. The basic subject matter, of course, grows out of the environment: figures in action, trees, houses, and simple items that children are able to fit into the pattern.

Developing interest in all of life is a major purpose. But even more important is to help create and develop in the child the awareness and the joy and satisfaction that come with creative expression and in coöperative group working and sharing.

Without the power to observe and to use that observation, without proper muscular coördination and manipulative control, all else is impossible. Whenever possible, we tie in the kinesthetic experiences of the art work, using the arms and body to parallel lines of direction and shapes which the children observe in their conscious activities, such as the walking trips we often take.

---

[9] Statement prepared by Margaret LaMorte, Supervisor of Art.

Two of the best experiences for the greatest number of children during the recent past were:

1. The Flower Show, in which the whole school-community effort fell into a beautiful, natural pattern of working, learning, and having fun together.
2. The coöperative development of the farm and community projects by two first-grade teachers. The remarkable construction of the farm and of a typical large market were worth-while experiences. The trips for purchasing and visiting and the interesting art work that resulted served as further stimulation for activity in art.

The evaluation by the children at Central School was a revelation. They decided that the winning of a ribbon at the Flower Show was not important in comparison to the fun they all had in making their own arrangements and in sharing.

Because children aim to please furnishes a natural form of motivation and, invariably, they succeed. Such was the case with the class that assumed responsibility for designing and making scenery for the Music Festival. This and other instances are continually coming up to make one aware that this method is worth while. It is evident that teachers are constantly developing their own rich background, and their growth and appreciation are the source on which the children build.

Teachers and coördinators try to develop something *special* in each building. Activities along this line are Christmas scenery in Roosevelt and Harrison Buildings, the Flower Show at Central, and the making of place mats for the Old Folks' Home and work for the Red Cross at Squiretown.

Next year, we are anxious to develop a series of workshops for teachers in order to help them with specific problems and in their understanding of the art program.

JUNIOR HIGH SCHOOL

We believe that being a "teen-ager" is particularly difficult, and that frequently the problem of growing up can assume overwhelming proportions. We believe sincerely that successful living is based upon personal integrity, a sense of responsibility, understanding, and coöperation. Therefore, a wide variety of classroom procedures are used to try to help individuals locate their particular niche and interest. The aims of our program at this level are these:

1. The development of greater awareness of the beauty which continually surrounds our lives; to broaden and enrich our experiences by opening our eyes to the well-designed and the lovely.
2. To coördinate awareness with keener observation.
3. To develop discrimination in selection.
4. To correlate observation with control and coördination.
5. To offer opportunity for expression in as many media as possible.
6. To encourage group work; to face problems and make decisions.
7. To stimulate active participation.
8. To stimulate and develop special art abilities.
9. To develop proper attitude toward self-discipline.
10. To offer young people pleasant, satisfactory, creative experiences in art.

Some methods used in achieving our aims are described below.

1. *Class discussions:* to locate and clarify the interest; to make available the "fine" and beautiful which might be unfamiliar and thus not understood; to stimulate thinking as part of and before a creative experience; to create a warm, satisfying relationship between teacher and pupil; to give opportunity for word expression and terminology experience as well as creative expression.
2. *Group work:* arrangement and selection of paintings to decorate the halls of the buildings; bulletin-board arrangements; scenery painting, stage construction, stage make-up, three-dimensional displays; cleaning and caring for equipment; making props for the various assembly programs; contributions to community groups and agencies.
3. *Individual contributions to the community:* Halloween windows; Poppy Day posters; decoration of bags for the Red Cross.
4. *Use of visual aids with discussion:* movies on various media; successful commercial posters; art magazines and books; displays of the work of some successful young artists from the initial layout through printed material or completed paintings; demonstration in oil painting of snowscape from art-room window, pointing up artists' prerogative of selection and deletion for purposes of beauty or composition.
5. *Research* in areas that tie art with home and life experience: interior decoration; clothing; color; theater.
6. *Experimentation:* awareness of design through experimentation with materials and with art elements and principles.
7. *Educational excursions:* planned museum visits; trips through town to identify architectural types; sketching trip to Flower Show; backstage visit to a theater; and other similar journeys.

Following the activities listed above, classes did critical written evaluations from which thoughtful suggestions for art work were gathered.

One of the strong beliefs we hold is to give all pupils opportunity to work with a wide range of materials: colored chalk, charcoal, crayon, tempera paint, water color, and oil. All should have experience in drawing from nature out of doors or through the art-room windows; working from the posed figure in action, from still-life, and imaginative expression. The many crafts are also made available and in the same spirit as the graphic experiences.

MINNEAPOLIS, MINNESOTA[10]

The philosophy that governs the art program in the schools of Minneapolis is expressed in a unique manner: art as it affects or reflects the needs of pupils, parents, and the community.

OUR PUPILS

. . . respond to an aesthetically pleasant and permissive atmosphere.

. . . need opportunities to communicate their experiences, ideas, feelings and concerns.

. . . crave experiences that encourage exploration, responsibility, and independent thinking.

. . . want teacher and peer acceptance, support, stimulation, guidance, praise, and respect.

. . . need to discover their own personal growth, interests, and capacities.

. . . like to see, feel, arrange, collect, express, and imagine.

. . . desire group activity as well as individual activity.

. . . have a variety of needs, interests, and capacities.

. . . desire success, satisfaction, and a sense of belonging.

OUR PARENTS

. . . recognize that art fulfills a basic human need.

. . . realize that all pupils have innate creative abilities.

. . . understand that pupils think and create differently than adults.

. . . see evidence of pupils' artistic abilities by work done in school as well as at home.

---

[10] This statement, reproduced by permission of Dr. Del Dosso, Director of Art, is in the form of an attractively designed folder.

. . . accept and encourage the pupils' independent thinking and solutions.

. . . encourage work and play experiences within the home.

. . . know that art can help to maintain natural creativity, resourcefulness, and sympathetic understanding.

. . . understand that art is personal rather than imitative.

. . . understand that the manipulation of art materials can foster physical, mental, social, and emotional development.

. . . like to see pupils' development and growth.

. . . enjoy pupils' work.

. . . know that art encompasses architecture, painting, sculpture, clothing, machine-made and handmade crafts.

. . . realize that discriminate tastes make everyday living more pleasant and convenient.

. . . realize the value of creative powers in adult life.

. . . know that beauty can bring spiritual uplift.

OUR COMMUNITY

. . . has many cultural resources.

. . . understands the importance of wholesome leisure-time activities.

. . . lives and worships within many fine examples of contemporary architecture.

. . . provides space for exhibits and opportunities for pupils to see, use, understand, and appreciate.

. . . has shops that handle contemporary man-made and machine-made forms.

. . . has much surrounding natural beauty and wildlife in parks, lakes, farms, and countrysides.

. . . sees pupils' experiences reflected in visual expression.

IN OUR SCHOOLS ART ACTIVITIES

. . . are based upon the pupils' needs, interests, and capacities.

. . . utilize the actual, imaginative, and vicarious experiences of pupils to stimulate individual thinking and resourcefulness.

. . . challenge explorative and creative powers by providing experiences in many two-and three-dimensional media.

. . . are based primarily on personal self-expression, but they also motivate appreciation, awareness, and sensitivity toward nature and man-made forms.

. . . provide pupils with the opportunity to achieve and enjoy success through participation in individual and group experiences.

. . . elevate self-esteem and self-confidence through pupil exhibitions, discussions, explorations, selections, and creations.

. . . encourage individuality through respectful praise of many ways of working and thinking.

. . . emphasize respect for machine and hand tools as well as a variety of media.

. . . help maintain open, flexible, and inquiring minds.

. . . help pupils to plan, discuss, and evaluate.

. . . help pupils to see, appreciate, understand, and apply.

. . . allow each pupil to set his own standard based on his capacities and progress.

. . . give teachers an opportunity to move among the pupils to give warm, friendly encouragement and praise.

. . . use family traditions, community resources, and our American heritage to vitalize the creative experience.

. . . accept flower and bulletin-board arrangement as art problems as well as the creation of a painting or sculpture.

. . . accept all pupils—the slow learners, the average, and the gifted.

. . . show that pupil growth is the important end product.

. . . belong to the pupils.

OKLAHOMA CITY, OKLAHOMA[11]

Belief in the inherent creativity of children is basic in the operations of the art department of the Oklahoma City public schools. And if creativity is inherent in children, then it must be a part of everyday living, of reactions to experiences, of associating and working with other people, and of developing all those innate individual powers which make life worthwhile.

In our elementary schools we no longer have specialists in art in each school, and so every classroom teacher is a potential art teacher. This presupposes, then, a continuing program of in-service education since

[11] Statement prepared by Grace Chadwick, Director of Art.

teachers, being human, cannot possibly possess a workable "know-how" in all subject areas; and after all, art education does require a teacher— an enthusiastic one, preferably, who believes in experimentation and in helping children develop and express *their* ideas and reactions to experiences in terms of form and color.

Generating belief in and enthusiasm for creative art expression on the part of the teacher becomes, then, a major issue in our elementary art-education program. Fortunately, we have three assistants in the elementary schools who go on call to help teachers with their art problems. They are booked solidly for weeks in advance. Teachers state the areas in which they want help, they know when the art assistant will be there, and they plan accordingly with their children. Schools love to have these assistants come. The confidence they inspire in teachers and children is of inestimable value. Our big problem is how adequately to serve a system the size of ours with so few assistants.

Our secondary schools, of course, have art teachers whose training enables them to guide adolescents in creative and appreciative activities in the space arts. These art departments operate with the idea of promoting art experiences for as many students as possible, offering opportunity for exploration and experimentation, and drawing inspiration from varied subject matters and life situations. Emphasis is placed upon acceptance of responsibility, development of taste and judgment, organization of ideas, emotional development of the individual student, and his relationship to the group at school, in the home, and in the community. For those with art career plans, an attempt is made to provide the basic needs for qualifying for subsequent training.

There are certain effective features of our art program which may be unique. We have just completed our third year of *Creative Crafts*, a thirty-minute weekly television program broadcast by WKY-TV over Channel 4. It is a public-service program produced by the Art Department of the Oklahoma City public schools and the Community Workshop of the Oklahoma City libraries. Scheduled on Saturday mornings, it is beamed directly to children in their homes, not only in Oklahoma City, but all over the state and sections of adjoining states.

A teacher who is doing good creative work in some chosen area assumes responsibility for a program. She produces a worksheet and trains the children for the presentation. The idea is to illustrate a number of ways of doing the craft, and then to suggest that "you try it your way." Over 500 worksheets are sent out on request each week by the Community Workshop. The effectiveness of the program in our own school system is very rewarding.

Artists Are People is an effective fifteen-minute weekly radio program prepared by a teacher and her group of children and broadcast over our school radio station KOKH-FM. It is usually biographical and in dialogue form.

At the Jefferson Building, our instructional center, we keep continuing exhibits of crafts and murals done in our schools.

At Inverness-Boyd Museum and Institute of Art, which is an old apartment house converted into a school museum and work center, we keep a continuous exhibit of the individual paintings and drawings of children in our schools.

OAK RIDGE, TENNESSEE[12]

Art education at Highland View Elementary School in Oak Ridge, Tennessee, is a composite of several circumscribing factors. The large enrollment of between 800 and 900, with 25 different class groups on six grade levels, has made periodic allocation of time one of the most limiting factors affecting the art program. The concept of the art teacher as a special teacher provides further limitation; notwithstanding the situation or circumstance, a genuinely creative art program can be had if the correct approach is employed.

In ascertaining that approach it is essential to determine what art is supposed to do for the child that no other subject can do. There are many overlapping contributions to child development when all the forces at work play upon him. But art plays a singular part when considered from the standpoint of a mode of expression through material. It seems that one of the most basic needs of life is the urge to express oneself and the accompanying need for acceptance, which is, in short, success. There are many avenues; some "say it with flowers," as the expression goes. Some use poetry, and all the various means of conveying ideas and concepts ensure success for all in some manner or other. Art provides an avenue of expression through material with acceptance for all in varying degrees of success depending upon aptitude and ability.

Consequently, an art program should provide a wide variety of ac-

---

[12] Statement prepared by George Wilson, Art Instructor.

620 tivities, experiences, and/or materials to meet the varied individual likes and dislikes within a group. Coupled with this concept is the dual pur-pose of also providing frequent exposure to the same media and ma-terial to develop facility or competency to achieve success. How often one hears the saying, "I know what I want to say but I don't know how to say it." A happy medium must be found between these two concepts.

However, it is not enough just to express oneself. There must be some-thing to say. It has been the author's personal experience in more ways than one that when once he has an idea or knows what he wants to say the rest seems relegated to a minor (though still important) role. Where do we get our idea for the things we do in art? Things we do, things we see, and things that happen to us. These form the subject matter for modeling, painting, etc.

These take in all the experiences that children have, which brings us to perhaps the most important aspect of the correct approach. There is a sense in which each child or individual conforms to the norm or to the group pattern. But there is also a counteracting force of self-selecting that is essential in the cycle of expressing and accepting necessary to success and the maintenance of the ego. There is a fine balance between imposition on the part of the adult and self-determination on the part of the child.

It is the responsibility of an art program to provide opportunity for adequate self-selecting or self-determining on the part of the child in all his experience through materials. The correct approach involves maxi-mum child participation on all stages of the process, from planning to evaluating—with adequate time, guidance, working space, and material to achieve maximum success for each child. Each activity and program should be evaluated on the basis of how far in this direction the particular activity is taking the individual and the group.

PITTSBURGH, PENNSYLVANIA[13]

The Foreword to the *Guide to Art Activities* in the Pittsburgh public schools, prepared by a committee of teachers and supervisors, states that the *Guide* is "based on an analysis of the child at each maturation level, his interests and his needs, both personal and social."

It further states that ideally the art activity grows out of teacher-

---

[13] Statement prepared by Mary Adeline McKibbin, Director of Art Education.

pupil planning in response to real needs. It is the obligation of the teacher to make children aware of needs not readily sensed, and continually to broaden their interests. Instead of following a set course of study, art activities in Pittsburgh develop in response to interests and needs, the scope and sequence of such art activities being determined by pupil-teacher identification of ways to satisfy those needs.

To care for children's individual differences, they are introduced to a variety of art media, both two- and three-dimensional, and encouraged to explore their possibilities. From kindergarten through twelfth grade this exploratory, creative attitude is encouraged. The quality of the child's experience is always considered more important than the quality of the art produced.

Art education is concerned both with the maximum development of the individual and with his adjustment to the social pattern of which he is an integral part. Use, therefore, is made of community resources— from zoos and supermarkets, planetarium and conservatories, community-development projects and the Arts and Crafts Center, to the Carnegie Institute and the International Art Exhibitions.

We plan art activities for all children, not for the talented few, for we believe that all human beings have a need for some form of creative expression. Art experiences, because they offer direct contacts with color, form, and texture, bring sensory response, develop sensitivity to these elements as they exist everywhere in life, and thus become sources of constant revelation and pleasure. Appreciation itself becomes a creative experience.

Coöperation rather than competition is characteristic of art activities. Children working together learn to value human differences and to appreciate the unique contribution of each to the group. Because of the informal atmosphere in the art class, tensions are resolved; individual self-control supplants imposed discipline. The good art teacher maintains a free but challenging classroom atmosphere.

We do not in Pittsburgh subscribe to a laissez-faire attitude toward art experiences; nor do we endorse teacher dictatorship, however well intentioned. Dictatorship is fatal to creativity; no leadership invites frustration.

Teachers, therefore, assume the role of democratic leadership. They attempt to understand child development and to consider the child's art product as evidence of growth at the child's own level.

They believe that sincere expression is more desirable than technical perfection or unfeeling documentation.

Good teachers promote the desire to use art materials creatively by furnishing challenging experiences and sensitizing children visually and emotionally to the possibilities for art expression inherent in these experiences.

They acquaint children with a variety of media, guide them in the use of materials, and help them acquire those skills for which children at any stage of their development sense the need.

Development of skills and understandings, however, represents only a part of the total development of the individual. There should be growth in the individual's capacities for satisfying self-expression and communication; increasing functional application of art values to control of the environment; an ever fuller understanding of the self and society.

This we believe and, in part, practice. Art is "for all" through the eighth grade. In grades 9–12 it is an elective, but, as such, is scheduled five periods a week and carries regular credit toward graduation. Not more than 25 percent of any high-school student body elects art. In large high schools there are specially equipped metalcrafts and ceramics rooms, as well as general art rooms. New junior-high-school art rooms are all-purpose studios, equipped for all types of two- and three-dimensional work.

Intermediate grades (4–6) in large elementary schools have art-trained teachers and fairly well-equipped art rooms.

Art activities in the primary grades are the responsibility of the classroom teacher, who, of course, has access to the art supervisor in the district. These teachers have responded enthusiastically to help in inservice workshops conducted by art supervisors.

As everywhere, the success or failure of an art program depends upon the teacher—his interest, his eagerness for growth, his understanding of both the child and art processes. We are fortunate in Pittsburgh in having a fine group of art teachers.

RICHMOND, VIRGINIA[14]

We have art in Richmond, for where there are children there is art. Children, teacher, and communities differ—so also do art experiences.

---

[14] Statement prepared by Helen Cynthia Rose, Supervisor of Art Education.

Our program provides the 35,000 children in Richmond schools with art experiences emphasizing:

Art for Good Living (at home, at school, and in the community)
Creating more attractive surroundings.
Developing a taste for good design in the things we see and use every day.
Acquiring a knowledge of our culture, past and present, so that we may be better able to appreciate and understand the art in our own lives and community.
Art for the Individual
Realizing emotional and moral satisfactions through the creative experience.
Developing skills and interests leading to hobbies and vocations through participation in the visual arts.
Art for the School Program
Giving the child an understanding of the world of which he is a vital part.
Helping the child to organize other areas of learning—science, history, geography, music, mathematics, physical education, and dramatics—in a visual, creative manner.

ANSWERS TO QUESTIONS

Is the elementary classroom teacher or the art teacher responsible for providing the child with art opportunities?

Both. Art teacher, classroom teacher, and children plan together. The art teacher works with the group in the activity for which it most needs his specialized help and the classroom teacher carries on the art program, which has been coöperatively planned on a long-range scale.

How does the elementary art consultant work, and what does he do?

He works best for the greatest number of people with a combination regular and "on call" schedule. This enables him to see all teachers and children periodically, and allows time to do the things requested of him when most needed.

The art consultant initiates long-range planning with the teacher, suggesting possible art activities; introduces new materials; keeps teachers informed of available visual material; initiates workshops for teachers and parents, arranges exhibitions; acts as adviser on bulletin-board and corridor displays; works with groups on scenery, props, and costumes for classroom and assembly performances; interprets the program to

624   P.T.A. and faculty groups; and helps all with whom he comes in contact to understand child characteristics in art.

How can art be available for all children on the secondary level?

Courses are offered which appeal to all students. Incorporated in these courses can be art for the consumer, specialized art, "hobby" art, art and culture, and the humanities and art. Exhibitions are displayed in the main corridors of schools from museums, local artists, and students.

Art study and art services may be a period for students who are or are not enrolled in art to come from other classes to work on an art project, to work on illustrations for school publications, scenery and costumes for dramatic productions, and other school needs. The art teacher may go to other classrooms to contribute to the program through the field of art during this period.

Is a course of study necessary in art?

A guide of some kind is highly desirable in a school system of this size where art teachers change and teacher training varies. Richmond has had an ever-changing guide in art over the years. For the past two years Richmond teachers have been working on a revision which will provide for continuous growth in art from junior primary through high school, but will be flexible enough to incorporate the interests and abilities of the child; the stages of development; the needs of the home, school, and community; the relation of art to other areas of learning; and the cultural implications of art.

What is unique and helpful about Richmond's art department?

We are particularly proud of the use by approximately 1100 teachers each year of the 1200 items, other than prints, available for loan through our department. These materials consist of books, folders, slides, exhibitions, display boards, textiles, posters, magazines, and prints.

In addition, over 36,000 children see exhibitions in their schools from the Virginia Museum each year. This is arranged by scheduling three exhibitions each month to as many as 12 schools. Our schools also use about 250 exhibitions from the Valentine Museum each year and 25,000 children enjoy them. The Richmond schools provide bus service and classes go continually to see exhibitions at both museums. The Valentine Museum sponsors a biennial show of our children's work of six weeks' duration.

What does the art supervisor do?

I have been asked to list the type of work which the art supervisor does. This seems a dull subject to anyone other than an art supervisor until it is realized that this work must be carried on by someone. Whether there is an art supervisor who is highly trained with experience on all grade levels or not, the size of the school system determines the need for one.

An art supervisor:

Is responsible for the quality of the art teaching of elementary classroom teachers, art teachers, and resource-room teachers.

Develops art curriculum with teachers and principals on all levels to provide continuous guidance for the child in art, relating it to other areas of learning.

Initiates in-service training program in art for elementary classroom teachers, art teachers, and resource-room teachers.

Interprets and stimulates the art program through faculty and P.T.A. meetings, speeches to community groups, exhibitions, newspaper publicity, and art bulletins.

Acts as museum coördinator in arranging traveling exhibitions, children's museum attendance, informing schools of offerings of the museum, and arranging museum workshops (Virginia Museum).

Supervises the development of visual loan material and its distribution.

Is responsible for art-room plans, furniture, and equipment planning and ordering for all schools.

Develops all art supply lists, consolidates orders, selects bids on large orders, keeps books on junior- and senior-high teacher allotments, and is a "coördinator" for distribution of supplies from warehouse.

SPECIAL FEATURES

Visual Materials

The Richmond schools have circulated three exhibitions from the Virginia Museum to as many as 12 schools each month, and as a result approximately 35,000 children have seen these exhibitions during the year.

The Valentine Museum has circulated 251 exhibitions to our schools and 25,848 children have seen them.

Children have enjoyed the exhibitions at the Virginia Museum. The Scandinavian show was considered particularly valuable for children, with 1190 attending.

Approximately 1100 teachers have used the 1200 items of visual materials, not including prints, which the Art Department has available for loan.

The Valentine Museum held the biennial exhibition "School Art on Parade" of the art work of children, September 23 through November 1, to which 3392 parents, children, teachers, and administrators came.

Exhibitions of student work have been held in the majority of the schools. Richmond students participated in the Junior Red Cross International School Art Program and an exhibition of the work was on display at Miller and Rhoads for one week in May.

Workshops

Workshops for teachers have been numerous this year. Many have been held on clay and glazes, Christmas, evaluation of the art program in individual schools, beautification of the school, better room arrangements, and various materials.

The Virginia Museum carried on a workshop for the "Better Use of Museum Materials," which fifty of our teachers attended.

Curriculum

The secondary art teachers of the city are working on a revision of curriculum material in staff meetings. Much of this material is being incorporated in the new state art guide for secondary schools. The elementary teachers have developed a bulletin, *Clay and Kiln in Your School,* and have produced innumerable visual aids this year.

Plans, Furniture, and Equipment

Plans for resource rooms and secondary-school art rooms have been developed. Furniture has been designed by the Art Department and produced by the state penitentiary. There are now thirty kilns being used in our schools.

Participation on State and National Levels

The Art Supervisor has been active as the representative of the National Art Education Association at the annual elementary-education conference in Washington, chairman of the Art Guide for the Art Section of VEA, chairman of the Curriculum Materials Committee of Southeastern Arts, member of the same committee for NAEA, and member of committees on articulation and teacher load in the city.

RIO VISTA, CALIFORNIA[15]

Rio Vista Joint Union High School has an enrollment of 230 young people, in a community of 2000, in a rich rural area seventy miles northeast of San Francisco. The area is self-sufficient to the extent of not even caring for city advantages or influences. Six big school buses carry two-thirds of the students on long daily commutes. This means that there can be almost no after-school activity.

In a staff of 22 teachers, there is one full-time art teacher. Crafts are taught as a part of the homemaking department. There are five art classes a day. One of these is reserved for third- and fourth-year art students. The other four classes are open to any student without prerequisite. These classes are held on the workshop idea. Sometimes as many as four activities are taking place simultaneously. The course of study has never been identical any two of the past 25 years, as the activities are planned to fit the interests and abilities of the students. Every student in high school is urged to take one year of art at some time during his four years, but it is not compulsory.

Freedom of expression is encouraged. As students show a need for basic drawing and a knowledge of structure, a group will work together for a few weeks on basic forms. Just as rapidly as the student shows some proficiency he moves on to another activity. Stragglers also progress, but into less-demanding mediums.

Over a four-year period students have an opportunity to participate in individual and group projects. Among the group activities are:

1. Murals for use at school or at the state or county fairs.
2. Puppets and or marionettes used at local organizations and on school exchange programs.
3. Stage settings for school musical and theatrical productions.
4. Art work for the school annual.
5. Illuminated cathedral-size "stained glass" windows as a backdrop for the Christmas concert.
6. School, class, and organization dance decorations.
7. Local-store Christmas decorations, for which students are paid.
8. A group trip once a year to either a Sacramento or San Francisco art museum. The museum trip also includes a look at store windows and store decorations.

---

[15] Statement prepared by Idella Church, Art Director.

Individual activities include:

1. Freehand sketching or designing while listening to music to establish the relation of form to sound and color.
2. Movement of abstract forms through space, both two- and three-dimensional.
3. Decorative designs: form, texture, and pattern.
4. Freehand brush drawing: form, line, and texture.
5. Lettering, posters, linoleum-block printing.
6. Pen and ink rendering.
7. Oil painting.
8. Crayon and/or water-color nature sketches: flower and animal forms.
9. All students attempt to paint a portrait for character studies.
10. Silk screen.
11. Three-dimensional work includes wire and paper sculpture, masks.

Each year there is one unit activity for all students on some period in the history of art. Each student reports orally to the class with an illustrated talk on the life and achievements of a recognized artist. In this manner a student who elects art for four years has a pretty fair view of the "masters," old and modern.

The general aims of the art classes are first of all to give students an opportunity for growth in art expression. Following that come developing skills in several art media to the end of hobby interests, and "creating for enjoyment." All classes at all times try to correlate art with good taste toward the end of a good shopping sense, and so that they will avoid shoddy and poorly designed merchandise.

The atmosphere of the art classes is organized, but students move about without unseemly confusion. With very few exceptions they enjoy their activities and usually produce something which they are interested in keeping. Unfortunately, the classes are the catchall for misfits from other school departments. Our aim is to give each child some experience in which he can succeed, show growth in performance, in appreciation, and have fun.

SEATTLE, WASHINGTON[16]

POINT OF VIEW

We have a planned program in art education because we believe it is a necessary part of a balanced education. We help children become more

---

[16] Statement prepared by Dale Goss, Director of Art Education.

inventive and resourceful so that they will become more confident of their own abilities and more able to express their ideas and feelings.

While there are many ways children learn to express themselves, in art we deal with the graphic processes of painting, drawing, constructing, modeling, and designing.

In addition to developing skill in graphic expression, we help children grow in aesthetic understanding and help them appreciate the values inherent in originality, simplicity, and tolerance.

CONDITIONS FOR ART EDUCATION

In best serving the creative interests of children we believe teachers and school administrators must recognize that every child is potentially a creative child, that every activity or experience is potential material for creative expression, that ways of expression are unimportant so long as they are within the range of children's abilities, and that the standards and values set must be within the range of the children's understanding and acceptance. Finally, we believe that techniques and skills must be adapted to the experiences and needs of the children and that, within the limits of the facilities, the children should participate in selecting their forms of expression.

ELEMENTARY ART EDUCATION

In the primary grades we develop skills in painting, modeling, and designing. Particular effort is made to stress originality and simplicity. The activities are closely integrated with the children's personal experience in and out of the classroom. At this level children are given experiences which will bring an awareness of color, space, and form.

During the intermediate years children expand their earlier design experiences with paper, paint, and scrap materials, but including design with wire, metal, fabrics, and wood among their activities. At the same time study is made which leads to a clearer understanding of such art elements as space, color, form, texture, and line. As the children's interest expand to include the community, the art projects allow expression of this interest.

When children leave our primary grades we assume that they will have gained a measure of confidence in their expressive powers, have acquired the beginning of a "graphic vocabulary," and come to accept art expression as a normal human activity. Upon leaving the elementary grades we trust that the children will have been successful in retaining their confidence, in increasing their expressive powers, in developing a tolerant attitude toward the creative efforts of other children, in broadening their aesthetic understanding, exploring the design potential of many materials, and in becoming awakened to the social and economic functions of art.

SECONDARY ART EDUCATION

The Junior High School

The junior high school encounters many problems related to child development and school organization not found in elementary schools. At the present time art education is required study for most children in the first half of grade 7 and the last half of grade 8. In the ninth year it is elected, but because of the requirements its availability to most children is remote.

In grade 7 we extend the objectives of the elementary schools and explore the place of art in our own community, including an introduction of its contributions to industry.

In grade 8 we teach more specific technical procedures and emphasize practical applications of the understandings acquired earlier. The aesthetic insecurity characteristic of adolescent youth can be reduced by specific design accomplishments with materials. We therefore include projects with the following materials: textiles, clay, light metals, and paper, and develop beginning skills in weaving, ceramics, jewelry, mobiles, gouache or water-color painting, silk-screen printing, and poster making. Included also in the eighth grade are activities leading to the understanding of art in America, with particular emphasis on a biographical study of selected contemporary artists.

Art students in grade 9 assume the major share of the art responsibility in the building. In this grade, therefore, we emphasize two aspects of our program. First, we encourage children to apply their skills and understandings to the everyday art requirements of their school. Second, we encourage them, in so far as time and facilities will allow, to advance their skills in one of the two- and one of the three-dimensional design areas.

Special attention is given to developing a more mature concept of design, composition, and color and to increasing drawing skills. Each child is encouraged to study the vocational aspects of a specific art area and to explore our community resources in this area.

Upon the completion of grade 9 we hope that the children will have continued to enjoy the discovery and invention of new processes, increased their mastery of drawing and design skills, broadened their understanding of color and composition, and recognized the extent to which art is a part of their everyday activities and those of other people throughout their community and nation.

Senior High School

The art-education classes in grades 10, 11, and 12 are elected. The students usually elect art because they have a vocational or an avocational interest. Most elect art in their eleventh or twelfth year.

Emphasis is placed on concrete application of design skills and understandings to everyday problems. Classes are formed in specific areas such as painting and drawing, commercial art, costume design and fashion illustration, ceramics, weaving, and sculpture.

Because of the differences in the students' backgrounds and experiences, effort is made to provide more individual instruction as well as more opportunity for pursuit of personal interests. Added to this are provisions for individual responsibility and leadership.

Nonetheless, coöperative activities in which two or three students work together are more a part of the general procedure than in earlier years.

Students are helped to understand the historical scope of art, its strands of development with their relationship to contemporary design. It is assumed, for example, that if students wish to make either a career or a hobby of art, they will understand the important influences which have preceded and molded the contemporary art of their particular interest. It is further assumed that they will learn the practical requirements, limits, and scope of their career area.

Because all students who take art in the high school can benefit from its avocational opportunities, we encourage exploration of one or more specific art areas in depth.

The attainments in art which we should expect from high-school graduates are difficult to state because of the relative uncertainty of a

632   continuous art program. Nevertheless, it is expected that students who come within the framework of an art program will develop sufficient skill, understanding, and interest in one or more areas to sustain them in continuous creative growth. Furthermore, it is expected that they will understand the broader influences on the contemporary arts and the specific influences on their areas of specialization.

STRATFORD, CONNECTICUT[17]

The pattern of art education to which we subscribe is creative and developmental. It uses many varied media and materials in a wide range of experiences appropriate to the level of the child.

This art program is developed at the elementary level by the classroom teacher with the guidance and help of an art resource person. At the junior-high level it is developed both in classrooms by classroom teachers and in art rooms by art specialists. At the senior-high-school level it is carried out entirely by art specialists.

ELEMENTARY LEVEL

The elementary classroom teacher makes the creative art experiences of the art program an integral part of the total program. Art activities are not superimposed upon other learning experiences; they are a part of them. Motivation, content, or inspiration for art projects develops out of whatever the child may be interested in or learning about at the time. It is easy and natural.

However, art education, as such, is not overlooked or neglected. Whatever the motivation for the art project, the necessary art learnings must be learned, and a line of continuity of learnings and experiences must be maintained if the art program is to remain successful past the primary levels.

A foundation of fundamental art skills and understandings is begun at an early level, and thereafter the growth and expansion of such skills and understandings in a continuous and continuing developmental process are a major objective of the art program.

The help of the resource person with specialized art training is essential to attain this objective, as well as the further objective of de-

---

[17] Statement prepared by Glen Ketchum Maresca, Supervisor of Art.

veloping a program of rich and varied interests and experiences, which will be and will continue to be satisfying to the needs of the child.

JUNIOR-HIGH LEVEL

In the junior high schools, all seventh- and eighth-grade pupils have classes in arts and crafts with art teachers. At the ninth grade such art classes become elective, but this is by no means the sum total of junior-high-school art experiences.

Art activities continue to be a very lively part of almost every classroom in the junior high schools. These are carried on under the guidance of classroom teachers with the advice and help of an art resource person when needed. Such art projects have a double value. They apply and utilize fundamentals and skills learned in the art room, and they bring an enriching interest and reality to the regular classroom work.

SENIOR-HIGH LEVEL

In the senior high school, art is entirely elective to a somewhat limited group and tends to become separated from the other subject areas.

We would like to see a definite program which would widen opportunities for integration of art appreciation, *with pupil participation,* in most of the other subject areas.

The possibilities for enrichment of subject matter in social studies, English, sciences, languages, and so on are far greater than is generally realized, and the potential value of such integration for the high-school-age youth remains generally unrecognized.

We are convinced that many problem areas in the senior high schools need never arise, and that they can be resolved through a more universal student participation in carefully and understandingly guided art projects, activities, and appreciation experiences.

TORONTO, CANADA[18]

In keeping with the philosophy of modern education, the art program in the schools of the city of Toronto is more concerned with the natural growth and development of the child than with formulas for art prod-

---

[18] Statement prepared by H. C. Dierlam, Supervisor of Art.

ucts. Through active participation in creative art activities, through exploration and experimentation with chosen media, sensitivity to art in everyday living is fostered. By providing experiences in group relationships an attitude of respect for the work of others is promoted with an awareness of the successes and limitations of the individual and the advantages of working coöperatively with others in a democratic society.

Believing that art experiences are essential to general education, art is a requisite for all children in the city up to and including grade 8 and is elective in subsequent grades. For the most part, where art is elective it is taught by an art specialist, but in other instances it is taught by the regular grade teacher.

The course of study in art for the elementary school and on the secondary level is not a prescribed course, but rather a teachers' guide to art activities to be used for reference in providing suitable art experiences for the various grades. A core of desirable outgrowths from the activities is suggested. The content is separated into certain areas for convenience of organization, but need not be followed specifically. Teachers are free to modify, adapt, or amplify the work in accordance to the varying interests and abilities of the pupils and in accordance with the needs of the local school situation. To plan a balanced program and provide for as wide a variety of art experiences as possible, it is suggested that teachers include both two- and three-dimensional activities, and that these should be related to the pupil's environment, the home, the school, and the community.

Since the Art Department is aware that teachers too have the capacity for growth and can profit by sharing experiences and thus become better teachers, their training in service is a regular feature, conducted in a specially designed and equipped studio-workshop. At this center exhibits of children's art of local, national, or foreign origin are on view at all times. In-service training includes teacher-pupil demonstrations, lectures by art educators, and "try your hand" classes, where teachers actively participate in creative art activities to gain firsthand knowledge of media and materials and processes which they propose to use with their pupils.

For teachers with a cultural interest in art and who wish to fraternize and meet socially with others of similar interests, an organization exists known as the Art Association of the Toronto Schools. For those who wish to develop some latent talent, a Sketch Club has been organized. Outdoor sketching trips are arranged from time to time, with special consideration for beginners and others who are more advanced. This organization has flourished for more than 15 years.

To make working conditions in the classroom more satisfactory for both teacher and pupils for carrying on a creative art program, one of the most recent developments in Toronto has been in art-room furniture. Realizing the need for adequate storage facilities and aware of lost space where conventional tables or desks are used, H. C. Dierlam designed the Art Room Sectional Furniture now used in many schools in city.

The unique feature of this furniture is that it can be used in any standard classroom as well as the special art room. It consists of three sections that are arranged in horseshoe fashion. Pupils sit on stools, or stand around the outside of the unit. Aisles are kept clear by moving the stools under the overhanging ledge of the furniture. Supplies for any particular activity are stored within the enclosure, which is fitted with deep shelves and drawers. Four such units will accomodate the average class. This furniture has proven very successful where several activities are engaged in at one time and many supplies and art materials are required. Traffic about the room has been reduced to a minimum and the clean-up period is more efficiently handled, with a great saving of time.

While noteworthy advances have been made in art education in Toronto, no feelings of self-sufficiency exist. There is an ever-searching spirit present that there is yet much to be accomplished, so that art might make its contribution to the development of well adjusted, happy, intelligent citizens through making the most of the abilities inherent in the children in our schools.

WALLKILL, NEW YORK[19]

An indirect way of injecting art is more effective. The child can apply art almost to everything he senses or experiences throughout his 12 years

---

[19] Statement prepared by Nuvart Bedrosian, Art Supervisor.

of school life. In this way art will prepare him to face life beyond schooldays and apply his knowledge of art to an artful living.

The art teacher can make the child aware of and sensitive to color, line, form, and organization, even in the early grades. This can be done in a simple way, without recourse to professional expressions and words. As the child grows according to his ability, this philosophy can be widened, each year, a little closer to natural expressions and techniques. The applications should include those on paper and in three-dimensional forms. No doubt these experiences will make children aware of how art touches their everyday life and will guide them constantly through the creative process. In the earlier school years this happens through emotional expression; in the higher grades inspiration can be motivated through informational guidance rather than copying habits.

However, whatever children learn, they should learn to apply to their everyday life. Very few can be artists, but all can live an artful life by interpreting the world around them by means of art which they experience during their school life.

ELEMENTARY ART EDUCATION

When the sense of color is developed from early childhood and children are constantly made aware that they are using their colors beautifully, they will have no difficulty later on, during the troubled adolescent period, in using color and design as an emotional outlet. While the child paints, very indirectly he learns what the basic or important colors are. Children express real excitement when they mix red, yellow, and blue, and when they discover the black. The same applies to the discovery of the secondary colors. They compare the mixed colors with the colors they have in their crayon boxes and actually sense that their mixed colors are brighter; this excitement increases when they actually experience it as they paint their pictures.

Materials growing out of the life of the child, especially the use of those experiences that are so vital and real to him, constitute the organized body of creative and appreciative experience of our elementary pupils.

This is religiously done by all our elementary teachers, not by dictated, general concepts, but through personal experience, and by making students sensitive to aesthetic values.

SECONDARY ART EDUCATION

The interests of junior-high students can be aroused by making them aware of the different arts that exist in life. Their interests can be easily aroused in works of architecture, sculpture, pottery, painting, industrial design, and advertising. These build in them a good foundation for their own experiment in color, form, and unity, which later forms the basis of the senior-high-school art expressions. In both stages the individual is important.

In all art expressions, good design is emphasized through significant information and activity experiences. Students should discuss intelligently the significance of art products, should learn how to choose, how to combine and arrange objects artistically, and how to paint artistic arrangements.

The historic developments are important to emphasize, because these often have recreational possibilities. It is important that children study man and his pattern of thought, its relationship with art and religions that create a way of living, and the fact that this living is a design and that design is life. This is an important phase to emphasize in the senior-high-school art program. Besides, because our human body is a monumental design itself, both inwardly and outwardly, we like to learn and live and create such forms of art as architecture, art for industry, art for the movies, fashion, window displays, art for magazines, art for interiors. And all these constitute the art of living.

SPECIAL FEATURES

1. As slides are rather expensive and our school cannot afford to buy them, we are preparing colored slides by photographing reproductions of world masterpieces and industrial designs. In addition to using them for regular class work, we make use of these in adult-education classes and our community groups. The Art Club helps to mount them, which is a good experience.

2. We have a new modern bank. Students decorate its windows during Christmas holidays with modern designs. We do the same for one of our grocery stores that has been renovated recently.

3. For our Open House, the advanced students exhibit their work in the art room. This helps them to learn how to display things in three-dimensional ways and also how to use wall space aesthetically.

4. Our sixth-graders made a mural painting. At the center of the given space they placed the Acropolis, at the right the Lincoln Memorial in Washington, D.C., and on the left their own Dutch Reformed Church, a classical structure over a century old. The entire class was excited and every day children brought to their classroom teachers examples of American buildings showing Doric, Ionic, and Corinthian columns. This is an example of awareness that leads to understanding of the heritage.

5. We join the Art Festival at the New York State University at New Paltz, New York. Each student's work of art is recognized by the awarding of certificates. This is a much more effective way than the contest idea of winning prizes.

WASHINGTON, PENNSYLVANIA[20]

Art appreciation, in its broadest sense, seems to me to be the first consideration in art education today. Students at all levels should become more aware of things of art and of beauty in their everyday lives. Life can become more meaningful and exciting when the beauty of nature and the creations of man begin to interest them. Through this awareness—whether it be of nature, fine paintings, architecture, outstanding illustration, industrial design, or whatever—combined with guidance by art educators, students can develop better taste, become better consumers of commercial products, and gain greater enjoyment from living.

The actual art activities used to develop this appreciation or awareness should be so planned that the student learns to *think*. Currently we say these activities must be creative, which to me means simply to think. Having the student reason out problems is more important than the finished project itself.

In the realization that students have a wide range of abilities, problems in both two and three dimensions should be presented. This variety of problems is helpful since some success is essential to continued interest as well as to help the student maintain his self-confidence.

---

[20] Statement prepared by John Grossman, Art Supervisor (now in Bethlehem, Pennsylvania).

ELEMENTARY ART EDUCATION

The integration of art with other subjects is an important function of art education at the elementary level. More interest and better understanding result from coupling of picture making, models, etc., with academic subjects.

Other phases of elementary art should include activities which more directly promote awareness and thought, mentioned earlier, through more abstract activities and those which do not tie in directly with other subjects. Study of fine art and emphasis on everyday art and design can begin at an early age. Provisions should be made for individual and group activities, and work should be keyed to child abilities so that reasonable success will result.

SECONDARY ART EDUCATION

Integration of art with other subjects can be encouraged, but is more difficult since groups are not in self-contained classrooms.

A wide variety of media and technique should be presented. With these as tools, problems in color and design—more abstract concepts— can be carried on. It is also desirable to have more practical final products in some cases, such as leather goods, paintings, and ceramic pieces.

Service to the school and community can be a part of the program, although the art department should not become a sign shop. Poster and other contests should be on an optional basis rather than a requirement.

The student who is interested in art as a career should be given every encouragement possible. The overall program should be one of helping young people learn to appreciate art and beauty. This may lead the student to an avocation, but, more important, should stimulate his interest in the world around life.

SPECIAL FEATURES

This year a bulletin called the *Art Co-op* was initiated. The art supervisor and the vocal and instrumental music supervisors all contribute material, which is then passed along to all elementary teachers. By this means, items of city-wide interest are quickly made known and policies can be set forth without hard-to-plan teachers' meetings.

When the county held its institute in our school, which is an independent district, our art department arranged an art meeting for the county teachers. This has since resulted in the forming of a county art organization as well as in furthering good relations between the city and county schools.

Rather than providing many signs as our contribution to the community, we have constructed and painted a large Christmas scene for all to enjoy, are presently working on four large murals for the Y.M.C.A., and generally try to make our presence known by more worth-while activities. A Halloween window-painting contest and better-quality play and dance scenery and decorations have brought art into the public eye.

INDEXES

INDEX OF NAMES

INDEX OF SUBJECTS